Public Relations
Strategies and Tactics

Eighth Edition

Dennis L. Wilcox
School of Journalism & Mass Communications
San Jose State University

Glen T. Cameron
School of Journalism
University of Missouri

PEARSON
A and B

Boston   New York   San Francisco
Mexico City   Montreal   Toronto   London   Madrid   Munich   Paris
Hong Kong   Singapore   Tokyo   Cape Town   Sydney

Series Editor: Molly Taylor
Series Editorial Assistants: Michael Kish, Suzanne Stradley
Senior Development Editor: Cheryl deJong-Lambert
Senior Marketing Manager: Mandee Eckersley
Composition and Prepress Buyer: Linda Cox
Manufacturing Manager: Megan Cochran
Text Designer: Carol Somberg
Photo Research: Helane M. Prottas, Posh Pictures
Cover Administrator: Linda Knowles
Editorial-Production Administrator: Anna Socrates
Editorial-Production Service: Modern Graphics, Inc.
Electronic Composition: Modern Graphics, Inc.

For related titles and support materials, visit our online catalog at www.ablongman.com

Between the time Web site information is gathered and then published, it is not unusual for some sites to have closed. Also the transcription of URLs can result in unintended typographical errors. The publisher would appreciate notification where these errors occur so that they may be corrected in subsequent editions.

Library of Congress Cataloging-in-Publication Data
Wilcox, Dennis L.
Public relations : strategies and tactics / Dennis L. Wilcox, Glenn T. Cameron—8th ed.
   p. cm.
  Includes bibliographical references and index.
  ISBN 0-205-44944-1
  1. Public relations. 2. Public relations—United States. I. Cameron, Glenn T. II. Title.
HM1221.W55 2005
659.2—dc22   2004065959

Photo credits appear on p. xx, which constitutes an extension of the copyright page.

Printed in the United States of America
10 9 8 7 6 5 4 3 2   VHP   10 09 08 07 06 05

Brief Contents

Contents

iv

4 Public Relations Departments and Firms   97

PART TWO: Process

5 Research   128

6 Program Planning   152

10 Conflict Management: Dealing with Issues, Risks, and Crises   242

11 The Audience and How to Reach It   270

PART FOUR: Tactics

14 New Releases, Newsletters, and Brochures   356

15   Radio, Television, and the Web

16   Speechwriting, Presentations, and Media Interviews

PART FIVE: Application

2 0 Nonprofit Organizations 540

2 1 Education 570

2 2 Entertainment, Sports, and Travel 587

Preface

This eighth edition of *Public Relations: Strategies and Tactics* is for students who want to understand the basic concepts of effective public relations and how they can prepare for the professional, ethical practice of public relations in today's fast-changing world.

The major strength of this edition, as in the previous editions, is the solid, understandable explanation of public relations theory and how basic principles are applied to current, real-world situations. Indeed, Holly Pieper of Ithaca College captures the essence of the book saying, "The style of writing is clear and concise. Appropriate examples are riddled throughout the text to exemplify concepts as well as to isolate support materials. The content is organized in a logical manner. It provides a conceptual framework for the students to follow, as each topic is uncovered."

This edition also builds upon its well-deserved reputation for being the most comprehensive introductory book in the field that successfully blends theory and practice in a format that is clear and easy to read for undergraduate students without being superficial or shallow. Its writing style and colorful design engages the interest of undergraduates and, at the same time, appeals to instructors who want their students to have an in-depth understanding of public relations as a strategic, problem-solving process involving the application of key principles.

New in the Eighth Edition

The authors have revised and reorganized major portions of the book to make basic information and case studies reflect daily headlines and current issues. In addition, there are several major changes in the eighth edition that have been suggested by adopters and reviewers of the previous edition. They include:

- A new chapter on **Conflict Management: Dealing with Issues, Risks, and Crises.** Increasingly, the professional practice of public relations deals with issues and organizational crises, and this new chapter gives students the theoretical framework to help them understand the complexities and variables involved in determining a course of action for their employers or clients.

- An expanded emphasis on public relations careers in the first chapter. Students immediately learn about the qualities needed for a successful career, the salaries of entry-level, as well as experienced professionals, and the areas of practice that are in demand today.

- A completely revised and expanded **Tactics** section that gives students "how-to" tips, checklists, and examples of actual public relations materials from successful campaigns.

- An updated and revised section on applications that is designed to give students an overview of such fields as government and politics, entertainment and sports, and international public relations.

- A new "On the Job" box in every chapter that features an ethical situation requiring student decision-making and classroom discussion.

- Other "On the Job" boxes in every chapter that give insights into the practice or discuss a public relations program conducted in other nations or on a global basis.

- A new "casebook" at the end of every chapter, which gives students an in-depth perspective on a particular project or campaign as it relates to the subject of the chapter.
- References throughout the book to various organizational Web sites that provide students with links to additional information about the topic.

Up-to-Date Coverage

This textbook has always been highly valued for its up-to-date coverage of events, issues, and situations that are relevant to today's students. This edition continues the tradition by adding new cases and discussion about the following topics:

- Current entry-level salaries in the field and those of more experienced professionals by practice area and geographical regions.
- Latest research about feminization of the field and the trend line for the future.
- Wal-Mart, one of the world's largest corporations, and its efforts to become a better corporate citizen.
- Current information about the size and scope of conglomerates that own multiple public relations firms, advertising agencies, and specialty companies.
- An account by a Burson-Marsteller account executive about her experiences representing Visa International at the Athens Olympics.
- Using meet-ups and flash mobs as a communications strategy.
- The National Rifle Association's (NRA) successful effort to defeat the renewal of a ban on assault weapons.
- Impact of the Sarbanes-Oxley Act regarding the disclosure of financial information and how it affects the practice of investor relations.
- Nike's corporate "free-speech" case that went all the way to the Supreme Court.
- Similarities and differences between plagiarism and copyright infringement.
- FCC's clampdown on "indecent" broadcasting after Janet Jackson's wardrobe "malfunction" at the Super Bowl.
- Martha Stewart's failure to win acquittal in the court of public opinion.
- The impact of Weblogs and bloggers on the practice of public relations.
- The global campaign to introduce the redesigned $20 bill.
- A creative campaign to publicize a new microwave popcorn.
- Pontiac's publicity bonanza by giving away free cars on the Oprah Winfrey show.
- The inside story on producing a video news release for the Segway human transportation device.
- The campaign by the People for Ethical Treatment of Animals (PETA) to change the policies of such corporations as KFC and Safeway.
- McDonald's response to the critical film, "Supersize Me."
- Coca-Cola and Samsung's sponsorship of the torch relay in the Athens Olympics.
- Bristol-Myers Squibbs' bicycle Tour of Hope for cancer research.
- Public relations efforts by the presidential campaigns of John Kerry and George Bush.

- Impact of the McCain-Feingold campaign finance reform act, and the rise of independent campaign groups, such as the Swift Boat Veterans and MoveOn.org, known as "527s."
- Food industry lobbying and public affairs efforts to influence the USDA's revision of the food pyramid.
- The Pentagon's public relations efforts to deal with the Abu Ghraib prison scandal in Iraq and other issues.
- American "public diplomacy" efforts around the globe to gain support for U.S. policies in Iraq.
- Saudi Arabia's efforts to polish its image in the United States after 9/11.
- An Australian school's efforts to cope with allegations of sexual abuse.
- The planning of West Point's 200th anniversary.
- China's public relations efforts to host the 2008 Olympics.
- Viral marketing and how it works.
- Development of corporate social responsibility (CSR) in today's environment of activist groups and governmental oversight.

Organization of the Book

The basic structure of the book remains the same, but there are three major changes in organization. First, the chapter on the "Individual in Public Relations" has been merged into Chapter 1 "What Is Public Relations?" Reviewers recommended that these two chapters be merged to give students a more integrated overview of the public relations field from the standpoint of what public relations is and what kind of careers are available.

The second major change, which has already been highlighted, is a new chapter in the **Strategy** section on "Conflict Management: Dealing with Issues, Risks, and Crises." This gives students a thorough grounding in understanding and coping with a host of situations that can drastically affect the reputation and bottom line of any organization.

These topics have traditionally been included in the "communication" process chapter, but both the reviewers and authors believe the topic is so important that it deserves an entire chapter. The chapter is unique because it includes both issues identification and risk management instead of just concentrating on what an organization should do after the crisis has reached the headline stage. The chapter also presents new theories about crises and the complex variables that determine how an organization responds to a situation.

The third major change is placement of the **Tactics** section in the middle of the book to directly follow the chapters on **Strategy**. The authors agree with adopters and reviewers that "tactics" should logically follow the section on "strategy." Adopters also indicated a desire for more "how-to" information, checklists, and illustrations to better prepare students for actually writing and producing various public relations materials. This has been accomplished in this edition.

The section with chapters about specific areas of practice **(Applications)** is now the last part of the book. This accomplishes two objectives. First, the core of the book is in the first 16 chapters, which easily can be assigned in a quarter or semester course. Second, it allows both professors and students to use the last section of the book as supplemental reading if they wish.

In sum, the book remains divided into five parts:

Part One: Role
Part Two: Process
Part Three: Strategy
Part Four: Tactics
Part Five: Application

Part One: Role

This section of the book gives students a thorough grounding in public relations as a pervasive, fully-developed field of activity in today's society and global economy. It properly defines the broad scope of public relations, its societal value, and the workplace settings where public relations is practiced.

Chapter 1: What Is Public Relations?   An explanation of what public relations is, and what it isn't. A number of operational definitions are given, and students gain an understanding of public relations as a systematic, problem-solving process. It discusses the differences and similarities between public relations, journalism, advertising, and marketing. There is also a discussion of integrated marketing communications (IMC) and public relations as a global activity found in virtually all nations. The chapter ends with a through discussion about careers in public relations.

Chapter 2: The Evolution of Public Relations.   A completely reorganized chapter that succinctly gives a short history of public relations in terms of major eras of development and the individuals that made a significant contribution to the field. Emphasis is placed on the last half of the twentieth century, and how the role and function of public relations have evolved over the years. The chapter ends with current and future trend lines in the practice of public relations, including feminization of the field and workforce diversity.

Chapter 3: Ethics and Professionalism.   Students, early in the book, are exposed to the ethical and professional standards of today's practice. The codes of conduct for several professional organizations are discussed and compared with emphasis on what kinds of activities would be considered unethical. There is also discussion of individual ethics and whether public relations is a "profession." A global perspective is offered, and the problem of media bribery in some nations is discussed.

Chapter 4: Public Relations Departments and Firms.   The structure of public relations departments and their role in various organizational structures are discussed. Line and staff functions, access to management, and areas of friction with other departments are highlighted. Public relations firms are discussed from the standpoint of the services they provide, global outreach, the rise of communication conglomerates, and how fees are calculated.

Part Two: Process

The four chapters in this part form a unified whole, taking students in sequence through the basic steps involved in a public relations program—research, planning, communication, and evaluation. In this way, students gain a deeper understanding and appreciation of public relations as a multiple-step process. To explain the process, the chapters follow the public relations programs of several organizations from conception to evaluation.

Chapter 5: Research.   The essential first step in public relations programming. Students are exposed to different levels of qualitative and quantitative research and how to construct a basic questionnaire. Piggy-back questions on national surveys and Web-based surveys are discussed. The use of the World Wide Web and the Internet for research are thoroughly discussed.

Chapter 6: Program Planning.   The importance of setting goals and objectives for a public relations program. It also gives the eight essential parts of a public relations plan, including information on how to identify target audiences, create budgets, do timelines, and evaluate the effort.

Chapter 7: Communication.   Students get a brief overview of major communication theories as they apply to various techniques for accomplishing everything from making individuals aware of a message to actually changing their behavior in terms of opinions or product purchase. Basic charts give the appropriate communication vehicle depending on the situation.

Chapter 8: Evaluation.   The pros and cons of various measurement methods are discussed. Techniques are clearly defined for measuring message exposure, audience awareness, audience attitudes, and audience action. The chapter ends with a discussion of how to do communication audits.

Part Three: Strategy

This part discusses the fundamental concepts of strategy from the standpoint of acquainting student with broad-based concepts such as persuasion, audience characteristics, law, and new technologies.

Chapter 9: Public Opinion and Persuasion.   The influence of opinion leaders is discussed, and various factors such as source credibility, timing and context, and appeal to self-interest are explained. The chapter ends with guidelines about the ethics of persuasion and the obligation of professionals to always act in the public interest.

Chapter 10: Conflict Management: Dealing with Issues, Risks, and Crises. This new chapter provides a basic, easy-to-understand theoretical framework so students can systematically go through a decision-tree in terms of how an organization should respond to risks and crises. Various real-life situations are discussed, such as the Catholic Church's response to allegations of sexual abuse by priests.

Chapter 11: The Audience and How to Reach It.   Students learn that the "general public" is really a group of "publics" with specific characteristics. Ethnic audiences, such as the growing Hispanic population, are discussed in addition to the influential "senior" and teen-age markets. Various media, and how they can be used by public relations practitioners to reach these audiences, are outlined.

Chapter 12: Public Relations and the Law.   Libel, privacy, copyright, plagiarism, and trademarks are explained. The chapter also outlines the rules and regulations of such regulatory agencies as the FTC, SEC, FCC, and the FDA that affect the content of public relations materials. New material includes the Sarbanes-Oxley Act on financial disclosure and Nike's corporate "free-speech" lawsuit that reached the Supreme Court.

Chapter 13: New Technologies in Public Relations. The rapid rise of the Internet is outlined within the context of how it has radically changed the distribution of public relations materials. E-mail, desktop publishing, Webconferencing, electronic distribution services, blogs, personal digital assistants (PDAs), satellite distribution of video news releases, and even new advances in voice recognition software are discussed.

Part Four: Tactics

This revised and expanded section focuses on "how-to" skills that the student needs to actually produce and write public relations materials.

Chapter 14: News Releases, Newsletters, and Brochures. Students also learn how to write and produce media advisories, pitch letters, media kits, annual reports, and institutional ads. There are numerous "how to" checklists, samples from various public relations campaigns, and even a section on what makes a good publicity photo.

Chapter 15: Radio, Television, and the Web. Students are exposed to broadcast news writing, arranging a guest on talk shows, satellite media tours, and the components of a video news release. The basics of an organizational Web site are discussed, with special emphasis on "pressrooms."

Chapter 16: Speechwriting, Presentations, and Media Interviews. Students learn how to write a speech, give a speech, and use PowerPoint in presentations. The basics of preparing for a one-on-one media interview are covered, as well as how to organize a news conference and a media tour.

Part Five: Application

The next logical step is for students to learn the practical ways in which the process, strategies, and tactics are applied in major areas of practice. These chapters, which make the text so comprehensive, build upon the basics that students have learned in the first 16 chapters.

Chapter 17: Corporations. The completely revised chapter on corporations that outlines the public relations challenges facing today's modern, global corporation. Such topics as media relations, consumer boycotts, multicultural marketing, investor relations, cause-related marketing, environmental activism, philanthropy, and corporate sponsorship of events are covered.

Chapter 18: Politics and Government. New sections discuss campaign finance legislation, the 2004 presidential election, the rise of "527" political groups, and public relations in the Bush White House. Lobbying and the problems of influence peddling are discussed, as well the nature of governmental public relations work at the federal, state, and city level.

Chapter 19: International Public Relations.   Students gain an appreciation of global public relations and the challenges of cross-cultural communications. The rise of NGOs and their influence, public relations development in other nations, opportunities for international work, and U.S. efforts in influence global public opinion about Iraq are explored.

Chapter 20: Nonprofit Organizations.   The nature of public relations work in trade groups, labor unions, professional associations, charities, social agencies, and activist groups. Resource development and how to conduct a fund-raising campaign are explored.

Chapter 21: Education.   The public relations activities of universities, grade school, and high schools are highlighted. Students learn about how to reach special publics to accomplish goals and objectives.

Chapter 22: Entertainment, Sports, and Travel.   Students learn about "celebrity" publicity and promotion, and the techniques of conducting "personality" campaigns for rock groups, professional sports, and movie stars. Tourism, a large industry, also is highlighted as a career area.

Student Learning Aids

Every chapter includes several learning tools to (l) help students better understand and remember the principlesÏ of public relations, and (2) give students the practice they need to apply those principles to real-life situations.

- **Chapter opening previews.** The preview, in outline format, gives students the major sections and structure of the chapter so they have a learning framework.
- **Boxed inserts.** Each chapter includes "On the Job" boxes that highlight additional insights, global programs, and ethical considerations. They supplement information in the regular text and also challenge students to formulate their own solutions and opinions.
- **Casebook.** A real-life case study of a public relations program is provided that encapsulates and elaborates upon the chapter topic. The objective is to show students how the concepts and principles are used in actual practice.
- **End-of-chapter summaries.** The major themes and issues are summarized for the student at the end of each chapter.
- **End-of-chapter "What Would You Do?"** A public relations situation or dilemma, based on actual cases, is posed and students are asked to apply what they have just read to a real-life situation.
- **Questions for review and discussion.** There is a list of questions to help students prepare for tests and to also stimulate classroom discussion.
- **Suggested readings.** End-of-chapter readings give students additional references for exploring topics brought up in the chapter.

Supplements

Instructors and students have a variety of ancillary tools available to them that help make teaching and learning with *Public Relations: Strategies and Tactics* easier.

- **Web site to accompany *Public Relations: Strategies and Tactics*** This exciting Web site contains an impressive collection of resources for both students and instructors. The Web site's features complement the coverage and organization of the text, yet extend beyond the book to offer further study tools and enrichment. Features include chapter summaries, sample text questions, Web links, and a variety of other rich resources to enhance your learning experience. Please visit us online at www.ablongman.com/wilcox8e.

- **Instructor's Resource Manual/Test Bank with PowerPoint Slides** This manual includes chapter outlines, lecture topics, sample syllabi, class activities, multiple choice and essay questions, PowerPoint slides of major concepts, and a section on using media and software in the classroom. In addition, the manual helps professors incorporate PUBLICS: PR Research Software into their lesson plans. Details are provided in the Instructor's Resource Manual. Instructors can access the instructor's manual, test bank, and PowerPoint slides for the eighth edition of *Public Relations: Strategies and Tactics* by registering online at Allyn and Bacon's Central Supplements Web site: http://suppscentral.ablongman.com/login.php.

- **Computerized Test Generator** The test bank portion of the Instructor's Resource Manual is available on our computerized testing system, TestGen-EQ 2.0. This fully networkable testing software is available on a cross-platform CD-ROM. TestGen EQ's friendly graphical interface enables instructors to view, edit, and add questions; transfer questions to tests; and print tests in a variety of fonts and forms. Search-and-sort features help instructors locate questions quickly and arrange them in a preferred order. QuizMaster-EQ allows instructors to create and save tests to a network so that students can take them at any networked computer terminal. Instructors can set preferences for how and when tests are administered. QuizMaster-EQ automatically grades the exams and allows instructors to view or print a variety of reports for individual students or courses.

- **PowerPoint Presentation on CD-ROM** Slides giving key points of a chapter, in addition to being available online, are also available on CD-ROM. Contact your Allyn and Bacon campus representative.

Acknowledgments

We express our gratitude to those who reviewed drafts of the manuscript for previous editions.

We also express our deep appreciation to many of our academic colleagues who reviewed the seventh edition and made many suggestions that we have incorporated into this new edition. Thank you: Josh Boyd, Purdue University; Stephen Firth, William Patterson University; Maria Ivancin, American University; Teresa Mastin, Michigan State University; Michelle O'Malley, Kansas State University; Maureen Taylor, Rutgers University; and Beth Wood, Indiana University. A special thank you to Josh Boyd, Teresa Mastin, Maureen Taylor, and Beth Wood, for reviewing the eighth edition.

D. L. W.
G. T. C.

Credits

p. 2, PR Week; p. 12, Julie Jacobson/AP/Wide world Photos; p. 13, © PhotoFest; p.14, © The New Yorker Collection 2004/ Mick Stevens from cartoonbank.com. All Rights Reserved; p. 21, Richard Drew/AP/Wide World Photos; p. 28, PR Week; p. 30, PR Week; p. 38, Kim Christensen/The Facts/AP/ Wide World Photos; p. 48, © Culver Photos; p. 50, U.S. Library of Congress; p. 53, © Bettmann/CORBIS; p. 54, © 2004 Metropolitan Transit Authority; p. 55, Courtesy Edward L. Bernays; p. 60, AP/Wide World Photos; p. 66, Bob Evans Farms, AARP, Avery Dennison, Best Buy, Inc. Reebok International, SAP/AG, Porter Novelli, Marriot International, Northwest Airlines; p. 77, 79, 88, Public Relations Society of America; p. 79, International Association of Business Communicators; p. 107, Frank Gunn/Canadian Press/AP/Wide World Photos; p. 108, PR Week; p. 110, Fleishman-Hillard; p. 111, Pablo Martinez Monsivais/ AP/Wide World Photos; p, 121, Home Depot Corporation; p. 124, Amanda Karmin/Aldo Montano; p. 137, © Jeff Greenberg/PhotoEdit; p. 138, Right Idea, Inc.; 155. Marriot Corporation; p. 165, © Leon Santow/Stone/GettyImages; p. 183, Courtesy of the Advertising Council; p. 216, AP Photo/Lockheed Martin Aeronautics Co./AP/Wide World Photos; p. 218, Amy Sancetta/AP/Wide World Photos; p. 227, PhotoFest; p. 228, Frederick M. Brown/Getty-AFP; p. 229, Paul Sakuma/AP/Wide World Photos; p. 233, Courtesy of Defenders of Wildlife; photo credit: © 1998 Tom Soucek/AlaskStock; p. 246, Michael O'Neill/Sports Illustrated; p. 255, Glenn T. Cameron and Sooyoung Cho; p. 287, Peter Kramer/© 2004 GettyImages; p. 310, Courtesy of Federal Express Corporation; p. 318, Awout David Phillip/AP/Wide World Photos; p. 320, Susan Walsh/AP/Wide World Photos; p. 322, Bebeto Matthews/AP/Wide World Photos; p. 330, Edward Parsons/UNHCR/AP/Wide World Photos; p. 333, Courtesy Edelman Public Relations Worldwide; p. 335, © Morgan/Greenpeace; p. 336, United Nations High Commission for Refugees; p. 373, AP Photo/Treasury Department/AP/Wide World Photos; p. 375, Nesnady + Schwartz: Cleveland + New York + Toronto; p. 381, Texas Association Against Sexual Assault (TAASA); p. 396, Courtesy Pepsi-Cola Company; p. 404, Brad Barket/ © 2004 Getty-Images; p. 414, Lisa Poole/AP/Wide World Photos; p. 420, Aramco; p. 427, Lisa Poole/AP/Wide World Photos; p. 439, Kevin Winter/© 2004 GettyImages; p. 440, Jennifer Szymaszek/AP/Wide World Photos; p. 457, Anat Givon/AP/Wide World Photos; p. 467, PR Week; p. 470, Frederic Brown/AP/Wide World Photos; p. 484, © Wesley Bedrosian. Used with permission; p. 486, stopthenra.com; p. 490, Scott Olson/© 2004 GettyImages; p. 492, Joe Marquette/AP/Wide World Photos; p. 493, MoveOn.org; p. 500, Laurent Rebours/AP/Wide World Photos; p. 504, J. Scott Applewhite/AP/Wide World Photos; p. 507, California Department of Health Services; p. 518, Ralph Radford/AP/Wide World Photos; p. 522, Federal Express Corporation; p. 526, Burhan Ozbilici/AP/Wide World Photos; p. 534, IRPA Frontline; p. 536, Cathay Pacific Airlines; p. 548, Courtesy of Mothers Against Drunk Driving (MADD); p. 551, Courtesy of the American Cancer Society; p. 552, Craig Taylor/AP/Wide World Photos; p. 555, Gerald Herbert/AP/Wide World Photos; p. 556, Lynne Sladky/AP/Wide World Photos; p. 558, Courtesy of University of California Museum of Paleontology, Berkeley; p. 572, Courtesy of St. Bonaventure University; p. 577, Kevork Diansezian/AP/Wide World Photos; p. 584, West Point Museum Collections; p. 595, Arturo Mari/AP/Wide World Photos; p. 597, Julia Malakie/AP/Wide World Photos; p. 600, Copyright 2004 NBAE (Photo by Jennifer Pottheiser/NBAE via GettyImages); p. 605, Diane Bondareff/AP/Wide World Photos

chapter 1

What Is Public Relations?

Topics covered in this chapter include:

The Challenge of Public Relations

It is 9 A.M. and Anne-Marie, an account executive in a San Francisco public relations firm, is at her computer working on a news release about a client's new software product. She finishes it, gives it a once-over, and e-mails it to the client for approval. She also attaches a note that an electronic news service can deliver it to newspapers across the country later in the day.

Her next activity is a brainstorming session with other staff members to generate creative ideas about a campaign to raise funds for the local AIDS foundation. When she gets back to her office, she finds a number of telephone messages. A reporter for a trade publication needs background information on a story he is writing; a graphic designer has finished a rough draft of a client's brochure; a catering manager has called about making final arrangements for a reception at an art gallery; and a video producer asks if she can attend the taping of a video news release next week.

Lunch is with a client who wants her counsel on how to announce the closing of a plant in another state. After lunch, Anne-Marie heads back to the office. She asks her assistant to check arrangements for a news conference next week in New York. She telephones a key editor to "pitch" a story about a client's new product. Anne-Marie also touches base with other members of her team, who are working on a 12-city media tour by an Olympic champion representing an athletic shoe manufacturer.

At 4 P.M., Anne-Marie checks several computer databases to gather information about the industry of a new client. She also checks online news updates to determine if anything is occurring that involves or affects her firm's clients. At 5 P.M., as she winds down from the day's hectic activities, she reviews news stories from a clipping service about her client, an association of strawberry producers. She is pleased to find that her feature story, which included recipes and color photos, appeared in 150 dailies.

As this scenario illustrates, the challenge of public relations is multi-faceted. <u>A public relations</u>

A career in public relations has variety and interesting projects. This "Day in the Life" feature published in *PR Week* gives insight to the types of jobs and activities that a public relations professional does on a daily basis.

A DAY IN THE LIFE

Brandee Brooks

Position
PR director
Company
TNT and TBS
Location
Atlanta

How long have you been working there?
Since 1995.

What time do you start your day?
It varies, depending on where the projects are filming, and if the talent's representatives are based on the East or West Coast.

What are your responsibilities?
I work on original programming from pre-production through domestic premiere. Most of my time is spent securing a variety of advertising, marketing, and PR needs for the life of the project, everything from setting up the unit/gallery photo shoots to coordinating all press interviews with the cast and crew.

What projects have you most recently worked on?
I just finished a project-managing assignment for our new limited series *The Grid*. In addition, I spent a lot of time on-set for the original film *The Wool Cap* and preparing for our original movie *Evel Knievel*, which premiered on July 30.

What makes you good at your job?
I thrive off of change. Production schedules change, talent wraps early, locations move, weather conditions are in constant flux, all of which contribute to having to think on your feet and not let any windows of opportunity pass.

Where did you go to school? What did you study?
I graduated from Pepperdine University with a double major in PR and advertising, with a minor in business.

What is your greatest professional achievement?
Going to lunch with my academic advisor and greatest, toughest teacher, Dr. Robert Woodruff, prior to his passing away. I told him all about my career accomplishments and mistakes. He just beamed with pride and respect.

Name one thing about your past that would surprise people
I used to raise and train guide dogs for the blind.

professional must have skills in written and interpersonal communication, research, negotiation, creativity, logistics, facilitation, and problem solving.

Indeed, those who want a challenging career with plenty of variety often choose the field of public relations. The U.S. Bureau of Labor Statistics estimates that the field already employs 200,000 nationwide and that it will be one of the fastest-growing industries through 2006. In addition, a *Fortune* magazine survey ranks public relations number 8 on a list of "where the best jobs will be."

Global Scope

It's difficult to estimate worldwide figures, but *Reed's Directory of Public Relations Organizations* lists more than 150 national and regional public relations associations. The Global Alliance (www.globalpr.org), with 60 associations representing some 150,000 members, estimates that some 3 million people worldwide practice public relations as their main professional activity. Conservatively, about one-twelfth (360,000) probably belong to some professional organization.

Included in such groups are the Public Relations Institute of Southern Africa (PRISA), the Public Relations Association of Mauritius (PRAM), the Public Relations Institute of Australia (PRIA), the Italian Federation of Public Relations (FERPI), the Canadian Public Relations Society (CPRS), the Public Relations Society of Tanzania (PRAT), the Institute of Public Relations (United Kingdom), the Association of Public Relations Practitioners in Thailand, the Public Relations Association of Romania, and the Agencies Association of Mexico (PRAA).

Large numbers of students around the world are studying public relations as a career field. In the United States, almost 200 universities have sequences or majors in public relations, and about 80 European universities also offer studies in the subject. Many Asian universities, particularly those in Thailand, Singapore, and Malaysia, also offer major programs. China claims that more than 500,000 students are studying aspects of public relations in colleges and training institutions. In sum, public relations is a well-established academic subject that is taught throughout the world.

In terms of economics, the public relations field is most extensively developed in the United States, where organizations spend an estimated $141 billion annually on public relations, in-store promotions, direct mail, and sponsorships. Another $176 billion is spent on advertising, according to estimates by Vernonis Suhler Stevenson, a specialty banker in the communications industry. Public relations is expected to grow almost 9 percent by 2008, more than any other communications practice except event planning and sponsorships.

Figures for the rest of the world are somewhat sketchy. European companies spend about $3 billion a year on public relations, compared with corporate public relations spending in the United States of about $3.5 billion. European figures continue to increase because of the expansion of the European Union (EU) and the developing market economies of Russia and the newly independent nations of the former Soviet Union.

Another region of major growth is Asia. China's economy is increasing at the rate of 10 percent annually, and the public relations industry is thriving (see the Global box on page 4). Other nations, such as Malaysia, Korea, Thailand, Singapore, Indonesia, and even India, are also rapidly expanding their free market economies, which creates a fertile environment for increased public relations activity. Latin America and Africa also present growth opportunities. A more detailed discussion of international public relations is found in Chapter 19.

A Variety of Definitions

People often define public relations by some of its most visible techniques and tactics, such as publicity in a newspaper, a television interview with an organization's spokesperson, or the appearance of a celebrity at a special event.

What people fail to understand is that public relations is a process involving many subtle and far-reaching aspects. It includes research and analysis, policy formation, programming, communication, and feedback from numerous publics. Its practitioners operate on two distinct levels—as advisers to their clients or to an organization's top management and as technicians who produce and disseminate messages in multiple media channels.

A number of definitions have been formulated over the years. One of the early definitions that gained wide acceptance was formulated by the newsletter *PR News*: "Public relations is the management function which evaluates public attitudes, iden-

ON THE JOB global

China: The New 500-Pound Gorilla on the Block

China has the fastest-growing public relations market in the world. The country, with 1.3 billion people, now has about 10,000 public relations practitioners and a host of international public relations firms in residence as it becomes a major economic power.

The China International Public Relations Association (CIPRA) estimated public relations revenues to be at least $300 million in 2002, and the percentage of growth continues to experience double-digit increases every year. In fact, it is estimated that China's public relations industry will accelerate its growth momentum, and the market could reach about $1.8 billion by 2010. Currently, China is the second-largest market in Asia after Japan.

The growth of Chinese public relations began to take off in the early 1990s as the country began to develop a market economy. The gross domestic product (GDP) has rapidly expanded in recent years, and the central government has also given a boost to the public relations industry by initiating massive reforms in the mass media industry, which has led to a more friendly environment for business news and product publicity.

China also has joined the World Trade Organization (WTO), and this has brought more public relations activity by international companies who are fiercely competing for customers. The biggest development, according to the *Economist*, is the soaring demand for public relations among Chinese companies as they actively seek local consumers, foreign investment, and international outlets for their goods.

China will host the 2008 Olympics in Beijing and the 2010 Shanghai World Expo; these events also are expected to fuel the dynamic growth of public relations in China.

tifies the policies and procedures of an individual or an organization with the public interest, and plans and executes a program of action to earn public understanding and patience."

Rex Harlow, a pioneer public relations educator who founded what eventually became the Public Relations Society of America (PRSA), once compiled more than 500 definitions from almost as many sources. After mulling over them and talking with leaders in the field, Harlow came up with this definition:

> Public relations is a distinctive management function which helps establish and maintain mutual lines of communication, understanding, acceptance, and cooperation between an organization and its publics; involves the management of problems or issues; helps management keep informed on and responsive to public opinion; defines and emphasizes the responsibility of management to serve the public interest; helps management keep abreast of and effectively utilize change, serving as an early warning system to help anticipate trends; and uses research and sound ethical communication techniques as its principal tools.

More succinct definitions are provided by theorists and textbook authors. Scott M. Cutlip, Allen H. Center, and Glen M. Broom state in *Effective Public Relations* that "public relations is the management function that identifies, establishes, and maintains mutually beneficial relationships between an organization and the various publics on whom its success or failure depends." The management function is also emphasized in *Managing Public Relations* by James E. Grunig and Todd Hunt. They state that public relations is "the management of communication between an organization and its publics." A European perspective on the dimensions of public relations is provided on page 7.

The best definition for today's modern practice is offered by Professors Lawrence W. Long and Vincent Hazelton, who describe public relations as "a communication function of management through which organizations adapt to, alter, or maintain their environment for the purpose of achieving organizational goals." Their approach represents the somewhat newer theory that public relations is more than persuasion. It should also foster open, two-way communication and mutual understanding with the idea that an organization also changes its attitudes and behaviors in the process—not just the target audience.

Inherent in this newer philosophy of public relations is the basic idea that the objective is to build mutually beneficial relationships between the organization and its various publics. In other words, organizational policies and actions should be a win-win situation for both the organization and the public.

A good example of a win-win situation was the decision by various apparel and footwear manufacturers (Nike, Reebok, GEAR for Sports, Tommy Hilfiger, etc.) to engage in a dialogue with labor and human rights groups about working conditions in their overseas factories after considerable negative publicity on their use of "sweatshop" labor. The result was the creation of the Fair Labor Association, which created a uniform code of conduct and a monitoring process to document whether member companies were in compliance.

In this instance, the companies improved their corporate reputations and avoided consumer boycotts by activist college groups, human rights groups, and labor unions. The workers in these factories got better working conditions in terms of wages, health, and safety. And consumers felt somewhat less guilty about wearing expensive sneakers and name-brand clothes made by exploited Third World labor.

National and international public relations organizations, including the PRSA, also have formulated definitions. Here is a sampling of definitions from around the world:

- "Public relations is the deliberate, planned, and sustained effort to establish and maintain mutual understanding between an organization and its publics." (British Institute of Public Opinion, whose definition has also been adopted in a number of Commonwealth nations)
- "Public relations is the management, through communication, of perceptions and strategic relationships between an organization and its internal and external stakeholders." (Public Relations Institute of Southern Africa)
- "Public relations is the sustained and systematic managerial effort through which private and public organizations seek to establish understanding, sympathy, and support in those public circles with which they have or expect to obtain contact." (Dansk Public Relations Klub of Denmark, which also uses the English term)
- "Public relations practice is the art and social science of analyzing trends, predicting their consequences, counseling organization leaders, and implementing planned programs of action which serve both the organization's and the public's interest." (A definition approved at the World Assembly of Public Relations in Mexico City in 1978 and endorsed by 34 national public relations organizations)

Careful study of these explanations should enable anyone to formulate a definition of public relations; committing any single one to memory is unnecessary. The key words to remember in defining public relations follow:

Part of interactive process known as "public relations activity"

1. **Deliberate.** Public relations activity is <u>intentional.</u> It is designed to influence, gain understanding, provide information, and obtain *feedback* (reaction from those affected by the activity).

2. **Planned.** Public relations activity is <u>organized.</u> Solutions to problems are discovered and logistics are thought out, with the activity taking place over a period of time. It is systematic, requiring research and analysis.

3. **Performance.** Effective public relations is based on <u>actual policies and performance.</u> No amount of public relations will generate good will and support if the organization is unresponsive to community concerns. A Pacific Northwest timber company, despite a campaign with the theme "For Us, Every Day Is Earth Day," became known as the villain of Washington State because of its insistence on logging old-growth forests and bulldozing a logging road into a prime elk habitat.

4. **Public interest.** Public relations activity <u>should be mutually beneficial to the organization and the public;</u> it is the alignment of the organization's self-interests with the public's concerns and interests. For example, the Mobil Corporation sponsors quality programming on public television because it enhances the company's image; by the same token, the public benefits from the availability of such programming.

5. **Two-way communication.** Public relations is more than one-way dissemination of informational materials. It is equally important to solicit feedback. As Jim

ON THE JOB global

A European Perspective on Public Relations

In the United States, public relations is often described as "relationship management," but European academics and practitioners have a somewhat different view. According to a survey sponsored by the European Association of Public Relations Education and Research, in Europe there is a strong belief that ". . . public relations is not only about relations with the public, but it is relations in the public and for the public."

The study, conducted as part of a compilation for the European Public Relations Body of Knowledge project, identified four roles, or dimensions, of European public relations:

Managerial: To develop strategies to maintain relations with public groups in order to gain public trust and/or mutual understanding. This role is concerned with the organizational mission and strategy and is aimed at commercial or other (internal and external) public groups.

Operational: To prepare a means of communication for the organization (and its members) in order to help the organization formulate its communications. This role is concerned with communication plans developed by others and is aimed only at the implementation and evaluation of the communication processes.

Reflective: To analyze changing standards and values in society and discuss these with members of the organization in order to adjust the standards and values of the organization regard-ing social responsibility and legitimacy. This role is concerned with organizational standards and values and is aimed at the dominant coalition in the organization.

Educational: To help all members of the organization to become communicatively competent in order to respond to social demands. The role is concerned with the mentality and behavior of the members of the organization and is aimed at internal public groups.

Source: Vercic, Dejan, Van Ruler, Betteke, Butschi, Gerhard, and Flodin, Bertil. "On the Definition of Public Relations: A European View." *Public Relations Review,* Vol. 27, No. 4, 2001, pp. 373–387. An updated article by the same authors titled "A First Look for Parameters of Public Relations in Europe" was published in the *Journal of Public Relations Research,* Vol. 16, No. 1, 2004, pp. 35–63.

Osborne, former vice president of public affairs at Bell Canada, says, "The primary responsibility of the public relations counselor is to <u>provide (management) a thorough grasp of public sentiment.</u>"

- **Management function.** Public relations is most effective when it is an <u>integral part of decision making by top management</u>. Public relations involves counseling and problem solving at high levels, not just the dissemination of information after a decision has been made.

To summarize, a person can grasp the essential elements of public relations by remembering the following words and phrases: *deliberate . . . planned . . . performance . . . public interest . . . two-way communication . . . management function.*

The elements of public relations just described are part of an interactive process that makes up what is called *public relations activity.* In the following section, public relations as a process is discussed.

ON THE JOB insights

Public Relations Society of America Official Statement on Public Relations

Public relations helps our complex, pluralistic society to reach decisions and function more effectively by contributing to mutual understanding among groups and institutions. It serves to bring private and public policies into harmony.

Public relations serves a variety of institutions in society such as businesses, trade unions, government agencies, voluntary associations, foundations, hospitals, and educational and religious institutions. To achieve their goals, these institutions must develop effective relationships with many different audiences or publics such as employees, members, customers, local communities, shareholders, and other institutions, and with society at large.

The managements of institutions need to understand the attitudes and values of their publics in order to achieve institutional goals. The goals themselves are shaped by the external environment. The public relations practitioner acts as a counselor to management, and as a mediator, helping to translate private aims into reasonable, publicly acceptable policy and action.

As a management function, public relations encompasses the following:

- Anticipating, analyzing, and interpreting public opinion, attitudes, and issues which might impact, for good or ill, the operations and plans of the organization.
- Counseling management at all levels in the organization with regard to policy decisions, courses of action and communication, and taking into account their public ramifications and the organization's social or citizenship responsibilities.
- Researching, conducting, and evaluating, on a continuing basis, programs of action and communication to achieve informed public understanding necessary to the success of an organization's aims. These may include marketing, financial, fund-raising, employee, community or government relations, and other programs.

- Planning and implementing the organization's efforts to influence or change public policy.
- Setting objectives, planning, budgeting, recruiting and training staff, and developing facilities—in short, *managing* the resources needed to perform all of the above.
- Examples of the knowledge that may be required in the professional practice of public relations include communication arts, psychology, social psychology, sociology, political science, economics, and the principles of management and ethics. Technical knowledge and skills are required for opinion research, public issues analysis, media relations, direct mail, institutional advertising, publications, film/video productions, special events, speeches, and presentations.

In helping to define and implement policy, the public relations practitioner utilizes a variety of professional communication skills and plays an integrative role both within the organization and between the organization and the external environment.

Public Relations as a Process

Public relations is a *process*—that is, a series of actions, changes, or functions that bring about a result. One popular way to describe the process, and to remember its components, is to use the RACE acronym, first articulated by John Marston in his book

The Nature of Public Relations. Essentially, RACE means that public relations activity consists of four key elements:

- *Research.* What is the problem or situation?
- *Action (program planning).* What is going to be done about it?
- *Communication (execution).* How will the public be told?
- *Evaluation.* Was the audience reached and what was the effect?

Part Two of this text discusses this key four-step process.

Another approach is to think of the process as a never-ending cycle in which six components are links in a chain. Figure 1.1 shows the process.

The public relations process also may be conceptualized in several steps:

Level 1

a. Public relations personnel obtain insights into the problem from numerous sources.
b. Public relations personnel analyze these inputs and make recommendations to management.
c. Management makes policy and action decisions.

FIGURE 1.1

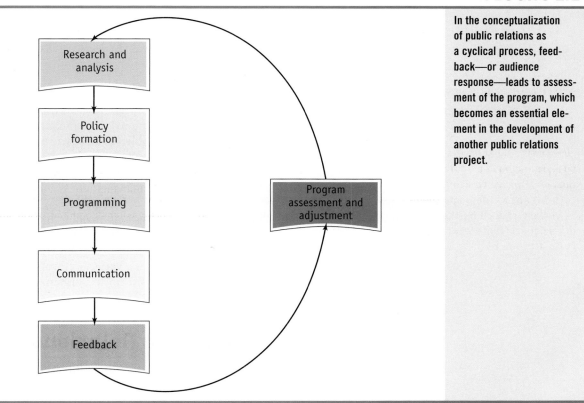

In the conceptualization of public relations as a cyclical process, feedback—or audience response—leads to assessment of the program, which becomes an essential element in the development of another public relations project.

ON THE JOB

insights

Public Relations Explained in Four Easy Steps

Public relations is a multi-faceted field that is difficult to describe in simple terms. James Hutton, a public relations educator and counselor at the College of Business at Fairleigh Dickinson University, gives the following succinct overview:

Definition

Managing strategic relationships

Situational Roles

Persuader, advocate, educator, crusader, information provider, reputation manager

Primary Functions Performed

Research, image making, counseling, managing, early warning, interpreting, communicating, negotiating

Tactics/Tools Used

Publicity, product placement, news releases, speeches, interpersonal communication, Web sites, publications, trade shows, corporate identity programs, corporate advertising programs, etc.

Source: Hutton, James G. "The Definition, Dimensions, and Domain of Public Relations." *Public Relations Review*, 1999, No. 2, pp. 199–214.

Level 2

d. Public relations personnel execute a program of action.
e. Public relations personnel evaluate the effectiveness of the action.

Step A consists of inputs that determine the nature and extent of the public relations problem. These may include feedback from the public, media reporting and editorial comment, analysis of trend data, other forms of research, personal experience, and government pressures and regulations.

In Step B, public relations personnel assess these inputs, establish objectives and an agenda of activity, and convey their recommendations to management. As previously noted, this is the adviser role of public relations.

After management makes its decisions in Step C, public relations personnel execute the action program in Step D through such means as news releases, publications, speeches, and community relations programs. In Step E, the effect of these efforts is measured by feedback from the same components that made up Step A. The cycle is then repeated to solve related aspects of the problem that may require additional decision making and action.

Note that public relations plays two distinct roles in this process, thus serving as a "middle ground" or "linking agent." On Level 1, public relations interacts directly with external sources of information, including the public, media, and government, and relays these inputs to management along with recommendations. On Level 2, public relations becomes the vehicle through which management reaches the public with assorted messages.

Diffusion-of-knowledge theorists call public relations people "linking agents." Sociologists refer to them as "boundary spanners" that act to transfer information between two systems. As the last lines of the official statement on public relations by the PRSA note: "The public relations practitioner utilizes a variety of professional communication skills and plays an integrative role both within the organization and between the organization and the external environment."

The Components of Public Relations

The basic components of public relations, according to a monograph issued by the PRSA Foundation, include:

- **Counseling.** Providing advice to management concerning policies, relationships, and communications.
- **Research.** Determining attitudes and behaviors of publics in order to plan public relations strategies. Such research can be used to (1) generate mutual understanding or (2) influence and persuade publics.
- **Media relations.** Working with mass media in seeking publicity or responding to their interests in the organization.
- **Publicity.** Disseminating planned messages through selected media to further the organization's interests.
- **Employee/member relations.** Responding to concerns, informing, and motivating an organization's employees or members.
- **Community relations.** Planned activity with a community to maintain an environment that benefits both the organization and the community.
- **Public affairs.** Developing effective involvement in public policy and helping an organization adapt to public expectations. The term is also used by government agencies to describe their public relations activities and by many corporations as an umbrella term to describe multiple public relations activities.
- **Government affairs.** Relating directly with legislatures and regulatory agencies on behalf of the organization. *Lobbying* can be part of a government affairs program.
- **Issues management.** Identifying and addressing issues of public concern that affect the organization.
- **Financial relations.** Creating and maintaining investor confidence and building good relationships with the financial community. Also known as *investor relations* or *shareholder relations*.
- **Industry relations.** Relating with other firms in the industry of an organization and with trade associations.
- **Development/fund-raising.** Demonstrating the need for and encouraging the public to support an organization, primarily through financial contributions.
- **Multicultural relations/workplace diversity.** Relating with individuals and groups in various cultural groups.
- **Special events.** Stimulating an interest in a person, product, or organization by means of a focused "happening;" also, activities designed to interact with publics and listen to them.
- **Marketing communications.** Combination of activities designed to sell a product, service, or idea, including advertising, collateral materials, publicity, promotion, direct mail, trade shows, and special events.

These components, and how they function, constitute the substance of this textbook.

Other Terms for Public Relations

Public relations is used as an umbrella term on a worldwide basis. Sixty-four of the 69 national membership associations, from the Arab Public Relations Society to the Zimbabwe Institute of Public Relations, identify themselves with that term.

Special event planning, promotion, and publicity are important activities in public relations work. Here, fireworks burst over the stadium during the opening ceremonies of the Summer 2004 Games in Athens.

Some Positive Descriptive Terms

Individual companies and other groups, however, often use other terms to describe the public relations function. *O'Dwyer's PR Services Report* surveyed *Fortune* magazine's list of the largest 500 corporations and found that the most common name, used by 165 companies, is *corporate communications*. The term *public relations* is a distant second, with 64 companies using it. Other popular names, in descending order, were *public affairs, communication, corporate relations*, and *corporate public affairs*. Some companies link public relations with marketing. Chase Manhattan, for example, has a *corporate marketing and communications* unit.

   Public information is the term most widely used by social service agencies, universities, and government agencies. The implication is that only information is being disseminated, in contrast to persuasive communication, generally perceived as the purpose of public relations. Social services agencies often use the term *community relations*, and the military is fond of *public affairs*.

   In many cases, it is clear that companies and organizations use *public information, public affairs,* or *corporate communications* as euphemisms for *public relations*. This, in part, is a reaction to the misuse of the original term by the public and the media. On occasion, a reporter or government official will use the term *public relations gimmick* or *ploy* to imply that the activities or statements of an organization are without substance or sincerity.

   The popularity of *corporate communications* is also based on the idea that the term is broader than *public relations*, which is often incorrectly perceived as only *media relations*. Corporate communications, many contend, encompasses all communications of the company, including advertising, marketing communications, public affairs, community relations, and employee communications.

   Other organizations use a term that better describes the primary activity of the department. It is clear, for example, that a department of investor relations deals primarily with stockholders, institutional investors, and the financial press. Likewise, a department of environmental affairs, community relations, or employee communications is self-explanatory. A department of marketing communications primarily emphasizes product publicity and promotion. The organization and functions of communications departments are discussed in Chapter 4.

Like departments, individuals specialize in subcategories of public relations. A person who deals exclusively with placement of stories in the media is, to be precise, a *publicist*. A *press agent* is also a specialist, operating within the subcategory of public relations that concentrates on finding unusual news angles and planning events or "happenings" that attract media attention—a stunt by an aspiring Hollywood actress, for example, or an attempt to be listed in the *Guinness Book of Records* by baking the world's largest apple pie.

Some Stereotypes and Less Flattering Terms

Unfortunately, the public and the press often have a much different image of public relations as a profession. A common stereotype is that public relations is a great field because you meet exciting and interesting people, go to parties, and generally spend the day doing a lot of schmoozing.

Many people gain these perceptions from television programs such as *Sex and the City*. Ellen Tashie Frisna, a professor at Hofstra University, writes in *Tactics*, "Samantha Jones (Kim Cattrall), the sexiest of the show's characters, owns a PR agency. And she is—shall we say—experienced. She talks about her career as a way to meet men. (Her conquests include clients and temps.) Sorry, kids—the real world of public relations isn't like that." And Diane Krider, a professor of public relations at Central Michigan University, adds, "the show doesn't seem to show Samantha actually working."

Of course, other television programs and movies also give somewhat negative stereotypes about public relations. ABC's *Spin City*, for example, featured Michael Fox as the deputy mayor of New York who protected his bumbling boss from the media and public. The movies *Phone Booth* and *People I Know* also add to the portrayals of sleazy publicists who have virtually no personal moral compass or sense of social responsibility.

Other negative stereotypes are perpetuated by journalists. Christopher Spicer conducted a content analysis of images of public relations in the print media for an article in the *Journal of Public Relations Research* (1993) and found that public relations was consistently equated with manipulation of the truth to a dubious end. A more re-

Entertainment programs often present a misleading image about the nature of public relations work. Samantha Jones (Kim Cattrall) portrays the owner of a public relations firm in the television series "Sex in the City." Real public relations work, however, requires more than dressing up and going to dinner parties.

cent study (2004) by Carma International found a more favorable portrayal of public relations by the media. Of the almost 700 articles analyzed, 57 percent mentioned public relations in a favorable way, whereas 43 percent mentioned the field in an unfavorable way. Slightly more than 15 percent of the articles said that public relations helps the bottom line, and 5 percent said that public relations educates the public on worthwhile causes. However, just over 10 percent said public relations was just publicity stunts.

A study of jokes and cartoons in the media about public relations showed about the same results in terms of negative impressions. Candace White of the University of Tennessee and Karen Russell Miller of the University of Georgia found that many jokes/cartoons exaggerated stereotypes of public relations practice as lying, hype, spin, and cover-up. Consequently, it is still not uncommon for journalists to describe public relations people as "flacks" or "spin doctors."

A *flack*, or *flak*, is a derisive slang term that journalists often use for a press agent or anyone else working in public relations. Although in recent years most publications, including the *Wall Street Journal*, have refrained from using the "F" word in print, trade publications such as *Editor & Publisher* still use it on a regular basis.

The term has an interesting history. According to Wes Pedersen, director of communications for the Public Affairs Council, the term *flack* originated in 1939 in *Variety*, the show business publication. It began using *flack* as a synonym for *press agent*, he says, "in tribute to the skills of Gene Flack in publicizing motion pictures." Others say the word *flak* was used during World War I to describe heavy ground fire aimed

Public relations is often stereotyped as simply "image building" as expressed in this somewhat humorous *New Yorker* cartoon. The image of an organization, however, is made up of many factors and public relations is only one of them. (Copyright © The New Yorker Collection 2004. Mick Stevens from cartoonbank .com. All rights reserved.)

at aircraft. At times, journalists consider the barrage of daily news releases they receive a form of flak that interferes with their mission of informing the public.

The term *spin doctor* is a more recent entry into the lexicon of public relations. It first appeared in 1984, according to *Safire's Political Dictionary* by William Safire, in a *New York Times* editorial about the activities of President Reagan's reelection campaign. In the beginning, the meaning of *spin* was restricted to what often were considered the unethical and misleading activities and tactics of political campaign consultants. By the mid-1990s, however, the media widely used the term to describe any effort by public relations personnel to put a positive slant on an event or issue.

Robert Dilenschneider, president of his own public relations firm in New York, wrote in a *Wall Street Journal* article: "I think the time has come for public relations professionals to condemn 'spin' and label 'spin doctors' for what they are: purveyors of deception, manipulation, and misinformation. Spin is antithetical to legitimate public relations, which aims to enhance the image of companies and individuals to generate public approval for the programs and policies they advance . . . Spin is to public relations what pornography is to art. . . ."

Indeed, *spin* seems to have well established itself as a popular slang term for any information with a point of view. It has even become popular as a title in books about public relations, as in *PR: A Social History of Spin*, by Stuart Ewan; *The Father of Spin: Edward L. Bernays & The Birth of Public Relations*, by Larry Tye; *Spin Man: The Topsy-Turvy World of Public Relations*, by Thomas Madden; *Spin Cycle: How the White House and the Media Manipulate the News*, by Howard Kurtz; and *Spin: How to Turn the Power of the Press to Your Advantage*, by Michael Sitrick.

Within the public relations community, feeling also exists that *PR* is a slang term that carries a somewhat denigrating connotation. The late Sam Black, a public relations consultant in the United Kingdom and author of several books on public relations, says, "The use of 'PR' was probably originated as a nickname for 'press relations,' " the primary activity of public relations in its early years (see Chapter 2).

Although PR is now more than press relations, the nickname is commonly used in daily conversation and is widely recognized around the world. A good compromise, which this book uses, is to adopt a style of spelling out "public relations" in the body of a text or article but to use the shorter term, "PR," if it is used in a direct quote.

How Public Relations Differs from Journalism

Writing is a common activity of both public relations professionals and journalists. Both also do their jobs in many of the same ways: They interview people, gather and synthesize large amounts of information, write in a journalistic style, and are trained to produce good copy on deadline. In fact, many reporters eventually change careers and become public relations practitioners.

This has led many people, including journalists, to the incorrect conclusion that little difference exists between public relations and journalism. For many, public relations is simply being a "journalist-in-residence" for a nonmedia organization.

However, despite the sharing of many techniques, the two fields are fundamentally different in scope, objectives, audiences, and channels.

Scope

Public relations, as stated earlier, has many components, ranging from counseling to issues management and special events. Journalistic writing and media relations, although important, are only two of these elements. In addition, effective practice of public relations requires strategic thinking, problem-solving capability, and other management skills.

Objectives

Journalists gather and select information for the primary purpose of providing the public with news and information. As Professors David Dozier and William Ehling explain, ". . . communication activities are an end in themselves." Public relations personnel also gather facts and information for the purpose of informing the public, but the objective is different. Communication activity is only a means to the end. In other words, the objective is not only to inform but to change people's attitudes and behaviors in order to further an organization's goals and objectives.

Whereas journalists are objective observers, public relations personnel are advocates. Harold Burson, chairman of Burson-Marsteller, makes the point:

> To be effective and credible, public relations messages must be based on facts. Nevertheless, we are advocates, and we need to remember that. We are advocates of a particular point of view—our client's or our employer's point of view. And while we recognize that serving the public interest best serves our client's interest, we are not journalists. That's not our job.

Audiences

Journalists write primarily for a mass audience—readers, listeners, or viewers of the medium for which they work. By definition, mass audiences are not well defined, and a journalist on a daily newspaper, for example, writes for the general public. A public relations professional, in contrast, carefully segments audiences into various demographic and psychological characteristics. Such research allows messages to be tailored to audience needs, concerns, and interests for maximum effect.

Channels

Most journalists, by nature of their employment, reach audiences through one channel—the medium that publishes or broadcasts their work. Public relations professionals use a variety of channels to reach the audiences previously described. The channels employed may be a combination of mass media outlets—newspapers, magazines, radio, and television. Or they may include direct mail, pamphlets, posters, newsletters, trade journals, special events, and posting messages on the Internet.

How Public Relations Differs from Advertising

Just as many people mistakenly equate publicity with public relations, there is also some confusion about the distinction between *publicity* (one area of public relations) and advertising.

Although publicity and advertising both utilize mass media for dissemination of messages, the format and context are different. Publicity—information about an event, an individual or group, or a product—appears as a news item or feature story in the mass media. Material is prepared by public relations personnel and submitted to the news department for consideration. Editors, known as *gatekeepers*, determine whether the material will be used or simply thrown away.

Advertising, in contrast, is paid space and broadcast time. Organizations and individuals typically contract with the advertising department of a mass media outlet for a full-page ad or a one-minute commercial. An organization writes the advertisement, decides the type and graphics, and controls where and when the advertisement will be run. In other words, advertising is simply renting space in a mass medium. The lion's share of revenue for all mass media comes from the selling of advertising space.

Other differences between public relations activities and advertising include:

- Advertising works almost exclusively through mass media outlets; public relations relies on a number of communication tools—brochures, slide presentations, special events, speeches, news releases, feature stories, and so forth.

- Advertising is addressed to external audiences—primarily consumers of goods and services; public relations presents its message to specialized external audiences (stockholders, vendors, community leaders, environmental groups, and so on) and internal publics (employees).

- Advertising is readily identified as a specialized communication function; public relations is broader in scope, dealing with the policies and performance of the entire organization, from the morale of employees to the way telephone operators respond to calls.

- Advertising is often used as a communication tool in public relations, and public relations activity often supports advertising campaigns. Advertising's function is to sell goods and services; the public relations function is to create an environment in which the organization can thrive. The latter calls for dealing with economic, social, and political factors that can affect the organization.

The major disadvantage of advertising, of course, is the cost. Typically, a full-page ad in *Parade* magazine, distributed weekly in almost 350 dailies, costs $421,000. Advertising campaigns on network television can run into the millions of dollars. For example, advertisers paid an average of $2.4 million for a Super Bowl ad in 2005. Because of this, companies are increasingly using a tool of public relations—product publicity—that is more cost effective and often more credible because the message appears in a news context. One national study, for example, found that almost 70 percent of consumers place more weight on media coverage than advertising when determining their trust of companies and buying a product or service.

How Public Relations Differs from Marketing

Public relations is distinct from marketing in several ways, although their boundaries often overlap.

The functions overlap, for example, because both deal with an organization's relationships and employ similar communication tools to reach the public. Both have the ultimate purpose of assuring an organization's success and economic survival. Public relations and marketing, however, approach this task from somewhat different perspectives or worldviews.

This difference is illustrated by the descriptions of each field that a distinguished panel of educators and practitioners in public relations and marketing developed during a colloquium at San Diego State University. After a day of debate, they formed this definition of public relations:

> Public relations is the management process whose goal is to attain and maintain accord and positive behaviors among social groupings on which an organization depends in order to achieve its mission. Its fundamental responsibility is to build and maintain a hospitable environment for an organization.

The group defined marketing's goal in different terms:

> Marketing is the management process whose goal is to attract and satisfy customers (or clients) on a long-term basis in order to achieve an organization's economic objectives. Its fundamental responsibility is to build and maintain markets for an organization's products or services.

In other words, public relations is concerned with building relationships and generating goodwill for the organization; marketing is concerned with customers and selling products and services.

James E. Grunig, editor of *Excellence in Public Relations and Communication Management*, put the differences between public relations and marketing in sharp contrast:

> . . . the marketing function should communicate with the markets for an organization's goods and services. Public relations should be concerned with all the publics of the organization. The major purpose of marketing is to make money for the organization by increasing the slope of the demand curve. The major purpose of public relations is to save money for the organization by building relationships with publics that constrain or enhance the ability of the organization to meet its mission.

In this passage, Grunig points out a fundamental difference between marketing and public relations in terms of how the public is described. Marketing and advertising professionals tend to speak of "target markets," "consumers," and "customers." Public relations professionals tend to talk of "publics," "audiences," and "stakeholders." These groups may be any publics that are affected by or can affect an organization. According to Grunig, "Publics can arise within stakeholder categories—such as employees, communities, stockholders, governments, members, students, suppliers, and donors, as well as consumers."

Public relations theorists point out another fundamental difference between public relations and marketing. In their view, "excellent" public relations is devoid of persuasion; its ideal purpose is to create mutual understanding and cooperation through two-way dialogue. Marketing, by definition, is persuasive in intent and purpose—to sell products and services. The four models of public relations are discussed in Chapter 2.

How Public Relations Supports Marketing

Philip Kotler, professor of marketing at Northwestern University and author of a leading marketing textbook, says public relations is the fifth "P" of marketing strategy, which includes four other Ps—Product, Price, Place, and Promotion. As he wrote in the *Harvard Business Review*, "Public relations takes longer to cultivate, but when energized, it can help pull the company into the market."

When public relations is used to support directly an organization's marketing objectives, it is called *marketing communications*. This was identified as a component of public relations earlier in the chapter. Another term, coined by Thomas Harris in his book *The Marketer's Guide to Public Relations*, is *marketing public relations*. He says:

> I make a clear distinction between those public relations functions which support marketing, which I call Marketing Public Relations (MPR) and the other public relations activities that define the corporation's relationships with its non-customer publics, which I label Corporate Public Relations (CPR).

Dennis L. Wilcox, in his text *Public Relations Writing and Media Techniques*, lists eight ways in which public relations activities contribute to fulfilling marketing objectives:

1. Developing new prospects for new markets, such as people who inquire after seeing or hearing a product release in the news media

2. Providing third-party endorsements—via newspapers, magazines, radio, and television—through news releases about a company's products or services, community involvement, inventions, and new plans

3. Generating sales leads, usually through articles in the trade press about new products and services

4. Paving the way for sales calls

5. Stretching the organization's advertising and promotional dollars through timely and supportive releases about it and its products

6. Providing inexpensive sales literature, because articles about the company and its products can be reprinted as informative pieces for prospective customers

7. Establishing the corporation as an authoritative source of information on a given product

8. Helping to sell minor products that don't have large advertising budgets

Harris summarizes:

> In its market-support function, public relations is used to achieve a number of objectives. The most important of these are to raise awareness, to inform and educate, to gain understanding, to build trust, to make friends, to give people reasons to buy and finally to create a climate of consumer acceptance.

Toward an Integrated Perspective

Although well-defined differences exist among the fields of advertising, marketing, and public relations, there is an increasing realization that an organization's goals and objectives can be best accomplished through an integrated approach.

This understanding gave rise in the 1990s to such terms as *integrated marketing communications*, *convergent communications*, and *integrated communications*. Don Schulz, Stanley Tannenbaum, and Robert Lauterborn, authors of *Integrated Marketing Communications*, explain the title of their book as follows:

> A concept of marketing communication planning that recognizes the added value of a comprehensive plan that evaluates the strategic roles of a variety of communication

disciplines—e.g., General Advertising, Direct Response, Sales Promotion, and Public Relations—and combines these disciplines to provide clarity, consistency, and maximum communication impact.

Several factors have fueled the trend toward integration. First is the downsizing and reengineering of organizations. Many of them have consolidated departments and have also reduced staff dedicated to various communication disciplines. As a result, one department, with fewer employees, is expected to do a greater variety of communication tasks.

Second, organizational marketing and communication departments are making do with tighter budgets. Many organizations, to avoid the high cost of advertising, look for alternative ways to deliver messages. These may include (1) building buzz word of mouth, (2) targeting influentials, (3) Web marketing, (4) grassroots marketing, (5) media relations and product publicity, and (6) event sponsorship.

Third is the increasing realization that advertising, with its high costs, isn't the silver bullet that it used to be. Part of the problem is the increasing clutter of advertising (one estimate is that the American consumer is exposed to 237 ads a day, or about 86,000 annually) and its general lack of credibility among consumers.

Al and Laura Ries, authors of the popular book (at least among public relations people) *The Fall of Advertising and The Rise of PR*, write, "We're beginning to see research that supports the superiority of PR over advertising to launch a brand. A recent study of 91 new product launches shows highly successful products are more likely to use PR-related activities than less successful ones." They go on to say, ". . . PR creates the brand. Advertising defends the brand."

Fourth, it is now widely recognized that the marketing of products and services can be affected by public and social policy issues. Environmental legislation influences packaging and the content of products, a proposed luxury tax on expensive autos affects sales of those cars, and a company's support of Planned Parenthood or health benefits for same-sex partners may spur a product boycott.

The impact of such factors, not traditionally considered by marketing managers, has led many professionals to believe that organizations should do a better job of integrating public relations and public affairs into their overall marketing considerations. In fact, David Corona, writing in the *Public Relations Journal* some years ago, was the first one to advance the idea that marketing's sixth "P" should be *public policy*.

ON THE JOB
insights

The Value of Public Relations in the Marketing Mix

PRWeek, in its annual survey of marketing executives, asked them to rate the effectiveness of *advertising, direct marketing*, and *public relations* in terms of accomplishing certain marketing objectives. The respondents rated public relations as the "most effective" in the following categories:

Premarket conditioning
Strategy development
Generating word-of-mouth
Message development
Building a brand's reputation
Building corporate reputation

Cultivating industry thought leaders
Overcoming a crisis

Direct marketing was rated most effective in (1) launching a new product/service, (2) promoting a new product/service, (3) acquiring customers, (4) retaining customers, and (5) targeting niche audiences. Advertising was rated most effective in only one category: building awareness.

Source: "Marketing Professionals Reveal the Role PR Plays in the Marketing Mix: Marketing Management Survey 2004." *PRWeek*, May 17, 2004, pp. 1, 13–21.

PR CASEBOOK

Microsoft Introduces XP

The headline in a major daily newspaper said it all: "XP hits street with plenty of hoopla." Microsoft's long-awaited XP operating system had its coming-out party during two days of special events in New York City, with the public relations objective of generating a great deal of media publicity.

Bill Gates, of course, was on hand to personally introduce and demonstrate his newest product at a Broadway theatre with 1,500 guests in attendance. A white-robed gospel choir sang

Microsoft chairman Bill Gates stands in Times Square, surrounded by Windows billboards, announcing the introduction of the XP operating system. A public relations campaign is often the first step in launching a new product.

"God Bless America" in front of the Windows blue-sky banner. New York mayor Rudolph Giuliani strode on stage with Gates to personally thank him for deciding to keep the product's coming-out party in New York after the September 11, 2001 terrorist attack on the World Trade Center. And there was even a concert by the rock singer Sting.

Afterwards, TV host Regis Philbin held a live video chat with Gates as the software mogul roamed around Times Square. There were also plenty of photo opportunities for the press; one picture that appeared in many dailies was of Gates playing a video game with a teenager at a local arcade. Meanwhile, a 1,200-pound cow lounged all day on a Manhattan street corner outside the Gateway Country retail shop, which just happened to be selling the new XP operating system.

Public relations techniques, such as events, are often used as part of a company's integrated marketing strategy to introduce a new product. The objective is to build awareness among the media, consumers, and the trade by generating excitement about the product. The XP introduction had a marketing budget of $200 million. The company, however, expected to sell 70 million copies of XP in the first year.

Jack Bergen, senior vice president of corporate affairs and marketing for Siemens Corporation, agrees. He told *PRWeek* that public relations is the best place for leading strategy in marketing. He continued, "In developing strategy, you have multiple stakeholders. PR people understand the richness of the audience that have an interest in the company; advertising just focuses on customers. Strategy is the development of options to accomplish an objective. PR people can develop these as they have the multiplicity of audiences and channels to use to reach them."

The concept of integration, therefore, is the increasing sophistication of organizations to use a variety of strategies and tactics to convey a consistent message in a variety of forms. The metaphor might be the golfer with a variety of clubs in her bag. She may use one club (public relations) to launch a product, another club (advertising) to reinforce the message, and yet another club (Web marketing) to actually sell the product or service to a well-defined audience. See the Insights box on page 20.

The concept of integration is less controversial than its implementation. It makes sense for an organization to coordinate its messages and communication strategies, but considerable discord arises on exactly how to accomplish this.

According to the consulting firm Osgood O'Donnell & Walsh, "The single biggest obstacle is company structure." In an article for *The Strategist*, the firm's principals wrote, "The communications functions—corporate communications, advertising, investor relations, and governmental affairs—are usually in different silos within companies, and interaction between their leaders is, for the most part voluntary (i.e., not required by senior management) and informal."

In other organizations, the marketing department is the dominant voice. Public relations is relegated to only a support function in terms of techniques instead of playing a role in overall strategy development. This often means that public relations is responsible only for tactical work such as creating product publicity, planning event promotions, and arranging media interviews at a trade show. Problems also arise when advertising agencies attempt to do integrated programs. In many cases, 90 percent of the budget is spent on advertising and 10 percent or less is spent on public relations. Patrick Sherwood, formerly CEO of D'Arcy North America, once summarized the ad agency approach to integration as follows: "The ad people take off and make a 30-second ad, and then invite other organizations in to see what they can do with the remaining budget."

Fortunately, such stories are becoming rarer as an increasing number of organizations emphasize the team approach to integrated communications. Experts in the various disciplines (advertising, public relations, direct promotion, marketing) now work as a team from the very beginning of a project. (See Figure 1.2.)

FIGURE 1.2

This illustration shows the interplay of messages and feedback in an integrated marketing communications campaign. The targeted database includes customers, media, and sales personnel.

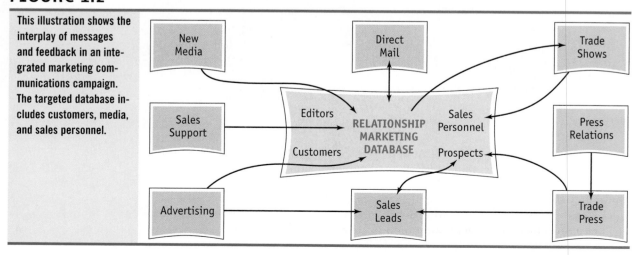

Careers in Public Relations

A person entering public relations may develop a career in numerous areas of this increasingly diverse field. Similarly, the variety of personal traits and skills that bring success is wide. Although certain abilities, such as writing well, are basic for all areas, experienced public relations practitioners may go on to develop increased skills in a particular practice area, such as investor relations, governmental affairs, or brand management.

A Changing Focus in Public Relations

Traditionally, it was widely believed that public relations practitioners should begin their careers as newspaper reporters or wire service correspondents to polish their writing skills and to learn firsthand how the media function. In an earlier era (see Chapter 2), a large percentage of public relations people did indeed have newspaper or broadcast experience. In fact, many of the leading pioneers in public relations were originally journalists.

This, however, is no longer true for several reasons. First, the field of public relations has broadened far beyond the concept of "media relations" and placing publicity in the mass media. Today, much writing in public relations is done for controlled media such as company publications, direct mail campaigns to key audiences, speech writing, brochures, and material posted on the organization's Web site. No media savvy or contacts are necessary. Writing skill and knowledge of the media are still vital, but so is training in management, logistics, event management, coalition building, budgeting, and supervision of personnel. Consequently, a *PRWeek* survey found that less than a third of current practitioners are former journalists.

Journalists still go into public relations, primarily for increased salaries and the opportunity to have a greater variety of job duties, but the successful ones must have the ability to adapt and be quick learners. Peter Himler, executive vice president of Burson Marsteller, told *PRWeek* that many journalists fail to make the switch to public relations. He said, "They may not come into the PR field knowing how to create consensus among clients and PR teams and, while they may know how to write, they may lack an understanding of how to use PR tools appropriately—when to use a press release, when to have a press conference, or when to use a video news release, for example."

The growth of public relations as a career field distinctly separate from journalism has spawned any number of public relations courses, sequences, and majors. The Commission on Public Relations Education, which includes public relations educators and representatives from all of the major professional organizations, has set the standard by saying that the ideal curriculum should have seven basic courses: (1) introduction to public relations, (2) case studies in public relations, (3) public relations research, measurement, and evaluation, (4) public relations writing and production, (5) public relations planning and management, (6) public relations campaigns, and (7) supervised public relations internship.

Increasingly, many universities are offering joint public relations/advertising programs, in part because of the growing trend in integrated marketing communications, which was discussed earlier in this chapter.

The 40th annual survey of programs, *Where Shall I Go to Study Advertising and Public Relations?* (www.whereshalligo.com) by Billy I. Ross of Louisiana State University and Keith F. Johnson of the University of Southern Mississippi, reported in 2004 that the number of advertising and public relations majors in the country totaled more than 43,000 students at almost 200 colleges and universities. These schools represented 279 programs: 95 in advertising, 136 in public relations, and 48 with joint advertising/public relations programs. About 18,000 undergraduates were majoring in public relations, which was a 7 percent increase from the previous year. At the graduate level, there were about 650 master's degree candidates and about 70 doctoral students.

Fortunately, the number of public relations jobs continues to increase as the field expands. The Bureau of Labor Statistics predicts a 31 to 35 percent increase in employment through 2008 for public relations specialists versus a 0 to 9 percent increase in journalism work. See the Insights box on page 25 for examples of public relations campaigns.

According to the experts, some specialty areas of public relations will be particularly "job-rich" over the next five years. The industry group most often cited is

ON THE JOB insights

Nine Ways Public Relations Contributes to the Bottom Line

It is often said that public relations is a management process, not an event. Patrick Jackson, active in the top leadership of the PRSA for many years and one of the best-known public relations counselors in the United States, formulated the following chart showing how public relations can contribute to the success of any organization.

PROCESS	PRINCIPAL ACTIVITIES	OUTCOMES
1. Awareness and information	Publicity, promotion, audience targeting, publications	Pave the way for sales, fundraising, stock offerings, etc.
2. Organizational motivation	Internal relations and communications, OD interventions	Build morale, teamwork, productivity, corporate culture; work toward One Clear Voice Outreach
3. Issue anticipation	Research, liaison with all publics, issue anticipation teams	Early warning of issues, social/political change, constituency unrest
4. Opportunity identification	Interaction with internal and external audiences, "knowing the business"	Discover new markets, products, methods, allies, positive issues
5. Crisis management	Respond to or blanket issues, disasters, attacks; coalition building	Protect position, retain allies and constituents, keep normal operations going despite battles
6. Overcoming executive isolation	Counseling senior managers about what's really happening, research	Realistic, competitive, enlightened decisions
7. Change agentry	Corporate culture, similar techniques, research	Ease resistance to change, promote smooth transition, reassure affected constituencies
8. Social responsibility	Social accountancy, research, mount public interest projects and tie-ins, volunteerism, philanthropy	Create reputation, enhance economic success through "double bottom line," earn trust
9. Influencing public policy	Constituency relations, coalition building, lobbying, grassroots campaigns	Public consent to activities, products, policies; political barriers removed

ON THE JOB insights

The Wonderful World of Public Relations

Public relations is an exciting field that offers variety, creativity, and the opportunity to work on any number of projects. Here's a sampling of projects and campaigns that required the expertise of public relations specialists.

Society for the Prevention of Cruelty to Animals (SPCA), Richmond, Virginia

The organization, through a public relations firm, organized the Fur Ball, a gala dinner/auction fundraiser, to provide financial support for its new 64,000-square-foot facility. Through effective media publicity and the event itself, almost $400,000 was raised to support the care of homeless animals.

Cold Stone Creamery

The popular ice cream company, through its public relations firm, generated extensive media publicity for the opening of its flagship store in New York's Times Square.

On the first day, lines ran out the doors and sales were 10 times that of the average operating store.

Statue of Liberty

After several years of being closed to the public, the Statue of Liberty in New York Harbor was opened to the public. The National Park Service hired a public relations firm to handle media previews and press coverage of the event.

Ford Mustang's 40th Anniversary

The Ford Motor Company planned a series of events across the country to celebrate the 40th anniversary of the classic car.

9/11 Commission

A major public relations firm was retained to generate public and political support for the recommendations of the 9/11 Commission, such as the creation of a

Cabinet-level intelligence czar and increasing U.S. defenses against terrorism. The Commission report, unlike most government documents, became a best seller.

Gillette Company

The new M3Power razor was launched with the help of a public relations firm that came up with the idea of having a popular Red Sox baseball player, with a real need for a shave, get rid of his beard at a public shaving. A thousand fans attended, and all the local media covered the event, creating local, and even national, coverage of the new product.

State of California

The California Department of Transportation enlisted the services of a public relations firm to conduct a 22-month campaign aimed at reducing litter on the state's highways and freeways. The theme: "Don't Trash California."

the pharmaceutical/biotechnology industry. The spotlight also is on financial services, media companies, health care, and security segments of the technology industry.

Belinda Hulin, writing in *Tactics*, notes "Knowing government protocols and procedures can provide an edge to both biotech and financial PR practitioners as Enronera scrutiny of public companies and their accounting practices has created a demand for such expertise."

Another expanding area of public relations practice is crisis communication counseling, but this is an area that requires considerable professional experience.

The Range of Public Relations Work

Women and men entering public relations may work in company departments, public relations firms that serve clients, or a wide range of organizations that require public relations services. The major areas of public relations work they will find include:

- **Corporations.** Departments seek to protect and enhance a company's reputation. They provide information to the public as well as to special audiences such as stockholders, financial analysts, and employees. Their work also includes community relations and often marketing communications.

- **Nonprofit organizations.** These range from membership organizations, such as trade and environmental associations, to social and cultural groups, hospitals, and other health agencies. Fund-raising often is involved.

- **Entertainment, sports, and travel.** Practitioners in these areas often are concerned with publicity for individuals and promotion of events ranging from football games to motion pictures.

- **Government and politics.** This area includes promotion of political issues, sometimes through lobbying, work with politicians, dissemination of information about government activities to citizens, and distribution of information about the armed forces.

- **Education.** At the college level, public relations people work primarily with alumni, faculty and administration, students, and the public to promote the school's image, recruit students, and raise funds. Secondary schools frequently have specialists to handle community relations.

- **International public relations.** The immense expansion of almost instantaneous global communications has opened an intriguing new area, especially for practitioners with language skills and familiarity with other cultures.

Detailed discussion of these areas appears in later chapters.

Personal Qualifications and Attitudes

Any attempt to define a single public relations type of personality is pointless, because the field is so diverse that it needs people of differing personalities. Some practitioners deal with clients and the public in person on a frequent basis; others work primarily at desks, planning, writing, and researching. Many do both.

Five Essential Abilities

Those who plan careers in public relations should develop knowledge and ability in five basic areas, no matter what area of work they enter. These are (1) writing skill, (2) research ability, (3) planning expertise, (4) problem-solving ability, and (5) business/economics competence.

1. Writing skill. The ability to put information and ideas onto paper clearly and concisely is essential. Good grammar and good spelling are vital. Misspelled words and sloppy sentence structure look amateurish. The importance of writing skill is emphasized in a career advice column in *Working Woman*: "I changed careers, choosing public relations as having the best potential, but found it difficult to per-

FIGURE 1.3

REQUIRED READING

The first thing I listen to is **CNN's American Morning** while I'm getting ready for work. On my commute, I feed my addiction to **NPR** by listening to **Bob Edwards**. When I arrive at the office, I pick up **The Wall Street Journal** and head for my website portal, where I look over news headlines from **The New York Times**, **AP**, and **Reuters**. Denver is fortunate enough to be a two-newspaper town, and I also scan both of our dailies—**The Denver Post** and **Rocky Mountain News**.

On weekends, **The Economist** and **The Sunday New York Times** are my media habits of choice. I catch up on celebrity gossip and lifestyle stories in the grocery store line with **People** and **Oprah**.

As far as the tube goes, if I'm home early enough, I love catching

NewsNight with Aaron Brown on **CNN**. I try to catch the Sunday morning news programs and **60 Minutes** and take a peek at what the latest reality TV show is.

Because I miss my Chicago girl-

friends, I was addicted to **Sex and the City** and nearly jumped for joy when I learned it's now in syndication. And because I miss seeing my mom, who lives in my Ohio hometown, I watch **Judging Amy** so I can see the mother/daughter team at work.

• *Dawn Doty is an account director with Linhart McClain Finlon Public Relations in Denver. Her accounts include the Colorado Department of Transportation, AAA Colorado, and Red Robin Gourmet Burgers.*

Public relations pros must be voracious consumers of media just to keep track of current events and situations that may affect their employers or clients. This feature, from *PRWeek*, shows what one public relations pro considers "Required Reading."

suade employers that my *writing and interpersonal skills* were sufficient for an entry-level job in the profession."

2. Research ability. Arguments for causes must have factual support instead of generalities. A person must have the persistence and ability to gather information from a variety of sources, as well as to conduct original research by designing and implementing opinion polls or audits. Too many public relations programs fail because the organization does not assess audience needs and perceptions. Skillful use of the Internet and computer databases is an important element of research work. Reading current newspapers and magazines also is important. See Figure 1.3.

3. Planning expertise. A public relations program involves a number of communication tools and activities that must be carefully planned and coordinated. A person needs to be a good planner to make certain that materials are distributed in a timely manner, events occur without problems, and budgets are not exceeded. Public relations people must be highly organized, detail-oriented, and able to see the big picture.

4. Problem-solving ability. Innovative ideas and fresh approaches are needed to solve complex problems or to make a public relations program unique and memorable. Increased salaries and promotions go to people who show top management how to solve problems creatively.

5. Business/economics competence. The increasing emphasis on public relations as a management function calls for public relations students to learn the "nuts and bolts" of business and economics. According to Joel Curren, senior vice president of CKPR in Chicago, "The greatest need PR people have is understanding how a business and, more importantly, how a public company operates." Elizabeth Allen, vice president of corporate communications for Dell Computer, agrees. She says, "You really have to be a business person first and a communicator second. If you don't understand the business, you can't make a direct link between business goals and what you're doing. Then you're just a fluffy publicist." In sum, students preparing for careers in public relations should obtain a solid grounding by taking elective courses in economics, management, and marketing.

It should be noted, of course, that all jobs in public relations don't require all five essential abilities in equal proportion. It often depends on your specific job responsi-

ON THE JOB insights

What Employers Want: 10 Qualities

PR Tactics, the monthly publication of the PRSA, asked job-placement experts what set of skills and experience was needed in today's employment market. Here are the top suggestions.

Good Writing

Excellent writing skills are more necessary now than ever before.

Intelligence

Although the descriptions vary from "bright," "clever," and "quick-witted," all placement executives agree that modern public relations isn't a refuge for those with a mediocre mind and only a good personality.

Cultural Literacy

Employers want individuals who are well rounded and well educated about the arts, humanities, and current events. According to *PR Tactics*, "You can't expect management to take your advice if you have no shared frame of reference."

Know a Good Story When You See One

The ability to manage your organization's image—in both large and small ways—starts with the identification and management of good stories that give the organization visibility, build brand recognition, and enhance the organization's reputation.

Media Savvy

Media convergence means that there are now multiple platforms—print media, Webcasts, Internet news sites, radio and television, and so on. Each platform has different deadlines, formats, and needs. Understanding this and being able to work with editors in each area is essential.

Contacts

"Cordial relationships with people in media, government, industry groups, and nonprofits, as well as colleagues in other companies will serve you well. The ability to pick up the phone and get crucial information or make things happen is essential."

Good Business Sense

The best companies weave public relations into their overall business strategy. To work at that level, however, public relations practitioners need to have a firm understanding of how the business operates in general and an employer's industry in particular.

Broad Communications Experience

All midlevel and senior positions require the individual to have familiarity with all aspects of communications, from the in-house newsletter to media relations and investor relations.

Specialized Experience

After getting some general experience, the individual should consider developing a specialty. Health care, finance, and technology are some of the promising areas.

Avoid Career Clichés

If the only reason for getting into the business is because you "like people" and enjoy organizing events, you should think about another field. Employers are looking for broad-based individuals with multiple communication and problem-solving skills.

Source: Hulin, Belinda. "10 Things You Need to Succeed in 2004—and Beyond." *Tactics*, April 2004, p. 11.

bilities and assignments. See the Insight box above for more tips from employment specialists.

Systematic research has shown that there is a hierarchy of roles in public relations practice. Professors Glen Broom and David Dozier of San Diego State University

ON THE JOB insights

Job Levels in Public Relations

- **Entry-Level Technician** Use of technical "craft" skills to disseminate information, persuade, gather data, or solicit feedback
- **Supervisor** Supervises projects, including planning, scheduling, budgeting, organizing, leading, controlling, and problem solving
- **Manager** Constituency and issue-trend analysis; departmental management, including organizing, budgeting, leading, controlling, evaluating, and problem solving
- **Director** Constituency and issue-trend analysis; communication and operational planning at departmental level, including planning, organizing, leading, controlling, evaluating, and problem solving
- **Executive** Organizational leadership and management skills, including developing the organizational vision, corporate mission, strategic objectives, annual goals, businesses, broad strategies, policies, and systems

Source: Adapted from the *Public Relations Professional Career Guide.* Public Relations Society of America, 33 Maiden Lane, New York, NY 10038.

were among the first researchers to identify organizational roles ranging from the communication technician to the communication manager.

Practitioners in the technician role, for example, are primarily responsible for producing communication products and implementing decisions made by others. They take photographs, write brochures, prepare news releases, and organize events. They function primarily at the "tactical" level of public relations work; they do not participate in policy decision making, nor are they responsible for outcomes. Many entry-level positions in public relations are at the technician level, but there are also many experienced practitioners whose specialty is "tactical" duties such as writing and editing newsletters, maintaining information on the company's intranet or Web site, or even working primarily with the media in the placement of publicity.

At the other end of the scale is the communication manager. Practitioners playing this role are perceived by others as the organization's public relations experts. They make communication policy decisions and are held accountable by others and themselves for the success or failure of communication programs. Managers counsel senior management, oversee multiple communication strategies, and supervise a number of employees who are responsible for "tactical" implementation.

Other studies conducted since Broom and Dozier's have indicated that the differences between managers and technicians aren't that clear-cut. In smaller operations, a public relations professional may perform daily activities at both the manager and the technician level.

Another way of looking at job levels in public relations is given in the Insights box on this page. In addition, see the AstraZeneca job ad (Figure 1.4) to see the kinds of skills and experience that employers are seeking.

FIGURE 1.4

This is a typical advertisement for a public relations manager and the qualifications that are sought in a candidate.

The Value of Internships

Internships are extremely popular in the communications industry, and a student whose résumé includes practical work experience along with a good academic record has an important advantage. The Commission on Public Relations Education believes the internship is so important that it is one of the seven basic courses it recommends for any quality college or university public relations curriculum.

An internship is a win-win situation for both the student and the organization. The student, in most cases, not only receives academic credit, but also gets firsthand knowledge of work in the professional world. This gives the student an advantage in getting that all-important first job after graduation. In many cases, recent graduates often are hired by their former internship employers because they have already proven themselves.

Indeed, *PRWeek* reporter Sara Calabro says:

Agencies and corporate communications departments are beginning to see interns as the future of their companies, not merely as gophers that they can pass the grunt work off to. While a few years ago, it was typical for an intern to work for nothing, it is almost unheard of for an internship to be unpaid these days. Examples of the essential work now entrusted to interns include tasks such as media monitoring, writing press releases, financial estimating, and compiling status reports. In many cases, interns are being included in all team and client meetings, as well as brainstorming sessions.

Many major public relations firms have formal internship programs. At Edelman Worldwide, for example, students enroll in "Edel-U," an internal training program

ON THE JOB insights

Public Relations Personality Checklist

This checklist, based on careful evaluation, can measure the effectiveness of your personality in terms of the public relations profession.

Rate each item "yes" or "no." Each "yes" counts for 4 points. A "no" doesn't count. Anything below 60 is a poor score. A score between 60 and 80 suggests you should analyze your weak areas and take steps to correct them. Scores above 80 indicate an effective public relations personality.

✓ Good sense of humor
___ Positive and optimistic
✓ Friendly, meet people easily

✓ Can keep a conversation going with anybody
___ Take frustration and rejection in stride
___ Able to persuade others easily
___ Well-groomed, businesslike appearance
___ Flair for showmanship
✓ Strong creative urge
✓ Considerate and tactful
✓ Adept in use of words
___ Able to gain management's confidence
___ Enjoy being with people
✓ Enjoy listening
✓ Enjoy helping other people resolve problems

✓ Curious about many things
✓ Enjoy reading in diverse areas
✓ Determined to complete projects
___ High energy level
✓ Can cope with sudden emergencies
___ See mistakes as learning experiences
✓ Factual and objective
✓ Respect other people's viewpoints
✓ Perceptive and sensitive
✓ Quickly absorb and retain information

Source: PRSSA Forum, Spring 1990.

that exposes them to all aspects of agency work. The summer internship program at Weber Shandick in Boston is called "Weber University." Calabro cites Jane Dolan, a senior account executive, who says that upper management is always incredibly impressed with the work that interns do for their final projects. "It is amazing to see them go from zero to 100 in a matter of months," says Dolan.

Hill & Knowlton also has an extensive internship training program in its New York office, taking about 40 interns a year from an applicant pool of about 600 to 700 students. In its view, the internship program is "the cheapest and most effective recruiting tool available." Ketchum also places great emphasis on finding outstanding interns and making sure they are actively involved in account work rather than spending most of their time running the photocopier or stuffing media kits.

It's not always possible, of course, for a student to do an internship in Chicago or New York. However, many opportunities are available at local public relations firms, businesses, and nonprofit agencies. It is important, however, that the organization have at least one experienced public relations professional who can mentor a student and ensure that he or she gets an opportunity to do a variety of tasks to maximize the learning experience.

Although national and international firms routinely pay interns, this is not usually the case at the local level. Many smaller companies claim that they cannot afford to pay an intern or that the opportunity to gain training and experience should be more than adequate compensation. Dave DeVries, a senior PR manager for the PCS Division of Sprint, disagrees. He wrote in PRSA's *Tactics*, "Unpaid internships severely limit the field of potential candidates" because, as he points out, the best and brightest students will always gravitate to employers who pay. Former *Fortune* 500 executive Tom Hagley also argued in *Tactics* that paying interns enables the student to focus effort and maintain high performance standards, resulting in an excellent return on any salary investment by the company.

Indeed, there seems to be a strong correlation between paid internships and starting salaries in the field. Most public relations firms and departments usually provide some level of paid internships, and entry-level salaries are comparatively high. On the other hand, television stations are notorious for not paying interns, and entry-level salaries are the lowest ($22,000) in the communications field. Salaries will be discussed shortly.

In sum, students should make a concentrated effort to negotiate paid internships. In general, these internships provide more meaningful experience and the employers have higher expectations.

Salaries in Public Relations

Public relations work pays relatively well compared to other communications professions. Many practitioners say they like the income and opportunities for steady advancement, and they also enjoy the variety and fast pace that the field provides.

Entry-Level Salaries

Several surveys have attempted to pinpoint the national average salary for recent graduates in their first full-time job in the public relations field. Probably the most definitive survey is the one conducted by Lee Becker and his associates at the University of Georgia. They work with journalism and mass communications programs throughout the nation to compile a list of recent graduates who are then surveyed (www.grady.uga.edu/annualsurveys/).

The latest data available, published in 2004, shows that the median annual salary for recent graduates working in public relations was $28,000. This is higher than the median national average for all communication fields, which is $26,000. The median yearly salaries reported by recent graduates for other communication fields are as follows:

Daily newspapers	$25,000
Weeklies	$24,000
Radio	$24,000
Television	$22,000
Cable television	$28,000
Advertising	$27,000
Consumer magazines	$25,000
Newsletters/trades	$27,000
World Wide Web	$32,000

ON THE JOB ethics

Problems with a Celebrity Endorser

The Slim-Fast Company has used actor Whoopi Goldberg as a celebrity endorser for several years. During the 2004 presidential campaign, Whoopi participated in a fundraiser at Radio City Music Hall for John Kerry in which she made some rather pointed criticisms of President George W. Bush.

After the event, a customer wrote the company complaining that Whoopi's remarks had offended him and wondered why Slim-Fast would use such a person as their spokesperson.

A customer relations representative wrote the following letter to the offended customer.

Dear Edwin

Thank you for contacting us recently about our use of Whoopi Goldberg, specifically regarding her remarks made at the recent fundraiser at Radio City Music Hall. The manner in which Ms. Goldberg chose to express her personal beliefs at this event do not reflect the views and values of Slim-Fast Foods Company.

Slim-Fast selected Whoopi Goldberg as its spokesperson because of her commitment to losing weight, which we applaud.

We are disappointed by the manner in which Ms. Goldberg chose to express herself and sincerely regret that her recent remarks offended you. Advertisements featuring Ms. Goldberg will no longer be on the air.

We appreciate you sharing your views with us and we hope you will continue to use Slim-Fast as your partner in healthy weight management.

What do you think of the company's response? Was it an ethical decision to withdraw the advertisements because of Whoopi's remarks as an individual, or did the company simply "cave in"? Does Whoopi have any ethical responsibility to the company to stay out of politics?

Another survey, conducted by *PRWeek*, places a more optimistic figure on starting salaries in public relations. Its 2004 survey of salaries, for example, found that entry-level salaries—professionals with less than two year's experience—averaged $33,506. The publication quotes one professor in the Minneapolis area saying that entry-level salaries ran from $32,000 to $36,000. Another recent graduate, now working for a public relations firm in the San Francisco area, said that entry-level salaries were about $30,000 to $35,000, despite some major downturns due to the sluggish U.S. economy.

Salaries for Experienced Professionals

Key components of *PRWeek*'s 2004 salary survey are listed in the Insights box on page 34, but the national average for all practitioners is about $63,000. Salaries are somewhat higher for those with 20 or more years experience. Men average $103,000 while women average about $81,000. Gender disparities in salary will be discussed shortly.

Salaries, of course, depend on a number of factors, including geographic location, job title, the industry, and even the type of public relations specialty. Major metropolitan areas, for example, generally have higher salaries, but there are some regional differences. Professionals get an average salary of $74,852 in New York, but $76,286

An Overview of Salaries in the Public Relations Field

PRWeek conducts an annual survey of salaries. The following tables are excerpted from its 2004 survey, which polled 2,546 practitioners in the field.

Average Overall Salaries

Total (Average)	$63,590
Men	$79,307
Women	$56,820
Men (age 21–26)	$36,571
Women (age 21–26)	$35,100
Men (age 27–30)	$59,146
Women (age 27–30)	$53,202

Salary by Job Title

Senior Vice President	$133,691
Executive Vice President	$107,222
Vice President	$106,624
Director/Managing Director	$90,914
Public Relations Manager	$64,007
Account Supervisor	$61,034
Senior Account Executive	$50,050
Account Executive/PR officer	$36,286

Salary by Sector

Utilities and Power	$80,650
Industry/Manufacturing	$79,191
Hi-Tech/Internet	$72,884
Financial Services	$71,469
Healthcare/Pharmaceuticals	$67,717
Food and Beverage	$65,250
Telecommunications	$59,733
Retail	$57,712
Government/Public Service	$57,230
Arts/Entertainment Media	$55,856
Travel	$53,477
Education	$52,252
Sports	$51,737
Nonprofit/Charity	$48,444

Salary by Public Relations Discipline

Crisis Management	$93,583
Financial/Investor Relations	$86,923
Reputation Management	$79,649
Brand Management	$66,969
Public Affairs/Governmental Relations	$65,479
International/External Communications	$66,205
Marketing Communications	$60,623
Community Relations	$44,596

Source: PRWeek, "Salary Survey 2004." February 23, 2004, pp. 15–21.

in Minneapolis and $82,759 in San Francisco. By the same token, professionals get an average salary of $62,229 in Denver, $61,773 in St. Louis, and $58,452 in Atlanta.

Job title also means a lot. A senior vice president gets an average of $133,691, whereas an account executive at a public relations firm gets $36,286. In addition, individuals who work for utility and power companies make an average of $80,650, but working for a nonprofit nets only $48,444. Some glamour areas, such as sports, also don't pay very well, comparatively speaking.

In terms of specialty areas, crisis management pays the most, with an average salary of $93,583, but financial/investor relations is close behind at $86,923. Community relations work pays the least, with an average salary of $44,596.

You should be aware that these salary figures are based on a poll of 2,546 practitioners, and the salaries reported may or may not be indicative of the entire field. For example, the average salary for crisis management was based on only 50 responses. The average salary for a senior vice president was based on 44 responses. In the absence of more complete salary data, however, surveys by publications such as *PRWeek* have become the standard reference in the industry.

The Arthur W. Page Society, a group of senior communication executives representing many of America's *Fortune* 500 corporations, also conducts an annual survey of its members regarding budgets and executive compensation. In general, compensation for the top communications officer in the organization ranges from $269,000 to almost $500,000. In general, salaries increase with the size of the corporation.

A good source for checking current salaries for public relations in major cities throughout the United States and around the world is www.workinpr.com. It posts current openings and also provides the salary ranges for various job classifications. In Minneapolis, for example, the salary range for a director of public relations is $101,000 to $137,000. The salary range for a public relations specialist, on the other hand, is $36,000 to $44,000.

Salaries for Women: The Gender Gap

The *PRWeek* survey clearly shows a gender gap in salaries across the board. The average salary for men was $79,307, whereas women made $56,820, or about 28 percent less than their male counterparts.

Indeed, this discrepancy in salaries exists across all age groups. The smallest gender gap was in the 21 to 26 age group, or at the entry level. Men earned more than a thousand dollars more than women, $36,571 versus $35,100. By ages 27 to 30, however, the gap becomes much more pronounced. Men earn an average of $59,146, compared to $53,202 for women. By the time men and women reach 41 to 50 years of age, the difference is $103,600 versus $80,926—a gap of about 22 percent.

The salary advantage for men over women is not unique to public relations. It is widespread in most of American business and throughout the world. The American Federation of Labor Congress of Industrial Organizations (AFL-CIO) reports that women continue to be paid about 75 cents for every dollar men receive, a figure that hasn't changed much over the past 10 years.

A number of studies have probed the pay differential between men and women in public relations. The first studies, starting in the 1980s, simply noted the gap without taking into consideration the multiple factors that could lead to discrepancies. Some of these factors included (1) the number of years in the field, (2) technician duties versus managerial responsibilities, (3) the nature of the industry, (4) the size of the organization, and (5) women's attempts to balance work and family.

Some studies, for example, concluded that women were relatively new to the field and didn't have the experience yet to compete with men who had been in the field for some years. Inherent in this finding was that women traditionally are assigned low-paying "technician" roles. Julie O'Neil, a professor at Texas Christian University, summarizes the conclusion of several studies in the *Journal of Public Relations Research*: "Women are segregated into the lower-level technician role, spending time on routine activities such as writing, editing, and handling media relations. Conversely, more men are promoted into the more powerful managerial role, engaging in such activities as counseling senior management, and making key policy decisions."

Others have tried to explain the salary differential in other ways. *PRWeek*, in its survey, pointed out that it found that its female respondents tended to take more time off than men to raise children or for other personal reasons. Others have pointed out that women have a tendency to work in areas of public relations that traditionally have low salaries, such as community relations, employee communications, or nonprofits. In contrast, a large percentage of practitioners in finance and investor relations—which pay well—are men.

Professors Linda Aldoory (University of Maryland) and Elizabeth Toth (formerly of Syracuse University and now at the University of Maryland) also explored discrepancies in salaries in an article for the *Journal of Public Relations Research* (2002). They explored a number of factors, but essentially concluded:

> The difference in the average salary of male respondents compared to female respondents was statistically significant. Regression analysis revealed that years of public relations experience accounted for much of the variance, but that gender and job interruptions also accounted for the salary difference. Age and education level were not found to be a significant influence on salary.

The role of women in public relations, and the increased feminization of the field (70 percent of the practitioners in the United States are women), will be discussed as a major trend line in the next chapter.

The Value of Public Relations

This chapter has outlined the size and global scope of public relations, provided some definitions, discussed the various activities of public relations, and explored how it differs from and is similar to journalism, advertising, and marketing. The case for an organization integrating all of its communications for maximum effectiveness has also been made. We've also discussed careers in public relations, the qualities needed in public relations professionals, and the salaries that can be earned in the field of public relations.

Today more than ever, the world needs not more information but sensitive communicators and facilitators who can explain the goals and aspirations of individuals, organizations, and governments to others in a socially responsive manner. Experts in communication and public opinion must provide their employers and clients with knowledge of what others are thinking to guide them in setting their policies for the common good.

Indeed, in this era of accountability and transparency, no organization exists solely for its own purposes; it must also serve society as a whole. Another way of expressing this point is the idea that no organization can exist without the express permission of its various publics.

Tom Glover, writing in *Profile*, the magazine of the Institute of Public Relations in the United Kingdom, believes "Clear and consistent communication helps organizations achieve their goals, employees to work to their potential, customers to make informed choices, investors to make an accurate assessment of an organization, and society to form fair judgments of industries, organizations, and issues."

Public relations provides businesses and society with a vital service. On a practical level, Laurence Moskowitz, chairman and CEO of Medialink, says that public relations is ". . . informative. It's part of the news, the program, the article, the stuff readers and viewers want. It's relevant. Positive messaging through the news lifts other forms of marketing, too. Good PR increases the effectiveness of ads, direct mail, sponsorship, and all other forms of 'permission' marketing."

PR CASEBOOK

Firestone versus Ford: An Epic Public Relations Battle

The reputation and credibility of a major corporation can be seriously damaged if it doesn't take the proper corrective action and public relations steps to solve a problem. Firestone/Bridgestone and Ford Motor Company learned this lesson the hard way.

Firestone had to recall 6.5 million of its tires after the National Highway Traffic Safety Administration (NHTSA) began investigating reports that 46 deaths and more than 300 accidents were linked to its tires. Later, it was determined that the number of deaths was actually 148, with an additional 525 injured. Of the tires recalled, more than 60 percent were used on Ford vehicles, primarily the Explorer.

Firestone's announcement followed basic public relations concepts. The company said that it was working closely with regulatory agencies, apologized for the lack of information in previous weeks before the recall, and made assurances that "nothing is more important to us than the safety of our customers." Ford, in the meantime, announced a separate public relations and advertising campaign notifying customers about possible tire problems with the Ford Explorer, but assuring them that the vehicles were completely safe.

Critics, including Congressional investigators, challenged both Firestone's and Ford's assertions that they were doing everything possible to ensure the safety of their customers. Ford, for example, continued to use Firestone tires on their vehicles, even though evidence suggested that Ford knew the tires were subject to blow out on vehicles that already had a reputation for instability and rolling over.

Firestone was also criticized for the way it handled the public relations element of the recall. Paul Hicks, head of corporate practice at Ogilvy Public Relations, said "I have yet to see a senior officer from the parent company quoted in any fashion. It's a grievous error in strategy that will cost them millions, if not hundreds of millions in the long run."

In addition, Firestone committed another public relations blunder before the voluntary recall because it tried to blame the consumer. Company spokespersons said the tires shredded or peeled because consumers didn't maintain proper inflation and drove on poor roads. As Paul Holmes of *Inside PR* pointed out, "By blaming the consumers, the company appeared to be shirking its own responsibility for the problem."

Although Firestone seemed to come across as highly defensive, Ford decided on a more proactive public relations strategy. In addition to using Ford's CEO as a major spokesperson on the crisis, about 30 members of the company's internal public relations staff worked on the automaker's crisis team. Ford PR chief Jason Vines was widely quoted, and Ford announced that new purchasers of Ford Explorers could choose any brand of tire they wanted.

The stakes for both Firestone and Ford were extremely high. Both companies saw a decline in sales of its products, and stock prices plunged as a result of both companies spending almost $1.3 billion on the recall. Bridgestone shareholders saw two-thirds of their stock value vanish practically overnight, whereas Ford experienced a $4 billion loss in shareholder value. Both companies were highly vulnerable to multiple lawsuits, and it was important to wage defense in the court of public opinion, which could have some impact on the number of lawsuits filed and the predisposition of juries to award large damages.

(continued)

PR CASEBOOK *(continued)*

Ford's public relations strategy was relatively simple. It understood that it was necessary to allay customer's concerns as well as those of Congressional investigators, so the legal department's intent to paint Firestone as the responsible party was highly supported. Firestone took major exception to Ford projecting itself as the "good guy." The stage was set for an epic public relations battle for the hearts and minds of the American consumer.

Firestone used reports, surveys, and statistics to make the case that Ford had known for several years that the Explorer was unstable and subject to rollover in the case of a tire blowout. Ford countered by trotting out internal memos from Firestone about the failure rate of its tires and noting that the company had opposed Ford's recall of Explorers with Firestone tires in other nations. Firestone raised the ante by announcing at a news conference that it would no longer do business with the automaker.

Ford then announced that it would spend between about $3 billion of its own money to replace Firestone tires on its Explorer model. It again blamed Firestone for any problems, but it had its own public relations problems in trying to explain new design changes in the Explorer without admitting that the older models were unsafe.

Public relations experts thought the "finger-pointing" and the "blame game" were not effective strategies for either company. One public

The expression of public opinion affects the corporate reputation of a company. Here, a woman lets everyone know that she is unhappy with the Firestone tires on her vehicle after it was announced that the tires had a high rate of failure on Ford Explorers.

relations veteran said, "This is a no-win for both sides. The more they fight, the more uncertain the public becomes." Indeed, one opinion poll indicated that Firestone had made some headway in eroding consumer confidence in Ford, but its own corporate reputation and consumer confidence continued to be at an all-time low.

Both Firestone and Ford, several years after the tire recall, have yet to regain the consumer confidence they had before what one newspaper called "one of the biggest and deadliest auto safety problems in U.S. history."

Patrick Jackson, a former president of the PRSA and publisher of *PR Reporter*, said it best:

> As soon as there was Eve with Adam, there were relationships, and in every society, no matter how small or primitive, public communication needs and problems inevitably emerge and must be resolved. Public relations is devoted to the essential function of building and improving human relationships.

SUMMARY

Global Scope

Public relations is well established in the United States and throughout the world. Growth is strong in Europe and Asia, particularly China.

A Variety of Definitions

Common terms in most definitions of public relations are *deliberate, planned, performance, public interest, two-way communication*, and *management function*. Also popular is the concept of building and maintaining mutually beneficial relationships.

Public Relations as a Process

The public relations process can be described with the RACE acronym: *Research, Action, Communication, Evaluation*. The process is a constant cycle; feedback and program adjustment are integral components of the overall process.

The Components of Public Relations

Public relations work includes the following components: *counseling, media relations, publicity, community relations, governmental affairs, employee relations, investor relations, development/fund-raising, special events*, and *marketing communications*.

Other Terms for Public Relations

Public relations is an umbrella term; many large organizations prefer such terms as *corporate communications, corporate affairs, public affairs*, or even *global communications* to describe the public relations function. Less flattering terms include *flack* and *spin doctor*.

How Public Relations Differs from Journalism

Although writing is an important activity in both public relations and journalism, the scope, objectives, and channels are different for each field.

How Public Relations Differs from Advertising

Publicity, one area of public relations, uses mass media to disseminate messages, as does advertising. The format and context, however, differ. Publicity goes through media gatekeepers that make the ultimate decision whether to use the material as part of a news story. Advertising involves paid space and time and is easily identified as being separate from news/editorial content.

How Public Relations Differs from Marketing

The functions of public relations often overlap with marketing, but the primary purpose of public relations is to build relationships and generate goodwill with a variety of publics. Marketing focuses on customers and the selling of products/services. Public relations can be part of a marketing strategy; in such cases, it is often called *marketing communications*.

Toward an Integrated Perspective

An organization's goals and objectives are best achieved by integrating the activities of advertising, marketing, and public relations to create a consistent message. Integration requires teamwork and the recognition that each field has strengths that complement and reinforce one another.

The Changing Face of Public Relations

In the past, those entering public relations were often former journalists, but that is no longer the case because public relations has evolved beyond publicity and media relations. In addition, public relations is now widely recognized as its own distinct academic discipline in colleges and universities throughout the world.

The Range of Work

Public relations professionals are employed in a variety of fields: corporations, nonprofits, entertainment and sports, politics and government, education, and international organizations and businesses.

Five Essential Abilities

Those who plan careers in public relations should have the following abilities: *writing skill, research ability, planning expertise, problem-solving ability*, and *business/economic competence*.

Internships are Valuable

Students should participate in internships throughout college as part of their preprofessional training in public relations.

Salaries in Public Relations

Entry-level salaries are higher in public relations than in many other communications fields. A person with one or two years' experience can earn a salary in the mid-30s, whereas a more experienced professional can earn into the six figures. Although the gender gap has somewhat narrowed, in general women earn less than men.

The Value of Public Relations

The world today doesn't need more information; it needs sensitive, well-educated individuals who can interpret the information and determine why and how it is relevant to people's lives. Public relations people must explain the goals and objectives of their clients and employers to the public and, at the same time, provide them with guidance about their responsibility to the public interest.

Case Activity: **What Would You Do?**

Cold Stone Creamery is a relatively new ice cream company that faces stiff competition in the marketplace from such established brands as Ben & Jerry's, Baskin-Robbins, and Häagen-Dazs.

The first store was established in Tempe, Arizona, in 1998. Since then, the company has expanded to more than 500 stores (franchises) nationwide. Its market niche is that customers can personalize their serving by choosing a base flavor and then mixing it with a number of toppings. Employees do the mixing by hand on a frozen granite stone (hence the company name).

The challenge, of course, is to generate more store revenue and to increase market share. Research shows that the typical Cold Stone customer is a woman between the ages of 24 and 35, but that she also brings her friends and other family members with her.

The company has decided to do an integrated communications program for the next year that would involve *public relations, advertising*, and *in-store marketing promotions* for some new products, such as ice cream cakes and nonfat flavors. The focus would be on enhancing the visibility of its stores at the local level and making it a distinct brand among the clutter of other ice cream franchises in the community. Do some brainstorming. What ideas and activities would you suggest? You have to be creative because you don't have a big budget.

QUESTIONS for Review and Discussion

1. How many people are estimated to work in public relations around the world? Is public relations growing as a field in terms of employees and revenues?

2. There are many definitions of public relations. Of those listed, which one do you prefer? Why?

3. Review the Insights box on the European Perspective on Public Relations. Do the four points reinforce other concepts (primarily American) of public relations, or do you see some major differences?

4. What key words and phrases are found in most definitions of public relations?

5. What does the acronym *RACE* stand for?

6. Public relations is described as a loop process. What component makes it a loop rather than a linear process?

7. Review the official statement on public relations by the PRSA. In what way did it change your initial perception of public relations as a field?

8. What are the components of basic public relations practice? Which one sounds the most interesting to you as a possible career specialty?

9. What other terms are used by organizations to describe the public relations function? Do you have any preference for any of them? Explain.

10. How do you think portrayals of various careers in films and television shows shape public perceptions? Do you think series like *Sex and the City* paint a negative or positive image of public rela-

tions as a career? Or do such portrayals make public relations appear to be more glamorous than it actually is?

11. What is *spin*? To some, it has negative connotations that conjure up images of manipulation and dishonesty. To others, it's simply a slang word for telling the organization's perspective on an issue or product. What do you think? Would you like to be called a "spin doctor"?

12. Do you consider "PR" to be a slang term that should be avoided? Why or why not?

13. How does public relations differ from the fields of journalism, advertising, and marketing?

14. How does public relations support marketing? Some experts say that public relations can launch a new product or service better than advertising. Do you agree or disagree? It's also asserted that public relations creates brands, and that advertising can only reinforce and defend a brand. What are your thoughts?

15. What is the concept of *integrated communications*, which some people also call *integrated marketing communications* (IMC)? What four factors have led to the growth of integrated campaigns?

16. The casebook discusses the Firestone versus Ford tire-recall controversy. What company probably did the best job at public relations?

17. The text says that former journalists often don't make a good transition to public relations work. What reasons were given as to why this is so?

18. Public relations people work for a variety of organizations. What type of organization would you prefer if you wanted to work in public relations?

19. The text mentions five essential qualities for working in public relations. On a scale of 1 to 10, how would you rate yourself on each ability?

20. Several job listings are illustrated in the chapter. Are there any common themes that run through them in terms of what employers are seeking?

21. Why is it important for a student to complete an internship in college? Do you think interns should be paid?

22. Job placement directors say that employers are looking for 10 qualities in applicants. Can you name at least 5 of the 10 qualities?

23. Discuss entry-level salaries in public relations. Do you think they are too low, or are they about what you expected? What about the salaries for experienced professionals?

24. Is there still a gender gap in salaries? If so, do you think that it is caused by overt discrimination or do other factors explain the salary gap?

SUGGESTED READINGS

Blaney, Joseph R., Benoit, William L., and Brazeal, LeAnn. "Blowout! Firestone's Image Restoration Program." *Public Relations Review*, Vol. 28, No. 4, 2002, pp. 379–392.

Bowen, Shannon A. "I Thought It Would Be More Glamorous; Perceptions and Misconceptions Among Students in the Public Relations Principles Course." *Public Relations Review*, Vol. 29, No. 2, 2003, pp. 199–214.

Calabro, Sara. "Poll Says People Base Trust on Media over Advertising." *PRWeek*, August 23, 2003, p. 5.

Calabro, Sara. "Jump-starting the Juniors: Working with Interns." *PRWeek*, October 29, 2001, p. 28.

Chu, Kenneth. "Dynamic Growth in China's PR Industry." *The Strategist*, Winter 2004, pp. 44–46.

Deptolla, Carol. "Looking for a Few Good Careers." *Writer*, April 2002, pp. 34–40. (U.S. Bureau of Labor Statistics projections for careers in communications.)

DeVries, Dave. "Paid Internships: Why They're Worth the Cost." *Tactics*, March 2003, p. 11.

Frank, John N. "Learning the Business: Today's PR Students Need to Know How Businesses Communicate and How They Work." *PRWeek*, March 29, 2004, p. 15.

Frisina, Ellen Tashie. "Addressing the 'Sex and the City' Syndrome." *Tactics*, August 2003, p. 19.

Gordon, Andrew. "Winning Teams: Integrated Marketing Is More than a Vague Concept or a Buzzword." *PRWeek*, March 29, 2004, p. 17.

Hulin, Belinda. "Where the Jobs Are." *Tactics*, April 2004, p. 10.

Mogel, Leonard. *Making It in Public Relations: An Insider's Guide to Career Opportunities*. Mahwah, NJ: Lawrence Erlbaum, 2002.

Molleda, Juan-Carlos. "Partners in an Alliance with a Global Reach." *The Strategist*, Winter 2004, pp. 48–51.

"Paying to Avoid Ads: It's Getting Harder to Reach Consumers." *Economist*, August 7, 2004, p. 52.

Quenqua, Douglas. "Survey Predicts 8 Percent Climb for PR Spending by 2008." *PRWeek*, August 9, 2004, p. 1.

Ruler, Betteke van, Vercic, Dejan, Butschi, Gerhard, and Flodin, Bertil. "A First Look for Parameters of Public Relations in Europe." *Journal of Public Relations Research*, Vol. 16, No. 1, 2004, pp. 35–63.

Somerick, Nancy M. "A Practical Approach That Can Help Organizations Recruit and Select Public Relations Interns." *Public Relations Quarterly*, Spring 2004, pp. 44–45.

Trickett, Eleanor. "Marketing Management Survey Reveals More Opportunity for PR Pros." *PRWeek*, May 17, 2004, p. 1. (This issue also contains the full results of the Marketing Management Survey, pp. 14–21.)

Trickett, Eleanor. "New Era for Integration." *PRWeek*, June 23, 2003, p. 15.

Walsh, Larry, O'Donnell, Joe, and Osgood, Peter. "Integrated Communications: Frequently Discussed, Seldom Realized." *The Strategist*, Winter 2004, pp. 56–58.

Warschawski, David. "PR Is Assuming Top Status in the Brand-building Arena." *PRWeek*, April 28, 2003, p. 8.

Weidlich, Thom. "Salary Survey Reveals Steep Drop in 2003 PR Paychecks." *PRWeek*, February 28, 2004, p. 1. (This issue contains survey report on salaries, pp. 15–20.)

chapter **2**

The Evolution
of Public Relations

Topics covered in this chapter include:

A Short History of Public Relations

The practice of public relations is probably as old as human communication itself. In many ancient civilizations, such as those of Babylonia, Greece, and Rome, people were persuaded to accept the authority of government and religion through common public relations techniques: interpersonal communication, speeches, art, literature, staged events, publicity, and other such devices. None of these endeavors were called public relations, of course, but the purpose and effect were often the same as today's modern practice.

Ancient Beginnings

It has often been said that the Rosetta Stone, which provided the key to modern understanding of ancient Egyptian hieroglyphics, was basically a publicity release touting the Pharaoh's accomplishments. Similarly, the ancient Olympic Games used promotional techniques to enhance the aura of athletes as heroes in much the same way as the 2004 Athens games. Even speech writing in Plato's time was similar to speech writing today. The speechwriter must know the composition of the audience, never talk down to it, and impart information that is credible and persuasive.

Julius Caesar was probably the first politician to publish a book, *Commentaries*, which he used to further his ambitions to become emperor of the Roman Empire. He also organized elaborate parades whenever he returned from a successful battle to burnish his image as an outstanding commander and leader. After Caesar became a consul of Rome in 59 B.C., he had clerks make a record of senatorial and other public proceedings and post them on walls throughout the city. These *Acta Diurna*, or "Daily Doings," were probably one of the world's first newspapers. Of course Caesar's activities got more space than his rivals.

Saint Paul, the New Testament's most prolific author, also qualifies for the public relations hall of fame. In fact, R. E. Brown of Salem State College says, "Historians of early Christianity actually regard Paul, author and organizer, rather than Jesus himself, as the founder of Christianity." He goes on to quote James Grunig and Todd Hunt, who wrote in *Managing Public Relations*:

> It's not stretching history too much to claim the success of the apostles in spreading Christianity through the known world in the first century A.D. as one of the great public relations accomplishments of history. The apostles Paul and Peter used speeches, letters, staged events, and similar public relations activities to attract attention, gain followers, and establish new churches. Similarly, the four gospels in the New Testament, which were written at least 40 years after the death of Jesus, were public relations documents, written more to propagate the faith than to provide a historical account of Jesus' life.

The Middle Ages

The Roman Catholic Church was a major practitioner of public relations throughout the Middle Ages. Pope Urban II persuaded thousands of followers to serve God and gain forgiveness of their sins by engaging in the Holy Crusades against the Muslims. Six centuries later, the church was among the first to use the word *propaganda*, with the establishment by Pope Gregory XV of the College of Propaganda to supervise foreign missions and train priests to propagate the faith.

Meanwhile, in Venice, bankers in the 15th and 16th centuries practiced the fine art of investor relations and were probably the first, along with local Catholic bishops, to adopt the concept of corporate philanthropy by sponsoring such artists as Michelangelo.

Early Beginnings in America

The United States was first settled by immigrants, primarily those from England, and various land companies with a license from the Crown actively promoted colonization to generate revenues from what the colonists were able to manufacture or grow. In other words, colonization in many cases was strictly a commercial proposition. The Virginia Company in 1620, for example, distributed flyers and brochures throughout Europe offering 50 acres of free land to anyone willing to migrate.

An early example of promotion in the New World was Sir Walter Raleigh's attempts to convince settlers to move to Virginia. In 1584, Raleigh sent back glowing accounts to England of what was actually a swamp-filled Roanoke Island. Eric the Red did the same thing back in 1000 A.D. when he discovered a land of ice and rock and named it Greenland. The Spanish explorers publicized the never-discovered Seven Cities of Gold and even the fabled Fountain of Youth to attract willing participants for further exploration and colonization.

After the American colonies were well established, publicity and public relations techniques were used to promote various institutions. In 1641, Harvard College published a fund-raising brochure. King's College (now Columbia University) issued its first news release in 1758, which announced its commencement exercises.

Public relations also played an active role in American independence. The Boston Tea Party, which *PRWeek* has called the "... the greatest and best-known publicity stunt of all time ...," was the inspiration of Samuel Adams, a man with a refined sense of how symbolism can sway public opinion. The colonists threw crates of tea leaves from a British trade ship into Boston harbor to protest excessive British taxation, and the rest is history. Adams and his colleagues also labeled the killing of several colonists by British troops at a demonstration as the "Boston Massacre" and further persuaded the American colonists to revolt against Great Britain.

Also instrumental in bringing lukewarm citizens into the Revolutionary movement was Tom Paine's *Common Sense*; more than 120,000 copies of the pamphlet were sold in three months. Influencing the makeup of the new political system were the *Federalist Papers*, which comprised 85 letters written by Alexander Hamilton, James Madison, and John Jay.

American Development in the 19th Century

The 1800s was a period of growth and expansion in the United States. It also was the golden age of the press agent, which *Webster's New World Dictionary* defines as "a person whose work is to get publicity for an individual, organization, etc." The period was also the age of *hype*, which is the shrewd use of the media and other devices to promote an individual, a cause, or even a product or service, such as a circus.

Press agents were able to glorify Davy Crockett as a frontier hero to draw political support from Andrew Jackson, attract thousands to the touring shows of Buffalo Bill and sharpshooter Annie Oakley, make a legend of frontiersman Daniel Boone, and promote hundreds of other personalities.

ON THE JOB global

The Beginnings of Public Relations in Other Nations

The British scholar J. A. R. Pimlott once wrote, "Public relations is not a peculiarly American phenomenon, but it has nowhere flourished as in the United States. Nowhere else is it so widely practiced, so lucrative, so pretentious, so respectable and disreputable, so widely suspected, and so extravagantly extolled."

It's important to realize, however, that other nations have their own histories. The following is a representative sample.

Germany

Railroads and other large business enterprises began publicity efforts as far back as the mid-19th century. Alfred Krupp, who founded the Krupp Company, the premier industrial firm in Germany and eventually the base of the Nazi war power, wrote in 1866, "We think . . . it is time that authoritative reports concerning factory matters, in accordance with the facts should be propagated on a regular basis through newspaper reports which serve an enlightened public."

Great Britain

The Marconi Company, a world leader in wireless telegraphy, established a department in 1910 to distribute news releases about its achievements and operations. In 1911, the first government public relations campaign was launched by the Insurance Commission to explain the benefits of the National Insurance Act, an unpopular measure that had attracted much adverse publicity.

The Air Ministry appointed the first government press officer in 1919, and a year later the Ministry of Health selected Sir Basil Clarke, a former Reuters correspondent, as director of information. By 1922, the government launched the British Broadcasting Service (BBC) as a way to communicate British values and viewpoints to its colonies and other nations.

Professional public relations counseling for business was introduced in the country in 1924, when Sir Basil Clarke, a former government press officer, established a firm in London. For his first client, a dairy group, he promoted the idea of milk pasteurization, an innovation that had met with some resistance from the public. A year later, Sir John Elliott was appointed a public relations officer of the Southern Railway Company.

Australia

Public relations in Australia largely consisted of publicity efforts until after World War II. When U.S. General Douglas MacArthur arrived after his escape from Corregidor in 1942, he introduced the term *public relations* and, with a highly skilled staff, demonstrated numerous ways of promoting his image and the war effort.

The industry grew steadily and, in 1960, the Public Relations Institute of Australia (PRIA) was formed. Notable practitioners have included George Fitzpatrick, credited with being the first Australian to conduct public relations, and Eric White who, according to one source, "virtually created the public relations industry" in Australia. As early as the 1960s, White oversaw extensions of his firm to six Pacific Rim countries.

Taiwan

In Taiwan, as in many nations, the government was the first entity to utilize public relations tactics. In the 1950s, the Taiwanese government used public relations to conduct "nation building." Several government information offices were formed to release government news to

ON THE JOB global, *continued*

the public. The Public Relations Foundation, a professional body of practitioners, was established in 1956. In 1958, the group announced a policy for government agencies and private organizations to promote public relations. One of the organization's vehicles is *Public Relations Magazine*, which is used to promote professionalism in the field.

Philippines

The public relations industry in the Philippines was transplanted from the West in the 1940s. In fact, the country is considered the "Pacific birthplace of public relations." U.S. Army public information officers regularly issued news releases to the Philippine press during World War II. After the war, the concept spread to local businesses, and the Business Writers Association of the Philippines was organized to promote the idea of corporate social responsibility.

Notable of the early Filipino pioneers are Pete Teodoro and Jose Carpio. Teodoro, then public relations director of Elizalde & Company, a paint manufacturer, is credited with undertaking the first organized public relations campaign to generate goodwill and business from local contractors and architects. Carpio managed the country's first association campaign. He helped a business association restore a favorable investment climate in the country.

In 1966, the San Miguel Corporation, one of the country's largest and most famous companies, known worldwide for its San Miguel beer, established the first public relations department.

Spain

The growth of public relations in Spain started in the 1950s and paralleled political, economic, and media developments in Spain. An advertising agency, Danis Advertising of Barcelona, launched a public relations campaign in 1955 to build community goodwill for a corporate client and its product. One of the directors of that campaign, Joaquin Maestre, started his own public relations firm in 1960. According to one historian, the advent of public relations consultancies, "marked the beginning of a 'dynamic consumer market' for public relations services, which led to setting up the first public relations agencies as a direct response to the 'market demand for services.' "

The Russian Federation

The collapse of the Soviet Union in 1991 ushered in a free-market economy and democratic reforms that caused the rapid growth of the public relations field in government and private business. With the new openness, global companies began selling products and services in the new Russia with the assistance of Western-style advertising, public relations, and promotion.

In addition, Russian companies began to understand the importance of publicizing their products and services. Before that time, most "public relations" was conducted by the government. In the mid-1990s, a Russian association of public relations professionals was organized to promote standards and provide continuing education. Most observers think public relations will develop as the economy stabilizes and democratic institutions become stronger.

Thailand

Public relations in Thailand, as in many nations, dates back to the 1950s. Esko Pajasalmi from Finland is credited with starting the first public relations firm. He started his firm, Presko, after serving more than a decade as a Christian missionary in northern Thailand. Presko eventually became that nation's largest public relations firm and set the standard for other firms that followed.

One early Presko campaign was for Colgate-Palmolive, after its toothpaste was falsely accused of containing pork fat. The Muslim community was horrified, and Colgate immediately lost 100 percent of the market in southern Thailand. Pajasalmi contacted Muslim leaders and took them to inspect the factories, managing to convince them that the rumors were unfounded. Business boomed again.

Phineas T. Barnum, a master of "hype," created pseudo-events, such as the beautiful baby show promoted in this poster. Notice how it appeals to two human instincts: the desire to win money and to look at something unusual such a triplets and quaterns (called quadruplets in modern usage).

These old-time press agents and the show people they most often represented played on the credulity of the public in its longing to be entertained. Advertisements and press releases were exaggerated to the point of being outright lies. Doing advance work for an attraction, the press agent dropped tickets on the desk of a newspaper editor, along with the announcements. Voluminous publicity generally followed, and the journalists and their families flocked to their free entertainment with scant regard for the ethical constraints that largely prohibits such practices today.

Small wonder then that today's public relations practitioner, exercising the highly sophisticated skills of evaluation, counseling, communications, and influencing management policies, shudders at the suggestion that public relations grew out of press agentry. And yet some aspects of modern public relations have their roots in the practice.

The Ultimate Showman. Phineas T. Barnum, the great American showman of the 19th century, was the master of what historian Daniel Boorstin calls the *pseudoevent*, which is a planned happening that occurs primarily for the purpose of being reported. Barnum, who was born in 1810, used flowery language and exaggeration to promote his various attractions in an age when the public was hungry for any form of entertainment.

Thanks to Barnum, Tom Thumb became one of the sensations of the century. He was a midget, standing just over two feet and weighing 15 pounds, but he was exceptional at singing, dancing, and performing comedy monologues. Barnum made a public relations event of the marriage of General Tom Thumb to another midget. He even got extensive European booking for Thumb by introducing him first to society leaders in London, who were enchanted by him. An invitation to the palace followed, and from then on Thumb played to packed houses every night. Barnum, even in his day, knew the value of third-party endorsement.

Another Barnum success was the promotion of Jenny Lind, the "Swedish Nightingale." Lind was famous in Europe, but no one in America knew about her beautiful voice until Barnum took her on a national tour and made her a pop icon even before the Civil War. He obtained full houses on opening nights in each community by donating part of the proceeds to charity. As a civic activity, the event attracted may of the town's opinion leaders, whereupon the general public flocked to attend succeeding performances—a device still employed today by entertainment publicists.

Westward Expansion.   Throughout the 19th century, publicity and promotion helped to populate the western United States. Land speculators distributed pamphlets and publicity that described almost every community as "the garden spot of the West," which one critic of the time called "downright puffery, full of exaggerated statements, and high-wrought and false-colored descriptions." One brochure about Nebraska, for example, described the territory as the "Gulf stream of migration . . . bounded on the north by the 'Aurora Borealis' and on the south by the Day of Judgment." Other brochures were more down-to-earth, describing the fertile land, the abundant water, and the opportunity to build a fortune.

American railroads, in particular, used extensive public relations and press agentry to attract settlers and expand operations. As Andy Piasecki, lecturer at Queen Margaret University College in Edinburgh describes it:

> The expansion of the railroads was dependent on publicity and promotion. This is hardly surprising that any investment in western expansion was dependent on finding a population. Many railroad companies were colonization agencies as much as they were transport companies. Without people, no railroads could be sustained and because there were, at this time, few people out West, they had to be brought in. . .

Consequently, such companies as the Burlington and Missouri Railroad took it upon themselves to promote Western settlement from England and other places. The Burlington and Missouri Railroad set up an information office in Liverpool that distributed fact sheets and maps and placed stories in the local press. In addition, the railroad promoted lectures about migrating to the American West. According to Piasecki, "The *pièce de resistance* for the Burlington was a kind of early road show . . . an elaborately illustrated lecture with 85 painted views, each covering 250 square feet." In addition, the railroad solicited the services of "independent" observers who wrote and spoke about the glories of the American West as the land of opportunity.

The publicity and promotion paid off. Piasecki notes, "During the 1870s and the 1880s, the railroads attracted something like 4.5 million people to the Midwestern states, and they were responsible for the establishment there of almost 2 million farms. None of this could have been achieved without complex communication strategies closely linked to business objectives . . ."

Near the end of the 19th century, the Santa Fe Railway launched a campaign to lure tourists to the Southwest. It commissioned dozens of painters and photographers to depict the dramatic landscape and show romanticized American Indians weaving, grinding corn, and dancing.

Politics and Activism.   The early 19th century also saw the development of public relations tactics on the political and activist front. Amos Kendall, a former Kentucky newspaper editor, became an intimate member of President Andrew Jackson's "kitchen cabinet" and probably was the first presidential press secretary.

Kendall sampled public opinion on issues, advised Jackson, and skillfully interpreted his rough ideas, putting them into presentable form as speeches and news releases. He also served as Jackson's advance agent on trips, wrote glowing articles that he sent to supportive newspapers, and probably was the first to use newspaper reprints in public relations; almost every complimentary story or editorial about Jackson was reprinted and widely circulated. Article reprints are still a standard tactic in today's modern practice.

Supporters and leaders of such causes as abolition, suffrage, and prohibition employed publicity to maximum effect throughout the century. One of the most influential publicity ventures for the abolition movement was the publication of Harriet Beecher Stowe's *Uncle Tom's Cabin*. Sarah J. Hale, editor of *Godey's Ladies Book*, a best-selling magazine, ardently promoted women's rights. Amelia Bloomer, a women's rights advocate, got plenty of media publicity by wearing loose-fitting trousers in protest of the corset. Noted temperance crusader Carrie Nation became nationally known by invading saloons with an axe. Her name lives on; a bar in California is named Carrie Nation's.

Professor Carolyn M. Byerly of Ithaca College says that these campaigns for social reform qualify as public relations operations and deserve a place in the history of the field. She cites Genevieve Gardner McBride, who points out that in Wisconsin support for a Constitutional amendment giving women the right to vote was carried out through a carefully managed information campaign that included "publicity, press agentry, publications, petition drives, advertising, merchandising, lobbying, membership recruitment and training, special events, fund-raising, issues management, and crisis PR."

Corporate Development. A wave of industrialization and urbanization swept the nation after the Civil War. Concentrations of wealth developed throughout manufacturing and trade. Amid the questioning of business practices, which intensified in the early 20th century, in 1888 the Mutual Life Insurance Company hired a journalist to write news releases designed to improve its image. In 1889, Westinghouse Corporation established what is thought to be the first in-house publicity department. In 1897, the term *public relations* was first used by the Association of American Railroads in a company listing.

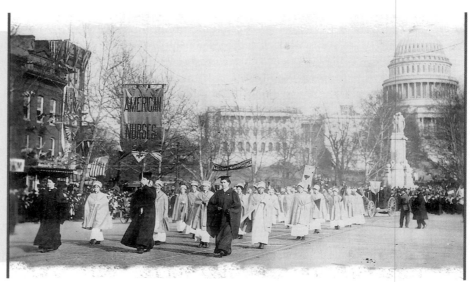

Groups advocating the right of women to vote in the United States used a variety of public relations tactics to press their cause. Here, a group of suffragists participate in a 1914 parade in Washington, D.C. Through such parades and demonstrations, they received media coverage and informed the public about their cause. Today, other groups representing various causes still continue to hold demonstrations, parades, and rallies.

1900 to 1950: The Age of Pioneers

As the use of publicity gained increased acceptance, the first publicity agency, known as the Publicity Bureau, was established in Boston in 1900. Harvard College was its most prestigious client. George F. Parker and Ivy Ledbetter Lee opened a publicity office in New York City in 1904. Parker remained in the publicity field, but Lee went on to become an advisor and counselor to individuals and companies.

At the corporate level, the Chicago Edison Company broke new ground in public relations techniques under the skillful leadership of its president, Samuel Insull. Well aware of the special need for a public utility to maintain a sound relationship with its customers, Insull created a monthly customer magazine, issued a constant stream of news releases, and even used films for public relations purposes. In 1912, he started the "bill stuffer" by inserting company information into customer bills—a technique used by many utilities today. Meanwhile, Theodore N. Vail, president of AT&T, greatly expanded that company's press and customer operations.

Henry Ford.   Henry Ford was America's first major industrialist, and he was among the first to use two basic public relations concepts. The first was the notion of *positioning*, the idea that credit and publicity always go to those who do something first. The second idea was being accessible to the press. Joseph Epstein, author of *Ambition*, says, "He may have been an even greater publicist than mechanic."

In 1900, Ford obtained coverage of the prototype Model T by demonstrating it to a reporter from the *Detroit Tribune*. By 1903, Ford achieved widespread publicity by racing his cars—a practice still used by today's automakers. Ford hired Barney Oldfield, a champion bicycle racer and a popular personality, to drive a Model T at a record speed of about 60 miles per hour. The publicity from these speed runs gave Ford financial backing and a ready market.

Ford also positioned himself as the champion of the common man and was the first automaker to envision that a car should be affordable to everyone. He produced his first Model T in 1908 for $850, and by 1915 he had reduced the selling price to $360. Such price reductions made Ford dominant in the auto industry and on newspaper front pages. He garnered further publicity and became the hero of working men and women by being the first automaker to double his worker's wages to $5 per day.

Ford became a household word because he was willing to be interviewed by the press on almost any subject, including the gold standard, evolution, alcohol, foreign affairs, and even capital punishment. A populist by nature, he once said, "Business is a service, not a bonanza," an idea reiterated by many of today's top corporate executives who believe in what is now called *corporate social responsibility* (CSR).

Teddy Roosevelt.   As president, Theodore Roosevelt proved to be a master at generating publicity. He was the first president to make extensive use of news conferences and interviews to drum up support for projects. He knew the publicity value of the presidential tour. For example, on a trip to what eventually became Yosemite National Park, Roosevelt was accompanied by a large group of reporters and photographers who wrote glowing articles about Roosevelt's pet project—the need to preserve areas for public recreational use.

President Franklin D. Roosevelt apparently took notes from Teddy. His supporters organized nationwide birthday balls in 1934 to celebrate his birthday and raise funds for infantile paralysis research. This led to the creation of the March of Dimes.

The campaign by Carl Byoir & Associates orchestrated 6000 events in 3600 communities and raised more than $1 million.

Ivy Lee: The First Public Relations Counsel.   The combination of stubborn management attitudes and improper actions, labor strife, and widespread public criticism produced the first public relations counselor, Ivy Ledbetter Lee. Although, as previously noted, the Princeton graduate and former business reporter for the *New York World* began as a publicist, he shortly expanded that role to become the first public relations counsel.

When Lee opened his public relations firm, he issued a declaration of principles that signaled a new model of public relations practice: *public information*. Lee's emphasis was on the dissemination of truthful, accurate information rather than the distortions, hype, and exaggerations of press agentry. Lee's declaration, which stemmed from his journalistic orientation, said, in part, "This is not a secret press bureau. All our work is done in the open. We aim to supply news. . . . In brief, our plan is, frankly and openly, in behalf of business concerns and public institutions, to supply to the press and the public of the United States prompt and accurate information concerning subjects which is of value and interest to the public . . ."

In 1906, at the grand age of 29, Lee was retained by the Pennsylvania Railroad as a "publicity counselor" to handle media relations. His first task was to convince management that the policy of operating in secret and refusing to talk with the press, typical of many large corporations at the time, was a poor strategy for fostering goodwill and public understanding. When the next rail accident occurred, Lee provided press facilities, released all available information, and took reporters to the accident site. Although such action appeared to the conservative railroad directors to be reckless indiscretion, they were pleasantly surprised that the company received fairer press comment than on any previous occasion. It wasn't long before other railroads also adopted a more open information policy.

Lee counseled a number of companies and charitable organizations during his lifetime, but he is best known for his work with the Rockefeller family. In 1914, John D. Rockefeller, Jr. hired Lee in the wake of the vicious strike-breaking activities known as the Ludlow Massacre at the Rockefeller family's Colorado Fuel and Iron Company plant. Lee went to Colorado to do some fact-finding (research) and talked to both sides. He found that labor leaders were effectively getting their views out by freely talking to the media, but that the company's executives were tight-lipped and inaccessible. The result, of course, was a barrage of negative publicity and public criticism directed at CF&I and the Rockefeller family.

Lee proposed a series of informational bulletins by management that would be distributed to opinion leaders in Colorado and around the nation. The leaflets were designed to be thought pieces about various issues concerning mining, manufacturing, and labor. In all, 19 bulletins were produced over a period of several months and sent to a mailing list of 19,000. Even at this early time, Lee recognized the value of directly reaching opinion leaders who, in turn, were highly influential in shaping public discussion and opinion.

Lee organized a number of other public relations activities on behalf of CF&I during 1914 and 1915, including convincing the governor of Colorado to write an article supporting the position taken by the company. Lee also convinced Rockefeller to visit the plant and talk with miners and their families. Lee made sure the press was there to record Rockefeller eating in the worker's hall, swinging a pickax in the mine, and having a beer with the workers after hours. The press loved it. Rockefeller was portrayed as being seriously concerned about the plight of the workers, and the visit led to policy changes and more worker benefits.

All of these activities, of course, also prevented the United Mine Workers from gaining a foothold. George McGovern, a former Democratic Party candidate for president, wrote his doctoral dissertation on the Ludlow Massacre and commented, "It was the first time in any American labor struggle where you had an organized effort to use what has become modern public relations to sell one side of a strike to the American people."

Lee continued as a counselor to the Rockefeller family and its various companies, but he also counseled a number of other clients, too. For example, he advised the American Tobacco Company to initiate a profit-sharing plan, the Pennsylvania Railroad to beautify its stations, and the movie industry to stop inflated advertising and form a voluntary code of censorship. See the PR Casebook box on page 54 for his work with New York's first subway.

He is remembered today for his four important contributions to public relations: (1) advancing the concept that business and industry should align themselves with the public interest, (2) dealing with top executives and carrying out no program unless it had the active support of management, (3) maintaining open communication with the news media, and (4) emphasizing the necessity of humanizing business and bringing its public relations down to the community level of employees, customers, and neighbors.

George Creel. The public information model that Lee enunciated in his counseling was also used by George Creel, who was also a former newspaper reporter. He was asked by President Woodrow Wilson to organize a massive public relations effort to unite the nation and to influence world opinion during World War I.

In their book *Words That Won the War*, James O. Mock and Cedric Larson write: "Mr. Creel assembled as brilliant and talented group of journalists, scholars, press agents, editors, artists, and other manipulators of the symbols of public opinion as America had ever seen united for a single purpose." Among its numerous activities, the Creel Committee persuaded newspapers and magazines to contribute volumes of news and advertising space to encourage Americans to save food and to invest heavily in Liberty Bonds, which were purchased by more than 10 million people. Thousands of businesses set up their own groups of publicity people to expand the effort.

President Wilson accepted Creel's advice that hatred of the Germans should be played down and that loyalty and confidence in the government should be emphasized. The committee also publicized the war aims and ideals of Woodrow Wilson—to make the world safe for democracy and to

Public relations counselor Ivy Lee convinced John D. Rockefeller that he should visit miners at the family's Colorado Fuel & Iron Company, the site of considerable labor unrest and union organizing activity that led to the "Ludlow Massacre." Here, Rockefeller watches children of miners marching into school.

PR CASEBOOK

Constructive Public Relations for the New York Subway

Ivy Lee, known as the first public relations counselor, was retained by the New York subway system in 1916 to foster public understanding and support.

The Interborough Rapid Transit Company (IRT) faced many new challenges as it began its second decade of service. It was completing construction and expanding service, but it also faced competition from a rival system, the Brooklyn Rapid Transit Company (later known as BMT).

Under Lee's direction, the IRT took an innovative approach, communicating directly with its passengers through pamphlets, brochures, and posters "to establish a close understanding of its work and policies." The most famous and influential products of Lee's campaign were two concurrently appearing poster series: *The Subway Sun* and *The Elevated Express*.

Between 1918, when the first posters appeared, and 1932, when the series ended, these posters became New York institutions. They entertained and informed millions of subway commuters during the First World War and through the Great Depression.

Posters, for example, were used to announce the introduction of coin-operated turnstiles, which Lee called "a change which revolutionized the daily habits of millions of people." They were also used to explain the need for fare increases in the 1920s and to extol fast and direct train service to baseball games at Yankee Stadium and the Polo Grounds. Posters also offered riders information on how to get to other city institutions. The poster shown promotes

the Museum of Natural History and provides directions.

Designed to resemble the front page of a newspaper, *The Subway Sun* and *The Elevated Express* announced the opening of the 42nd Street shuttle between Grand Central Station and Times Square; asked riders to not block the doors; and urged them to visit the city's free swimming pools. As the subways became more crowded, the IRT used these posters to promote its "open air" elevated lines as a more comfortable alternative.

Today, more than 90 years later, Lee's idea of communicating directly to passengers through posters, pamphlets, and brochures is still being used by public transit systems around the world. And many of the themes are the same as in Lee's day—public safety, system improvements, travel advisories, subway etiquette, and public service announcements.

make World War I the war to end all wars. The American Red Cross, operating in co-operation with the Creel Committee, enrolled more than 19 million new members and received more than $400 million in contributions during the period.

This massive publicity effort had a profound effect on the development of public relations by demonstrating the success of these techniques. It also awakened an awareness in Americans of the power of mediated information in changing public attitudes and behavior. This, coupled with postwar analysis of British propaganda devices, resulted in a number of scholarly books and college courses on the subject. Among these books was Walter Lippmann's classic, *Public Opinion* (1922), in which he pointed out how people are moved to action by "the pictures in our heads."

Edward B. Bernays: Father of Modern Public Relations. The Creel Committee was the training ground of many individuals who went on to become successful and widely known public relations executives and counselors. One such person was Edward B. Bernays who, through brilliant campaigns and extensive self-promotion, became known as the "father of modern public relations" by the time of his death in 1995 at the age of 103.

Bernays, who was the nephew of Sigmud Freud, conceptualized a third model of public relations that emphasized the application of social science research and behavioral psychology to formulate campaigns and messages that could change people's perceptions and encourage certain behaviors. Unlike Lee's public information model that emphasized the accurate distribution of news, Bernays' model was essentially one of advocacy and scientific persuasion. It included listening to the audience, but the purpose of feedback was to formulate a better persuasive message. James Grunig at the University of Maryland, a major theorist in public relations, has labeled this the *two-way asymmetric* model. See the Insights box on page 63.

Bernays became a major spokesperson for the "new" public relations through his book *Crystallizing Public Opinion*, which was published in 1923. His first sentence announced: "In writing this book I have tried to set down the broad principles that govern the new profession of public relations counsel." In the following pages, Bernays outlined the scope, function, methods, techniques, and social responsibilities of a *public relations counsel*—a term that was to become the core of public relations practice.

The book, published a year after Walter Lippmann's insightful treatise on public opinion, attracted much attention, and Bernays was even invited by New York University to offer the first public relations course in the nation. However, not everyone was happy with Bernays or his book. The editor of the *New York*

Edward L. Bernays, a legendary figure in public relations with a career spanning about three-quarters of a century, died at the age of 103 in 1995. He outlived all his contemporaries and became known as the "father of modern public relations."

Herald Tribune wrote, "Bernays has taken the sideshow barker and given him a philosophy and a new and awesome language. He is no primitive drum-beater . . . He is devoid of swank and does not visit newspaper offices (as did the circus press agents); and yet, the more thoughtful newspaper editors . . . should regard Bernays as a menace, and warn their colleagues of his machinations."

Clients, however, did not seem to share such concerns and Bernays, over the course of his long career, had many successful campaigns that have become classics. Here is a sampling:

● **Ivory Soap.** Procter & Gamble sold its Ivory Soap by the millions after Bernays came up with the idea of sponsoring soap sculpture contests for school-aged children. In the first year alone, 22 million schoolchildren participated in the contest, which eventually ran for 35 years. Bernays' brochure with soap sculpture tips, which millions of children received in their schools, advised them to "use discarded models for face, hands, and bath, adding, "You will love the feeling of cleanliness that comes from Ivory soap bath once a day." Thomas Harris, a Chicago counselor, quotes Bernays, "Soap sculpture became a national outlet for children's creative instincts and helped a generation that enjoyed cleanliness."

● **Ballet Russe.** The challenge was to build a following for a Russian dance troupe in the middle of World War I, when ballet was considered a scandalous form of entertainment. According to *PRWeek*, "Bernays used magazine placements, created a publicity guide, and used overseas reviews to make men in tights respectable and put ballerina dreams into the heads of little girls."

● **Light's Golden Jubilee.** To celebrate the 50th anniversary of Thomas Edison's invention of the electric light bulb, Bernays arranged the worldwide attention-getting Light's Golden Jubilee in 1929. It was his idea, for example, that the world's utilities would shut off their power all at one time, for one minute, to honor Edison. President Herbert Hoover and many dignitaries were on hand, and the U.S. Post Office issued a commemorative two-cent postage stamp. Bill Moyers, in an interview with Bernays in 1984, asked, "You know, you got Thomas Edison, Henry Ford, Herbert Hoover, and masses of Americans to do what you wanted them to do. You got the whole world to turn off its lights at the same time. That's not influence, that's power." Bernays responded, "But you see, I never thought of it as power. I never treated it as power. People want to go where they want to be led."

Journalist Larry Tye has outlined a number of campaigns conducted by Bernays in his book *The Father of Spin: Edward B. Bernays and the Birth of Public Relations.* Tye credits Bernays with having a unique approach to solving problems. Instead of thinking first about tactics, Bernays would always think about the "big idea" on how to motivate people. The bacon industry, for example, wanted to promote its product, so Bernays came up with the idea of doctors across the land endorsing a hearty breakfast. No mention was made of bacon, but sales soared anyway as people took the advice and started eating the traditional breakfast of bacon and eggs.

Bernays, as previously mentioned, is widely acknowledged as the founder of modern public relations. One historian even described him as "the first and doubtless the leading ideologist of public relations." Bernays constantly wrote about the profession of public relations and its ethical responsibilities—even to the point of advocating the licensing of public relations counselors. He also eventually advocated that public relations should be a two-way street of mutual understanding and interaction with the public rather than just scientific persuasion.

Although he was named by *Life* magazine in 1990 as one of the 100 most important Americans of the 20th century, it should be noted that he had a powerful partner in his wife, Doris E. Fleischman, who was a talented writer, ardent feminist, and former Sunday editor of the *New York Tribune*.

Fleischman was an equal partner in the work of Bernays' firm, interviewing clients, writing news releases, editing the company's newsletter, and writing and editing books and magazine articles. Bernays called Fleischman "the brightest woman I've ever met in my life" and the "balance wheel of our operation."

Other Pioneers. A number of individuals, either through the force of their personality, their expertise, or their professional success, also have contributed to the history and lore of public relations.

● **Arthur W. Page.** Page became vice president of the American Telephone & Telegraph Company in 1927 and is credited with establishing the concept that public relations should have an active voice in higher management. Page also expressed the belief that a company's performance, not press agentry, comprises its basis for public approval. More than any other individual, Page is credited with laying the foundation for the field of corporate public relations. He served on the boards of numerous corporations, charitable groups, and universities. After his death in 1960, a group of AT&T associates established a society of senior communication executives in his name. The Arthur W. Page Society, comprising about 300 executives, has several meetings a year and publishes various monographs on communications management. See the Insights box on page 58 for a list of Page principles.

● **Benjamin Sonnenberg.** It was Sonnenberg who suggested that Texaco sponsor performances of the Metropolitan Opera on national radio. Sponsorship of the Saturday afternoon series, which began in 1940, continued for a half-century. He believed that a brief mention of the client in the right context is better than a long-winded piece of flattery. He proposed Texaco's sponsorship as a way to reach opinion leaders and position the company as a patron of the arts. Biographer Isadore Barmash described Sonnenberg as "the most influential publicist of the mid-twentieth century." He had an opulent townhouse in New York and entertained many of America's most powerful men and women. Asked what the secret of his success was, he quipped, "I build large pedestals for small people."

● **Jim Moran.** Moran was a publicist and press agent who became famous for his media-grabbing stunts. He publicized the book *The Egg and I* by sitting on an ostrich egg for 19 days until it hatched. On another occasion, he walked a bull though an exclusive New York china shop.

● **Rex Harlow.** Considered by many to be the "father of public relations research," Harlow was probably the first full-time public relations educator. As a professor at Stanford University's School of Education, he taught public relations courses on a regular basis and also conducted multiple workshops around the nation. Harlow also founded the American Council on Public Relations, which later became the Public Relations Society of America (PRSA). In 1952, he founded *Social Science Reporter*, one of the first newsletters in the field.

ON THE JOB insights

Principles of Public Relations Management

Noted counselor Arthur W. Page practiced six principles of public relations management as a means of implementing his philosophy:

1. *Tell the truth.* Let the public know what's happening and provide an accurate picture of the company's character, ideals, and practices.

2. *Prove it with action.* Public perception of an organization is determined 90 percent by doing and 10 percent by talking.

3. *Listen to the customer.* To serve the company well, understand what the public wants and needs. Keep top decision-makers and other employees informed about public reaction to company products, policies, and practices.

4. *Manage for tomorrow.* Anticipate public reaction and eliminate practices that create difficulties. Generate goodwill.

5. *Conduct public relations as if the whole company depends on it.* Corporate relations is a management function. No corporate strategy should be implemented without considering its impact on the public. The public relations professional is a policy maker capable of handling a wide range of corporate communications activities.

6. *Remain calm, patient, and good-humored.* Lay the ground-work for public relations miracles with consistent, calm, and reasoned attention to information and contacts. When a crisis arises, remember that cool heads communicate best.

Page recognized an additional truth: A company's true character is expressed by its people. This makes every active and retired employee a part of the public relations organization. So it is the responsibility of the public relations function to support each employee's capacity to be an honest, knowledgeable ambassador to customers, friends, and public officials.

Source: Membership Directory, The Arthur W. Page Society, New York.

● **Leone Baxter.** Baxter and her partner, Clem Whitaker, are credited with founding the first political campaign management firm in the United States. The firm handled several California governor and U.S. Senate campaigns, advised General Dwight Eisenhower when he ran for president in 1952, and counseled Richard Nixon on the famous "Checkers" speech that saved his career as vice president. Her basic advice, "Never wage a campaign defensively. The only successful defense is a spectacular, hard-hitting crushing offensive."

● **Henry Rogers.** In the mid-1930s, Rogers, with Warren Cowan, established a highly successful public relations firm in Hollywood to serve the movie industry. One of his early clients was an unknown starlet named Rita Hayworth who needed some publicity. Rogers, in the true tradition of the press agent, convinced *Look* magazine to do a feature with the news angle that Hayworth spent every cent she earned on clothes. He even produced a telegram from the Fashion Couturiers Association of America (a fictitious organization) that declared Hayworth the best-dressed off-screen actress. *Look* assigned the photographer, Rogers convinced the clothiers to provide the wardrobe, Hayworth struck a seductive pose that made the cover, and her career was on its way. Rogers later became a corporate counsel. Of his image-building years, he said, "Dog food and movie stars are much alike because they are both products in need of exposure."

● **Eleanor Lambert.** The "grande dame" of fashion public relations, Lambert is credited with putting American designers such as Bill Blass and Calvin Klein on the map when European brands dominated the industry. She also compiled the "Best-Dressed" list for 62 years, which always received extensive media publicity. Lambert was active in New York fashion and the arts. She, for example, was the public relations counsel for the introduction of the Whitney Museum in 1930.

● **Elmer Davis.** President Franklin D. Roosevelt appointed Davis head of the Office of War Information (OWI) during World War II. Using the Creel Committee as a model, Davis mounted an even larger public relations effort to promote the sale of war bonds, obtain press support for wartime rationing, encourage the planting of "victory gardens," and spur higher productivity among American workers to win the war. The Voice of America (VOA) was established to carry news of the war to all parts of the world, and the movie industry made a number of feature films in support of the war. The OWI was the forerunner of the U.S. Information Agency (USIA), which was established in 1953.

1950 to 2000: Public Relations Comes of Age

During the second half of the 20th century, the practice of public relations became firmly established as an indispensable part of America's economic, political, and social development.

The booming economy after World War II produced rapid growth in all areas of public relations. Companies opened public relations departments or expanded existing ones. Government staffs increased in size, as did those of nonprofits, such as educational institutions and health and welfare agencies. Television emerged in the early 1950s as a national medium and as a new challenge for public relations expertise. New counseling firms sprang up nationwide.

The growth of the economy was one reason for the expansion of public relations, but there were other factors, too. They included (1) major increases in urban and suburban populations; (2) the growth of a more impersonalized society represented by big business, big labor, and big government; (3) scientific and technological advances, including automation and computerization; (4) the communications revolution in terms of mass media; and (5) bottomline financial considerations often replacing the more personalized decision making of a previous, more genteel, society.

Many citizens felt alienated and bewildered by such rapid change, cut off from the sense of community that characterized the lives of previous generations. They sought power through innumerable pressure groups, focusing on causes such as environmentalism, working conditions, and civil rights. Public opinion, registered through new, more sophisticated methods of polling, became increasingly powerful in opposing or effecting change.

Both physically and psychologically separated from their publics, American business and industry turned increasingly to public relations specialists for audience analysis, strategic planning, issues management, and even the creation of supportive environments for the selling of products and services. Mass media also became more complex and sophisticated, so specialists in media relations who understood how the media worked were also in demand.

ON THE JOB insights

Classic Campaigns Show the Power of Public Relations

During the last half of the 20th century, a number of organizations and causes have used effective public relations to accomplish highly visible results. *PRWeek* convened a panel of public relations experts and came up with some of the "greatest campaigns ever" during this time period.

● **The Civil Rights Campaign.** Martin Luther King, Jr. was an outstanding civil rights advocate and a great communicator. He organized the 1963 civil rights campaign and used such techniques as well-written, well-delivered speeches; letter writing; lobbying; and staged events (nonviolent protests) to turn a powerful idea into reality.

● **NASA.** From the very beginning NASA fostered media accessibility at Houston's Johnson Space Center. For example, NASA director Chris Kraft insisted that television cameras be placed on the lunar lander in 1969, and in later years reporters were invited inside mission control during the Apollo 13 mission. According to *PRWeek*, "Those historic moments have helped the public overlook the huge taxpayer expense and numerous technical debacles that could otherwise have jeopardized the future of the organization."

● **Cabbage Patch Kids.** Public relations launched the craze for the adoptable dolls and created a "must have" toy. The campaign set the standard for the introduction of a new product and showed what a strong media relations program can do for a product.

● **Seat Belt Campaign.** In the 1980s, the U.S. automotive industry got the nation to "buckle up" through a public relations campaign. Tactics included winning the support of news media across the country, interactive displays, celebrity endorsements, letter-writing campaigns, and several publicity events, such as buckling a 600-foot-wide safety belt around a Hollywood sign. Notes *PRWeek*, "The results of one of the biggest public relations campaigns of all time were phenomenal, with the number of people 'buckling up' rising from 12 to 50 percent—it is now even higher."

● **Hands Across America.** The largest human gathering in history was a public relations stunt in 1986 that saw 7 million people across 16 states join hands to form a human chain to raise money for the hungry and the homeless. Even President Ronald Reagan participated.

● **StarKist Tuna.** When negative media coverage threatened

The power of public relations was used in the civil rights movement to create public awareness and support. Here, Martin Luther King, Jr. addresses a massive rally in Washington, D.C. and delivers his "I have a dream" speech.

the tuna industry because dolphins were getting caught in fishermen's nets, StarKist led the industry in changing fishing practices with conferences, videos, and an Earth Day coalition. About 90 percent of the public heard about the company's efforts, and StarKist was praised as an environmental leader.

● **Tylenol Crisis.** This has become the classic model for a product recall. When Johnson & Johnson found out that several

ON THE JOB insights, *continued*

people had died from cyanide-laced Tylenol capsules, a national panic erupted. Many thought the company would never recover from the damage caused by the tampering. However, the company issued a complete recall, redesigned the packaging so that it was tamper-proof, and launched a media campaign to keep the public fully informed. The result was that Tylenol sur-

vived the crisis and again became a best seller.

- **Windows 95 Launch.** This campaign is easily in the product launch hall of fame. Microsoft, through media relations and publicity, achieved a unprecedented 99 percent awareness level among consumers even before the product hit the shelves.
- **Understanding AIDS.** This successful health education cam-

paign changed the way that AIDS was perceived by Americans. In addition to a national mailing of a brochure titled *Understanding AIDS*, there were grassroots activities that specifically targeted African Americans and Hispanics.

Source: "The Greatest Campaigns Ever." *PRWeek*, July 15, 2002, pp. 14–15.

By 1950, an estimated 17,000 men and 2,000 women were employed as practitioners in public relations and publicity. Typical of the public relations programs of large corporations at mid-century was that of the Aluminum Company of America (ALCOA). Heading the operation was a vice president for public relations-advertising, who was aided by an assistant public relations director and advertising manager. Departments included community relations, product publicity, motion pictures and exhibits, employee publications, the news bureau, and speech writing. The *Alcoa News* magazine was published for all employees, and separate publications were published for each of the 20 plants throughout the United States. The company's main broadcast effort was sponsorship of Edward R. Murrow's *See It Now* television program.

By 1960, the U.S. Census counted 23,870 men and 7,271 women in public relations, although some observers put the figure at approximately 35,000. Since 1960, the number of public relations practitioners has increased dramatically to about 200,000 nationwide. The latest estimate from the U.S. Department of Labor predicts that public relations will be one of the fastest-growing fields (36 percent or more), and that from 2000 to 2010 there will be a demand for public relations specialists and managers.

Evolving Practice and Philosophy. The period from 1950 to 2000 marked distinct changes in the practice and philosophy of public relations. To place these changes in context, it's probably prudent to review some of what has been presented so far. First, the 1800s were marked by the press agentry model, which was best represented by the hype and exaggerations of P. T. Barnum and various land developers. By the early 20th century, however, public relations began to reinvent itself along journalistic lines, mainly because former newspaper reporters such as Ivy Lee started to do public relations work and counseling. Cynthia Clark of Boston University picked up the evolution in a succinct review that appeared in the *Public Relations Review*.

Clark says that before the 1920s, public relations was simply an extension of the journalistic function and was focused on "the dissemination of information or one-way communication models in which the quality of information was important but audience feedback had yet to be fully considered." James Grunig, in his interpretation of the evolutionary models of public relations (see the Insight box on page 63, called this the *public information* model of public relations.

In the 1920s, thanks to breakthroughs in social science research, the focus of public relations shifted to the psychological and sociological effects of persuasive communication on target audiences. Both Rex Harlow and Edward Bernays, among others, believed that any campaign should be based on feedback and an analysis of an audience's dispositions and value system so messages could be structured for maximum effect. Grunig labeled this the *two-way asymmetric* model because it involved scientific persuasion based on the research of the target audience.

The 1960s saw Vietnam War protests, the Civil Rights movement, the environmental movement, interest in women's rights, and a host of other issues. Antibusiness sentiment was high, and corporations adjusted their policies to generate public goodwill and understanding. Thus, the idea of issues management was added to the job description of the public relations manager. This was the first expression of the idea that public relations should be more than persuading people that corporate policy was correct. During this period, the idea emerged that perhaps it would be beneficial to have a dialogue with various publics and adapt corporate policy to their particular concerns. Grunig labeled this approach *two-way symmetrical communication* because there's balance between the organization and its various publics; the organization and the public can influence each other.

The 1970s was an era of reform in the stock market and investor relations. The Texas Gulf Sulfur case changed investor relations forever by establishing the idea that a company must immediately disclose any information that may affect the value of its stock. The field of investor relations boomed.

By the 1980s, the concept that public relations was a management function was in full bloom. The term *strategic* became a buzzword, and the concept of Management by Objective (MBO) was heavily endorsed by public relations practitioners as they sought to prove to higher management that public relations did indeed contribute to the bottom line. Many definitions from this time emphasized public relations as a management function. As Derina Holtzhausen of the University of Florida notes, "Public relations *management* highlights organizational effectiveness, the *strategic* management of the function through *strategic* identification of publics, and issues management to prevent crisis."

Reputation, or *perception*, management was the buzzword of the 1990s. Burson-Marsteller, one of the largest public relations firms, decided that its business was not public relations but, rather, "perception management." Other firms declared that their business was "reputation management." However, there was some debate as to whether reputations can be managed, because reputation is the cumulative effect of numerous actions and activities.

The basic idea, however, was that public relations people worked to maintain credibility, to build solid internal and external relationships, and to manage issues. Inherent in this was the idea that public relations personnel should use research to do (1) environmental monitoring, (2) public relations audits, (3) communication audits, and (4) social audits. By doing these things, it would be possible to enhance corporate social responsibility (CSR).

By 2000, a number of scholars and practitioners began to conceptualize the practice of public relations as "relationship management," the basic idea being that public relations practitioners are in the business of building and fostering relationships with an organization's various publics. The idea has also caught on in marketing; *re-lation-ship marketing* is an effort to form a solid, ongoing relationship with the purchaser of a product or service.

ON THE JOB insights

Four Classic Models of Public Relations

A four-model typology of public relations practice was presented by Professors James Grunig of the University of Maryland and Todd Hunt of Rutgers State University in their 1984 book *Managing Public Relations*. The models, which have been used widely in public relations theory, help to explain how public relations has evolved over the years. Although all four models are practiced today in varying degrees, the "ideal" one is the two-way symmetric model.

Press Agentry/Publicity

This is one-way communication, primarily through the mass media, to distribute information that may be exaggerated, distorted, or even incomplete to "hype" a cause, product, or service. Its purpose is advocacy, and little or no research is required. P. T. Barnum was the leading historical figure during this model's heyday from 1850 to 1900. Sports, theater, music, film, and the classic Hollywood publicist are the main fields of practice today.

Public Information

One-way distribution of information, not necessarily with a per-

suasive intent, is the purpose. It is based on the journalistic ideal of accuracy and completeness, and the mass media is the primary channel. There is fact-finding for content, but little audience research regarding attitudes and dispositions. Ivy Lee, a former journalist, is the leading historical figure during this model's development from about 1910 into the 1920s. Government, nonprofit groups, and other public institutions are primary fields of practice today.

Two-Way Asymmetric

Scientific persuasion is the purpose, and communication is two-way, with imbalanced effects. The model has a feedback loop, but the primary purpose of the model is to help the communicator better understand the audience and how to persuade it. Research is used to plan the activity and establish objectives as well as to learn whether an objective has been met. Edward Bernays is the leading historical figure during the model's beginning in the 1920s. Marketing and advertising departments in competitive businesses and public re-

lations firms are the primary places of practice today.

Two-Way Symmetric

Gaining mutual understanding is the purpose, and communication is two-way with balanced effects. Formative research is used mainly to learn how the public perceives the organization and to determine what consequences organizational actions/policy might have on the public. The result may be counseling management to take certain actions or change policies. Evaluative research is used to measure whether a public relations effort has improved public understanding. This idea, also expressed as "relationship building" is to have policies and actions that are mutually beneficial to both parties. Edward B. Bernays, later in his life, supported this model and is considered a leading advocate of this approach. Educators and professional leaders are the main proponents of this model, which has been used by many professionals since the 1980s. The fields of practice today include organizations that engage in issue identification, crisis and risk management, and long-range strategic planning.

Relationship management builds on Grunig's idea of two-way symmetrical communication, but goes beyond this by recognizing that an organization's publics are, as Stephen Bruning of Capital University notes, "active, interactive, and equal participants of an ongoing communication process." Bruning continues, "Typically, organizations are fairly effective at fulfilling content communication needs (communicating to key public members what is happening), but often fall short of fulfilling key public member relational communication needs (making the key public member feel they are valued in the relationship)."

An extension of relationship management is the *dialogic* (dialogue) model of public relations that has emerged since 2000. Michael Kent of Montclair University and Maureen Taylor of Rutgers University wrote in a *Public Relations Review* article that "A theoretical shift, from public relations reflecting an emphasis on managing communication, to an emphasis on communication as a tool of negotiating relationships, has been taking place for some time." Kent and Taylor say that good dialogic communication requires skills such as the following:

> . . . listening, empathy, being able to contextualize issues within local, national and international frameworks, being able to identify common ground between parties, thinking about long-term rather than short-term objectives, seeking out groups and individuals with opposing viewpoints, and soliciting a variety of internal and external opinions on policy issues.

The concept of dialogue places less emphasis on mass media distribution of messages and more on interpersonal channels. Kent and Taylor, for example, say that the Internet and World Wide Web are excellent vehicles for dialogue if the sites are interactive. They write, "The Web can be used to communicate directly with publics by offering real-time discussions, feedback loops, places to post comments, sources for organizational information, and postings of organizational member biographies and contact information."

Although there has been a somewhat linear progression in public relations practice and philosophy as the field has expanded, today's practice represents a mixture of public relations models. The Hollywood publicist/press agent and the public information officer for the government agency are still with us. We also still have marketing communications, which almost exclusively uses the concept of scientific persuasion and two-way asymmetric communication. However, when it comes to issues management and relationship building, the two-way symmetric and dialogue models seem to be the most appropriate.

Trend Lines in Today's Practice

Technological and social changes continue to transform aspects of public relations practice during the first decade of the 21st century. The following sections discuss the feminization of the field, the search for more ethnic and cultural diversity, and other trends that will shape the practice in the years to come.

Feminization of the Field

In terms of personnel, the most dramatic change has been the transformation of public relations from a male-dominated field to one in which women now constitute 70 percent of practitioners.

The shift has been going on for several decades. In 1979, women made up 41 percent of the public relations field. By 1983, they became the majority (50.1 percent) of the public relations workforce. A decade later, the figure stood at 66.3 percent. By 2000, the percentage had leveled off at about 70 percent, where it remains today. In contrast, the total number of women in the U.S. workforce was about 42 percent in 2001, according to the U.S. Bureau of Labor Statistics.

The national organizations also reflect the trend. About 75 percent of the membership in the International Association of Business Communicators (IABC) are now women, and the PRSA says that more than 50 percent of its members are now women. However, the Arthur W. Page Society, which is composed of senior-level communication executives, still has a majority of males (70 percent).

About 65 percent of all majors in journalism and mass communications programs are now women, and 70 to 75 percent of public relations majors are female. It's worth noting that women also constitute the majority of students in law school, veterinary programs, and a number of other academic disciplines. Engineering is not one of them.

A number of reasons are given for the major influx of women into the field of public relations. Some of these reasons include the following: (1) women find a more welcoming environment in public relations and see more opportunities for advancement than in other communications fields, such as newspaper work; (2) women still make more money in public relations than comparable female-dominated fields, such as teaching and social work; (3) a woman can start a public relations firm without a lot of capital; (4) women tend to have better listening and communication skills than men; and (5) women are more sensitive than men in facilitating two-way communication.

Marina Maher, founder and president of her own public relations firm, echoed some of these ideas in a *PRWeek* article. She writes, "Women thrive in this industry because we're good at it—it taps into our natural abilities. We're highly intuitive, detail-oriented, and have a strong service mentality. We're good at finding the common ground and creating emotional bonds, which is the essence of a brand-target relationships."

At the same time, a number of studies show that the majority of women in public relations earn less money than their male counterparts (see the salary survey information in Chapter 1) and are usually found at the tactical level of public relations practice rather than the management/counseling role.

The optimists say that women are still relatively new to the field and, with time, will eventually rise to their fair share of top posts. Feminist scholars refer to this assimilation model as *liberal feminism*. Radical feminists, however, disagree with this reasoning. They say that increasing the number of women in management is not enough, and that nothing less than a complete restructuring of society and its institutions will end gender discrimination and bias.

University of Maryland professors Linda Aldoory and Elizabeth Toth, writing in the *Journal of Public Relations Research*, say "Surveys and focus groups continue to offer valid and reliable statistics and experiences attesting to the fact that, although the public relations profession is almost 70 percent women today, men are often favored for hiring, higher salaries, and promotions to management positions."

Indeed, women in higher levels of management are still unusual in business and industry. A study by D. Meyerson and J. Fletcher that was published in the *Harvard Business Review* found that women only constituted 10 percent of the senior managers in *Fortune* 500 companies and less than 4 percent of the uppermost ranks of CEOs, presidents, and executive vice presidents. Another interesting statistic is that women earn about 76 cents for every dollar earned by a man. In fact, the actual figure actually dropped to 75 cents in 2004.

Some women in public relations have become the top communications officers of their corporation. However, Professor Laurie Grunig of the University of Maryland

This group of high-ranking executives exemplifies the rise of women to senior positions in large corporations and public relations firms. From left to right, *top row:* Mary Cusick, SVP, Bob Evans Farms; Lisa Davis, Director of Communications, AARP; Diane Dixon, SVP of Worldwide Communications, Avery Dennison. *Second row:* Susan Hoff, SVP, Best Buy, Inc.; Denise Kaigler, SVP and Chief Communications Officer, Reebok International; and Anne McCarthy, SVP of Global Communications, SAP AG. *Third row:* Helen Ostrowski, CEO of Porter Novelli; Charlotte Sterling, EVP of Communications, Marriott International; and Mary Linder, SVP of Corporate Communications, Northwest Airlines.

is concerned about highlighting women who have made it to the top, calling it *compensatory feminism*. According to Grunig, it gives women the false idea that progress is being made.

A number of feminist scholars have explored the dimensions and impact of women in public relations, and some of their works are listed in the Suggested Readings at the end of the chapter. Over the years, more empirical evidence and insights have accumulated.

As early as the 1970s, there was passionate debate about the large influx of women into the field. Many public relations leaders (men, of course) expressed a deep concern that feminization of the field would lower the status of the public relations as a management function and that salaries in the field would drop given the history of other female-dominated fields, such as nursing, education, and social work.

Some alleged that business and industry were simply hiring women in public relations to show a commitment to affirmative action. Indeed, the Velvet Ghetto study of 1978 by the International Association of Business Communicators (IABC) found that companies did tend to load up their public relations departments with women to compensate for their scarcity in other professional and managerial capacities that lead to top management. The idea was that a company could have a woman vice president of public relations as "window dressing" without giving her any real management authority.

These arguments and fears have somewhat dissipated over the years. Public relations as a high status occupation still has mixed reviews, but the power and influence of women in the management suite is stronger today than it has ever been. Also, salaries remain fairly high compared to other female-dominated fields. As for the Velvet Ghetto, most women who now occupy top positions reject the idea that they were hired as "window dressing." Aedhmar Hynes, CEO of Text 100, told *PRWeek*, "I have worked damned hard to get to where I am, but so have all the men who are in senior management positions."

Statistics and surveys still show, however, that there continues to be a gender gap in salaries as well as fewer women than men in senior management. A number of reasons have been offered, but the most recent research seems to indicate that the biggest factor is years of experience in the field. Youjin Choi and Linda Childers Hon of the University of Florida found that "The number of years of respondents' professional experience was the single significant predictor of income." Aldodry and Toth also found years of experience to be a significant factor in income inequity, but they also cited evidence that gender and interrupting a career also had an effect on salaries and job advancement.

ON THE JOB ethics

Affirmative Action for Men?

There's a shortage of men in the public relations field. About 70 percent of today's practitioners are women, and this has created a considerable gender imbalance in many corporate departments and public relations firms.

Many managers say that such an imbalance is not a healthy workplace situation. Consequently, some feel that

something like reverse affirmative action is needed to attract more men into the public relations field. Given the law of supply and demand, for example, some firms may offer a man more pay than a woman for doing the same job. In some quarters, some believe that a less-qualified man should be hired over a more-qualified

female applicant. By the same token, it is claimed that men get promoted faster than women in order to retain them.

What do you think? Should a public relations firm offer men more pay and opportunities for advancement in order to achieve some degree of gender equity in the office? Does the end justify the means in this case?

The organizational environment also may affect a female's rise to top management. This theory is called the *structionalist perspective*. Toth argues that more women than men fulfill the technician role—a less powerful role than the managerial role—because of different experiences received on the job. Choi and Hon also say organizational structure is a problem because women in many organizations are excluded from influential networks, have a paucity of role models, and must work in male-dominated environments.

Choi and Hon, however, did find that organizations (such as many public relations firms) where women occupied 40 to 60 percent of the managerial positions were "gender integrated" and more friendly environments for the advancement of women than male-dominated organizational structures. In other words, organizations committed to gender equity were those organizations that practiced the most excellent public relations.

The Search for Diversity

According to the U.S. Census Bureau, minorities now constitute 33 percent of the 285 million people in the United States. The fastest growing, and now largest group, is Hispanics. Hispanics are now 13.4 percent of the population, compared with 13.3 percent for Blacks/African Americans—a statistical difference of about 500,000 people. Asian/Pacific Islanders make up 4.9 percent, and Native Americans comprise 1.5 percent of the population.

The number of minorities in public relations falls considerably short of equaling the population at large, and one major goal is to somehow make the field of public relations more representative of the population as a whole. In previous decades, public relations was literally a "lily white" preserve and was considered, more or less, to be a white, upper-middle-class occupation—in much the same way as journalism was perceived.

Indeed, in 1997, the membership profile for the PRSA showed that 93 percent of the members were white, 3 percent black, 2 percent Hispanic, and 1 percent Asian. Since that time, there has been some improvement. In 2003, a *PRWeek* survey found that professionals in public relations firms were 81 percent Caucasian, 7 percent African American, 7 percent Hispanic, and 4 percent Asian or Pacific Islander. Company public relations department reported about the same statistics for ethnic groups but, for some reason, registered a large percentage of Native Americans (20 percent).

Many public relations employers express the desire to hire more minority candidates, but they have difficulty doing so because they receive so few applications. One problem is the education pipeline. About 182,000 undergraduates are studying journalism and mass communications (including public relations) across the country. Of that number, less than 30 percent are minorities. Hispanics, which are the largest minority in the general population, at 13.4 percent, constitute only 6.4 percent of journalism enrollments. African Americans make up 13.7 percent of journalism enrollments, Asian Americans are 3.2 percent, and Native Americans comprise 2 percent.

Admittedly, the percentage of ethnic groups in public relations has improved over the past decade, but there is now a concentrated effort to attract more minorities. Hispanics, in particular, constitute a major audience for marketers and public relations specialists because of their spending power. It's estimated that the Hispanic market is now worth about $400 billion to $500 billion annually, and will climb to more than $900 billion by 2010. Reaching this audience, and other major ethnic audiences, will require specialized knowledge and messages tailored to their particular cultures and values.

The PRSA (www.diversity.prsa.org) and other major public relations organizations are increasing minority scholarships, organizing career fairs, and giving awards to local chapters that institute diversity programs. In a more recent development, Tyco Corporation has funded a $300,000 three-year program with the Lagrant Foundation in Los Angeles to set up an internship program for minorities in public relations and advertising.

In addition, groups such as the National Black Public Relations Society (BPRS), the Hispanic Public Relations Association (HPRA), and the Asian American Advertising and Public Relations Association (AAAPRA) are being asked to help public relations firms and companies identify aspiring job applicants. Leaders of these minority associations, however, say that employers must make a more concerted effort to recruit minorities to public relations by going to traditionally black colleges, participating in more college career fairs, enlisting the aid of college professors to identify good candidates, and even placing job ads in publications that reach a variety of ethnic groups.

The globalization of public relations has also created a strong need for diversified ethnic staffs. Staff members are needed with language skills, personal knowledge of other nations, and sensitivity to the customs and attitudes of others. Knowledge of Spanish and Asian languages, such as Chinese, will be especially valuable.

Other Major Trends

Feminization of the field and the recruitment of a more diverse workforce are major trends, but other issues also will impact the practice of public relations in the coming years.

The Advent of Transparency. Instant global communications, corporate finance scandals, government regulation, and the increased public demand for accountability have made it necessary for all society's institutions, including business and industry, to be more transparent in their operations.

A position paper by Vocus, a communications software firm, says it best: "An organization's every action is subject to public scrutiny. Everything—from the compensation provided to a departing CEO to the country from which a manufacturing plant orders its materials—is considered open to public discourse."

The Institute of Public Relations (IPR) in the United Kingdom says that the role of public relations has changed considerably over the last decade: "Instead of being used primarily as a way to influence and secure media coverage, organizations are using public relations to communicate with their stakeholders as society demands more transparency."

Expanding the Role of Public Relations. Professionals have already repositioned public relations as being more than media relations and publicity, but those hard-fought gains will need to be reinforced in the coming years as marketing and management consultants enter the field offering the ability to also build relationships with various publics. Tom Gable, a public relations counselor in San Diego, says, "Our challenge and opportunity will be to own the areas of positioning, branding, reputation management, and building relationships for the long term with multiple constituencies." Increasingly, public relations personnel will play an even greater role in planning and executing integrated communications campaigns.

Increased Emphasis on Evaluation.   Public relations professionals will continue to improve measurement techniques for showing management how their activities actually contribute to the bottom line.

One dimension is the *return on investment* (ROI). According to Kathy Cripps, chair of the Council of Public Relations Firms, two other important dimensions of measurement are (1) measuring outcomes—the long-term effectiveness of a public relations program and (2) measuring outputs—how well a program was executed and how effective its tactics were.

Management increasingly demands better measurement, and Ed Nicholson, director of media relations at Tyson Foods, says, "We're compelled to create measurable objectives and evaluation that goes beyond clip counts and impressions and demonstrate delivered value to the organization."

Managing the 24/7 News Cycle.   The flow of news and information is now a global activity that occurs 24 hours day, 7 days a week. This means that public relations personnel must constantly update information, answer journalists' inquiries at all hours of the day, and be aware that any and all information is readily available to a worldwide audience.

New media and technology make it possible to disseminate news and information 24 hours a day, but the effect is often information overload. In addition to the proliferation of traditional media outlets, there are virtually millions of Web sites. A major challenge to today's practitioners is how to cope with the cascade of information and how to give it shape and purpose so that it's relevant to multiple audiences.

New Directions in Mass Media.   Traditional media isn't what it used to be. Circulation of English-language dailies in the United States has dropped 11 percent since 1990. Network evening news ratings have fallen 34 percent since 1993. Local news share is down 16 percent since 1997. Even cable news ratings have been flat since late 2001.

In other words, public relations personnel are now expanding their communication tools to account for the fact that no single mass media, or combination of them, will be a good vehicle for reaching key publics.

One new avenue is the ethnic press, whose growth has been particularly dramatic. Over the past 13 years, Spanish-language newspaper circulation has nearly quadrupled to 1.7 million. Another avenue is the Internet, which has seen its audience dramatically increase in just a few years. More than 55 percent of Internet users aged 18 to 34 obtain news online in a typical week, according to a UCLA Internet study.

Another trend line is the electronic preparation of media materials. The printed news release and media kit are rapidly becoming artifacts of the past. An IABC study found that electronic newsletters, e-mail notices, Web sites, and even CDs or DVDs are rapidly replacing print materials.

Outsourcing to Public Relations Firms.   The outsourcing trend developed some years ago, but now it's almost universal. A survey by Ian Mitroff, Gerald Swerling, and Jennifer Floto published in *The Strategist* notes, "The use of agencies is now the norm in American business across all revenue categories and industries in this study: 85 percent of respondents (corporate executives) work with outside PR firms." This is not to say that corporate public relations departments are disappearing, but increasingly such tactics as media relations, annual reports, and sponsored events are being outsourced to public relations firms.

The Need for Life-Long Learning. Public relations personnel, given the rapid additions to knowledge in today's society, will need to continually update their knowledge base just to stay current. New findings in a variety of fields are emerging that can be applied to public relations practice. Some of these fields are behavioral genetics, evolutionary social psychology, economics, the physics of information, social network analysis, semiotic game theory, and the use of technology to create relationships and dialogue with various publics.

In addition, the need to specialize in a particular field or area of public relations will increase because it's becoming almost impossible for a generalist to master the detailed knowledge required for such areas as health care and financial relations. One growing specialty area is environmental communication.

Increased Emphasis on Financial Relations. The corporate scandals involving Enron, WorldCom, and Tyco have prompted a whole new series of government regulations. One new regulation is the Sarbanes-Oxley Act of 2002, which dictates how companies must disclose information (see Chapter 12).

Donna Stein, managing partner of Brainerd Communications in New York, says, "Understanding Sarbanes-Oxley and keeping pace with the ever-changing Securities and Exchange Commission regulations is at the top of every financial communicator's to-do list." But understanding the regulations is not just the province of financial relations; Stein says that all public relations practitioners must understand the law and how it might impact their assigned communication duties.

SUMMARY

The Roots of Public Relations
Although *public relations* is a 20th-century term, the roots of the practice go back to ancient Egyptian, Greek, and Roman times.

Early Beginnings in America
Private companies attracted immigrants to the New World through promotion and glowing accounts of fertile land. The American Revolution, in part, was the result of such staged events as the Boston Tea Party and the writing of the Federalist Papers.

The Age of Press Agentry and Hype
The 1800s were the golden age of the press agent. P. T. Barnum used many techniques that are still used today. In addition, the settlement of the West was due in large part to promotions by land developers and American railroads. Toward the end of the 19th century, corporations began to use public relations as a response to public criticism of their policies and actions.

The Age of Public Relations Pioneers
From 1900 to 1950, the practice of public relations was transformed by individuals such as Henry Ford, Ivy Lee, George Creel, Edward B. Bernays, and Arthur Page. The concept moved from press agentry to the more journalistic approach of distributing accurate public information.

Public Relations Comes of Age
The period from 1950 to 2000 saw the consolidation of public relations as a major established force in American society. As the U.S. population grew, the economy expanded, and big business became the norm, organizations found it necessary to employ public relations specialists to effectively communicate with the mass media and a variety of publics. This was the age of scientific persuasion, management by objective, and strategic thinking.

Evolving Practice and Philosophy
At the turn of the century, public relations was widely considered to be a management function. Its purpose

was to engage in "reputation management" and to build mutually beneficial relationships with various constituencies. Public relations also took an increased role in launching new products, building brands, and positioning the organization in the marketplace.

Females Become the Majority

A major trend in public relations has been the influx of women into the field. Women now comprise 70 percent of public relations practitioners in America. This has raised questions about gender discrimination, why women hold more tactical than managerial positions, and whether there is still a "glass ceiling."

The Search for Diversity

The public relations workforce is still overwhelmingly white. Efforts are being made to diversify the workforce to better represent ethnic/minority groups. Hispanics now constitute the largest minority in the United States, but are poorly represented in public relations practice.

Other Trends

Public relations professionals will face a host of challenges during the first decade of the 21st century, including facilitating organizational transparency, owning brand management, doing a better job of measurement and evaluation, managing the 24/7 news cycle, and engaging in lifelong learning.

Case Activity: **What Would You Do?**

The latter part of this chapter identified a number of trends in public relations, including the feminization of the field and the drive for a more diversified workforce. Other trends include the decline of the mass media, the need for lifelong olearning, and the public's demand for organizational transparency.

Select one of these issues and do some additional research. White a short paper or make a presentation from the standpoint of what a public relations person should know about this issue and how it may affect working in public relations.

An alternative is to do more research on one of the pioneers in public relations and give a short report.

QUESTIONS for Review and Discussion

1. The roots of public relations extend deep into history. What were some of the early antecedents to today's public relations practice?
2. The Boston Tea Party has been described as the "greatest and best-known publicity stunt of all time." Would you agree? Do you feel that staged events are a legitimate way to publicize a cause and motivate people?
3. Which concepts of publicity and public relations practiced by P. T. Barnum should modern practitioners use? Which should they reject?
4. Describe briefly the publicity strategies employed by Henry Ford and Theodore Roosevelt.

5. What are the four important contributions Ivy Lee made to public relations?
6. Arthur W. Page enunciated six principles of public relations management. Do you think these "principles" are as relevant today as they were in the 1930s?
7. What's your assessment of Ivy Lee's work for the Rockefeller family in the Colorado Fuel & Iron Company labor strife? Do you think his approach was sound? What would you have done differently?
8. What effect did the Creel Committee have on the development of public relations?

9. Edward B. Bernays, who has been called the "father of modern public relations," had many innovative, successful campaigns. Of those listed in the book, which one is your favorite? Why?

10. Benjamin Sonnenberg once said, "I build large pedestals for small people" as an explanation of what he did in public relations. Would you agree that this is the essence of public relations? Why or why not?

11. Name at least three women who made major contributions to the development of public relations in the United States.

12. Summarize the major developments in the philosophy and practice of public relations from the 1920s to 2000.

13. James Grunig outlined four models of public relations practice. Name and describe each one? Do the models help explain the evolution of public relations theory?

14. Public relations is now described as "relationship management." How would you describe this concept to a friend? A newer concept is the idea that the purpose of public relations is to establish a "dialogue" with individuals and various publics. Is this a worthy concept?

15. Females now constitute the majority of public relations personnel. How do you personally feel about this? Does it make the field of public relations more attractive or less attractive to you?

16. Public relations is still considered a "lily white" profession. How do you think more minorities can be attracted to the field?

SUGGESTED READINGS

Aldoory, Linda, and Toth, Elizabeth. "Leadership and Gender in Public Relations: Perceived Effectiveness of Transformational and Transactional Leadership Styles." *Journal of Public Relations Research*, Vol. 16, No. 2, 2004, pp. 157–183.

Aldoory, Linda, and Toth, Elizabeth. "Gender Discrepancies in a Gendered Profession: A Developing Theory for Public Relations." *Journal of Public Relations Research*, Vol. 14, No. 2, 2002, pp. 103–126.

Anderson, William B. "We Can Do It: A Study of the Women's Field Army Public Relations Efforts." *Public Relations Review*, Vol. 30, No. 2, pp. 187–196.

Brody, E. W. "Have You Made the Transition? Are You Practicing Public Relations in the 21st Century Rather Than the 20th?" *Public Relations Quarterly*, Spring 2004, pp. 7–8.

Brown, R. E. "St. Paul as a Public Relations Practitioner: A Metatheoretical Speculation on Messianic Communication and Symmetry?" *Public Relations Review*, Vol. 29, No. 2, 2003, pp. 229–240.

Bruning, Stephen D. "Relationship Building as a Retention Strategy: Linking Relationship Attitudes and Satisfaction Evaluation to Behavioral Outcomes." *Public Relations Review*, Vol. 28, No. 1, 2002, pp. 39–48.

Calabro, Sara. "The Ceiling Breakers: Women Who Have Gained CEO Status, but Does That End All Gender Talk?" *PRWeek*, September 9, 2002, p. 15.

Choi, Youjin, and Hon, Linda Childers. "The Influence of Gender Composition in Powerful Positions on Public Relations Practitioners' Gender-Related Perceptions." *Journal of Public Relations Research*, Vol. 14, No. 3, 2002, pp. 229–263.

Cutlip, Scott M. *The Unseen Power: A History of Public Relations*. Mahwah, NJ: Lawrence Erlbaum, 1994.

Gable, Tom. "Five Major PR Issues for the Next Decade." *The Strategist*, Spring 2003, pp. 18–21.

Grunig, Larissa A., Toth, Elizabeth L., and Hon, Linda C. *Women in Public Relations: How Gender Influences Practice*. New York: Guilford Publications, 2001.

Hallahan, Kirk. "Ivy Lee and the Rocefellers' Response to the 1913–1914 Colorado Coal Strike." *Journal of Public Relations Research*, Vol. 14, No. 4, 2002, pp. 265–315.

Harrison, Shirley, and Moloney, Kevin. "Comparing Two Public Relations Pioneers" American Ivy Lee and British John Elliott." *Public Relations Review*, Vol. 30, No. 2, 2004, pp. 205–214.

Hutton, James G., Goodman, Michael B., Alexander, Jill B., and Genest, Christina M. "Reputation Management: The New Face of Corporate Public Relations?" *Public Relations Review*, Vol. 27, No. 3, 2001, pp. 247–261.

"In the year 2014 . . ." *Public Relations Tactics*, July 2004. (Entire issue is devoted to exploring public relations in the next decade.)

Karpf, Jason. "Adams, Paine, and Jefferson: A PR Firm." *Public Relations Tactics*, January 2002, pp. 12–14.

Kent, Michael L., and Taylor, Maureen. "Toward a Dialogic Theory of Public Relations." *Public Relations Review*, Vol. 28, No. 1, 2002, pp. 21–37.

O'Neil, Julie. "An Analysis of the Relationship Among Structure, Influence, and Gender: Helping to Build a Feminist Theory of Public Relations." *Journal of Public Relations Research*, Vol. 15, No. 2, 2003, pp. 151–179.

Piasecki, Andy. "Blowing the Railroad Trumpet: Public Relations on the American Frontier." *Public Relations Review*, Vol. 26, No. 1, 2000, pp. 53–65.

Pompper, Donnalyn. "Linking Ethnic Diversity and Two-Way Symmetry: Modeling Female African American Practitioner Roles." *Journal of Public Relations Research*, Vol. 16, No. 3, 2004, pp. 269–299.

Shortman, Melanie, and Bloom, Jonah. "The Greatest Campaigns Ever? *PRWeek*, July 15, 2002, pp. 14–15.

Van Ruler, Betteke.: The communication grid: an introduction of a model of four communication strategies." *Public Relations Review*, Vol. 30, No. 2, 2004, pp. 123–143.

Weidlich, Thom. "Diversity Survey 2003: Gauging the Efforts of the PR Industry to Diversify the Workforce." *PRWeek*, December 1, 2003, pp. 14–19.

Wrigley, Brenda J. "Glass Ceiling? What Glass Ceiling? A Qualitative Study of How Women View the Glass Ceiling in Public Relations and Communications Management." *Journal of Public Relations Research*, Vol. 14, No. 1, 2002, pp. 27–55.

chapter 3

Ethics and Professionalism

Topics covered in this chapter include:

What Is Ethics?

J. A. Jaksa and M. S. Pritchard provide a good definition of *ethics* in their book *Methods of Analysis*. "Ethics," they say, "is concerned with how we should live our lives. It focuses on questions about what is right or wrong, fair or unfair, caring or uncaring, good or bad, responsible or irresponsible, and the like."

A person's conduct is measured not only against his or her conscience, but also against some norm of acceptability that has been determined by society, professional groups, and a person's employer. The difficulty in ascertaining whether an act is ethical lies in the fact that individuals have different standards and perceptions of what is "right" or "wrong." Most ethical conflicts are not black or white, but fall into a gray area.

A person's belief system can also determine how that person acts in a specific situation. Philosophers say that the three basic value orientations are (1) *absolutist*, (2) *existentialist*, and (3) *situationalist*. The absolutist believes that every decision is either "right" or "wrong," regardless of the consequences. The existentialist, whose choices are not made in a prescribed value system, decides on the basis of immediate practical choice. The situationalist believes that each decision is based on what would cause the least harm or the most good. This often is called the *utilitarian* approach.

Others slice and dice value orientations into finer detail. There's the *fairness*, or *social justice*, approach, which posits that everyone should be treated equally or, if unequally, then fairly, based on some inequality that is defensible. The *virtue* approach assumes that individuals will achieve their highest potential if they practice such virtues as honesty, courage, compassion, generosity, fidelity, integrity, fairness, self-control, and prudence.

Public relations professionals have the burden of making ethical decisions that satisfy (1) the public interest, (2) their employer, (3) their professional organization's code of ethics, and (4) their personal values. In an ideal world, these four spheres would not conflict. In reality, however, they often do.

Perhaps you will be asked to keep news of an impending layoff secret from your co-workers. Maybe you will be asked to defend company practices that despoil the environment. Or maybe you will be asked to make claims for a product or service that can't be substantiated. The responses to these thorny issues usually depend on the individual's interpretation of truth-telling, promise-keeping, loyalty, and what is morally right.

The Ethical Advocate

Another issue of concern to students, as well as public relations critics, is whether a public relations practitioner can ethically communicate at the same time he or she is serving as an advocate for a particular client or organization. To some, traditional ethics prohibits a person from taking an advocacy role because that person is "biased" and trying to "manipulate" people.

David L. Martinson of Florida International University makes the point, however, that the concept of *role differentiation* is important. This means that society, in general, expects public relations people to be advocates, just as they expect advertising copywriters to make a product sound attractive, journalists to be objective, and attorneys to defend someone in court. Because of this concept, Martinson believes that "Public relations practitioners are justified in disseminating persuasive information so long as objective and reasonable persons would view those persuasive efforts as truthful." He continues, in a monograph published by the public relations division of the Association for Education in Journalism & Mass Communications:

> Reasonable persons recognize that public relations practitioners can serve important societal goals in an advocacy (role defined) capacity. What reasonable persons require, however, is that such advocacy efforts be directed toward genuinely informing impacted publics. Communication efforts . . . will not attempt, for example, to present false/deceptive/misleading information under the guise of literal truth no matter how strongly the practitioner wants to convince others of the merits of a particular client/organization's position/cause. . . . Role differentiation is not a license to "lie, cheat, and/or steal" on behalf of clients whether one is an attorney, physician, or public relations practitioner.

The Role of Professional Organizations

Professional organizations such as the Public Relations Society of America (PRSA) and the International Association of Business Communicators (IABC) have done much to develop the standards of ethical, professional public relations practice and to help society understand the role of public relations. Because of their influence in setting ethical standards for and fostering professionalism among public relations practitioners, the following section gives a thumbnail sketch of the largest professional groups serving the public relations profession.

The Public Relations Society of America

The largest national public relations organization in the world is the Public Relations Society of America (PRSA); the group's Web site can be found at www.prsa.org. PRSA is headquartered in New York City. It has almost 20,000 members organized into 116 chapters nationwide. It also has 18 professional interest sections that represent such areas as business and industry, counseling firms, independent practitioners, the military, government agencies, associations, hospitals, schools, nonprofit organizations, and even educators.

PRSA has an extensive professional development program that offers short courses, seminars, teleconferences, and Webcasts throughout the year. Some typical topics from a recent listing of events included seminars on strategic management planning, media relations building, crisis communication strategy, employee communication programs, and emerging trends in reputation management. Topical workshops have included "The Role of Public Relations in the Michael Jackson Case" and "Lessons from Martha (Stewart): Going to Jail Is Bad for Business."

In addition to workshops and seminars, PRSA holds an annual meeting and publishes two major periodicals. *Tactics* is a monthly tabloid of current news and professional tips. *The Strategist* is a quarterly magazine that contains in-depth articles about the profession and on issues touching on contemporary public relations practice. The organization also sponsors the Silver Anvil and Bronze Anvil awards that recognize outstanding public relations campaigns. According to PRSA, "In the 57 years since the inception of the Silver Anvil Awards program, more than 1,000

ON THE JOB insights

PRSA's Code of Ethics

The Public Relations Society of America (PRSA) has a fairly comprehensive code of ethics for its members. The group believes that "professional values are vital to the integrity of the profession as a whole."

Its six core values are as follows:

- **Advocacy:** Serving the public interest by acting as responsible advocates for clients or employers.
- **Honesty:** Adhering to the highest standards of accuracy and truth in advancing the interests of clients and employers.
- **Expertise:** Advancing the profession through continued professional development, research, and education.
- **Independence:** Providing objective counsel and being accountable for individual actions.
- **Loyalty:** Being faithful to clients and employers, but also honoring an obligation to serve the public interest.
- **Fairness:** Respecting all opinions and supporting the right of free expression.

The following is a summary of the major provisions and the kinds of activities that would constitute improper conduct.

Free Flow of Information

The free flow of accurate and truthful information is essential to serving the public interest in a democratic society. You should not give an expensive gift to a journalist as a bribe so that he or she will write favorable stories about the organization or its products/services. Lavish entertainment and travel junkets for government officials, beyond the limits set by law, also are improper.

Competition

Healthy and fair competition among professionals should take place within an ethical framework. An employee of an organization should not share information with a public relations firm that is in competition with other firms for the organization's business. You should not disparage your competition or spread malicious rumors about them to recruit business or to hire their employees.

Disclosure of Information

Open communication is essential to informed decision making in a democratic society. You should not conduct grassroots and letter-writing campaigns on behalf of undisclosed interest groups. In addition, you should not deceive the public by employing people to pose as "volunteers" at a public meeting. This also applies to booking "spokespersons" on talk shows without disclosing that they are being paid by an organization or special interest for their appearance. Intentionally leaving out essential information or giving a false impression of a company's financial performance is considered "lying by omission." If you do discover that inaccurate information has been given out, you have a responsibility to correct it immediately.

Safeguarding Confidences

Client trust requires appropriate protection of confidential and private information. You should not leak proprietary information that could adversely affect some other party. If you change jobs, you should not use confidential information from your previous employer to benefit the competitive advantage of your new employer.

Conflicts of Interest

Avoid real, potential, or perceived conflicts of interest among clients, employers, and the public. A public relations firm should inform a prospective client that it already represents a competitor or has a conflicting interest. A firm, for example, should not be doing public relations for two competing fast-food restaurant chains.

Enhancing the Profession

Public relations professionals should work constantly to strengthen the public's trust in the profession. You should not say a product is safe when it isn't. If it's unsafe under certain usage or conditions, you have an obligation to disclose this information.

For the complete code, please consult PRSA's Web site at www.prsa.org.

organizations have received awards for excellence in strategic public relations planning and implementation." The 2004 awards, for example, generated 650 entries in 54 categories.

PRSA is also the parent organization of the Public Relations Student Society of America (PRSSA), whose Website can be found at www.prssa.org. This group is the world's largest preprofessional public relations organization, having 248 campus chapters and more than 8400 student members.

The student group serves its members at the local chapter level through a variety of programs and maintains a close working relationship with the local professional PRSA chapter. It has a national publication, *Forum*, and sponsors a national case study competition so that students have the opportunity to exercise the analytical skills and mature judgment required for public relations problem solving. In 2004, for example, the case problem involved Ford Motor Credit Company. The PRSSA chapter at the University of South Carolina took first place honors. PRSSA members, after graduation, are eligible to become associate members of PRSA.

The International Association of Business Communicators

The second-largest organization of communication and public relations professionals is the International Association of Business Communicators (IABC). The group's Web site can be accessed at www.iabc.com. It has more than 13,000 members in 60 nations. Most members live in the United States, but it has many members in Canada, the United Kingdom, and Hong Kong. The Toronto chapter, for example, has about 1300 members, or about 10 percent of the entire IABC membership.

IABC, headquartered in San Francisco, has similar objectives as the PRSA. Its mission is to "provide lifelong learning opportunities that give IABC members the tools and information to be the best in their chosen disciplines." It does this through year-round seminars and workshops and an annual meeting. The organization also has an awards program, The Gold Quill, that honors excellence in business communication. Of the 920 entries received in 2004, 109 entries were selected to receive top awards for excellence. Approximately 22 percent of the Quill winners were from outside North America.

The IABC publication is *Communication World*; it features professional tips and in-depth articles on current issues. IABC also sponsors student chapters on various campuses, but it is not comparable to PRSSA in size, organizational structure, or scope.

The International Public Relations Association

A third organization, thoroughly global in scope, is the International Public Relations Association (IPRA), which is based in London. The group's Web site is available at www.ipra.org. IPRA has 1000 members in 96 nations. Its membership is primarily senior international public relations executives, and its mission is "to provide intellectual leadership in the practice of international public relations by making available to our members the services and information that will help them to meet their professional responsibilities and to succeed in their careers."

IPRA organizes regional and international conferences to discuss issues in global public relations, but it also reaches its widespread membership through its Web site

ON THE JOB insights

IPRA's Code of Ethics

The following code of professional conduct, based on the charter of the United Nations, has been published in 20 languages:

IPRA Members Shall Endeavor:

1. To contribute to the achievement of the moral and cultural conditions enabling human beings to reach their full stature and enjoy the indefeasible rights to which they are entitled under the "Universal Declaration of Human Rights."

2. To establish communication patterns and channels which, by fostering the free flow of essential information, will make each member of the group feel that he/she is being kept informed, and also gives him/her an awareness of his/her own personal involvement and responsibility, and of his/her solidarity with other members.

3. To conduct himself/herself always and in all circumstances in such a manner as to deserve and secure the confidence of those with whom he/she comes in contact.

4. To bear in mind that, because of the relationship between his/her profession and the public, his/her conduct—even in private—will have an impact on the way in which the profession as a whole is appraised.

IPRA Members Shall Undertake:

5. To observe, in the course of his/her professional duties, the moral principles and rules of the "Universal Declaration of Human Rights."

6. To pay due regard to, and uphold, human dignity, and recognize the right of each individual to judge for himself/herself.

7. To establish the moral, psychological, and intellectual conditions for dialogue in its true sense, and to recognize the right of the parties involved to state their case and express their views.

8. To act, in all circumstances, in such a manner as to take account of the respective interests of the parties involved: both the interests of the organization which he/she serves and

the interests of the publics involved.

9. To carry out his/her undertakings and commitments, which shall always be so worded as to avoid any misunderstanding, and to show loyalty and integrity in all circumstances so as to keep the confidence of his/her employers, past or present, and of all the publics that are affected by his/her actions.

IPRA Members Shall Refrain From:

10. Subordinating the truth to other requirements.

11. Circulating information which is not based on established and ascertainable facts.

12. Taking part in any venture or undertaking which is unethical or dishonest or capable of impairing human dignity or integrity.

13. Using any manipulative methods or techniques designed to create subconscious motivation which the individual cannot control of his/her own free will and so cannot be held accountable for the action taken on them.

and *Frontline*, its major magazine, which is available online. It also issues Gold Papers on public relations practice, conducts an annual awards competition (Golden World Awards), and is currently conducting a media transparency campaign to encourage media in various nations not to accept bribes in exchange for news coverage. See the Insights box on page 92.

Other Groups

The PRSA, IABC, and IPRA are the largest broad-based organizations for communicators and public relations professionals. In addition, there are smaller, more specialized organizations. Three of the better known ones in the United States include the Council for the Advancement and Support of Education (CASE), the National Investor Relations Institute (NIRI), and the National School Public Relations Association. There also are a number of statewide groups, such as the Florida Public Relations Association, the Maine Public Relations Council, the Texas Public Relations Association, and the Puerto Rico Public Relations Association (Asociacion de Relacionistas Profesionales de Puerto Rico).

Professional Codes of Conduct

Practically every national public relations organization has a code of ethics, and the codes of such organizations as the Canadian Public Relations Society (CPRS), the Public Relations Institute of Southern Africa (PRISA), and the Public Relations Institute of Australia (PRIA) are very similar to the PRSA code (see the Insights box on page 78).

Most national organizations place heavy emphasis on educating their members on professional standards rather than having a highly structured grievance process in place. They do exercise the right, however, to censure or expel members who violate the organization's code or who are convicted of a crime in a court of law. PRSA, at one time, did have a judicial process, but in 33 years, only about 10 members were ever disciplined by the organization.

The IABC's code is based on the principle that professional communication is not only legal and ethical, but also in good taste and sensitive to cultural values and beliefs. Members are encouraged to be truthful, accurate, and fair in all of their communications.

According to IABC, the organization "fosters compliance with its code by engaging in global communication campaigns rather than through negative sanctions." The code is published in several languages, and IABC bylaws require that articles on ethics and professional conduct be published in the organization's monthly publication, *Communication World*. In addition, the organization includes sessions on ethics at its annual meeting, conducts workshops on ethics, and encourages chapters to include discussions of ethics in their local programs. PRSA and other organizations have similar programs.

Critics often complain that such codes of ethics "have no teeth" because there's really no punishment for being unethical and unprofessional. About the only penalty that an organization can impose is to expel a person from the organization; however, that person can continue to work in public relations.

Problems with code enforcement, however, are not unique to public relations groups. Professional organizations, including the Society for Professional Journalists,

ON THE JOB insights

Use of "Front Groups" Poses Ethical Concerns

The proliferation of so-called "front groups" waging purported "grassroots" campaigns to achieve public relations goals has created much debate in the field in recent years.

The establishment of dozens of such groups evoked a strongly worded statement from the board of directors of the PRSA.

> PRSA specifically condemns the efforts of those organizations, sometimes known as "front groups," that seek to influence the public policy process by disguising or obscuring the true identity of their members or by implying representation of a much more broadly based group than exists.

Almost every "save the environment" organization has spawned a counter group. For example, the Forest Alliance of British Columbia posed as a grassroots movement opposing the International Coalition to Save British Columbia's

Rainforests, composed of 25 "green" groups. It was later revealed that the Canadian timber industry paid Burson-Marsteller $1 million to create the alliance, whose aim was to convince the public that environmental destruction has been exaggerated and to persuade lawmakers to abolish unprofitable environmental regulations.

Names given to many of the organizations are confusing, if not downright deceptive. Northwesterners for More Fish was the name chosen for a "grassroots" coalition of utilities and other companies in the Northwest under attack by environmental groups for depleting the fish population.

In California's Riverside County, a public relations firm organized Friends of Eagle Mountain on behalf of a mining company that wanted to create the world's largest landfill in an abandoned iron ore pit.

A prohunting group that works to convince people that wildlife is so plentiful that there is no reason not to kill some of it is known as the Abundant Wildlife Society of North America.

A Gallup Poll once showed that the majority of Americans considered themselves environmentalists. In the face of such findings, "People sometimes create groups that try to fudge a little bit about what their goals are," said Hal Dash, president of Cerrell Associates, a Los Angeles public relations firm that has represented clients with environmental problems.

Questioned about the tactics used in so-called grassroots campaigns, more than half of professionals surveyed by *PRNews* said that it is unethical for parties to fail to mention that their impetus for contacting a government official or other organization is due to a vested interest or membership in another organization sponsoring the campaign.

are voluntary organizations, and they don't have the legal authority to ban members from the field because no licensing is required to practice, which will be discussed shortly. Such organizations run a high risk of being sued for defamation or restricting the First Amendment guarantee of free speech if they try to expel a member or restrict their occupation.

Consequently, most professional groups believe that the primary purpose of establishing codes of ethics is not enforcement, but rather education and information. They seek to enunciate standards of conduct that will guide members in their professional lives. It seems to work. Several studies have shown that the members of PRSA and other organizations have a much higher awareness of ethics and professional standards than nonmembers.

Codes for Specific Situations

Various organizations, as noted, have established codes for the general practice of public relations, but various groups have also endorsed codes of conduct for specific situations and issues, such as the distribution of video news releases, the use of the Internet, environmental sensitivity, and even corporate practice.

Video News Releases. Occasionally, a controversy breaks out over the use of video news releases (VNRs) by television stations and whether the viewing public has been informed about the source of the information. One survey by *TV Guide*, for example, found that almost half of TV station news directors failed to identify the source of VNRs on their news programs.

"Don't blame the makers of VNRs," said Bob Kimmel, senior vice president of the News/Broadcast Network, a producer and distributor of such releases. Kimmel continued, "We are doing everything we can by putting the source of the material on the VNR. We can't control what happens at the news level, however." Many stations apparently don't like to admit that they use video material that is not produced by their own staffs.

Six video news producers, members of the Public Relations Service Council in New York, decided that a Code of Good Practice was needed to assure the public and TV industry critics that all VNRs produced by them contained accurate information and were clearly labeled as coming from a corporate sponsor. The key components of the code are as follows:

- Information contained in a VNR must be accurate and reliable. Intentionally false and misleading information must be avoided.

- A video news release must be identified as such, both on the video's opening slate and on any advisory material and scripts.

- The sponsor of the release must be clearly identified on the tape. The name and phone number of the sponsor must be provided on the video for journalists to contact for further information.

ON THE JOB

ethics

Ford/Firestone Tire Recall

Can public relations gloss over a lack of corporate responsibility? The Firestone/Ford tire recall controversy, detailed in Chapter 1, raises serious ethical questions about each company's failure to take action until the glare of publicity apparently forced them to admit there was a problem.

For nearly two years before the recall, for example, Ford had received complaints from overseas about possible problems with Firestone tires on its Explorers in such nations as Venezuela and Saudi Arabia. Yet, Ford continued to sell Explorers with Firestone tires in the U.S. market. Firestone also had indications that the tread was separating from some of its models as early as 1994, because there already was a pattern of lawsuits.

Even when the National Highway Traffic Safety Administration (NHTSA) launched an investigation in May of 2000 after receiving numerous reports of accidents and fatalities, it took another three months before Firestone voluntarily recalled 6.5 million tires. This has led many critics to charge that both Firestone and Ford were more interested in preserving their image and corporate reputation than in saving lives.

But hiding information, or refusing to act swiftly in the public interest, is no doubt the worst public relations strategy. Both Firestone and Ford saw their reputations and credibility plummet in the wake of disclosures about what they knew and when. Corporate credibility also declined when both companies actively blamed each other for the problem. Kirk O. Hanson, a senior lecturer in business ethics at the Stanford Business School, wrote: "In the long run, sound ethical behavior makes good business sense, allowing companies to protect their reputations and their bottom line. Acting ethically is also the right thing to do."

- Persons interviewed on the VNR must be accurately identified by name, title, and affiliation in the video.

Internet Public Relations. Should public relations personnel covertly build a buzz for their client or employer's products in online chat rooms without revealing that they are being paid for praising the product?

This question was raised by Richard Edelman, president and CEO of Edelman Worldwide, when he found out some of his staff were doing just that. "They were going in on an unattributed basis and saying, 'Well, the Game Cube—or whatever— is the world's greatest thing,' and, meanwhile, not revealing that 'Hi, I work for Nintendo,' " Edelman told *PRWeek*. His conclusion, "No, we can't do that. It's wrong, and it ruins our credibility."

Because of such practices, the Arthur W. Page Society, an organization of senior-level communication executives, and 10 other major public relations organizations decided it was time to establish a set of principles for public relations on the Web. In addition to calling for truth and accuracy in all Web content, the organizations also endorsed adherence to the following guidelines:

- Disclose any affiliations in chat room postings
- Offer opportunities for dialogue and interaction with experts
- Reveal the background of experts, disclosing any potential conflicts of interest or anonymous economic support of content
- Practice principled leadership in the digital world, adhering to the highest standards

Corporate Practice. Many public relations firms and companies also have established standards of conduct for their employees.

Ketchum tells its employees, as do many other firms, "We will deal with clients in a fair and businesslike fashion, providing unbiased, professional recommendations to move their business ahead." Ketchum's code deals with (1) truth and accuracy in communications, (2) how to handle confidential information, (3) what gifts and entertainment are acceptable and not acceptable, (4) fair dealings with suppliers and vendors, (5) safeguarding of client proprietary information, and (6) abuse of "inside" information. (See also Chapter 18 for Ketchum's problem with government contracts.)

Of course, it is one thing to have codes of conduct printed in the employee handbook and framed on the wall and another to actually practice what is being preached. As Samuel Petok, senior vice president of communications at Rockwell International Corp., wrote in an Arthur W. Page Society newsletter, "Media perceptions of business increasingly are distorted and adversarial. We can't change public perceptions solely by advertising and public relations; perception is a function of the day-to-day performance of the business."

Professionalism, Licensing, and Accreditation

Is public relations a profession? Should its practitioners be licensed? Does the accreditation of practitioners constitute a sufficient guarantee of their talents and integrity? These and other such questions are addressed in this section.

Professionalism

Among public relations practitioners, there are considerable differences of opinion about whether public relations is a craft, a skill, or a developing profession. Certainly, at its present level, public relations does not qualify as a profession in the same sense that medicine and law do. Public relations does not have prescribed standards of educational preparation, a mandatory period of apprenticeship, or state laws that govern admission to the profession.

Adding to the confusion about professionalism is the difficulty of ascertaining what constitutes public relations practice. John F. Budd, Jr., a veteran counselor, wrote in *Public Relations Quarterly*: "We *act* as publicists, yet we *talk* of counseling. We *perform* as technologists in communication, but we *aspire* to be decision-makers dealing in policy."

On the other hand, there is an increasing body of literature about public relations—including this text and many others in the field. PRSA has compiled a Body of Knowledge abstract that contains more than 100 references, available on computer disk or hard copy. Substantial progress also is being made in developing theories of public relations, conducting research, and publishing scholarly journals.

There is also the idea, advanced by many professionals and PRSA itself, that the most important thing is for the individual to *act like a professional* in the field. This means that a practitioner should have:

- A sense of independence.
- A sense of responsibility to society and the public interest.
- Manifest concern for the competence and honor of the profession as a whole.
- A higher loyalty to the standards of the profession and fellow professionals than to the employer of the moment. The reference point in all public relations activity must be the standards of the profession and not those of the client or the employer.

Unfortunately, a major barrier to professionalism is the attitude that many practitioners themselves have toward their work. As James Grunig and Todd Hunt state in their text *Managing Public Relations*, practitioners tend to hold more "careerist" values than professional values. In other words, they place higher importance on job security, prestige in the organization, salary level, and recognition from superiors than on the values just listed. For example, 47 percent of the respondents in a survey of IABC members gave a neutral or highly negative answer when asked if they would quit their jobs rather than act against their ethical values. And 55 percent considered it "somewhat ethical" to present oneself misleadingly as the only means of achieving an objective. Almost all agreed, however, that ethics is an important matter, worthy of further study.

On another level, many practitioners are limited in their professionalism by what might be termed a "technician mentality." These people narrowly define professionalism as the ability to do a competent job of executing the mechanics of communicating (preparing news releases, brochures, newsletters, and so on) even if the information provided by management or a client is in bad taste, is misleading, lacks documentation, or is just plain wrong.

The *Wall Street Journal* once highlighted the pitfalls of the technician mentality. The story described how Jartran, Inc., used the services of the Daniel J. Edelman, Inc., public relations firm to distribute a press packet to the media. The packet included a letter offering information about wheels falling off trucks owned by U-Haul, its archrival. When the newspaper reporter asked about the ethics of this approach, an Edelman junior account executive was quoted as saying, "It was their idea. We're merely the PR firm that represents them."

In other words, readers may get the impression that the public relations expertise of a firm is available to the highest bidder, regardless of professional values, fair play, and ultimately, the public interest. When public relations firms and departments take no responsibility for what is communicated—only *how* it is communicated in terms of techniques—they reinforce the perception that public relations is more flackery than profession.

Some practitioners defend the technician mentality, however, arguing that public relations people are like lawyers in the court of public opinion. Everyone is entitled to his or her viewpoint and, whether the public relations person agrees or not, the client or employer has a right to be heard. Thus, a public relations representative is a paid advocate, just as a lawyer is. The only flaw in this argument is that public relations people are not lawyers, nor are they in a court of law where judicial concepts determine the roles of defendant and plaintiff. In addition, lawyers have been known to turn down clients or resign from a case because they doubted the client's story.

In Chapter 12, which concerns legal aspects of public relations, it is pointed out that courts are increasingly holding public relations firms accountable for information disseminated on behalf of a client. Thus, it is no longer acceptable to say, "The client told me to do it."

Licensing

Proposals that public relations practitioners be licensed were discussed before PRSA was founded. One proponent, Edward L. Bernays, who was instrumental in formulating the modern concept of public relations (see Chapter 2), believed that licensing would protect the profession and the public from incompetent, shoddy opportunists who do not have the knowledge, talent, or ethics required of public relations professionals.

The problem is stated by PRSA's task force on demonstrating professionalism:

> Pick up any metropolitan newspaper and scan the employment ads. Under the "public relations" classification, you are likely to find opportunities for door-to-door salespersons, receptionists, used-car salesmen, singles bar hostesses and others of less savory reputation. The front pages of the newspapers are full of stories about former government employees peddling influence and calling it public relations.

Thus, under the licensing approach, only those individuals who pass rigid examinations and tests of personal integrity could call themselves "public relations" counselors. Those not licensed would have to call themselves "publicists" or adopt some other designation.

Several arguments for licensing and registration have been advanced. Advocates say that it would help (1) define the practice of public relations, (2) establish uniform educational criteria, (3) set uniform professional standards, (4) protect clients and employers from imposters and charlatans, (5) protect qualified practitioners from unfair competition from the unethical and unqualified, and (6) raise the overall credibility of public relations practitioners. One survey, for example, found that a company public relations representative was next to the bottom as a credible spokesperson, ranking slightly above athletes and entertainers.

Opponents of licensing say that it won't work and that it is unfeasible for the following reasons: (1) any licensing in the communications field would violate the First Amendment guarantee of freedom of speech; (2) civil and criminal laws already exist to deal with malpractice; (3) licensing is a function of state governments, and public relations people often work on a national and international level; (4) licensing ensures only minimum competence and professional standards, it doesn't necessarily ensure high ethical behavior; (5) the credibility and status of an occupation are not necessarily ensured through licensing (attorneys, for example, don't enjoy particularly high status and prestige because they are licensed, nor do licensed practical nurses); and (6) setting up the machinery for licensing and policing would be very costly to the American taxpayer.

The opponents seem to have won the day. Today, there is no particular interest on the part of the public relations industry, the consumer movement, or even state governments to initiate any form of legislated licensing. An alternative to licensing is accreditation, which many public relations groups do actively endorse and promote.

Accreditation

The major effort to improve standards and professionalism in public relations around the world has been the establishment of accreditation programs. This means that practitioners voluntarily go through a process in which they are "certified" by a national organization that they are competent, qualified professionals.

PRSA, for example, began its accreditation program more than 40 years ago. In 2003, it completely revamped its testing process for members to earn Accredited in Public Relations (APR) status. Other national groups, including the IABC, the Canadian Public Relations Society (CPRS), the British Institute of Public Relations (BIPR), the Public Relations Institute of Australia (PRIA), and the Public Relations Institute of Southern Africa (PRISA), to name just a few, also have established accreditation programs.

The approach used by most national groups is to have written and oral exams and to have candidates submit a portfolio of work samples to a committee of professional peers. IABC, for example, places a major emphasis on the individual's portfolio of accomplishments as part of its ABC (Accredited Business Communicator) certification. The candidate also must outline the objectives of a campaign, present the overall communications strategy, and provide evaluation of the results. About 10 percent of IABC's 1,300 members have the ABC designation.

Most groups also have guidelines as to how many years of experience are required before a person can apply for accredited or membership status. IABC, for example, requires a minimum of five years' experience and a bachelor's degree. South Africa's PRISA, on the other hand, ensures some knowledge of the field by requiring that each candidate first complete a Certificate in Public Relations Management before taking the exam.

Some groups are beginning to require continuing education as a prerequisite for professional certification. The PRIA, for example, requires members to earn Certified Practitioner (CP) status by completing 40 hours of continuing education each year, but most national groups—including PRSA—have been less than successful in requiring continuing education for their members.

The PRSA Approach.   PRSA was one of the first public relations organizations to develop an accreditation program for its members in 1965. For many years, the accreditation process included both an oral and a written exam, but not a portfolio of professional work.

In 2003, the entire accreditation process was completely restructured to better reflect the growing body of knowledge and diversity in the field. Candidates are now required to take a preview course (available online), complete a "readiness" questionnaire, and show a portfolio of work to a panel of professional peers before taking the written exam, which is available at test centers throughout the United States. In addition, the member must have five years of professional experience.

The 2.5-hour exam tests knowledge of the field and gives proportional weight to various core topics: research, planning, execution, and evaluation of programs (30 percent); ethics and law (15 percent); communication models and theories (15 percent); business literacy (10 percent); management skills (10 percent); crisis communication management (10 percent); media relations (5 percent); information technology (2 percent); history and current issues in public relations (2 percent); and advanced communication skills (1 percent).

Candidates who pass earn the credential "APR" (Accredited in Public Relations). To date, about 5,000 practitioners have earned APR status, or about 25 percent of the PRSA's membership.

Administration of the APR exam falls under the auspices of the Universal Accreditation Board (UAB), which was created by PRSA in 1998. It allows non-PRSA members from other professional groups who have joined the UAB to take the accreditation exam. The consortium of groups, however, is not exactly "universal." It mainly consists of various state organizations, such as the Florida Public Relations Association, and specialized groups, such as the National School Public Relations Association, that don't have their own accreditation programs.

Other Steps Toward Professionalism

PRSA, IABC, and other national groups have various programs designed to advance the profession of public relations. They include (1) working with universities to standardize curricula, (2) implementing research projects, and (3) recognizing outstanding practitioners who mentor and serve as role models.

Education. PRSA, IABC, and other organizations, such as the National Communication Association (NCA), have worked with the public relations division of the Association for Education in Journalism and Mass Communications (AEJMC) to improve and standardize the curricula of public relations at the undergraduate and master's degree levels.

One result of this cooperation was the 1999 Commission on Public Relations Education, which consisted of leading educators and practitioners representing a number of professional communication groups. The commission's report, *A Port of Entry: Public Relations Education for the 21st Century*, pointed out that a strong background in liberal arts and social sciences is a necessary foundation for public relations majors.

The commission recommended that coursework in public relations should comprise 25 to 40 percent of all undergraduate credit hours. Of those, at least half should be clearly identified as public relations courses covering such topics as (1) principles, (2) case studies, (3) research and evaluation, (4) writing and production, (5) planning and management, (6) campaigns, and (7) supervised internships. The commission also recommended that students complete a minor or a double major in another discipline, such as business or the behavioral sciences.

At the graduate level, the commission recommended public relations courses in such areas as (1) theory, (2) law, (3) research methods, (4) management, (5) programming and production, (6) communication theory, (7) integrated marketing, (8) social psychology and cultural anthropology, and (9) ethics.

Research.   Various groups have added to the body of knowledge of public relations through the commissioning of research studies, monographs, books, and reports. IPRA, for example, has issued a number of "gold papers" over the years. Recent papers have included *Green Communication in the Age of Sustainable Development, Quality Customer Satisfaction Public Relations, Public Relations Evaluation—Professional Accountability*, and *Corporate Social Responsibility*.

Measurement and evaluation have been a major focus of the Institute for Public Relations (IPR) in recent years (www.instituteforpr.com). Some of the papers it has commissioned have included titles such as *Guidelines and Standards for Measuring the Effectiveness of PR Programs and Activity, Public Relations Research for Planning and Evaluation*, and *What You Need to Know to Measure Investor Relations*. Meanwhile, IABC has published a number of books and monographs on such topics as *The Intranet Advantage: Your Guide to Understanding the Total Intranet and the Communicator's Role, Managing the Communication Function: Capturing Mindshare for Organizational Performance*, and *Face-to-Face: Communicating for Leadership*.

Recognition of Senior Professionals.   Several national groups, such as PRSA and IABC, have established "Fellow" programs that recognize career achievement and contributions to the profession. PRSA, for example, has a College of Fellows that has grown to about 500 members. In addition, annual awards by both PRSA and IABC honor educators and practitioners who are leaders in the field.

Ethics in Individual Practice

Despite codes of professional practice and formalized accreditation, ethics in public relations boils down to deeply troubling questions for the individual practitioner: Will I lie for my employer? Will I rig a doorprize drawing so a favorite client can win? Will I deceive in order to gain information about another agency's clients? Will I cover up a hazardous condition? Will I issue a news release presenting only half the truth? Will I seek to bribe a reporter or a legislator? Will I withhold some information in a news conference and provide it only if a reporter asks a specific question? Will I quit my job rather than cooperate in a questionable activity? In other words, to what extent, if any, will I compromise my personal beliefs?

These and similar questions plague the lives of many public relations people, although a number hold such strong personal beliefs and/or work for such highly principled employers that they seldom need to compromise their personal values. If employers make a suggestion that involves questionable ethics, the public relations person often can talk them out of the idea by citing the possible consequences of such an action—adverse media publicity, for example.

"To thine own self be true," advised New York public relations executive Chester Burger at an IABC conference. A fellow panelist, Canadian politician and radio commentator Stephen Lewis, commented: "There is a tremendous jaundice on the part of the public about the way things are communicated. People have elevated superficiality to an art form. Look at the substance of what you have to convey, and the honesty used in conveying it." With the audience contributing suggestions, the panelists formulated the following list of commendable practices:

- Be honest at all times.
- Convey a sense of business ethics based on your own standards and those of society.
- Respect the integrity and position of your opponents and audiences.
- Develop trust by emphasizing substance over triviality.
- Present all sides of an issue.
- Strive for a balance between loyalty to the organization and duty to the public.
- Don't sacrifice long-term objectives for short-term gains.

Adherence to professional standards of conduct—being truly independent—is the chief measure of a public relations person. Faced with such personal problems as a mortgage to pay and children to educate, practitioners may be strongly tempted to become yes men (or yes women) and decline to express their views forcefully to an employer, or to resign. J. Kenneth Clark, vice president of corporate communications, Duke Power Company, Charlotte, North Carolina, once gave the following advice to an IABC audience:

> If the boss says newspapers are no damn good, the yes man agrees.
> If the boss says to tell a reporter "no comment," the yes man agrees.
> If the boss says the company's employees get a paycheck and don't really need to be informed about anything else, the yes man agrees.
> If the boss says the public has no right to pry into what's going on inside a company—even though that company is publicly held and is dependent upon public support and public sales—the yes man nods his head agreeably and starts work on the corporate version of a Berlin Wall.
> The fate of the yes man is as inevitable as it is painful. Although your boss may think you're the greatest guy in the world for a while, you're going to lose your internal credibility because you never really state your professional opinions. And you're talking to a person who dotes on strong opinions and does not think highly of people who fail to offer them.

Allen H. Center, professor emeritus at San Diego State University and a long-time corporate public relations executive, has written: "Public relations has emerged more as an echo of an employer's standards and interests than that of a professional discipline applied to the employer's problems." Yet many a practitioner has resigned rather than submit to a compromising situation.

In some cases practitioners have been arbitrarily fired for refusing to write news releases that are false and misleading. This happened to an accredited PRSA member in the San Francisco Bay area. The company president wanted him, among other things, to write and send a news release giving a list of company clients when, in fact, none of the companies had signed a contract for services. When the practitioner refused, on the grounds that the PRSA code would be violated, he was fired. In turn, the practitioner sued the company for unlawful dismissal and received almost $100,000 in an out-of-court settlement.

Thus, it can be readily seen that ethics in public relations really begins with the individual—and is directly related to his or her own value system as well as to the good of society. Although it is important to show loyalty to an employer, practitioners must never allow a client or an employer to rob them of their self-esteem.

Ethical Dealings with News Media

The most practical consideration facing a public relations specialist in his or her dealings with the news media is that anything less than total honesty will destroy credibility and, with it, the practitioner's usefulness to an employer.

Trust is maintained even when practitioners say "no comment" and refuse to answer questions that go beyond information reported in the news releases, according to a study by Professors Michael Ryan and David L. Hartinson, published in *Journalism Quarterly*. Practitioners and journalists tend to agree on how they define lying; both, for example, believe that giving evasive answers to reporters' questions constitutes lying.

Gifts

Achieving trust is the aim of all practitioners, and it can only be achieved through highly professional and ethical behavior. It is for this reason that public relations practitioners should not undermine the trust of the media by providing junkets of doubtful news value, extravagant parties, expensive gifts, and personal favors for media representatives. Journalists, for the most part, will think you are trying to bribe them to get favorable coverage. See also the Insights box on page 78.

Gifts of any kind, according to PRSA, can contaminate the free flow of accurate and truthful information to the public. Although the exact words, "corrupting the channels of communication," are no longer used in the PRSA code, there are still the same strictures about gifts of products, travel, and services to reporters.

Coca-Cola, for example, got roundly criticized by public relations practitioners and journalists for sending sample cans of Coke Classic stuffed with $5 bills to 200 consumer and trade reporters as part of a nationwide promotion. The public relations newsletter, *Bulldog Reporter*, quoted a number of newspeople and public relations executives who, for the most part, pointed out that the sending of cash to news sources—even as a gimmick—raised questions of whether a bribe was intended. The Global box on page 92 discusses the problem of gifts for coverage in other countries.

Another area of ethical concern is when a company or organization pays a reporter's expenses for covering its event or news conference. U.S. journalists, as a rule, don't expect their expenses to be paid for by the company or organization that they are covering. However, the practice is quite common in other nations. In one survey, almost a third of European journalists expected public relations people to pay their expenses. The percentage rises to almost 60 percent in Asian nations.

Shades of Gray in the News Business

Although it may be presumed that public relations representatives would benefit from being able to influence journalists with gifts or offers of paid advertising, this is not the case. A major selling point of public relations work is the third-party credibility of reporters and editors. The public trusts journalists to be objective and to be somewhat impartial in the dissemination of information. If the public loses that trust because

ON THE JOB global

Cash for News Coverage Raises Ethical Concerns

In Russia and Eastern Europe, it's not uncommon for companies and public relations practitioners to bribe journalists to get a news release or a product photo published in the news columns of a newspaper or mentioned on a television news program. The Russians call this practice "zakazukha."

A survey by the IPRA also found that "pay-for-play" was practiced extensively in Africa, the Middle East, and Southern Europe. To a much lesser extent, it occurs in Asia, Western Europe, Australia, and the United States.

IPRA and five other global organizations have joined forces to support a set of principles designed to foster greater transparency between public relations professionals and the media in an attempt to end bribery for media coverage throughout the world. The other organizations are the International Press Institute, the International Federation of Journalists, Transparency International, the Global Alliance for Public Relations and Communications Management, and the Institute for Public Relations Research and Education.

The guidelines call for the following:

- News material should appear as a result of the news judgment of journalists and editors, not as a result of any payment in cash or in kind or any other inducements.
- Material involving payment should be clearly identified as advertising, sponsorship, or promotion.
- No journalist or media representative should ever suggest that news coverage will appear for any reason other than its merit.
- When samples or loans of products or services are necessary for a journalist to render an objective opinion, the length of time should be agreed in advance and loaned products should be returned.
- The media should institute written policies regarding the receipt of gifts or discounted products and services, and journalists should be required to sign the policy.

"In too many countries, bribery of the news media robs citizens of truthful information that they need to make individual and community decisions," says Don Wright, president of IPRA. He continues, "We started this campaign with the goal of creating greater transparency and eliminating unethical practices in dealings between news sources and the media."

IPRA and the Institute for Public Relations Research and Education (IPR) have also started a biennial international index of bribery and the media to monitor progress in the reduction of media corruption around the world.

they feel the media can be "bought," the information provided by public relations sources also becomes less trusted.

The relationship between automotive journalists and car manufacturers is already questionable, according to the *Wall Street Journal*. It is not unusual, for example, for an editor at *Car and Driver* to write reviews for autos made by an automaker that also employs the journalist as a consultant. As the author of the *Wall Street Journal* article notes, "Welcome to the world of automotive enthusiast journalism where the barriers that separate advertisers from journalists are porous enough for paychecks to pass

PR CASEBOOK

Political Pay-offs or Relationship Building?

Should a public relations firm interested in government contracts give gifts and political contributions to elected officials? And, if they do, does it raise any ethical concerns?

At least three public relations firms have received negative publicity and criticism because of gift-giving and political contributions. Edelman Worldwide in Chicago, for example, received intense media scrutiny after it was revealed that it had contributed $32,600 to Gov. Rod Blagojevich (D-IL) and had been successful in receiving the renewal of a $6.2 million state tourism contract.

In Colorado, Peter Webb Public Relations had a three-year $400,000 annual contract with the state lottery, but it was also revealed by the *Rocky Mountain News* that the firm had given 23 gifts to lottery officials, which included meals and sports tickets. In the uproar, the Colorado Lottery cancelled the contract with the public relations firm and the state legislature considered a bill that would bar vendor gifts to lottery employees.

Meanwhile, in Los Angeles, the mayor cancelled all contracts with public relations firms working for various city agencies because Fleishman-Hillard's $3 million contract with the LA Department of Water and Power also involved the firm's contributions to elected officials. It is not illegal to make such contributions, as long as they are publicly reported, but the media and the public often perceive such contributions as influence peddling to get government contracts.

Doug Downie, general manager of the Fleishman office in Los Angeles, was unapologetic. He told *PRWeek*, "The way to understand this dynamic is that contributions allow you to build relationships with elected officials and while they are not necessarily required in order to do public affairs work, they are door openers, and they are certainly something that is appreciated by people who need to raise money in order to seek higher office or to win office in the first place. . . . This is how our political system works."

Edelman Chicago general manager Cathleen Johnson agrees that contributions are a valid strategy. She told *PRWeek*, "It's really part of doing business. We have made contributions throughout the history of the company really because we're a part of the community."

What do you think? Should government agencies hire public relations firms in the first place? Are political contributions, legally reported, part of pursuing government business? Do you think it is a part of "relationship building" or simply a method to get favorable treatment for contracts? What do such controversies do to the image of public relations as a whole?

through." There's also considerable suspicion that the maker of the *Car of the Year* on the cover of an auto magazine has placed extensive paid advertising in that particular issue. Is this just coincidence, or part of an "understanding"?

Magazines, in particular, are increasingly blurring the line between news features and advertisements. Tony Silber, who writes about the magazine industry, told *PRWeek*, "If you look at shelter magazines, they are going to have advertisers' products in their decorated spreads of homes." Product placements are discussed in detail in Chapters 11 and 15.

Transparency is another problem. Should a spokesperson on a television talk show reveal his or her employer? This question came to the forefront when it was revealed in the press that the Toy Guy (Christopher Byrne), who appears on scores of local and national television shows with his selections of the best and hottest toys for the Christmas season, is actually paid hundreds of thousands of dollars by various toy companies to promote their products.

Byrne, who bills himself as an objective consumer advocate, says that he appears on radio talk shows and television programs for free and that he doesn't charge the manufacturers for his appearances. At the same time, however, the toy companies pay large fees to the public relations firm that employs him. The manufacturers, according to published reports, pay for his participation in a national media tour and other public relations efforts on their behalf.

A *New York Daily News* reporter asked Shannon Eis, spokeswomen for the Toy Industry Association, if television viewers should be informed that Byrne is paid. She responded, "I don't know if it's right. I can't say yes or no." Representatives of several toy companies were more definitive. They said that there was nothing wrong with what Byrne was doing and that it was a long-established industry practice.

Paul Holmes, a columnist for *PRWeek*, took a different view. He wrote, "It's hard to read this kind of thing and not conclude that the entire toy industry is corrupt, united in its shared contempt for consumers and by its denial that this kind of sleazy practice is acceptable."

Celebrities appearing on talk shows such as NBC's *Today* show also raise the issue of transparency. Actress Kathleen Turner, for example, told Diane Sawyer on ABC's *Good Morning America* about her battle with rheumatoid arthritis and mentioned that a drug, Enbrel, helped ease the pain. What Turner didn't reveal, however, was that she was being paid to appear by the company that manufactured the drug.

The *New York Times* broke the story, and the networks responded that they would initiate a policy that viewers will be told of a celebrity's ties to corporations. A CNN spokesperson, quoted in *Jack O'Dwyer's PR Newsletter*, said, "We decided it was important for our viewers to be aware of that as part of any future interviews or features about a celebrity."

SUMMARY

What Is Ethics?

Ethics refers to a person's value system and how he or she determines right or wrong. The three basic value orientations are (1) absolutist, (2) existentialist, and (3) situationalist.

The Ethical Advocate

Even if one is an advocate for a particular organization or cause, one can behave in an ethical manner. Because of the concept of *role differentiation*, society understands that the advocate is operating within an assigned role, much like a defense lawyer or prosecuting attorney in court.

Professional Organizations

Groups such as PRSA, IABC, and IPRA provide an important role in setting the standards and ethical behavior of the profession. Most professional organizations have published codes of conduct and educational programs.

Front Groups Are Unethical

It is the responsibility of public relations professionals to disclose the funding and identity of individuals who claim to be "citizen groups" but actually represent the disguised interests of their actual sponsors.

Professionalism

True public relations professionals have a loyalty to a higher standard and to the public interest. They are more than "careerists" and practice public relations with more than a "technician mentality." They are not hired guns who just parrot whatever the client or organization wants them to say.

Licensing and Accreditation

Freedom of speech concerns severely limit the concept of licensing in the communication fields, includ-ing public relations. Accreditation programs for practitioners, plus continuing education, is an attractive alternative.

Media Relations

Public relations practitioners should be fair, honest, and open with the media. Such behavior builds trust and credibility. Advertising influences on media coverage, plus the giving of gifts, tend to undermine public trust of the media.

Case Activity: **What Would You Do?**

Here's hypothetical situation. A well-known professional basketball player is charged with cocaine possession and the rape of a contestant in a local beauty contest. His attorney asks you to advise and assist him in handling the intense media interest in the case. He wants you to try to place favorable stories about the athlete in the media and create a positive pretrial environment for him. If convicted, it would mean the end of his professional basketball career.

You are not asked to do anything unethical. The money is quite good, and you know the publicity from working on the case will probably help your public relations consulting career, especially if the athlete is found innocent. Would you take the account? The lawyer tells you confidentially that the athlete has admitted that he snorted cocaine and raped the woman, but the plea will be "not guilty." Does this information affect your decision? What are the ethics of the situation as you see them?

QUESTIONS for Review and Discussion

1. What is ethics? How can two individuals disagree about what constitutes an ethical dilemma or concern?

2. What key points do the PRSA, IABC, and IPRA codes of conduct have in common? In what ways are they different?

3. Some critics say voluntary codes of ethics "have no teeth" because they can't be enforced. Are there other reasons for having codes of ethics?

4. IPRA and other global organizations have formed a set of guidelines to reduce "pay-for-play" in the world's media. What are five guidelines for public relations–media relationships?

5. Why do "careerism" and the "technician mentality" undermine efforts to establish professional standards in public relations?

6. Should public relations practitioners be licensed? What are the pros and cons of licensing?

7. What is the primary goal of most professional codes in public relations? Is it enforcement or education?

8. Is it unethical to set up a "front group" as a citizens organization when, in fact, the group is organized and funded by special or corporate interests?

9. What makes an occupation a profession?

10. When companies operate in other nations, should they adhere to the standards of their home country or adapt to the ethical standards of the host nation? For example, should American companies pay bribes to journalists in Russia if that is the standard operating practice?

11. Public relations practitioners often have conflicting loyalties. Do they owe their first allegiance to their client or employer or to the standards of their professional organization, such as PRSA?

12. Some celebrities on television talk shows endorse products, but the viewers don't know that they are being paid by the manufacturer. Is this the fault of the news media or the organization making the product?

13. Some argue that there is such a thing as an "ethical advocate." What reasons do they give?

14. It is important for an individual to act like a professional. What are four qualities of professionals?

15. What do membership groups, such as PRSA, do to encourage their members to be professionals?

16. What is the ideal undergraduate public relations curriculum?

17. Why are gifts to the media considered unprofessional and, at times, unethical?

SUGGESTED READINGS

Baker, S., and Martinson, D. "Out of the Red Light District: Five Principles for Ethically Proactive Public Relations." *Public Relations Quarterly*, Fall 2002, pp. 15–20.

Bowen, Shannon A. "Expansion of Ethics as the Tenth Generic Principle of Public Relations Excellence: A Kantian Theory and Model for Managing Ethical Issues." *Journal of Public Relations Research*, Vol. 16, No. 1, 2004, pp. 65–92.

Burnett, James. "Internet Ethics for PR Professionals." *PRWeek*, January 7, 2002, p. 18.

Chabria, Anita. "Pay-to-Play Political Deals Could Cost PR Public's Trust." *PRWeek*, March 1, 2004, p. 9.

Creamer, Matthew. "The Rise of Pay-for-Play." *PRWeek*, June 14, 2004, p. 13.

David, Prabu. "Extending Symmetry: Toward a Convergence of Professionalism, Practice, and Pragmatics in Public Relations." *Journal of Public Relations Research*, Vol. 16, No. 2, 2004, pp. 185–211.

Gorney, Carole. "PR Ethics: Changing Thinking Within Your Organization." *Public Relations Tactics*, February 2002, pp. 27–28.

Holmes, Paul. "In Paying for Its Television Experts, the Toy Industry Is Playing U.S. Consumers for Fools." *PRWeek*, January 5, 2004, p. 8.

Hood, Julia. "Fleischman's LA Controversy Raises Questions for All Firms." *PRWeek*, August 2, 2004, p. 9.

Hutchison, Liese L. "Teaching Ethics Across the Public Relations Curriculum." *Public Relations Review*, Vol. 28, No. 3, 2002, pp. 301–309.

Kim, Yungwook, and Choi, Youjin. "Ethical Standards Appear to Change with Age and Ideology: A Survey of Practitioners." *Public Relations Review*, Vol. 29, No. 1, 2003, pp. 79–89.

Lukaszewski, J., and Frause, R. "Surviving the Moral and Ethical Jungle: How to Build the Definitive Ethical Compass." *Public Relations Tactics*, February 2002, pp. 18–21.

Martinson, David L. "Ethical Decision Making in Public Relations: What Would Aristotle Say?" *Public Relations Quarterly*, Fall 2000, pp. 18–21.

McGraw, Mike. "Fighting Editorial Corruption." *IPRA Frontline*, June 2003, pp. 12–13.

Mercer, Laura. "For Those Entering Public Relations: How to Be Recognized as a True Professional." *Public Relations Tactics*, April 2004, p. 24.

Mindezenthy, Bart J. "Ten Rules for the Practice of Public Relations in the New Century." *Public Relations Tactics*, January 2000, p. 29.

Weidlich, Thom. "The Ethics of Entertaining Journalists: In Building Media Relationships, Knowing Each Outlet's Rules as to What They Accept and Expect Is Key, But the Gift They Still Prefer Most Is a Solid Story." *PR Week*, August 23, 2004 p. 20.

Williams, Dean. "Weaving Ethics into Corporate Culture." *Communication World*, June/July 2002, pp. 38, 48.

chapter 4

Public Relations Departments and Firms

Topics covered in this chapter include:

Public Relations Departments

Public relations departments serve various roles and functions within companies and organizations. The following sections discuss the public relations function in organizational structures, names of departments, line and staff functions, sources of friction with other departments, and the pros and cons of working in a department.

Role in Various Organizational Structures

For over a century, public relations departments have served companies and organizations. George Westinghouse is reported to have created the first corporate public relations department in 1889 when he hired two men to publicize his pet project, alternating current (AC) electricity. Their work was relatively simple compared to the mélange of physical, sociological, and psychological elements that contemporary departments employ. Eventually Westinghouse won out over Thomas A. Edison's direct current (DC) system, and his method became the standard in the United States. Westinghouse's public relations department concept has also grown into a basic part of today's electronic world.

Today, public relations is expanding from its traditional functions, which have expanded over the years, as explained in Chapter 2, to exercise its influence in the highest levels of management.

Importance in Today's World.   In a changing environment, and faced with the variety of pressures previously described, executives increasingly see public relations not as publicity and one-way communication, but as a process of negotiation and compromise with a number of key publics. James Grunig, professor of public relations at the University of Maryland, calls the new approach "building good relationships with strategic publics," which will require public relations executives to be "strategic communication managers rather than communication technicians."

Grunig, head of a six-year IABC Foundation research study on *Excellence in Public Relations and Communications Management*, continues:

> When public relations helps that organization build relationships, it saves the organization money by reducing the costs of litigation, regulation, legislation, pressure campaign boycotts, or lost revenue that result from bad relationships with publics—publics that become activist groups when relationships are bad. It also helps the organization make money by cultivating relationships with donors, customers, shareholders and legislators.

The results of the IABC study seem to indicate that chief executive officers (CEOs) consider public relations to be a good investment. A survey of 200 organizations showed that CEOs gave public relations operations a 184 percent return on investment (ROI), a figure just below that of customer service and sales/marketing.

Ideally, professional public relations people assist top management in developing policy and communicating with various groups. Indeed, the IABC study emphasizes that CEOs want communication that is strategic, based on research, and involves two-way communication with key publics.

Dudley H. Hafner, executive vice president of the American Heart Association (AHA), echoed these thoughts:

In the non-profit business sector, as well as in the for-profit business of America, leadership needs to pay close attention to what our audiences (supporters or customers as well as the general public) want, what they need, what their attitudes are, and what is happening in organizations similar to ours. Seeking, interpreting, and communicating this type of critical information is the role of the communications professional.

Importance of Organizational Structure.   Research indicates, however, that the role of public relations in an organization often depends on the type of organization, the perceptions of top management, and even the capabilities of the public relations executive.

Research studies by Professor Larissa Grunig at the University of Maryland and Mark McElreath at Towson State University, among others, show that large, complex organizations have a greater tendency than do smaller firms to include public relations in the policy-making process. Companies such as IBM and General Motors, which operate in a highly competitive environment, are more sensitive than many others to policy issues and public attitudes and to establishing a solid corporate identity. Consequently, they place more emphasis on news conferences, formal contact with the media, writing executive speeches, and counseling management about issues that could potentially affect the corporate bottom line.

In such organizations, which are classified as *mixed organic/mechanical* by management theorists, the authority and power of the public relations department are quite high. Public relations is part of what is called the "dominant coalition" and has a great deal of autonomy.

In contrast, a small-scale organization of low complexity that offers a standardized product or service feels few public pressures and little governmental regulatory interest. It has scant public relations activity, and staff members are relegated to such technician roles as producing the company newsletter and issuing routine news releases. Public relations in what is called the *traditional organization* has little or no input into management decisions and policy formation.

Research also indicates that the type of organization involved may be less significant in predicting the role of its public relations department than are the perceptions and expectations of its top management. In many organizations, top-level management perceives public relations as primarily a journalistic and technical function— media relations and publicity. In large-scale mechanical organizations of low complexity, there is also a tendency to think of public relations as only a support function of the marketing department.

Such perceptions by top management severely limit the role of the public relations department as well as its power to take part in management decision making. Instead, public relations is relegated to being a tactical function, simply preparing messages without input on what should be communicated. In many cases, however, public relations personnel self-select technician roles because they lack a knowledge base in research, environmental scanning, problem solving, and managing total communications strategies.

The most admired *Fortune* 500 corporations, in terms of reputation, tend to think of public relations as more of a strategic management tool. A study by the University of Southern California (USC) Annenberg Strategic Public Relations Center and the Council of Public Relations Firms found that these companies dedicated a larger percentage of their gross revenues to public relations activities, extensively used outside public relations firms to supplement their own large staffs, and didn't have public relations reporting to the marketing department.

PRWeek, summarizing the survey, said, "PR Departments that closely align their own goals with their companies' strategic business goals receive greater executive support, have larger budgets, and have a higher perceived contribution to their organizations' success."

A survey of corporations by *PRWeek* reinforces the idea that public relations has gained a seat at the management table. *PRWeek* found that 55 percent of respondents reported that public relations reported directly to the chairman/CEO or the Chief Operating Officer (COO) of the organization. However, a relatively large percentage (39 percent) reported to the head of marketing.

Julie O'Neil of Texas Christian University researched the sources of influence for corporate public relations practitioners. She reported in a *Public Relations Review* article that influence was based on four factors: (1) perception of value by top management, (2) practitioners taking on the managerial role, (3) reporting to the CEO, and (4) years of professional experience. In terms of value, Ken Plowman of Brigham Young University found that public relations practitioners secure "value" based on their ability to solve problems for the organization.

Names of Departments

A public relations department in an organization goes by many names. And most often it is not "public relations." In the largest corporations (the *Fortune* 500), the terms *corporate communications* or *communications* outnumber *public relations* by almost four to one.

O'Dwyer's PR Services Report, in a survey of the *Fortune* 500 companies, found 200 such departments and only 48 public relations departments. Among those switching from "public relations" to "corporate communications" in recent years are Procter & Gamble and Hershey Candies. In both cases, the companies say that the switch occurred because the department had expanded beyond "public relations" to include such activities as employee communications, shareholder communications, annual reports, consumer relations, and corporate philanthropy.

Such activities, however, are considered subcategories of modern public relations, so consultant Alfred Geduldig has offered another reason. He told *O'Dwyer's PR Services Report* that the term *public relations* had suffered from repeated derogatory usage, causing companies to move away from the term. He also thought that the term *corporate communications* was a sign that public relations people were doing many more things in a company than in the past, reflecting an integration of communications services.

Echoing this thought is Linda Ambrose, director of corporate affairs for Tenneco. She says that the company changed the name from "public relations" to "elevate the function of the department." The unit now handles internal relations, speech writing, and community affairs. It is headed by a vice president who reports to the chairman of the company. "So corporate affairs is precisely what it is," Ambrose told *O'Dwyer's PR Services Report*.

Other names used for public relations departments in the corporate world include *corporate relations, investor relations, public affairs, marketing communications, public and community relations*, and *external affairs*.

Government agencies, educational institutions, and charitable organizations use such terms as *public affairs, community relations, public information*, and even *market services*.

Organization of Departments

The head executive of a public relations or similarly named department usually has one of three titles: manager, director, or vice president. A vice president of corporate communications may have direct responsibility for the additional activities of advertising and marketing communications.

A department usually is divided into specialized sections that have a coordinator or manager. Common sections found in a large corporation are media relations, investor relations, consumer affairs, governmental relations, community relations, marketing communications, and employee communications.

The organizational chart of IBM's corporate communications department is shown in Figure 4.1.

One of the world's largest corporations, General Motors, has more than 300 public relations personnel and a wide range of job titles based on geography and operating divisions. Each division, such as Buick or the Saginaw Steering Gear Division, has its own director of public relations. General Electric, another corporate giant, has several hundred persons in various public relations functions.

These examples should not mislead you about the size and budget of public relations departments. The USC study found that *Fortune* 500 companies typically have 24 professionals in the corporate communications/public relations department and an average annual budget of $8.5 million.

ON THE JOB insights

Expertise Required in a Department

The *Excellence in Public Relations and Communication Management* study, funded by IABC, identified 15 areas of specialized expertise that should be present in a public relations department:

Strategic and Operational Management Knowledge

- Develop strategies for solving problems
- Manage organizational response to issues
- Develop goals and objectives for department
- Prepare budgets
- Manage people

Research Knowledge

- Perform environmental scanning
- Determine public reactions to your organization

- Use research to segment publics
- Conduct evaluation research

Negotiation Knowledge

- Negotiate with activist publics
- Help management understand opinions of publics
- Use conflict resolution theories with publics

Persuasion Knowledge

- Persuade a public that your organization is right
- Use attitude theory in a campaign
- Get publics to behave as your organization wants

Source: Dozier, David, with Grunig, James, and Grunig, Larissa. *The Manager's Guide to Excellence in Public Relations and Communication Management.* Mahwah, NJ: Lawrence Erlbaum, 1995, p. 64.

Another study by the Conference Board of other large U.S. corporations found that the typical public relations department had nine professionals. The USC study found that the average annual budget for *Fortune* 501 to 1000 companies was $2.2 million. Of course, thousands of even smaller companies employ only one or two public relations practitioners.

Public relations personnel may also be dispersed throughout an organization in such a manner that an observer has difficulty in ascertaining the extent of public relations activity. Some may be housed under marketing communications in the marketing department. Others may be assigned to the personnel department as communication specialists producing newsletters and brochures. Still others may be in

FIGURE 4.1

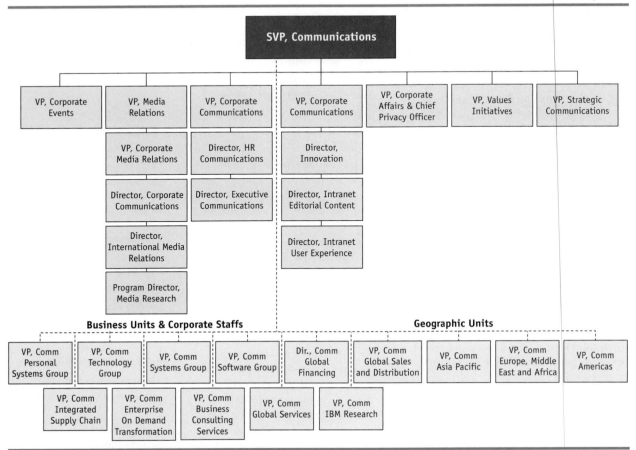

This chart shows the overall organization of IBM's global communications team. It shows delegation of responsibilities by function, business unit, and geography under a senior vice president of communications. Courtesy of Jon Iwata, IBM Corporation.

marketing, working exclusively on product publicity. Decentralization of the public relations function, and the frictions it causes, will be discussed later in this chapter.

Line and Staff Functions

Traditional management theory divides an organization into *line* and *staff* functions. A line manager, such as a vice president of manufacturing, can delegate authority, set production goals, hire employees, and directly influence the work of others. Staff people, in contrast, have little or no direct authority. Instead, they indirectly influence the work of others through suggestions, recommendations, and advice.

According to accepted management theory, public relations is a staff function. Public relations people are experts in communication; line managers, including the chief executive officer, rely on them to use their skills in preparing and processing data, making recommendations, and executing communication programs to implement the organization's policies.

Public relations staff members, for example, may find through a community survey that people have only a vague understanding of what the company manufactures. To improve community comprehension and create greater rapport, the public relations department may recommend to top management that a community open house be held at which product demonstrations, tours, and entertainment would be featured.

Notice that the department *recommends* this action. It would have no direct authority to decide arbitrarily on an open house and to order various departments within the company to cooperate. If top management approves the proposal, the department may take responsibility for organizing the event. Top management, as line managers, has the authority to direct all departments to cooperate in the activity.

Although public relations departments can function only with the approval of top management, there are varying levels of influence that departments may exert. These levels will be discussed shortly.

Access to Management. The power and influence of a public relations department usually result from access to top management, which uses advice and recommendations to formulate policy. That is why public relations, as well as other staff functions, is located high in the organizational chart and is called upon by top management to make reports and recommendations on issues affecting the entire company. In today's environment, public acceptance or nonacceptance of a proposed policy is an important factor in decision making—as important as costing and technological ability. This is why the former president of RJR Nabisco, F. Ross Johnson, told the *Wall Street Journal* in an interview that his senior public relations side was "Numero Uno" and quipped, "He is the only one who has an unlimited budget and exceeds it every year."

Levels of Influence. Management experts state that staff functions in an organization operate at various levels of influence and authority. On the lowest level, the staff function may be only *advisory:* Line management has no obligation to take recommendations or even request them.

When public relations is purely advisory, it is often not effective. A good example is the Enron scandal. The energy company generated a great deal of public, legislative, and media criticism because public relations was relegated to a low level and was, for all practical purposes, nonexistent.

ON THE JOB
insights

The Functions of a Corporate PR/Communications Department

A 2004 survey of corporations by *PRWeek* asked respondents what activities their departments performed. Listed below is the percent of in-house departments responsible for the following public relations functions.

Media Relations	96%
Crisis Management	75%
Special Events	68%
Reputation Management	65%
Employee Communications	64%
Product/Brand Communication	63%
Community Relations	60%
Messaging	45%
Annual/Quarterly Reports	37%
Marketing	35%
Measurement and Analysis	29%
Public Affairs/Governmental Relations	28%
Product/Brand Advertising	16%

Source: "Corporate Survey 2004." PRWeek, March 15, 2004, p. 19.

Johnson & Johnson, on the other hand, gives its public relations staff function higher status. The Tylenol crisis, in which seven persons died after taking capsules containing cyanide, clearly showed that the company based much of its reaction and quick recall of the product on the advice of public relations staff. In this case, public relations was in a *compulsory-advisory* position.

Under the compulsory-advisory concept, organization policy requires that line managers (top management) at least listen to the appropriate staff experts before deciding on a strategy. Don Hellriegel and John Slocum, authors of the textbook *Management*, state: "Although such a procedure does not limit the manager's decision-making discretion, it ensures that the manager has made use of the specialized talents of the appropriate staff agency."

Another level of advisory relationship within an organization is called *concurring authority*. For instance, an operating division wishing to publish a brochure cannot do so unless the public relations department approves the copy and layout. If differences arise, the parties must agree before work can proceed. Many firms use this mode to prevent departments and divisions from disseminating materials that do not conform with company standards. In addition, the company must ascertain that its trademarks are used correctly to ensure continued protection (see Chapter 12).

Concurring authority, however, may also limit the freedom of the public relations department. Some companies have a policy that all employee magazine articles and external news releases must be reviewed by the legal staff before publication. The material cannot be disseminated until legal and public relations personnel have agreed upon what will be said. The situation is even more limiting on public relations when the legal department has *command authority* to change a news release with or without the consent of public relations. This is one reason that newspaper editors find some news releases so filled with "legalese" as to be almost unreadable.

Sources of Friction

Ideally, public relations is part of the managerial subsystem. It is, say professors James and Larissa Grunig "the management of communication between an organization and its publics." However, other staff functions also are involved in the communication process with internal and external publics. And, almost invariably, friction occurs. The four areas of possible friction are legal, human resources, advertising, and marketing.

Legal.   The legal staff is concerned about the possible effect of any public statement on current or potential litigation. Consequently, lawyers often frustrate public relations personnel by taking the attitude that any public statement can potentially be used against the organization in a lawsuit. Conflicts over what to release and when often have a paralyzing effect on decision making, causing the organization to seem unresponsive to public concerns. This is particularly true in a crisis, when the public demands information immediately.

Human Resources.   The traditional personnel department has now evolved into the expanded role of "human resources," and there are often turf battles over who is responsible for employee communications. Human resources personnel believe they should control the flow of information. Public relations administrators counter that satisfactory external communications cannot be achieved unless effective employee relations are conducted simultaneously. Layoffs, for example, affect not only employees, but also community and investor relations.

Advertising. Advertising and public relations departments often collide because they compete for funds to communicate with external audiences. Philosophical differences also arise. Advertising's approach to communications is, "Will it increase sales?" Public relations asks, "Will it make friends?" These differing orientations frequently cause breakdowns in coordination of overall strategy.

Marketing. Marketing, like advertising, tends to think only of customers or potential buyers as key publics. Public relations, on the other hand, defines *publics* in a broader way—any group that can have an impact on the operations of the organization. These publics include governmental agencies, environmental groups, neighborhood groups, and a host of other publics that marketing would not consider customers.

This led James Grunig, editor of the IABC study, to conclude, "We believe, then, that public relations must emerge as a discipline distinct from marketing and that it must be practiced separately from marketing in the organization." Logic dictates, however, that an organization needs a coordinated and integrated approach to communications strategy. Indeed, one survey found that 65 percent of corporate managers were now spending more time on developing integrated communications programs.

The following suggestions may help achieve this goal:

- Representatives of departments should serve together on key committees to exchange information on how various programs can complement each other to achieve overall organizational objectives.

- Heads of departments should be equals in job title. In this way, the autonomy of one department is not subverted by another.

- All department heads should report to the same superior, so that all viewpoints can be considered before an appropriate strategy is formulated.

- Informal, regular contacts with representatives of other departments help dispel mind-sets and create understanding and respect for each other's viewpoint.

- Written policies should be established to spell out the responsibilities of each department. Such policies are helpful in settling disputes over which department has authority to communicate with employees or alter a news release.

Some organizational charts for public relations and other departments are shown in Figure 4.2.

The Trend Toward Outsourcing

A major trend for American corporations has been the outsourcing of services, whether telecommunications, accounting, customer service, software engineering, or even legal services. Increasingly, much of this outsourcing has been to India, and it was an emotionally charged economic issue in the 2004 presidential election.

Public relations services, to date, haven't been outsourced to Bangalore, India, but the trend line is for more organizations to outsource their communication activities to public relations firms and outside contractors. Indeed, the USC and Council of

FIGURE 4.2

This chart depicts three examples of corporate management organization, showing the important position of public relations.

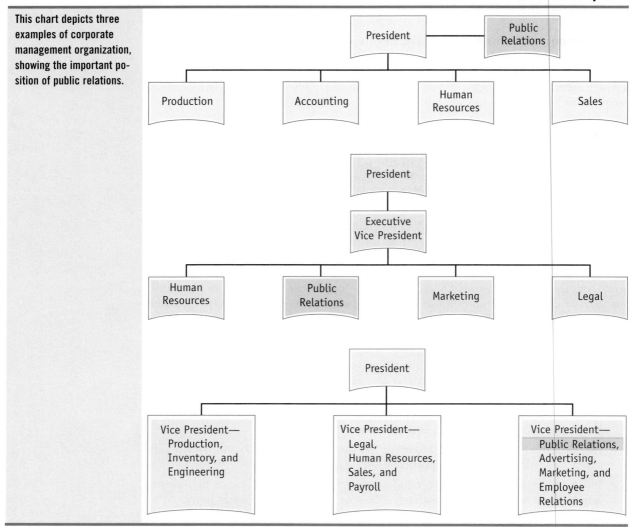

Public Relations Firms study found that *Fortune* 500 companies now spend 25 percent of their public relations budgets on outside firms. Almost 90 percent of the companies use outside public relations counsel to varying degrees.

A national survey by *PRWeek* found that companies of all sizes spent an average of more than 40 percent of their public relations budget on the services of outside firms. In high technology, the percentage was even higher—a whopping 66 percent of the corporate budget. In contrast, nonprofits allocated an average of 38 percent of their budgets for external public relations services.

The most frequent reason given for outsourcing is to bring expertise and resources to the organization that can't be found internally. A second reason is the need to supplement internal staffs during peak periods of activity. The most frequently outsourced activities, according to a study by Bisbee & Co. and Leone Marketing

Public relations firms often are commissioned to organize media tours, news conferences, and photo opportunities for celebrities. Here, Britney Spears smiles during a photo op in Toronto after a news conference to promote a new album.

Research were, in descending order, (1) writing and communications, (2) media relations, (3) publicity, (4) strategy and planning, and (5) event planning.

The trend toward outsourcing, say many experts, follows what has occurred in advertising. Today, about 90 percent of corporate and institutional advertising is handled by agencies rather than by in-house departments. In the beginning of the 21st century, it appears that the major beneficiary of this trend will be public relations firms, which are discussed next.

Public Relations Firms

Public relations firms are found in every industrialized nation and most of the developing world.

With regard to size, public relations firms range from one- or two-person operations to global giants such as Weber-Shandwick, which employs almost 3,000 professionals in 80 offices around the world (www.webershandwick.com). The scope of services provided to clients varies, but there are common denominators. Big or small, each firm gives counsel and performs technical services required to carry out an agreed-upon program. The firm may operate as an adjunct to an organization's public relations department or, if no department exists, conduct the entire effort. Examples of work done by firms in other nations are given in Chapter 19.

The United States, because of its large population and economic base, has the world's most public relations firms (about 9,000, according to one count) and generates the most fee income. In fact, the international committee of the Public Relations Consultancies Association reported in a worldwide study that the fee income of U.S. firms "plainly dwarfs those in all other regions."

A survey by the Council of Public Relations Firms in 2000, for example, found that U.S. industry revenues grew 33 percent over 1999 to $3 billion. Worldwide revenues were $4.6 billion. About 50 percent of the U.S. revenues were generated by the 10 largest firms. The major sectors of growth in 2000, according to the survey, were

PR CASEBOOK

Wal-Mart Tries to Polish Its Image

Wal-Mart is the world's largest retailer with sales of $256 billion from about 3600 stores worldwide. It's also the largest corporate employer in the United States, with 1.1 million people on its payroll. Everything is fine, except that the giant retailer has a terrible image problem.

First, the media extensively reported that federal agents raided 60 Wal-Mart stores and arrested 250 illegal immigrants employed by a Wal-Mart contractor to clean the stores. Then, a federal judge put in motion the largest workplace-bias suit in history by extending a discrimination complaint by several female employees to about 1.6 million current and former employees.

On top of this, Wal-Mart regularly receives extensive news coverage, often negative, when various citizen groups try to block the building of new superstores in their communities. In California, the giant retailer worked to get a new store on the ballot in Inglewood, and the voters turned it down by a large margin. Add labor unions' complaints that Wal-Mart pays substandard wages, and you have a major public relations problem, which can ultimately affect the corporation's bottom line.

Wal-Mart has, more or less, admitted that it has a negative image. H. Lee Scott, Jr., chief executive, told a retail conference that the view of many people ". . . is what they read in the newspaper and what they see on TV. We have decided it is important for us to reach out to this group." And company spokesperson Mona Williams told the *New York Times*, "We probably didn't realize soon enough how important it was to work with the media. It is an acknowledgment that the media and others offer important venues for

telling our story, and we need to continue doing a better job of that."

In addition to doing a better job of telling its story and improving media relations, Wal-Mart has also decided on several initiatives to change its image and become known as a good corporate citizen.

After spending millions on television ads, without much effect, Wal-Mart is now a sponsor of National Public Radio (NPR). This medium was chosen because it has an audience of highly educated and intelligent listeners who tend to be active in community affairs. And, as Wal-Mart spokesperson Williams says, the goal is to "reach community leaders and help them understand the value we bring to their areas."

Another initiative is Wal-Mart's award of $500,000 in scholarships to minority students in journalism programs around the country. Although media companies usually fund such scholarships, Wal-Mart apparently believes that such an action will help journalists have a better image of the retailer and generate more "balanced" coverage. The plan is to have the scholarship winners attend the company's annual meeting and tour the corporation's offices in Arkansas.

These initiatives, at a time of intense media scrutiny of Wal-Mart's operations, leave some skeptics somewhat less than impressed. John Siegenthaler, founder of the First Amendment Center at Vanderbilt University, told the *New York Times,* "Wal-Mart is doing what most corporations do: When they feel pain, they try to salve the wound. They may get less out of it than they expect to."

Wal-Mart's public relations firm is Fleischman-Hillard. However, the company is also looking for some good in-house senior public relations managers. See the employment ad on the previous page that was placed in *PRWeek.*

technology, 46 percent; financial products and services, 37 percent; industry, 36 percent; government and nonprofit, 36 percent; health care, 30 percent; and consumer and retail, 22 percent. Fueling all this growth, as already mentioned, was the increased outsourcing of work by corporations.

American public relations firms have proliferated in proportion to the growth of the global economy. As American companies expanded after World War II into booming domestic and worldwide markets, many corporations felt a need for public relations firms that could provide them with professional expertise in communications.

Also stimulating the growth of public relations firms were increased urbanization, expansion of government bureaucracy and regulation, more sophisticated mass media systems, the rise of consumerism, international trade, and the demand for more information. Professionals were needed to maintain lines of communication in an increasingly complicated world and to provide much of the material to be distributed. Executives of public relations firms predict future growth as more countries adopt free market economies and more international outlets such as CNN are established. In addition, the skyrocketing use of the Internet has fueled the global reach of public relations firms. Also expected is an increasing demand for public relations in the high-technology, health care, financial, sports, and entertainment fields.

Services They Provide

Counseling firms today offer services far more extensive than those provided by the nation's first firm, the Publicity Bureau, founded in 1900 in Boston. Today, public relations firms provide a variety of services:

- *Marketing communications.* This involves promotion of products and services through such tools as news releases, feature stories, special events, brochures, and media tours.
- *Executive speech training.* Top executives are coached on public affairs activities, including personal appearances.
- *Research and evaluation.* Scientific surveys are conducted to measure public attitudes and perceptions.
- *Crisis communication.* Management is counseled on what to say and do in an emergency such as an oil spill or a recall of an unsafe product.
- *Media analysis.* Appropriate media are examined for targeting specific messages to key audiences.

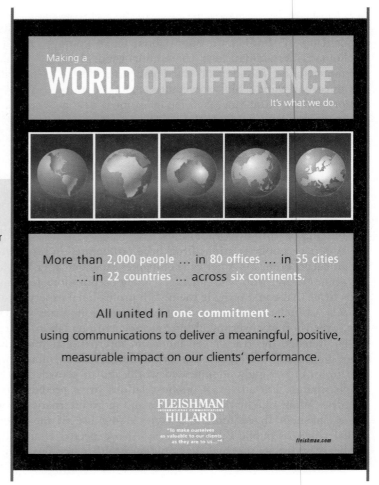

Public relations firms with global reach offer prospective clients a variety of services. This advertisement for Fleishman-Hillard emphasizes the number of staff and offices around the world.

- *Community relations*. Management is counseled on ways to achieve official and public support for such projects as building or expanding a factory.
- *Events management*. News conferences, anniversary celebrations, rallies, symposiums, and national conferences are planned and conducted.
- *Public affairs*. Materials and testimony are prepared for government hearings and regulatory bodies, and background briefings are prepared.
- *Branding and corporate reputation*. Advice is given on programs that establish a company brand and its reputation for quality.
- *Financial relations*. Management is counseled on ways to avoid takeover by another firm and effectively communicate with stockholders, security analysts, and institutional investors.

Public relations firms also offer specialty areas of service as trend lines are identified. Burson-Marsteller now has a practice specialty in labor to help corporations deal with unions. Earlier, in 1989, the firm set up a specialty area in environmental communications. After September 11, Fleischman-Hillard set up a practice in homeland security. Other firms offer specialty services in such areas as litigation public relations to help organizations give their side of the story when a major lawsuit is filed.

Public relations firms are also beginning to discard the term *public relations* from their official names. Thus, it's "Burson-Marsteller," and not "Burson-Marsteller Public Relations." Other firms use the term *communications*. For example, Fenton Communications describes itself as a "public interest communications firm."

Increasingly, public relations firms emphasize the counseling aspect of their services, although most of their revenues come from implementing tactical aspects, such as writing news releases, organizing special events, and organizing media tours. The transition to counseling is best expressed by Harold Burson, chairman of Burson-Marsteller, who once told an audience, "In the beginning, top management used to say to us, 'Here's the message, deliver it.' Then it became, 'What should we say?' Now, in smart organizations, it's 'What should we do?' "

A public relations firm was retained to publicize and organize the grand opening of the Smithsonian's National Museum of the American Indian. The ceremonies, which generated extensive media coverage, featured representatives from various tribes in full regalia.

Because of the counseling function, we use the phrase *public relations firm* instead of *agency* throughout this book. Advertising firms, in contrast, are properly called *agencies* because they serve as agents, buying time or space on behalf of a client.

A good source of information about public relations counseling is the Council of Public Relations Firms, which has about 100 member firms. The group provides information on its Web site (www.prfirms.org) about trends in the industry and how to select a public relations firm as well as a variety of other materials. It also offers the popular publication *Careers in Public Relations: Opportunities in a Dynamic Industry*. The group also operates a career center and posts résumés on its Web site of individuals looking for employment with a public relations firm. See the organization's code of ethics on page 112.

Global Reach

Public relations firms, large and small, usually are found in metropolitan areas. On an international level, firms and their offices or affiliates are situated in most of the world's major cities and capitals. Fleischman-Hillard, for example, has more than 2000 employees in 83 offices across six continents. Edelman Worldwide, the world's largest independently owned firm, has almost 2,000 employees in 27 offices abroad.

ON THE JOB insights

Code of Ethics for the Council of Public Relations Firms

More than 100 public relations firms are members of the Council of Public Relations Firms. These firms have pledged to support the following code of ethics:

Code of Ethics

Members of the Council commit to standards of practice that assure clients, the public and media, employees, and business partners and vendors the highest level of professionalism and ethical conduct in every relationship with a Council member. This commitment is a requirement for application and continued membership in the Council.

Member firms will serve their **clients** by applying their fullest capability to achieve each client's business objectives, and charging a fair price for that service. Members will avoid representing any conflicting or competing client interests without the expressed approval of those concerned. Council firms and their employees will respect client confidences and the privacy of client employees, and will refrain from recruiting employees of their clients.

In communicating with the **public** and **media**, member firms will maintain total accuracy and truthfulness. To preserve both the reality and perception of professional integrity, information that is found to be misleading or erroneous will be promptly corrected and the sources of communications and sponsors of activities will not be concealed.

Council members will respect the personal rights of their **employees** and former employees. They will provide employees the necessary tools to serve their clients and opportunities to develop their professional skills. They will safeguard the privacy and protect the professional reputation of current and former employees.

Commercial relationships with business **partners** and **vendors** will be handled in a businesslike manner, and credit will be given for ideas and services provided by others.

Source: Council of Public Relations Firms, New York (www.prfirms.org).

The importance of international operations is reflected in the fact that most of the major public relations firms generate substantial revenues from international operations. Edelman, for example, had $206 million in revenues in 2003, but 33 percent of this revenue came from its international offices. Burson-Marsteller, with 47 offices abroad, generates about 40 percent of its revenues from international operations. London-based Incepta/Citigate generates almost 70 percent of its income from international operations.

International work isn't only for large firms. Small and medium-sized firms around the world have formed working partnerships with each other to serve client needs. The largest such group is Worldcom, with 100 firms in 35 nations. Other major groups include Pinnacle, with 60 firms in 31 nations, and Iprex, with 52 firms in 20 nations.

Essentially, firms in an affiliation cooperate with each other to service clients with international needs. A firm in India may call its affiliate in Los Angeles to handle the details of news coverage for a visiting trade delegation from India. One of Worldcom's accounts is Bausch & Lomb, which involves 17 affiliates in 20 separate markets. Bob Oltmanns, head of Iprex, told *PRWeek*, "One of the reasons we started in the first place was to provide clients with a need for reach beyond their own markets with a viable alternative to the large multinational agencies."

Areas of Growth. The large international firms, as well as affiliated local and national firms, were first established in English-speaking countries. These countries remain the most developed public relations marketplaces on a global basis. The public relations industries in Australia and Canada, for example, are much larger than those found in countries with much larger economies.

Western Europe, however, has had a well-developed public relations market for a number of years, and prospects are relatively bright with the expansion of the European Union (EU) to 25 nations. Brussels has become the capital of the EU, and many international companies, as well as lobbyists, are relocating there. Burson-Marsteller, for example, says that 90 percent of its Belgian business is now related to promoting EU policies and EU–U.S. relations.

Increased opportunities for public relations work are now available in the new members of the EU, such as Estonia, Latvia, Poland, and Hungary. Ogilvy PR Worldwide, for example, opened an office in Warsaw after Poland joined EU. Paul

ON THE JOB global

Firms Win Golden World Awards

Public relations firms around the world handle a variety of assignments. Here are some that have received a Golden World award from the International Public Relations Association (IPRA):

● **Sigma International (Poland).** Conducted a heart disease prevention campaign to encourage high-risk individuals to get screened by medical personnel. Over 300,000 Poles underwent examination and received counseling.

● **Ruder Finn Asia (Singapore).** Organized a series of events celebrating Citigroup's 100 years of business in Asia. One event was sponsorship of 21 concerts by the New York Philharmonic in 14 Asian cities. As a result, Citigroup gained new business.

● **Strategic Objectives (Canada).** Developed a campaign to increase brand awareness of Guinness beer and increase sales. One initiative was to create

grassroots support for declaring St. Patrick's Day a national holiday in Canada.

● **Weber-Shandwick (Germany).** Coordinated a campaign by McDonald's in Germany to celebrate World Children's Day by having children use tray liners to pen their wishes for the future. The top two wishes: peace/no war and better schools and playgrounds.

● **United Partners Ltd. (Bulgaria).** The firm, on behalf of Procter & Gamble, organized and publicized a "Teen Information Center" Web site. Experts in psychology, sex education, drug abuse, and personal relationships were trained to answer inquiries from teenagers via the Web site. Procter & Gamble's objective was corporate citizenship.

● **Kaizo (United Kingdom).** Developed a campaign to increase printer manufacturer Epson's market share by showing small businesses how the use of a color printer could enhance their sales materials and improve sales.

Taaffe, CEO of Hill & Knowlton, also says the public relations business in Russia, France, Germany, Sweden, and Italy will expand substantially over the next 3 to 5 years.

In Latin America, Chile is a good candidate for expansion of the public relations marketplace because of its strong economy. Brazil and Argentina, because of their size, also are good growth prospects. The Middle East is considered a potential market for expansion because it consists of 22 nations and 300 million people. Consumer public relations in the region is growing, but Iraq and various calls for boycotts of American products are potential obstacles.

Asia also has good growth prospects, and the rapid growth of the public relations industry in China has already been noted. Other nations, such as India, Thailand, Malaysia, Singapore, and Japan, continue to suffer from economic downturns, but knowledgeable experts are optimistic. The SARS virus scare in 2003 caused a considerable downturn in business and public relations activity throughout Asia.

On the African continent, South Africa is the continent's largest public relations market. Nigeria and Kenya, however, are considered bright spots for expansion of public relations work. International public relations is discussed further in Chapter 19.

The Rise of Communication Conglomerates

Until the 1970s, the largest public relations firms were independently owned by their founders or, in some cases, by employee stockholders. A significant change began in 1973 when Carl Byoir & Associates, then the largest U.S. public relations firm, was purchased by the advertising firm of Foote, Cone, & Belding. In short order, other large public relations firms were purchased by major advertising agencies.

Today, both public relations firms and advertising agencies have become part of large, diversified holding companies with global reach. Interpublic Group (IPG) not only owns Foote, Cone & Belding (now called FCB Worldwide) and other advertising agencies, but also six major public relations firms. They include the world's largest, Weber-Shandwick, as well as Golin/Harris International, Carmichael Lynch Spong, DeVries PR, MWW Group, and Tierney Communications.

IPG, despite total 2003 revenues of $5.9 billion, is only the third-largest holding company. The largest is Omnicom, with $8.6 billion in revenues, which generates almost 60 percent of its revenues outside of advertising (see Insights box on page 117). It owns, like the other communication conglomerates, a host of companies specializing in such areas as advertising, marketing, billboards, direct mail, special event promotion, graphic design studios, survey research firms, and public relations firms. For example, it owns seven major firms, including Brodeur, Porter Novelli, Fleischman-Hillard, Cone, Ketchum, Gavin Anderson, and Clark & Weinstock.

WPP, which is based in London, is the second-largest holding company, with revenues of $7.6 billion. Among its holdings are three advertising agencies: J. Walter Thompson, Ogilvy & Mather, and Y&R Advertising. It also owns six leading public relations firms, including Burson-Marsteller, Hill & Knowlton, and Cohn & Wolfe. In late 2004, WPP acquired another holding company, Grey Global, and added the public relations firm CGI Group to its stable.

Large conglomerates acquire public relations firms for several reasons. One is the natural evolutionary step of integrating various communication disciplines into "total communication networks." Supporters of integration say that no single-function agency or firm is equipped with the personnel or resources to handle complex, often

ON THE JOB ethics

Conflict of Interest Is Often in the Eye of the Beholder

Public relations firms, for business and ethical reasons, should not represent conflicting or competing interests. A firm that has Baskin-Robbins for a client, in general, should not also work for a competing ice cream chain.

Oftentimes, however, conflict of interest is a bit more complicated. Ketchum was accused of "blatantly unethical" conflict of interest by Public Interest Watch because it represented both the Centers for Medicare & Medicaid Services (CMS), which sets payment levels for drugs, and the American Society of Clinical Oncology (ASCO), which opposes some of that group's proposed cuts in payments.

According to Public Interest Watch, a watchdog group for the abuse of public funds, Ketchum has a conflict of interest. However, a spokeswoman for ASCO didn't think that there was any conflict of interest, because both groups had a common goal of improving care. And Ketchum issued a statement saying, "Both of our clients are working together on the Medicare Modernization Act, and neither one of them is considering it a conflict of interest."

Meanwhile, the Natural Resources Defense Council, an environmental group, charged that the public relations firm Stratacomm set up a "front" group for the auto industry by organizing the Sport Utility Vehicle Owners of America. The "front" group is opposed to proposed clean-air regulations in California that would limit emissions from large vehicles, such as SUVs.

Stratcomm, whose main partner is also communications director of the SUV group, claims that there is no connection with the auto industry. But critics say the firm has many automakers as clients, who also advertise on the group's Web site. This, in their minds, constitutes a conflict of interest or at least a failure to disclose the real sponsors of the SUV group, which claims 23,000 members.

Another form of conflict of interest is when employees of a public relations firm also represent themselves as actual employees of a client. Fleischman-Hillard (F-H) touched off an ethical controversy when a columnist with the *San Francisco Chronicle* discovered that the vice president of corporate communications at SBC, the telephone company, was actually a F-H employee. Seven other F-H staffers also had corporate titles and business cards to match.

The columnist argued that the actual employer of the individuals should be disclosed and that he had been misled. Although the Counselor's Academy of PRSA and the Council of Public Relations Firms waffled as to whether an employee of a public relations firm could also hold a corporate title in a client's organization, Thomas Martin of the Arthur W. Page Society was more definitive. He said that the press and the public should be told in all materials, including business cards, who the person's actual employer is.

Other public relations professionals thought that carrying a corporate title compromised a public relations firm's ability to offer independent and objective advice to a client. SBC, given the criticism, dropped corporate titles for F-H employees.

global, integrated marketing functions efficiently for a client. In addition, joint efforts by public relations and advertising professionals can offer prospective clients greater communications impact, generate more business, and expand the number of geographical locations around the world.

A second reason is pure business. Holding companies find public relations firms to be attractive investments. According to *PRWeek*, revenues from advertising clients have remained somewhat static over the years, whereas public relations firms have experienced double-digit growth in the same time frame. Increasingly, because of good profit margins, public relations firms are becoming the "glittering jewels" in holding company portfolios, says the publication.

For the past several years, however, it has been difficult to find out exactly how much these "jewels" are worth. The major conglomerates have refused to break out revenues from their public relations operations because they say such disclosures would violate the Sarbanes-Oxley Act passed by the U.S. Congress, which, ironically, called for more corporate financial disclosures in the wake of the Enron and Worldcom scandals. Consequently, the old standard of ranking the top 20 public relations firms by revenues is no longer possible. Instead, the Insights box on page 117 gives the total revenues of the holding companies and the percent of total revenues that is generated outside of advertising.

Toward More Integration. Although earlier efforts to create "total communication networks" for clients often met with limited success, there is now increasing evidence that the strategy may be working. One promising area is joint pitches for business. Interpublic's McCann-Erickson and Weber Shandwick, for example, got a multimillion-dollar advertising and public relations account from Aon Insurance Company after making a joint presentation. Considerable new business is also generated when units of the same conglomerate refer customers to each other. As communication campaigns become more integrated, even more synergy will become commonplace.

Holding companies originally started out primarily as a stable of advertising agencies under one umbrella, but they have evolved considerably beyond that with the acquisition of public relations firms and other specialty communication companies. London-based WPP, for example, now employs 69,000 people in more than 100 nations.

Sir Martin Sorrell, chairman of WPP (London), told a *Wall Street Journal* interviewer:

> If you want to upset me, call me an advertising agency. The strategic objective is for two-thirds of our revenue to come from nontraditional advertising in 5 to 10 years. Because of fragmentation, TiVo, and Sky Plus, clients and ourselves have to look at everything. Instead of focusing on network television, we have to look at public relations and radio and outdoor and mobile messaging and satellite. Media planning becomes more important.

Sir Martin also makes the point that one size doesn't fit all when it comes to global communications strategies and campaigns. Campaigns still have to be tailored to local customs, ethnic groups, and religious preferences. Muslims now constitute 26 percent of the world's population and, by 2014, they will be 30 percent. By the same year, two-thirds of the world's population will be Asian.

Structure of a Counseling Firm

A small public relations firm may consist only of the owner (president) and an assistant (vice president) who are supported by an administrative assistant. Larger firms have a more extended hierarchy.

Major Public Relations Firms Are Owned by Conglomerates

An estimated 60 percent of the global business in public relations is conducted by firms that are owned by communication conglomerates that also own advertising agencies, marketing firms, billboard companies, direct mail firms, and special event specialty shops. The following is a list of the major holding companies by 2003 total revenues and what percentage came from nonadvertising sources.

Omnicom

Total revenue: $8.6 billion
Percent of revenue not from advertising: 57%
Public relations firms owned: Brodeur, Porter Novelli, Fleischman-Hillard, Cone, Ketchum, Gavin Anderson, and Clark & Weinstock

WPP

Total revenue: $7.6 billion
Percent of revenue not from advertising: 40%
Public relations firms owned: Hill & Knowlton; Cohn & Wolfe; Burson-Marsteller; Ogilvy PR; Robinson, Lerer & Montgomery; and the GCI Group (acquired September 2004)

Interpublic Group

Total revenue: $5.9 billion
Percent of revenue not from advertising: Not given

Public relations firms owned: Weber-Shandick, Golin/Harris International, Carmichael Lynch Spong, DeVries PR, MWW Group, and Tierney Communications

Publicis Groupe

Total revenue: $4.79 billion
Percent of revenue not from advertising: 40%
Public relations firms owned: Publicis Dialog, Publicis Consultants, Rowland Communications, and MS&L

Havas

Total revenue: $2 billion
Percent of revenue not from advertising: 60%
Public relations firms owned: Euro RSCG MVBMS Partners, Euro RSCG Life NRP, Euro RSCG Magnet, and Abernathy MacGregor

Incepta

Total revenue: $305 million
Percent of revenue not from advertising: 50%
Public relations firms owned: Citigate Technology, Citigate Broadcast, Citigate Dewe Rogerson, Citigate Sard Verbinnen, Citigate Cunningham, and Citigate Public Affairs

Source: "Agency Business Report 2004." *PRWeek*, April 19, 2004, pp. 25–29.

The organization of Ketchum in San Francisco is fairly typical. The president is based in Ketchum's New York office, so the executive vice president is the on-site director in San Francisco. A senior vice president is associate director of operations. Next in line are several vice presidents who primarily do account supervision or special projects.

An *account supervisor* is in charge of one major account or several smaller ones. An *account executive*, who reports to the supervisor, is in direct contact with the client and handles most of the day-to-day activity. At the bottom of the list is the *assistant account executive*, who does routine maintenance work compiling media lists, gathering information, and writing rough drafts of news releases.

Recent college graduates usually start as assistant account executives. Once they learn the firm's procedures and show ability, promotion to account executive may occur within 6 to 18 months. After two or three years, it is not uncommon for an account executive to become an account supervisor.

Executives at or above the vice-presidential level usually are heavily involved in selling their firm's services. In order to prosper, a firm must continually seek new business and sell additional services to current clients. Consequently, the upper management of the firm calls on prospective clients, prepares proposals, and makes new business presentations. In this very competitive field, a firm not adept at selling itself frequently fails.

Firms frequently organize account teams, especially to serve a client whose program is multifaceted. One member of the team, for example, may set up a nationwide media tour in which an organization representative is booked on television talk shows. Another may supervise all materials going to the print media, including news stories, feature articles, background kits, and artwork. A third may concentrate on the trade press or perhaps arrange special events.

Pros and Cons of Using a Public Relations Firm

Because public relations is a service industry, a firm's major asset is the quality of its people. Potential clients thinking about hiring a public relations firm usually base their decisions on that fact, according to a survey of *Fortune* 500 corporate vice presidents.

Thomas L. Harris, a consultant who conducted a survey of corporate communication directors, found that clients believe that meeting deadlines and keeping promises are the most important criteria for evaluating firms. Other important considerations were, in descending order: (1) client services; (2) honest, accurate billing; (3) creativity; and (4) knowledge of the client's industry.

Advantages.   Public relations firms offer:

- *Objectivity*. The firm can analyze a client's needs or problems from a new perspective and offer fresh insights.

- *A variety of skills and expertise*. The firm has specialists, whether in speechwriting, trade magazine placement, or helping with proxy battles.

- *Extensive resources*. The firm has abundant media contacts and works regularly with numerous suppliers of products and services. It has research materials, including data information banks, and experience in similar fields.

- *Offices throughout the country*. A national public relations program requires coordination in major cities. Large firms have on-site staffs or affiliate firms in many cities and even around the world.

- *Special problem-solving skills*. A firm may have extensive experience and a solid reputation in desired areas. For example, Burson-Marsteller is well known for expertise in crisis communications, health and medical issues, and international coordination of special projects. Hill & Knowlton is known for expertise in public affairs, and Ketchum is the expert in consumer marketing.

- *Credibility*. A successful public relations firm has a solid reputation for professional, ethical work. If represented by such a firm, a client is likely to get more attention among opinion leaders in mass media, government, and the financial community.

On the Minus Side.   Despite many successes, not everything always goes smoothly between a firm and its client. There are several drawbacks to using public relations firms:

- *Superficial grasp of a client's unique problems.* Although objectivity is gained from an outsider's perspective, there is often a disadvantage in the public relations firm's not thoroughly understanding the client's business or needs.

- *Lack of full-time commitment.* A public relations firm has many clients to service. Therefore, no single client can monopolize its personnel and other resources.

- *Need for prolonged briefing period.* Some companies become frustrated because time and money are needed for a public relations firm to research the organization and make recommendations. Consequently, the actual start of a public relations program may take weeks or months.

- *Resentment by internal staff.* The public relations staff members of a client organization may resent the use of outside counsel because they think it implies that they lack the ability to do the job.

- *Need for strong direction by top management.* High-level executives must take the time to brief outside counsel on specific objectives sought.

- *Need for full information and confidence.* A client must be willing to share its information, including the skeletons in the closet, with outside counsel.

- *Costs.* Outside counsel is expensive. In many situations, routine public relations work can be handled at lower cost by internal staff.

Fees and Charges

A public relations firm charges for its services in several ways. The three most common methods, also used by law firms and management consultants, are:

1. *Basic hourly fee, plus out-of-pocket expenses.* The number of hours spent on a client's account is tabulated each month and billed to the client. Work by personnel in the counseling firm is billed at various hourly rates. Out-of-pocket expenses, such as cab fares, car rentals, airline tickets, and meals, are also billed to the client. In a typical $100,000 campaign, about 70 percent of the budget is spent on staff salaries.

2. *Retainer fee.* A basic monthly charge billed to the client covers ordinary administrative and overhead expenses for maintaining the account and being "on call" for advice and strategic counseling. Many clients have in-house capabilities for executing communication campaigns but often need the advice of experts during the planning phase. Many retainer fees also specify the number of hours the firm will spend on an account each month. Any additional work is billed at normal hourly rates. Out-of-pocket expenses are usually billed separately.

3. *Fixed project fee.* The public relations firm agrees to do a specific project, such as an annual report, a newsletter, or a special event, for a fixed fee. For example, a counseling firm may write and produce a quarterly newsletter for $30,000 annually. The fixed fee is the least popular among public relations firms because it is difficult to predict all work and expenses in advance. Many clients, however, like fixed fees for a specific project because it is easier to budget and there are no "surprises."

ON THE JOB ethics

When It's Time to Resign an Account

Credibility and a reputation for integrity are important assets to a public relations firm in terms of keeping clients and adding new ones. Because of this, a firm will sometimes resign an account for ethical reasons.

Patrice Tanaka, CEO of PT& Co., resigned her agency's biggest account after the client adopted an antigay position. She told *PRWeek*, "We tried to explain that it wasn't smart business practice, and we didn't think it was ethical to not welcome any segment of the population."

Fleischman-Hillard resigned from the Firestone tire account after deciding the firm could not ethically defend Firestone's position regarding the safety of its tires during a tire-recall controversy and allegations that Firestone failed to act on information that defective tires were causing a number of injuries and deaths.

In Washington, D.C, three executives of Qorvis Communications left the firm because, according to press reports, they felt uneasy defending the government of Saudi Araba against accusations that Saudi leaders had turned a blind eye to terrorism. Following 9/11, the firm had a $200,000 monthly retainer with Saudi Araba to help to improve that country's image with the American public. According to the *New York Times*, friends said that the three executives were concerned that the firm's reputation was being tarnished by its work for the Saudi government.

On occasion, a public relations firm finds it necessary to resign an account because of client behavior. A Michigan firm, for example, decided to terminate a contract with a resort client because the point of contact was rude and abusive to agency staff and even to their own employees. In such a situation, the firm didn't feel it could service the client in an effective manner.

Many public relations firms, before taking on a possibly controversial client, will discuss the situation with their employees to determine if any staff would feel uncomfortable working with the client. Hill & Knowlton, some years ago, made the mistake of signing on the Catholic Bishops for an antiabortion campaign. Several employees quit, and others said they would refuse to work on the account.

Public relations firms may also resign from accounts if the client asks them to distribute misleading or incorrect information. The code of ethics for the Council of Public Relations Firms notes, "In communicating with the public and media, member firms will maintain total accuracy and truthfulness. To preserve both the reality and perception of professional integrity, information that is found to be misleading or erroneous will be promptly corrected. . . . "

A fourth method, not widely used, is the concept of *pay-for-placement*. Clients don't pay for hours worked but for actual placements of articles in the print media and broadcast mentions. Fees for a major story can range anywhere from $1,500 to $15,000 depending on the prestige, circulation, or audience size of the media outlet that uses a story proposed by a pay-for-placement firm. One firm in Florida, for example, charges clients $5,000 if they are successful in getting a client's spokesperson or a product featured on a national television show such as ABC's *Good Morning America*.

The vast majority of public relations firms don't use this business model for several reasons. First, it reduces public relations to simply media relations and media

Build a career with the youngest retailer ever to reach $60 billion in revenues. The Home Depot is seeking individuals who are passionate about creating or broadening a career with a company that is experiencing unprecedented growth.

Public Relations Manager for Professional Business

Based in our Atlanta headquarters, the Manager of PR will lead communication efforts aimed at a variety of professional customers. This individual will also manage all proactive & reactive media relations in new and existing markets to enhance the position of The Home Depot.

Candidates should have 10+ years of experience, to include media relations and counseling senior management. PR agency and/or industry experience with builders, building products, contractors, and other professional trades large and small is required. Bachelor's degree in Journalism, PR, Communications or English is preferred.

The Home Depot offers competitive compensation, bonus plans plus excellent benefits including Medical, Dental, Vision, 401(k), Tuition Reimbursement, Stock Plans and more.

Apply online at: careers.homedepot.com   Equal Opportunity Employer
Requisition #6956

Media relations is an important part of public relations as this advertisement for Home Depot indicates.

placement, when it is a much broader field. Second, it presents cash-flow problems because payment isn't made until a placement is made. Third, media gatekeepers ultimately decide what to use and what not to use; placement is never guaranteed despite countless hours spent by a staff person "pitching" the story.

The primary basis of the most common methods—the basic hourly fee, the retainer fee, and the fixed project fee—is to estimate the number of hours that a particular project will take to plan, execute, and evaluate. The first method—the basic hourly fee—is the most flexible and most widely used among large firms. It is preferred by public relations people because they are paid for the exact number of hours spent on a project and because it is the only sound way that a fee can be determined intelligently. The retainer fee and the fixed project fee are based on an estimate of how many hours it will take to service a client.

A number of variables are considered when a public relations firm estimates the cost of a program. These may include the size and duration of the project, geographical locations involved, the number of personnel assigned to the project, and the type of client. A major variable, of course, is billing the use of the firm's personnel to a client at the proper hourly rate.

An account supervisor, for example, may earn $60,000 annually and receive benefits (health insurance, pension plan, and so on) that cost the firm an additional $13,000. Thus, the annual cost of the employee to the firm totals $73,000. Using 1,600 billable hours in a year (after deducting vacation time and holidays), the account executive makes $45.63 per hour.

The standard industry practice, however, is to bill clients at least three times a person's salary. This multiple allows the firm to pay for office space, equipment, insurance, supplies, and try to operate at a profit level of about 10 to 20 percent before taxes. Thus, the billing rate of the account supervisor (3 × $45.63) rounds off at $137 per hour. The principals of a counseling firm, because of their much higher salaries, often command $175 to $500 per hour, depending on the size and capabilities of the firm. On the other hand, an assistant account executive may be billed out at only $85 per hour. One nationwide survey conducted by an executive search

ON THE JOB insights

A Job at a Corporation or a PR Firm?

Recent college graduates often ponder the pros and cons of joining a corporate department or going to work for a PR firm. The following summarizes some of the pluses and minuses:

PR FIRM: BREATH OF EXPERIENCE	CORPORATE PR: DEPTH OF EXPERIENCE
Experience gained quickly; tip—find a mentor you can learn from.	Jobs more difficult to find without experience; duties more narrowly focused.
Variety. Usually work on several clients and projects at same time. Possibility of rapid advancement.	Sometimes little variety at entry level.
Fast-paced, exciting.	Growth sometimes limited unless you are willing to switch employers.
Seldom see the impact of your work for a client; removed from "action."	Can be slower paced.
Abilities get honed and polished. (This is where a mentor really helps.)	Heavy involvement with executive staff; see impact almost instantly. You are an important component in the "big picture."
Networking with other professionals leads to better job opportunities.	Strength in all areas expected. Not a lot of time for coaching by peers.
Learn other skills, such as how to do presentations and budgets and establish deadlines.	Sometimes so involved in your work, you don't have time for networking.
Intense daily pressure on billable hours, high productivity. Some firms are real "sweat shops."	Same "client" all the time. Advantage: Get to know organization really well. Disadvantage: Can become boring.
	Less intense daily pressure; more emphasis on accomplishing longer-term results.
Somewhat high employment turnover.	Less turnover.
Budgets and resources can be limited.	More resources usually available.
Salary traditionally low at entry level.	Salaries tend to be higher.
Insurance, medical benefits can be minimal.	Benefits usually good, sometimes excellent.
Little opportunity for profit-sharing, stock options.	More opportunities available.
High emphasis on tactical skills, production of materials.	Can be more managerial and involved in strategic planning.

firm found that the average hourly rate, across all public relations firm sizes and billable titles, was $213.

The primary income of a public relations firm comes from the selling of staff time, but some additional income results from markups on photocopying, telephone, fax, and artwork the firm supervises. The standard markup in the trade is between 15 and 20 percent.

PR CASEBOOK

Olympics PR: The Greatest Show on Earth

Public relations firms often handle special events for clients, and the ultimate event may be representing a corporate sponsor at the Olympics. Amanda Kamin, an associate account director at Burson-Marsteller compiled the following diary of her work with Visa International at the Athens Olympics.

2004 Olympics Diary; Week One

Sunday 8 August
After months of phone calls, planning and preparation, the on-the-ground work begins even as we arrive at Heathrow for the flight to Athens. Waiting with the Visa team in the lounge, we bump into the Bermuda Olympic team and Sean Kerly, winner of a gold medal with the British hockey team in 1988. We invite him to our first media reception on Tuesday.

Monday 9 August
We arrive at the Visa press office, with every piece of communications kit—mobiles, Blackberries, laptops—and ring the media to get journalists to our press reception tomorrow evening. We then visit event venues to check the display materials we have designed, then back to the office to work the phones till 1 A.M.

Tuesday 10 August
We begin preparations for tonight's media reception. The journalists show up as soon as it kicks off—we have everyone from Shanghai TV to *The Wall Street Journal* and EuroSport. Many are hoping for interviews with athletes that we can organise. Others, from Bloomberg and Reuters, are looking for a business angle and we inform them about the special briefing on sponsorship we have organised.

Wednesday 11 August
Today we opened the Visa Olympians Reunion Center (VORC) at the Athens Tennis Club with 350 guests and camera crews. Even at night it's hot in Athens, so we organised for water misters for the terrace earlier on.

Carl Lewis turns up, as does Prince Albert of Monaco, much to the media's interest. We have to make sure the journalists have the proper accreditation before letting them in and facilitate introductions to people such as Visa head of sponsorship Tom Shepard. There's one stressful moment: running around with two Italian journalists desperate to speak to Lewis, who left 20 minutes earlier. We track him down and the Carl Lewis story is on the front page of La Gazzetta dello Sport the next day.

Thursday 12 August
Today we have the first Team Visa lunch. Team Visa is a sponsorship and mentoring programme and the lunch features Sir Steve Redgrave, the mentor for the UK Team Visa athletes. My colleague disappears to VORC to help manage the event, while I hit the phones again to drum up media attendance for tomorrow's big event—the awards ceremony for the Visa Olympics of the Imagination (VOI) children's art contest. The finalists are from 17 countries, and even with five people it takes us hours to contact them all. I know the result of the contest and have to encourage the Chinese media to attend without revealing the winner. At 10 P.M. it's time for another meeting, over dinner, then back to the office at 1 A.M. to load up for tomorrow.

Friday 13 August
We spend two hours setting up the venue and by 11 A.M. It's 40°C, so we've organised to have 200 bottles of water sent to the venue. A journalist from EuroSport rings and asks if Prince Faisal of

(continued)

PR CASEBOOK *(continued)*

Jordan can attend with some guests. Redgrave and Prince Albert will be handling out medals to the kids and the VIP room also holds EU commissioner for culture and sport Viviane Reding, and about 12 bodyguards for both princes. Camera crews from Mexico, Greece, Poland, Russia and China begin to arrive, as does a Polish radio station and UK journalists. We're pleased at the turnout because we were concerned the big story about the Greek sprinters would undermine all our efforts.

Saturday 14 August

My first day off. I've been given tickets for the swimming and men's gymnastics events, so I watch the sports for a while before heading to the beach. Hosting four major events in five days is no easy task and I'm glad we did so much preparation in London. Now it's begun, there are fewer sponsor events because the journalists are covering the sports.

I can see why it's important to reach them during the first week as we're beginning to build up a large clippings file, including hits in The *Daily Telegraph*, *The Sun,* and on ITN and Sky News.

2004 Olympics Diary; Week Two

Sunday 15 August

The finalists from VOI are scheduled to appear on Rendezvous Athens, a late-night talk-show on Greek National Broadcast TV, so we head down to the TV station with the children and their guardians.

The programme features their artwork, along with a B-roll of the grand opening of VORC, which is an excellent result.

Monday 16 August

It's time to get ready for tonight's event to celebrate the Torino 2006 Winter Games. The close contact we've had with the Torino organising committee PR team will be very useful for us in two years. Turismo Torino has laid on Italy's premier bartender and an extensive Italian buffet, which pleases the business and travel journalists we've invited.

Public relations does have it glamour moments. Amanda Karmin, an account executive for Burson-Marsteller (London) was assigned to the Athens Olympics on behalf of client Visa International. Here, she poses with Aldo Montano, Italian gold medal athlete in fencing.

Tuesday 17 August

Visa is holding a briefing about the business of sponsorship for some of the non-sporting journalists who have been sent to Athens in case of a crisis. With little to report on so far, they are grateful for a business-based story. We now have good relationships with them all because we've seen them at our other events, and we're in a position to help Visa get positive coverage.

The rest of the second week is focused on preparation for the major events next week, although we still have to get hold of some national media for Team Visa lunches. We also get some time off and tickets for the Games.

2004 Olympics Diary; Week Three

Sunday 22 August

Swimmer Michael Phelps is sponsored by Visa USA and will be at VORC today for a press conference with Visa USA head of sponsorship Michael Lynch.

We've had less than a day to prepare, but it's been an easy sell. We focus on the stage dressing, getting Phelps to and from the event and how to handle all the questions we're expecting from the media.

Monday 23 August
Today we help Visa Europe with the Italian Team Visa lunch. Later Cherie Blair pays a visit to VORC.

Thursday 26 August
For the past couple of days, we've been preparing for the Team Visa party, which is held today for all the athletes and their mentors, including Rosa Mota, Sara Simeoni, Redgrave, and the media.

Friday 27 August
We get a call at short notice about former Olympic gymnastic gold medallist Nadia Comaneci visiting VORC. The team is fully occupied with calls for our Beijing 2008 event tomorrow, but fortunately I know from a contact at *The Times* that Alastair Campbell is looking for interviews with prominent Olympians. My colleague Sujit ends up chatting to Campbell over a drink while arranging an interview with Comaneci.

Saturday 28 August
Tonight is our last event. We've been working with the Visa China PR team and the Chinese National Tourism Agency on a press briefing for the next Olympic Games in Beijing. The Visa Olympians Reunion Center will be decorated throughout with red lanterns and there will be a Chinese dance performance after the briefing.

Although there will be a symbolic hand-over of the Games from Athens to Beijing at the closing ceremony tomorrow, tonight is the business hand-over and it's a great way to finish. We'll be heading home on Monday after three action-packed weeks, but we'll be doing it all again in mid-September at the Paralympics.

Source: Kamin, Amanda. "Event PR: The Greatest Show on Earth." *PRWeek*, September 20, 2004. www.PRWeek.com

SUMMARY

Public Relations Departments

Most organizations have public relations departments. Such departments may also be called by other names, such as *corporate communications*. Organizations, depending on their culture and the wishes of top management, structure the public relations function in various ways. Public relations professionals often serve at the tactical and technician level, but others are counselors to the top executive and have a role in policy making. In management theory, public relations is a staff function rather than a line function.

Public Relations Firms

Public relations firms come in all sizes and are found worldwide, providing a variety of services. In recent decades, many public relations firms have either merged with advertising agencies or become subsidiaries of diversified holding companies. Advantages of using outside firms include versatility and extensive resources, among other considerations; but they can also lack the full-time commitment of an in-house department, need a lot of direction, and are often more expensive.

Case Activity: **What Would You Do?**

You will graduate from college in several months and plan a career in public relations. After several interviews, you receive two job offers.

One is with a high-technology company that makes inkjet printers and scanners for the consumer market. The corporate communications department has about 20 professionals, and it is customary for beginners to start in employee publications or product publicity. Later, with more experience, you might be assigned to do marketing communications for a product group or work in a spe-

cialized area such as investor relations, governmental affairs, or even community relations.

The second job offer is from a local office of a large, national public relations firm. You would begin as an assistant account executive and work on several accounts, including a chain of fast-food restaurants and an insurance company. The jobs pay about the same, but the corporation offers better insurance and medical plans. Taking into consideration the pros and cons of working for public relations firms versus corporations, what job would best fit your abilities and preferences? Explain your reasons.

QUESTIONS for Review and Discussion

1. How have the role and function of public relations departments changed in recent years?
2. In what ways do the structure and culture of an organization affect the role and influence of the public relations department?
3. What kinds of knowledge does a manager of a public relations department need today?
4. Many departments are now called *corporate communications* instead of *public relations*. Do you think the first term is more appropriate? Why or why not?
5. What is the difference between a line and a staff function? To which function does public relations belong, and why?
6. Why is a compulsory-advisory role within an organization a good one for a public relations department to have?
7. What four areas of the organization cause the most potential for friction with public relations? Explain.
8. In your opinion, should public relations or human resources be responsible for employee communications?
9. Public relations people express a fear that they

will lose influence and be relegated to purely technical functions if they are controlled by the marketing department. Do you think their fears are justified? Why or why not?

10. Name at least seven services that a public relations firm offers clients.
11. What are the three largest communications conglomerates in the world?
12. How important is international business to American public relations firms?
13. Why do large holding companies find the acquisition of public relations firms so attractive?
14. What are the pros and cons of using a public relations firm?
15. What are the standard methods used by a public relations firm to charge for its services?
16. Review the Wal-Mart PR casebook on page 108. Do you think the company is taking the right steps to improve its image? What other policies and programs would be appropriate? The company is seeking public relations personnel. Would you apply? Why or why not?
17. Under what circumstances should a public relations firm resign from an account?

SUGGESTED READINGS

"Burson-Marsteller's Global Pilot." *IPRA Frontline*, March 2001, pp. 18–21.

Chabria, Anita. "Most-Admired Firms Put More Stock in PR." *PRWeek*, May 25, 2002, p. 3.

Creamer, Matthew. "Global Expansion Requires Local Familiarity." *PRWeek*, December 8, 2003, p. 20.

Goldstein, Richard. "Charging Clients: Find the Best Method to Suit Your Needs." *O'Dwyer's PR Services Report*, December 2003, pp. 29, 33.

Hays, Constance. "Wal-Mart Tries to Shine Its Image By Supporting Public Broadcasting: Money for the Media From a Company Under the Microscope." *New York Times*, August 8, 2004, pp. C1, C6.

Hood, Julia. "Agency Excellence Survey: Clients Reveal What Agencies Can Do to Make a Difference." *PRWeek*, May 3, 2004, pp. 17–24.

Hood, Julia. "Agency Business Report 2004." *PRWeek*, April 19, 2004, pp. 3–34.

Hood, Julia. "Corporate PR Professionals Reveal What Tough Times Can Teach a Team: Corporate Survey." *PRWeek*, March 15, 2004, pp. 17–24.

Hood, Julia. "The Global Report: War, SARS, and Recession Have Hurt Global PR, but Firms Remain Optimistic." *PRWeek*, July 21, 2003, pp. 14–22.

Hood, Julia. "The World is Their Roster: Agency Networks Have a Lot to Offer." *PRWeek*, March 18, 2002, pp. 14–15.

Lewis, Tanya. "Wary Resignation: When to Quit an Account." *PRWeek*, August 25, 2003, p. 16.

Mitroff, Ian, Swerling, Gerald, and Floto, Jennifer. "Study Proves Value of Public Relations and Finds Self-Doubt Within the Profession." *The Strategist*, Winter 2003, pp. 32–34.

O'Dwyer, Jack. "F-H Snagged in Two-Title Flap." *O'Dwyer's PR Services Report*, June 2004, pp. 1, 12.

O'Neil, Julie. "An Investigation of the Sources of Influence of Corporate Public Relations Practitioners." *Public Relations Review*, Vol. 29, No. 2, 2003, pp. 159–169.

"Profiles of International Firms." *O'Dwyer's PR Services Report*. June 2004, pp. 16–23.

Richter, Lisa, and Steen, Robert. "Getting Senior Management Buy-in for PR Return on Investment." *The Strategist*, Fall 2003, pp. 46–47.

Shenon, Philip. "Three Partners Quit Firm Handling Saudis' PR." *New York Times*, December 6, 2002, p. A12.

Sudhaman, Arun. "Asia's PR Industry Bounces Back from Troubles in 2003." *PRWeek*, July 19, 2004, p. 7.

Taaffe, Paul. "The Future of Global Public Relations: An Agency Perspective." *The Strategist*, Winter 2004, pp. 22–23.

White, Erin, and Trachtenberg, Jeffrey. "One Size Doesn't Fit All: At WPP, Sir Martin Sorrell Sees Limits to Globalization." *Wall Street Journal*, October 1, 2003, p. B1.

chapter 5

Research

Topics covered in this chapter include:

The Importance of Research

Effective public relations is a process, and the essential first step in the process is *research*. Today, research is widely accepted by public relations professionals as an integral part of the planning, program development, and evaluation process.

Defining the Research Role

In basic terms, research is a form of listening. Broom and Dozier, in their book *Using Research in Public Relations*, say, "Research is the controlled, objective, and systematic gathering of information for the purpose of describing and understanding."

Before any public relations program can be undertaken, information must be gathered and data must be collected and interpreted. Only by performing this first step can an organization begin to make policy decisions and map out strategies for effective communication programs. This research often becomes the basis for evaluating the program once it has been completed. The results of an evaluation can lead to greater accountability and credibility with upper management. (See Chapter 8 for details.)

Various types of research can be used to accomplish an organization's objectives and meet its need for information. The choice of what type of research to use really depends on the particular subject and situation. As always, time and budget are major considerations, as is the perceived importance of the situation. Consequently, many questions should be asked before formulating a research design:

- What is the problem?
- What kind of information is needed?
- How will the results of the research be used?
- What specific public (or publics) should be researched?
- Should the organization do the research in-house or hire an outside consultant?
- How will the research data be analyzed, reported, or applied?
- How soon will the results be needed?
- How much will the research cost?

These questions will help the public relations person determine the extent and nature of the research needed. In some cases, only informal research may be required, because of its low cost or the need for immediate information. In other cases, a random scientific survey may be selected, despite its costs and time requirement, because a political candidate may want to know exactly where he or she stands in the polls. The pros and cons of each research method will be discussed later in the chapter.

Using Research

Research is a multipronged tool that is involved in virtually every phase of a communications program. In general, studies show that public relations departments spend about 3 to 5 percent of their budget on research. Some experts contend that it should be 10 percent. Public relations professionals use research in the following ways:

- **To achieve credibility with management.** Executives want facts, not guesses and hunches. The inclusion of public relations personnel in an organization's policy and decision making, according to the findings of IABC's research on excellence in communication management, is strongly correlated with their ability to do research and relate their findings to the organization's objectives.

- **To define audiences and segment publics.** Detailed information about the demographics, lifestyles, characteristics, and consumption patterns of audiences helps to ensure that messages reach the proper audiences. A successful children's immunization information campaign in California was based on State Health Department statistics that showed that past immunization programs had not reached rural children and that Hispanic and Vietnamese children were not being immunized in the same proportion as other ethnic groups.

- **To formulate strategy.** Much money can be spent pursuing the wrong strategies. Officials of the New Hampshire paper industry, given the bad press about logging and waterway pollution, thought a campaign was needed to tell the public what it was doing to reduce pollution. An opinion survey of 800 state residents by a public relations firm, however, indicated that the public was already generally satisfied with the industry's efforts. Consequently, the new strategy focused on reinforcing positive themes such as worker safety, employment, and environmental responsibility.

- **To test messages.** Research is often used to determine what particular message is most salient with the target audience. According to one focus group study for a campaign to encourage carpooling, the message that resonated the most with commuters was saving time and money, not air quality or environmental concerns. Consequently, the campaign emphasized how many minutes could be cut from an average commute by using car pool lanes and the annual savings in gasoline, insurance, and car maintenance.

- **To help management keep in touch.** In a mass society, top management is increasingly isolated from the concerns of employees, customers, and other important publics. Research helps bridge the gap by periodically surveying key publics about problems and concerns. This feedback is a "reality check" for top executives and often leads to better policies and communication strategies.

- **To prevent crises.** An estimated 90 percent of organizational crises are caused by internal operational problems rather than by unexpected natural disasters. Research can often uncover trouble spots and public concerns before they become page-one news. (See the section on issues management in Chapter 10.) Analyzing complaints made to a toll-free number or monitoring chat rooms on the Internet often can tip off an organization that it should act before a problem attracts media attention.

- **To monitor the competition.** Savvy organizations keep track of what the competition is doing. This is done through surveys that ask consumers to comment on competing products, content analysis of the competition's media coverage, and reviews of industry reports in trade journals. Such research often helps an organization shape its marketing and communication strategies to counter a competitor's strengths and capitalize on its weaknesses.

- **To sway public opinion.** Facts and figures, compiled from a variety of primary and secondary sources, can change public opinion. Shortly before an election in Ohio, 90 percent of the voters supported a state ballot measure that would require cancer warnings on thousands of products from plywood to peanut butter. A coalition called Ohioans for Responsible Health Information, which opposed the bill, commissioned universities and other credible outside sources to research the economic impact of such legislation on consumers and major industries. The research, which was used as the basis of the grass-roots campaign, caused the defeat of the ballot measure, with 78 percent of the voters voting "no."

● **To generate publicity.** Polls and surveys can generate publicity for an organization. Indeed, many surveys seem to be designed with publicity in mind. Simmons Mattress once polled people to find out if they slept in the nude. And Kiwi Brands, a shoe polish company, obtained extensive media coverage about a survey it commissioned that showed a high correlation between ambition and shiny shoes. The study found that 97 percent of self-described "ambitious" young men believe that polished shoes are important.

● **To measure success.** The bottom line of any public relations program is whether the time and money spent accomplished the stated objective. As one of its many programs to boost brand awareness, Miller Genuine Draft sponsored a "reunion ride" on Harley Davidson Corporation's 90th anniversary. Ketchum generated extensive media publicity about the "ride" and Miller's sponsorship that was 98 percent positive. Perhaps more importantly, sales increased in all but two of the cities included in the event. Evaluation, the last step of the public relations process, is discussed in Chapter 8. The following sections will discuss ways of doing research.

ON THE JOB insights

Rules for Publicizing Surveys and Polls

The Council of American Survey Research Organizations (CASRO), a nonprofit national trade organization of more than 150 survey research companies, states that survey findings released to the public should contain the following information:

● The sponsor of the study
● The name of the research company conducting the study
● A description of the study's objectives
● A description of the sample, including the size of the sample and the population to which the results are intended to be generalized
● The dates of data collection
● The exact wording of the questions asked
● Any information that the researcher believes is relevant to help the public make a fair assessment of the results

In addition, CASRO recommends that other information should be readily available in case anyone asks for it. This information includes the following: (1) the type of survey conducted, (2) the methods used to select the survey sample, (3) how respondents were screened, and (4) the procedure for data coding and analysis.

Research Techniques

When the term *research* is used, people tend to think only of scientific surveys and complex statistical tabulations. In public relations, however, research techniques are used to gather data and information.

In fact, a survey of practitioners by Walter K. Lindenmann, former senior vice president and director of research for Ketchum, found that three-fourths of the respondents described their research techniques as casual and informal rather than scientific and precise. The research technique cited most often by the respondents was literature searches/database information retrieval.

This technique is called *secondary research*, because it uses existing information in books, magazine articles, electronic databases, and so on. In contrast, with *primary research*, new and original information is generated through a research design that is directed to answer a specific question. Some examples of primary research are in-depth interviews, focus groups, surveys, and polls.

Another way of categorizing research is by distinguishing between *qualitative* and *quantitative* research. Lindenmann contrasts the basic differences between qualitative and quantitative research in Table 5.1. In general, qualitative research affords the researcher rich insights and understanding of a situation or a target public. It also provides "red flags" or warnings when strong or adverse responses occur. These responses may not be generalizable, but they provide the practitioner with an early warning. Quantitative research is often more expensive and complicated, but it enables a greater ability to generalize to large populations. If enormous amounts of money are to be spent on a national campaign, an investment in quantitative research may be necessary.

The following sections briefly describe the most common research techniques.

Organizational Materials

Robert Kendall, in his book *Public Relations Campaign Strategies*, calls researching organizational materials *archival research*. Such materials may include an organization's policy statements, speeches by key executives, past issues of employee newsletters and magazines, reports on past public relations and marketing efforts, and news clippings. Marketing statistics, in particular, often provide the baseline data for public relations firms that are hired to launch a new product or boost awareness and sales for an existing product or service.

Kendall observes, "Archives provide the resources for background research, which is the essential first step in most other research techniques." Archival research also is a major component in most audits that are intended to determine how the organization communicates to its internal and external publics. (See Chapter 8 for more information on audits.)

TABLE 5.1

Qualitative versus Quantitative Research

QUALITATIVE RESEARCH	QUANTITATIVE RESEARCH
"Soft" data	"Hard" data
Usually uses open-ended questions, unstructured	Usually uses close-ended questions, requires forced choices, highly structured
Exploratory in nature; probing, fishing-expedition type of research	Descriptive or explanatory type of research
Usually valid, but not reliable	Usually valid and reliable
Rarely projectable to larger audiences	Usually projectable to larger audiences
Generally uses nonrandom samples	Generally uses random samples
Examples: Focus groups; one-on-one, in-depth interviews; observation; participation; role-playing studies; convenience polling	Examples: Telephone polls, mail surveys, mall-intercept studies, face-to-face interviews, shared cost, or omnibus, studies; panel studies

Library and Online Database Methods

Reference books, academic journals, and trade publications are found in every library. In many cases, these materials also are on CD-ROM. Many databases are available online that contain abstracts or full-text articles of thousands, or even millions, or articles. Two such services are Proquest (www.proquest.com), which indexes thousands of current periodicals and newspapers, and INFOTRAC (infotrac .thomsonlearning.com), which indexes 15 million full-text articles from over 5,000 scholarly and popular periodicals.

Some common reference sources used by public relations professionals include the *Statistical Abstract of the United States*, which summarizes census information; the Gallup Poll and the Gallup Index, which provide an index of public opinion on a variety of issues; *American Demographics*, which reports on population shifts and lifestyle trends; and *Simmons' Media and Markets*, an extensive annual survey of households on product usage by brand and exposure to various media.

Literature searches, the most often used informal research method in public relations, can tap an estimated 1,500 electronic databases that store an enormous amount of current and historical information.

Public relations departments and firms use online databases in a number of ways:

- To research facts and figures to support a proposed project or campaign that requires top management approval
- To keep up-to-date with news about clients and their competitors
- To track an organization's media campaigns and a competitor's press announcements
- To locate a special quote or impressive statistic for a speech or report
- Tracking the press and business reaction to an organization's latest actions
- To locate an expert who can provide advice on an issue or a possible strategy
- To keep top management apprised of current business trends and issues
- To learn the demographics and attitudes of target publics

Online databases are available on a subscription basis and usually charge by the minute in the same way that a telephone company charges for long-distance calls. The following are some of the online databases commonly used in public relations:

- **Burrelle's Broadcast Database.** This database contains the full-text transcripts of radio and television programs within 24 hours after they are transmitted. Sources include ABC, NBC, CBS, CNN, National Public Radio, and selected syndicated programs.

- **Dow Jones News/Retrieval.** This massive business library electronically transmits up-to-the-second global coverage of business news, economic indicators, and industry and market data. In includes approximately 45 million documents drawn from nearly 3,000 key business and financial publications, including the *Wall Street Journal* and the *New York Times*.

- **Lexis/Nexis.** This database, available at www.lexis/nexis.com, includes 8 million full-text articles from more than 125 magazines, newspapers, and news services as well as the full text of the *New York Times* and the *Washington Post*. Abstracts also are available from leading international publications.

ON THE JOB

global

Database Research Can Track Media Coverage

What sports events generate the most news coverage? Practitioners can use online search engines to access electronic databases that store thousands of print and broadcast stories to answer such a question.

Delahaye Medialink, a measurement and evaluation firm, used the names of several major sporting events around the world as keywords and came up with the following numbers of news stories:

The British Open	5,237
Women's World Cup Soccer	4,635
The French Open	3,598
The NBA Draft	3,218
The Stanley Cup Finals	2,996
The WNBA All-Star Game	1,474
The Tour de France	1,296
The NBA Championships	720

In addition to database research, the tried and true method of using library holdings and books remains a valuable research tool. With the rise of electronic versions of books, and even entire libraries online, background research about a situation, client, or business category can be done quickly and efficiently. Questia (Questia.com), which claims to be the world's largest online library, describes its holdings as follows:

Now with over 50,000 books and 399,000 journal, magazine, and newspaper articles—see the newest titles in our online library

All books and articles are available in their entirety—search every page

Credible content not found anywhere else on the Internet

The service is fast and relatively inexpensive, offering many of the basic library resources that enable a practitioner to be informed and up-to-date.

Public relations practitioners must follow current events and public affairs issues so that they can provide thoughtful counsel in their organizations. Reading newspapers and watching television news programs is a habit that young professionals must embrace.

A number of relatively new delivery systems are appearing that offer magazines (zinio.com) or newspapers (pressdisplay.com and newsstand.com) that are formatted like their print counterparts, but also include online LINKs and video. These services may appeal to the next generation of professionals. Other new media include services such as Audible.com, which delivers audio to MP3 players, including the daily reading of the *New York Times*. This enables commuters to multitask.

Innovative newspapers are developing interactive versions of their daily paper that can be read to the car commuter through satellite radio. The user can then save or forward the stories to colleagues. Listeners of NPR can forward stories or order transcripts or broadcasts.

This wide array of information resources, both offline and online, enables public relations practitioners to be current and knowledgeable about their own organization and its place in the larger world.

The Internet and World Wide Web

The Internet is a powerful research tool for the public relations practitioner. Any number of corporations, nonprofits, trade groups, special interest groups, foundations, universities, think tanks, and government agencies post reams of data on the Internet, usually in the form of home pages on the World Wide Web.

Online search engines are essential for finding information on the Internet and the World Wide Web. With literally millions of possible Web sites, search engines make it possible for a researcher to simply type in a keyword or two, click "Go," and in a few seconds receive all of the links that the search engine has found that relate to a given topic. Search engines such as Google also have become locations for sharing expertise and problem-solving skills regarding a wide array of topics. In the Google Groups section of the Google Web site (groups-beta.google.com), helpful information can be found on everything from recreation to business to the arts.

One of the more popular search engines is Yahoo!, which in one month alone had 36.2 million visitors. Other popular engines include Google, Go.com, MSN Search, AOL Search, and Ask Jeeves. Researchers also can use specialized search engines or search tools to locate audio and video content or content of topical interest, such as sports or business news. Reviews and directories of search engines are available at searchenginewatch.com. Public relations professionals should visit such sites from time to time to stay current on search capabilities as well as to monitor changes in search engines' policies, such as fees required for high placement in search results.

Researchers can use newsgroups such as PRFORUM, a newsgroup dedicated to public elations topics, to request information from others. The researcher posts a request to the newsgroup, and then people who know something about the subject respond to the researcher by sending him or her an e-mail message. An extensive discussion of the Internet's development and operation appears in Chapter 13.

Content Analysis

Content analysis is the systematic and objective counting or categorizing of content. In public relations, content often is selected from media coverage of a topic or organization. This research method can be relatively informal or quite scientific in terms of random sampling and establishing specific subject categories. It is often applied to news stories about an organization.

At a basic level, a researcher can assemble news clips in a scrapbook and count the number of column inches. Robert Kendall says that content analysis involves ". . . systematic analysis of any of several aspects of what a communication contains, from key words or concept references, such as company name or product; to topics, such as issues confronting the organization; to reading ease of company publications; or to all elements of a company video production."

A good example of content analysis is the way one company evaluated press coverage of its publicity campaign to celebrate its

ON THE JOB

insights

Surfing the Internet

Public relations requires research and fact-finding skills. Here's a sample of helpful sites for public relations professionals.

- **Statistical Abstract of the United States:** www.census.gov/stat_abstract
- **The PR Survey Observer:** www.clientize.com/home.asp
- **Bureau of Labor Statistics:** bls.gov
- **Environmental News Network:** www.enn.com
- **A list of home pages of various public relations firms:** www.prweb.com/prfirms.php
- **International Association of Business Communicators (IABC):** www.iabc.com
- **Public Relations Society of America (PRSA):** www.prsa.org
- **Business Wire (hyperlinks to corporate home pages):** www.hnt.com/bizwire
- **Zinio Magazine Reader:** www.zinio.com
- **NewsStand, Inc.:** www.home.newsstand.com
- **Vanderbilt Television News Archive:** tvnews.vanderbilt.edu/

100th anniversary. "A low-budget content analysis was carried out on 427 newspaper, magazine, radio, and television placements referring both to the client and its product. The research found that the client's principal themes and copy points were referred to in most of the media coverage the company had received."

Another use of content analysis is to determine if a need exists for additional public relations efforts. Faneuil Hall Marketplace in Boston stepped up its public relations activities after it discovered that the number of travel articles about it had decreased. An anniversary celebration of the Marketplace helped to generate increased coverage.

Content analysis also can be applied to letters and phone calls. They provide good feedback about problems with the organization's policies and services. A pattern of letters and phone calls pointing out a problem is evidence that something should be done.

Interviews

As with content analysis, interviews can be conducted in several different ways. Almost everyone talks to colleagues on a daily basis and calls other organizations to gather information. In fact, public relations personnel faced with solving a particular problem often "interview" other public relations professionals for ideas and suggestions.

If information is needed on public opinion and attitudes, many public relations firms will conduct short interviews with people in a shopping mall or at a meeting. This kind of interview is called an *intercept interview*, because people are literally intercepted in public places and asked their opinions.

The intercept interview does not use a rigorous sampling method, but it does give an organization a sense of current thinking or exposure to certain key messages. For example, a health group wanted to find out if the public was actually receiving and retaining crucial aspects of its message. To gather such information, intercept interviews were conducted with 300 adults at 6 malls. Both unaided and aided recall questions were asked to assess the overall impact of the publicity.

Intercept interviews last only two to five minutes. At other times, the best approach is to do in-depth interviews to get more comprehensive information. Major fund-raising projects by charitable groups, for example, often require in-depth interviews of community and business opinion leaders. The success of any major fund drive, those seeking $500,000 or more, depends on the support of key leaders and wealthy individuals.

This more in-depth approach is called *purposive interviewing*, because the interviewees are carefully selected based on their expertise, influence, or leadership in the community. For example, the Greater Durham, North Carolina, Chamber of Commerce interviewed 50 "movers and shakers" to determine support for an extensive image-building and economic development program.

Focus Groups

A good alternative to individual interviews is the *focus group*. The focus group technique is widely used in advertising, marketing, and public relations to help identify attitudes and motivations of important publics. Another purpose of focus groups is to formulate or pretest message themes and communication strategies before launching a full campaign.

The Paging Services Council used six focus groups in three cities to plan a campaign that would help consumers understand that beepers were more than little black boxes worn only by doctors and drug dealers. The groups helped the coun-

Surveys of public opinion, often taken by researchers on the street or in shopping malls, help public relations practitioners target audiences they wish to reach and to shape their messages.

cil and its public relations firm (1) define target audiences, (2) test program messages, (3) explore consumer attitudes about paging, and (4) evaluate product positioning statements.

Focus groups usually consist of 8 to 12 people who represent the characteristics of the target audience, such as employees, consumers, or community residents. The Paging Services Council chose baby boomers and users of pagers.

During the interview, a trained facilitator uses nondirective interviewing techniques that encourage group members to talk freely about a topic or give candid reactions to suggested message themes. The setting is usually a conference room, and the discussion is informal. A focus group may last one or two hours, depending on the subject matter.

A *focus group*, by definition, is an informal research procedure that develops qualitative information rather than hard data. Results cannot be summarized by percentages or even projected onto an entire population. Nevertheless, focus groups are useful in identifying the range of attitudes and opinions among the participants. Such insights can help an organization structure its messages or, on another level, formulate hypotheses and questions for a quantitative research survey.

Increasingly, focus groups are being conducted online. The online technique can be as simple as posing a question to a chat or interest group online. Researchers also are using more formal selection processes to invite far-flung participants to meet in a prearranged virtual space. In the coming years, techniques and services will be well developed for cost-effective, online focus group research.

In another adaptation of new media, engineering management professor Hal Nystrom recently conducted focus groups for a Monsanto subsidiary that were then Webcast to the client. The focus group files remained available for review via password on the Web. Time and location are becoming less relevant to conducting focus groups, increasing the potential of this research method.

Copy Testing

All too often, organizations fail to communicate effectively because they produce and distribute materials that the target audience can't understand. In many cases, the material is written above the educational level of the audience. Consequently, representatives of the target audience should be asked to read or view the material in draft form before it is mass-produced and distributed. This can be done one-on-one or in a small group setting.

A brochure about employee medical benefits or pension plans, for example, should be pretested with rank-and-file employees for readability and comprehension. Executives and lawyers who must approve the copy may understand the material, but a worker with a high school education might find the material difficult to follow.

Another approach to determine the degree of difficulty of the material is to apply a readability formula to the draft copy. Fog, Flesch, and similar techniques relate the number of words and syllables per sentence or passage with reading level.

Focus groups are an effective tool that can be utilized to collect qualitative data about public opinion and attitudes about products and services.

Right Ideas, Inc.

| About Us | Areas of Expertise | Research Methods | Success Stories | Contact Us |

Focus Groups   Mail Studies   Phone Surveys   Mall Intercepts

Focus Groups

Focus groups are an effective tool that can be utilized to collect qualitative marketing data. The groups usually consist of 8-12 respondents who are led through a targeted discussion of a particular product or service by a skilled moderator. A one-way mirror or a videoconferencing unit allows clients the opportunity to observe the respondents' reactions. (Due to the small sample involved, focus group results cannot be generalized to a larger population.) However, they are a very popular method for gathering opinions, ideas, and for measuring a specific group's reaction to possible new products.

Utilizing videoconference technologies, it is possible to view groups conducted at any of more than 1,000 locations around the country in real time. Our current clients enjoy the cost savings and the time-efficiency it provides. They are no longer out of the office for days at a time traveling to focus group facility sites in far-flung cities.

Highly complex sentences and multisyllabic words require an audience with a college education.

Other Research Techniques

Several new techniques deserve at least brief mention. Web sites have become one of the more important public relations tools for information dissemination and for establishing exchange with publics. Web sites can be reviewed and refined through usability research, which often involves a think-aloud technique for testing Web pages and Web functionality. Subjects typically are recruited at random and then invited to a comfortable, home-like research location with a computer workstation. The subjects begin with a practice session to become accustomed with the assigned task of vocalizing their every move and their impressions while they browse Web sites. After a sufficient practice session, the think-aloud process usually becomes quite fluid and natural, and the subjects then evaluate the Web site being tested. The transcripts or videotapes of the session can then be content analyzed to guide changes in the Web site's design, content, and function.

Experiments, especially those related to persuasion and information processing, may soon be a new frontier in public relations research. With persuasion and information-processing experiments, subjects process information while certain conditions of the session are manipulated. For example, two versions of a health message may be created, one including gross details about the health consequences of smoking and the other appealing to a person's vanity. In this example, sorting out the effects of fear appeals and vanity appeals can help to guide message development.

The theater, or perception analyzer, technique, has been effective in pretesting political speeches. With this technique, the audience views video or slides of print content while turning a dial higher or lower to reflect how well they like the material. Such dial-turning (called *analog data collection* in research jargon) enables close tracking of the viewer's response to each segment of the speech, video, or print materials that are presented.

Scientific Sampling

The research techniques discussed thus far can provide good insights to public relations personnel and help them formulate effective programs. Increasingly, however, public relations professionals need to conduct polls and surveys, as well as more rigorous content analyses, using highly precise scientific sampling methods. Such sampling is based on two important factors: randomness and a large number of respondents.

Random Sampling

Effective polls and surveys require a random sample. In statistics, this means that everyone in the targeted audience (as defined by the researcher) has an equal or known chance of being selected for the survey. This is also called a *probability sample*.

In contrast, a *nonprobability survey* is not random at all. Mall-intercept interviews, for example, are usually restricted only to shoppers in the mall at the time the interviewers are working. A number of factors affect exactly who is interviewed, including the time of day and the location of the intercept interviews. Researchers doing interviews in the morning may have a disproportionate number of home-makers, whereas interviews after 5 P.M. may include more high school students and office workers. Also, if the researcher stands outside a record store or athletic shoe outlet, the average age of those interviewed may be much younger than that of the general population.

A random sample could be accomplished if researchers were present at all hours and conducted interviews throughout the mall. This would ensure a more representative sampling of mall shoppers, particularly if a large number of shoppers were interviewed.

Researchers must be careful, however, about projecting results to represent an entire city's population. Market surveys show that the demographic characteristics of shoppers vary from mall to mall. In other words, the selection of malls for random intercept interviewing often depends on how the researcher defines the target audience.

A survey sponsored by the International Franchise Association shows how sample selection can distort results. The organization touted its findings that "92 percent of franchise owners were successful." The survey, however, involved only franchises still operating, not those that had failed.

ON THE JOB

ethics

Is This News Release Misleading?

Organizations often publicize the favorable findings of survey research, and the International Franchise Association (IFA) is no exception. It sent out a news release quoting a Gallup survey with the headline, "Gallup Survey: 92 Percent of Franchise Owners Successful." The text continued, "Whether you're serving burgers or bagels, tending to taxes or helping the bereaved select a casket, franchise owners consider themselves successful . . . ."

The news release didn't include the fact that the survey involved only those still operating and not those who failed. It also didn't specify how the sample was derived or whether bagel owners were even sampled. The IFA also grouped two categories of the survey results together—those who said "very successful" and those who said "somewhat successful"—to come up with the 92 percent.

If you were the public relations director for IFA, would you have allowed this news release to be distributed? Why or why not?

The most precise random sample is one generated from lists that have the name of every person in the target audience. This is relatively simple when conducting a random survey of an organization's employees or members, because the researcher can randomly select, for example, every 25th name on a list. However, care must be taken to avoid patterns in the lists based on rank or employee category. It is always advisable to choose large intervals between selected names so that the researcher makes numerous passes through the list. In addition, computerized lists may enable random selection of a specified number of names.

Another common method to ensure representation is to draw a random sample that matches the characteristics of the audience. This is called *quota sampling*. Human resource departments usually have breakdowns of employees by job classification, and it is relatively easy to proportion a sample accordingly. For example, if 42 percent of the employees work on the assembly line, then 42 percent of the sample should be assembly-line workers. A quota sample can be drawn on any number of demographic factors—age, sex, religion, race, income—depending on the purpose of the survey.

Random sampling becomes more difficult when comprehensive lists are not available. In those cases, researchers surveying the general population often use telephone directories or customer lists to select respondents at random. A more rigorous technique employs random generation of telephone numbers, assuring that new and unlisted numbers are included in the sample.

A travel company used this, random digit dialing (RDD) method for a nationwide telephone survey of 1,000 adult Americans to determine if the hurricane that devastated the island of Kauai affected vacation plans to visit the other Hawaiian islands not struck by the hurricane. On the basis of the results, the travel company restructured its advertising and public relations messages to emphasize that resorts on the other islands were open for business as usual.

Sample Size

In any probability study, sample size is always a big question. National polling firms usually sample 1,000 to 1,500 people and get a highly accurate idea of what the U.S. adult population is thinking. The average national poll samples 1,500 people, and the margin of error is within 3 percentage points 95 percent of the time. In other words, 19 out of 20 times that the same questionnaire is administered, the results should be within the same 3 percentage points and reflect the whole population accurately.

In public relations, the primary purpose of poll data is to get indications of attitudes and opinions, not to predict elections. Therefore, it is not usually necessary or practical to do a scientific sampling of 1,500 people. A sample of 250 to 500 will give relatively accurate data—with a 5 or 6 percent variance—that will help determine general public attitudes and opinions. A sample of about 100 people, accurately drawn according to probability guidelines, will include about a 10 percent margin of error.

This percentage of error would be acceptable if a public relations person, for example, asked employees what they want to read in the company magazine. Sixty percent may indicate that they would like to see more news about opportunities for promotion. If only 100 employees were properly surveyed, it really doesn't matter if the actual percentage is 50 or 70 percent. The larger percentage, in either case, would be sufficient to justify an increase in news stories about advancement opportunities.

This is also true in ascertaining community attitudes. If a survey of 100 or fewer citizens indicates that only 25 percent believe that an organization is a good community citizen, it really doesn't matter whether the result is 15 or 35 percent. The main point is that the organization must take immediate steps to improve its performance.

Questionnaire Construction

Although correct sampling is important in gaining accurate results, pollsters generally acknowledge that sampling error may be far less important than the errors that result from the wording and order of questions in a survey and even the timing of a survey.

The Problem of Semantics

Wording the questions on a questionnaire is a time-consuming process, and it is not unusual for a questionnaire to go through multiple drafts to achieve maximum clarity. The question "Is it a good idea to limit handguns?" differs from "Do you think registration of handguns will curtail crime?" On first glance, the two questions seem to be asking the same thing. On closer examination, however, one can realize that a respondent could easily answer "yes" to the first question and "no" to the second.

The first question asks if limiting handguns is a good idea. The second asks if people think it will curtail crime. A third question that might elicit a different response would be, "Do you think that laws curtailing the use of handguns would work?" Thus, the questions emphasize three different aspects of the problem. The first stresses the value of an idea, the second explores a possible effect, and the third examines the practicality of a proposed solution. Research shows that people often think something is a good idea, but do not think it would work. Another related problem is how respondents might interpret the words *limit* and *curtail*. To some, these words may refer to a total ban on handguns, whereas others may think they suggest that guns should be kept away from people with criminal records.

Avoid Biased Wording

Questionnaires should avoid questions that use highly charged words to elicit a particular response. Such a question was used by Republican Party pollsters who asked respondents whether they agreed or disagreed that "We should stop excessive legal claims, frivolous lawsuits, and overzealous lawyers." Not surprisingly, an overwhelming majority of the respondents agreed. Another example of a loaded question is one by U.S. English, Inc., a group advocating English as the official language of the United States. It asked, "Do you think American taxpayers should be forced to pay for special voter registration drives for those who insist on or want to vote in a language other than English?"

In a survey, such statements and questions are an indication that *advocacy research* is being conducted. That is, the questionnaire is intentionally skewed to promote a cause or product. Such studies tarnish the reputation of legitimate research and make the public increasingly skeptical of the results of any survey.

Timing and Context

Responses to survey questions are influenced by events, and this should be taken into consideration when reviewing the results of a survey. The public's esteem for an airline, for example, will be lower if a survey is conducted just after a plane crash. Intel's corporate reputation took a dip in company surveys just after major news coverage about a flaw in its Pentium microchip.

On the positive side, surveys by Coca-Cola about its reputation and corporate citizenship showed very favorable public attitudes just after its massive investment in the Atlanta Olympic Games.

Consequently, polls and surveys should be conducted when the organization isn't in the news or connected to a significant event that may influence public opinion. In neutral context, a more valid survey can be conducted about an organization's reputation, products, or services.

Large organizations, such as Exxon/Mobil, General Electric, and Microsoft, counterbalance the effects of one-time events by conducting quarterly surveys. This technique, called *benchmarking*, is discussed in Chapter 8.

Political Correctness

Another problem with questionnaire design involves questions that tend to elicit the "correct" response. This is also called a *courtesy bias*. Respondents often choose answers that won't offend the interviewer and that reflect mainstream thinking. For example, surveys show that 80 percent of Americans consider themselves "environmentalists." As skeptics point out, however, would anyone admit that he or she was not concerned about the environment?

Surveys of public relations practitioners about the value of research also show a degree of courtesy bias in choosing the politically correct answer. Almost 90 percent of public relations practitioners agree that research is a necessary and integral part of public relations work. Almost the same percentage, however, agree that research is talked about more often than it is done.

Those conducting employee surveys also fall into the "courtesy" trap by posing such questions as "How much of each newsletter do you read?" or "How well do you like the column by the president?" Employees may never read the newsletter or think that the president's column is ridiculous, but they know the "correct" answer should be that they read the "entire issue" and that the president's column is "excellent."

Researchers try to avoid politically correct answers by making questionnaires confidential and by promising anonymity to the people who are surveyed. Because employees often perceive the public relations department to be part of management, it is often best to employ an outside research firm to conduct employee surveys.

Answer Categories

Answer categories also can skew a questionnaire. It is important that answer choices are provided that cover a range of opinions. Several years ago, a national polling organization asked the question, "How much confidence do you have in business corporations?" but provided only the following answer categories: (a) a great deal, (b) only some, and (c) none at all. A large gap exists between "a great deal" and the next category, "only some." Such categories invariably skew the results to show very little confidence in business. A better list of answers might have been (a) a great deal, (b) quite a lot, (c) some, (d) very little, and (e) none. Perhaps an even better approach would have been to provide the answer categories (a) above average, (b) average, and (c) below average. The psychological distance between the three choices is equal, and there is less room for the respondent's interpretation of what "quite a lot" means.

In general, "yes or no" questions are not very good for examining respondents' perceptions and attitudes. An answer of "yes" or "no" provides little feedback on the strength or weakness of a respondent's opinion. A question such as "Do you agree with the company's policy of requiring drug testing for all new employees?" can be answered by "yes" or "no," but more useful information would be obtained by setting up a Likert-type scale—(a) strongly agree, (b) agree, (c) undecided, (d) disagree, and (e) strongly disagree. These types of answers enable the surveyor to probe the depth of feeling among respondents and may serve as guidelines for management in making major changes or just fine-tuning the existing policy.

Another way of designing a numeric scale to pinpoint a respondent's beliefs or attitudes is to use a 5-point scale. Such a scale might look like this:

Question:

How would you evaluate the company's efforts to keep you informed about job benefits? Please circle one of the following numbers ("1" being a low rating and "5" being a high rating).

Answer:

1   2   3   4   5

The advantage of numeric scales is that medians and means can be calculated. In the previous example, the average from all respondents might be 4.25, which indicates that employees think the company does keep them informed about job benefits, but that there is still room for communication improvement.

Questionnaire Guidelines

The following are some general guidelines for the construction of questionnaires:

- Determine the type of information that is needed and in what detail.
- State the objectives of the survey in writing.
- Decide which group(s) will receive the questionnaire.
- Decide on the size of the sample.
- State the purpose of the survey and guarantee anonymity.
- Use closed-end (multiple-choice) answers as often as possible. Respondents find it easier and less time-consuming to select answers than to compose their own.
- Design the questionnaire in such a way that answers can be easily coded for statistical analysis.
- Strive to make the questionnaire no more than 25 questions. Long questionnaires put people off and reduce the number of responses, particularly in print questionnaires, because it is easy to see how long the survey will take to complete.
- Use categories when asking questions about education, age, and income. People are more willing to answer when a category or range is used. For example, what category best describes your age? (a) Under 25, (b) 26 to 40, and so on.
- Use simple, familiar words. Readability should be appropriate for the group being sampled. At the same time, don't talk down to respondents.
- Avoid ambiguous words and phrases that may confuse the respondents.
- Edit out leading questions that suggest a specific correct response or bias an answer.
- Remember to consider the context and placement of questions. A question placed before another can influence response to the later question.
- Provide space at the end of the questionnaire for respondents' comments and observations. This allows them to provide additional information or elaboration that may not have been covered in the main body of the questionnaire.
- Pretest the questions for understanding and possible bias. Representatives of the proposed sampling group should read the questionnaire and be asked to make comments as to how it can be improved.

Designing a questionnaire and analyzing the results can be time-consuming, but a software program is available that can make the task much easier. The software, *Publics PR Research Software*, was developed by Glen T. Cameron at the University of Missouri and Tim Herzog of Kno Technology. The software helps the public relations personnel create questionnaires by providing ready-made questions that can be tailored to fit any situation. In addition, the program also helps conduct data analysis to identify target publics. This component is a modest artificial intelligence module that draws on judgments from statistics to generate advice. Cameron describes it as artificial intelligence, but with a low I.Q.

Reaching Respondents

A questionnaire is only as good as the delivery system that gets it to respondents. This section presents the pros and cons of (1) mail questionnaires, (2) telephone surveys, (3) personal interviews, (4) piggyback, or omnibus, surveys, and (5) Web and e-mail surveys.

Mail Questionnaires

Questionnaires may be used in a variety of settings. They may be handed out at a manufacturing plant, at a county fair, or even in a bank lobby. However, for several different reasons, most survey questionnaires are mailed to respondents:

- Because the researchers have better control as to who receives the questionnaire, they can make sure that the survey is representative.
- Large geographic areas can be covered economically.
- It is less expensive to administer paper-based questionnaires than to hire interviewers to conduct personal interviews.
- Large numbers of people can be included at minimal cost.

However, mail questionnaires do have some disadvantages. The biggest is the low response rate. A mail questionnaire by a commercial firm sent to the general public usually produces a response rate of 1 to 2 percent. If the survey concerns issues considered highly relevant to the general public, the response rate might increase to 5 to 20 percent. A much better response rate would be generated, however, if a questionnaire were mailed by an organization to its members. In this case, the response rate may be 30 to 80 percent. The more closely people identify with the organization and the questions, the better the response.

The response rate to a mail questionnaire can be increased, say the experts, if all the guidelines of questionnaire construction are followed. In addition, researchers should keep the following suggestions in mind:

- Include a stamped, self-addressed return envelope and a personally signed letter explaining the importance of participating in the survey.
- Provide an incentive. Commercial firms often encourage people to fill out questionnaires by including a token amount of money or a discount coupon. Other researchers promise to share the results of the survey with the respondents.
- Mail questionnaires by first-class mail. Some research shows that placing special issue stamps on the envelope attracts greater interest than simply using a postage meter.
- Mail a reminder postcard three or four days after the questionnaire has been sent.
- Do a second mailing (either to nonrespondents or to the entire sample) two or three weeks after the first mailing. Again, enclose a stamped, self-addressed re-

turn envelope and a cover letter explaining the crucial need for the recipient's participation.

Telephone Surveys

Surveys by telephone, particularly those that are locally based, are used extensively by research firms. The telephone survey has several advantages:

- The response or nonresponse is immediate. A researcher doesn't have to wait several weeks for responses to arrive by mail.
- A telephone call is personal. It is effective communication, and it is much cheaper than a personal interview.
- A telephone call is less intrusive than going door-to-door and interviewing people. Surveys have found that many people are willing to talk on the phone for up to 45 minutes, but they will not stand at a door for more than 5 or 10 minutes and are unwilling to admit strangers to their homes.
- The response rate, if the survey is properly composed and the phone interviewers trained, can reach 80 to 90 percent.

The major disadvantage of telephone surveys is the difficulty in getting access to telephone numbers. In many urban areas, as many as one-third to one-half of all numbers are unlisted. Although researchers can let a computer program pick numbers through random dialing, this method is not as effective as actually knowing who is being called. Another barrier is convincing respondents that a legitimate poll or survey is being taken. Far too many salespeople attempt to sell goods by posing as researchers.

Personal Interviews

The personal interview is the most expensive form of research because it requires trained staff and travel. If travel within a city is involved, a trained interviewer may only be able to interview 8 or 10 people a day, and salaries and transportation costs make it expensive. Considerable advance work is required to arrange interviews and appointments and, as previously noted, residents are reluctant to admit strangers into their homes.

However, in some instances personal interviews can be cost-effective. They can generate a wealth of information if the setting is controlled. Many research firms conduct personal interviews at national conventions or trade shows, where there is a concentration of people with similar interests. An equipment company, for example, may hire a research firm to interview potential customers at a national trade show.

Piggyback Surveys

An alternative method of reaching respondents is the piggyback survey, also known as the *omnibus survey*. In basic terms, an organization "buys" a question in a national survey conducted by a survey organization such as Gallup or Harris. For example, General Mills may place one or two questions in a national poll that ask respondents what professional athlete they most admire as a way to find new endorsers for its breakfast foods. In the same survey, the American Cancer Society may place a question asking how the public feels about sporting events sponsored by tobacco companies.

This method is attractive to public relations people for two reasons. One is cost. An organization pays much less to participate in a piggyback poll than to conduct its own survey. A second reason is expertise. Firms such as Gallup or Harris have the skill and organization to do a survey properly and efficiently; few public relations departments or firms do.

Piggyback surveys, however, do have limitations. An organization can only get a small snapshot of public opinion with one or two questions, and the subject matter must be relevant to the general public.

Web and E-Mail Surveys

The newest way to reach respondents is through electronic communications. One such method is to post a questionnaire on an organization's Web site and then ask visitors to complete it online. The advantage of this is that once the visitor completes the survey, his or her response is immediately available and the results can be added to the running tabulation. For example, an undergraduate campaign team sought to test messages about the National Wildlife Foundation's travel program, which was targeted at those over age 50. The students sampled from an e-mail list of university alumni by year of graduation so that they reached the appropriate age group. They invited the alumni to visit a Web site and rate several of the travel program's message strategies.

Researchers use several methods to attract respondents to a Web site, including (1) banner ads announcing the survey on other Web sites or online networks, (2) sending e-mail invitations to members of the target audience, (3) telephoning individuals with an invitation to participate, and (4) sending a postcard. The major disadvantage of Web surveys is that it is difficult to control the exact characteristics of the respondents, because a Web site is accessible to virtually anyone with a computer and a modem. It is also very important to control repeated participation by the same respondent by identifying the unique identifying number of the computer (called the IP address) and only allowing one submission. One of the biggest problems for online surveys is the low response rate due to the impersonal nature of the survey and the ease of leaving the survey's Web site with a single mouse click. For this reason, many online surveys begin with the most crucial questions to be asked and the key demographics needed for analysis.

If reaching the exact audience is important, another approach is an e-mail survey that is sent to a list of known respondents. Organizations can compile e-mail lists of clients or customers, but it's also now possible to purchase e-mail address lists from a variety of sources. Full-service Web survey companies can target populations, collect responses, and deliver data to the client. The costs of such surveys can be low if an online survey service such as freeonlinesurveys.com, which is more of a do-it-yourself service, is used. Zoomerang (info.zoomerang.com) and Harris Interactive recruit and maintain pools of respondents to fit profiles that clients want to survey. Gender, income, and political persuasion are examples of characteristics that can be selected for Web survey purposes. If a politician wants to refine how best to appeal to conservative, well-to-do, female prospects for fund-raising, a sample can be quickly drawn and surveyed by these services.

PR CASEBOOK

Getting Under the Surface: Applying Anthropology to Public Relations Research

Although much attention and significant budgets are allocated to quantitative research in public relations, the value of qualitative research should not be overlooked. A public relations research pioneer, Dr. Walter Lindenmann, formerly director of public relations for Ketchum, praised a basic research technique that he called "walking-around research." This is the process of getting a sense of the place and the people who make up the target public, whether they be a company's employees or donors to an opera company.

The company Context-Based Research (CBR) takes a more systematic approach to qualitative research, employing principles of anthropology to gain richer insights and develop strategies that may not be possible with quantitative methods. CBR claims that the difference between what people say and what they do is where focus groups, surveys, and other conventional research methods fail. In the words of CBR principals, here is the rationale for using anthropological methods:

- "Traditionally we think of anthropology as studying people in some remote part of the world." Brian Lewbart, marketing and communication director of CBR, told *pr reporter*. However, CBR uses ethnography to analyze consumer behaviors.
- "Ethnography is basically a study of the structure of how people act," partner Chuck Donofrio told *pr reporter*, " 'Ethno' meaning people, and 'graph'—chart or structure." Lewbart and Donofrio offered

pr reporter several additional strengths of ethnographic methodology:

- "When you observe people, you see them doing things that they don't tell you about."
- "Anthropologists are trained to observe behavior and pull information based on the observations. Watching behavior and then talking to subjects about what is observed can give you a better sense of behavior."
- One tool of ethnography takes observation a step further through actual participant observation: "You go to where they are and take part. Doing things with them gives you another insight." This can lead to delicate issues about disclosure of purposes and confidentiality that must be considered for the well-being of the research subjects.
- Other tools include having subjects chart their own behavior: "Over the course of a week or a month, that data can show you how this group works, put a structure to their experience."
- "What we are finding is that we can help clients fit into the lives of the people they're trying to serve."

Women in the Outdoors: A Sample Anthropological Study

In one of CBR's first studies, documented in *pr reporter*, a retailer of outerwear had two research objectives:

- Defining patterns of outdoor activity in the target audience—40 women from 4 major cities categorized as either "enthusiasts" or "casual users" of the outdoors
- Developing contextual insight into the connection between these experiences

and their choice of outerwear and outdoor gear, with an emphasis on product development.

Methodologies

CBR developed rapport by engaging the women in "naturalistic," open-ended interviews. Researchers explained the goals and methods of the project and collected data on each participant's occupation, salary, and marital status to build profiles. Participants were asked to do some of the work:

1. Participants were asked to describe their lives, incorporating thoughts about work, leisure, friends, family, responsibilities, and weekend versus workday routines.
2. They were asked to discuss how the outdoors fits into their lives, including where they go to be outdoors, whether they are with others or alone, what preparation is required, and how they feel when they are outdoors.
3. They were asked to talk about the clothing and equipment they use, what relationship their "outdoors self" has on their everyday work or leisure wardrobe, and how their wardrobe selection relates to both self-image and the perception they believe others have of them.
4. Participants were asked to keep photo diaries. CBR provided each participant with a camera for a two-week period. Participants snapped pictures on their commutes to work, on daily walks with their dogs or children, and in their closets to document their favorite, and perhaps least favorite, activewear.

In addition, each participant took part in a one-on-one, semi-structured in-depth interview at her home or locale of her choice. This goes beyond the reach of traditional focus groups by engaging participants in their own environments, where they're most comfortable. Researchers had the participant's photo diary photos in hand for discussion.

The researchers also used a secure Web area on the Internet. During the interview process, researchers uploaded their field notes to the secure Web area where the management team reviewed, analyzed, and interpreted the incoming information.

Farmer's Markets, Fido, and Country Chic

CBR shared its findings with *pr reporter* about the distinct profiles that emerged. "One of the things we discovered about women in general is that they have a strong affinity for the outdoors and how they connect with it is very telling," says Lewbart.

In the city, women display a connection with farmers' markets, outdoor produce marts, and rustic shopping environments where vendors sell everything from potato knishes to dried flowers. Says Lewbart, "They took pictures of where they had been, and farmers' markets always popped up. You don't learn that from a focus group or survey." This offered the retailer a signal for product placement and the kinds of designs that might appeal to their target public. Also, it showed that the women seek nature and simplicity in an urban environment.

Another linkage that emerged was the women's relationships with their dogs. Women in all of the survey cities connect with the outdoors by walking their dogs and playing with them in parks.

CBR concluded that these women want style and good looks combined with purpose in their outerwear. "There is a growing market for stylish, casual outerwear," Lewbart says, "They are seeking functionality, but it doesn't have to be for hiking."

The sorts of profiles derived from ethnography are insightful and offer a rich source of inspiration for those planning communications directed to a target audience.

Source: pr reporter, February 21, 2000; jim & lauri grunig's research, a supplement of pr reporter, February 25, 2002.

SUMMARY

The Importance of Research

Research is the basic groundwork of any public relations program. It involves the gathering and interpretation of information. Research is used in every phase of a communications program.

Research Techniques

Secondary research uses information from library sources and, increasingly, from online and Internet sources. Primary research involves gathering new information through interviews or sampling procedures.

Sampling

The sampling method used constrains the extent to which the findings can be analyzed in detail and generalized to a larger population. When possible, probability samples generate the best results, particularly when doing quantitative research.

Questionnaire Construction

The design of a questionnaire—wording and the order of the questions—is probably at least as important as correct sampling. Timing and context also affect responses.

Reaching Respondents

Survey respondents may be reached by mail, e-mail, telephone, the Web, personal interviews, or through piggyback (omnibus) surveys.

Case Activity: **What Would You Do?**

Universal Manufacturing Corporation is located in a Midwestern city of 500,000 people. At 6000 employees, it is one of the largest employers in the county, and the company has been at its present location for the past 50 years. Despite this record, management believes that the company doesn't have a strong identity and lacks visibility in the community.

The director of public relations has been asked to prepare a new public relations plan for the coming fiscal year. She recommends that the company first conduct research to determine exactly what its image is in the community.

If you were the public relations director, what informal research methods would you use? What more formal research methods could be used? What kinds of information about the company's image should be researched?

QUESTIONS for Review and Discussion

1. Why is research important to public relations work?
2. What questions should a person ask before formulating a research design?
3. Identify at least five ways that research is used in public relations.
4. How can survey research be used as a publicity tool?
5. List at least five informal research methods.
6. What are online databases? How are they used by public relations professionals?
7. How can the Internet and World Wide Web be used as research tools?
8. What is the procedure for organizing and conducting a focus group? What are the pros and cons of using focus groups?

9. What is an intercept interview?
10. What is the difference between probability (random) and nonprobability samples?
11. What guidelines should be followed when releasing the results of a survey to the media and the public?
12. What percentage margin of error is associated with various sample sizes? What size sam-

ples are usually adequate for public relations work?
13. Identify at least five guidelines that should be followed when preparing a questionnaire.
14. What are the pros and cons of each of the following: mail questionnaires, telephone surveys, personal interviews, and piggyback surveys?

SUGGESTED READINGS

Austin, Erica, and Pinkleton, Bruce. *Strategic Public Relations Management*. Mahwah, NJ: Erlbaum Associates, 2001.

Broom, Glen, and Dozier, David. *Using Public Relations Research*. Upper Saddle River, NJ: Prentice Hall, 1990.

Charland, Bernie. "The Mantra of Metrics: A Realistic and Relevant Approach to Measuring the Impact of Employee Communications." *The Strategist*, Fall 2004, pp. 30–32.

Creamer, Matthew. "Sharing Intelligence: PR People Should Be Pushing for More Access to Better Research," *PRWeek*, February 9, 2004, p. 17.

Dysart, Joe. "Building Web Traffic With On-Site Polls." *Public Relations Tactics*. April 2003, p. 6.

Eschrich, Jim. "Establishing a Comport Level: Rapport Is the Root of Qualitative Research," *tips & tactics, a supplement to pr reporter*, June 10, 2002, pp. 1–2.

Green, Sherri Deatherage. "Strategy by Numbers: Up-Front Research Doesn't Yet Have a Permanent Place in PR." *PRWeek*, August 4, 2003, p. 15.

Grunig, Larissa A., and Grunig, James. "Ethical Relationships in the Conduct of PR Research," *jim & lauri grunig's research, a supplement of pr reporter*, No. 15, February 25, 2002, pp. 1–4.

Grunig, Larissa A., and Grunig, James. "When Conventional Wisdom Meets Research: The Myth of Implied Third-Party Endorsement," *jim & lauri grunig's research, a supplement of pr reporter*, No. 8, May 22, 2000, pp. 1–4.

"How to Measure Relationships? Grunig/Hon Study for Institute Measurement Commission Lays Groundwork." *pr reporter*, Vol. 42, No. 40, October 11, 1999, pp. 1–3.

Rockland, David. "PR Research and Measurement at a Crossroads." *The Strategist*, Fall 2003, pp. 35–39.

Stacks, Don W. *Primer of Public Relations Research*. New York: Guilford Press, 2002.

Wimmer, Roger D., and Dominick, Joseph R. *Mass Media Research: An Introduction*, 7th ed. Belmont, MA: Wadsworth, 2003.

6

Program Planning

Topics covered in this chapter include:

The Value of Planning

The second step of the public relations process, following research, is *program planning*. Before any public relations activity can be implemented, it is essential that considerable thought be given to what should be done and in what sequence to accomplish an organization's objectives.

A good public relations program should be an effective tool to support an organization's business, marketing, and communications objectives. As Larry Werner, executive vice president of Ketchum, points out, "No longer are we simply in the business of putting press releases out; we're in the business of solving business problems through communications."

In other words, public relations planning should be strategic. As Glen Broom and David Dozier say in their text *Using Public Relations Research*, "Strategic planning is deciding where you want to be in the future (the goal) and how to get there (the strategies). It sets the organization's direction proactively, avoiding 'drift' and routine repetition of activities." A practitioner must think about a situation, analyze what can be done about it, creatively conceptualize the appropriate strategies and tactics, and determine how the results will be measured. Planning also involves the coordination of multiple methods—news releases, special events, Web pages, press kits, CD-ROM distribution, news conferences, media interviews, brochures, newsletters, speeches, and so on—to achieve specific results.

Systematic planning prevents haphazard, ineffective communication. Having a blueprint of what is to be done and how it will be executed makes programs more effective and public relations more valuable to the organization.

Approaches to Planning

Planning is like putting together a jigsaw puzzle. Research, which was discussed in Chapter 5, provides the various pieces. Next, it is necessary to arrange the pieces so that a coherent design, or picture, emerges. The best planning is systematic; that is, gathering information, analyzing it, and creatively applying it for the specific purpose of attaining an objective.

This section presents two approaches to planning. In both cases, the emphasis is on asking and answering questions to generate a roadmap for success.

Management by Objective

One popular approach to planning is a process called *management by objective (MBO)*. MBO provides focus and direction for formulating strategy to achieve specific organizational objectives. According to Robert E. Simmons, author of *Communication Campaign Management*, the use of MBO in planning ensures the "production of relevant messages and establishes criteria against which campaign results can be measured."

In their book *Public Relations Management by Objectives*, Norman R. Nager and T. Harrell Allen discuss nine basic MBO steps that can help a practitioner conceptualize everything from a simple news release to a multifaceted communications program. The steps can serve as a planning checklist that provides the basis for strategic planning.

1. Client/employer objectives. What is the purpose of the communication, and how does it promote or achieve the objectives of the organization? Specific objectives such as "to make consumers aware of the product's high quality" are more meaningful than "to make people aware of the product."

2. Audience/publics. Who exactly should be reached with the message, and how can that audience help achieve the organization's objectives? What are the characteristics of the audience, and how can demographic information be used to structure the message? The primary audience for a campaign to encourage carpooling consists of people who regularly drive to work, not the general public.

3. Audience objectives. What is it that the audience wants to know, and how can the message be tailored to audience self-interest? Consumers are more interested in how a new computer will increase their productivity than in how it works.

4. Media channels. What is the appropriate channel for reaching the audience, and how can multiple channels (news media, brochures, special events, and direct mail) reinforce the message among key publics? An ad may be best for making consumers aware of a new product, but a news release may be better for conveying consumer information about the product.

5. Media channel objectives. What is the media gatekeeper looking for in a news angle, and why would a particular publication be interested in the information? A community newspaper is primarily interested in a story with a local angle.

6. Sources and questions. What primary and secondary sources of information are required to provide a factual base for the message? What experts should be interviewed? What database research should be conducted? A quote from a project engineer about a new technology is better than a quote from the marketing vice president.

7. Communication strategies. What environmental factors will affect the dissemination and acceptance of the message? Are the target publics hostile or favorably disposed to the message? What other events or pieces of information negate or reinforce the message? A campaign to conserve water is more salient if there has been a recent drought.

8. Essence of the message. What is the planned communication impact on the audience? Is the message designed merely to inform, or is it designed to change attitudes and behavior? Telling people about the values of physical fitness is different from telling them how to achieve it.

9. Nonverbal support. How can photographs, graphs, films, and artwork clarify and visually enhance the written message? Bar graphs or pie charts are easier to understand than columns of numbers.

A Strategic Planning Model

By working through the checklist adapted from Nager and Allen's book, a practitioner has in place the general building blocks for planning. These building blocks serve as background to create a specific plan. Ketchum offers more pointed questions in its "Strategic Planning Model for Public Relations." Ketchum's organizational model makes sense to professionals and clients alike, moving both parties

One of the most common and important planning specialties in public relations is meeting and special event planning. When these events are located at major hotels and convention centers, the hotels offer a variety of excellent services. Even when your event will not be held at a site that specializes in event planning and facilitation, you can make use of excellent planning tools. Marriott's step-by-step process, for example, is available to you at http//:marriott.com/meeting.

toward a clear situation analysis needed to make planning relevant to the client's overall objectives.

Facts

- **Category facts.** What are recent industry trends?
- **Product/service issues.** What are the significant characteristics of the product, service, or issue?
- **Competitive facts.** Who are the competitors, and what are their competitive strengths, similarities, and differences?
- **Customer facts.** Who uses the product and why?

Goals

- **Business objectives.** What are the company's business objectives? What is the time frame?
- **Role of public relations.** How does public relations fit into the marketing mix?
- **Sources of new business.** What sectors will produce growth?

Audience

- **Target audiences.** What are the target audiences? What are their "hot" buttons?
- **Current mindset.** How do audiences feel about the product, service, or issue?
- **Desired mindset.** How do we want them to feel?

Key Message

- **Main point.** What one key message must be conveyed to change or reinforce mindsets?

These two approaches to planning, MBO and Ketchum's model, lead to the next important step—the writing of a strategic public relations plan. The next section explains the elements of such a plan.

Elements of a Program Plan

A public relations program plan identifies what is to be done, why, and how to accomplish it. By preparing such a plan, either as a brief outline or as an extensive document, the practitioner can make certain that all the elements have been properly considered and that everyone involved understands the "big picture."

It is common practice for public relations firms to prepare a program plan for client approval and possible modification before implementing a public relations campaign. At that time, both the public relations firm and the client reach a mutual understanding of the campaign's objectives and how to accomplish them. Public relations departments of organizations also map out a particular campaign or show the department's plans for the coming year.

Although there can be some variation, public relations plans include eight basic elements:

1. Situation
2. Objectives
3. Audience
4. Strategy
5. Tactics
6. Calendar/timetable
7. Budget
8. Evaluation

This section will elaborate on these elements and give examples from campaigns that received PRSA Silver Anvil Awards for excellence.

ON THE JOB

insights

Capstone Courses for Public Relations Majors Offer Excellent Examples of Campaign Planning

If you are a public relations major, you will likely complete your undergraduate degree in a capstone campaigns course. According to Benigni, Cheng, and Cameron's national study of public relations curricula, most programs arrange for teams of four students to work for a real client over the term. Operated like agencies with teams reporting to the professor, the main task is to define a problem/opportunity for the client and then develop a strategic campaign plan book for the client. Usually, the plan is presented to the client during a 20–30-minute persuasive business pitch. These plans and pitches serve to illustrate how thorough and astute planning documents can be developed on a small budget by students. See the Web site provided for this textbook to examine complete digital copies of campaign plans and related PowerPoint presentations.

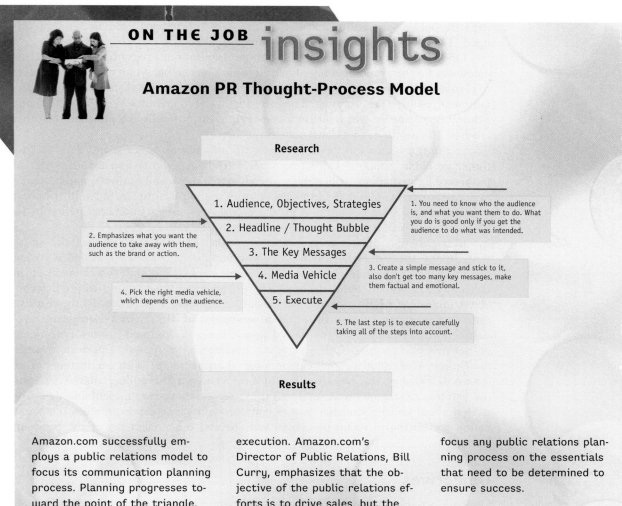

ON THE JOB insights

Amazon PR Thought-Process Model

Research

1. Audience, Objectives, Strategies

2. Headline / Thought Bubble

3. The Key Messages

4. Media Vehicle

5. Execute

1. You need to know who the audience is, and what you want them to do. What you do is good only if you get the audience to do what was intended.

2. Emphasizes what you want the audience to take away with them, such as the brand or action.

3. Create a simple message and stick to it, also don't get too many key messages, make them factual and emotional.

4. Pick the right media vehicle, which depends on the audience.

5. The last step is to execute carefully taking all of the steps into account.

Results

Amazon.com successfully employs a public relations model to focus its communication planning process. Planning progresses toward the point of the triangle, and results are measured after execution. Amazon.com's Director of Public Relations, Bill Curry, emphasizes that the objective of the public relations efforts is to drive sales, but the model works equally well to focus any public relations planning process on the essentials that need to be determined to ensure success.

Source: pr reporter, April 1, 2002

Situation

Valid objectives cannot be set without a clear understanding of the situation that led to the conclusion that a public relations program was needed. Three situations often prompt a public relations program: (1) The organization must conduct a remedial program to overcome a problem or negative situation; (2) the organization needs to conduct a specific one-time project; or (3) the organization wants to reinforce an ongoing effort to preserve its reputation and public support.

Loss of market share and declining sales often require a remedial program. Mack Trucks, for example, initiated an extensive public relations campaign after seeing its market share decline from 21 percent in the 1980s to less than 9 percent in the 1990s. Other organizations launch such campaigns to change public perceptions. The

Turkish government conducted an extensive tourism campaign designed to combat negative public perceptions that the country was "uncivilized" and an "underdeveloped, Third-World Middle Eastern country."

One-time specific events often lead to public relations programs. One such campaign was for the grand opening of San Antonio's new public library. It was important to plan a celebration that showcased the facility as an educational, cultural, and entertainment resource for everyone. The introduction of Microsoft's Windows XP Media Edition operating system was also a one-time event; it required a program plan that covered 20 months of prelaunch activities.

In the third situation, program plans are initiated to preserve and develop customer or public support. Department 56, a leading designer and manufacturer of miniature lighted village collectibles, already had a successful business, but it wanted new customers. Its public relations program to accomplish this included distribution of brochures on home decoration for the Christmas holidays and participation by its dealers in local efforts to decorate Ronald McDonald houses.

In a program plan, relevant research often is included as part of the situation. In the case of Department 56, consumer market analysis revealed a strong link between consumers interested in home decorating and those involved in collecting. Microsoft found that in focus groups consumers would respond favorably to messages about a "faster and easier" computing experience. In the Turkish campaign, research showed little public awareness of Turkey as a European travel destination, and a content analysis of press clippings disclosed a large percentage of negative stereotypes. Other research portrayed the typical American traveler to Turkey as a sophisticated person over the age of 40 with an income of at least $50,000. For the repositioning of Levi jeans for the college market, media-use patterns of students were analyzed using secondary research, including data collection about college students' use of computers. Such research provides the foundation for setting program objectives and shaping other elements of the program plan.

Objectives

Once the situation or problem is understood, the next step is to establish objectives for the program. A stated objective should be evaluated by asking: (1) Does it really address the situation? (2) Is it realistic and achievable? (3) Can success be measured in meaningful terms?

An objective is usually stated in terms of program outcomes rather than inputs. Or, put another way, objectives should not be the "means" but the "end." A poor objective, for example, is to "generate publicity for a new product." Publicity is not an "end" in itself. The actual objective is to "create consumer awareness about a new product." This is accomplished by such tactics as news releases, special events, and brochures.

It is particularly important that public relations objectives complement and reinforce the organization's objectives. Professor David Dozier of San Diego State University expressed the point well in a *Public Relations Review* article: "The prudent and strategic selection of public relations goals and objectives linked to organizational survival and growth serves to justify the public relations program as a viable management activity."

Basically, objectives are either informational or motivational.

PR CASEBOOK

The 100th Anniversary of Jell-O

A public relations plan contains eight basic elements. The following is an outline of a plan that Kraft Foods and its public relations firm, Hunter & Associates, developed for Jell-O's 100th anniversary celebration.

Situation

Sales of this famous dessert were flat. Brand research showed that Jell-O, on the eve of its 100th anniversary celebration, was not top-of-mind with consumers, who were moving to "newer" desserts. Research in company archives provided extensive historical information and graphics about the use and promotion of Jell-O through the years.

Objectives

- Increase brand awareness in order to increase sales.
- Generate widespread awareness of Jell-O's 100th anniversary in high-profile media.

Target Audience

- Current and lapsed Jell-O consumers; women, aged 25–44, with families.

Strategies

- Use the nostalgic appeal of the brand to capture major media interest.
- Develop many story angles around three key messages for a broad range of media.
- Introduce a new Jell-O product to convey the idea that the brand is still in sync with the times.
- Involve LeRoy, New York, where Jell-O was invented, in the anniversary celebration
- Involve Kraft Food employees with anniversary celebrations at each plant and corporate location.
- Generate stories emphasizing three key messages: (1) Jell-O is fun, (2) Jell-O is contemporary, and (3) Jell-O is an American and Canadian icon.

Tactics

- Host a gala event with Bill Cosby, Jell-O spokesperson, as master of ceremonies.
- Introduce a new flavor—champagne.
- Publish a new cookbook.
- Open a new museum and tour exhibits around the country.
- Use Jell-O's hometown, LeRoy, New York, to host a Jell-O Jubilee.
- Establish a new Web site.
- Provide print and broadcast media with press kits that include historical backgrounders and artwork.

Calendar

- 18 months for the entire campaign.
- Three months for research, planning.
- Four months for preparing press kits, media lists, etc.
- 11 months of scheduled events and news releases at quarterly intervals:
  - First Quarter—Jell-O celebrates its 100th anniversary.
  - Second Quarter—Champagne flavor is introduced, cookbook is promoted.
  - Third Quarter—Jell-O museum opens and begins touring the nation.
  - Fourth Quarter—Jell-O builds new float for Macy's Thanksgiving Parade.

Budget

- $450,000 for 18 months

(continued)

PR CASEBOOK *(continued)*

Evaluation

- Brand awareness was established through much extensive media coverage. Research showed 6617 positive stories, 7893 minutes of TV time, and 101 minutes of radio time. This included extensive stories in the *New York Times*, inclusion of Jell-O in a Jay Leno monologue, and a Jell-O feature on Oprah Winfrey's Mother's Day Special.

- Survey research showed 48 percent of respondents heard about the anniversary from television, while another 37 percent found out about it from newspapers or magazines.

- Sales of Jell-O increased more than 5 percent from the previous year.

Informational Objectives. Many public relations plans are designed primarily to expose audiences to information and to increase awareness of an issue, an event, or a product. The five objectives of public relations activity will be discussed in Chapter 7. The first two of these—message exposure and accurate dissemination of messages—are the most common. Many communication and marketing professionals believe that the major criteria for public relations effectiveness are (1) an increase in public awareness and (2) delivery of key messages.

The following are some examples of informational objectives:

- **Mack Trucks:** "Increase awareness and understanding of Mack highway vehicles and engine technology."
- **Levi Jeans:** "Double teen traffic to Levi.com."
- **National Association of Manufacturers (NAM):** "Educate target audiences on the fundamental importance of manufacturing to our nation's current competitiveness and future prosperity."

One difficulty with informational objectives is measuring how well a particular objective has been achieved. Public awareness and the extent of education that takes place are somewhat abstract and difficult to quantify. Survey research often is required, as will be explained in Chapter 8; many organizations, however, infer "awareness" by counting the number of media placements. In reality, message exposure doesn't necessarily mean increased public awareness.

Motivational Objectives. Although changing attitudes and influencing behavior are difficult to accomplish in a public relations campaign, motivational objectives are easier to measure. That's because they are bottom-line oriented and are based on clearly measurable results that can be quantified. This is true whether the goal is an increase in product sales, a sellout crowd for a theatrical performance, or expanded donations to a charitable agency.

The following are some examples of motivational objectives:

- **Duracell Batteries:** "Distribute all of the branded 'guidebooks' [*Together We Can Become Safe Families*] and coupons to consumers in the major metropolitan cities."

- **CheckFree:** "To increase awareness and confidence in online bill paying among women by securing at least 15 articles in target publications, with each article including at least two key CheckFree messages or research statistics."
- **Council for Biotechnology Information:** "Halt the trend of negative news coverage of the topic."
- **Cingular:** "Create awareness of the dangers of distracted driving among 3 million teens over a three-year period (2002–2004)."
- **Levi Jeans:** "Reverse Levi's stodgy image with young consumers by generating upbeat media coverage."

A public relations program will often have both informational and motivational objectives. A good example is the Fighting Hunger in Wisconsin campaign. Its objectives were to (1) increase public awareness of hunger in Wisconsin, (2) enlist additional volunteers, and (3) raise more money than in the previous year to support hunger relief programs around the state.

Objectives, and how to measure their accomplishment, will be discussed in Chapter 8.

Audience

Public relations programs should be directed toward specific and defined audiences or publics. Although some campaigns are directed to a general public, such instances are the exception. Even the M&M's Chocolate Candies national "election" campaign to select a new color (blue) for its famous mix was designed to reach consumers 24 years of age or under.

In other words, public relations practitioners target specific publics within the general public. This is done through market research that can identify key publics by such demographics as age, income, social strata, education, existing ownership or consumption of specific products, and where people live. For example, market research told M&M's Candies that young people were the primary consumers of its product. On a more basic level, a water conservation campaign defines its target audience by geography—people living in a particular city or area.

In many cases, common sense is all that is needed to adequately define a specific public. Take, for example, the Ohio vaccination program for children under the age of two. The primary audience for the message is parents with young children. Other audiences are pregnant women and medical professionals who treat young children.

ON THE JOB

global

An Indian View of Public Relations

A public relations plan, to be strategic, must be tied to the organization's overall business plan and organizational objectives. This is how Aarohan Communications of Bombay, India, expresses it:

> A PR program contributes toward achieving corporate objectives by using various communication tools. A professional develops and manages such a program.

The effectiveness of the professional depends on whether he/she is able to analyze the situation, understand the issues involved, properly identify the target audiences, and use the correct communication tools that would support the accomplishment of corporate objectives. The results must be measured to assure that all of the above have been done effectively.

Perhaps a more complex situation involves a company that wants to increase the sale of a CD-ROM program on home improvement for do-it-yourselfers. Again, the primary audience is not the general public, but those persons who actually have CD-ROM players and enjoy working around the house. Such criteria exclude a large percentage of the American population.

The following are examples of how the organizations already mentioned have defined target audiences:

- **Cingular:** "We have reached 5.6 million teens to date, significantly surpassing our three-year goal . . ."
- **CheckFree:** "Female Americans who are not early adopters of technology, but who are Internet users and pay the household bills."
- **Duracell:** ". . . target audience—women, ages 25–54 with children, who are the primary shoppers for their households."
- **Levi Jeans:** "(1) College-age consumers; (2) youth-focused media."

As previously noted, some organizations identify the media as a "public." On occasion, in programs that seek media endorsements or that try to change how the media report on an organization or an issue, editors and reporters can become a legitimate "public." In general, however, mass media outlets fall in the category of a means to an end. They are channels to reach defined audiences that need to be informed, persuaded, and motivated.

A thorough understanding of the primary and secondary publics is essential if a program's objectives are to be accomplished. Such knowledge also provides guidance on the selection of appropriate strategies and tactics that would reach these defined audiences.

The manufacturer of the CD-ROM on home improvement, for example, might completely bypass the general press and concentrate on specialized publications in the home improvement and CD-ROM fields. Cost is a driving factor; spending large sums to reach members of the general public on matters in which they have no stake or interest is nonproductive and a waste of money.

Strategy

A strategy statement describes how, in concept, an objective is to be achieved, providing guidelines and themes for the overall program. Strategy statements offer a rationale for the actions and program components that are planned. One general strategy may be outlined or a program may have several strategies, depending on the objectives and the designated audiences.

The public relations programs for Help Heal Florida's Healthcare and Levi Jeans illustrate the basic concept of formulating and writing a strategy. Note that the following strategies are broad statements; specific activities are part of tactics, to be covered in the next section.

The health-care reform group summarized its strategies as follows:

1. Convert feelings of discontent with health-care costs into a willingness to listen and support medical liability reform.
2. Focus on problem consensus before offering solution specifics.
3. Build a broad-based coalition that includes the insurance industry, but don't walk hand-in-hand with them.

4. Avoid turning off consumers by resorting to the "same old fight between doctors and lawyers."

5. Communicate impact on patients rather than health-care providers, but insist on credible fact-based communications without resorting to "scare tactics" over access.

The following were Levi Jeans' strategies:

1. Build an online community for college-age kids about college-age kids that's entertaining and interactive.

2. Creatively capitalize on the e-commerce explosion to engage target media.

3. Stimulate ongoing coverage via newsworthy moments-in-time.

The anchor for these three strategies was the Levi's Online Challenge: Levi's would select three college students who would purchase everything online that they needed to live for one semester.

Key Messages/Themes. The strategy element of a program plan should state key themes and messages to be reiterated throughout the campaign on all publicity materials. The Ohio juvenile immunization program, for example, was based on the concept that parents love their children and want them to be healthy. Thus, a key message was to tell parents how important vaccinations were to keep their children out of danger. Carrying out this message was the theme of the campaign, "Project L.O.V.E.," with the subhead "Love Our Kids Vaccination Project."

In the Turkish tourism campaign, the strategy of combating "negative stereotypes and lack of knowledge about Turkey" included key messages designed to reinforce historical/cultural sites, natural beauty, upscale accommodations, great shopping, excellent cuisine, ideal weather, and friendly people. In an effort to position Turkey as part of Europe instead of the Middle East, the themes "Center of World History" and "Where Europe Becomes Exotic" were used.

Tactics

Tactics is the nuts-and-bolts part of the plan that describes, in sequence, the specific activities that put the strategies into operation and help to achieve the stated objectives. Tactics involves using the tools of communication to reach primary and secondary audiences with key messages. Chapters 14 through 16 discuss communication tools in greater detail.

The Tactics of Cox Cable. In many cases, each strategy is supported by specific tactics. In a Cox Cable campaign, strategies to educate audiences about rising charges for programming from ESPN and Fox were supported by the following tactics:

Ready to Rumble

Strategy 1

Educate audiences and move them to Cox's side of the ring: We briefed targets on Capitol Hill. Emphasizing sports TV networks' excessive price increases, we built notable support. We briefed leaders of major national consumer organizations to build their understanding. CEO Robbins threw jabs at major industry forums, reaching other cable companies as well as industry analysts. We provided a campaign toolkit to Cox's local cable systems, helping local Cox executives land body blows at the grassroots level to further soften the opponent. We produced PSA-style television ads in which local Cox executives told the story. Print ads in key markets helped early, and a political-style TV ad helped late. We also communicated directly with Cox customers and Cox employees. An e-mail campaign targeted sports enthusiasts and reached 97 sports fan organizations. And the best publicity of our careers—from national and local business, sports, and consumer media—has generated 364 million consumer impressions to date. With near universal consistency, our messages were well reported in all media.

Strategy 2

Incite audiences to take action against sports programmers: The centerpiece of our campaign was www.MakeThemPlayFair.com. We marketed the site in all of our communications. The site allows consumers to send grassroots e-mails on the issue to their members of Congress and to the CEOs of FOX and ESPN. We made it easy for them, and consumers sent more than 100,000 e-mails! The team also worked the phones with politically active Americans and secured 600 custom-written letters to members of Congress. We identified 60 "grass tops," leaders across America to send letters to Congress. We partnered with the American Cable Association, a group of 1,000 independent cable operators serving rural and small-town America; this partnership paid off when ACA mailed letters to their 14 million cable customers on our behalf. We helped members of Congress understand the public support for Cox's position.

Strategy 3

Maintain control of the match by striking quickly, remaining on the offensive, and anticipating the opponent's moves. Team Cox/Ketchum conducted a weekly "War Room" to evaluate developments and determine which tactics to unleash. For example, ESPN responded to Cox's allegations by launching www.keepespn.com, which encouraged consumers to leave Cox for satellite TV. Our team counterpunched the very same day by developing and launching www.satelliteTVmyths.com, a Web site that we had developed weeks prior in anticipation of ESPN's move. Another example: A journalist we work with tipped us off to an ESPN press conference that was planned at the National Press Club. Mindful of ESPN's likely messages, we swarmed the Press Club with our countermessages as the ESPN executive spoke and chose that moment to launch www.MakeThemPlayFair.com. The resulting media coverage credited Cox for its tenacity and preparedness ("Ah, but Cox was ready"—Cablefax).

The Tactics of Levi Jeans.   Levi used a number of tactics to support its objectives and strategies in its program to reposition Levi Jeans as a hip brand in the college-age market. The Levi's Online Challenge was kicked off by a contest to select three "point-and-click pioneers" who would make all necessary purchases online for a semester. Contestants answered questions such as: "What was the wackiest online purchase you ever made?" and "If you named your computer and mouse, what would you call them?" Other tactics included:

- Announcement of winners and "freshman orientation" for publicity.
- The semester of online shopping, including Levi outfits, was documented on the personal Web pages of the three shoppers with digital photos, virtual diaries, and personal anecdotes.
- Creation of a weekly Web show using Webcams and headsets to broadcast online shopping experiences as well as chat on issues from cars to safe sex with thousands of teens logged on to Levi.com.
- Levi Jeans made a $1 donation to the brand's ongoing beneficiary, the music industry's cause against AIDS called LIFEbeat, for every viewer who logged on to the final show.

Planning a public relations program requires conferences like this one, at which participants weigh information on such diverse topics as objectives, graphics, media selection, demographics, and timing.

Calendar/Timetable

The three aspects of timing in a program plan are (1) deciding when a campaign should be conducted, (2) determining the proper sequence of activities, and (3) compiling a list of steps that must be completed to produce a finished product. All three aspects are important to achieve maximum effectiveness.

The Timing of a Campaign. Program planning should take into account the environmental context of the situation and the time when key messages are most meaningful to the intended audience. A campaign to encourage carpooling, for example, might be more successful if it follows a major price increase in gasoline or a government report that traffic congestion has reached gridlock proportions.

Some subjects are seasonal. Department 56, the designer and manufacturer of miniature lighted village collectibles and other holiday giftware, timed the major bulk of its campaign for November to take advantage of the Christmas holidays, when there was major interest in its product lines. Charitable agencies, such as the Wisconsin Project on Hunger, also gear their campaigns around Christmas when there is increased interest in helping the unfortunate.

By the same token, strawberry producers increase public relations efforts in May and June, when a crop comes to market and stores have large supplies of the fruit. Similarly, a software program on income tax preparation attracts the most audience interest in February and March, just before the April 15 filing deadline. In another situation, a vendor of a software program designed to handle personal finances launched a public relations/marketing program in January. The timing was based on research indicating that people put "getting control of personal finances" high on their list of New Year's resolutions.

Other kinds of campaigns depend less on environmental or seasonal context. The Mack Truck and Levi Jeans' campaigns, for example, could be conducted at almost any time.

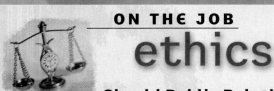

ON THE JOB

ethics

Should Public Relations Writers Join In?

Microsoft, under attack from the U.S. Department of Justice and its major competitors for monopolistic business practices, asked a public relations firm for a plan to tell its side of the story and influence public opinion. One suggestion from the firm was for Microsoft to ask influential supporters to write op-ed pieces and letters to the editor in states where regulators were considering possible antitrust violations.

A copy of this memo was leaked to the *Los Angeles Times*, and an article appeared accusing Microsoft of secretly trying to place articles or editorials. A *Washington Post* columnist called it "a phony grass-roots campaign" in the same league as the tactics used by "Big Tobacco." Other critics accused Microsoft of unethical behavior. However, others wondered what the big fuss was about. They say it's standard practice for PR firms to solicit articles from opinion leaders and even assist in the writing of them.

What do you think? Should this practice be a legitimate part of a public relations plan? Why or why not?

Scheduling of Tactics. The second aspect of timing is the scheduling and sequencing of various tactics or activities. A typical pattern is to concentrate the most effort at the beginning of a campaign, when a number of tactics are implemented. The launch phase of a campaign, much like that of a rocket, requires a burst of activity just to break the awareness barrier. After the campaign has achieved orbit, however, less energy and fewer activities are required to maintain momentum.

To further the rocket analogy, public relations campaigns often are the first stage of an integrated marketing communications program. Once public relations has created awareness and customer anticipation of a new product, the second stage may be an advertising and direct mail campaign.

Compiling a Calendar. An integral part of timing is advance planning. A video news release, a press kit, or a brochure often takes weeks or months to prepare. Arrangements for special events also take considerable time. Practitioners must take into account the deadlines of publications. Monthly periodicals, for example, frequently need information at least six to eight weeks before publication. A popular talk show may book guests three or four months in advance.

In other words, the public relations professional must think ahead to make things happen in the right sequence, at the right time. One way to achieve this goal is to compile time lines and charts that list the necessary steps and their required completion dates.

Calendars and time lines take various forms. One simple method is to post activities for each day on a large monthly calendar. The public relations manager of Kendall-Jackson Winery used this method to plan a luxury wine tasting and dinner. Figure 6.1 shows an excerpt from one day from the April calendar (initials in the left column indicate the person responsible for the activity).

Gantt charts are also used for planning purposes. Essentially, a Gantt chart is a column matrix that has two sides. The left side has a vertical list of activities that must be accomplished, and the top has a horizontal line of days, weeks, or months. Figure 6.2 is a simplified example of a Gantt chart.

Budget

No program plan is complete without a budget. Both clients and employers ask, "How much will this program cost?" In many cases, the reverse approach is taken.

FIGURE 6.1

A page from the April calendar used to plan an event.

> ### Wednesday, April 12
>
> M   Begin development of invitation, RSVP,
> envelopes, tickets, program, nametags,
> placards, etc.
>
> J/M   Review printing costs and options
>
> T   Investigate possibility of having palette
> tasting trays
>
> T   Reserve Stars' Grill Room for evening of event
> (asking Jess)
>
> T   Determine RSVP voice mail #
>
> **ALL   2 p.m. Committee Meeting at SF War
> Memorial and Performing Arts Center**

Organizations establish an amount they can afford and then ask the public relations staff or firm to write a program plan that reflects the amount allocated.

Some budgets of campaigns already discussed were as follows:

- **Cox Cable:** $880,000 ($690,000 fee; $190,000 out-of-pocket expenses)
- **Turkish Government Tourism:** $650,000 for 15-month program: $450,000 in public relations firm fees and $200,000 in expenses
- **Florida Healthcare:** $585,000 (excluding paid advertising) for 11 months
- **Duracell:** $600,000, including both the agency fee and out-of-pocket expenses. Program budget skewed heavily toward out-of-pocket expenses, because it accounted for production of 150,000 guidebooks and 300,000 coupons, Web site development, market research, the 10-city preparedness survey, a $250,000 donation to the American Red Cross and all other miscellaneous expenses related to the program.
- **Levi Jeans:** $600,000: $460,000 in public relations firm fees and $140,000 in out-of-pocket expenses

A budget can be divided into two categories: staff time and out-of-pocket (OOP) expenses. Staff and administrative time usually takes the lion's share of any public relations budget. In a $100,000 campaign done by a public relations firm, for example, it is not unusual for 70 percent to be salaries and administrative fees. Information about how public relations firms charge fees is presented in Chapter 4.

One method of budgeting is to use two columns. The left column will list the staff cost for writing a pamphlet or compiling a press kit. The right column will list the

FIGURE 6.2

A typical Gantt Chart.

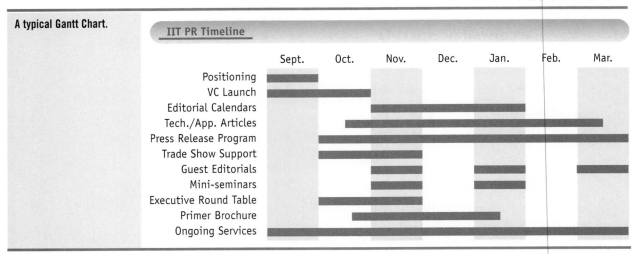

actual OOP expense for having the pamphlet or press kit designed, printed, and delivered. Internal public relations staffs, whose members are on the payroll, often complete only the OOP expenses. It is good practice to allocate about 10 percent of the budget for contingencies or unexpected costs.

In a program plan, budgets are usually estimated on the basis of experience and requests from vendors for estimates. After the program is completed, part of the evaluation (see Chapter 8) is to compile a form that shows estimated expenses versus actual expenses.

Evaluation

The evaluation element of a plan relates directly back to the stated objectives of the program. As discussed earlier, objectives must be measurable in some way to show clients and employers that the program accomplished its purpose.

Consequently, evaluation criteria should be realistic, credible, specific, and in line with client or employer expectations. The evaluation section of a program plan should restate the objectives and then name the evaluation methods to be used.

Evaluation of an informational objective often entails a compilation of news clips and an analysis of how often key message points were mentioned. Other methods might be to determine how many brochures were distributed or the estimated number of viewers who saw a video news release. Motivational objectives often are measured and evaluated by increases in sales or market share, the number of people who called an 800 number for more information, or by benchmark surveys that measure people's perceptions before and after a campaign.

Chapter 8 discusses evaluation techniques and refers to many of the campaigns mentioned here.

SUMMARY

The Value of Planning

After research, the next step is program planning. Such planning must be strategic.

Approaches to Planning

Two approaches to planning are management by objective (MBO) and Ketchum's strategic planning model. Both involve asking and answering many questions.

Elements of a Program Plan

A program plan is either a brief outline or an extensive document identifying what is to be done and how. Firms prepare these for client approval. They usually include the eight elements of situation, objectives, audience, strategy, tactics, a calendar or timetable, budget, and evaluation.

Case Activity: **What Would You Do?**

Sunshine Cafe, a chain of coffee houses, did some market research and found that college students would be an excellent audience to reach. To this end, Sunshine Cafe has contacted your public relations firm and asked that you develop a comprehensive plan to (1) create brand awareness among college students and (2) increase walk-in business at their local stores in college towns.

Using the eight-point planning outline described in this chapter, write a public relations program for Sunshine Cafe. You should consider a variety of communication tools, including campus events. However, no money has been allocated for advertising.

QUESTIONS for Review and Discussion

1. Why is planning so important in the public relations process?

2. What is MBO, and how can it be applied to public relations planning?

3. Name the eight elements of a program plan.

4. Identify the three situations that often require a public relations campaign.

5. Explain the difference between an informational objective and a motivational objective.

6. Should a practitioner define an audience as the "general public?" Why or why not?

7. What is the difference between a strategy and an objective?

8. Review the Levi Jeans company's strategies and tactics for reversing its stodgy image. Do you think it was a well-conceived campaign?

9. Why are timing and scheduling so important in a public relations campaign?

10. What is the largest expense in a campaign conducted by a public relations firm?

SUGGESTED READINGS

"Ads Entertain but PR Builds the Brand." *O'Dwyer's PR Services Report,* Vol. 16, No. 3, 2000, pp. 1, 16, 32.

Ahles, Catherine B. "Campaign Excellence: A Survey of Silver Anvil Award Winers Compares Current PR Practice With Planning Campaign Theory." *The Strategist*, Summer 2003, pp. 46–53.

Austin, Erica, and Pinkleton, Bruce. *Strategic Communication Management: Planning and Managing Effective Communication Programs.* Mahwah, NJ: Lawrence Erlbaum, 2001.

Barker-Plummer, Bernadette. "Producing Public Voice: Resource Mobilization and Media Access in the National Organization for Women." *Journalism and Mass Communication Quarterly*, Vol. 79, Spring 2002, pp. 188–205.

Daughtery, Emma. "Strategic Planning in Public Relations: A Matrix That Ensures Tactical Soundness," *Public Relations Quarterly*, Spring 2003, pp. 21–26.

Duncan, Tom, and Mulhern, Frank. "A White Paper on the Status, Scope, and Future of IMC." Denver: McGraw-Hill Publishing, 2004.

Gelphman, Rob. "Positioning: A Big Hand for the Brand." *PRWeek*, May 6, 2002, p. 15.

Gibbs, Nancy. "Cause Celeb." *Time*, June 17, 1996, pp. 28–30.

"Got an Idea for a PR Campaign? Ask Your Audience First." *Ragan's Interactive Public Relations*, April 2004, pp. 5–6.

Kendall, Robert. *Public Relations Campaign Strategies.* New York: HarperCollins, 1996.

McElreath, Mark P. *Managing Systematic and Ethical Public Relations Campaigns.* Madison, WI: Brown & Benchmark, 1996.

Nager, Norman R., and Allen, T. Harrell. *Public Relations Management by Objectives.* New York: Longman, 1983.

"No Time to Lose: Your Event Draws Near. The Reporter Bailed. Where Do You Go Next?" *Ragan's Media Relations Report*, September 2004, p. 7.

"PR Thought Process Model Earns Amazon Its Mega Stature Through Branded Messages, Targeted Publics." *pr reporter*, April 1, 2002, p. 1.

Samansky, Arthur W. "Successful Strategic Communications Plans Are Realistic, Achievable, and Flexible," *Public Relations Quarterly*, Summer 2003, pp. 24–26.

Temple, K. B. "Setting Clear Goals: The Key Ingredient to Effective Communication Planning," *Public Relations Quarterly*, Summer 2003, pp. 32–35.

Therkeisen, David J., and Fiebich, Christina L. "Message to Desired Action: A Communication Effectiveness Model." *Journal of Communication Management*, Vol. 5, No. 4, 2001, pp. 374–390.

chapter 7

Communication

Topics covered in this chapter include:

The Goals of Communication

The third step in the public relations process, after research and planning, is *communication*. This step, also called *execution*, is the most visible part of public relations work.

Implementing the Plan

In a public relations program, as pointed out in Chapter 6, communication is the implementation of a decision, the process and the means by which objectives are achieved. A program's strategies and tactics may take the form of news releases, news conferences, special events, brochures, viral marketing, speeches, bumper stickers, newsletters, Webcasts, rallies, posters, and the like.

The goals of the communication process are to inform, persuade, motivate, or achieve mutual understanding. To be an effective communicator, a person must have basic knowledge of (1) what constitutes communication and how people receive messages, (2) how people process information and change their perceptions, and (3) what kinds of media and communication tools are most appropriate for a particular message.

Concerning the last point, Kirk Hallahan of Colorado State University makes the point that today's communication revolution has given public relations professionals a full range of communication tools and media, and the traditional approach of simply obtaining publicity in the mass media—newspapers, magazines, radio, and television—is no longer sufficient, if it ever was. He writes:

> PR program planners need to reexamine their traditional approaches to the practice and think about media broadly and strategically. PR media planners must now address some of the same questions that confront advisers. What media best meet a program's objectives? How can media be combined to enhance program effectiveness? What media are most efficient to reach key audience?

Hallahan's concept of an integrated public relations media model, which outlines five categories of media, is shown in Table 7.1. Many of these media are discussed in Part 4, Tactics.

A Public Relations Perspective

A number of variables must be considered when planning a message on behalf of an employer or client. Patrick Jackson, who was editor of *pr reporter* and a senior counselor, believes that the communicator should ask whether the proposed message is (1) appropriate, (2) meaningful, (3) memorable, (4) understandable, and (5) believable to the prospective recipient. According to Jackson, "Many a wrongly directed or unnecessary communication has been corrected or dropped by using a screen like this."

In addition to examining the proposed content, a communicator should determine exactly what objective is being sought through the communication. James Grunig, professor of public relations at the University of Maryland, lists five possible objectives for a communicator:

1. **Message exposure.** Public relations personnel provide materials to the mass media and disseminate other messages through controlled media such as newsletters and brochures. Intended audiences are exposed to the message in various forms.

TABLE 7.1

An Integrated Public Relations Media Model The variety and scope of media and communication tools available to public relations professionals runs the spectrum from mass media (public media) to one-on-one communication (interpersonal communication). Here, in chart form, is a concept developed by Professor Kirk Hallahan at Colorado State University.

CHARACTERISTIC	PUBLIC MEDIA	INTERACTIVE MEDIA	CONTROLLED MEDIA	EVENTS/GROUPS	ONE-ON-ONE
Key use	Build awareness	Respond to queries; exchange information	Promotion; provide detailed information	Motivate attendees; reinforce attitudes	Obtain commitments; resolve problems
Examples	Newspapers, magazines, radio, television	Computer based: World Wide Web, databases, e-mail listservs, newsgroups, chat rooms, bulletin boards	Brochures, newsletters, sponsored magazines, annual reports, books, direct mail, point-of-purchase displays, video-brochures	Speeches, trade shows, exhibits, meetings/conferences, demonstrations, rallies, sponsorships, anniversaries	Personal visits, lobbying, personal letters, telephone calls, telemarketing
Nature of communication	Nonpersonal	Nonpersonal	Nonpersonal	Quasi-personal	Personal
Direction of communication	One-way	Quasi-two-way	One-way	Quasi-two-way	Two-way
Technological sophistication	High	High	Moderate	Moderate	Low
Channel ownership	Media organizations	Common carrier or institution	Sponsor	Sponsor or other organization	None
Messages chosen by	Third parties and producers	Receiver	Sponsor	Sponsor or joint organization	None
Audience involvement	Low	High	Moderate	Moderate	High
Reach	High	Moderate-low	Moderate-low	Low	Low
Cost per impression	Extremely low	Low	Moderate	Moderate	High
Key challenges to effectiveness	Competition, media clutter	Availability, accessibility	Design, distribution	Attendance, atmosphere	Empowerment, personal dynamics

2. **Accurate dissemination of the message.** The basic information, often filtered by media gatekeepers, remains intact as it is transmitted through various media.

3. **Acceptance of the message.** Based on its view of reality, the audience not only retains the message, but accepts it as valid.

4. **Attitude change.** The audience not only believes the message, but makes a verbal or mental commitment to change behavior as a result of the message.

5. **Change in overt behavior.** Members of the audience actually change their current behavior or purchase the product and use it.

Grunig says that most public relations experts usually aim at the first two objectives: exposure to the message and accurate dissemination. The last three objectives depend in large part on a mix of variables—predisposition to the message, peer reinforcement, feasibility of the suggested action, and environmental context, to name a few. The first two objectives are easier to accomplish than attitude change (see Chapter 9).

A Behavioral Communication Model

The behavioral communication model, suggests *pr reporter*, is better than traditional communication models because it forces practitioners to think in terms of what behaviors they are trying to motivate in target publics, rather than on what information is being communicated. The process is described as follows:

1. **Awareness.** Salience or relevance is the key to reaching awareness. The purpose of communication here is to create awareness, which is the start of any behavioral process.

2. **Latent readiness.** Either positive or negative readiness to behave in a certain way starts to form, often subconsciously (latently). People get ready to act by accumulating and developing experience, information, word-of-mouth, beliefs, opinions, and emotions.

3. **Triggering event.** The triggering event step gives people a chance to act on their latent readiness. Triggering events may be an election day, a store sale, distribution of a company's annual report, or even a major event announcing a new product or service. Public relations people should build triggering events into their planning: This moves the emphasis from communication to behavior motivation.

4. **Behavior.** Although the ultimate goal is to motivate people to buy something or act in a certain way, they may adopt intermediate behaviors, such as requesting more literature, visiting a showroom, or trying the product or idea experimentally.

Although the communicator cannot always control the outcome of a message, researchers recognize that effective dissemination is the beginning of the process that leads to opinion change and adoption of products or services. Therefore, it is important to review all components of the communication process.

David Therkelsen, now CEO of the American Red Cross in St. Paul, Minnesota, succinctly outlines the process:

> To be successful, a message must be received by the intended individual or audience. It must get the audience's attention. It must be understood. It must be believed. It must be remembered. And ultimately, in some fashion, it must be acted upon. Failure to accomplish any of these tasks means the entire message fails.

Therkelsen appropriately places the emphasis on the audience and what it does with the message. The following sections elaborate on the six elements he enumerates.

Receiving the Message

Several communication models explain how a message moves from the sender to the recipient. Some are quite complex, attempting to incorporate an almost infinite number of events, ideas, objects, and people that interact among the message, channel, and receiver.

Five Communication Elements

Most communication models, however, incorporate four basic elements. David K. Berlo's model is an example. It has a sender/source (encoder), a message, a channel, and a receiver (decoder). A fifth element, feedback from the receiver to the sender, is now incorporated in modern models of communication.

Mass media researcher Wilbur Schramm's early models (see Figure 7.1) started with a simple communication model (top), but he later expanded the process to include the concept of "shared experience" (middle diagram). In other words, little or no communication is achieved unless the sender and the receiver share a common language and even an overlapping cultural or educational background. The importance of this "shared experience" becomes apparent when a highly technical news release about a new computer system causes a local business editor to shake his or her head in bewilderment.

Schramm's third model (bottom) incorporates the idea of continuous feedback. Both the sender and the receiver continually encode, interpret, decode, transmit, and receive information. The loop process also is integral to models that show the public relations process of research, planning, communication, and evaluation. This concept was illustrated in Chapter 1, which showed public relations as a cyclical process. Communication to internal and external audiences produces feedback that is taken into consideration during research, the first step, and evaluation, the fourth step. In

FIGURE 7.1

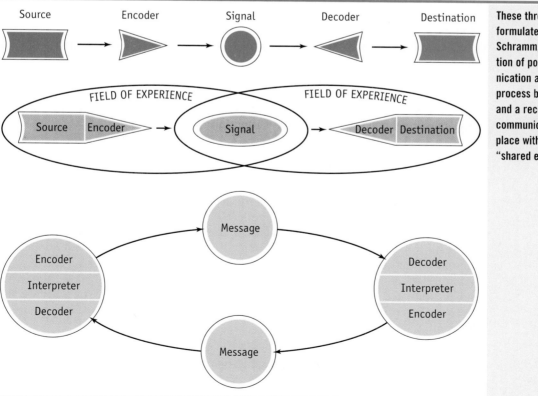

These three models, formulated by Wilbur Schramm, show the evolution of portraying communication as an interactive process between a sender and a receiver. Effective communication takes place within a sphere of "shared experience."

this way, the structure and dissemination of messages are continuously refined for maximum effectiveness.

The Importance of Two-Way Communication

Another way to think of feedback is two-way communication. One-way communication, from sender to receiver, only disseminates information. Such a monologue is less effective than two-way communication, which establishes a dialogue between the sender and receiver.

Grunig goes even further to postulate that the ideal public relations model is two-way symmetrical communication. That is, communication is balanced between the sender and the receiver. He says: "In the symmetric model, understanding is the principal objective of public relations, rather than persuasion."

In reality, research shows that most organizations have mixed motives when they engage in two-way communication with targeted audiences. Although they may employ dialogue to obtain a better sense of how they can adjust to the needs of an audience, their motive often is asymmetrical—to convince the audience of their point of view through dialogue.

The most effective two-way communication, of course, is two people talking to each other. Small-group discussion also is effective. In both forms, the message is fortified by gestures, facial expressions, intimacy, tone of voice, and the opportunity for instant feedback. If the listener asks a question or appears puzzled, the speaker has an instant cue and can rephrase the information or amplify a point.

Barriers to communication tend to mount as one advances to large-group meetings and, ultimately, to the mass media. Organizational materials can reach thousands and, through the mass media, even millions of people at the same time, but the psychological and physical distance between sender and receiver is considerably lengthened. Communication is less effective because the audience no longer is involved with the source. No immediate feedback is possible, and the message may undergo distortion as it passes through mass media gatekeepers.

Models of communication emphasize the importance of feedback as an integral component of the process. As they implement communication strategies, public relations personnel need to give it careful attention.

Paying Attention to the Message

Sociologist Harold Lasswell has defined the act of communication as "Who says what, in which channel, to whom, with what effect?"

Although in public relations much emphasis is given to the formation and dissemination of messages, this effort is wasted if the audience pays no attention. It is therefore important to remember the axiom of Walt Seifert, professor emeritus of public relations at Ohio State University. He says: "Dissemination does not equal publication, and publication does not equal absorption and action." In other words, "All who receive it won't publish it, and all who read or hear it won't understand or act upon it."

Some Theoretical Perspectives

Seifert and social psychologists recognize that the majority of an audience at any given time are not particularly interested in a message or in adopting an idea. This doesn't mean, however, that audiences are merely passive receivers of information. Werner Severin and James Tankard, in their text *Communication Theories*, quote one researcher as saying:

> The communicator's audience is not a passive recipient—it cannot be regarded as a lump of clay to be molded by the master propagandist. Rather, the audience is made up of individuals who demand something from the communication to which they are exposed, and who select those that are likely to be useful to them.

This is called the *media uses and gratification theory* of communication. Its basic premise is that the communication process is interactive. The communicator wants to inform and even persuade; the recipient wants to be entertained, informed, or alerted to opportunities that can fulfill individual needs.

In other words, audiences come to messages for very different reasons. People use mass media for such purposes as (1) surveillance of the environment to find out what is happening, locally or even globally, that has some impact on them; (2) entertainment and diversion; (3) reinforcement of their opinions and predispositions; and (4) decision making about buying a product or service.

The media uses and gratification theory assumes that people make highly intelligent choices about which messages require their attention and fulfill their needs. If this is true, as research indicates it is, the public relations communicator must tailor messages that focus on getting the audience's attention.

One approach is to understand the mental state of the intended audience. Grunig and Hunt, in *Managing Public Relations*, suggest that communication strategies be designed to attract the attention of two kinds of audiences, those who actively seek information and those who passively process information.

Passive audiences may initially pay attention to a message only because it is entertaining and offers a diversion. They can be made aware of the message through brief encounters: a billboard glimpsed on the way to work, a radio announcement heard in the car, a television advertisement broadcast before a show begins, and information available in a doctor's waiting room. In other words, passive audiences use communication channels that can be utilized while they are doing little else.

For this reason, passive audiences need messages that have style and creativity. The person must be lured by photos, illustrations, and catchy slogans into processing information. Press agentry, the dramatic picture, the use of celebrities, radio and television announcements, and events featuring entertainment can make passive audiences aware of a message. The objectives of a communication, therefore, are simply exposure to and accurate dissemination of a message. In most public relations campaigns, communications are designed to reach primarily passive audiences.

A communicator's approach to audiences that actively seek information is different. These people are already at the interest stage of the adoption process (discussed later) and seek more sophisticated supplemental information. The tools may include brochures, in-depth newspaper and magazine articles, slide presentations, videotape presentations, symposiums and conferences, major speeches before key groups, and demonstrations at trade shows.

At any given time, of course, the intended audience has both passive and active information seekers in it. It is important, therefore, that multiple messages and a variety of communication tools be used in a full-fledged information campaign.

Public relations personnel have two ways by which to determine strategies. First, research into audience attitudes can give insight into the extent of group interest in, or apathy toward, a new product or idea. Second, more efficient communication can be achieved if the intended audience is segmented as much as possible. After dividing an audience into segments, a practitioner can select the appropriate communication tools.

Other Attention-Getting Concepts

Communicators should think in terms of the five senses: sight, hearing, smell, touch, and taste. Television and film or videotape are the most effective methods of communication because they engage an audience's senses of sight and hearing. They also offer attractions of color and movement. Radio, on the other hand, relies on only the sense of hearing. Print media, although capable of communicating a large amount of information in great detail, rely only on sight.

Individuals learn through all five senses, but psychologists estimate that 83 percent of learning is accomplished through sight. Hearing accounts for 11 percent. Fifty percent of what individuals retain consists of what they see and hear. For this reason, speakers often use visual aids.

These figures have obvious implications for the public relations practitioner. Any communication strategy should, if possible, include vehicles of communication designed to tap the senses of sight or hearing or a combination of the two. In other words, a variety of communication tools is needed, including news releases, publicity photos, slide presentations, videotapes, billboards, newsletters, radio announcements, video news releases, media interviews, and news conferences. This multiple approach not only assists learning and retention, it also provides repetition of a message in a variety of forms that accommodate audience needs.

Other research suggests that audience attention can be generated if the communicator raises a "need" level first. The idea is to "hook" an audience's attention by beginning the message with something that will make its members' lives easier or benefit them in some way. An example is a message from the Internal Revenue Service. It could begin with a reminder about the necessity of filing tax returns on time, but it would get far more audience attention if it opened by urging people to take all the exemptions for which they were eligible. The prospect of paying less taxes would be alluring to most people.

Public relations writers also should be aware that audience attention is highest at the beginning of a message. Thus, it is wise to state the major point at the beginning, give details in the middle, and end with a summary of the message.

Another technique to garner audience attention is to begin a message with a statement that reflects audience values and predispositions. This is called *channeling* (see

ON THE JOB

global

Different Worlds of Value Systems

Many theories that explain the communication process are applicable around the world. The application of communication theory, however, is closely tied to the values of a particular culture. A. H. Tobaccowala of Voltas Limited in India makes this observation:

> While galloping modernization and the impact of global value systems will accelerate, as of now the idols and heroes of most people in Asia are not the highly successful wealthy industrialists or the stars of the entertainment world or the record breakers in sports. Those who are most honored, admired, and almost worshipped are the Gandhis, the Mandelas, the Mother Theresas, the monks, and the ascetics. This is a world of very different value systems that the western PR person must deal with.

Chapter 9). According to social science research, people pay attention to messages that reinforce their predispositions.

Prior knowledge and interest also make people pay more attention to messages. If a message taps current events or issues of public concern already in the news, there is an increased chance that the audience will pay attention.

Understanding the Message

Communication is the act of transmitting information, ideas, and attitudes from one person to another. Communication can take place, however, only if the sender and receiver have a common understanding of the symbols being used.

Effective Use of Language

Words are the most common symbols. The degree to which two people understand each other is heavily dependent on their common knowledge of word symbols. Anyone who has traveled abroad can readily attest that very little communication occurs between two people who speak different languages. Even signs translated into English for tourists often lead to some confusing and amusing messages. A brochure for a Japanese hotel, for example, said, "In our hotel, you will be well fed and agreeably drunk. In every room there is a large window offering delightful prospects."

Even if the sender and receiver speak the same language and live in the same country, the effectiveness of their communication depends on such factors as education, social class, regional differences, nationality, and cultural background.

Employee communication specialists are particularly aware of such differences as a multicultural workforce becomes the norm for most organizations. One major factor is the impact of a global economy in which organizations have operations and employees in many countries. A second factor is the increasing multicultural composition of the American workforce. One study says that 85 percent of new entrants in the workforce are now white women, immigrants, African Americans, Hispanics, and Asians. For many of these workers, English will be a second language.

These statistical trends will require communicators to be better informed about cultural differences and conflicting values in order to find common ground and build bridges between various groups. At the same time, a major task will be to communicate in clear and simple terms. A national survey by the Educational Testing Service found that 42 million American adults fall within the lowest category of literacy. Other studies show that one in eight employees reads at no better than a fourth-grade level.

Writing for Clarity

The nature of the audience and its literacy level are important considerations for any communicator. The key is to produce messages that match, in content and structure, the characteristics of the audience.

The Illinois Public Health Department had the right idea when it commissioned a song in rap music style as one way to inform low-income, poorly educated groups about the dangers of AIDS. The words and music of the "Condom Rag," however, were offensive to elected officials, who cancelled the song.

ON THE JOB insights

Selective Management—Engaging on Your Own Terms

Noted consultant and public relations strategist, Jim Lukaszewski, offers an intriguing approach to communication planning. In his regular *pr reporter* insert, he states that selective management is a mindset "stressing focus, control, and patterns of action that target the most appropriate audiences and constituencies in the most useful and appropriate ways (from their perspectives)." In other words, *you choose* when and with whom to communicate.

The Principles of Selective Engagement

1. Act to control, to contain, and to manage your own communication.
   - Recognize when a story is national or international in nature or when a story is simply much larger than its location.
   - Keep the visibility as close to the site of the problem as possible.
2. Always let opponents and critics speak for themselves. (Avoid media goading to make a comment.)
   - Critics need your negative, defensive responses to generate energy.
   - There is no obligation to respond to anything said by any critic, opponent, or antagonist.
   - Avoid needless rebuttal, commentary, or response. Shut up.
3. Concentrate your preparation on only the toughest questions.
   - Focus on what is truly important, only the killer questions.
   - Avoid listing every conceivable question someone could possibly be asked.
   - Clients can't absorb all the information anyway.
4. Focus on your communications goal—no matter what.
   - Define and verbalize your own achievable goals.
   - Write down your communication objectives.
   - Say them out loud and say them often.
   - Refuse to be distracted.
   - Refuse to be irritated.
   - Refuse to be rushed.
   - Work relentlessly, but incrementally.
5. Avoid mindless visibility.
   - Force the issues, the messages, and the players to be small in number.
   - Solid information simply presented is a key ingredient of victory.
   - The vast majority of news stories produced during high-profile incidents are repetitive.
   - The more focus you have, the more focus commentators, critics, and others will have.
   - Feeding the mindless visibility machine is one reason management is reluctant to trust the public relations practitioner.
6. Keep your friends, relatives, and bosses on the script or quiet.
   - Script everyone.
   - Script the sequence of events and the time line of communication.
   - Media believe that the truth comes from surprise, often deceptive, questioning.
   - Neither deception nor surprise produce truth, maybe interesting stories and sensational information, but rarely the truth.
   - Stick to your scripts.
   - The boss or someone the boss trusts must be a part of the script development and participate in its execution.
7. Let entropy occur.
   - Allow the energy of events to dissipate through appropriate nonaction.
   - Before taking counteractive measures, first assess where events are heading.

- Doing nothing is often a very powerful and successful strategy.
- The strategy of doing nothing needs to be fully evaluated.
- Practice laggership, the art of responding promptly, just not immediately.
- Mention the strategic options of laggership or doing nothing before the attorney or CFO does.

8. Monitor the media aggressively, but avoid letting reporters, critics, and commentators drive your strategy.
   - Monitor the media aggressively to search for questions and issues to which you can respond directly.
   - If something you do negatively affects people, animals, or living systems, have a more-than-prompt media approach.

9. Respond to or through the media only when the message needs of those affected are served.
   - If you and your organization are acting honorably, you have the greatest range of options for communicating.
   - The rule is that useful, positive action must always precede communication.

- Communication without action is spin.
- On the other hand, the media tend to ignore positive actions.

10. Use a limited set of brief, positive messages.
    - Initial messages are the final messages even though they become muddled or are attacked and vetted throughout the time line of response.
    - Altering messages tends to expand and extend problems.
    - Keep messages consistent across all affected audiences.
    - Avoid negative words and phrases; they become the headline and focus of the story every time.
    - Negative language sends the discussion out of control and creates defensive verbal perpetrators who respond in ever more negative ways. The media love it.
    - Positive language is the most powerful relationship-managing tool.
    - Negative language creates angry, victimized, and injured audiences and gives the media free negative premises on which to continue their questions and incorrect perceptions.

11. Use non-news media direct communications tools.
    - Talk directly to employees, customers, suppliers, victims, and others.
    - The more directly you speak, the more likely it is that actual communication will occur.
    - The next best method is communicating with larger groups, but still face-to-face.
    - Use other unfiltered techniques as well: e-mail, videoconferencing, mass fax, and special, rather than general, news media.

12. Prompt, honorable action on the ground is always the most crucial strategic ingredient, not media coverage.
    - What makes selective engagement a powerful positive strategy is its basis in honor, trust-worthiness, prompt ethi-cal action, and credible behavior.
    - Without these attributes, this strategy will clearly fail.
    - Stay the course; you will prevail.
    - In the end, you'll achieve less than you expect, but accomplish more than you need to make your goals.

For more information and lengthier discussion of this subject, explore Mr. Lukaszewski's Web site at www.e911.com.

This example poses the classic dilemma for the expert communicator. Should the message be produced for supervisors, who may be totally different in background and education from the intended audience, or should it be produced with the audience in mind? The obvious answer is the latter, but it is often difficult to convince management of this. One solution is to copy-test all public relations materials on a target audience. This helps convince management—and communicators—that what they like isn't necessarily what the audience wants, needs, or understands.

Another approach is to apply readability and comprehension formulas to materials before they are produced and disseminated. Learning theory makes the case: The simpler the piece of writing, the easier it will be for audiences to understand.

The most widely known readability formula is by Rudolph Flesch. Another is by Barr, Jenkins, and Peterson. Both are based on average sentence length and the number of one-syllable words per 100 words. If a randomly selected sample of 100 words contains 4.2 sentences and 142 syllables, it is ranked at about the ninth-grade level. This is the level for which most news releases and daily newspapers strive. In other words, long, complex sentences (more than 19 words) and multi-syllabic words ("compensation" instead of "pay") reduce comprehension for the average reader.

The Cloze procedure, developed by William Taylor, also tests comprehension. The concept comes from the idea of closure, the human tendency to complete a familiar but incomplete pattern. In the Cloze procedure, copy is tested for comprehension and redundancy by having test subjects read passages in which every fifth or ninth word is removed. Their ability to fill in the missing words determines whether the pattern of words is familiar and people can understand the message.

Audience understanding and comprehension also can be increased by applying some of the following concepts.

Use Symbols, Acronyms, and Slogans.   Clarity and simplicity of message are enhanced by the use of symbols, acronyms, and slogans. Each is a form of shorthand that quickly conceptualizes an idea and travels through extended lines of communication.

The world is full of symbols, such as the Christian cross, the Jewish Star of David, and the crusading sword of the American Cancer Society. Corporate symbols such as the Mercedes Benz star, the Nike swoosh, and the multicolored, now holographic, apple of Apple Computer are known throughout the world. The concept is called *branding*, and corporations invest considerable time and money to make their names and logos a symbol for quality and service.

A symbol should be unique, memorable, widely recognized, and appropriate. Organizations spend considerable time and energy searching for unique symbols that convey the essence of what they are or what they hope to be. Considerable amounts of money are then spent on publicizing the symbols and creating meanings for them.

Acronyms are another shorthand for conveying information. An acronym is a word formed from the initial letters of other words. The Group Against Smokers' Pollution goes by the acronym GASP; Juvenile Opportunities in Business becomes JOB. And the National Organization for Women has the acronym NOW, which says a great deal about its political priorities.

In many cases, the acronym—because it is short and simple—becomes the common name. The mass media continually use the term *AIDS* instead of *Acquired Immune Deficiency Syndrome*. And *UNESCO* is easier to write and say than *United Nations Educational, Scientific, and Cultural Organization*.

Slogans help condense a concept. Massive advertising and promotion have made "Don't Leave Home without It" readily identified with American Express. "The Ultimate Driving Machine" is strongly identified with BMW, which is an acronym for Bavarian Motor Works.

Avoid Jargon. One source of blocked communication is technical and bureaucratic jargon. Social scientists call it *semantic noise* when such language is delivered to a general audience. Jargon interferes with the message and impedes the receiver's ability to understand it. An example of a useless news release is the following, which was actually sent to business editors of daily newspapers. This is how it began:

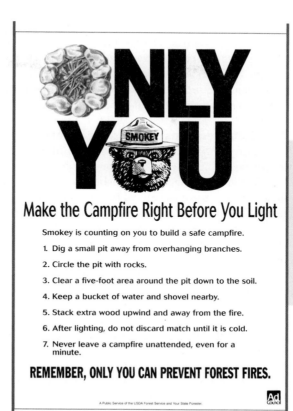

Make the Campfire Right Before You Light

Smokey is counting on you to build a safe campfire.

1. Dig a small pit away from overhanging branches.
2. Circle the pit with rocks.
3. Clear a five-foot area around the pit down to the soil.
4. Keep a bucket of water and shovel nearby.
5. Stack extra wood upwind and away from the fire.
6. After lighting, do not discard match until it is cold.
7. Never leave a campfire unattended, even for a minute.

REMEMBER, ONLY YOU CAN PREVENT FOREST FIRES.

A Public Service of the USDA Forest Service and Your State Forester.

Smokey Bear is a familiar symbol in the campaign to prevent forest fires. Some advertisements for Smokey merely carry the slogan "Only You," while others, like this one, include a detailed list of prevention measures. The Advertising Council prepares the campaign.

Versatec, a Xerox Company, has introduced the Graphics Network Processor-SNA (Model 451). The processor, operating as a 377x RJE station, sends and receives EBCDIC or binary data in IMB System Network Architecture (SNA) networks using Synchronous Data LINK Control (SDLC) protocol . . . .

This news release may be perfectly appropriate for an engineering publication serving a particular industry, but the information must be written in simple terms for the readers of a daily newspaper. A failure to understand the audience means a failure in communication.

Avoid Clichés and Hype Words. Highly charged words with connotative meanings can pose problems, and overuse of clichés and hype words can seriously undermine the credibility of the message.

The *Wall Street Journal*, for example, mocked the business of high-technology public relations with a story titled, "High-Tech Hype Reaches New Heights." A reporter analyzed 201 news releases and compiled a "Hype Hit Parade" that included the 11 most overused and ineffective words. They were *leading, enhanced, unique, significant, solution, integrated, powerful, innovative, advanced, high performance*, and *sophisticated*.

Similar surveys have uncovered overused words in business and public relations. A New York firm, John Rost Associates, compiled a list of words and phrases used excessively in business letters and reports. The list included: *agenda, proactive, interface, networking, finalize, done deals, impact, bottomline, vis-à-vis, world class, state-of-the-art, user-friendly, competitive edge, know-how, win–win, breakthrough, fast track, hands-on, input, dialogue,* and *no-brainer.*

A survey of corporate annual reports also revealed the overuse of certain words. Robert K. Otterbourg, president of a company that does annual reports for corporations, said the most overused words were *challenge, opportunity, fundamental achievements, pioneering efforts,* and *state-of-the-art.*

Avoid Euphemisms.   According to Frank Grazian, founding editor of *Communication Briefings,* a *euphemism* is "an inoffensive word or phrase that is less direct and less distasteful than the one that represents reality."

Public relations personnel should use positive, favorable words to convey a message, but they have an ethical responsibility not to use words that hide information or mislead. Probably little danger exists in substituting positive words, such as saying a person has a disability rather than using the word *handicapped.* Some euphemisms can even cause amusement, such as when car mechanics become *automotive internists,* and luxury cars are called *preowned* on the used car lot.

More dangerous are euphemisms that actually alter the meaning or impact of a word or concept. Writers call this *doublespeak*—words that pretend to communicate but really do not. Governments are famous for doublespeak. In the Persian Gulf War, U.S. military briefing officers described civilian casualties and destruction as *collateral damage.* And Serbian authorities used the term *ethnic cleansing* to sanitize the murder of thousands in Kosovo. A government economist once called a recession "a meaningful downturn in aggregate output."

Corporations also use euphemisms and doublespeak to hide unfavorable news. Reducing the number of employees, for example, is often called *right-sizing, skill mix adjustment,* or *career assignment and relocation.* An airline once called the crash of a plane "the involuntary conversion of a 727."

Use of euphemisms to hide or mislead obviously is contrary to professional public relations standards and the public interest. As William Lutz writes in *Public Relations Quarterly,* "Such language breeds suspicion, cynicism, distrust, and, ultimately, hostility."

Avoid Discriminatory Language.   In today's world, effective communication also means *nondiscriminatory* communication. Public relations personnel should double-check every message to eliminate undesirable gender, racial, and ethnic connotations.

With regard to gender, it is unnecessary to write about something as being *man-made* when a word like *synthetic* or *artificial* is just as good. Companies no longer have *manpower,* but rather *employees, personnel,* and *workers.* Most civic organizations have *chairpersons* now, and cities have *firefighters* instead of *firemen* and *police officers* instead of *policemen.* Airlines, of course, have *flight attendants,* not *stewardesses.*

Writers also should be careful about descriptive phrases for women. *Bulldog Reporter,* a West Coast public relations newsletter, once criticized a Chicago public relations firm for describing a female company president as "a tall, attractive blonde who could easily turn heads on Main Street [but] is instead turning heads on Wall Street."

Nor is it appropriate in professional settings to say that a woman is the wife of someone also well known. A female vice president of a public relations firm cried foul when a local newsletter described her as the wife of a prominent journalist. The newsletter editor apologized in the next issue.

Messages should not identify any individual by ethnic designation, but it may be necessary in some situations to designate a particular ethnic or racial group. Although fashions and preferences change, today's writers use *Asian American* instead of the now-pejorative *Oriental*. And the term *Hispanic* is now more acceptable than the politically charged *Spanish-speaking*. The term *Latino*, however, raises some controversy; some women say that it is sexist because the "o" in Spanish is male.

The term *black* seems to be making a comeback, according to the U.S. Department of Labor, which surveyed 60,000 households several years ago about the names of race and ethnic categories to use in job statistics. Forty-four percent of the blacks preferred this designation, whereas another 28 percent preferred *African American* and 12 percent chose *Afro-American*. As a matter of policy, many newspapers use *African American* on first reference and *black* on second reference. Headlines almost always use *black* because it is short.

Believing the Message

One key variable in the communication process, discussed further in Chapter 9, is *source credibility*. Do members of the audience perceive the source as knowledgeable and expert on the subject? Do they perceive the source as honest and objective or as representing a special interest? Audiences, for example, ascribe lower credibility to statements in an advertisement than to the same information contained in a news article, because news articles are selected by media gatekeepers.

Source credibility is a problem for any organizational spokesperson because the public already has a bias. In one study conducted for the GCI Group, Opinion Research Corporation found that more than half of Americans surveyed are likely to believe that a large company is probably guilty of some wrongdoing if it is being investigated by a government agency or if a major lawsuit is filed against the company. At the same time, only one-third would trust the statements of a large company.

The problem of source credibility is the main reason that organizations, whenever possible, use respected outside experts or celebrities as representatives to convey their messages.

The *sleeper effect* also influences source credibility. This concept was developed by Carl Hovland, who stated: "There is decreased tendency over time to reject the material presented by an untrustworthy source." In other words, even if organizations are perceived initially as not being very credible sources, people may retain the information and eventually separate the source from the opinion. On the other hand, studies show that audiences register more constant opinion change if they perceive the source to be highly credible in the first place.

A second variable in believability is the *context* of the message. Action (performance) speaks louder than a stack of news releases. A bank may spend thousands of dollars on a promotion campaign with the slogan, "Your Friendly Bank—Where Service Counts," but the effort is wasted if employees are not trained to be friendly and courteous.

Incompatible rhetoric and actions can be somewhat amusing at times. At a press briefing about the importance of "buying American," the U.S. Chamber of Commerce passed out commemorative coffee mugs marked in small print on the bottom, "Made in China."

Another barrier to the believability of messages is the audience's predispositions. This problem brings to mind the old saying, "Don't confuse me with the facts, my mind is already made up."

ON THE JOB

ethics

How Do You Write This News Release?

You work in public relations for a large medical center, and one of your duties is publicizing major research studies by the staff.

One study that comes across your desk shows that postmenopausal women taking estrogen experience a 30 percent increase in the risk of breast cancer. You talk with the head of the research study, and she says that this percentage—when you consider other factors—actually means that a woman who doesn't take estrogen increases her odds of avoiding cancer by only about 1 percent—to 96 percent from 95 percent.

You know the media won't be very interested in the latter figure because there is no psychological effect of an impressive number. So what do you do? Would you just go ahead and use the 30 percent figure, which is technically correct, or would you write a news release emphasizing the minimal difference?

In this case, Leon Festinger's theory of *cognitive dissonance* should be understood. In essence, it says that people will not believe a message contrary to their predispositions unless the communicator can introduce information that causes them to question their beliefs.

Dissonance can be created in at least three ways. First, make the target audience aware that circumstances have changed. "In other words," says Patrick Jackson of *pr reporter*, "they needn't rationalize any longer; it's safe and OK to change because the situation has changed." Second, give information about new developments or discoveries. This is an unthreatening way to break through a person's opinions. Third, use an unexpected spokesperson. Chevron, for example, sought to overcome opposition to some of its oil exploration policies by getting endorsements from several respected leaders in the conservation movement.

Involvement is another important predisposition that impacts how messages are processed by audience members. Involvement can be described in simple terms as interest or concern for an issue or a product. Those with higher involvement often process persuasive messages with greater attention to detail and to logical argument (central processing), whereas those with low involvement for the topic are impressed more by incidental cues, such as an attractive spokesperson, humor, or the number of arguments given. The public relations professional can use the involvement concept to devise messages that focus more on "what is said" for high-involvement audiences and more attention to "who says it" for low-involvement audiences.

Remembering the Message

For several reasons, many messages prepared by public relations personnel are repeated extensively:

- Repetition is necessary because all members of a target audience don't see or hear the message at the same time. Not everyone reads the newspaper on a particular day or watches the same television news program.
- Repetition reminds the audience, so there is less chance of a failure to remember the message. If a source has high credibility, repetition prevents erosion of opinion change.
- Repetition helps the audience remember the message itself. Studies have shown that advertising is quickly forgotten if not repeated constantly.

● Repetition can lead to improved learning and increase the chance of penetrating audience indifference or resistance.

Researchers say that repetition, or redundancy, also is necessary to offset the "noise" surrounding a message. People often hear or see messages in an environment filled with distractions—a baby crying, the conversations of family members or office staff, a barking dog—or even while daydreaming or thinking of other things.

Consequently, communicators often build repetition into a message. Key points may be mentioned at the beginning and then summarized at the end. If the source is asking the receiver to call for more information or write for a brochure, the telephone number or address is repeated several times. Such precautions also fight entropy, which means that messages continually lose information as media channels and people process the information and pass it on to others. In one study about employee communications, for example, it was found that rank-and-file workers got only 20 percent of a message that had passed through four levels of managers.

The key to effective communication and retention of the message is to convey information in a variety of ways, using multiple communication channels. This helps people remember the message as they receive it through different media and extends the message to both passive and active audiences.

A good example of using multiple communication tools is a campaign to get a bond issue passed for Macomb Community College in Michigan. The message was quite simple: Vote "Yes." A nonprofit citizens group used 13 communication tools to put the message across: news releases, media interviews, news conferences, rallies, debates, campaign buttons, speaker's bureau, posters, direct mail, flyers, newsletters, phone calls to registered voters, and an essay contest. The bond issue passed.

Acting on the Message

The ultimate purpose of any message is to have an effect on the recipient. Public relations personnel communicate messages on behalf of organizations to change perceptions, attitudes, opinions, or behavior in some way. Marketing communications, in particular, has the objective of convincing people to buy goods and services.

The Five-Stage Adoption Process

Getting people to act on a message is not a simple process. In fact, research shows that it can be a somewhat lengthy and complex procedure that depends on a number of intervening influences. One key to understanding how people accept new ideas or products is to analyze the adoption process. The five stages, shown in Figure 7.2, are summarized as follows:

1. **Awareness.** A person becomes aware of an idea or a new product, often by means of an advertisement or a news story.
2. **Interest.** The individual seeks more information about the idea or the product, perhaps by ordering a brochure, picking up a pamphlet, or reading an in-depth article in a newspaper or magazine.
3. **Evaluation.** The person evaluates the idea or the product on the basis of how it meets specific needs and wants. Feedback from friends and family is part of this process.

FIGURE 7.2

This graph shows the steps through which an individual or other decision-making unit goes in the innovation-decision process from first knowledge of an innovation to the decision to adopt it, followed by implementation of the new idea and confirmation of the new decision.

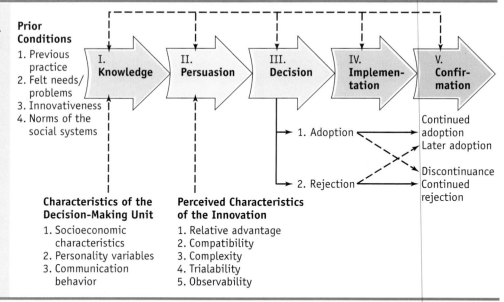

Prior Conditions
1. Previous practice
2. Felt needs/ problems
3. Innovativeness
4. Norms of the social systems

I. Knowledge
II. Persuasion
III. Decision
IV. Implementation
V. Confirmation

1. Adoption
2. Rejection

Continued adoption
Later adoption
Discontinuance
Continued rejection

Characteristics of the Decision-Making Unit
1. Socioeconomic characteristics
2. Personality variables
3. Communication behavior

Perceived Characteristics of the Innovation
1. Relative advantage
2. Compatibility
3. Complexity
4. Trialability
5. Observability

4. **Trial.** Next, the person tries the product or the idea on an experimental basis, by using a sample, witnessing a demonstration, or making qualifying statements such as, "I read . . ."

5. **Adoption.** The individual begins to use the product on a regular basis or integrates the idea into his or her belief system. The "I read . . ." becomes "I think . . ." if peers provide support and reinforcement of the idea.

It is important to realize that a person does not necessarily go through all five stages with any given idea or product. The process may be terminated after any step. In fact, the process is like a large funnel. Although many are made aware of an idea or a product, only a few will ultimately adopt it.

A number of factors affect the adoption process. Everett Rogers, author of *Diffusion of Innovation*, lists at least five:

1. **Relative advantage.** The degree to which an innovation is perceived as better than the idea it replaces.

2. **Compatibility.** The degree to which an innovation is perceived as being consistent with the existing values, experiences, and needs of potential adopters.

3. **Complexity.** The degree to which an innovation is perceived as difficult to understand and use.

4. **Trialability.** The degree to which an innovation may be experienced on a limited basis.

5. **Observability.** The degree to which the results of an innovation are visible to others.

The communicator should be aware of these factors and attempt to implement communication strategies that will overcome as many of them as possible. Repeating a message in various ways, reducing its complexity, taking into account competing messages, and structuring the message to meet the needs of the audience are ways to do this.

The Time Factor

Another aspect that confuses people is the amount of time needed to adopt a new idea or product. Depending on the individual and situation, the entire adoption process can take place almost instantly if the result is of minor consequence or requires low-level commitment. Buying a new brand of soft drink or a bar of soap is relatively inexpensive and often done on impulse. On the other hand, deciding to buy a new car or vote for a particular candidate may involve an adoption process that takes several weeks or months.

Rogers's research shows that people approach innovation in different ways, depending on their personality traits and the risk involved. "Innovators" are venturesome and eager to try new ideas, whereas "Laggards" are traditional and the last to adopt anything. Between the two extremes are "Early Adopters," who are opinion leaders; "Early Majority," who take the deliberate approach; and "Late Majority," who are often skeptical but bow to peer pressure.

Psychographics, discussed in Chapter 9, can often help communicators segment audiences that have "Innovator" or "Early Adopter" characteristics and would be predisposed to adopting new ideas.

How Decisions Are Influenced

Of particular interest to public relations people is the primary source of information at each step in the adoption process. Mass media vehicles such as advertising, short news articles, feature stories, and radio and television news announcements are most influential at the awareness stage of the adoption process. A news article or a television announcement makes people aware of an idea, event, or new product. They also are made aware through such vehicles as direct mail, office memos, and simple brochures.

Individuals at the interest stage also rely on mass media vehicles, but they are actively seeking information and pay attention to longer, in-depth articles. They rely more on detailed brochures, specialized publications, small-group seminars, and meetings to provide details. At the evaluation, trial, and adoption stages, group norms and opinions are the most influential. Feedback, negative or positive, from friends and peers may determine adoption. If a person's friends generally disapprove of a candidate, a movie, or an automobile brand, it is unlikely that the individual will complete the adoption process even if he or she is highly sold on the idea. If a person does make a commitment, mass media vehicles become reinforcing mechanisms. Studies show, for example, that owners of a new car are the most avid readers of that car's advertising. The complexities of the adoption process show that public relations communicators need to think about the entire communication process—from the formulation of the message to the ways in which receivers ultimately process the information and make decisions. By doing so, communicators can form more effective message strategies and develop realistic objectives for what can actually be accomplished.

PR CASEBOOK

Meet-ups and Flash Mobs Might Just Be "Unplanned" Public Relations Bonanzas

Two related uses of new technology have caught on with 20- and 30-somethings: flash mobs and meet-ups. Using cell phones, e-mail, Web sites, and text messaging, large groups of young people are spontaneously coordinating meetings and gatherings called *flash mobs*. Often the point behind the rendezvous is either vague or nonexistent, silly, or just plain fun. *PRWeek*'s Matthew Creamer put it well: "It's easy to see flash mobs as downright Shakespearean in their meaninglessness. If anything's full of sound and fury signifying nothing, it's a bunch of urbanites gathering at a toy store to scream and point at a single toy and fall to the ground—which actually happened this summer at a Toys-R-Us in New York."

Meet-ups are a related, more deliberate variation that uses the same technologies to bring young adults together. Meet-ups involve the organization of meetings or events at a grassroots level, but toward some goal or end. One of the best examples was the use of Meetup.com by the Howard Dean for President Campaign to organize Dean supporters and potential supporters. Not only was the facilitation of grassroots organizing and meeting a success, but the technique garnered extensive media attention, which led to additional fundraising and recruitment opportunities. Meetup.com continues to function, long after the Dean campaign has become a historical footnote. The site helps people find others who share a particular interest or cause and form lasting, influential, local community groups that regularly meet face-to-face. According to the site:

Meet-up groups help people:

- Find the others
- Get involved locally
- Learn, teach, and share things
- Make friends and have fun
- Rise up, stand up, unite, and make a difference
- Be a part of something bigger—both locally and globally

The site is nonpartisan and nondenominational, holding that everyone should have access to a Meet-up group about almost anything. Exceptions are hate groups and adult-related topics.

As a public relations communication tool, the picture is mixed. Experts caution that events are difficult to manage so that the client's message comes through. The technique may be most effective for niche audiences, dilettantes, and those with lots of free time. On the other hand, Tom Grow, who runs MobProject.com, sees promise for flash mobs and meet-ups as public relations tools: ". . . I think the potential is there to take guerilla marketing to a whole new level. I believe that people will use this eventually to promote a new product or event, even political leanings or specific agendas. There's a lot of potential when you can get that many people together." Recently, Nokia and an Australian museum have tried the technique.

PRWeek offers the following guidelines for the use of meet-ups and flash mobs:

- Do consider your client's audience. Meet-ups and flash mobs will be most successful in reaching younger consumers.
- Do be diligent in monitoring campaigns that use these tactics, because these uncontrolled communications environments can easily get out of hand.

- Do be wary of your messages getting lost in the hype that surrounds the communications vehicle.
- Don't rely solely on these largely untried methods of communicating.
- Don't go into these campaigns without being prepared for a backlash.

- Don't lose sight that a clear messaging strategy is still necessary.

Check out the following Web sites to learn more about meet-ups and flash mobs:

- www.friendster.com
- www.meetup.com

Source: PRWeek, October 20, 2003, p. 20.

SUMMARY

The Goals of Communication

Communication, also called *execution*, is the third step in the public relations process. Five possible objectives at this stage are message exposure, accurate dissemination of the message, acceptance of the message, attitude change, and change in overt behavior.

Receiving the Message

Successful communication involves interaction, or shared experience, because the message must be not only sent but received. The larger the audience, the greater the number of barriers to communication.

Paying Attention to the Message

Because audiences have different approaches to receiving messages, communicators must tailor the message to get the recipient's attention. They need to understand the audience's mental state. Messages for passive audiences must have style and creativity, whereas messages for an audience actively seeking information must have more sophisticated content. In either case, the effective message will raise the audience's "need" level by providing some obvious benefit.

Understanding the Message

The most basic element of understanding between communicator and audience is a common language. This is becoming a greater issue with the emphasis on multiculturalism. Public relations practitioners must

consider their audiences and style their language appropriately, taking into consideration literacy levels, clarity and simplicity of language, and avoidance of discriminatory language.

Believing the Message

Key variables in believability include source credibility, context, and the audience's predispositions, especially their level of involvement.

Remembering the Message

Messages are often repeated extensively to reach all members of the target audience and to help them remember and enhance their learning. One way to do this is to convey information in several ways, through a variety of channels.

Acting on the Message

The success of a message is in its effect on the recipient. Five steps in acceptance of new ideas or products are awareness, interest, evaluation, trial, and adoption. The adoption process is affected by relative advantage, compatibility, complexity, trialability, and observability. The time needed to adopt a new idea or product can be affected by the importance of the decision as well as the personality of the person receiving the message. The primary source of information varies at each step of the adoption process.

Case Activity: **What Would You Do?**

Extensive information campaigns are being mounted throughout the world to inform people of the dangers of Acquired Immune Deficiency Syndrome (AIDS). Information specialists must utilize a variety of communication strategies and tactics to create public awareness and change individual behavior patterns.

At the same time, the communication process is very complex because a number of variables must be considered. Using this chapter as a guide, how would you apply the various communication concepts and theories to the task of informing people about AIDS?

QUESTIONS for Review and Discussion

1. Kirk Hallahan lists five categories of media and communication tools. What are they, and what are some of the pros and cons of each?

2. James Grunig says that there are at least five possible objectives for a communicator. What are they? What two objectives do most public relations campaigns try to achieve?

3. What are the five basic elements of a communication model?

4. Why is two-way communication (feedback) an important aspect of effective communication?

5. What are the advantages and disadvantages, from a communication standpoint, of reaching the audience through mass media channels?

6. Explain the behavioral communication model. What is the importance of the "triggering event?"

7. What is the premise of the media uses and gratification theory?

8. What kinds of messages and communication channels would you use for a passive audience? An active information-seeking audience?

9. Why is it necessary to use a variety of messages and communication channels in a public relations program?

10. Why is it important to write with clarity and simplicity? How can symbols, acronyms, and slogans help?

11. Explain the concept behind readability formulas.

12. Why is it important to build repetition into a message?

13. Explain the five steps of the adoption process. What are some of the factors that affect the adoption of an idea or product?

SUGGESTED READINGS

Andsager, Julie L. "How Interest Groups Attempt to Shape Public Opinion With Conpeting News Frames." *Journalism & Mass Communications Quarterly*, Vol. 77, No. 3, 2000, pp. 577–592.

Creamer, Matthew. "Turning Crowds into Customers." *PRWeek*, October, 20, 2003, p. 20.

DeVito, Joseph. *Essentials of Human Communication*, 5th ed. Boston: Allyn & Bacon, 2004.

Hallahan, Kirk. "Strategic Media Planning: Toward an Integrated Public Relations Media Model." In *Handbook of Public Relations*, edited by Robert Heath. Thousand Oaks, CA: Sage, 2000.

Hood, Julia. "Poll: CEOs Boost Role in External Comms." *PR Week*, November 8, 2004, p. 1, 22.

Lukaszewski, Jim. "Overcoming Destructive Management Communication Behavior." *strategy, a supplement of pr reporter*, April 14, 2003, pp. 1–4.

Lukaszewski, Jim. "Selective Management: A Powerful Strategy for Managing Your Communications Destiny." *strategy, a supplement of pr reporter*, March 20, 2000, pp. 1–4.

Perloff, Richard M. *The Dynamics of Persuasion*, 2d ed. Mahwah, NJ: Lawrence Erlbaum, 2003.

Rice, Ronald E., and Atkin, Charles K., editors. *Public Communication Campaigns*. Thousand Oaks, CA: Sage, 2001.

chapter 8

Evaluation

Topics covered in this chapter include:

The Purpose of Evaluation

The fourth step of the public relations process is *evaluation*. It is the measurement of results against established objectives set during the planning process discussed in Chapter 6.

Evaluation is well described by Professor James Bissland of Bowling Green State University. He defines it as "the systematic assessment of a program and its results. It is a means for practitioners to offer accountability to clients—and to themselves."

Results and accountability also are themes of Professors Glen Broom and David Dozier of San Diego State University. In their text *Using Research in Public Relations*, they state, "Your program is intended to cause observable impact—to change or maintain something about a situation. So, after the program, you use research to measure and document program effects."

Frank Wylie, emeritus professor at California State University in Long Beach, summarizes: "We are talking about an orderly evaluation of our progress in attaining the specific objectives of our public relations plan. We are learning what we did right, what we did wrong, how much progress we've made and, most importantly, how we can do it better next time."

The desire to do a better job next time is a major reason for evaluating public relations efforts, but another equally important reason is the widespread adoption of the management-by-objectives system by clients and employers of public relations personnel. They want to know if the money, time, and effort expended on public relations are well spent and contribute to the realization of an organizational objective, such as attendance at an open house, product sales, or increased awareness of ways to prevent the spread of AIDS.

Objectives: A Prerequisite for Evaluation

Before any public relations program can be properly evaluated, it is important to have a clearly established set of measurable objectives. These should be part of the program plan (discussed in Chapter 6), but first some points need to be reviewed.

First, public relations personnel and management should agree on the criteria that will be used to evaluate success in attaining objectives. A Ketchum monograph simply states, "Write the most precise, most results-oriented objectives you can that are realistic, credible, measurable, and compatible with the client's demands on public relations."

Second, don't wait until the end of the public relations program to determine how it will be evaluated. Albert L. Schweitzer at Fleishman-Hillard public relations in St. Louis makes the point: "Evaluating impact/results starts in the planning stage. You break down the problem into measurable goals and objectives, then after implementing the program, you measure the results against goals."

If an objective is informational, measurement techniques must show how successfully information was communicated to target audiences. Such techniques fall under the rubrics of "message dissemination" and "audience exposure," but they do not measure the effect on attitudes or overt behavior and action.

Motivational objectives are more difficult to accomplish. If the objective is to increase sales or market share, it is important to show that public relations efforts caused the increase rather than advertising or other marketing strategies. Or, if the objective is to change attitudes or opinions, research should be done before and after the public relations activity to measure the percentage of change.

Although objectives may vary, the following checklist contains the basic evaluation questions that any practitioner should ask:

- Was the activity or program adequately planned?
- Did the recipients of the message understand it?
- How could the program strategy have been more effective?
- Were all primary and secondary audiences reached?
- Was the desired organizational objective achieved?
- What unforeseen circumstances affected the success of the program or activity?
- Did the program or activity fall within the budget set for it?
- What steps can be taken to improve the success of similar future activities?

Current Status of Measurement and Evaluation

During the 1990s, public relations professionals made considerable progress in evaluation research and the ability to tell clients and employers exactly what has been accomplished. Sophisticated techniques are being used, including computerized news clip analysis, survey sampling, quasi-experimental designs in which the audience is divided into groups that see different aspects of a public relations campaign, and attempts to correlate efforts directly with sales.

Today, the trend toward more systematic evaluation is well established. Katherine Delahaye Paine, founder of her own public relations measurement firm, says that the percentage of a public relations budget devoted to measurement and evaluation was about 1 percent a decade ago, but is now closer to 5 percent. By 2010, it is projected that the amount will increase to 10 percent. One reason: There is increasing pressure on all parts of the organization—including public relations—to prove their value to the "bottom line."

There are, however, still those who say that public relations is not an exact science and is extremely difficult to measure. Walter K. Lindenmann, a former senior vice president and director of research at Ketchum, takes a more optimistic view. He wrote in *Public Relations Quarterly*: "Let's get something straight right off the bat. First, it is possible to measure public relations effectiveness. . . . Second, measuring public relations effectiveness does not have to be either unbelievably expensive or laboriously time-consuming."

Lindenmann suggests that public relations personnel use a mix of evaluation techniques, many borrowed from advertising and marketing, to provide more complete evaluation. In addition, he notes that there are at least three levels of measurement and evaluation (see Figure 8.1).

On the most basic level are compilations of message distribution and media placement. The second level, which requires more sophisticated techniques, deals with the measurement of audience awareness, comprehension, and retention of the message. The most advanced level is the measurement of changes in attitudes, opinions, and behavior.

FIGURE 8.1

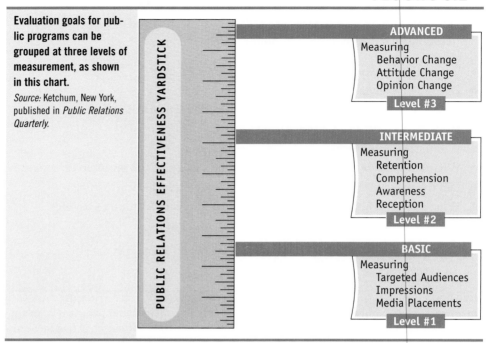

Evaluation goals for public programs can be grouped at three levels of measurement, as shown in this chart.
Source: Ketchum, New York, published in *Public Relations Quarterly.*

The following sections outline the most widely used methods for evaluating public relations efforts. These include measurement of production, message exposure, audience awareness, audience attitudes, and audience action. Supplemental activities such as communication audits, readability tests, event evaluation, and split messages also are discussed. In most cases, a skilled practitioner will use a combination of methods to evaluate the effectiveness of a program.

Measurement of Production

One elementary form of evaluation is simply to count how many news releases, feature stories, photos, letters, and the like are produced in a given period of time. This kind of evaluation is supposed to give management an idea of a staff's productivity and output. Public relations professionals, however, do not believe that this evaluation is very meaningful, because it emphasizes quantity instead of quality. It may be more cost-effective to write fewer news releases and spend more time on the few that really are newsworthy. It may, for example, be more important for a staff person to spend five weeks working on an article for the *Wall Street Journal* or *Fortune* than to write 29 routine personnel releases.

Another side of the production approach is to specify what the public relations person should accomplish in obtaining media coverage. One state trade association evaluated its director of media relations on the expectation that (1) four feature stories would be run in any of the 11 largest newspapers in the state and (2) news releases would be used by at least 20 newspapers, including 5 or more among the 50 largest.

Such evaluation criteria not only are unrealistic, they are almost impossible to guarantee, because media gatekeepers—not the public relations person—make such decisions. Management may argue, however, that such placement goals provide incentive to the public relations staff and are tangible criteria in employee performance evaluation.

Closely allied to the production of publicity materials is their distribution. Thus, a public relations department might report, for instance, that a total of 756 news releases were sent to 819 daily newspapers, 250 weeklies, and 137 trade magazines within one year or that 110,000 copies of the annual report were distributed to stockholders, security analysts, and business editors.

Measurement of Message Exposure

The most widely practiced form of evaluating public relations programs is the compilation of press clippings and radio–television mentions. Public relations firms and company departments working primarily on a local basis often have a staff member scan and clip the area newspapers. Large companies with regional, national, or even international outreach usually hire clipping services to scan large numbers of publications. It also is possible to have electronic clipping services monitor and tape major radio and television programs on a contractual basis. Burrelle's, for example, monitors nearly 400 local TV stations in 150 cities. Web tracking systems and firms are discussed in Chapter 11.

Strategic research by Hallmark Cards and its public relations firm, Fleishman-Hillard, identified the need for a line of less expensive cards to compete with deep discount card companies and to increase occasions for sending a card to a friend, colleague, or relative. Hallmark used media clips as one measure of its Warm Wishes campaign. According to Fleishman-Hillard's report, which was the basis for the firm's receipt of a Silver Anvil award from PRSA:

> The public relations strategies and tactics generated nearly 107 million trackable impressions. The television outreach resulted in 71 known placements and 12.8 million impressions nationwide, with many stations showing footage of the BigBox Color production process, furthering the quality message. Warm Wishes was even included in the Tonight Show monologue by Jay Leno. The story proved to be an "evergreen," with hits in March, April, May, and June.

The agency not only noted the total impressions, but alluded to the importance of the key message being included as part of the coverage. Similar analysis was provided for print coverage. Such a compilation measures media acceptance of the story and shows that Hallmark received massive coverage. Clearly, the publicity effort accomplished the first stage of the adoption process by making people aware of the Warm Wishes line of cards.

Media Impressions

In addition to the number of media placements, public relations departments and firms report how many people may have been exposed to the message. These numbers are described as *media impressions*, the potential audience reached by a periodical or a broadcast program.

ON THE JOB

global

Airline's Employees Spread the Word

A decade after it was privatized, British Airways (BA) was one of the world's leading airlines. However, it decided to reinforce its mission "To Be the Undisputed Leader in World Travel" by launching a new corporate identity program on a worldwide basis.

The objective was to reach 70 percent of the 55,000 staff members worldwide prior to the public launch of the new corporate identity program. It was reasoned that if the employees were aware of the key messages behind the campaign, they could also convey the key messages to various publics, including customers. British Airways used 13 satellites to link 30,000 guests and employees at 126 locations in 63 countries for a simultaneous, all-time-zone launch.

This is how the airline evaluated the results:

An average of 89 percent of overseas employees, ahead of the 70 percent target, saw the new BA prior to June 10. Almost 80 percent of 444 articles from 49 countries were positive, and 48 percent used visuals. Key messages were conveyed in 78 percent of the articles.

It is no simple task to gather news clips for global campaigns. Imagine trying to buy and then read all of the major newspapers around the world that might pick up your public relations work. Obtaining a valid and reliable sample of news clips from around the world is indeed a challenge. An international trade association called FIBEP represents clipping services worldwide. It is a good reference for securing foreign clipping services. As a quality check, you may also want to scan news Web sites or hire a company such as Factiva to do the work for you.

If, for example, a story about an organization appears in a local daily that has a circulation of 130,000, the media impressions are 130,000. If another story is published the next day, this counts for 130,000 more impressions. Estimated audiences for radio and television programs, certified by auditing organizations, also are used to compile media impressions.

A regional or national news story can generate millions of impressions by simple multiplication of each placement by the circulation or audience of each medium. Two examples:

- The American College of Obstetricians and Gynecologists organized a public relations campaign to celebrate the 35th anniversary of the birth control pill. According to its report, total media impressions were almost 61 million from print, radio, and television stories.

- M&M's Chocolate Candies conducted a national contest to name a new color for M&M's Candies. Public relations activities generated 1.06 billion impressions from 10,000 TV, radio, and print placements; these included 36,000 print column inches, 12 hours of television news coverage, and 74 hours of radio broadcast time.

Media impressions are commonly used in advertising to document the breadth of penetration of a particular message. Such figures give a rough estimate of how many people are exposed to a message. They don't, however, disclose how many people actually read or heard the stories and, more important, how many absorbed or acted on the information. Other techniques needed for this kind of evaluation are discussed later in this chapter.

Hits on the Internet

A cyberspace version of media impressions is the number of people reached via an organization's World Wide Web site or home page. Each instance of a person accessing a site is called a *hit* or a *visit*.

A good example is Purple Moon, a software developer of girls' interactive entertainment. It used a Web site to promote its CD-ROM product, "Friendship Adventures." According to the company and its public relations firm, Ketchum, "Media relations and grassroots online programs helped drive traffic resulting in 700,000 visitors in the first six months and an average of 6 million impressions per month, equaling or surpassing those of top kids' sites including Disney.com and Sports Illustrated for Kids."

A third example is the Florida health-care reform campaign designed by Hill & Knowlton. The campaign included coordination of Floridians to send daily e-mail messages to legislators with a "headline of the day so they (legislators) were aware of the kind of coverage the issue was receiving in different areas of the state. The effect was one of a brush fire that could not be extinguished without reform." The Web-based system generated 163,128 constituent e-mails to legislators.

In another example, MCI launched a Web site to make consumers aware of its Internet services. The Web site provided information and also included a test that visitors could take to measure their Internet skills. According to the company and its public relations firm, Ruberry Communications, "More than 2.3 million hits were recorded for the Web test site. More than 16,500 people actually completed the test and recorded a score. The test was taken by people from 12 countries."

Advertising Equivalency

Another approach is to calculate the value of message exposure. This is done by converting stories in the regular news columns or on the air into equivalent advertising costs. In other words, a 5-inch article in a trade magazine that charges $100 per column inch for advertising would be worth $500 in publicity value.

Mack Trucks, for example, evaluated its public relations campaign to improve its image in the trucking industry by using advertising equivalency. It reported, "The program generated more than 9,000 inches of editorial coverage with an advertising equivalency of more than $1.2 million—more than five times the company's investment in the program."

Some practitioners even take the approach of calculating the cost of advertising for the same amount of space and then multiplying that total three to six times to reflect a number of research studies that show that a news story has greater credibility than an advertisement. Consequently, if Mack Trucks multiplied the equivalent advertising space by three, it could say that the editorial space was worth $3.6 million in publicity.

Although such dollar amounts may impress top management, the technique of calculating advertising equivalency is really comparing apples with oranges. In fact, Ron Levy, president of North American Precis Syndicate, told *Jack O'Dwyer's Public Relations Newsletter* that he thought the technique was "blatantly ridiculous."

One reason why the two can't be compared is the fundamental difference between advertising and publicity. Advertising copy is directly controlled by the organization and can be oriented to specific objectives. The organization also controls the size and placement of the message. News mentions, on the other hand, are determined by media gatekeepers and can be negative, neutral, or positive. In addition, a news release can be edited to the point that key corporate messages are deleted. In other words, the organization can't control size, placement, or content.

It thus becomes a question of what is being measured. Should an article be counted as equivalent advertising space if it is negative? It also is questionable whether a 15-inch article that mentions the organization only once among six other organizations is comparable to 15 column inches of advertising space. And the numbers game doesn't take into account that a 4-inch article in the *Wall Street Journal* may be more valuable in reaching key publics than a 20-inch article in the *Denver Post*.

In summary, the dollar-value approach to measuring publicity effectiveness is somewhat suspect, and there has been a rapid decline of such statistics in PRSA award entries. The equating of publicity with advertising rates for comparable space also does not engender good media relations. The technique reinforces the opinion of many media gatekeepers that all news releases are just attempts to get free advertising.

Systematic Tracking

As noted earlier, message exposure traditionally has been measured by sheer bulk. New advances in computer software and databases, however, now make it possible to track media placements in a more sophisticated way.

Computer databases can be used to analyze the content of media placements by such variables as market penetration, type of publication, tone of coverage, sources quoted, and mention of key copy points. Ketchum, for example, can build up to 40 variables into its computer program, including the tracking of reporter bylines to determine if a journalist is predisposed negatively or positively to the client's key messages. Other firms, such as Carma International and Delahaye MediaLink, do extensive analysis for clients using databases such as LEXIS/NEXIS. Table 8.1, prepared by Delahaye MediaLink for a client, illustrates the type of analysis that can be done.

The value of systematic tracking is manifested in several ways. One is continuing, regular feedback during a campaign to determine if an organization's publicity efforts are paying off in terms of placements and mention of key messages. Tracking coverage and comparing it over a period of time is called *benchmarking*.

An example of benchmarking is the campaign that Capitoline/MS&L public relations conducted on behalf of the Turkish government to make Americans more aware of Turkey as a travel destination. By comparing the number of stories before and after the campaign was launched, Carma International found that articles with Turkey as the primary destination increased 400 percent. Favorable articles on Turkey increased 90 percent from the previous year.

At other times, an organization may wish to do a systematic analysis comparing its media coverage with the competition's. Is a major competitor getting more favorable publicity? Is the company being portrayed as an innovative leader, or is its size the only major message being mentioned? Such evaluation allows an organization to fine-tune its public relations efforts and concentrate on problem areas.

Another form of analysis is comparing the number of news releases sent with the number actually published and in what kinds of periodicals. Such analysis often helps a public relations department determine what kinds of publicity are most effective and earn the most return on investment (ROI).

As Katharine Paine, former president of Delahaye MediaLink, says, "The world doesn't need more data. What it needs is analyzed data."

TABLE 8.1

Total Coverage	
	TOTAL
Total impressions	89,641,378
Percent of positive impressions	26.98%
Percent of negative impressions	19.85%
Total articles	1,049
Percent of positive articles	35.65%
Percent of negative articles	16.02%
Percent of articles containing one or more positive messages	52.43%
Percent of articles containing one or more negative messages	18.78%

Requests and 800 Numbers

Another measure of media exposure is to compile the number of requests for more information. A story in a newspaper or an appearance of a company spokesperson on a broadcast often provides information as to where people can get more information about a subject.

In many cases, a toll-free 800 number is provided. Dayton Hudson Corporation, owner of several department store chains, used a toll-free hotline number as part of its "Child Care Aware" program to help educate parents about quality child care and how to get it. In a six-month period, 19,000 calls were received from people seeking advice and copies of a brochure. Dole Food Company, through its toll-free 800 number, got requests for more than 100,000 copies of its brochure titled, "Fun with Fruits and Vegetables: Kid's Cookbook."

Requests for materials also can show the effectiveness of a public relations program. An information program by the U.S. Centers for Disease Control on AIDS prevention, for example, received nearly 2,000 phone calls on its information hotline after its "Safe Sex" program on the Public Broadcasting Service (PBS). In addition, the program and resulting publicity generated 260 requests for videotapes and 400 requests for "Smart Sex" organization kits.

Cost per Person

Another way to evaluate exposure to the message is to determine the cost of reaching each member of the audience. The technique is commonly used in advertising to place costs in perspective. Although a 30-second commercial during the 2004 Super Bowl telecast cost $2.4 million, advertisers believed it was well worth the price because an audience of more than 145 million would be reached for less than a half-cent each. This was a relatively good bargain, even if several million viewers probably visited the refrigerator while the commercial played. Professor Dean Krugman at the University of Georgia conducts viewer behavior research that suggests that television ratings used in advertising offer a false precision. His findings indicate that public relations professionals should use caution in adapting such ratings to estimates of media coverage.

ON THE JOB

ethics

Measuring Use of a Client's Name

You've been hired as an intern at a public relations firm for the summer. One of your duties is to go through recent issues of trade magazines and clip any article in which the name of a client appears. You are then asked to look up advertising rates for these publications and calculate what the comparable space in advertising would cost. The idea, says the account supervisor, is to count entire articles even if the client's name is only mentioned once. "The client is impressed with big numbers," she says, "so count anything you can find." You ask whether you should also try to judge whether the coverage is favorable or not. Your supervisor says that all the client really wants is to be visible—and besides, it's really hard to decide what is favorable or unfavorable coverage.

Does this approach raise any ethical concerns on your part? Why or why not? How would you handle the assignment?

Cost-effectiveness, as this technique is known, also is used in public relations. *Cost-per-thousand* (CPM) is calculated by taking the cost of the publicity program and dividing it by the total media impressions (discussed earlier). SkyTel, for example, spent $400,000 to publicize its new two-way paging and messaging system and obtained 52 million impressions, about seven-tenths of a cent per impression. According to counselor Ford Kanzler, "CPMs for print publicity programs usually fall well below media space advertising and about 100 percent above direct mail promotions."

In another example, a campaign by the Virginia Department of Tourism to attract Canadian visitors cost $5,500, but generated 90,000 consumer inquiries. This made the cost per inquiry only six cents. The same approach can be done with events, brochures, and newsletters. Nike produced a sports video for $50,000, but reached 150,000 high school students, for a per-person cost of 33 cents.

Audience Attendance

Counting attendance at events is a relatively simple way of evaluating the effectiveness of pre-event publicity. The New York Public Library centennial day celebration, for example, attracted a crowd of 10,000 for a sound and laser show and speeches. In addition, 20,000 visitors came to the library on the designated centennial day and more than 200,000 people from around the world visited the library's exhibitions during the year.

Poor attendance at a meeting or event can indicate inadequate publicity and promotion. Another major cause is lack of public interest, even when people are aware that a meeting or event is taking place. Low attendance usually results in considerable finger-pointing; thus an objective evaluation of exactly what happened—or didn't happen—is a good policy.

Measurement of Audience Awareness

Thus far, techniques of measuring audience exposure and accurate dissemination have been discussed. A higher level of evaluation is to determine whether the audience actually became aware of the message and understood it.

Walter Lindenmann calls this the second level of public relations evaluation. He notes:

At this level, public relations practitioners measure whether target audience groups actually received the messages directed at them: whether they paid attention to those messages, whether they understood the messages, and whether they have retained those messages in any shape or form.

The tools of survey research are needed to answer such questions. Members of the target audience must be asked about the message and what they remember about it. Public awareness of what organization sponsors an event also is important. BayBank found that only 59 percent of the spectators recognized the bank as sponsor of the Head of the Charles Regatta. Through various innovations, increased publicity efforts, and more signage at the following year's regatta, BayBank raised public awareness to 90 percent. (The bank has since been absorbed by another banking firm.)

Another way of measuring audience awareness and comprehension is day-after recall. Under this method, participants are asked to view a specific television program or read a particular news story. The next day they are then interviewed to learn which messages they remembered.

Ketchum, on behalf of the California Prune Board, used this technique to determine if a 15-city media tour was conveying the key message that prunes are a high-fiber food source. Forty women in Detroit considered likely to watch daytime television shows were asked to view a program on which a Prune Board spokesperson would appear. The day after the program, Ketchum asked the women questions about the show, including their knowledge of the fiber content of prunes. Ninety-three percent remembered the Prune Board spokesperson, and 65 percent, on an unaided basis, named prunes as a high-fiber food source.

Measurement of Audience Attitudes

Closely related to audience awareness and understanding of a message are changes in an audience's perceptions and attitudes. A major technique to determine such changes is the *baseline study*. Basically, a baseline study is a measurement of audience attitudes and opinions before, during, and after a public relations campaign. Baseline studies, also called *benchmark studies*, graphically show the percentage difference in attitudes and opinions as a result of increased information and publicity. A number of intervening variables may account for changes in attitude, of course, but statistical analysis of variance can help pinpoint how much the change is attributable to public relations efforts.

The insurance company Prudential Financial regularly conducts baseline studies. One survey found that the company scored high in respondent familiarity, but achieved only a 29 percent favorable rating in fulfilling its corporate social responsibilities.

As a result, the company launched "The Prudential Helping Hearts Program." This effort provided $2 million in matching grants to volunteer emergency medical squads (EMS) to help purchase portable cardiac arrest equipment used to treat heart attack victims before they reach the hospital. After a year of publicizing the program and making grants, Prudential found that its overall corporate image had risen to 29 percent.

The American Iron and Steel Institute did a baseline study to determine the effectiveness of its campaign to inform the public about the industry's recycling efforts. Before the program, only 52 percent of the respondents in Columbus, Ohio, were aware that steel cans are recyclable. After the campaign, the percentage had risen to 64 percent.

ON THE JOB insights

Sales: For Many Companies, This Is the Ultimate Outcome

In the corporate world, one behavioral outcome of company performance is almost always measured daily and with great precision. It is sales of products and services. Sabrina Horn calls for a shift in thinking about the role of public relations in driving sales figures: "To those outside marketing, public relations is frequently misunderstood as nothing more than a tactical press release machine. Unfortunately, PR is often an afterthought to strategic planning."

By being involved in the strategic plan, the role of public relations can be broader, and objectives can be set that are clearly linked to sales, for example, "increase sales leads by 50 percent in financial services through precision public relations efforts targeted at the new customer base." It is essential to then plan strategies that can impact this objective and, finally, to devise measures that evaluate impact on sales performance.

BUSINESS GOAL	PR STRATEGY	MEASUREMENT TOOLS
Increase sales leads by 50 percent in financial services for new customers.	Product launches, including tours, press releases, a customer testimonial program, direct mail of CD-ROM presenting services, and repeated urging of new prospective customers to call the toll-free number and ask for Operator 39 to receive special discounts	1. Telemarketing staff maps source of incoming calls back to articles published as the result of press releases. 2. Sales lead tracking system is programmed to track callers' requests for Operator 39—the marker for the public relations effort.

With early participation in the planning process and some clever techniques, it is possible for public relations to contribute to the sales figures that are already being captured by your company.

Source: O'Dwyer's PR Services Report, March 2002; *tips & tactics, pr reporter,* March 4, 2002.

The value of the baseline survey is underscored by Frank R. Stansberry, former manager of guest affairs for Coca-Cola and now at the University of Central Florida. He told the *Public Relations Journal:* "The only way to determine if communications are making an impact is by pre- and posttest research. The first survey measures the status quo. The second one will demonstrate any change and the direction of that change."

Measurement of Audience Action

The ultimate objective of any public relations effort, as has been pointed out, is to accomplish organizational objectives. As David Dozier of San Diego State University aptly points out, "The outcome of a successful public relations program is not a hefty stack of news stories . . . . Communication is important only in the effects it achieves among publics."

The objective of an amateur theater group is not to get media publicity; the objective is to sell tickets. The objective of an environmental organization such as

Greenpeace is not to get editorials written in favor of whales, but to motivate the public (1) to write elected officials, (2) to send donations for its preservation efforts, and (3) to get protective legislation passed. The objective of a company is to sell its products and services, not get 200 million media impressions. In all cases, the tools and activities of public relations are a means, not an end.

Thus, public relations efforts ultimately are evaluated on how they help an organization achieve its objectives. Cingular Wireless and its public relations firm, Ketchum, employed a variety of primary and secondary research methods, including data analysis of highway traffic safety statistics that showed that teens are four times more likely to be in distraction-related accidents and focus groups with educators to better understand how to communicate with teens. In their winning PRSA Silver Anvil award application, Ketchum recounted how the measurable objectives that were developed for the "Be Sensible! Cingular Wireless Helps Teens Manage Driving Distractions" were addressed. The evaluation recap illustrates rigorous measurement of both awareness and audience actions:

Evaluation

Objective One: Create awareness of the dangers of distracted driving among 3 million teens over a three-year period (2002–2004):

- More than 10,000 high schools and 4,200 private driving schools have requested and received the teen-driving program.
- We have reached 5.6 million teens to date, significantly surpassing our three-year goal with 11 months still to go!
- From the 1,000 educator surveys received to date:
    - 93 percent of teachers strongly agree/agree that this program gives students a new perspective on the role of driver distraction in vehicle collisions.
    - 92 percent strongly agree/agree that the program generated student interest in the topic of driver distraction.
    - 99 percent of instructors said they would use the program again.

Objective Two: Integrate Be Sensible: Don't Drive Yourself to Distraction video into five state driver education programs by 2004:

- Maryland, Virginia, Maine, Ohio, Georgia, New Jersey, New York, Indiana, Kansas, Alabama, and Florida state driver education administrators have embraced the Be Sensible teen program by distributing the program to all driver education teachers statewide.

Cingular's Be Sensible: Don't Drive Yourself to Distraction program has been the recipient of several education awards, including the CINE Golden Eagle and U.S. International Film and Video Festival Silver Screen.

Measurement of Supplemental Activities

Other forms of measurement can be used in public relations activities. This section discusses (1) communication audits, (2) pilot tests and split messages, (3) meeting and event attendance, and (4) newsletter readership.

Communication Audits

The entire communication activity of an organization should be evaluated at least once a year to make sure that every primary and secondary public is receiving appropriate messages. David Hilton-Barber, past president of the Public Relations Institute of South Africa (PRISA), has written: "The most important reasons for an audit are to help establish communication goals and objectives, to evaluate long-term programs, to identify strengths and weaknesses, and to point up any areas which require increased activity."

A communication audit, as an assessment of an organization's entire communication program, could include the following:

- Analysis of all communiation activities—newsletters, memos, policy statements, brochures, annual reports, position papers, mailing lists, media contacts, personnel forms, graphics, logos, advertising, receptionist contacts, waiting lounges for visitors, and so on.
- Informal interviews with rank-and-file employees and middle management and top executives.
- Informal interviews with community leaders, media gatekeepers, consumers, distributors, and other influential persons in the industry.

A number of research techniques, as outlined in Chapter 5, can be used during a communication audit, including mail and telephone surveys, focus groups, and so forth. The important point is that the communications of an organization should be analyzed from every possible angle, with the input of as many publics as possible. Security analysts may have something to say about the quality of the company's financial information; municipal leaders are best qualified to evaluate the company's efforts in community relations. Consumers, if given a chance, will make suggestions about quality of sales personnel and product instruction booklets.

Pilot Tests, Split Messages, Perception Analyzers, and Think-Aloud Techniques

Evaluation is important even before a public relations effort is launched. If exposure to a message is to be maximized, it is wise to pretest it with a sample group from the targeted audience. Do its members easily understand the message? Do they accept the message? Does the message motivate them to adopt a new idea or product?

A variation of pretesting is the *pilot test*. Before going national with a public relations message, companies often test the message and key copy points in selected cities to learn how the media accept the message and how the public reacts. This approach is quite common in product marketing because it limits costs and enables the company to revamp or fine-tune the message for maximum exposure. It also allows the company to switch channels of dissemination if the original media channels are not exposing the message to the proper audiences.

The *split-message* approach is common in direct mail campaigns. Two or three different appeals may be prepared by a charitable organization and sent to different audiences. The response rate is then monitored (perhaps the amount of donations is totaled) to learn what message and graphics seemed to be the most effective.

With *perception analyzer systems*, sometimes called *theater systems*, selected subjects are asked to view speeches, public service announcements, or video news releases while turning a dial up or down to offer their ratings of favorability as the message is presented. This dynamic system enables the public relations firm to identify which passages of a tape work the best or which message strategies are most effective.

Increasingly, Web development professionals are seeking to refine the content of organizational Web sites. Among Web publishers, the refrain often heard is: "Content is king." This means that it is insufficient for public relations professionals to be satisfied with simply having a Web site or relying on bells and whistles, such as flashing elements and animation, to jazz up a site. The content needs to be compelling and effective to meet organizational objectives. A relatively new research technique, called the *think-aloud method*, can be used to assess Web content in a similar fashion to the perception analyzers. With the think-aloud method, a person is encouraged to vocalize his or her comments while examining a Web site.

Meeting and Event Attendance

It has already been pointed out that meetings can be evaluated to some degree by the level of attendance. Such data provide information about the number of people exposed to a message, but it doesn't answer the more crucial question of what they thought about the meeting.

Public relations people often get an informal sense of an audience's attitudes by its behavior. A standing ovation, spontaneous applause, complimentary remarks as people leave, and even the expressions on people's faces provide clues as to how a meeting was received. On the other hand, if people are not responsive, if they ask questions about subjects supposedly explained, if they express doubts or antagonism, the meeting can be considered only partly successful.

Public relations practitioners use a number of information methods to evaluate the success of a meeting, but they also employ more systematic methods. The most common technique is an evaluation sheet that participants fill out at the end of the meeting.

A simple form asking people to rate such items as location, costs, facilities, and program on a 1-to-5 scale (1 being the best) can be used. Other forms may ask people to rate aspects of a conference or meeting as (1) excellent, (2) good, (3) average, (4) poor, or (5) very poor.

Evaluation forms also can ask how people heard about the program and what suggestions they have for future meetings.

Newsletter Readership

Editors of newsletters should evaluate readership annually. Such an evaluation can help ascertain (1) reader perceptions, (2) the degree to which stories are balanced, (3) the kinds of stories that have high reader interest, (4) additional topics that should be covered, (5) the credibility of the publication, and (6) the extent to which the newsletter is meeting organizational objectives.

Note that systematic evaluation is not based on whether all the copies of a newsletter have been distributed or picked up. This information doesn't tell the editor what the audience actually read, retained, or acted upon.

A newsletter, newspaper, or even a brochure can be evaluated in a number of ways. The methods include (1) content analysis, (2) readership interest surveys,

(3) readership recall of articles actually read, (4) application of readability formulas, and (5) the use of advisory boards.

Content Analysis.   Based on a representative sample of past issues, stories may be categorized under general headings such as (1) management announcements, (2) new product developments, (3) new personnel and retirements, (4) features about employees, (5) corporate finances, (6) news of departments and divisions, and (7) job-related information.

Such a systematic analysis will show what percentage of the publication is devoted to each category. It may be found that one division rarely is covered in the employee newsletter or that management pronouncements tend to dominate the entire publication. Given the content-analysis findings, editors may decide to shift the content.

Readership Interest Surveys.   The purpose of these surveys is to get feedback about the types of stories employees are most interested in reading. The most common survey method is simply to provide a long list of generic story topics and have employees rate each as (1) important, (2) somewhat important, or (3) not important. The International Association of Business Communicators (IABC) conducted such a survey on behalf of several dozen companies and found that readers were not very interested in "personals" about other employees (birthdays, anniversaries, and the like).

A readership interest survey becomes even more valuable when it is compared with the content analysis of a publication. Substantial differences signal a possible need for changes in the editorial content.

Article Recall.   The best kind of readership survey occurs when trained interviewers ask a sampling of employees what they have read in the latest issue of the publication. Employees are shown the publication page by page and asked to indicate which articles they have read. As a check on the tendency of employees to report that they have read everything, interviewers also ask them (1) how much of each article they have read and (2) what the articles were about. The results are then content-analyzed to determine which kinds of articles have the most readership.

A variation of the readership-recall technique involves individual evaluation of selected articles for accuracy and clarity. For example, an article about a new production process may be sent before or after publication to the head of production for evaluation. On a form with a rating scale of excellent, good, fair, and deficient, the person may be asked to evaluate the article on the basis of such factors as (1) technical data provided, (2) organization, (3) length, (4) clarity of technical points, and (5) quality of illustrations.

Advisory Boards.   Periodic feedback and evaluation can be provided by organizing an employee advisory board that meets several times a year to discuss the direction and content of the publication. This is a useful technique because it expands the editor's feedback network and elicits comments that employees might be hesitant to tell the editor face-to-face.

A variation of the advisory board method is periodically to invite a sampling of employees to meet to discuss the publication. This approach is more systematic than just soliciting comments from employees in the hallway or cafeteria.

PR CASEBOOK

Changing Health Behaviors in Hispanic Communities

The American Heart Association (AHA) launched "The Heart of Diabetes: Understanding Insulin Resistance" (THOD) to educate at-risk Hispanics on how insulin resistance, cardiovascular disease, and diabetes are related. To reach the Hispanic community, THOD used bilingual patient materials and publicity, a Hispanic celebrity, and bilingual physicians to drive patient enrollment in the program.

The goal of the campaign was to inform people with Type-2 diabetes and their families about the link between diabetes and cardiovascular disease. THOD provided participants with educational materials and a free subscription to *Diabetes Positive*, which people could request by telephone or over the Internet.

With the help of Rita Moreno and bilingual physicians, in 2003 more than 76 million media impressions drove 58,000 calls to the AHA call center, putting more than 15,000 Hispanic patients on the path to better health.

Research

The objectives for the campaign were based on varied and extensive research:

- **Web-based research.** No pharmaceutical companies or competing patient groups, such as the American Diabetes Association, were prepared to develop a program focused on cardiovascular disease and diabetes.
- **Media audits.** Reporters were not focusing on the disease triangle of insulin resistance, diabetes, and cardiovascular disease.
- **Industry analysis.** Because the Hispanic population is a high-risk group for diabetes and related cardiovascular complications, the team consulted with a Hispanic/Latino health-care consulting firm to better understand this community and plot an approach to effectively reach the target population.
- **Roper Starch Survey.** Roper Starch Worldwide was commissioned to conduct a telephone survey of people with diabetes (with an over-sampling of Hispanics) to determine specific levels of awareness/behavior. Results showed that:
  - Patients were frustrated by a lack of bilingual materials.
  - More than 60 percent of patients surveyed had cardiovascular disease, but only 33 percent considered it among the most serious diabetes-related complications.
  - Many patients did not know what insulin resistance was or how it related to diabetes and cardiovascular disease.

Planning

Audience

Hispanic men and women with Type-2 diabetes who are at risk for cardiovascular disease.

Objectives

1. **Education:** Increase awareness of the relationship between insulin resistance/diabetes/cardiovascular disease among the at-risk population (GOAL: 50 million media impressions).
2. **Action:** Help at-risk patients recognize and reduce their risk of cardiovascular disease (GOAL: 7,500 enrollees) and drive traffic to the Spanish-language Web site.

(continued)

PR CASEBOOK *(continued)*

Strategies

1. Leverage survey results to demonstrate the need for increased awareness.
2. Offer free Spanish–English health information (handbook, journal, Web site) through the AHA.
3. Engage a celebrity with ties to the Hispanic community.

Messages

1. Heart disease and stroke are the leading causes of death for people with diabetes, particularly Latinos/Hispanics.
2. Diabetes dramatically increases a person's risk for heart disease. Common underlying risk factors for diabetes are obesity, elevated cholesterol levels, high blood pressure, and physical inactivity. An emerging risk factor is insulin resistance, a condition in which the body doesn't efficiently respond to the insulin that it makes.
3. The American Heart Association's "The Heart Of Diabetes: Understanding Insulin Resistance" program can help people with Type-2 diabetes learn more about the connection between diabetes and heart disease and understand what they can do to minimize their risks.

Execution

Patient Education Materials

Produced and distributed patient education materials in both Spanish and English. Patient education materials included the following:

- The handbook "Getting to the Heart of Diabetes," which was widely distributed through an alliance of organizations (i.e., American Association of Diabetes Educators, National Black Nurses Association, and the American Stroke Association).
- The "Thriver" journal, which patients could use to track blood glucose, blood pressure, cholesterol, diet, and exercise routines.
- The "Shape Your Family History" chart, which was designed to encourage families to map out their health problems and

discuss them with their health-care providers.
- The THOD consumer Web site at americanheart.org/diabetes.

The National Campaign Launch

The national campaign launch featured the following:

- Rita Moreno joined THOD as the national celebrity spokesperson, sharing her personal story of losing her mother and sister-in-law to diabetes-related heart disease.
- As part of the national launch, a reception was held at Restaurant Noche in New York City where Ms. Moreno revealed the Hispanic-specific survey statistics.
- A national radio public service announcement (available in English and Spanish) featuring Ms. Moreno was produced and distributed.
- Ms. Moreno and the national physician spokesperson were featured in a three-hour television satellite media tour and a two-hour radio media tour.

Local Activities

The following activities were conducted at the local/regional level:

- Ms. Moreno toured cities with high Hispanic populations, including Chicago, Los Angeles, Miami, and San Antonio, teaming up with local bilingual cardiologists to reach Hispanic patients with Type-2 diabetes.
- Worked with local AHA chapters to generate excitement in the market by tapping their local media contacts and coordinating special appearances for Ms. Moreno in heavily populated settings (e.g., Hispanic senior centers).

Evaluation

The evaluation component of the campaign focused on two major objectives: one focusing on message *outputs*, with concomitant media exposure, and the other focusing on the *impacts* of the campaign.

Objective 1

1. **Education:** Increase awareness of the relationship between insulin resistance/diabetes/cardiovascular disease among the at-risk population (GOAL: 50 million media impressions).
2. **Results:** Through targeted media outreach, the program generated 76 million media impressions, exceeding the goal by more than 50 percent. Coverage included Telemundo, Univision's national morning show *Despierta America, Newsday*, the *Chicago Sun-Times*, and the *San Antonio Express-News*.

Objective 2

1. **Action:** Help at-risk patients recognize and reduce their risk of cardiovascular disease (GOAL: 7,500 enrollees) and drive traffic to the Spanish-language Web site.
2. **Results:** (1) More than 15,000 people enrolled in the program in 2003, doubling the goal set at the beginning of the year, representing the strongest determinant for the program's effectiveness. (2) In 2002, the total number of participation cards returned by Hispanics was 287. In contrast, the 2003 Hispanic program resulted in 1,631 returned cards, representing more than a 500 percent response increase. (3) The Rita Moreno radio public service announcement reached more than 62 million listeners with more than 15 percent of the total number of airings in top-10 local markets. (4) More than 58,000 people contacted the AHA call center, and 246,000 patient education handbooks were distributed. (5) Numerous "Thrivers" have posted their personal testimonials on how following the program's guidelines has helped them live a healthier lifestyle.

Note the large numbers from the target audience who actually took action as a result of the campaign—enrolling in programs, returning participation cards, making calls to a help center, and posting testimonials. It is one thing to estimate the size of the audience that was exposed to the message, with some purported increased awareness resulting from the exposure, but the documentation of Objective 2 makes a far more impressive case for the good done by the campaign in improving the health of at-risk Hispanics.

Sources: The American Heart Association, in partnership with Takeda Pharmaceuticals North America, Eli Lilly and Company, and Manning Selvage & Lee, garnered a highly prized Public Relations Society of America Silver Anvil Award for this campaign.

SUMMARY

The Purpose of Evaluation

Evaluation is the measurement of results against objectives. This can enhance future performance and also establish whether the goals of management by objective have been met.

Objectives: A Prerequisite for Evaluation

Objectives should be part of any program plan. There must be agreed-upon criteria used to evaluate success in obtaining these objectives.

Current Status of Measurement and Evaluation

The proportion of public relations budgets devoted to measurement and evaluation grew over the 1990s to about 5 percent. On the most basic level, practitioners can measure message distribution and media placements. The second level would be measurement of audience awareness, comprehension, and retention. The most advanced level is the measurement of changes in attitudes, opinions, and behaviors.

Measurement of Production

Measurement of production gives management an idea of a staff's productivity and output.

Measurement of Message Exposure

Several criteria can be used to measure message exposure, including the compilation of press clippings and radio–television mentions; media impressions, or the potential audience reached; Internet hits on a Web site; advertising equivalency, which is calculated by converting news stories to the cost of a comparable amount of paid space; systematic tracking by use of computer databases; requests for additional information, often through a toll-free telephone number; and audience attendance at special events. Sometimes exposure is evaluated by determining how much it cost to reach each member of the target audience.

Measurement of Audience Awareness

The next level of evaluation is whether the audience became aware of and understood the message. Audience awareness can be measured through survey research.

Measurement of Audience Attitudes

Changes in audience attitudes can be evaluated through a baseline or benchmark study, measuring awareness and opinions before, during, and after a public relations campaign.

Measurement of Audience Action

Ultimately, public relations campaigns are evaluated based on how they help an organization achieve its objectives through changing audience behavior, whether it involves sales, fund-raising, or the election of a candidate.

Measurement of Supplemental Activities

A yearly communication audit is necessary to ensure that all publics are receiving appropriate messages. A number of techniques can be used to pretest a public relations effort: pilot tests, the split-message approach, perception analyzer systems, or the think-aloud method. Meeting and event attendance can be measured both by the number of attendees and by their behavior, which is an indicator of their acceptance of a message. Newsletter readership can be evaluated by content analysis, interest surveys, and article recall.

Case Activity: **What Would You Do?**

The Ohio Department of Transportation, with 17 rideshare groups, is planning a Rideshare Week. The objective is to increase participation in carpooling and use of mass transit during this special week. A long-term objective, of course, is to increase the number of people who use carpools or mass transit on a regular basis.

Your public relations firm has been retained to promote Ohio Rideshare Week. Your campaign will include a news conference with the governor encouraging participation, press kits, news releases, interviews on broadcast talk shows, special events, and distribution of Rideshare information booklets at major businesses.

What methods would you use to evaluate the effectiveness of your public relations efforts on behalf of Ohio Rideshare Week?

QUESTIONS for Review and Discussion

1. What is the role of stated objectives in evaluating public relations programs?
2. What primary method of evaluation do public relations people use? Is there any evidence that other methods increasingly are being used?
3. What are some general types of evaluation questions that a person should ask about a program?
4. List four ways that publicity activity is evaluated. What, if any, are the drawbacks of each one?

5. Do you think news stories about a product or service should be evaluated in terms of comparable advertising costs? Why or why not?

6. What are the advantages of systematic tracking and content analysis of news clippings?

7. How are pilot tests and split messages used to determine the suitability of a message?

8. How does measurement of message exposure differ from measurement of audience comprehension of the message?

9. How are benchmark studies used in the evaluation of public relations programs?

10. What is a communication audit?

11. What methods can be used to evaluate a company newsletter or magazine?

SUGGESTED READINGS

Austin, Erica, and Pinkleton, Bruce. *Strategic Communication Management: Planning and Managing Effective Communication Programs*. Mahwah, NJ: Lawrence Erlbaum, 2001.

Cameron, Glen T. "Does Publicity Outperform Advertising? An Experimental Test of the Third-Party Endorsement." *Journal of Public Relations Research*, Vol. 6, No. 3, 1994, pp. 185–207.

Creamer, Matthew. "Life Beyond the Clip Book." *PRWeek*, October 6, 2003, p. 17.

Creamer, Matthew. "Firms Put Emphasis on ROL Amid Competitive Climate," *PRWeek*, October 6, 2003, p. 11.

Eveland, W. P., Jr., and Dunwoody, S. "Examining Information Processing on the World Wide Web Using Think Aloud Protocols." *Media Psychology*, No. 2, 2000, pp. 219–244.

Hon, Linda Childers. "Demonstrating Effectiveness in Public Relations: Goals, Objectives, and Evaluation." *Journal of Public Relations Research*, Vol. 10, No. 2, 1998, pp. 103–135.

Hon, Linda Childers. "What Have You Done for Me Lately? Exploring Effectiveness in Public Relations." *Journal of Public Relations Research*, Vol. 9, No. 1, 1997, pp. 1–30.

Hood, Julia. "The Value of Measurement: What's the ROL on Measurement and Who Foots the Bill?" *PRWeek*, February 3, 2003, p. 15.

Hood, Julia. "Evaluating the Landscape on PR Measurement Tools." *PRWeek*, February 18, 2002, p. 7.

Iacono, Erica. "Making Measurement Count: Research and Measurement Play a Strategic Role in Defining the Success of Companies' Campaigns," *PRWeek*, November 15, 2004, pp. 1819.

Jeffrey, Angela, and Getto, Gary. "Measuring To Show the Positive Value of Public Relations," *Public Relations Tactics*, October 2003, p. 10.

Kim, Yungwook. "Measuring the Bottom-Line Impact of Corporate Public Relations." *Journalism and Mass Communication Quarterly*, Vol. 77, Summer 2000, pp. 273–291.

Lindenmann, Walter K. "Setting Minimum Standards for Measuring Public Relations Effectiveness." *Public Relations Review*, Winter 1997, pp. 391–401.

Lindenmann, Walter K., editor. *Guidelines and Standards for Measuring and Evaluating PR Effectiveness*, Gainesville, FL: Institute for Public Relations Research, University of Florida, 2003. (www.instituteforpr.com)

"More Clients, Agencies Find the Value in Measurement." *PRWeek*, May 31, 2004, p. 7.

Slater, Michael D. "Operationalizing and Analyzing Exposure: The Foundation of Media Effects Research." *Journalism and Mass Communication Quarterly*, Vol. 81, No. 1, Spring 2004, pp. 168–183.

"Still Counting Clips? More Companies Employ Metrics to Measure Their PR and Compare Themselves to the Competition." *pr reporter*, October 14, 2003, pp. 23.

"Weighing In on Pluses and Problems of Measurement." *PRWeek*, March 15, 2004, p. 7.

c h a p t e r 9

Public Opinion and Persuasion

Topics covered in this chapter include:

What Is Public Opinion?

Americans talk about public opinion as if it were a monolithic entity overshadowing the entire landscape. Editorial cartoonists humanize it in the form of John or Jane Q. Public, characters who symbolize what people think about any given issue. The reality is that public opinion is somewhat elusive and extremely difficult to measure at any given moment.

In fact, to continue the metaphor, public opinion is a number of monoliths perceived by John and Jane Q. Public, all existing at the same time. Few issues create unanimity of thought among the population, and public opinion on any issue is split in several directions. It also may come as a surprise to note that only a small number of people at any given time take part in public opinion formation on a specific issue. But once people and the press begin to speak of public opinion for an issue as an accomplished fact, it can take on its own momentum. According to Elisabeth Noelle-Neumann's spiral-of-silence theory, public opinion can be an almost tangible force on people's thinking. Noelle-Neumann defines *public opinion* as opinions on controversial issues that one can express in public without isolating oneself. This implies the element of conformity that public opinion can impose on individuals who want to avoid alienation.

There are two reasons for the profound influence of vocal segments of society and public-opinion momentum. First, psychologists have found that the public tends to be passive. It is often assumed that a small, vocal group represents the attitude of the public when, in reality, it is more accurate to say that the majority of the people are apathetic because an issue doesn't interest or affect them. Thus, "public" opposition to such issues as nuclear power, gay marriage, abortion, and gun control may really be the view of a small but significant number of concerned people.

Second, one issue may engage the attention of one part of the population, whereas another arouses the interest of another segment. Parents, for example, may form public opinion on the need for improved secondary education, whereas senior citizens constitute the bulk of public opinion on the need for increased Social Security benefits.

These two examples illustrate the most common definition of *public opinion:* "Public opinion is the sum of individual opinions on an issue *affecting* those individuals." Another popular definition states: "Public opinion is a collection of views held by persons *interested* in the subject." Thus, a person unaffected by or uninterested in (and perhaps unaware of) an issue does not contribute to public opinion on the subject.

Inherent in these definitions is the concept of *self-interest.* The following statements appear in public opinion research:

● Public opinion is the collective expression of opinion of many individuals bound into a group by common aims, aspirations, needs, and ideals.

● People who are interested or who have a vested or self-interest in an issue—or who can be affected by the outcome of the issue—form public opinion on that particular item.

● Psychologically, opinion basically is determined by self-interest. Events, words, or other stimuli affect opinion only insofar as their relationship to self-interest or a general concern is apparent.

- Opinion does not remain aroused for a long period of time unless people feel their self-interest is acutely involved or unless opinion—aroused by words—is sustained by events.

- Once self-interest is involved, opinion is not easily changed.

ON THE JOB global

Public Diplomacy: Crisis Public Relations on the Global Stage

With the rapid growth of international news media and globalization, disputes and conflicts between countries are now more than ever subject to the shaping influence of increasingly diverse publics. To examine public diplomacy, Professor Juyan Zhang and colleagues identified factors affecting international dispute resolution on the part of the U.S. government.

The dispute in question was sparked by the supposedly accidental collision of a U.S. Navy reconnaissance plane with a Chinese fighter jet that had been sent to intercept it and tail it over the South China Sea. After the collision, the U.S. spy plane made an emergency landing on the Chinese island of Hainan; the Chinese fighter jet crashed into the sea, resulting in the death of its pilot.

The collision led to a tense standoff between the two countries. China demanded an apology; the United States demanded the return of its plane and crew members. In the beginning, neither side was willing to shift toward a more accommodative stance.

The conflict was ultimately resolved after public positioning of the issue in the media and face-to-face negotiations between the two parties. Cordial relations between the two powers resumed after several months of tension. Throughout the dispute, both sides employed a welter of public relations techniques to advance the rhetoric for its side. Public opinion on both sides was enflamed as the countries competed on the world stage for credence and respect.

This dispute provides an ideal case study for understanding framing theory and conflict resolution under the dynamics of international public diplomacy, as played out in major media outlets. The following selection of headlines charts the shift from recalcitrant demands by the United States in early April to negotiation and "apology without guilt" to the ultimate joint agreement and transport of the plane from China to the United States on July 3, 2001.

- "U.S. Plane in China after It Collides with Chinese Jet."

Technicians from Lockheed Martin dismantle the American spy plane that was forced down by Chinese jet fighters. Although the Chinese government released the crew after intense negotiations with the U.S. government, part of the agreement also called for the plane to be dismantled instead of flying out of a Chinese airfield.

ON THE JOB global, *continued*

(*New York Times*, April 2, 2001, p. A1)

- "Bush Is Demanding a 'Prompt' Return of Plane and Crew." (*New York Times*, April 3, 2001, p. A1)
- "Delicate Passage with China." [Editorial] (*New York Times*, April 3, 2001, p. A18)
- "Anti-China Coalition in Congress Is Emboldened." (*New York Times*, April 4, 2001, p. A1)
- "Powell Sees No Need for Apology; Bush again Urges Return of Crew." (*New York Times*, April 4, 2001, p. A1)
- "U.S. Shies Away from Threats in Plane Standoff with China."

(*New York Times*, April 9, 2001, p. 1)

- "Powell Warns of Damage to Ties as Crisis Drags On." (*New York Times*, April 9, 2001, p. A10)
- "The Semantics; U.S. and China Look for a Way to Say 'Sorry.'" (*New York Times*, April 9, 2001, p. A1)
- "China Policy, Without Regrets." (*New York Times*, April 12, 2001, p. A29)
- "China's Bonus: Attention, and Respect." (*New York Times*, April 12, 2001, p. A13)
- "Delicate Diplomatic Dance Ends Bush's First Crisis." (*New York Times*, April 12, 2001, p. A1)

- "Ending the Spy Plane Deadlock." (*New York Times*, April 12, 2001, p. 28)
- "Flight Pattern? U.S. Claims Chinese Pilots 'maneuvering aggressively.'" (*China Online*, April 15, 2001)
- "How Bush Had to Calm Hawks in Devising a Response to China." (*New York Times*, April 13, 2001, p. A1)
- "Hitting the Great Brick Wall: U.S.–China Talks Stalled after First Day." (*China Online*, April 18, 2001)

Source: Juyan Zhang, Qi Qiu, and Glen T. Cameron. "Contingency Approach to International Dispute Resolution: A Case Study," *Public Relations Review*, Vol. 30, No. 1, Spring 2004.

Research studies also emphasize the importance of *events* in the formation of public opinion. Social scientists, for example, have made the following generalizations:

- Opinion is highly sensitive to *events* that have an impact on the public at large or a particular segment of the public.

- By and large, public opinion does not anticipate *events*. It only reacts to them.

- *Events* trigger formation of public opinion. Unless people are aware of an issue, they are not likely to be concerned or have an opinion. Awareness and discussion lead to crystallizing of opinions and often a consensus among the public.

- *Events* of unusual magnitude are likely to swing public opinion temporarily from one extreme to another. Opinion does not stabilize until the implication of the event is seen with some perspective.

One event that triggered the formation of public opinion, causing people to swing from apathy to outrage, was the French government's decision to conduct nuclear bomb tests on Mururoa Atoll in the South Pacific. After President Jacques Chirac announced the tests, an outpouring of public condemnation resounded around the world. Nations in the South Pacific, among them Australia and New Zealand, announced a boycott of French goods. The French Polynesian Independence Movement conducted massive demonstrations in Tahiti and motivated thousands of Polynesians to sign petitions. Greenpeace gained thousands of new members. Nevertheless, the French conducted the tests. A year later, public outrage over the tests was no longer a subject of media attention.

Demonstrations and rallies play a major role in creating public awareness and persuading individuals that their cause is valid. Here, supporters of John Kerry wait for results during an election night rally.

People also have more opinions, and are able to form them more easily, with respect to goals than with the methods necessary to reach those goals. For example, according to polls, there is fairly strong public opinion for improving the quality of the nation's schools. However, there is little agreement on how to do this. One group advocates higher salaries for "master" teachers, another endorses substantial tax increases for school operations. A third group urges more rigorous standards, such as the No Child Left Behind Act. All three groups, plus others with still more solutions, make up public opinion on the subject.

Opinion Leaders as Catalysts

Public opinion on an issue may have its roots in self-interest or in events, but the primary catalyst is public discussion. Only in this way does opinion begin to crystallize, and pollsters can measure it.

Serving as catalysts for the formation of public opinion are people who are knowledgeable and articulate about specific issues. They are called *opinion leaders*. Sociologists describe them as (1) highly interested in a subject or issue, (2) better informed on an issue than the average person, (3) avid consumers of mass media, (4) early adopters of new ideas, and (5) good organizers who can get other people to take action.

Types of Leaders

Sociologists traditionally have defined two types of leaders. First are the *formal opinion leaders*, so called because of their positions as elected officials, presidents of companies, or heads of membership groups. News reporters often ask them for statements when a specific issue relates to their areas of responsibility or concern. People in formal leadership positions also are called *power leaders*.

Second are the *informal opinion leaders*, those who have clout with peers because of some special characteristic. They may be role models who are admired and emulated or opinion leaders who can exert peer pressure on others to go along with something. In general, informal opinion leaders exert considerable influence on their peer groups by being highly informed, articulate, and credible on particular issues.

A survey of 20,000 Americans by the Roper Organization found that only 10 to 12 percent of the general public are opinion leaders. These "influentials," those whom other people seek out for advice, fit the profile of (1) being active in the community, (2) having a college degree, (3) earning relatively high incomes, (4) regularly reading newspapers and magazines, (5) actively participating in recreational activities, and (6) showing environmental concern by recycling.

Regis McKenna, a marketing communications expert responsible for the original launch of the Apple Macintosh, likes to think of opinion leaders as luminaries because "There are about 20 to 30 key people in every industry who have major influence on trends, standards, and an organization's reputation." He also knows that journalists seek quotes from key opinion leaders in an industry whenever a new product is introduced.

The Flow of Opinion

Many public relations campaigns, particularly those in the public affairs area, concentrate on identifying and reaching key opinion leaders who are pivotal to the success or failure of an idea or project. In the 1940s, sociologists Elihu Katz and Paul Lazarsfeld discovered the importance of opinion leaders during a study of how people chose candidates in an election. They found that the mass media had minimal influence on electoral choices, but voters did rely on person-to-person communication with formal and informal opinion leaders.

These findings became known as the *two-step flow theory of communication*. Although later research confirmed that it really was a multiple-step flow, the basic idea remained intact. Public opinion is really formed by the views of people who have taken the time to sift information, evaluate it, and form an opinion that is expressed to others.

The *multiple-step flow model* is graphically illustrated by a series of concentric circles. In the epicenter of action are opinion makers. They derive large amounts of information from the mass media and other sources and then share that information with people in the adjoining concentric circle, who are labeled the "attentive public." The latter are interested in the issue but rely on opinion leaders to provide synthesized information and interpretation. The outer ring consists of the "inattentive public." They are unaware of or uninterested in the issue and remain outside the opinion-formation process. The multiple-step flow theory, however, means that some will eventually become interested in, or at least aware of, the issue.

The Life Cycle of Public Opinion

Public opinion and persuasion are important catalysts in the formation of a public issue and its ultimate resolution. The natural evolution of an issue involves five stages:

1. **Definition of the issue.** Activist and special interest groups raise an issue, perhaps a protest against scenic areas being threatened by logging or strip mining. These groups have no formal power but serve as "agenda stimuli" for the media that cover controversy and conflict. Visual opportunities for television coverage occur when activists hold rallies and demonstrations.

2. **Involvement of opinion leaders.** Through media coverage, the issue is put on the public agenda and people become aware of it. Opinion leaders begin to discuss the issue and perhaps see it as being symbolic of broader environmental issues. According to research in Roper Reports, 10 to 12 percent of the population that the magazine calls "The Influentials" drive public opinion and consumer trends.

3. **Public awareness.** As public awareness grows, the issue becomes a matter of public discussion and debate, garnering extensive media coverage. The issue is simplified by the media into "them versus us." Suggested solutions tend to be at either end of the spectrum.

4. **Government/regulatory involvement.** Public consensus begins to build for a resolution as government/regulatory involvement occurs. Large groups identify with some side of the issue. Demand grows for government to act.

5. **Resolution.** The resolution stage begins as people with authority (elected officials) draft legislation or interpret existing rules and regulations to make a statement. A decision is made to protect the scenic areas or to reach a compromise with advocates of development. If some groups remain unhappy, however, the cycle may repeat itself.

The Role of Mass Media

One traditional way that public relations personnel reach opinion leaders and other key publics is via the mass media—radio, television, newspapers, and magazines. *Mass media*, as the term implies, means that information from a public relations source can be efficiently and rapidly disseminated to literally millions of people.

Although journalists often argue that they rarely use public relations materials, one has only to look at the daily newspaper to see the quote from the press officer at the sheriff's department, the article on a new computer product, the statistics from the local real estate board, or even the after-game interview with the winning quarterback. In almost all cases, a public relations source at the organization provided the information or arranged the interview. Indeed, Oscar H. Gandy, Jr., of the University of Pennsylvania says that up to 50 percent of what the media carry comes from public relations sources in the form of "information subsidies."

Gandy and other theorists have concluded that public relations people—via the mass media—are major players in forming public opinion because they often provide the mass media with the information in the first place. This opinion also is echoed by Elizabeth L. Toth and Robert L. Heath, authors of *Rhetorical and Critical Approaches to Public Relations*. They say, "Few professions have so many skilled and talented individuals contributing to the thoughts, actions, and policies of our nation."

To better understand how public relations people inform the public and shape public opinion via the mass media, it is necessary to review briefly several theories about mass media effects.

Agenda-Setting Theory

One of the early theories, pioneered by Max McCombs and Don Shaw, contends that media content sets the agenda for public discussion. People tend to talk about what they see or hear on the 6 o'clock news or read on the front page of the newspaper. Media, through the selection of stories and headlines, tell the public what to think about, but not necessarily what to think. The U.S. invasion of Iraq, for example, was high on the media agenda for many months, but public opinion polls indicated a variety of viewpoints on the subject.

Social scientist Joseph Klapper calls this the *limited-effects model* of mass media. He postulates, "Mass media ordinarily does not serve as a necessary and sufficient cause for audience effects, but rather functions among and through a nexus of mediating factors and influence." Such factors may include the way that opinion leaders analyze and interpret the information provided by the mass media. More recently, Wayne Wanta and others have explored second-level agenda-setting effects, finding evidence that the media not only set an agenda, but also convey a set of attributes about the subject of the news. These positive or negative attributes are remembered and color public opinion.

From a public relations standpoint, even getting a subject on the media agenda is an accomplishment that advances organizational goals. Sales of Apple's iPod rose as the media reported its success and the public became aware of this "hot" item. Research is under way to document how public relations efforts can build the media agenda, and thus affect public opinion.

Media-Dependency Theory

Although the agenda-setting function of the media is generally valid, other research indicates that mass media can have a "moderate" or even "powerful" effect on the formation of opinions and attitudes. When people have no prior information or attitude disposition regarding a subject, the mass media play a role in telling people what to think.

Mass media effects also are increased when people cannot verify information through personal experience or knowledge. They are highly dependent on the media for information. This tendency is particularly evident in crisis situations, which also often leave reporter and editor dependent on official spokespersons for information as the story breaks. Researchers Debbie Steele and Kirk Hallahan found: "Official sources enjoy an advantage in the early phases of a crisis or issue, particularly when media and others are still in the discovery phase of coverage and the primary emphasis is merely to identify the extent of the problem." Therefore, if much of this crucial initial information comes from official spokespersons of organizations, it's an opportunity for public relations to shape the tone and content of a story, to put a particular emphasis on the story. In sum, media dependency often occurs when the media are, in turn, quite dependent on public relations sources.

Framing Theory

The term *framing* has a long history in mass media research. Traditionally, framing was related to journalists and how they selected certain facts, themes, treatments, and even words to "frame" a story. According to researchers Julie L. Andsager at Washington State University and Angela Powers at Northern Illinois University, "Mass media scholars have long argued that it is important to understand the ways in which journalistic framing of issues occurs because such framing impacts public understanding and, consequently, policy formation." For example, how media frame the debate over health care and the role of HMOs often plays a major role in public perceptions of the problem.

Increasingly, however, scholars are applying framing theory to public relations efforts. One research paper by James Tankard and Bill Israel of the University of Texas was titled, "PR Goes to War: The Effects of Public Relations Campaigns on Media Framing of the Kuwait and Bosnian Crises." Their basic contention was that the governments involved in the conflicts used public relations professionals to help frame the issues involved. The issues, as framed by public relations professionals were then picked up by the press.

Tankard and Israel point out that the media dependency of most Americans—who often have little direct knowledge of these places or the complex issues involved—means that they accept the media's version of reality, which originally came from what the two researchers describe as "special interest groups or other groups with particular causes."

Most public relations personnel rarely find themselves framing the issues of an international conflict, but they do exercise framing or positioning strategies on any number of products and services. When Edelman Worldwide, for example, was considering strategy for the launch of Apple's iMac computer, one of the strong themes (or frames) was that Apple was on the way back to prosperity after several years of massive losses and erosion of customer support. Indeed, one headline in a daily newspaper proclaimed, "Apple Regains Its Stride." Such framing obviously bolsters investor and consumer confidence in the company.

Persuasion: Pervasive in Our Lives

Persuasion has been around since the dawn of human history. It was formalized as a concept more than 2,000 years ago by the Greeks, who made *rhetoric*, the art of using language effectively and persuasively, part of their educational system. Aristotle was the first to set down the ideas of *ethos*, *logos*, and *pathos*, which roughly translate as "source credibility," "logical argument," and "emotional appeal."

More recent scholars, such as Richard Perloff, author of *The Dynamics of Persuasion*, say, "Persuasion is an activity or process in which a communicator attempts to induce a change in the belief, attitude, or behavior of another person or group of persons through the transmission of a message in a context in which the persuadee has some degree of free choice."

Such a definition is consistent with the role of public relations professionals in today's society. Indeed, Professor Robert Heath of the University of Houston says:

> . . . public relations professionals are influential rhetors. They design, place, and repeat messages on behalf of sponsors on an array of topics that shape views of government, charitable organizations, institutions of public education, products and con-

sumerism, capitalism, labor, health, and leisure. These professionals speak, write, and use visual images to discuss topics and take stances on public policies at the local, state, and federal levels.

The Dominant View of Public Relations

The dominant view of public relations, in fact, is one of persuasive communication actions performed on behalf of clients, according to Professors Dean Kruckeberg at the University of Northern Iowa and Ken Starck at the University of Iowa. Oscar Gandy, Jr., adds that ". . . the primary role of public relations is one of purposeful, self-interested communications." And Edward Bernays even called public relations the "engineering" of consent to create "a favorable and positive climate of opinion toward the individual, product, institution or idea which is represented." See Chapter 2 for definitions by Edward L. Bernays.

To accomplish this goal, public relations personnel use a variety of techniques to reach and influence their audiences. At the same time, persuasion or rhetoric should be considered more than a one-way flow of information, argument, and influence. In the best sense, Toth and Heath say that persuasion should be a dialogue between points of view in the marketplace of public opinion, where any number of persuaders are hawking their wares.

Indeed, persuasion is an integral part of democratic society. It is the freedom of speech used by every individual and organization to influence opinion, understanding, judgment, and action.

Uses of Persuasion

Persuasion is used to (1) change or neutralize hostile opinions, (2) crystallize latent opinions and positive attitudes, and (3) conserve favorable opinions.

The most difficult persuasive task is to turn hostile opinions into favorable ones. There is much truth to the adage, "Don't confuse me with the facts; my mind is made up." Once people have decided, for instance, that HMOs are making excessive profits or that a nonprofit agency is wasting public donations, they tend to ignore or disbelieve any contradictory information. Everyone, as Walter Lippmann has described, has pictures in his or her head based on an

ON THE JOB

insights

A Sampler on Persuasion

A number of research studies have contributed to a basic understanding of persuasion concepts. Here are some basic ideas from the text *Public Communication Campaigns*, edited by Ronald E. Rice and William J. Paisley:

- Positive appeals are generally more effective than negative appeals for retention of the message and actual compliance.

- Radio and television messages tend to be more persuasive than print, but if the message is complex, better comprehension is achieved through print media.

- Strong emotional appeals and fear arousal are most effective when the audience has minimal concern about or interest in the topic.

- High fear appeals are effective only when a readily available action can be taken to eliminate the threat.

- Logical appeals, using facts and figures, are better for highly educated, sophisticated audiences than strong emotional appeals.

- Altruistic need, like self-interest, can be a strong motivator. Men are more willing to get a physical checkup to protect their families than to protect themselves.

- A celebrity or an attractive model is most effective when the audience has low involvement, the theme is simple, and broadcast channels are used. An exciting spokesperson attracts attention to a message that would otherwise be ignored.

individual perception of reality. People generalize from personal experience and what peers tell them. For example, if a person has an encounter with a rude clerk, the inclination is to generalize that the entire department store chain is not very good.

Persuasion is much easier if the message is compatible with a person's general disposition toward a subject. If a person tends to identify Toyota as a company with a good reputation, he or she may express this feeling by purchasing one of its cars. Nonprofit agencies usually crystallize the public's latent inclination to aid the less fortunate by asking for a donation. Both examples illustrate the reason that organizations strive to have a good reputation—it is translated into sales and donations. The concept of message channeling will be discussed in more detail later in the chapter.

The easiest form of persuasion is communication that reinforces favorable opinions. Public relations people, by providing a steady stream of reinforcing messages, keep the reservoir of goodwill in sound condition. More than one organization has survived a major problem because public esteem for it tended to minimize current difficulties. Continual efforts to maintain the reservoir of goodwill is called *preventive public relations*, and it is the most effective type of public relations.

Factors in Persuasive Communication

A number of factors are involved in persuasive communication, and the public relations practitioner should be knowledgeable about each one. The following is a brief discussion of (1) audience analysis, (2) source credibility, (3) appeal to self-interest, (4) clarity of message, (5) timing and context, (6) audience participation, (7) suggestions for action, (8) content and structure of messages, and (9) persuasive speaking.

Audience Analysis

Knowledge of audience characteristics such as beliefs, attitudes, concerns, and lifestyles is an essential part of persuasion. It helps the communicator tailor messages that are salient, answer a felt need, and provide a logical course of action.

Basic demographic information, readily available through census data, can help determine an audience's gender, income level, education, ethnic background, and age groupings. Other data, often prepared by marketing departments, give information on a group's buying habits, disposable income, and ways of spending leisure time.

Polls and surveys, discussed in Chapter 5, tap a target audience's attitudes, opinions, and concerns. Such research tells about the public's resistance to some ideas, as well as its predisposition to support others. Recycling programs, for example, made a slow start in the early 1990s because the public resisted changing its habit of throwing everything into the same garbage container. Yet surveys showed that although the public was concerned about the environment, "convenience" was king. The only way to change habits was to make it easy for homeowners to recycle by providing sorting bins that were regularly picked up. Many cities also opened neighborhood recycling centers that paid people for bottles and cans. Today, recycling is the norm. The concepts of making suggestions for action and self-interest will be discussed shortly.

Another audience-analysis tool is *psychographics*. This method attempts to classify people by lifestyle, attitudes, and beliefs. The Values and Lifestyle Program, popularly known as VALS, was developed by SRI International, a research organization in Menlo Park, California. VALS is routinely used in public relations to help communicators structure persuasive messages to different elements of the population. A good illustration is the way Burson-Marsteller used VALS for its client, the National Turkey Foundation. The problem was simple: how to encourage turkey consumption throughout the year, not just at Thanksgiving and Christmas.

One element of the public was called "Sustainers and Survivors;" VALS identified them as low-income, poorly educated, often elderly people who ate at erratic hours, consumed inexpensive foods, and seldom ate out. Another element was the "Belongers," who were highly family oriented and served foods in traditional ways. The "Achievers" were those who were more innovative and willing to try new foods.

Burson-Marsteller tailored a strategy for each group. For Survivors and Sustainers, the message stressed bargain cuts of turkey that could be stretched into a full meal. The message for Belongers focused on cuts that signaled turkey, such as drumsticks. Achievers, who were better educated and had higher income levels, received the message about gourmet cuts and new, innovative recipes.

This segmentation of the consumer public into various VALS lifestyles enabled Burson-Marsteller to select appropriate media for specific story ideas. An article placed in *True Experience*, a publication reaching the demographic characteristics of Survivors and Sustainers, was headlined "A Terrific Budget-Stretching Meal." Articles in *Better Homes and Gardens* with such titles as "Streamlined Summer Classics" and stories about barbecued turkey on the Fourth of July were used to reach Belongers. Articles for Achievers in *Food and Wine* magazine and *Gourmet* included recipes for turkey salad and turkey tetrazzini.

Such audience analysis, coupled with suitably tailored messages in the appropriate media outlets, is the technique of *channeling*. Persuasive messages are more effective when they take into account the audience's lifestyles, beliefs, and concerns.

ON THE JOB

insights

Appeals That Move People to Act

Persuasive messages often include information that appeals to an audience's self-interest. Here is a list of persuasive message themes:

- Make money
- Save money
- Save time
- Avoid effort
- More comfort
- Better health
- Cleaner
- Escape pain
- Gain praise
- Be popular
- Be loved/accepted
- Keep possessions
- More enjoyment
- Satisfy curiosity
- Protect family
- Be stylish
- Have beautiful things
- Satisfy appetite
- Be like others
- Avoid trouble
- Avoid criticism
- Be an individual
- Protect reputation
- Be safe
- Make work easier
- Be secure

Source: Charles Marsh, "Fly Too Close to the Sun." *Communication World*, September 1992, p. 24.

Source Credibility

A message is more believable to the intended audience if the source has *credibility*. This was Aristotle's concept of *ethos*, mentioned earlier, and it explains why organizations use a variety of spokespeople, depending on the message and the audience.

The California Strawberry Advisory Board, for example, arranged for a home economist to appear on television talk shows to discuss nutrition and to demonstrate easy-to-follow strawberry recipes. The viewers, primarily homemakers, identified with the representative and found her highly credible. By the same token, a manufacturer of sunscreen lotion uses a professor of pharmacology and a past president of the State Pharmacy Board to discuss the scientific merits of sunscreen versus suntan lotions.

The Three Factors.   Source credibility is based on three factors. One is *expertise*. Does the audience perceive the person as an expert on the subject? Companies, for example, use engineers and scientists to answer news conference questions about how an engineering process works or whether an ingredient in the manufacturing process of a product presents a potential hazard.

The second component is *sincerity*. Does the person come across as believing what he or she is saying? Bono, leader of the Irish rockgroup U2, may not be considered an expert on all the products or causes he endorses, but he does get high ratings for sincerity.

The third component, which is even more elusive, is *charisma*. Is the individual attractive, self-assured, and articulate, projecting an image of competence and leadership?

Ideally, a source will exhibit all three attributes. Steve Jobs, president of Apple, is a good example. He is highly credible as an expert on Apple products because he is one of the company's founders and also a "geek" in his own right. In countless media interviews and trade show presentations, he comes across as a candid, open individual who really believes in the company's products. Jobs also has charisma; he is self-assured, confident, and articulate. His standard uniform—the open-neck shirt, the vest, and the designer jeans—gives him additional aura as a legendary figure in the computer industry.

Not every organization, however, has a Steve Jobs for its president. Depending on the message and the audience, various spokespersons can be used and quoted for source credibility. A news release for a new product, for example, might quote the director of research and development (R&D) for the company. If the information is about an organization's financial picture, the most credible person would be the chief executive officer (CEO) or the vice president of finance, primarily because of perceived expertise.

Expertise is less important than sincerity and charisma if celebrities are used as spokespersons. Their primary purpose is to call attention to the product or service. Another purpose is to associate the celebrity's popularity with the product. This technique is called *transfer*; it is discussed later in this chapter as a propaganda device.

Problems with Celebrities.   Using celebrities has its problems, however. One is the increasing number of celebrity endorsements to the point that the public sometimes can't remember who endorses what. A second problem can be overexposure of a celebrity, such as Tiger Woods, who earns millions of dollars annually from endorsing more than a dozen products.

The third problem occurs when an endorser's actions undercut the product or service. Singer Britney Spears, for example, had a $108 million contract to exclusively promote Pepsi, but British tabloids photographed her twice in one month swigging a Coca-Cola. The German unit of America Online also had a problem after signing up tennis legend Boris Becker for a series of commercials portraying him as a "family man" who discovers how easy it is to get hooked up with AOL. However, shortly after the campaign started, Becker divorced his wife. Another German company hired a famous soccer coach as a celebrity endorser, but then he flunked a drug test and was fired from the national team. "Anytime an advertiser pins its image to a star, whether an athlete or an actor, it takes a chance that reality won't live up to the storyboard," says Christina White, a reporter for the *Wall Street Journal*.

In summary, the use of various sources for credibility depends, in large part, on the type of audience being reached. That is why audience analysis is the first step in formulating persuasive messages.

Appeal to Self-Interest

Self-interest was described during an earlier discussion about the formation of public opinion. Publics become involved in issues or pay attention to messages that appeal to their psychological or economic needs.

Publicity for a personal computer can serve as an example. A news release to the trade press serving the computer industry might focus on the technical proficiency of the equipment. The audience, of course, consists of engineers and computer programmers. A brochure prepared for the public, however, may emphasize how the computer can (1) help people keep track of personal finances, (2) assist youngsters in becoming better students, (3) fit into a small space, and (4) offer good value. Consumers are interested in how the personal computer can make life easier for them.

PR CASEBOOK

Can Sex Sell Mutual Funds?

Financial surveys are not exactly stimulating reading, but adding a little sex appeal helps.

Even fictional figures such as Carrie Bradshaw, can become endorsers of products.

Oppenheimer Funds used the allure of *Sex and the City's* Carrie Bradshaw to enliven the results of a survey on the financial planning attitudes of Generation-X women.

According to the financial firm, many women are showing signs of "Carrie Bradshaw Syndrome" when it comes to their finances. The survey, for example, revealed that 54 percent of the single women surveyed are likely to acquire 30 pairs of shoes before saving $30,000 toward their retirement. Another 50 percent said at this time in life, money is for spending, not for saving.

Oppenheimer sent out a news release and a complete copy of the survey results to the media. One major result: the *New York Times* ran a feature story on the "Carrie Bradshaw Syndrome." Apparently, Carrie truly represents Generation-X women. A quick review of the new Web page for Carrie on the TBS cable channel's Web site showcases Carrie as a "Fashionista," not as a fiscally conservative investor (tbssuperstation.com/series/sexandthecity).

Charitable organizations don't sell products, but they do need volunteers and donations. This is accomplished by careful structuring of messages that appeal to self-interest. This is not to say that altruism is dead. Thousands of people give freely of their time and money to charitable organizations, but they do receive something

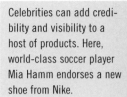
Celebrities can add credibility and visibility to a host of products. Here, world-class soccer player Mia Hamm endorses a new shoe from Nike.

in return, or they would not do it. The "something in return" may be (1) self-esteem, (2) the opportunity to make a contribution to society, (3) recognition from peers and the community, (4) a sense of belonging, (5) ego gratification, or even (6) a tax deduction. Public relations people understand psychological needs and rewards, and that is why there is constant recognition of volunteers in newsletters and at award banquets. (Further discussion of volunteerism appears in Chapter 20.)

Sociologist Harold Lasswell says that people are motivated by eight basic appeals. They are power, respect, well-being, affection, wealth, skill, enlightenment, and physical and mental vitality. Psychologist Abraham Maslow, in turn, says that any appeal to self-interest must be based on a hierarchy of needs. The first and lowest level involves basic needs such as food, water, shelter, and even transportation to and from work. The second level consists of security needs. People need to feel secure in their jobs, safe in their homes, and confident about their retirement. At the third level are "belonging" needs—people seek association with others. This is why individuals join organizations.

"Love" needs comprise the fourth level in the hierarchy. Humans have a need to be wanted and loved—fulfilling the desire for self-esteem. At the fifth and highest level in Maslow's hierarchy are self-actualization needs. Once the first four needs have been met, Maslow says that people are free to achieve maximum personal potential; for example, through traveling extensively or perhaps becoming experts on orchids.

Maslow's hierarchy helps to explain why some public information campaigns have difficulty getting the message across to people classified in the VALS lifestyle categories as "Survivors" and "Sustainers." Efforts to inform minorities and low-income groups about AIDS provide an example of this problem. For these groups, the potential danger of AIDS is less compelling than the day-to-day problems of poverty and satisfying the basic needs of food and shelter.

The challenge for public relations personnel, as creators of persuasive messages, is to tailor information to fill or reduce a need. Social scientists have said that success in persuasion largely depends on accurate assessment of audience needs and self-interests.

PR CASEBOOK

Gary Condit Flunks Persuasion 101

Rep. Gary Condit of California found himself the focus of national media attention after a student intern in Washington, D.C., who was intimately involved with the married man disappeared.

At the beginning, Condit said that he had only met Chandra Levy in a social setting. Then, as police gathered more information and the Levy family hired a detective (as well as a public relations firm to keep their daughter in the news), Condit decided to stonewall and not answer any media questions. The media had a field day; the story was a great circulation builder: a politician, a coed, an affair, and a mystery (What happened to Chandra?).

After some weeks, Condit's advisors (including lawyers and public relations professionals who were experts in damage control) finally convinced Condit that he should explain himself by doing a national interview on ABC's *PrimeTime* with a highly credible reporter, Connie Chung. The two questions on everyone's mind, including Chung's, were (1) Did you have an affair with Chandra Levy? and (2) Did you kill her?

Condit, within a few minutes, lost all credibility. He refused to answer the first question, nor did he express much sympathy or even remorse that she was missing. In terms of the second question, he insisted that he was not involved in her disappearance, but didn't offer much believable information. In sum, Condit was castigated by viewers for being evasive, robotic in his answers, and totally lacking in credibility.

Jeffrey Graubard, president of his own firm in New York, summed it up best in a letter to *PRWeek*. He said, "Condit should have affected a more informal and empathic pose, admitted adultery, and reminded Chung that philandering is a deeply troubling private issue, but not criminal. He could have apologized for withholding information, concluding that he'd seen his miscalculation and is now fully cooperating."

Sandra Sokoloff, senior vice president of Magnet Communications in New York, added, "While Condit's media trainers certainly hammered some key messages into his head, what they failed to realize is that messages are a means to help frame answers to questions, not a tactic to avoid them. . . . Condit's messages did not achieve any of this. Rather than reaching out and appeasing, his messages just raised another level of suspicion and negativity."

Rep. Gary Condit faces tough questioning from the press about the disappearance of Chandra Levy, a Washington intern, after he admits having a romantic relationship with her. Her body eventually was found in a local park.

Clarity of Message

Many messages fail because the audience finds the message unnecessarily complex in content or language. The most persuasive messages are direct, simply expressed, and contain only one primary idea. The management expert Peter Drucker once said, "An innovation, to be effective, has to be simple and it has to be focused. It should do only one thing, otherwise it confuses." The same can be said for the content of any message.

Public relations personnel should always ask two questions: "What do I want the audience to do with the message?" and "Will the audience understand the message?" Although persuasion theory says that people retain information better and form stronger opinions when they are asked to draw their own conclusions, this doesn't negate the importance of explicitly stating what action an audience should take. Is it to buy the product, visit a showroom, write a member of Congress, make a $10 donation, or what?

If an explicit request for action is not part of the message, members of the audience may not understand what is expected of them. Public relations firms, when making a presentation to a potential client, always ask for the account at the end of the presentation.

Timing and Context

A message is more persuasive if environmental factors support the message or if the message is received within the context of other messages and situations with which the individual is familiar. These factors are called *timing and context*.

Information from a utility on how to conserve energy is more salient if the consumer has just received the January heating bill. A pamphlet on a new stock offering is more effective if it accompanies an investor's dividend check. A citizens' group lobbying for a stoplight gets more attention if a major accident has just occurred at the intersection.

Political candidates are aware of public concerns and avidly read polls to learn what issues are most important to voters. If the polls indicate that crime and unemployment are key issues, the candidate begins to use these issues—and to offer his or her proposals—in the campaign.

Timing and context also play an important role in achieving publicity in the mass media. Public relations personnel, as pointed out earlier in the text, should read newspapers and watch television news programs to find out what media gatekeepers consider newsworthy. A manufacturer of a locking device for computer files got extensive media coverage about its product simply because its release followed a rash of news stories about thieves' gaining access to bank accounts through computers. Media gatekeepers found the product newsworthy within the context of actual news events.

The value of information and its newsworthiness are based on timing and context. Public relations professionals disseminate information at the time it is most highly valued.

Audience Participation

A change in attitude or reinforcement of beliefs is enhanced by *audience involvement and participation*.

An organization, for example, may have employees discuss productivity in a quality-control circle. Management may already have figured out what is needed, but if workers are involved in the problem solving, they often come up with the same solution or even a better one. And, from a persuasion standpoint, the employees are more committed to making the solution work because it came from them—not as a policy or order handed down by higher management.

Participation also can take the form of samples. Many companies distribute product samples so consumers can conveniently try them without expense. A consumer who samples the product and makes a judgment about its quality is more likely to purchase it.

Activist groups use participation as a way of helping people actualize their beliefs. Not only do rallies and demonstrations give people a sense of belonging, but the act of participation reinforces their beliefs. Asking people to do something—conserve energy, collect donations, or picket—activates a form of self-persuasion and commitment.

Suggestions for Action

A principle of persuasion is that people endorse ideas only if they are accompanied by a proposed action from the sponsor. Recommendations for action must be clear. Public relations practitioners must not only ask people to conserve energy, for instance, but also furnish detailed data and ideas on how to do it.

A campaign conducted by Pacific Gas & Electric Company provides an example. The utility inaugurated a Zero Interest Program (ZIP) to offer customers a way to implement energy-saving ideas. The program involved several components:

- **Energy kit.** A telephone hotline was established and widely publicized so interested customers could order an energy kit detailing what the average homeowner could do to reduce energy use.

- **Service bureau.** The company, at no charge, sent representatives to homes to check the efficiency of water heaters and furnaces, measure the amount of insulation, and check doors and windows for drafts.

- **ZIP.** The cost of making a home more energy efficient was funded by zero-interest loans to any qualified customer.

Content and Structure of Messages

A number of techniques can make a message more persuasive. Writers throughout history have emphasized some information while downplaying or omitting other pieces of information. Thus, they addressed both the content and structure of messages.

Expert communicators continue to use a number of devices, including (1) drama, (2) statistics, (3) surveys and polls, (4) examples, (5) testimonials, (6) mass media endorsements, and (7) emotional appeals.

Drama.   Because everyone likes a good story, the first task of a communicator is to get the audience's attention. This is often accomplished by graphically illustrating an event or situation. Newspapers often dramatize a story to get reader interest in an issue. Thus, we read about the family evicted from its home in a story on the increase in bankruptcies; the old man who is starving because of welfare red tape; or the worker disabled because of toxic waste. In newsrooms, this is called *humanizing an issue*.

Drama also is used in public relations. Relief organizations, in particular, attempt to galvanize public concern and donations through stark black-and-white photographs and emotionally charged descriptions of suffering and disease.

A more mundane use of drama is the so-called *application story*, sent to the trade press. This is sometimes called the *case study technique*, in which a manufacturer prepares an article on how an individual or a company is using the product. IBM, for example, provides a number of application stories about the unique ways in which its products are being used.

Statistics. People are impressed by statistics. Use of numbers can convey objectivity, size, and importance in a credible way that can influence public opinion. Caterpillar, for example, got considerable media publicity for its new 797 mining dump truck by combining statistics and some humor. In the news release for the largest truck in the world, it announced that the bed of the truck was so large that it could haul the following payloads: 4 blue whales, 217 taxicabs, 1,200 grand pianos, and 23,490 Furby dolls.

Surveys and Polls. Airlines and auto manufacturers, in particular, use the results of surveys and polls to show that they are first in "customer satisfaction," "service," and even "leg room" or "cargo space." The most credible surveys are those conducted by independent research organizations, but readers still should read the fine print to see what is being compared and rated. Is an American-made auto, for example, being compared only with other U.S. cars or with foreign cars as well?

Examples. A statement of opinion can be more persuasive if some examples are given. A school board can often get support for a bond issue by citing examples of how the present facilities are inadequate for student needs. Environmental groups tell how other communities have successfully established greenbelts when requesting a city council to do the same. Automakers promote the durability of their vehicles by citing their performance on a test track or in a road race.

Testimonials. A form of source credibility, testimonials can be either explicit or implied. A campaign to curtail alcohol and drug abuse may feature a pop singer as a spokesperson or have a young woman talk about being paralyzed and disfigured as the victim of a drunk driver. Implied testimonials also can be effective. Proclamations by mayors and governors establishing Red Cross Day or Library Week are implied testimonials. The testimonial as a propaganda device is discussed later in the chapter.

Endorsements. In addition to endorsements by paid celebrities, products and services benefit from favorable statements by experts in what is called a *third-party endorsement*. A well-known medical specialist may publicly state that a particular brand of exercise equipment is best for general conditioning. Organizations such as the American Dental Association and the National Safety Council also endorse products and services.

Media endorsements, usually unpaid, can come through editorials, reviews, surveys, and news stories. A daily newspaper may endorse a political candidate, review restaurants and entertainment events, and even compile a survey ranking the best coffeehouses. The media also produce news stories about new products and services

Dear Friend,

For polar bear cubs like Snowflake, life starts out as a nearly impossible challenge.

Snowflake

Born with her sister Aurora in the frigid darkness of the Arctic winter, Snowflake weighed only about a pound at birth, the size of a cell phone. For months, she and her sister didn't leave the den where they were born, a small cave that their mother had dug in a snow bank. Helpless, they depended on their mother for the essentials of life — her body warmth and her nutrient-rich milk.

Snowflake and her sister will stay with their mother for more than two years. She will feed them, teach them to hunt, and protect them from predators.

With the fierce maternal protection of her mother, cuddly little Snowflake will grow up to become one of the most awesome animals on Earth.

But now, a looming new threat could cut short the lives of precious little polar bear cubs like Snowflake.

You see, the powerful oil lobby and its political allies in Congress are pushing to open Snowflake's home — the Arctic National Wildlife Refuge — to environmentally destructive oil and gas drilling. The Refuge's coastal plain is America's most important on-shore polar bear nursery, and scientist warn that the habitat destruction, pollution and other impacts of the plan could be deadly to the bears.

That's why I'm asking you to please "adopt" a polar bear cub like Snowflake by joining Defenders of Wildlife today with a contribution of $15 or more.

Defenders of Wildlife is helping lead the fight to save America's greatest wildlife sanctuary for Snowflake and the other wild animals that call it home. But to succeed, we urgently need the help of concerned individuals like you to overcome the enormous money and political clout of the oil lobby.

And we must act now — because politicians are already moving to hand over this unique natural treasure to Big Oil. Congressman Don Young (R-Alaska) — who decorates his office with animal skins — has already introduced legislation to allow drilling. The pristine 19 million-acre Arctic Refuge is the last place in North America where Arctic wildlife is fully protected. And the Refuge's coastal plain, often referred to as "America's Serengeti," is the biological heart of this

(over, please)

Defenders of Wildlife • 1101 Fourteenth Street, N.W. • Room 1400 • Washington, D.C. 20005
www.defenders.org • www.kidsplanet.org

Your continued activism is important. Please call your representatives in Washington to let them know you support the preservation of wildlife and its habitat. You can contact them at 202-224-3121. Thank you.

Successful persuasion by direct mail depends heavily on an eye-catching opening that persuades the recipient to read on rather than toss the letter aside. Letters such as this have a strong emotional appeal and often stir a reader's high concern for a particular situation.

that, because of the media's perceived objectivity, are considered a form of third-party endorsement. The idea is that media coverage bestows legitimacy and newsworthiness on a product or service. When the *Washington Post* reported that President Clinton's favorite burger was a soybean-based vegetarian product made by Boca Burger Company, sales of the product immediately boomed.

Emotional Appeals.   Fund-raising letters from nonprofit groups, in particular, use this persuasive device. Amnesty International, an organization dedicated to human rights and fighting state terrorism, began one direct-mail letter with the following message in large red type:

"We Are God in Here . . . "
. . . That's what the guards taunted the prisoner with as they applied electrical shocks to her body while she lay handcuffed to the springs of a metal bed. Her cries were echoed by the screams of other victims and the laughter of their torturers.

Such emotional appeals can do much to galvanize the public into action, but they also can backfire. Such appeals raise ego defenses, and people don't like to be told that in some way they are responsible. A description of suffering makes many people uncomfortable, and, rather than take action, they may tune out the message. A relief organization once ran full-page advertisements in magazines with the headline "You Can Help Maria Get Enough to Eat . . . Or You Can Turn the Page." Researchers say that most people, their ego defenses raised, turn the page and mentally refuse to acknowledge that they even saw the ad. In sum, emotional appeals that attempt to lay a guilt trip on the audience are not very successful.

Strong fear arousals also can cause people to tune out, especially if they feel that they can't do anything about the problem anyway. Research indicates, however, that a moderate fear arousal, accompanied by a relatively easy solution, is effective. A moderate fear arousal is: "What would happen if your child were thrown through the windshield in an accident?" The message concludes with the suggestion that a baby, for protection and safety, should be placed in a secured infant seat.

Psychologists say the most effective emotional appeal is one coupled with facts and figures. The emotional appeal attracts audience interest, but logical arguments also are needed.

Persuasive Speaking

Psychologists have found that successful speakers (and salespeople) use several persuasion techniques:

● **Yes–yes.** Start with points with which the audience agrees to develop a pattern of "yes" answers. Getting agreement to a basic premise often means that the receiver will agree to the logically developed conclusion.

● **Offer structured choice.** Give choices that force the audience to choose between A and B. College officials may ask audiences, "Do you want to raise taxes or raise tuition?" Political candidates ask, "Do you want more free enterprise or government telling you what to do?"

● **Seek partial commitment.** Get a commitment for some action on the part of the receiver. This leaves the door open for commitment to other parts of the proposal at a later date. "You don't need to decide on the new insurance plan now, but please attend the employee orientation program on Thursday."

● **Ask for more, settle for less.** Submit a complete public relations program to management, but be prepared to compromise by dropping certain parts of the program. It has become almost a cliché that a department asks for a larger budget than it expects to receive.

ON THE JOB insights

Motivation–Ability–Opportunity Model for Enhancing Message Processing

The following chart summarizes the various communication strategies that can be used to reach publics who have little knowledge or interest in a particular issue, product, or service. The object, of course, is to structure persuasive messages that attract their attention.

ENHANCE MOTIVATION	ENHANCE ABILITY	ENHANCE OPPORTUNITY
Attract and encourage audiences to commence, continue processing	*Make it easier to process the message by tapping cognitive resources*	*Structure messages to optimize processing*
Create attractive, likable messages (create affect)	Include background, definitions, explanations	Expend sufficient effort to provide information
Appeal to hedonistic needs (sex, appetite, safety)	Be simple, clear	Repeat messages frequently
Use novel stimuli:	Use advance organizers (e.g., headlines)	Repeat key points within text—in headlines, text, captions, illustrations, etc.
• Photos	Include synopses	Use longer messages
• Typography	Combine graphics, text, and narration (dual coding of memory traces)	Include multiple arguments
• Oversized formats	Use congruent memory cues (same format as original)	Feature "interactive" illustrations, photos
• Large number of scenes, elements	Label graphics (helps identify which attributes to focus on)	Avoid distractions:
• Changes in voice, silence, movement	Use specific, concrete (versus abstract) words and images	• Annoying music
Make the most of formal features:	Include exemplars, models	• Excessively attractive spokespersons
• Format size	Make comparison with analogies	• Complex arguments
• Music	Show actions, train audience skills through demonstrations	• Disorganized layouts
• Color	Include marks (logos, logotypes, trademarks), slogans, and symbols as continuity devices	Allow audiences to control pace of processing
• Include key points in headlines	Appeal to self-schemas (roles, what's important to audience's identity)	Provide sufficient time
Use moderately complex messages	Enhance perceptions of self-efficacy to perform tasks	Keep pace lively and avoid audience boredom
Use sources who are credible, attractive, or similar to audience	Place messages in conducive environment (priming effects)	
Involve celebrities	Frame stories using culturally resonating themes, catchphrases	
Enhance relevance to audience—ask them to think about a question		
Use stories, anecdotes, or drama to draw into action		
Stimulate curiosity: Use humor, metaphors, questions		
Vary language, format, source		
Use multiple, ostensibly independent sources		

Source: Kirk Hallahan, "Enhancing Motivation, Ability, and Opportunity to Process Public Relations Messages." *Public Relations Review*, Vol. 26, No. 4, pp. 463–480.

A persuasive speech can either be one-sided or offer several sides of an issue, depending on the audience. A series of 1950s studies by Carl Hovland and his associates at Yale determined that one-sided speeches were most effective with persons favorable to the message, whereas two-sided speeches were most effective with audiences that might be opposed to the message.

By mentioning all sides of the argument, the speaker accomplishes three objectives. First, the speaker is perceived as having objectivity. This translates into increased credibility and makes the audience less suspicious of the speaker's motives. Second, the speaker is treating the audience as mature, intelligent adults. Third, including counterarguments allows the speaker to control how those arguments are structured. It also deflates opponents who might challenge the speaker by saying, "But you didn't consider . . ."

Panel discussions and debates present other problems. Psychologists say the last person on a panel to talk will probably be most effective in changing audience attitudes—or at least be longer remembered by the audience. But it has also been shown that the first speaker sets the standard and tone for the remainder of the discussion. Being first or last is better positioning than being between two presentations.

Propaganda

No discussion of persuasion would be complete without mentioning propaganda and the techniques associated with it.

Garth S. Jowett and Victoria O'Donnell in their book, *Propaganda and Persuasion*, say, "Propaganda is the deliberate and systematic attempt to shape perceptions, manipulate cognitions, and direct behavior to achieve a response that furthers the desired intent of the propagandist." Its roots go back to the 17th century, when the Roman Catholic Church set up the *congregatio de propaganda* ("congregation for propagating the faith"). The word took on extremely negative connotations in the 20th century.

In World Wars I and II, propaganda was associated with the information activities of the enemy. Germany and Japan were sending out "propaganda," whereas the United States and its allies were disseminating "truth." Today, *propaganda* connotes falsehood, lies, deceit, disinformation, and duplicity—practices that opposing groups and governments accuse each other of employing.

Some have even argued that propaganda, in the broadest sense of the word, also includes the advertising and public relations activity of such diverse entities as Exxon and the Sierra Club. Social scientists, however, say that the word *propaganda* should be used only to denote activity that sells a belief system or constitutes political or ideological dogma.

Advertising and public relations messages for commercial purposes, however, do use several techniques commonly associated with propaganda. The most common are the following:

● **Plain folks.** An approach often used by individuals to show humble beginnings and empathy with the average citizen. Political candidates, in particular, are quite fond of telling about their "humble" beginnings.

● **Testimonial.** A frequently used device to achieve credibility, as discussed earlier. A well-known expert, popular celebrity, or average citizen gives testimony about the value of a product or the wisdom of a decision.

- **Bandwagon.** The implication or direct statement that everyone wants the product or that the idea has overwhelming support; for example, "Millions of Americans support a ban on abortion" or "Every leading expert believes . . ."

- **Card stacking.** The selection of facts and data to build an overwhelming case on one side of the issue, while concealing the other side. The advertising industry says a ban on beer advertising would lead to enormous reductions in network sports programming and a ban on cigarette advertising would kill many magazines.

- **Transfer.** The technique of associating the person, product, or organization with something that has high status, visibility, or credibility. Many corporations, for example, paid millions to be official sponsors of the 2004 Olympic Games, hoping that the public would associate their products with excellence.

- **Glittering generalities.** The technique of associating a cause, product, or idea with favorable abstractions such as freedom, justice, democracy, and the American way. The White House named its military action in the Middle East "Operation Iraqi Freedom" and American oil companies argue for offshore drilling to keep "America energy independent."

ON THE JOB
ethics

Is Framing an Issue OK?

The chapter includes information about the efforts of public relations firms to frame issues that would, in turn, be reflected by media coverage. Others might call this kind of effort positioning or even putting a spin on a particular event. The objective, of course, is to define the issues involved for the media and subsequently for the public.

Hill and Knowlton, for example, helped to frame Iraq's invasion of Kuwait by using the theme of atrocity stories to generate anti-Iraq sentiment in the American people. In

the Global box on public diplomacy, the Bush administration framed the downing of its surveillance plane as an aggressive act by China. China framed the same event as a tragic defense of its sovereignty in disputed international airspace.

Is framing a legitimate and ethical aspect of today's public relations practice? Why or why not? Can you ever achieve an ethically irreproachable framing of events using public relations tools? What are the implications of your answer?

A student of public relations should be aware of these techniques to make certain that he or she doesn't intentionally use them to deceive and mislead the public. Ethical responsibilities exist in every form of persuasive communication; guidelines are discussed at the end of the chapter.

Persuasion and Manipulation

The discussion on previous pages examined ways in which an individual can formulate persuasive messages. The ability to use these techniques often leads to charges that public relations practitioners have great power to influence and manipulate people.

In reality, the effectiveness of persuasive techniques is greatly exaggerated. Persuasion is not an exact science, and no surefire way exists to predict that people or media gatekeepers will be persuaded to believe a message or act on it. If persuasive techniques were as refined as the critics say, all people might be driving the same make of automobile, using the same soap, and voting for the same political candidate.

This doesn't happen because several variables intervene in the flow of persuasive messages. Elihu Katz says the two major intervening variables are selectivity and interpersonal relations; these are consistent with the limited-effects model of mass communication.

For purposes of discussion, the limitations on effective persuasive messages can be listed as (1) lack of message penetration, (2) competing messages, (3) self-selection, and (4) self-perception.

Lack of Message Penetration

The diffusion of messages, despite modern communication technologies, is not pervasive. Not everyone, of course, watches the same television programs or reads the same newspapers and magazines. Not everyone receives the same mail or attends the same meetings. Not everyone the communicator wants to reach will be in the audience eventually reached, despite advances in audience-segmentation techniques. There is also the problem of messages being distorted as they pass through media gatekeepers such as reporters and editors. Key message points often are left out or the context of the message is changed.

Competing Messages

In the 1930s, before much was known about the complex process of communication, it was believed that people received information directly, without any intervening variable. This was called the *bullet theory* or the *hypodermic-needle theory* of communication.

Today, communication experts realize that no message is received in a vacuum. Messages are filtered through a receiver's entire social structure and belief system. Nationality, race, religion, gender, cultural patterns, family, and friends are among the variables that filter and dilute persuasive messages. In addition, people receive countless competing and conflicting messages daily. Social scientists say a person usually conforms to the standards of his or her family and friends. Consequently, most people do not believe or act on messages that are contrary to group norms.

Self-Selection

The people most wanted in an audience are often the least likely to be there. Vehement supporters or loyalists frequently ignore information from the other side. They do so by being selective in the messages that they want to hear. They read books, newspaper editorials, and magazine articles and view television programs that support their predispositions. This is why social scientists say that the media are more effective in reinforcing existing attitudes than in changing them.

Self-Perception

Self-perception is the channel through which messages are interpreted. People will perceive the same information differently, depending on predispositions and already formulated opinions. The newsletter *Inside PR* describes how people react to news stories: "If they believe something to be true and see a story affirming that belief, their belief is strengthened. If they believe something to be true and see a story challenging that belief, they assume the story is biased or just plain wrong."

Thus, depending on a person's views, an action by an organization may be considered a "great contribution to the community" or a "self-serving gimmick."

The Ethics of Persuasion

Public relations people, by definition, are advocates of clients and employers. The emphasis is on persuasive communication to influence a particular public in some way. At the same time, as Chapter 3 points out, public relations practitioners must conduct their activities in an ethical manner.

The use of persuasive techniques, therefore, calls for some additional guidelines. Professor Richard L. Johannnesen of Northern Illinois University, writing in *Persuasion, Reception and Responsibility*, a text by Charles Larson, lists the following ethical criteria for using persuasive devices that should be kept in mind by every public relations professional:

- Do not use false, fabricated, misrepresented, distorted, or irrelevant evidence to support arguments or claims.
- Do not intentionally use specious, unsupported, or illogical reasoning.
- Do not represent yourself as informed or as an "expert" on a subject when you are not.
- Do not use irrelevant appeals to divert attention or scrutiny from the issue at hand. Among the appeals that commonly serve such a purpose are smear attacks on an opponent's character, appeals to hatred and bigotry, innuendo, and "God" or "devil" terms that cause intense but unreflective positive or negative reactions.
- Do not ask your audience to link your idea or proposal to emotion-laden values, motives, or goals to which it actually is not related.
- Do not deceive your audience by concealing your real purpose, your self-interest, the group you represent, or your position as an advocate of a viewpoint.
- Do not distort, hide, or misrepresent the number, scope, intensity, or undesirable features of consequences.
- Do not use emotional appeals that lack a supporting basis of evidence or reasoning or that would not be accepted if the audience had time and opportunity to examine the subject itself.
- Do not oversimplify complex situations into simplistic, two-valued, either/or, polar views or choices.
- Do not pretend certainty when tentativeness and degrees of probability would be more accurate.
- Do not advocate something in which you do not believe yourself.

It is clear from the preceding list that a public relations professional should be more than a technician or a "hired gun." This raises the issue that public relations personnel often lack the technical and legal expertise to know whether information provided to them by the client or employer is accurate.

Robert Heath makes it clear that this doesn't excuse public relations professionals from ethical responsibility. He writes:

> The problem of reporting information that they cannot personally verify does not excuse them from being responsible communicators. Their responsibility is to demand that the most accurate information be provided and the evaluation be the best available.

Persuasive messages require truth, honesty, and candor for two practical reasons. First, Heath says that a message is already suspect because it is advanced on behalf of a client or organization. Second, half-truths and misleading information do not serve the best interests of the public or the organization.

SUMMARY

What Is Public Opinion?

Public opinion can be difficult to measure; there are few if any issues on which the public (which is in fact many publics) can be said to have a unanimous opinion. In fact, only a small number of people will have opinions on any given issue. Engaging the interest of a public will involve affecting its self-interest. Publics also react strongly to events.

Opinion Leaders as Catalysts

The primary catalyst in the formation of public opinion is public discussion. People who are knowledgeable and articulate on specific issues can be either formal opinion leaders (power leaders) or informal opinion leaders (role models). Opinion "flows" from these leaders to the public, often through the mass media.

Persuasion: Pervasive in Our Lives

The concept of persuasion has been around at least since the time of the ancient Greeks. The dominant view of public relations is of persuasive communications on behalf of clients. Persuasion can be used to change or neutralize hostile opinions, crystallize latent opinions and positive attitudes, and conserve favorable opinions.

Factors in Persuasive Communication

Factors involved in persuasion include audience analysis, source credibility, appeal to self-interest, mes-sage clarity, timing and context, audience participation, suggestions for action, content and structure of messages, and persuasive speaking.

Propaganda

Although the roots of the word *propaganda* go back to the 17th century, during the 20th century the word took on extremely negative connotations. During the World Wars, it was associated with the enemies' information activities. It is now used to refer to political or ideological persuasion, with emphasis on deceit and duplicity. Propaganda techniques can be the same as those used in advertising and other public relations messages.

Persuasion and Manipulation

Limitations on effective persuasion include lack of message penetration, competing messages, self-selection, and self-perception.

The Ethics of Persuasion

There are two practical reasons for an ethical approach to persuasive messages. First, publics will automatically have a level of suspicion because they know the communicator is promoting a client or organization. Second, the interests of that client or organization will not be well served by false or misleading communications.

Case Activity: **What Would You Do?**

The school system of a major city wants to draw attention to the need for more volunteer adult tutors in the city's 200 public schools. Budget cutbacks in teaching staff and other resources have made it a vital necessity to recruit volunteers who will work with students on an individual basis to improve reading and math skills.

Your public relations firm has volunteered to organize a public information campaign. Explain what you would do in each of the following categories that relate to the structure and content of persuasive messages: drama, statistics, examples, testimonials, endorsements, and emotional appeals.

QUESTIONS for Review and Discussion

1. Public opinion is highly influenced by self-interest and events. What are these concepts?
2. What is the importance of opinion leaders in the formation of public opinion?
3. What theories about mass media effects have relevance for public relations?
4. What are the stages of public opinion in the life cycle of an issue?
5. Name the three objectives of persuasion in public relations work. What objective is the most difficult to accomplish?
6. Can you name and describe the nine factors involved in persuasive communication?
7. What are three factors involved in source credibility?
8. What are the pros and cons of using celebrities for product endorsements?
9. What are the levels of Maslow's hierarchy of needs? Why is it important for public relations people to understand people's basic needs?
10. Why is audience involvement and participation important in persuasion?
11. What techniques can be used to write persuasive messages?
12. Name several propaganda techniques. Should they be used by public relations people?
13. What are some ethical responsibilities of a person who uses persuasion techniques to influence others?

SUGGESTED READINGS

Callison, Coy. "Do PR Practitioners Have a PR Problem? The Effect of Associating a Source with Public Relations and Client-Negative News on Audience Perception of Credibility." *Journal of Public Relations Research*, Vol. 13, No. 3, 2001, pp. 219–234.

De Burton, Simon. "Fancy a Touch of Start Status: The Relationship Between Brands and Celebrities." *Financial Times*, November 14, 2004, p. 5.

Dobrow, Larry. "Keeping Tabs on the Talent." *PRWeek*, September 3, 2001, p. 25.

Glasser, Theodore L., and Salmon, Charles T., editors. *Public Opinion and the Communication of Consent.* New York: The Guilford Press, 1995.

Gordon, Andrew. "Woods Tops Annual List of Overexposed Sports Stars." *PRWeek*, January 6, 2003, p. 2.

Green, Deatherage. "So, You Want (Your Spokesperson) to Be Famous?" *PRWeek*, September 4, 2000, p. 28.

Hallahan, Kirk. "Enhancing Motivation, Ability, and Opportunity to Process Public Relations Messages." *Public Relations Review*, Vol. 26, No. 4, 2000, pp. 463–480.

Hallahan, Kirk. "Inactive Publics: The Forgotten Publics in Public Relations." *Public Relations Review*, Vol. 26, No. 4, 2000, pp. 499–515.

Hiebert, Ray E. "Public Relations and Propaganda Framing the Iraq War: A Preliminary Review." *Public Relations Review*, Vol. 29, No. 4, pp. 243–255.

Keller, Ed, and Berry, Jon. *The Influentials: One American in Ten Tells the Other Nine How to Vote, Where to Eat, and What to Buy.* New York: Free Press, 2003.

Newman, Kelli B. "The Power of Emotion." *Public Relations Tactics*, July 2001, p. 27.

Perloff, Richard M. *The Dynamics of Persuasion*, 2d ed. Mahwah, NJ: Lawrence Erlbaum, 2003.

Wanta, Wayne, Golan, Guy, and Lee, Cheolhan. "Agenda Setting and International News: Media Influence on Public Perceptions of Foreign Nations." *Journalism & Mass Communication Quarterly*, Vol. 81, No. 2, 2004, pp. 364–377.

Zhang, Juyan, and Cameron, Glen T. "The Structural Transformation of China's Propaganda: An Ellulian Perspective." *Journal of Communication Management*, Vol. 8, No. 3, 2004, pp. 307–321.

Zhang, Juyan, Qiu, Qi, and Cameron, Glen T. "Contingency Approach to International Dispute Resolution: A Case Study." *Public Relations Review*, Vol. 30, No. 1, 2004, pp. 391–399.

chapter

10

Conflict Management: Dealing with Issues, Risks, and Crises

Topics covered in this chapter include:

Strategic Conflict Management

Conflict takes many forms, from warfare between nations to spats between kids at a daycare center. Any sharp disagreement or collision of interests and ideas can be defined as a *conflict*. Many societal conflicts fall under the purview of public relations. This means that the public relations professional must develop communication strategies and processes *to influence the course of conflicts to the benefit of the organization and, when possible, to the benefit of the organization's many constituents*. The use of public relations to influence the course of a conflict is called *strategic conflict management*.

The influence of public relations on the course of a conflict can take many forms. Sometimes conflict is escalated for activist purposes, such as when the Animal Liberation Front not only verbally attacks biological research laboratories, but also physically assaults research staff. Other strategies are less dramatic, such as oil industry advocates pushing to open parts of the Alaskan wilderness to exploration, striving to win approval over time in the marketplace of ideas—and ultimately in Congress. Sometimes an organization is able to catch a conflict at an early stage and reduce damage to the organization. However, in other cases, an issue may smolder and finally become a conflagration, such as the prison-abuse scandal at Abu Ghraib prison in Iraq. The Pentagon ignored adverse reports about the prison until the problem was in the hands of the media, and in the public's mind. Dealing with problems early on is not only more efficient, it is usually the right thing to do. Public relations professionals often have the opportunity to serve as the organization's conscience because of the importance of efficiency and ethics in managing a conflict.

Public relations professionals will often work to accommodate publics to obtain mutually beneficial results. (For more about the valuable role of public relations in building mutually beneficial outcomes, see Grunig's excellence model of public relations in Chapter 2.) But, at other times, professionals will need to make tough calls and advocate on behalf of their organization, such as when the public relations and legal staffs at the railroad giant CSX coordinated their efforts to orchestrate lawsuits and publicity to shift stockholder opinion concerning a handsome offer to take over Conrail's lines.

Making the right strategic moves will determine just how long a conflict will persist and how much damage or benefit it will cause. Figure 10.1 depicts the conflict life cycle and includes numerous techniques that public relations people use to deal with conflict.

The conflict management life cycle shown in Figure 10.1 shows the "big picture" of how to manage a conflict. Strategic conflict management can be divided into four general phases, but bear in mind that the lines between the phases are not absolute and that some techniques overlap in actual practice. Furthermore, in the exciting world of public relations, busy practitioners may be actively managing different conflicts in each of the four phases simultaneously. To better understand the conflict management life cycle, each phase will be briefly explained.

The Proactive Phase

The proactive phase includes activities and thought processes that can prevent a conflict from arising or from getting out of hand. The first step in the phase is **environmental scanning**—the constant reading, listening, and watching of

FIGURE 10.1

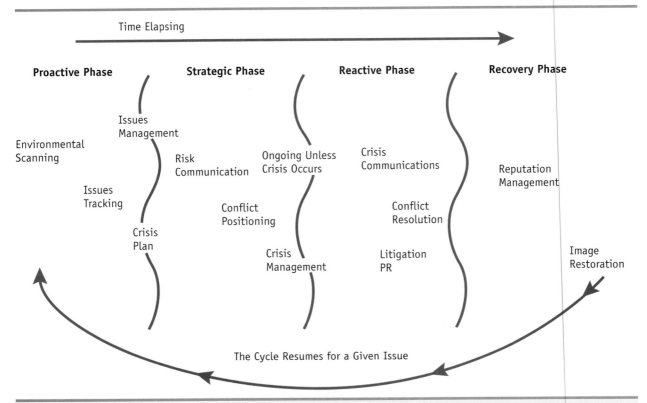

The Cycle of Conflict depicts the four phases in conflict management experienced by public relations professionals. The Cycle also includes a few of the numerous strategies in public relations that professionals employ to deal with conflict.

current affairs with an eye to the organization's interests. As issues emerge, **issues tracking** becomes more focused and systematic through processes such as the daily clipping of news stories. **Issues management** occurs when the organization makes behavioral changes or creates strategic plans in ways that address the emerging issue. In the proactive phase, well-run organizations will also develop a general **crisis plan** as a first step in preparing for the worst—an issue or an event that has escalated to crisis proportions.

The Strategic Phase

In the strategic phase, an issue that has become an emerging conflict is identified as needing concerted action by the public relations professional.

Three broad strategies take place in this phase. Through **risk communication**, dangers or threats to people or organizations are conveyed to forestall personal injury, health problems, and environmental damage. This risk communication continues so long as the risk exists or until the risk escalates into a crisis. **Conflict-positioning** strategies enable the organization to position itself favorably in anticipation of actions such as litigation, boycott, adverse legislation, elections, or similar events that will play out in "the court of public opinion." To be prepared for the

ON THE JOB insights

Strategic Conflict Management in the Real World

The following scenarios provide just a few examples of the conflict-related challenges public relations professionals tackle every day around the world.

- A public relations pro takes charge of the temporary press briefing room that was built near the site of a plant explosion, funneling all press and family inquiries through her makeshift operation and offering fax, phone, and Internet access for a flock of reporters.
- Recognizing the need for domestic fuel sources in an uncertain world, a D.C. lobbyist works with his PR firm to bolster arguments for federal subsidies to ethanol producers in the U.S. corn belt.

- As American waistlines bulge, the National Institutes of Health calls for the creation of centers to prevent obesity and related diseases.
- Anticipating a strike by Teamster truckers delivering products to a nonunion plant, the plant's public relations team launches a philanthropic campaign to aid widows of the Iraqi war in plant communities.
- Having allowed yet another instance of sexual harassment in the workplace, a spokesperson expresses mortification about the performance of her company and pledges to change the company culture.

These scenarios share a common theme: the strategic

management of conflict. Conflict management is one of the most interesting, vibrant, and essential functions of public relations.

Strategic efforts also run a wide gamut, corresponding to the four phases of the conflict management life cycle:

- Monitoring media for emerging issues (Proactive Phase)
- Taking preventive actions that forestall conflict (Strategic Phase)
- Dealing with crisis or disaster, whether caused by the organization or by nature (Reactive Phase)
- Repairing relations and public image in the aftermath of a conflict (Recovery Phase)

worst outcome—that is, an issue that resists risk communication efforts and becomes a conflict of crisis proportions—a specific **crisis management** plan is developed for that particular issue.

The Reactive Phase

Once the issue or imminent conflict reaches a critical level of impact on the organization, the public relations professional must react to events in the external communication environment as they unfold.

Crisis communications includes the implementation of the crisis management plan as well as the hectic 24/7 efforts to meet the needs of publics such as disaster victims, employees, government officials, and the media. When conflict has emerged but is not careening out of control, **conflict resolution** techniques are used to bring a heated conflict, such as collapsed salary negotiations, to a favorable resolution. The public relations practitioner may employ strategies to assist negotiation or arbitration efforts to resolve conflict.

Often, the most intractable conflicts end up in the courts. **Litigation public relations** employs communication strategies and publicity efforts in support of legal actions or trials (see Chapter 12 for details).

Recovery Phase

In the aftermath of a crisis or a high profile, heated conflict with a public, the organization should employ strategies either to bolster or repair its reputation in the eyes of key publics.

Reputation management includes systematic research to learn the state of the organization's reputation and then taking steps to improve it. As events and conflicts occur, the company responds with actions and communication about those actions. Poorly managed issues, imposing excessive risk to others, and callous responses to a crisis damage an organization's reputation. When this damage is extreme, **image restoration** strategies can help.

Not only do public relations practitioners face the challenge of addressing different conflicts in different phases of the life cycle, they no sooner deal with a conflict and then the cyclical process starts over again for that very same issue. Environmental scanning resumes to ensure that the conflict does not reemerge as an issue. Although challenging, conflict management is not impossible. Systematic processes described in the remaining sections of the chapter provide guidance and structure for this highly rewarding role played by public relations professionals in conflict management.

It Depends—A System for Managing Conflict

Olympic swimmer Natalie Coughlin embodies the view of public relations as strong and competitive in spirit, yet not macho or underhanded.

Each of the phases of the conflict management life cycle share an underlying process: A public relations professional or team must determine the stance its organization will take toward each public or stakeholder involved in the conflict situation. This concept, which is called the *contingency theory of conflict management*, began with the discovery that all practitioners shared an unstated, informal approach to managing conflict. Through graduate student interviews with top practitioners, Amanda Cancel and her advisor Glen Cameron of the University of Missouri heard a recurring theme: "It Depends." This short phrase became the title of a landmark article on conflict management in public relations. Public relations professionals said that pure accommodation, which means making concessions to a public, occurs mainly in philanthropic programs or community relations efforts. For the most part, the stance taken toward publics "depends" on many factors, which causes the stance to change in response to circumstances.

Subsequent studies on the contingency theory established that practitioners face a complex set of forces that must be monitored and considered to represent the best interests of the organization and, when possible, to attend to the well-being of publics that interact with the organization.

Contingency theory established that much of public relations management involves anticipating or managing conflict and that this function is among the most important areas of strategy for the profession. Managing conflict includes the ongoing challenge for public relations professionals to deal with competitors in the same line of business or with a similar mission. For example, corporations compete in the marketplace, nonprofit organizations seek volunteers from the same limited pool, and government communicators vie for limited funds.

Playing fair while competing for customers, members, or donors is part of what Cameron calls "muscular PR." He uses images such as Olympic swimmer Natalie Coughlin to embody the preparation, strength, and fair play required to contend against others. This image of public relations embraces competition and advocacy as sometimes necessary and usually healthy elements of public relations.

In free societies, competition is ongoing and fully accepted, but more dramatic conflict episodes are a significant force in shaping public relations practice. For example, conflict management occurs when a business or industry contends with government regulators or activist groups that seem determined to curtail operations because of what the industry considers excessive safety or environmental standards. At the same time, the regulatory body or the activists engage in their own public relations efforts to make the case for their position against the company and its practices and on behalf of workers or the ecosystem. Professor Jae-Hwa Shin of the University of Southern Mississippi describes this dialogue as the "wrangle in the marketplace of ideas." And much like Olympic swimmers striving in the pool to represent their own interests, this wrangle is inevitable and perfectly acceptable, according to Shin.

ON THE JOB

global

Lysistrata Project: A Worldwide Theatrical Act of Dissent

Conflict strategies can be earnest *and* fun. The Lysistrata Project called for performances or readings of the Greek classic *Lysistrata* on March 3, 2003. The basic plot of the Greek play is that the women of Athens barricade themselves in the Acropolis and go on a sex strike until their husbands stop the Peloponnesian War. The play is an extended metaphor for nonviolent resistance; the women view the city as a household that needs their healing approach to reconcile and reorganize the men's militaristic institutions.

With the Lysistrata Project, the politics of war are replaced with the politics of love. One or two performances were planned by actresses Kathryn Blume and Sharron Bower to make a statement. This wry approach to protesting the war on Iraq was initially a personal effort to raise voices against the war. The grassroots movement, fueled by the universal themes of the play, gathered immediate momentum. Ultimately, more than 300,000 people attended readings of the play at 1,029 locations around the world.

In the public relations world, competing stances and sometimes competing views of the world meet and even collide through strategic conflict management by multiple parties. At the extreme, moral conflicts such as the rhetoric of pro- and antiwar groups often become heated as each side is driven by deeply held principles to advocate a strong position. But as the Lystistrata Project illustrates, even deeply held values can sometimes be conveyed with a lighter touch to great effect (see the Global box on page 247).

Two Basic Contingency Principles

The contingency theory of public relations is complex, but two basic principles capture the essence of the theory. First, the public relations stance for dealing with a given audience or public is dynamic, changing as events unfold. This is represented by a continuum from pure accommodation to pure advocacy at a given time for a given public. Figure 10.2 shows the contingency continuum with some examples of the many conflict management strategies used in public relations practice.

Second, a matrix of factors drive the stance of an organization toward each of its publics, as shown in Figure 10.3. Professor Bryan Reber has statistically validated the original 86 contingency factors in the matrix that can be used to determine whether a specific public relations position will tend more toward the accommodation or advocacy end of the continuum.

FIGURE 10.2

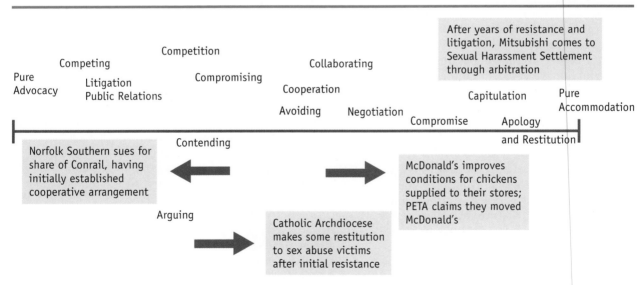

Note: PR professionals will change stance as events and factors emerge as is indicated in the real life examples.

Contingency Continuum This continuum from pure advocacy to pure accommodation forms the foundation for identifying the stance of an organization toward a given public at a given time. The diagram also illustrates the dynamism of strategic conflict management, citing some high profile instances of organizations shifting positions along the continuum as a conflict evolved.

FIGURE 10.3

An organization's stance toward any given public lies on a continuum from advocacy to accommodation. This stance is contingent upon the matrix of external and internal variables enumerated below.

External Variables

1. External Threats
2. Industry Specific Environment
3. General Political/Social Environment
4. External Public Characteristics
5. Issue Under Question

Internal Variables

1. General Corporate/Organizational Characteristics
2. PR Department Characteristics
3. Dominant Coalition Characteristics
4. Internal Threats
5. Personality Characteristics of Internal, Involved Persons
6. Relationship Characteristics

External Variables

1. Threats
   A. Litigation
   B. Government Regulation
   C. Potentially Damaging Publicity
   D. Scarring of Organization's Reputation in Community
   E. Legitimizing Activists' Claims

2. Industry Environment
   A. Changing (Dynamic) or Static
   B. # of Competitors/Level of Competition
   C. Richness or Leanness of Resources in the Environment

3. General Political/Social Environment/External Culture (level of constraint/uncertainty)
   A. Degree of Political Support of Business
   B. Degree of Social Support of Business

4. The External Public (Group, Individual, etc.)
   A. Size/# of Members
   B. Degree of Source Credibility/Powerful Members or Connections
   C. Past Successes or Failures of Public to Evoke Change
   D. Amount of Advocacy Practiced by Organization
   E. Level of Commitment/Involvement of Public's Members
   F. Whether the Public has Public Relations Counselors of Not
   G. Community's Perception of Public: Reasonable or Radical
   H. Level of Media Coverage the Public Has Received in Past

I. Whether Representatives of the Public Know or Like Representatives of the Organization
J. Whether Representatives of the Organization Know or Like Representatives from the Public
K. Public's Willingness to Dilute Its Cause/Request/Claim
L. Moves and Countermoves
M. Relative Power of Organization
N. Relative Power of Public

5. Issue Under Question
   A. Size
   B. Stakes
   C. Complexity

Internal Variables

1. Organization's Characteristics
   A. Open or Closed Culture
   B. Dispersed Widely Geographically or Centralized
   C. Level of Technology the Organization Uses to Produce Its Product or Service
   D. Homogeneity or Heterogeneity of Employees
   E. Age of the Organization/Value Placed on Tradition
   F. Speed of Growth in the Knowledge Level the Organization Uses
   G. Economic Stability of the Organization
   H. Existence or Non-Existence of Issues Management Personnel or Program
   I. Organization's Past Experiences with the Public
   J. Distribution of Decision-making Power
   K. Formalization: # of Rules or Codes Defining and Limiting the Job Descriptions of Employees
   L. Stratification/Hierarchy of Positions
   M. Existence or Influence of Legal Department
   N. Business Exposure (Product Mix and Customer Mix)
   O. Corporate Culture

2. Public Relations Department Characteristics
   A. Number of Practitioners Total and Number with College Degrees
   B. Type of Past Training of Employees: Trained in PR or Ex-Journalists, Marketing, Etc.
   C. Location of PR Department in Hierarchy: Independent or Under Marketing; Umbrella/Experiencing Encroachment of Marketing/Persuasive Mentality
   D. Representation in the Dominant Coalition
   E. Experience Level of PR Practitioners in Dealing with Conflict
   F. General Communication Competency of Department
   G. Autonomy of Department
   H. Physical Placement of Department in Building (Near CEO and other top decision-makers or not)

(continued)

FIGURE 10.3 *(continued)*

I. Staff Trained in Research Methods
J. Amount of Funding Available for Dealing with External Publics
K. Amount of Time Allowed to Use Dealing with External Publics
L. Gender: Percentage of Female Upper-Level Staff/Managers
M. Potential of Department to Practice Various Models of Public Relations

3. Characteristics of Dominant Coalition (Top Management)
   A. Political Values: Conservative or Liberal/Open or Closed to Change
   B. Management Style: Domineering or Laid-Back
   C. General Altruism Level
   D. Support and Understanding of PR
   E. Frequency of External Contact with Publics
   F. Departmental Perception of the Organization's External Environment
   G. Calculation of Potential Rewards or Losses Using Different Strategies with External Publics
   H. Degree of Line Manager Involvement in External Affairs

4. Internal Threats (How much is at stake in the situation)
   A. Economic Loss or Gain from Implementing Various Stances
   B. Marring of Employees' or Stockholders' Perception of the Company
   C. Marring of the Personal Reputations of the Company Decision Makers (Image in employees' perceptions and general public's perception)

5. Individual Characteristics (Public Relations Practitioner, Dominant Coalition, and Line Managers)
   A. Training in PR, Marketing, Journalism, Engineering, etc.
   B. Personal Ethics
   C. Tolerance of Ability to Deal with Uncertainty
   D. Comfort Level with Conflict or Dissonance
   E. Comfort Level with Change
   F. Ability to Recognize Potential and Existing Problems
   G. Extent of Openness to Innovation
   H. Extent to which Individual Can Grasp Other's World Views
   I. Personality: Dogmatic, Authoritarian
   J. Communication Competency
   K. Cognitive Complexity: Ability to Handle Complex Problems
   L. Predisposition Toward Negotiation
   M. Predisposition Toward Altruism
   N. How Individuals Receive, Process and Use Information and Influence
   O. Familiarity with External Public or Its Representative
   P. Like External Public or Its Representative
   Q. Gender: Female Versus Male

6. Relationship Characteristics
   A. Level of Trust Between Organization and External Public
   B. Dependency of Parties Involved
   C. Ideological Barriers Between Organization and Public

A Matrix of Contingency Factors in Conflict Management Many of the contingency factors that affect the stance of an organization are organized into this matrix. Depending on circumstances and the judgment of public relations professionals, the factors may move the organization toward or away from accommodation of a public.

Variables in contingency theory are categorized as being *external* or *internal*. External variables fall into subcategories such as external threats, industry environment, and the characteristics of the external publics fomenting the conflict. For example, if an activist group faces a powerful corporation, the stance and strategy will need to take into account how many resources the company can bring to bear on the issue. Internal variables include characteristics of the organization, the public relations department, and top management.

Variables also are categorized as being either *predisposing* or *situational*. Predisposing variables are always present in an organization and may set the tone for dealing with conflict. For example, a company led by a tough, hard-nosed CEO may begin its engagement with a public from a "take no prisoners" stance. Predisposing variables usually are more influential than situational variables. Situational variables are responsive to specific circumstances and settings and are therefore more dynamic and subject to rapid change. For example, when a tough CEO realizes that public has a fair claim, he or she may lead the company toward a more accommodative stance in light of the situational variables.

Suffice it to say that managing conflict is a subtle process of first judging the status of conflicts for the organization and then deciding what to do about them. Research suggests that power factors and certain threats to the organization, along with the approach of top management, appear to be profound, persistent factors in the way public relations professionals develop a stance and a set of strategies for dealing with a given public.

Experience helps professionals discern what the important issues are and what stance to take in the face of conflict. But by embracing the idea of "muscular public relations," a dynamic approach, and consideration of multiple contingency factors, even neophyte public relations practitioners can be effective conflict managers. Career progress is often furthered by this approach, making the public relations function invaluable to top management in organizations. As we will see, managing conflict can save untold costs to the organization's budget and to its position in society.

Issues Management

Identifying and then dealing with issues early on is one of the more important functions during the proactive phase of the conflict management life cycle. The interaction of organizations with various elements of society has led to the emergence of issues management as an important part of effective public relations and strategic planning. Essentially, *issues management* is a proactive and systematic approach to (1) predict problems, (2) anticipate threats, (3) minimize surprises, (4) resolve issues, and (5) prevent crises. Martha Lauzen, a professor at San Diego State University, says that effective issues management requires two-way communications, formal environmental scanning, and active sense-making strategies.

Another definition of issues management has been formulated by Coates, Coates, Jarratt, and Heinz in their book *Issues Management: How You Can Plan, Organize, and Manage for the Future.* They say, "Issues management is the organized activity of identifying emerging trends, concerns, or issues likely to affect an organization in the next few years and developing a wider and more positive range of organizational responses toward the future."

The basic idea behind issues management is proactive planning. Philip Gaunt and Jeff Ollenburger, writing in *Public Relations Review*, say, "Issues management is proactive in that it tries to identify issues and influence decisions regarding them before they have a detrimental effect on a corporation."

Gaunt and Ollenburger contrast this approach with crisis management, which is essentially reactive in nature. They note, "Crisis management tends to be more reactive, dealing with an issue after it becomes public knowledge and affects the company." In other words, active planning and prevention through issues management can often mean the difference between a noncrisis and a crisis, or, as one practitioner put it, the difference between little or no news coverage and a page-one headline. This point is particularly relevant because studies have shown that the majority of organizational crises are self-inflicted, because management ignored early warning signs.

The issue of the exploitation of women and children in Third World factories by American companies, for example, simmered for several years before it

ON THE JOB insights

An Issues Management Matrix

Issues management involves assessing an issue and determining its importance to the organization.

The Milwaukee-based firm of Bader Rutter & Associates uses

the following matrix to rate issues on their potential to affect a client's business. For example, if an issue gets a 10 on its potential impact on the business and

an 8 on the client's ability to influence the outcome, it will fall into the upper-right-hand quadrant of the matrix, meaning it should be high priority.

FIGURE 10.4

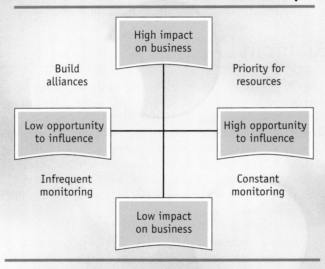

finally broke into the headlines after a worker activist group publicly accused Nike of using "sweatshop" labor to make its expensive and profitable athletic shoes and apparel.

Such revelations put the entire U.S. garment industry on the defensive. David Birenbaum, a consultant to the garment industry, wrote in the *Wall Street Journal* that the issue of using cheap Third World labor was not really new, but the public reaction to such practices was different. He wrote in an op-ed article, "What's changed is that for the first time human rights concerns could become a major marketing issue. . . . More and more importers are now considering safety and other conditions in Asian factories. Few can afford not to, because all it takes is one disaster to damage a label's reputation."

All of the publicity and public outrage, however, might have been avoided if the various clothing and athletic shoe manufacturers had paid attention to the concept of issues management.

Public relations counselors W. Howard Chase and Barrie L. Jones were among the first practitioners to specialize in issues management. They defined the process as consisting of five basic steps: (1) issue identification, (2) issue analysis, (3) strategy options, (4) an action plan, and (5) the evaluation of results. The following is an illustration of how these steps could have been used by the garment industry.

Issue Identification

Organizations should track the alternative press, mainstream media, online chat groups, and the newsletters of activist groups to learn what issues and concerns are being discussed. Of particular importance is establishing a trend line of coverage. Concern about the working conditions of women and children in the garment industry began showing up as an emerging issue several years before the Kathie Lee Gifford exposé.

Issue Analysis

Once an emerging issue has been identified, the next step is to assess its potential impact on the organization. Another consideration is to determine whether the organization is vulnerable on the issue. Are its policies exploitative? Is the company being ethical and socially responsible by turning a blind eye to violations of human rights in the interest of high profit margins? Can revelations about sweatshop conditions affect sales or damage a label's reputation?

Strategy Options

If the company decides that the emerging issue is potentially damaging, the next step is to consider what to do about it. One option might be to set higher standards for foreign contractors seeking the company's business. Another option: Work with human rights groups to monitor possible violations in foreign factories that produce the company's products. A third option might be to establish a new policy that would ensure that Third World workers receive decent pay and health benefits. The pros and cons of each option are weighed against what is most practical and economical for the company.

Action Plan

Once a specific policy has been decided on, the fourth step is to communicate it to all interested publics. These may include consumers, the U.S. Department of Labor, labor unions and worker activist groups, company employees, and the financial community. The action may be an opportunity to use the new policy as a marketing tool among consumers who make buying decisions based on a company's level of social responsibility.

Evaluation

With the new policy in place and communicated, the final step is to evaluate the results. Has news coverage been positive? Have activist groups called off product boycotts? Have the working conditions for women and children in the factories improved? Is the company being positioned as an industry leader? Have public perceptions of the company and the industry improved? If the company has acted soon

When organizations clash over a heated issue or a moral conflict such as embryonic stem cell research or capital punishment, charges leveled at the opposition often include impugning the ethics of the opponent. Oftentimes, such charges can be paraphrased as "We are just trying to tell the truth, but they are lying and twisting facts." Sometimes this "truth-telling" is contrasted with the "PR spin" practiced by the other side—even though both sides often use the same tactics and a full range of persuasive public relations strategies. When proponents embrace absolute moral values, they fail to reach out and understand the other side.

Do you find it ironic or perfectly appropriate for activists to garner publicity by accusing the opposition of using "PR ploys" when such publicity is a standard component of public relations? Watch for examples of this double bind in the media to share with your instructor and the class.

Most news conferences begin with an opening statement by the organization holding the news conference. Write an opening statement for a press conference on a current moral conflict some-where in the world. You might write the opening script for the Department of Defense or for a peace advocacy group. Write your statement for the side that you support most strongly. Then try to understand the worldview of the other side and sketch an opening statement for that group as well.

Having written both opening statements, consider how it is that both sides claim to be right. Discuss in class whether this exercise illustrates moral relativism or whether it shows that moral absolutes do exist, but that diametric values can be held by different groups.

enough, perhaps the greatest measurement of success is avoiding the media coverage that occurs when the problem eventually becomes a crisis.

Issues and situations can be managed or even forestalled by public relations professionals before they become crises or before their conflictual nature leads to significant losses for the organization, such as a diminished reputation, alienation of key stakeholders, and financial damage to the organization.

Risk Communication

Closely associated with and following upon issues management is risk communication. In essence, *risk communication* is any verbal or written exchange that attempts to communicate information regarding risk to public health and safety and the environment. The risk may be naturally occurring, such as undertows and riptides on beaches that require warning signs and flyers in hotel rooms. Or the risk may be associated with a product, such as an air bag or a lawn mower.

Organizations, including large corporations, increasingly engage in risk communication to inform the public of risks, such as those surrounding food products, chemical spills, radioactive waste disposal, or the placement of drug-abuse treatment centers or halfway houses in neighborhoods. These issues deserve public notice in fairness to the general populace. Such risks may also result in expensive lawsuits, restrictive legislation, consumer boycotts, and public debate if organizations fail to disclose potential hazards. As is often the case, doing the right thing in conflict management is quite often the least disruptive in the long run.

An example of somewhat unsuccessful risk communication was the 2003 "mad cow scare" in Canada. Despite assurances by Canadian health officials and the beef industry that the fatal cow disease posed an "extremely small" risk to consumers, many countries stopped buying Canadian beef, severely damaging the Canadian cattle industry and driving up beef prices worldwide. In contrast, Jeff Zucker of Burson-Marsteller points out that U.S. cattlemen have worked for years to get the message out that U.S. beef is the safest in the world. Thus, the discovery of a possibly infected cow in Washington State did not result in dire consequences for U.S. producers. Risk communication can minimize adverse effects on publics, but it also often reduces risk to the organization itself. When risk communication fails, however, the organization often faces a crisis.

The mad cow example illustrates the point that the dissemination of accurate information is insufficient in risk communication. Both the Canadian and U.S. cattle industries accomplished the informational objective, but the U.S. cattle industry was far more successful in limiting negative impacts of its mad cow scare on prices and world markets.

Risk communication is often complicated by the fact that scientific studies often contradict each other, leaving consumers somewhat uncertain about the amount of risk they face. Another problem is distortion of scientific findings by a portion of the mass media, such as when headlines imply a "cure" despite the qualifying details in the story.

As Marcia Angell, executive editor of the *New England Journal of Medicine*, wrote in the *New York Times Magazine*, "Most Americans are not very good at distinguishing big risks from little ones, or risks based on solid evidence from those that aren't. We are likely to react to all reported risks in the same way, or choose which to respond to, on the basis of irrational fears or the prominence given them on the 6 o'clock news."

Such situations pose considerable challenges to public relations personnel as they attempt to ascertain how the public perceives a risk. Because mad cow can cause death in humans, the public perceived the risk to be far greater than the statistical probability indicated, but they found U.S. claims of safety to be more credible than those from Canada.

Variables Affecting Risk Perceptions

Risk communication researchers have identified several variables that affect public perceptions:

● Risks voluntarily taken tend to be accepted better than those over which individuals have little or no control. Smokers have more control over their health situation, for example, than airline passengers do over their safety.

● The more complex a situation, the higher the perception of risk. Disposal of radioactive wastes is more difficult to understand than the dangers of cigarette smoking.

● Familiarity breeds confidence. If the public understands the problem and its factors, it perceives less risk. A study by Robert Heath, Shaila Seshadri, and Jaesub Lee at the University of Houston found that communities that are close to chemical plants have more favorable views of the chemical industry, probably because of the economic benefit of the plants to the community.

● Perception of risk increases when the messages of experts conflict.

● The severity of consequences affects risk perceptions. There is a difference between having a stomachache and getting cancer.

Suzanne Zoda, writing on risk communication in *Communication World*, gives some suggestions to communicators:

● Begin early and initiate a dialogue with publics that might be affected. Do not wait until the opposition marshals its forces. Vital to establishing trust is early contact with anyone who may be concerned or affected.

● Actively solicit and identify people's concerns. Informal discussions, surveys, interviews, and focus groups are effective in evaluating issues and identifying outrage factors.

● Recognize the public as a legitimate partner in the process. Engage interested groups in two-way communication and involve key opinion leaders.

● Address issues of concern, even if they do not directly pertain to the project.

● Anticipate and prepare for hostility. To defuse a situation, use a conflict-resolution approach. Identify areas of agreement and work toward common ground.

● Understand the needs of the news media. Provide accurate, timely information and respond promptly to requests.

● Always be honest, even when it hurts.

Health Communication: A Burgeoning Risk Communication Specialty

Public relations professionals specializing in health communication impact all Americans who are concerned about risks to their personal health as well as threats to their financial security from burdensome medical costs. Essentially, health communicators strive to convey health information and prevention measures as a means of reducing health risks. Because personal health and the related costs are so important to us, health issues and related policies often are leading stories in the news. Medical breakthroughs, high-profile drugs such as Viagra, the graying of 76 million baby boomers, and the ongoing controversies over health costs, medical malpractice reform and claims of excessive profits for doctors and health care companies guarantee robust opportunities to practice sophisticated public relations.

One recent multifaceted campaign dealt with a serious health scare. The issue was bacterial contamination of precut vegetables. Television news producers often aired "buyer beware" segments on the dangers of precut salad ingredients, citing lists of common, harmless bacteria normally found on the vegetables and suggesting that their presence could mean that dangerous bacteria may appear.

Having identified the emerging issue, the food industry hired the Londre Group and Fineman Associates to undertake communication efforts for the salad suppliers. Risk communication tactics included publicity that featured university food scientists debunking stories about the innocuous bacteria, video news releases to set forth the scientific facts, trade media briefings, face-to-face meetings with food editors, national opinion surveys, and an array of additional actions.

Also indicative of the growing sophistication of health-care public relations is the targeting of women as health-care consumers; 60 percent of doctor visits and 59 percent of prescription drug purchases are made by women, according to Kym White, Managing Director of Ogilvy PR Worldwide's Health & Medical Practice. Audience targeting also was the thrust of a study entitled "Femstat 3 Report: American Women and Self Care." The study found that 50 percent of women get information mainly from their primary care doctors, 24 percent from magazines and newspapers, 7 percent from television and radio, and 5 percent from self-help books. Much of the health information that women receive is from public relations sources.

The new frontier for health communication is tailored messaging—delivering messages to individuals based on their specific interests, concerns, and health conditions. Professor Matthew Kreuter at Saint Louis University employs a tailoring engine developed by his programming group in the Health Communication Research Laboratory to make tailoring feasible and efficient for large audiences.

Health information and advice on the Web has grown exponentially over the past several years. The National Cancer Institute has a single database with over 650 articles on cancer risk. According to *O'Dwyer's PR Services Report*, 55 percent of the adult population has online access, and 86 percent of them used the Internet to find health-related information. Some experts estimate that nearly 25 percent of all Web searching is health related. Public relations companies now produce video and audio programming on the Web for their health-care clients, providing doctors, medical reporters, investors, and patients with medical and pharmaceutical information.

The tension between health-care providers and those who pay for services is an ongoing source of conflict and the impetus for risk communication to reduce expenses through the prevention of illness. Federally financed Medicaid, which assists low-income patients, has been under recurring political attack. Older Americans sometimes struggle to obtain eligibility for Medicare, a form of government-operated insurance they help finance from their Social Security benefits. Health maintenance organizations (HMOs), in which individuals and families can buy memberships, seek to hold down medical costs by limiting their members' choice of doctors and reserving the right to refuse payment for certain procedures. Conflicting interests create the undertow that pulls politicians, officials, patients and doctors into the everpresent conflict over access and quality of care.

Crisis Management

In public relations, high-profile events such as accidents, terrorist attacks, disease pandemics, and natural disasters can dwarf even the best conflict positioning and risk management strategies. This is when crisis management takes over. The conflict management process, which includes ongoing issues management and risk communication efforts, is severely tested in crisis situations where a high degree of uncertainty exists. Unfortunately, even the most thoughtfully designed conflict management process cannot have a plan in place for specific crises, such as planes flying into the World Trade Center. And sometimes, in spite of risk communication to prevent an issue from becoming a major problem, that issue will grow into a crisis right before the professional's eyes. At such times, verifiable information about what is happening or has happened may be lacking.

This causes people to become more active seekers of information and, as research suggests, more dependent on the media for information to satisfy the human desire for closure. A crisis situation, in other words, puts a great deal of pressure on organizations to respond with accurate, complete information as quickly as possible. How an organization responds in the first 24 hours, experts say, often determines whether the situation remains an "incident" or whether it becomes a full-blown crisis.

What Is a Crisis?

Academics cite many dimensions of what constitutes a crisis for an organization. Ole R. Holsti, author of several articles on crisis theory, defines *crises* as "situations characterized by surprise, high threat to important values, and a short decision time." Thierry C. Pauchant and Ian J. Mitroff, authors of *Transforming the Crisis-Prone Organization*, use this definition: "A disruption that physically affects a system as a whole and threatens its basic assumptions, its subjective sense of self, its existential core." Steven Fink, author of *Crisis Management: Planning for the Inevitable*, states, "Crises are forewarning situations that run the risk of escalating in intensity, falling under close media or government scrutiny, interfering with normal operations, jeopardizing organizational image and damaging a company's bottom line."

Perhaps the best definition, however, is provided by Pacific Telesis, the parent company of Pacific Bell. Its manual on crisis communication says that a crisis is "an extraordinary event or series of events that adversely affects the integrity of the product, the reputation or financial stability of the organization; or the health or well-being of employees, the community, or the public at large."

In other words, an organizational crisis can constitute any number of situations. A *PRWeek* article makes the point: "Imagine one of these scenarios happening to your company: a product recall; a plane crash; a very public sexual harassment suit; a gunman holding hostages in your office; an *E. coli* bacteria contamination scare; a market crash, along with the worth of your company stock; a labor union strike; a hospital malpractice suit . . ."

Nor are crises always unexpected. One study by the Institute for Crisis Management found that only 14 percent of business crises were unexpected. The remaining 86 percent were what the Institute called "smoldering" crises in which an organization was aware of a potential business disruption long before the public found out about it. The study also found that management—or in some cases, mismanagement—caused 78 percent of the crises. "Most organizations have a crisis plan to deal with sudden crises, like accidents," says Robert B. Irvine, president of the Institute, "However, our data indicates many businesses are denying or ducking serious problems that eventually will ignite and cost them millions of dollars and lost management time." With proper issues management and conflict planning, perhaps many of the smoldering crises could be prevented from bursting into flames.

A Lack of Crisis Planning

Echoing Irvine's thought, another study by Steven Fink found that 89 percent of the chief executive officers of *Fortune* 500 companies reported that a business crisis was

ON THE JOB global

Public Nudity on South Korean Cell Phones

Sooyoung Cho, a doctoral student at the Missouri School of Journalism, presented a case study at an international conference in 2004 that showcases both cultural differences in mass media as well as universals surrounding conflict management and contingency theory.

A South Korean company named *Netian* markets its wireless phone services by producing edgy, nude, and partially nude photos of women. This reflects a cultural difference between South Korea and the United States, where nude photo screens on cell phones would probably not be deemed acceptable. According to Ms. Cho, here is how the Netian public relations campaign unfolded in South Korea:

> On February 12, 2004, in a morning press conference in Seoul, South Korea, Netian Entertainment Corporation announced the release of an ambitious serial nude photo project, which had just finished its first series in Palau Island a few days before. Seemingly, this was just another celebrity nude collection that has been so popular in Korea the last several months except the fact that the model posed nude in these photographs

is the top-class Miss Korea-turned-actress, Lee Seung-yeon. In the press conference, the corporation and the actress Lee announced that they would release the nude photos through the mobile phone service and Internet next month after completing the second and third shootings. The idea of providing nude photos through the cell phones so that people can watch naked pictures even in the commuting subways is a daring marketing method recently popular in South Korea.

However, as a few photographs were unveiled, everyone in the room was stunned because those pictures shown were not just ordinary nude photos picturing a woman's naked body. The nude photos were based on the

theme of Korean comfort women who were abducted, hurt, raped, and ruthlessly used by the Japanese army as sex slaves during World War II. Comfort women are a living symbol of sorrow and tragedy in Korea's history . . . . when the stories and a few photographs were released, many human rights groups, women's organizations and angry citizens expressed abhorrence against the photos through protests and Internet discussion, insisting the project be stopped. The corporation and actress faced acerbic criticism from the public accusing them of being traitors. They had to deal with this tremendous animosity from the public for the next several days . . . .

Based on Cameron's contingency theory of conflict management in public relations and Coomb's crisis management typology, the present study found that the corporation moved from an intransigent stance to a claim that all revenue was meant for surviving Comfort Women to final capitulation and apology. One of the main factors in this shift was the major grassroots effort on the Web.

Ms. Cho recommends that Netizen Pressure be added to the matrix of contingency factors shown in Figure 10.3.

almost inevitable; however, 50 percent admitted that they did not have a crisis management plan.

This situation has caused Kenneth Myers, a crisis consultant, to write, "If economics is the dismal science, then contingency planning is the abysmal science." As academics Donald Chisholm and Martin Landry have noted, "When people believe that because nothing has gone wrong, nothing will go wrong, they court disaster.

There is noise in every system and every design. If this fact is ignored, nature soon reminds us of our folly."

Here is a sampling of major crises that have hit various organizations:

● Nike became the archetype of the company that lacked a social conscience due to its exploitation of workers in foreign plants. The value of the company stock went down, the media wrote numerous unflattering stories, and human rights activists had a field day.

● Microsoft, caught in a battle with the U.S. Department of Justice and its competitors about monopolistic policies, received mostly unfavorable publicity throughout 1998 and 1999.

● Odwalla, the natural juice maker, had to recall about 70 percent of its product line after several cases of *E. coli* poisoning—including one death—were linked to its unpasteurized apple juice. The company pled guilty to criminal charges and agreed to pay a $1.5 million fine.

● McDonald's got negative publicity when an 81-year-old woman won a multi-million-dollar lawsuit against the company because she suffered third-degree burns from a scalding cup of coffee.

● Intel, the leading manufacturer of computer chips, faced a major credibility problem when flaws were found in its Pentium chip.

Each of these examples, as Irvine suggests, started as a "smoldering" crisis that management could have prevented if it had used more environmental scanning and issues management, leading to the development of a strategic management plan. Instead, it left the issue to fester and ultimately ignite in national headlines. In the McDonald's case, the company had received at least 700 complaints of coffee burns during the last decade and had settled more than $500,000 in claims from scalding injuries.

Intel worsened its problem by treating the Pentium flaw as a trivial matter and failing to offer customers an explanation or a replacement. Indeed, the Intel crisis finally got national attention when IBM announced its decision to halt the sale of Pentium-based personal computers. This decision was made six weeks after Intel knew there was a problem but failed to take corrective action. Alfonso Gonzalez-Herrero and Cornelius B. Pratt, writing about the Intel situation, said, "Intel possibly forgot two key principles of modern corporate communications: (a) image is perceptual reality, and (b) passiveness is a transitory state that can change when publics feel outraged."

How to Communicate During a Crisis

Many professionals offer advice on what to do during a crisis. Here's a compilation of good suggestions:

● Put the public first.
● Take responsibility. An organization should take responsibility for solving the problem.
● Be honest. Don't obscure facts and try to mislead the public.

- Never say, "No comment." A Porter/Novelli survey found that nearly two-thirds of the public feel that "no comment" almost always means that the organization is guilty of wrongdoing.
- Designate a single spokesperson.
- Set up a central information center.
- Provide a constant flow of information. When information is withheld, the cover-up becomes the story.
- Be familiar with media needs and deadlines.
- Be accessible.
- Monitor news coverage and telephone inquiries.
- Communicate with key publics.

How Various Organizations Respond to Crises

The list just presented offers sound, practical advice, but recent research has shown that organizations don't all respond to a crisis in the same way. Indeed, W. Timothy Coombs postulates that an organization's response may vary on a continuum from defensive to accommodative. Here is a list of crisis communication strategies that an organization may use:

- **Attack the accuser.** The party that claims a crisis exists is confronted and its logic and facts are faulted. Sometimes a lawsuit is threatened.

- **Denial.** The organization explains that there is no crisis.

- **Excuse.** The organization minimizes its responsibility for the crisis. Any intention to do harm is denied, and the organization says that it had no control over the events that led to the crisis. This strategy is often used when there is a natural disaster or product tampering.

- **Justification.** Crisis is minimized with a statement that no serious damage or injuries resulted. Sometimes, the blame is shifted to the victims, as in the case of the Firestone recall outlined in Chapter 1. This is often done when a consumer misuses a product or when there is an industrial accident.

- **Ingratiation.** Actions are taken to appease the publics involved. Consumers who complain are given coupons or the organization makes a donation to a charitable organization. Burlington Industries, for example, gave a large donation to the Humane Society after the discovery that it had imported coats from China with fur collars containing dog fur instead of "coyote" fur.

- **Corrective action.** Steps are taken to repair the damage from the crisis and to prevent it from happening again.

- **Full apology.** Organization takes responsibility and asks forgiveness. Some compensation of money or aid is often included.

The Coombs typology gives options for crisis communication management depending on the situation. He notes that organizations do have to consider more accommodative strategies (ingratiation, corrective action, full apology) if defensive strategies (attack accuser, denial, excuse) are not effective in repairing an organization's reputation or restoring previous sales levels. He says, "Accommodative strategies emphasize each repair, which is what is needed as image damage worsens. Defensive strategies, such as denial or minimizing, logically become less effective as organizations are viewed as more responsible for the crisis."

Often, however, an organization doesn't adopt an accommodative strategy because of corporate culture and other constraints included in the contingency theory of conflict management matrix. Organizations do not, and sometimes cannot, engage in two-way communication and accommodative strategies when confronted with a crisis or conflict with a given public. Some variables proscribing accommodation, according to Cameron, include: (1) management's moral conviction that the public is wrong; (2) moral neutrality when two contending publics want the organization to take sides on a policy issue; (3) legal constraints; (4) regulatory constraints such as the FTC or SEC; (5) prohibition by senior management against an accommodative stance; and (6) possible conflict between departments of the organization on what strategies to adopt.

In some cases, the contingency theory contends that the ideal of mutual understanding and accommodation doesn't occur because both sides have staked out highly rigid positions and are not willing to compromise their strong moral positions. For example, it is unlikely that the prolife and prochoice forces will ever achieve mutual understanding and accommodation. Taking an inflexible stance, however, can be a foolish strategy and a sign of unprofessionalism. At other times, conflict is a natural state between competing interests, such as oil interests seeking oil exploration in Alaskan wildlife refuges and environmental groups seeking to block that exploration. As the contingency theory declares, one's stance and strategies for conflict management entail the reading of many factors.

How Some Organizations Have Handled Crises

The crisis communication strategies outlined by Coombs are useful in evaluating how an organization handles a crisis. Intel, for example, first denied that there was a problem with its Pentium chip. As the crisis deepened and was covered in the mainstream press, Intel tried the strategy of justification by saying that the problem wasn't serious enough to warrant replacing the chips. It minimized the concerns of end-users such as engineers and computer programmers. Only after considerable damage had been done to Intel's reputation and IBM had suspended orders for the chip did Intel take corrective action to replace the chips, and Andy Grove, Intel's president, issued a full apology.

Exxon, still highly identified with the major oil spill in Prince William Sound, Alaska, also chose a defensive strategy when one of its ships, the Exxon Valdez, hit a reef in 1989 and spilled nearly 240,000 barrels of oil into a pristine environment. The disaster, one of history's worst environmental accidents, was badly mismanaged from the beginning.

Exxon management started its crisis communication strategy by making excuses. Management claimed that Exxon, as a corporation, wasn't at fault because (1) the weather wasn't ideal, (2) the charts provided by the U.S. Coast Guard were out of date, and (3) the captain of the ship was derelict in his duties by drinking while on duty. As clean-up efforts began, Exxon also tried to shift the blame by maintaining that government bureaucracy and prohibitions against the use of certain chemicals hampered the company's efforts.

Exxon also used the strategy of justification to minimize the damage, saying that environmentalists in the government were exaggerating the ill effects of the spill on bird and animal life. Meanwhile, negative press coverage was intense, and public outrage continued to rise. William J. Small of Fordham University, who researched the press coverage, wrote, "Probably no other company ever got a more damaging portrayal in the mass media." More than 18,000 customers tore up their Exxon credit cards, late-night talk show hosts ridiculed the company, and Congressional committees started hearings. Exxon dropped from eighth to 110th on *Fortune*'s list of most-admired companies.

Exxon's response to all of these developments was somewhat ineffective. It did try the strategy of ingratiation by running full-page advertisements stating that the company was sorry for the oil spill—but it didn't take responsibility for it. Instead of calming the storm, that approach only further enraged the public. Exxon also took corrective action and cleaned up the oil spill, spending about $3 billion in its efforts. The company received little credit for this action, however, because most of the public believed it was done only under government pressure. And by the time the cleanup was finished, public attitudes about Exxon had already been formed.

Odwalla and Pepsi provide examples of more successful crisis communication strategies.

Odwalla didn't bother with a defensive strategy when they got a phone call from Washington State health officials that the company's apple juice was implicated in several cases of *E. coli* poisoning. Twenty minutes after the call, Odwalla held a press conference announcing its recall of all of its products that contained unpasteurized apple juice.

Within 72 hours, the company set up a crisis-related Web site with the aid of its public relations firm, Daniel Edelman Worldwide. The company's Web site, which was widely publicized, contained links to the Food and Drug Administration (FDA) and the Centers for Disease Control and Prevention so consumers could get additional information about *E. coli* contamination.

Company management, from the very beginning, initiated an accommodative stance. The press conference and the Web site were an ingratiation strategy to retain consumer confidence; corrective action was taken immediately by recalling the product and taking steps to change the production process. Early in the crisis, the company president also issued a full apology and garnered much public support by announcing that the company would pay any medical bills of the approximately 70 people poisoned. The company also offered to replace any bottles of apple juice on consumer shelves. The result was widespread public approval, and in one survey almost 90 percent of consumers said they would continue to buy the product.

It is important to note, however, that not all successful crisis communication strategies need to be accommodative. Pepsi-Cola was able to mount an effective defensive crisis communication strategy and avoid a recall when a hoax of nationwide proportions created an intense but short-lived crisis for the soft-drink company.

The crisis began when the media reported that a man in Tacoma, Washington, claimed that he had found a syringe inside a can of Diet Pepsi. As the news spread, men and women across the country made similar claims of finding a broken sewing needle, a screw, a bullet, and even a narcotics vial in their Pepsi cans. As a consequence, demands for a recall of all Pepsi products arose, an action that would have had major economic consequences for the company.

Company officials were confident that insertion of foreign objects into cans on the high-speed, closely controlled bottling lines was virtually impossible, so they chose to defend their product. The urgent problem, then, was to convince the public that the product was safe, and that any foreign objects found had been inserted after the cans had been opened.

Company officials and their public relations staff employed several strategies. One approach was to attack the accuser. Pepsi officials said the foreign objects probably got into the cans after they were opened, and even explained that many people make such claims just to collect compensation from the company. The company also announced that it would pursue legal action against anyone making false claims about the integrity of the company's products.

Pepsi also took the strategy of denial, saying that there was no crisis. Pepsi president Craig E. Weatherup immediately made appearances on national television programs and gave newspaper interviews to state the company's case that its bottling lines were secure. Helping to convince the public was U.S. Food and Drug Administration Commissioner David Kessler, who said that a recall was not necessary.

These quick actions deflated the public's concern, and polls showed considerable acceptance of Pepsi's contention that the problem was a hoax. A week after the scare began, Pepsi ran full-page advertisements with the headline, "Pepsi is pleased to announce . . . Nothing." It stated, "As America now knows, those stories about Diet Pepsi were a hoax . . ."

These varied cases illustrate one emphasis of contingency theory: No single crisis communication strategy is appropriate for all situations. Therefore, as Coombs indicates, "It is only by understanding the crisis situation that the crisis manager can select the appropriate response for the crisis." Corporate culture and management mind-sets also influence how an organization responds to a developing crisis.

Reputation Management

Reputation is defined as the collective representation of an organization's past performance that describes the firm's ability to deliver valued outcomes to multiple stakeholders. Put in plain terms, reputation is the track record of an organization in the public's mind.

Public relations scholar Lisa Lyon makes the point that reputation, unlike corporate image, is *owned* by the publics. Reputation isn't formed by packaging or slogans. A good reputation is created and destroyed by everything an organization does, from the way it manages employees to the way it handles conflicts with outside constituents.

The Three Foundations of Reputation

Reputation scholars offer three foundations of reputation: (1) economic performance, (2) social responsiveness, and (3) the ability to deliver valuable outcomes to stakeholders. Public relations plays a role in all three foundations, but professionals who manage conflict effectively will especially enhance the latter two foundations of reputation. The social responsiveness of an organization results from careful issue tracking and effective positioning of the organization. It is further enhanced when risk communication is compelling and persuasive. The ability to make valuable contributions to stakeholders who depend on the organization results in part from fending off threats to the organization that would impair its mission.

Research techniques called *reputation audits* can be used to assess and monitor an organization's reputation. These can be as basic as *Fortune* magazine's list of "Most

Admired Companies" (www.fortune.com/fortune/mostadmired) to rigorous global reputation measures, such as the Reputation Quotient offered by the Reputation Institute (www.reputationinstitute.com) in conjunction with Harris Interactive. Of particular interest to public relations professionals is the Media Reputation Index (MRI), which measures the effects of media coverage on corporate reputations. Working with Delahaye Medialink, the project documents the important role of media in reputation management. This relationship is depicted in Figure 10.5. See Chapter 17 for more discussion of how corporations conduct reputation management.

In addition to tracking and dealing proactively with issues, conveying risks to publics, and managing crises as they arise, public relations practitioners also will be faced with the need to apologize when all efforts to manage conflict have fallen short. The future trust and credibility of the organization are at stake in how well this recovery phase of conflict management is handled.

The frequent platitude in postcrisis communication is that practitioners should acknowledge failings, apologize, and then put the events in the past as quickly as possible. However, Lyon has found that apology is not always effective because of the *hypocrisy factor*. When an organization has a questionable track record (i.e., a bad reputation), the apology may be viewed as being insincere and hypocritical. Coombs suggests a relational approach, which assumes that crises are episodes within a larger stakeholder–organizational relationship. Applying the contingency theory, considering how stakeholders perceive the situation can help communicators determine which strategy is best to rebuild the stakeholder–organization relationship and restore the organization's reputation.

FIGURE 10.5

This diagram shows many of the forces affecting corporate reputation, most notably how media coverage and performance of an organization impact reputation and, in turn, how reputation influences the health of the organization.

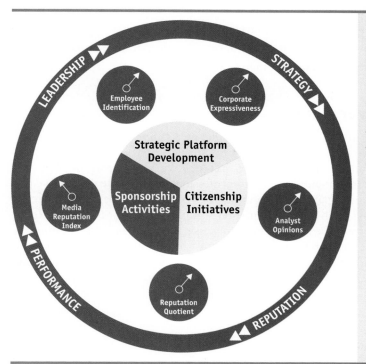

Image Restoration

Reputation repair and maintenance is a long-term process, but one of the first steps in the process is the final one in the conflict management life cycle discussed earlier in this chapter. Professor William Benoit of the University of Missouri offers five general strategies for image restoration and a number of substrategies, adding to the options available to the public relations professional that can be used when the worst of a crisis has passed:

1. Denial
   - Simple denial—Your organization did not do what it is accused of.
   - Shift the blame—Someone else did it.
2. Evade responsibility
   - Provocation—Your organization was provoked.
   - Defeasibility—Your organization was unable to avoid its actions.
   - Accident—The bad events were an accident.
   - Good intentions—Good intentions went awry.
3. Reduce offensiveness
   - Bolstering—Refer to the organization's clean record and good reputation.
   - Minimization—Reduce the magnitude of negative feelings.
   - Differentiation—Distinguish the act from other similar, but more offensive, acts
   - Transcendence—Justify the act by placing it in a more favorable context.
   - Attack the accuser—Reduce the credibility of the accusations.
   - Compensation—Reduce the perceived severity of the injury.
4. Corrective action—Ensure the prevention or correction of the action.
5. Mortification—Offer a profuse apology.

Déjà vu—All Over Again

Empirical evidence from Benoit's work is ongoing, but it appears that image restoration can be an effective final stage in the conflict management process. But to paraphrase Yogi Berra, conflict management is like déjà vu all over again. The best organizations, led by the best public relations professionals, will strive to improve performance by starting once again at the beginning of the conflict management life cycle (Figure 10.1) with tasks such as environmental scanning and issues tracking. Issues that are deemed important receive attention for crisis planning and risk communication. When preventive measures fail, the crisis must be handled with the best interests of all parties held in a delicate balance. Then reputation must be given due attention. At all times, the goal is to change organizational behavior in ways that minimize damaging conflict, not only for the sake of the organization, but also for its many stakeholders.

PR CASEBOOK

West Point Averts a Crisis

Charges of sexual harassment can seriously damage an organization's reputation and diminish public support. Officials at West Point knew they had a potential crisis on their hands when a group of women cadets on a "spirit run" were groped as they ran through a cordon of football players at a practice session.

After the women complained, the Academy triggered its crisis communications plan. Four objectives were established: (1) The Academy's investigation would be conducted swiftly, fairly, and openly; (2) the incident was an exception; (3) the complaint should not be equated with the infamous Tailhook scandal; and (4) West Point had zero tolerance for sexual harassment.

The Academy's superintendent, who acted as the spokesperson on this issue, reported the incident at a scheduled meeting with the *New York Times*. The Academy also communicated with the cadets, faculty, employees, alumni, parents, admission officers, the Pentagon, and members of Congress. The public relations staff coordinated media interviews with cadets and officials at the Academy.

Two weeks after the incident, the Academy issued a news release announcing the final results of the investigation and the punishment meted out to the guilty cadets. Media reports were uniformly positive about how West Point handled the problem.

By being open, forthright, and candid and by effectively communicating its policy that sexual harassment would not be tolerated, West Point got its key messages across and emerged from the incident with an enhanced reputation. In fact, acceptance of admission offers from women increased 50 percent from the previous year.

SUMMARY

Life Cycle of Conflict Management

Strategic conflict management can be broadly divided into four phases with specific techniques and functions falling into each phase. The life cycle emphasizes that conflict management is ongoing and cyclical in nature.

Contingency Theory of Conflict Management

Some of the most crucial roles played by public relations professionals involve the strategic management of conflict. The contingency theory argues for a dynamic and multifaceted approach to dealing with conflict in the field.

Issues Management

Issues management is a proactive and systematic approach to predict problems, anticipate threats, minimize surprises, resolve issues, and prevent crises. The five steps in the issues management process are issue identification, issue analysis, strategy options, an action plan, and the evaluation of results.

Risk Communication

Risk communication attempts to convey information regarding risk to public health and safety and the environment. It involves more than the dissemination of accurate information. The communicator must begin early, identify and address the public's concerns, recognize the public as a legitimate partner, anticipate hostility, respond to the needs of the news media, and always be honest.

Crisis Communications

The communications process is severely tested in crisis situations, which can take many forms. A common problem is the lack of crisis management plans even when a "smoldering" crisis is building. Organizations' responses may vary from defensive to accommodative. Corporate culture and other constraints may prevent adoption of an appropriate strategy.

Reputation Management

One of an organization's most valuable assets is its reputation. This asset is impacted by how the organization deals with conflict, particularly those crises that generate significant media attention. Using research to monitor reputation and making realistic responses after crises have passed can minimize damage to an organization's reputation. More importantly, returning to the proactive phase of conflict management to improve organizational performance will ultimately improve reputation.

Case Activity: **What Would You Do?**

Formed in response to the 9/11 terrorist attacks, the Department of Homeland Security (DHS) faces an array of threats—nuclear bombs, suicide bombers, biological weapons, and attacks on the nation's communications systems. One of the most devastating attacks would be if a terrorist succeeded in contaminating the U.S. food supply, resulting in either poisoning of the population or famine. A terrorist might introduce a disease or genetic modification that could destroy plants or animals, or perhaps worse, impact consumers eating food that they believe is safe

and healthful. Even a rumor of contamination or mad cow disease causes economic turmoil. Some consider rumor and economic embargo to be the major threats, even without an actual agroterrorist event. DHS has a four-stage strategy for agroterrorism: (1) prevention, (2) detection, (3) response, and (4) recovery. Applying concepts from this chapter and from Chapter 6, "Program Planning," outline a master strategic plan or tackle one of the four stages to develop a strategy for DHS. You may want to deal only with one aspect of conflict management, such as issue tracking or crisis management.

QUESTIONS for Review and Discussion

1. Do you accept the proposition that conflict management is one of the most important functions of public relations? Why or why not?
2. What are the five steps in the issues management process?
3. How can effective issues management prevent organizational crises?
4. Both Exxon and Pepsi used defensive crisis communication strategies. However, one succeeded and the other failed. What factors do you think made the difference?
5. What is risk communication?
6. How would you use the contingency theory of conflict management (the continuum from accommodation to advocacy and the matrix of factors) in advising management on a rising conflict situation?
7. Do you think that image restoration is merely a superficial fix or a substantive solution to adverse events? Support your view with some examples from current news stories.

SUGGESTED READINGS

Cancel, Amanda E., Cameron, Glen T., Sallot, Lynne M., and Mitrook, Michael. "It Depends: A Contingency Theory of Accommodation in Public Relations." *Journal of Public Relations Research*, Vol. 9, No. 1, 1997, pp. 31–64.

Coombs, Timothy W. "An Analytic Framework for Crisis Situations: Better Response from a Better Understanding of the Situation." *Journal of Public Relations Research*, Vol. 8, No. 2, 1996, pp. 79–106.

Frank, John N. "All Hands on Deck: When Crisis Hits, a Whole Host of People Are Needed to Pitch in and Help Out." *PRWeek*, February 16, 2004, p. 15.

Fombrun, Charles J., and van Riel, Cees. *Fame and Fortune: How Successful Companies Build Winning Reputations*. Upper Saddle River, NJ: Financial Times Prentice Hall, 2003.

Greer, Clark F., and Moreland, Kurt D. "United Airlines' and American Airlines' Online Crisis Communication Following the September 11 Terrorist Attacks." *Public Relations Review*, Vol. 29, No. 4, 2003, pp. 427–441.

Hallahan, Kirk. "The Dynamics of Issues Activation and Response: An Issues Process Model." *Journal of Public Relations Research*, Vol. 13, No. 1, pp. 27–59.

Hazley, Greg. "Beef Industry Passes Its First Run-in with Mad Cow." *O'Dwyer's PR Services Report*, February 2004, pp. 1, 15, 17.

Heath, Robert L., Seshardi, Shaila, and Lee, Jaesub. "Risk Communication: A Two-Way Community Analysis of Proximity, Dread, Trust, Involvement, Uncertainty, Openness/Accessibility, and Knowledge on Support/Opposition toward Chemical Companies." *Journal of Public Relations Research*, Vol. 10, No. 1, 1998, pp. 35–56.

Herskovits, Beth. "GlaxoSmithKline Launches Push to End Concerns about Drug Costs." *PR Week*, August 23, 2004, p. 1.

Herskovits, Beth. "US Vaccine Shortage Yields Widespread Crisis Outreach." *PR Week*, October 18, 2004, p. 1.

Leo, John. "I'm Terribly Sorry. Really." *U.S. News & World Report*, May 10, 2004, p. 13.

Lyon, Lisa, and Cameron, Glen T. "Fess Up or Stonewall? An Experimental Test of Prior Reputation and Response Style in the Face of Negative News Coverage." *Web Journal of Mass Communication Research*, Vol. 1, No. 4, September 1998, pp. 1–24 (www.scripps.ohiou.edu/wjmcr).

Lyon, Lisa, and Cameron, Glen T. "A Relational Approach Examining the Interplay of Prior Reputation and Immediate Response to a Crisis." *Journal of Public Relations Research*, Vol. 16, No. 3, 2004, pp. 213–241.

Palenchar, Michael J., and Heath, Robert L. "Another Part of the Risk Communication Model: Analysis of Communication Processes and Message Content." *Journal of Public Relations Research*, Vol. 14, No. 2, pp. 127–158.

Reber, Bryan H. and Cameron, Glen T. "Measuring Contingencies: Using Scales to Measure Public Relations Practitioner Limits to Accommodation." *Journalism and Mass Communication Quarterly*, Vol. 80, Summer 2003, pp. 431–446.

Seeger, Matthew W. "Chaos and Crisis: Propositions for a General Theory of Crisis Communication." *Public Relations Review*, Vol. 28, No. 4, 2002, p. 329–337.

Wan, Hua-Hsin, and Pfau, Michael. "The Relative Effectiveness of Inoculation, Bolstering, and Combined Approaches to Crisis Communication." *Journal of Public Relations Research*, Vol. 16, No. 3, pp. 301–328.

chapter 11

The Audience and How to Reach It

Topics covered in this chapter include:

Nature of the Public Relations Audience

If the audience on which public relations practitioners focus their messages was a monolithic whole, their work would be far easier—and far less stimulating. The audience, in fact, is just the opposite: It is a complex intermingling of groups with diverse cultural, ethnic, religious, and economic attributes whose interests coincide at times and conflict at others.

For the public relations professional, knowledge of these shifting audience dynamics is essential. A successful campaign must be aimed at those segments of the mass audience that are most desirable for its particular purpose, and it must employ those media most effective in reaching them. Some of these segments are easily identifiable and reachable as "prepackaged publics." They are well-organized groups whose members have banded together in a common interest; they constitute ready-made targets for practitioners who have projects of concern to them. Examples of such prepackaged publics are members of civic, educational, and charitable organizations.

Diversity is the most significant aspect of the mass audience in the United States. Differences in geography, history, and economy among regions of the sprawling country are striking; ranchers in Montana have different attitudes than residents in the heavily populated Eastern seaboard cities. Yet people in the two areas do have national interests in common. Ethnicity also shapes the audience segments that public relations practitioners address.

Computer technology can be used to conduct both secondary and primary research to identify target audiences. The rich source of geographic and social statistics found in Census Bureau reports provides a foundation. Much of this data can be broken down by census tract and ZIP code.

Data on automobile registrations, voter registrations, sales figures, mailing lists, and church and organization memberships also can be merged into computer databases. For example, one marketing research organization, Claritas Inc., has divided the Chicago metropolitan district into 62 lifestyle clusters. It has assigned a name to each cluster; for example, "Boomers & Babies," whose buying habits, Claritas says, include "rent more than five videos a month, buy children frozen dinners, read parenting magazines."

Public relations has become more strategic in practice; audiences are targeted precisely and in some instances messages are customized at the individual level. In health-care settings, e-mail messages can be tailored to the individual patient based on his or her most recent examination. Not only can the practitioner target a precise public, but in many cases the professional can actually bypass the media and communicate directly with the target audience. The use of communication channels that reach directly to the audience is called *controlled media*. Using a database, an organization can send letters directly to key decision makers, such as stockholders, for example. The same technique can be used by directing e-mail or broadcast faxes to key constituents.

Publications directed at employees and customers serve as examples of controlled media. Two of the most effective and popular controlled media are sponsored video and online media.

Senior and Ethnic Markets

As the demographic makeup of the United States continues to change, two major target audiences have emerged that deserve special attention. One is seniors. This group frequently is defined as men and women 65 years or older, although some sociologists and marketing experts include everyone over age 50. The other group consists of racial and ethnic minorities.

Similar audiences are developing to various degrees in other countries.

Seniors

Medical advances have improved life expectancy to the point that today almost 35 million Americans are age 65 or older, according to the U.S. Census Bureau. A heavy upsurge in the senior population will peak at 50 million by 2010, when the post–World War II "baby boomers" begin to reach age 65. These older citizens form an important opinion group and a consumer market with special interests.

When appealing to seniors, public relations people should try to ignore the stereotypes of "old folks" so often depicted in the movies and television. Some 80-year-old women sit in rocking chairs, knitting or snoozing, but others cheer and boo ardently while watching professional basketball on TV. Nor are all grandfathers crotchety complainers with quavering voices or kindly patriarchs who fly kites with their grandsons. As many differences in personality, interest, financial status, and living styles exist in the older audience as among their young-adult grandchildren.

Public relations practitioners should remember these characteristics of seniors:

● With the perspective of long experience, they often are less easily convinced than young adults, demand value in the things they buy, and pay little attention to fads.

● They vote in greater numbers than their juniors and are more intense readers of newspapers and magazines. Retirees also watch television heavily.

● They form an excellent source of volunteers for social, health, and cultural organizations because they have time and often are looking for something to do.

● They are extremely health-conscious, out of self-interest, and want to know about medical developments. A Census Bureau study showed that most people over age 65 say they are in good health; not until their mid-80s do they frequently need assistance in daily living.

Financially, the elderly are better off than the stereotypes suggest. The poverty rate among older Americans is slightly below that of the population at large. The Census Bureau found that people ages 65 to 74 have more discretionary income than any other group. In many instances, their homes are completely paid for, and they hold 70 percent of the country's assets. Although they are poor customers for household goods, they eat out frequently and do much gift buying. They travel frequently. In fact, seniors account for about 80 percent of commercial vacation travel, especially cruises.

Ethnic Groups

Historically, the United States has welcomed millions of immigrants and assimilated them into the cultural mainstream. They bring a bubbling mixture of personal values, habits, and perceptions that are absorbed slowly, sometimes reluctantly. The questions of assimilation—how much, how little?—also pertain to two minorities that have a long history in United States: African Americans and Native Americans. This diversity is a great strength of the United States, but also a source of friction and misunderstandings. Communication campaigns have been employed in other highly diverse societies such as Malaysia and the Middle East to build understanding and interaction among diverse ethnic groups. Called *nation-building*, this important public relations work will become invaluable in building a relevant new definition of nationhood in the United States as it embraces growing diversity and multiculturalism while also maintaining a national identity.

Recently, the easily identifiable ethnic groups—primarily Hispanics, African Americans, Asian Americans, and Native Americans—as a whole have been growing five times faster than the general population, with nonwhite ethnic groups now comprising a majority in some states. The U.S. Census Bureau predicts that by the year 2010 Hispanics and African Americans will make up 14.6 and 12.5 percent of the U.S. population, respectively, for a total of 27.1 percent, and Anglos 67.3 percent. Asian Americans and Native Americans will provide the remaining percentage. According to the Census Bureau, even greater changes will occur by 2050. Notably, Hispanics will comprise nearly one-fourth of the U.S. population. (See Figure 11.1.)

A basic point to remember is that minority populations form many target audiences, not a massive monolithic group whose members have identical interests. Asian Americans in San Francisco have different cultures and concerns from Hispanics in Miami. To be more precise, even the common terms for minority groups, such as Asian American, miss the cultural diversity among that racial group. For example, the lifestyles, values, and interests of fourth-generation Japanese Americans in Los Angeles are dramatically different from what is found among recent immigrants from

FIGURE 11.1

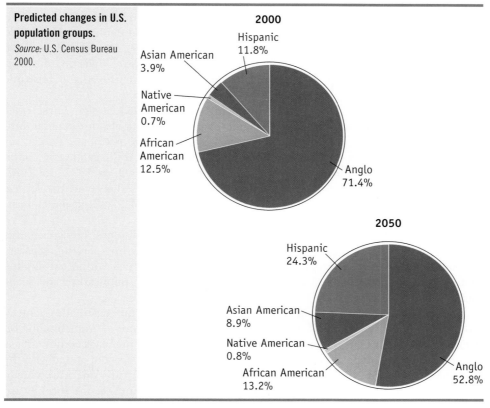

Predicted changes in U.S. population groups.
Source: U.S. Census Bureau 2000.

2000
Hispanic 11.8%
Asian American 3.9%
Native American 0.7%
African American 12.5%
Anglo 71.4%

2050
Hispanic 24.3%
Asian American 8.9%
Native American 0.8%
African American 13.2%
Anglo 52.8%

Vietnam or the Philippines. Thus, the practitioner must define the audience with particular care and sensitivity, taking into account race but increasingly considering the cultural and ethnic self-identity of many target audience segments.

Expanding populations have been accompanied by an increase in the number and strength of the minority media through which messages can be delivered. The *Gale Directory of Publications and Broadcast Media* lists 162 Hispanic publications and 245 African American publications; Spanish-language and African American radio stations also have increased in number. Two Spanish-language TV networks, Univision and Telemundo, serve millions of viewers. The Black Entertainment Television Network has a large national audience. A substantial number of outlets exist for public relations messages, provided news releases and story pitches are translated and culturally appropriate.

The swift expansion of the Hispanic population is a challenge for public relations practitioners. Merely translating messages into Spanish is not good enough. Practitioners must shape communications to the Hispanic culture. According to the U.S. Census Bureau, 12 million Hispanic children lived in the United States in 1996, up from 9.8 million six years earlier. This compares to 50.8 million Anglo children and 11.4 million non-Hispanic blacks. According to New America Strategies and DemoGraph Corporation, this family oriented culture is why Hispanic spending on health care and entertainment will be more than three times greater than white household expenditures.

Radio is an especially important way to reach this ethnic group. Surveys show that the average Hispanic person listens to radio 26 to 30 hours a week, about 13 percent more than the general population. Hispanic station KLVE-FM has the largest audience in Los Angeles, more than any English-language station.

Television also has a large, rapidly expanding Hispanic audience. The Nielsen rating service in 2004 estimated the number of Hispanic households in the United States with television sets at 10.57 million. Such households are defined as those in which the head of the household is of Hispanic descent. Univision, the predominant Spanish-language TV network, claims to reach three-fourths of Hispanic viewers.

Hispanic-owned businesses are multiplying in the United States. These offer new client possibilities, not only for Hispanic-owned firms, but also for general public relations firms that adapt their services to Hispanic needs. A Census Bureau report in 2001 showed an 83.7 percent increase in the number of Hispanic companies in the United States during the five-year period from 1992 to 1997. In 1997, Hispanics owned the largest number of minority businesses; however, the largest share of minority business revenue was earned by Asian and Pacific Islander business owners.

Business Wire, a major distributor of public relations messages, recognizes this diversity of interest among racial and ethnic minority groups by operating separate Hispanic, African American, and Asian American media circuits within the United States. As further indication of diversity, the *Gale Directory* lists publications in 48 languages other than English.

Public relations people should give particular attention to the sensitivities of racial and ethnic minority audiences. For example, the familiar figure of Aunt Jemima on packages of Quaker Oats food products was widely regarded in the black community as a patronizing stereotype. To change this perception, Quaker Oats cooperated with the National Council of Negro Women to honor outstanding African-American women in local communities, who then competed for a national award. At the local award

FIGURE 11.2

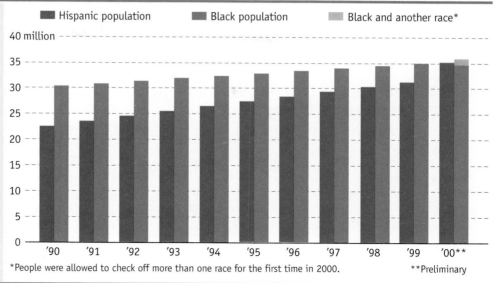

The Hispanic population is the fastest-growing minority group in the United States. Many public information campaigns now include brochures and radio spots in Spanish to reach this population.

*People were allowed to check off more than one race for the first time in 2000.

**Preliminary

breakfasts, all food served was Aunt Jemima brands, and Quaker Oats officials participated in the programs. The project generated an atmosphere of mutual understanding.

Audience Characteristics

Human drives have changed little over the centuries. As we move deeper into the 21st century, we continue to love, hate, worship, work for food and shelter, protect our families, and respond to our neighbors' needs much as our forefathers did 300 years ago. Knowing how to appeal to these basic emotions and needs is essential.

Even though these drives are constant, specific aspects and attitudes of the audience change over time. In numerous respects, current audience trends differ from those of previous generations in ways significant to the public relations practitioner:

● **The public is increasingly visually oriented.** The enormous impact of television on daily life has increased visual orientation, with many people obtaining virtually all of their news from the TV screen. Several studies indicate that local television is the most credible and frequently used news source, supplanting the local newspaper. Television news is told primarily in pictures presented briefly at a swiftly changing pace. Such exposure may lead to a shortened attention span for current events coverage. Political leaders' policies reach the public largely in 10-second "sound bites." Television also serves as a potent communicator of manners and mores.

● **Fervent support is generated for single issues.** Many individuals become so zealously involved in promoting or opposing a single favorite issue that they lose the social and political balance so needed in a country. Such vehement behavior may create severe public relations problems for the objects of their attacks.

ON THE JOB

global

American Web Sites Overlook European Audiences

Europe boasts nearly 200 million online users who share an emerging common identity as members of the European Union (EU). The European community even has its own Web domain name, ".eu." However, in a study conducted by APCO Online, the world's 50 largest companies in financial terms do not give Europe its due; three out of every four of these corporate Web sites do not offer a European link. Other findings:

- Fewer than one in three of the sites included a phone number for the European corporate division of the parent company.

- Only half answered an e-mail request for information about European operations of the company within one week.
- The majority failed to communicate in a language other than English.
- Of the 10 highest-scoring sites, four were European companies.

For a medium that claims to be customizable and interactive, corporate Web sites appear to be falling short of their potential.

Sources: pr reporter, April 15, 2002. www.apcoworldwide .com.

- **Heavy emphasis is placed on personality and celebrity.** Sports stars, television and movie actors, and rock music performers are virtually worshipped by some fans. When stars embrace causes, many people blindly follow them. More and more, celebrities are used as spokespersons and fund-raisers, even though their expertise as performers does not necessarily qualify them as experts or opinion leaders for complex issues, such as the environment or world trade.

- **Strong distrust of authority and suspicion of conspiracy can arise from sensationalistic investigative reporting.** People are so inundated with exaggerated political promises, see so much financial chicanery, and are exposed to so many misleading television advertisements that many of them distrust what they read and hear. They suspect evil motives and tend to believe rumors. The need for public relations programs to develop an atmosphere of justifiable, rational trust is obvious.

- **The international audience for public relations has expanded swiftly.** Growth of global corporations and expanded foreign marketing by smaller firms opens new public relations situations, as does increased foreign ownership of U.S. companies.

Many of these trends will continue well into the new century, creating an ongoing need for flexibility and growth among public relations practitioners. The variety and number of employment opportunities in public relations will be fueled in part by these changes in audience characteristics.

Matching the Audience with the Media

This chapter explains each of the major media—how each one functions and ways in which it can be used for public relations purposes. With such an array of printed, spoken, visual, and new media methods available, practitioners must make wise choices in order to use their time and budgets efficiently.

Before we look at each medium in more detail, some general guidelines can be given for matching the audience with the media:

● Print media are the most effective for delivering a message that requires absorption of details and contemplation by the receiver. Printed matter can be read repeatedly and kept for reference. The Internet, perhaps more like traditional print sources than like broadcast media, is the fastest to deliver breaking news. Newspapers also are fast and have the most widespread impact. Magazines, although slower, are better directed to special-interest audiences. Books take even longer but can generate strong impact over time.

● Television has the strongest emotional impact of all media. Its visual power makes situations seem close to the viewer. The personality of the TV communicator creates an influence that print media cannot match.

● Radio's greatest advantages are flexibility and the ability to reach specific target audiences. Messages can be prepared for and broadcast on radio more rapidly than on television, at much lower cost. Because there are nine times as many radio stations as TV stations, audience exposure is easier to obtain, but the audiences reached are smaller.

● The online media are usually used as a supplemental method of reaching a generally well-educated, relatively affluent audience interested in new ideas and fresh approaches. However, usage patterns are changing almost weekly, and major breaking news stories now reach a large audience online. The most striking recent example was the enormous attention by audiences to breaking news about the September 11 terrorist attacks.

In some campaigns, the most cost-effective results come from use of a single medium. Other campaigns work best when several types of media are used. Wise selection of media, based on the audience sought and the money available, is an important skill for public relations practitioners to develop.

Media Relations

Before examining the print, electronic, and film media individually, we need to look at the relationship between the media and public relations practitioners, who need to understand this sometimes sensitive interplay.

Editors and reporters and public relations people need each other. The media must have material and ideas from public relations sources, and practitioners must have the media as a place to tell their stories.

Public relations people should remember several things about editors and reporters:

● They are busy. When you approach them with a story idea, either verbally or on paper, make your sales pitch succinctly and objectively.

● Editors pride themselves on making their own decisions about what stories to run and how to run them. That is their job. Excessive hype of a story often turns them against it. An urgent demand that editors must run a story may lead to rejection.

● Stories submitted by nonprofits are better received by editors than are corporate news releases, which are perceived as attempts to obtain free advertising.

● Able editors and competent public relations people respect each other and work well together. A review of studies for *Communication Yearbook 20* found that over the decades, media respect for public relations has increased. The reviewers also noted that editorial distrust of the public relations profession in general co-existed with trust of individual public relations sources. If editors discover, however, that they have been misled or fed false information, they will never again fully trust the offending practitioner.

Practitioners also need to remember several things about themselves when dealing with the media:

● Your job is important in keeping the public informed. You are performing a service, not asking a favor, when you submit a story idea or a news release.

● You should assume that your story will be judged on its merits as seen by the editor, and you should not demean yourself by begging an editor to use it.

● Your role continues after the story or idea has been accepted. You cannot control the tone of the story that appears, but you can influence it by providing favorable story angles and additional information. A public relations person's helpful, pleasant personality does influence most writers, at least subtly.

For more information on dealing with the media, see Chapters 14 and 15.

The Print Media

Printed words can be kept indefinitely and can be reread. Messages delivered in printed form through newspapers, magazines, and books are a fundamental element in public relations work.

Newspapers

Every edition of a newspaper contains hundreds of news stories and pieces of information, in much greater number than the largest news staff can gather by itself. More than most readers realize, and more than many editors care to admit, newspapers depend upon information brought to them voluntarily.

The *Columbia Journalism Review* noted, for example, that in one edition the *Wall Street Journal* had obtained 45 percent of its 188 news items from news releases. Because of its specialized nature, the *Journal*'s use of news releases may be higher than that of general-interest daily newspapers. Public relations generates about 50 percent of the stories in New York City newspapers, according to Albert Scardino, press secretary for former Mayor David L. Dinkins.

Approximately 1,500 daily newspapers and 7,200 weekly newspapers are published in the United States. Most cities today have only one daily newspaper, resulting in little competition between newspapers. Television, direct mail, and the Internet are now the main challenges to newspapers. Although some metropolitan newspapers have circulations of more than 1 million copies a day, approximately two-thirds of daily newspapers have circulations of 20,000 or less.

Newspapers published for distribution in the late afternoon, called evening or P.M. papers, outnumber morning (A.M.) papers approximately three to one. However, especially in larger cities, a substantial trend toward morning publication is in progress. Knowledge of a newspaper's hours of publication and the deadlines it enforces for submission of copy is essential for everyone who supplies material to the paper.

Approximately three-quarters of American daily newspapers are owned by newspaper groups. The publishers and editors of a group-owned newspaper have broad local autonomy but must follow operating standards laid down by group headquarters.

A Commercial Institution. When dealing with a newspaper, public relations people should remember that it is a commercial institution, created to earn a profit as a purveyor of news and advertising. Although newspapers often are so deeply rooted in a community that they seem like public institutions, they are not. Their publishers and editors as a whole seek to serve the public interest and often succeed admirably in doing so. Like any other business, however, a newspaper that loses money soon disappears. Therefore, in the long run, and sometimes in the short run as well, management decisions about what appears in a newspaper must be made with the balance sheet in mind.

Newspapers receive nearly 80 percent of their income from advertising and about 20 percent from selling papers to readers. They cannot afford to publish press releases that are nothing more than commercial advertising; to do so would cut into their largest source of income. To be published, a release submitted to a newspaper must contain information that an editor regards as news of interest to a substantial number of readers.

Because newspapers are protected by the First Amendment to the Constitution, they cannot be forced to publish any material, including news releases, nor do they need to receive permission from the government or anyone else to publish whatever they desire. Editors resist pressure to suppress material they consider to be newsworthy and, conversely, to print material they do not believe to be newsworthy. However, the definitions of newsworthiness are abstract and fluctuating. What one newspaper considers to be news, another will not.

Organization of a Newspaper. Public relations professionals should know how a newspaper staff is organized so they can take story ideas or policy problems to the proper person. In most cases, the publisher is the director of all financial, mechanical, and administrative operations. Frequently the publisher also has ultimate responsibility for news and editorial matters.

The editor heads the news and editorial department. The associate editor conducts the editorial and commentary pages and deals with the public concerning their content. The managing editor is the head of news operations to whom the city editor and the editors of sections, such as sports, business, entertainment, and family living, answer. The city editor directs the local news staff of reporters. Some members of the city staff cover beats such as the police and city hall; others are on general assignment, meaning that they are sent to cover any type of story the city editor deems to be potentially newsworthy. (Submission of news releases to editors is discussed in Chapter 14.)

Weekly newspapers have a different focus from that of daily newspapers. The much smaller staff of the weekly concentrates exclusively on its own community. Weekly editors rely heavily on volunteered material. Although weekly newspapers often are overlooked in public relations programs, weeklies can be effective outlets for those who study how to meet their needs.

Public Relations Opportunities in Newspapers

Material for a newspaper should be submitted either as a news release ready for publication or as a fact sheet from which a reporter can develop a feature story or interview. When an invitation to a news conference is sent to a newspaper, it should include a fact sheet containing basic information. Frequently, the reporter to whom an editor assigns a news release for processing rewrites and expands it, developing additional story angles and background. When a public relations representative presents an important story idea in fact-sheet form rather than as a news release for publication, a personal conversation with the appropriate editor, if it can be arranged, helps to sell the concept and expand its potential. Such personal calls to editors should last no longer than is necessary to explain the idea adequately. Although some practitioners make a follow-up phone call shortly after the fact sheet has arrived, this practice irritates many editors. They dislike being interrupted. (Preparation of news releases and fact sheets is discussed in Chapter 14.)

Public relations representatives never should assume that editors and reporters are all-knowing about projects being planned in a community. A basic rule: When you have news to announce, tell the media; don't wait for them to come to you.

For large-scale projects such as a communitywide fund drive, make an appointment with the managing editor or city editor after the deadline hour has passed. A newspaper is more likely to give a major project sympathetic treatment if its editors receive background information before the first stories break. This allows them time to plan coverage.

At times, an organization's representative or other individual may need to discuss a policy issue with the newspaper management—a complaint against perceived mistreatment by the newspaper, for example, or an attempt to obtain editorial support. Usually this is done by appointment with the editor or associate editor or, in the case of a news story, with the managing editor.

Magazines

Magazines differ markedly from newspapers in content, time frame, and methods of operation. Therefore, they present different opportunities and problems to the public relations practitioner. In contrast with the daily newspaper, with its hurry-up deadlines, magazines are published weekly, monthly, or sometimes quarterly. Because these publications usually deal with subjects in greater depth than newspapers do, magazine editors may allot months for the development of an article. Those who seek to supply subject ideas or ready-to-publish material to them must plan much further ahead than is necessary with newspapers.

A newspaper is designed for family reading, with something for men, women, and children; its material is aimed at an audience of varying educational and economic levels. Its editors fire buckshot to hit the reading interests of as many people as possible. Magazine editors, on the other hand, in most instances aim carefully at special-interest audiences. They fire rifle bullets at limited, well-defined readership groups.

The more than 75,000 periodicals published in the United States may be classified in several ways. Periodicals generally are grouped into categories such as news

ON THE JOB insights

Created Events: Making News Happen

Some news stories happen. Other stories must be created. Successful public relations practitioners must do more than produce competent, accurate news releases about routine occurrences in the affairs of their clients or employers. They must use ingenuity and organization skills to create events that attract coverage in the news media. Historian Daniel Boorstin calls these projects "pseudoevents." This extra dimension of creativity is the difference between acting to make news and merely reacting to news that happens. We are not speaking here of feeding phony stories to the media or doing anything else unethical. We are talking about causing something to occur.

Such created events vary in scope from the huge antiabortion and prochoice marches in Washington, staged by ardent advocates of opposite positions, to small, clever publicity promotions that draw media coverage because they are unusual, involve prominent people, or are just plain fun.

According to Jarol B. Manheim at Northwestern University, created events play an important role in what he calls corporate campaigns, which are the organized assault on a company by an activist group centered around the media, an activist's attempt to redefine the image and reputation of the target company, based on the adversarial position toward the company that is held by the activist group.

The 100th anniversary of the invention of Jell-O gelatin dessert posed a challenge to Kraft Foods' public relations firm, Hunter and Associates: Celebrate the traditions of Jell-O in American life without contributing to a consumer percep-

tion in the 1990s that Jell-O was old-fashioned (see Chapter 6).

Every one of the events listed later in this chapter represents a legitimate news story that the local newspaper and other media might cover. But these stories exist only because a public relations adviser convinced the company to sponsor or conduct them. Once this decision is made, the practitioner must produce a flow of news releases with fresh angles, as well as use other techniques to build public interest.

Openings of stores and shopping centers, as well as groundbreakings, happen so frequently that the ingenuity of public relations representatives is challenged. Editors dislike pictures of the traditional, rigidly posed group of men in dark business suits and incongruous hard hats lined up behind one man with a shovel.

magazines, women's interest, men's interest, the senior market, and trade journals. Each has its own specialty interest.

Public Relations Opportunities in Magazines

Examination of the monthly periodical *Writer's Digest* will provide abundant information about individual magazines and the kinds of material each publishes. Every magazine has its special formula.

Operating with much smaller staffs than newspapers have, magazines are heavily dependent on material submitted from outside their offices. Some, especially the smaller ones, are almost entirely staff written. The staffs create ideas and cover some

ON THE JOB

ethics

Information Pollution in Trade Publications?

It is not uncommon in the trade press for an editor to make a subtle demand on a public relations person who wants to place a story in the magazine or newsletter. There often is a "linkage" between getting the story published and buying advertising space in the trade publication. If a company wants a good editorial spread, it must help "pay the freight" through an advertising buy. Some trade press publishers defend this "linkage," saying that the publication cannot survive without advertising—so it is only fair for the companies that want coverage to contribute to the financial stability of the publication. From another perspective, editors simply give preference to advertisers when selecting stories to cover. Either view violates the PRSA code of ethics, which says that the exchange of advertising for "good" copy is one form of "corrupting the media."

Say that you pitch a story by telephone to the editor of a trade publication. The editor knows that you really want coverage for your client, and she implies that you need to buy ad space to ensure that your story will be run.

What would you do? Do you think that advertiser influence on stories diminishes the value of public relations? In your mind, is there a qualitative difference between trade publications that require advertising and more independent publications such as newspapers? Which has more value for the practice of public relations?

stories; they also process public relations material submitted to them. The more carefully the submitted material is tailored to the particular periodical's audience and written in a style preferred by the editor, the more likely it is to be published, with or without rewriting by the staff. Many magazines purchase part or almost all of their material from freelance writers on a fee basis. An editor may buy a submitted article for publication if it fits the magazine's formula or the editor may commission a writer to develop an idea into an article along specified lines.

Editors are always looking for ideas. Many magazine articles have their origins in suggestions submitted by public relations practitioners. An article in a women's magazine on preventing sunburn, for example, may have resulted from a letter and a media kit sent to an editor by a sunscreen manufacturer or its public relations firm.

A public relations practitioner has four principal approaches for getting material into a periodical:

1. Submit a story idea that would promote the practitioner's cause, either directly or subtly, and urge the editor to have a writer, freelance or staff, develop the story on assignment.

2. Send a written query to the editor outlining an article idea and offering to submit the article in publishable form if the editor approves the idea.

3. Submit a completed article, written either by the practitioner or by an independent writer under contract, and hope that the editor will accept it for publication.

In this and the two previously mentioned instances, however, the editor should be made fully aware of the source of the suggestion or article. As pointed out in Chapter 3, allowing a freelance writer to place what presumably is an "independent" article is a violation of the PRSA Code of Professional Standards, which forbids using third parties who are purported to be independent but serve the special interests of the employer or client.

4. For trade journals and other periodicals that use such material, submit news releases in ready-to-publish form.

The size and nature of each magazine determines its content. Most common is a formula of several major articles, one or two short articles, and special departments. These may be personal commentary, a compilation of news items in a specific category (short items about new products in a trade journal, for example), or chitchat about personalities. Special departments offer excellent public relations opportunities.

Books

Because their writing and publication is a time-consuming process, often involving years from the conception of an idea until the appearance of the volume, books are not popularly recognized as public relations tools. Yet they can be. A book, especially a hardcover one, has stature in the minds of readers. They read it with respect and give attention to the message it carries.

Books are promulgators of ideas. As channels of communication, they reach thoughtful audiences, including opinion leaders. Publication of a book often starts a trend or focuses national discussion on an issue.

The standard method of book publishing is for an author and publisher to sign a contract describing the material the author will deliver to the publisher and the conditions under which the publisher will issue and sell the book. The publisher pays the cost of production and marketing. The author receives a royalty fee on each copy sold, perhaps 10 to 15 percent of the retail price. Publishers often make advance payments to authors against the royalties their books are expected to earn.

A book published in hardcover often requires a year from acceptance of the manuscript to publication. Thus, a public relations effort made through publication of a hardcover book must be long range in nature and aimed at the broad-stroke influencing of public opinion.

Although the fact is seldom mentioned publicly, companies and nonprofit organizations sometimes pay subsidies to both hardcover and paperback publishers to help defray production costs of a book they wish to see published. The subsidy may take the form of a guarantee to purchase a specific number of copies. The idea for a beautifully illustrated book on New England, to cite an example, might come from a state travel agency, which approaches the publisher either directly or through an author. The state agency pays part of the publisher's cost, knowing that the book will draw visitors to the area.

From the point of view of publishers, publicity for books and their authors is an important public relations function. The public relations departments of publishing houses use news releases, prepublication endorsements, interviews, and other standard techniques to create awareness of a forthcoming book. A writer may be taken on a tour of major cities for interviews and autograph parties or speak to reviewers nationwide by satellite.

Public Relations Opportunities in Books

Growth of paperback publishing has opened new avenues for use of books as public relations vehicles. An examination of nonfiction titles on the paperback shelves will show the range of opportunity that exists to promote products, ideological movements, personalities, and fads.

As indicated previously, books as public relations tools, both hardcover and paperback, usually are best suited to promote ideas and create a favorable state of mind. For example, the autobiography of Conrad Hilton, placed in hotel rooms, helps establish the character and tradition of Hilton Hotels. Political movements often are publicized through books by their proponents. On a more mundane level, every book published about gardening indirectly helps the sale of garden tools. Although a specific brand of tools may not be mentioned in such a book, it benefits from the book's existence. The manufacturer's public relations representative can help the company's cause by assisting the author in assembling material. Public relations efforts need not be overt to be effective. *The Complete Dairy Foods Cookbook*, by E. Annie Proues and Lew Nichols, inevitably helped promote the use of dairy products; *The Joy of Chocolate*, by Judith Olney, must have made chocolate manufacturers happy.

However, unless he or she knows the publishing industry well, a public relations representative seeking to publicize a client's cause through publication of a book is well advised to work through an agent.

The Spoken and Visual Media

Radio, television, motion pictures, and video have strong impact on virtually everyone. The messages they contain usually are delivered by individuals whose personality, expressed through voice and/or visual manner, adds emphasis to the words.

Radio

Speed and mobility are the special attributes that make radio unique among the major media. If urgency justifies such action, messages can be placed on the air almost instantly upon their receipt at a radio station. They need not be delayed by the time-consuming production processes of print. Because radio programming is more loosely structured than television programming, interruption of a program for an urgent announcement can be done with less internal decision making. Although most public relations material does not involve such urgency, moments of crisis do occur when quick on-the-air action helps a company or other organization get information to the public swiftly.

Radio benefits, too, from its ability to be heard almost anywhere. Reporters working from mobile trucks can be broadcasting from the scene of a large fire within minutes after it has been discovered. They can hurry from a press conference to a luncheon speech, carrying only a small amount of equipment. A disc jockey can broadcast an afternoon program from a table in a neighborhood shopping center. Flexibility is ever-present.

So is flexibility among listeners. Radios in automobiles reach captive audiences, enhancing the popularity of drive-time disc jockeys. Radio brings programs, news, and opinion to mail carriers on their routes, carpenters on construction sites, and homeowners pulling weeds in their gardens. In fact, according to *PRWeek*, radio is a pervasive medium, with 97 percent of adults listening to an AM or FM station at least once a week.

In many markets, a media company will own a group of stations, including both AM and FM formats, with perhaps one news director and one weathercaster serving all of the stations in the market. Both AM and FM stations in the group attempt to develop distinctive "sounds" by specializing in one kind of music or talk format. A public relations practitioner should study each station's format and submit material suitable to it. Don't send information about senior citizen recreational programs to the news director of a hard-rock station with an audience primarily of teenagers.

Public Relations Opportunities in Radio

Commercial radio is highly promotional in nature and provides innumerable opportunities for public relations specialists to further their causes. Radio programs may be divided into two general categories: news-talk and entertainment. The news director for a station or station group is responsible for the former, the program director for the latter. At least eight possible targets exist in radio:

1. Newscasts. Many stations have frequent newscasts, of which the five-minute variety is the most common. If the station has a network affiliation, some of the newscasts it carries will be national in content. Of much more interest to the public relations practitioner are the local newscasts. News releases sent to a radio station should cover the same newsworthy topics as those sent to a newspaper; they should follow identical rules of accuracy and timeliness. Brevity is fundamental on radio. See Chapter 15 for how to write a radio news release.

2. Community calendars. Many stations broadcast a daily program called the "Community Bulletin Board" or a similar title. This listing of coming events is an excellent place to circulate information about a program the practitioner is handling.

3. Actualities. Radio news directors brighten their newscasts by including actualities. These are brief reports from scenes of action, either live or on tape. Public relations representatives may supply stations with actualities from events or speeches to be used on newscasts.

4. Talk shows. Placement of a client on a talk show provides exposure for the individual and for the cause being espoused while avoiding the filtering of information by news staff. Talk shows may be news oriented, such as a discussion of a controversial issue, and produced by the news director; or they may be entertainment-oriented, controlled by the program director and handled by a staff producer. Midmorning homemaker hours have numerous spots for guest appearances.

5. Editorials. Powerful radio stations often broadcast editorials, comparable to newspaper editorials, that are usually delivered by the station manager. Public relations specialists may be able to persuade a station to carry an editorial of endorsement for their cause. They should stay alert, too, for editorials that condemn a cause they espouse. The representative should request equal time on the air for a rebuttal, usually given by a leading executive of the organization or cause under attack. Hundreds of smaller stations, however, do not carry editorials.

6. Disc jockey shows. On the entertainment side, disc jockeys in their programs of music and chitchat frequently air material provided by public relations sources. The DJs conduct on-the-air contests and promotions, give away tickets to shows, discuss coming local events, offer trivia quizzes—whatever they can think of to make their programs distinctive and lively. A disc jockey on the air several hours a day devours large amounts of material. After studying a program's style, an able practitioner can supply material that the DJ welcomes.

7. Community events. At times, radio stations sponsor community events such as outdoor concerts or long-distance runs. Repeated mention of such an event on the air for days or weeks usually turns out large crowds. Here, too, is an opportunity for the public relations person to convince a station either to sponsor such an event or to develop tie-ins with it.

8. Public service announcements (PSAs). These commercials promoting public causes such as health care and civic programs are run free of charge by stations, usually in unsold time slots during scheduled commercial breaks. PSA scripts should be written to run 20, 30, or 60 seconds. Use of celebrity voices is common. See Chapter 15 for how to write a PSA.

Television

Our lives feel the impact of television more than that of any other communication medium. More than 1,600 television stations project over-the-air visual programming. According to estimates provided by the A. C. Nielsen Company, the major rating firm for national programming, more than 102 million American households own television sets. According to Nielsen statistics, the average American family watches television about seven hours a day. Little wonder that public relations specialists look upon television as an enormous arena in which to tell their stories!

The fundamental factor that differentiates television from the other media and gives it such pervasive impact is the visual element. Producers of entertainment shows, newscasts, and commercials regard movement on the screen as essential. Something must happen to hold the viewer's attention. Persons talking on the screen for more than a brief time without movement, or at least a change of camera angle, are belittled as "talking heads."

Because of this visual impact, television emphasizes personality. Entertainment programs are built around stars. Only on television do news reporters achieve "star quality." When public relations people plan material for television, they should remember the importance of visual impact and personality.

Television shows live and die by their ratings. A scorecard mentality dominates the selection of programs and program content, especially on the networks. The viewing habits of a few thousand Americans, recorded by the Nielsen, Arbitron, and other rating services, determine what programs all TV watchers can see. The explanation is money. Networks and local stations determine the prices they charge to show commercials by the estimated size of the audience watching a program when the commercial is shown. Thus, the larger the audience, the higher the price for commercial time, and the higher the profit. Even nonprofit television stations keep a close watch on the size of their audiences, because their income comes in part from the grants that corporations give them to show certain programs.

A tremendous battle for admission to the home viewer's screen has developed among satellite dish, cable TV, video, and the traditional over-the-air stations and networks. In the mid-1970s, the three basic commercial networks were viewed by 92 percent of the audience during prime-time evening hours. This figure has fallen to below one-third of the total television audience. The fragmenting of the television audience has led to the rise of cable news competitors that challenge the supremacy of network news.

This turmoil has opened enormous new programming potential and a consequent increase in public relations opportunities. When a cable system offers hundreds of channels, the need for program material is voracious.

Cable Television.   Because television networks and individual stations, especially those in major cities, gear their programming to large audiences, public relations practitioners often have difficulty obtaining airtime for projects lacking mass appeal. Cable television, however, often presents valuable opportunities.

More than 69 million U.S. households were wired for cable TV as of 2001. However, the number of viewers for an individual cable channel is usually relatively small, because the total TV audience is fragmented among the numerous competing channels. On the plus side, the public relations specialist faces fewer editing and management barriers in getting a program or short segment broadcast.

Municipal authorities have the right to demand that cable systems to which they grant operating franchises include an *access channel* for public, educational, or government programming, without advertising. Public relations directors for cultural, social, and other nonprofit agencies—and even for commercial interests—can use these so-called PEG channels effectively to promote public-service causes by creating interesting programs.

Some cable systems also produce *local origination* (LO) programming. LO programs may carry advertising. They offer an outlet for public relations material that provides substantial information without being obviously commercial in tone.

Public Relations Opportunities in Television

The possibilities for the public relations specialist to use television are so numerous that they are worth examining on two levels: network and local.

Early-morning and late-night television talk shows are often a string of promotional appearances by various celebrities who have a new album, a new movie, or a new product to endorse. Here, the singers of "Destiny's Child" are interviewed on ABC's "Good Morning America." Such appearances are considered the Holy Grail by publicists for their clients.

The Network Level. Six public relations methods are commonly used at the network level:

1. Guest appearances on news and talk shows. Placement of clients on such programs as the *Tonight* and *Today* shows allows the clients to plug new products, books, films, and plays and to advocate their causes. For entertainment personalities in particular, these interviews provide a setting in which to display their skills. National leaders are interviewed in depth on the Sunday discussion panel shows such as *Meet the Press*. See Chapter 15 for more information.

2. News releases and story proposals to network news departments. This process is identical to that followed with radio stations. If a story or an idea is accepted, the assignment editor gives it to a reporter for visual development. Letters with story suggestions often are sent directly to popular TV personalities. When a client is criticized in a controversial news situation or editorial, a representative should submit the client's response and urge that it be used on the air. If the response is submitted in concise videotape form, the likelihood of a quick airing is increased.

3. Video news releases (VNRs). These are ready-to-broadcast tapes or satellite feeds with background footage for use in news programs. News programs will use VNRs in some form if they are well done and avoid delivering an obvious commercial message. (VNRs are discussed in Chapter 15.)

4. Program ideas. The representative of an important cause may propose to a network that it build an episode in a dramatic or situation comedy series around the cause. Activist groups apply considerable pressure on television producers and the networks to include social issues such as environmental cleanups, drunk driving, and AIDS in their program scripts. Characters in situation comedies or dramas quite frequently take strong advocacy positions in the plotline, thus delivering a message to viewers.

5. Silent publicity. There are almost subliminal impacts in entertainment programs that quietly publicize a representative's cause. In a private detective show, for example, the star may be shown chasing the villain through an airport terminal past a Delta sign. Or the automobiles used by the lead characters may be Ford products exclusively. Sometimes a program's credits include a mention such as "Transportation provided by American Airlines." Another way to generate silent publicity, especially valuable for the tourist industry, is to convince network show producers to shoot their programs in a client's city or region, showing the scenery there. The network series *Chicago Hope*, *NYPD Blue*, and *Seinfeld*, all set in New York, and *Wings*, based in Nantucket, provided those localities with publicity.

6. Public service announcements. Stations nationwide run about one in three of the spots they receive as public relations gestures. The Advertising Council prepares material for national nonprofit organizations as a public service.

The Local Station Level. The methods listed for network public relations apply just as effectively on the local level; indeed, even more so in some instances, because competition for time on local stations often is less intense. The more intimate nature of local programming increases public relations opportunities. Even a diaper-changing contest at a shopping mall can gain airtime.

The four most frequently used techniques are:

1. Guest appearances on local talk shows. Visiting experts in such fields as homemaking crafts, sponsored by companies and trade associations, demonstrate their skills for the moderator and audience. National public relations firms send such clients around well-established circuits of local television and radio shows in each city they visit.

2. Protest demonstrations. Filmed demonstrations are such a staple on some television stations in large cities to the point that they are a visual cliché. A group supporting or opposing a cause notifies a station that it will march at a certain time and place. Carrying placards, the marchers parade before the camera, and a representative is shown explaining the group's cause. Although, for fairness, stations should put on an advocate for the other side in the same sequence, some stations neglect this responsibility, and so the marching group's point of view dominates. Many group demonstrations are so much alike, however, that their impact is minimized. Stations use them primarily because they involve movement.

3. Videotapes for news shows. Smaller TV stations, in particular, lack enough staff to cover all potentially newsworthy events in their areas. Practitioners can fill the gaps by delivering videotapes of events they handle for inclusion in newscasts. Excerpts from a local speech by a prominent client may be incorporated in an evening news show. Arrival or departure at the local airport of a client in the news might be used, too, if the person says something newsworthy on camera.

4. General-interest films. Local cable channels sometimes will show films of 15- or 20-minute duration produced by corporations in which the direct commercial message is nonexistent or muted. The purpose of such films is to strengthen a company's image as a good community citizen. Films explaining large civic programs by nonprofit organizations also may be used.

Motion Pictures

Mention of motion pictures brings to mind, first and inevitably, the commercial entertainment films turned out by that nebulous place called Hollywood. From a public relations point of view, possibilities for influencing the content of commercial motion pictures for client purposes are relatively limited. Practitioners who know their way through the labyrinth of Hollywood financing and production can make deals for silent publicity through use of brand-name merchandise, negotiating how the product will be used and whether there will be a fee. Firms such as Pepsi and Coca-Cola make deals to show their products in a movie, often tied in with an off-screen promotion of the item.

Public relations counselors and corporate departments occasionally serve as advisers on films that involve their areas of expertise. Filmmakers seek this advice to prevent embarrassing technical errors on the screen and to protect themselves from inadvertently angering a group that might retaliate by denouncing the picture. In terms of specific public relations results similar to those obtainable from the other mass media, however, commercial films are a minor channel.

Sponsored Films and Videotape

In other forms, the film is an important public relations tool.

ON THE JOB

ethics

The National Rifle Association Offers Its Own Online News Channel

An increasingly common strategy in public relations is to use controlled media such as direct mail, direct e-mail, Web sites, and brochures or information kiosks placed in high-traffic areas. But can the use of controlled media lead to confusion about the vested interests of the sponsor of the message? What happens when the medium looks and acts a lot like an independent news medium. And what about the rights of organizations who think that the news industry frames its cause incorrectly, inaccurately, and with inherent bias? The National Rifle Association (NRA) offers one answer to this question.

The NRA works actively to get its position in defense of the Second Amendment, the right to bear arms, before the American public. Recently, the NRA shifted some of its resources from pitching stories to news media to starting its own television news channel on the Web at www.nranews.com. The Web site does more than offer

links to stories and information sites, it actually broadcasts news and interviews and takes calls from the Web audience. Susan E. Tifft, writing a guest editorial in *USA Today*, decried the development: "The NRA is one of the biggest magazine publishers in the country and trumpets its views through ads, news releases, newspapers, and a slickly produced Web site. What it doesn't do—and shouldn't do—is pretend it is providing 'news.' " What do you think?

In the 19th Century, news sources were more overtly political, aligning with either corporate or worker interests. Some say this move back to standpoint journalism is a good thing because more voices are being heard. This would be the position of the conservative NRA, and perhaps also that of former Vice President Al Gore, who recently acquired a small cable news channel called Newsworld International. Should we hope for a

media landscape that is more diverse? Or should we hope for one that is less fragmented, but that strives to be balanced in its treatment of issues? And what of the many recent scandals at newspapers such as the *New York Times, Boston Globe*, and, yes, *USA Today* over faked sources and facts or the use of stringers to research stories?

Why shouldn't the NRA generate its own perspective in public space? Is it a matter of effective labeling, making sure that the source of the news is known? Again, what do you think? Is labeling a panacea or a solution?

Finally, what if the newscast does not deal with politics? Companies such as Williams Energy offer Webcasts of industry news. Williams Energy News is intended to position Williams as the best-informed and most-credible company in the energy sector. Is this sort of focused information service acceptable to you? Why or why not?

Corporations and nonprofit organizations use films and videotapes for internal purposes as part of audiovisual programs to train and inform their employees or for external purposes to inform and influence the public and the financial community.

When, for example, Levi Strauss & Co. needed to explain to its employees a new personnel management program called Teamwork, it prepared a video for them. Like some other corporations, San Diego Gas & Electric Company produces a periodic Employee Video News Magazine. The topics covered range from the company's annual meeting to an employees' campaign against graffiti.

Online Media

The personal computer is a significant, swiftly expanding tool for public relations practitioners. Its ability to deliver information about client projects, to establish contacts with reporters, and to exchange ideas through the commercial online services and the global Internet is fascinating and not yet fully realized. The World Wide Web portion of the Internet, which provides on-screen graphics, photographs, audio, and video clips along with text, is an especially effective form of cyberspace public relations.

Home pages on the World Wide Web offer an unusual opportunity to reach an audience with a message in the exact form a public relations practitioner conceives it, because the Web is not subject to editing by any media gatekeeper. Tens of thousands of companies, nonprofit organizations, and individuals maintain sites on the World Wide Web on which they explain and promote their services. Specific examples of how the Web is used in public relations appear in Chapter 13. By participating in online discussion groups and similar online interchanges, public relations people often reach opinion leaders in specific fields with facts and opinions favorable to their cause. Among these key online contacts are reporters and editors of Web-based publications that increasingly offer breaking news faster than print or broadcast outlets. The pace of media relations has increased as public relations professionals monitor online news, striving for what Professor Stephen Thomsen of Brigham Young University calls "real-time response." The public relations person hopes to catch errors or offer balancing comments for stories as they break online and before they pick up momentum through print and broadcast dispersion.

PR CASEBOOK

Teen Audience Offers Novel Challenges to Public Relations Pros

Generalizing is always dangerous, especially for large segments of the population just emerging from childhood to independent living. Nevertheless, today's teens and young adults, conveniently grouped by some media under the rubric Generation Y (GY) or Generation.com, comprise an interesting and powerful force in modern life. Accounting for over $150 billion in annual purchases, the youth market represents significant disposable income. In a *pr reporter* article, Marianne Friese of Ketchum succinctly stated the importance of the youth audience: "They rival the baby boom in sheer size and their global purchasing power is enormous." Like every new generation before them, they cause adults to fret about their character but show signs that they, too, will rise to the challenges that come with maturity.

Generation Y (GY) Might Better Be Labeled the E-Generation

The Fortino Group (Pittsburgh) projects that GY will spend 23 years online. Spending one-third of their lives online will have interesting impacts:

- GY will spend equal time interacting with friends online and in person.

(continued)

PR CASEBOOK *(continued)*

- Initial interaction online will precede most dating and marriages.
- GY time online will exceed interaction with parents tenfold.
- GY will be more reserved in social skills.
- GY will be savvy and skeptical about online identities such as chat participants.
- Print forms, slow application processes, and archaic systems will not be tolerated by GY.

GY will share this propensity for online pastimes with retired seniors. Their world will be diverse and global in perspective, and, like no previous generation, they will understand world cultures and markets.

Generation Y Values Relationships and Trust

In a survey of 1,200 teens worldwide, Ketchum's Global Brand Marketing Practice found:

- Parents still rule when it comes to advice about careers and drugs, and even for product decisions.
- Trust in information is derived from relationships.
- The top five sources of advice are parents, doctors, clergy, friends, and teachers.
- As avid and skilled Internet users, GY remains savvy about unfiltered and unpoliced content.

- Teens also recognize the credibility of editorial content compared to ads and even public service announcements, with television being the most trusted medium for them.
- Garnering publicity for products and issues will impact GY, whether directed at them or at those to whom they look for advice.

This active consumer market instills trust in cause-oriented companies and rewards companies that do what is perceived as right. Work such as Liz Claiborne's activism against dating violence and Valvoline Instant Oil Change's service centers hiring young women for traditionally male-dominated jobs serve as good examples of corporate responsibility that is appreciated by GY.

Music pervades their waking hours, accompanying other media use such as Web surfing and gaming. Although 64 percent of respondents in an Ogilvy PR survey would rather go a day without food than without music, the message effects of music are subtle.

Sources: PRWeek, January 14, 2002; pr reporter, May 21, 2001; November 13, 2000; February 7, 2000; and November 22, 1999.

SUMMARY

The Nature of the Public Relations Audience

The public relations practitioner must reach a diverse and constantly changing audience. One of the most important aspects of the job will be identifying the target audience in order to customize communications appropriately.

Senior and Ethnic Markets

Two increasingly important publics are seniors and racial and ethnic minorities. The senior group has grown in number as life span has increased. It has also grown in affluence. The population of ethnic groups is increasing at five times the rate of the general population, and such groups constitute many different target audiences. Language is only one of the challenges in reaching them. The public relations practitioner must be sensitive to the special issues of different ethnic audiences.

Characteristics of the Audience

Current trends include an increase in the public's visual orientation, fervent support for single issues, emphasis on personality and celebrity, a strong distrust of authority, and an expanding international audience.

Matching the Audience with the Media

Each of the media has different strengths for different types of communication. The practitioner must be careful to use the appropriate media (or, sometimes, single medium) for each campaign.

Media Relations

Although public relations practitioners and editors need one another, public relations people can be more effective by remembering that media people can be busy and resistant to hype. At the same time, public relations practitioners provide a service by keeping the public informed.

The Print Media

Print media—newspapers, magazines, other periodicals, and books—are appropriate for communications that should be kept over time and reread. Both newspapers and magazines are commercial institutions that depend heavily on advertising for their income, but magazines are published less frequently and often deal with subjects at greater length and depth than is possible in a daily newspaper. Magazines also are more likely to be targeted at a special-interest audience. Books are published on much longer schedules than either magazines or newspapers, but can still be useful as public relations tools.

The Spoken and Visual Media

Radio is one of the quickest and most flexible means of communicating a message, reaching a variety of audiences through such types of programming as newscasts, community calendars, talk shows, and public service announcements. Television has a tremendous impact on society because of its pervasiveness and visual impact. The growth of cable television has provided new venues for public relations with access channels and local-origination programming. Public relations opportunities exist in television on both the network and the local level. Product placement is an example of public relations at work in the motion-picture industry. Sponsored films and videotapes can also be important public relations tools.

Online Media

Internet home pages provide an opportunity for the public relations practitioner to communicate directly with an audience without the filter of editors and journalists. Online news sources are growing in stature, especially when big stories are breaking and developing throughout the workday.

Case Activity: **What Would You Do?**

Cygna Labs, a medium-sized pharmaceutical firm located in Salt Lake City, has developed a sunscreen lotion. The product, Sun-Cure, joins a number of similar products on store shelves. Independent laboratory testing shows that Sun-Cure is particularly effective in blocking UVB rays, which cause burning and even premature aging of the skin. It is a good product and gets high ratings from dermatologists.

Unfortunately, the public still shows confusion about the differences between sunscreens and suntan lotions, as well as the merits of competing brands. Your public relations firm has been retained to develop a product publicity program for Sun-Cure that would reach daily newspapers, selected magazines, radio, and television. What communication strategies would you develop for getting coverage in each medium?

QUESTIONS for Review and Discussion

1. Why is the senior audience so important in the United States? What are some of the characteristics of this audience?

2. On what basis do newspaper editors select the news releases they publish?

3. A good public relations person knows how to create news events. Why is this important?

4. What significant differences between magazines and newspapers must a public relations practitioner keep in mind when submitting material to them?

5. Why are special-audience magazines and trade journals such important targets for many public relations people?

6. How do you think the various changes in the racial and ethnic makeup of the United States will impact future practice of public relations?

7. What two special attributes make radio distinctive among the major media of mass communication?

8. Do local radio newscasts have good potential as an outlet for news releases? If so, why?

9. Ratings determine which television programs survive and which die. Why do ratings have such power?

10. How should public relations representatives go about trying to place their clients on television interview shows?

11. Can you describe three ways in which public relations practitioners use online media?

SUGGESTED READINGS

Bollinger, Lee. "Public Relations, Business and the Press." *Public Relations Quarterly*, Summer 2003, pp. 20–23.

Cameron, Glen T., Sallot, Lynne, and Curtin, Patricia A. "Public Relations and the Production of News: A Critical Review and a Theoretical Framework." *Communication Yearbook 20*, 1997, pp. 111–155.

Cameron, Glen T., and Shin, Jae-Hwa. "The Potential of Online Media: A Coorientational Analysis of Conflict between PR Professionals and Journalists in South Korea." *Journalism and Mass Communication Quarterly*, Vol. 80, Autumn 2003, pp. 583–602.

Durham, Deborah. "How to Get the Biggest Bang Out of Your Next Spokesperson Campaign." *Public Relations Quarterly*, Spring 1997, pp. 38–41.

"Getting Beyond Stereotypes: Grassroots PR Campaign Works to Give Media a Truer Picture of Native Americans." *Ragan's Media Relations Report*, January 2005, pp. 3, 7.

Green, Sherri. "And Finally . . . How to Get Your Kicker on Air." *PRWeek*, September 8, 2003, p. 18.

Lubove, Seth. "Get Smart: A Reporter's Take on Good PR Practices." *PR Tactics*, October 1998, p. 20.

Manheim, Jarol B. *The Death of a Thousand Cuts: Corporate Campaigns and the Attack on the Corporation*. Mahwah, NJ: Lawrence Erlbaum, 2001.

Morton, Linda P. "Targeting Hispanic Americans." *Public Relations Quarterly*, Fall 2002, pp. 46–48.

Pfau, Michael, Moy, Patricia, Holbert, R. Lance, Szabo, Erin A., Lin, Wei-Kuo, and Zhang, Weiwu. "The Influence of Political Talk Radio on Confidence in Democratic Institutions." *Journalism and Mass Communication Quarterly*, Vol. 75, Winter 1998, pp. 730–745.

Rabin, Phil. "How to Create a Top-Notch PSA." *PRWeek*, July 26, 1999, p. 21.

Shin, Jae-Hwa, and Cameron, Glen T. "Informal Relations: A Look at Personal Influence in Media Relations." *Journal of Communication Management*, Vol. 7, No. 3, 2003, pp. 239–253.

Walker, Jerry. "The Internet Brings New Trends to Media-PR Relations." *O'Dwyer's PR Services Report*, May 2002, pp. 36–37.

Ward, David. "Youth-Targeted Publications Have Truly Come of Age." *PRWeek*, January 14, 2002, p. 12.

chapter **12**

Public Relations and the Law

Topics covered in this chapter include:

A Sampling of Legal Problems

The law and its many ramifications are somewhat abstract to the average person. Many people may have difficulty imagining exactly how public relations personnel can run afoul of the law or generate a suit simply by communicating information.

To bring things down to earth and to make this chapter more meaningful, we provide here a sampling of recent government regulatory agency cases and lawsuits that involved public relations materials and the work of practitioners:

● Porter Novelli sued two employees who left to start another public relations firm, claiming that they had planned the new firm on company time and took a client with them.

● A public relations counselor was quizzed in a California courtroom regarding his role in writing a misleading news release stating that all of the Oakland Raiders's games were sold out for the season. The lawsuit was between the football team and the Oakland Coliseum.

● Bonner & Associates and its client, the Pharmaceutical Research and Manufacturers of America, were charged with violating Maryland's lobbying disclosure laws. A citizens group claimed that the firm used "deceptive tactics in the guise of a consumer-based organization to do the bidding of the pharmaceutical industry."

● The Securities and Exchange Commission (SEC) fined a former employee of Ogilvy PR Worldwide $34,000 for passing "material, nonpublic information" to his father who used the information to purchase stock in Wells Fargo Bank before it was publicly announced that it was acquiring another company.

● The Federal Trade Commission (FTC) filed charges against three national diet firms after they failed to provide factual evidence in their advertising and publicity that clients actually achieved weight-loss goals or maintained them.

● A Chicago man sued for invasion of privacy after he appeared in a video news release for a cholesterol-lowering drug because the company and video producer didn't tell him the actual purpose of the taping.

● The Los Angeles city attorney filed a civil suit against Fleischman-Hillard charging that the LA office inflated invoices, claimed work that was not done, and double-charged for other activities when the firm worked for the city's Department of Water and Power.

● A San Francisco public relation practitioner who was fired by his employer for refusing to write misleading news releases won a lawsuit against his former employer for "unlawful dismissal."

● An 81-year-old man sued the United Way of America for using his picture on campaign posters and brochures without his permission.

These examples provide some idea of the legal pitfalls that a public relations person may encounter. Many of the charges were eventually dismissed or settled out of court, but the organizations paid dearly for the adverse publicity and the expense of defending themselves.

Public relations personnel must be aware that they can be held legally liable if they provide advice or tacitly support an illegal activity of a client or employer. This area of liability is called *conspiracy*. A public relations person can be named as a co-conspirator with other organizational officials if he or she:

- Participates in an illegal action such as bribing a government official or covering up information of vital interest to the public health and safety
- Counsels and guides the policy behind an illegal action
- Takes a major personal part in the illegal action
- Helps establish a "front group" whereby the connection to the public relations firm or its clients is kept hidden
- Cooperates in any other way to further an illegal action

These five concepts also apply to public relations firms that create, produce, and distribute materials on behalf of clients. The courts have ruled on more than one occasion that public relations firms cannot hide behind the defense of "the client told me to do it." Public relations firms have a legal responsibility to practice "due diligence" in the type of information and documentation supplied by a client. Regulatory agencies such as the FTC (discussed shortly) have the power under the Lanham Act to file charges against public relations firms that distribute false and misleading information.

Libel and Defamation

Public relations professionals should be thoroughly familiar with the concepts of libel and slander. Such knowledge is crucial if an organization's internal and external communications are to meet legal and regulatory standards with a minimum of legal complications.

Traditionally, *libel* was a printed falsehood and *slander* was an oral statement that was false. Today, as a practical matter, there is little difference in the two, and the courts often use *defamation* as a collective term.

Essentially, defamation is any false statement about a person (or organization) that creates public hatred, contempt, ridicule, or inflicts injury on reputation. A person filing a libel suit usually must prove that: (1) the false statement was communicated to others through print, broadcast, or electronic means; (2) the person was identified or is identifiable; (3) there is actual injury in the form of money losses, loss of reputation, or mental suffering; and (4) the person making the statement was malicious or negligent.

ON THE JOB

global

In China, Product Liability Depends on News Coverage

Public relations professionals, when operating in any nation, must be familiar with local laws that can affect their activities. In China, for example, press reports can be introduced as evidence to prove claims of product liability.

So, if a person wants to sue a company for a faulty product, one common strategy is to get the story in the press. Defendants in such cases have no choice but also to get press coverage or convince Chinese editors not to run a story.

A *Wall Street Journal* article on product liability in China notes: "Building good relations with the press is one way to head off potential lawsuits. When a Shanghai fast-food customer took a fly in his fish fillet to the newspaper because the U.S. restaurant chain refused to compensate him, the restaurant's manager called local editors to explain his side of the story. No article ran and no suit was filed."

In general, private citizens have more success winning defamation suits than public figures or corporations. With public figures—government officials, entertainers, political candidates, and other newsworthy personalities—there is the extra test of whether the libelous statements were made with actual malice (*New York Times v. Sullivan*).

Corporations, to some degree, also are considered "public figures" by the courts for several reasons: (1) They engage in advertising and promotion offering products and services to the public, (2) they are often involved in matters of public controversy and public policy, and (3) they have some degree of access to the media—through regular advertising and news releases—that enables them to respond and rebut defamatory charges made against them.

This is not to say that corporations don't win lawsuits regarding defamation. A good example is General Motors, which filed a multimillion-dollar defamation suit against NBC after the network's *Dateline* news program carried a story about gas tanks on GM pickup trucks exploding in side-impact collisions.

GM's general counsel, in a news conference, meticulously provided evidence that NBC had inserted toy rocket "igniters" in the gas tanks, understated the vehicle speed at the moment of impact, and wrongly claimed that the fuel tanks could be easily ruptured. Within 24 hours after the suit was filed, NBC caved in. It agreed to air a nine-minute apology on the news program and pay GM $2 million to cover the cost of its investigation.

Increasingly, corporations are using fraud and contract law to sue news organizations, instead of pursuing harder-to-prove libel claims. In *Food Lion v. Capital Cities/ABC* (1995), for example, the grocery chain was awarded $315,000 after it sued ABC News for fraud and trespassing; two TV producers had lied on job applications and hidden cameras in their wigs to report an exposé on alleged health violations at several stores. In another case, a federal judge in Cincinnati ruled that a *Business Week* reporter lied and breached a contract with a credit-reporting agency while writing a cover story on privacy.

Avoiding Libel Suits

There is little investigative reporting in public relations, but libel suits can be filed against organizational officials who make libelous accusations during a media interview, send out news releases that make false statements, or injure someone's reputation.

Some executives have been sorry that they lost control during a news conference and called the leaders of a labor union "a bunch of crooks and compulsive liars." Suits have been filed for calling a news reporter "a pimp for all environmental groups." Such language, although highly quotable and colorful, can provoke legal retaliation, merited or not.

Accurate information, and a delicate choice of words, must be used in news releases. For example, a former employee of J. Walter Thompson advertising agency claimed she was libeled in an agency news release that stated she had been dismissed because of financial irregularities in the department she headed. Eventually, the $20 million lawsuit was dismissed because she couldn't prove that the agency acted in a "grossly irresponsible manner."

In situations involving personnel, organizations often try to avoid lawsuits by saying that an employee left "for personal reasons" or to "pursue other interests," even if the real reason was incompetence or a record of sexual harassment. News releases and product publicity should also be written in accordance with FTC and SEC regulations, to be discussed shortly.

Another potentially dangerous practice is making unflattering comments about the competition's products. Although comparative advertising is the norm in the United States, a company must walk a narrow line between comparison and "trade libel," or "product disparagement." Statements should be truthful, with factual evidence and scientific demonstration available to substantiate them. Companies often charge competitors with overstepping the boundary between "puffery" and "factual representation."

An organization can offer the opinion that a particular product or service is the "best" or "a revolutionary development" if the context clearly shows that the communication is a statement of opinion attributed to someone. Then it is classified as "puffery" and doesn't require factual evidence.

Along the same line, a statement of opinion also has a degree of legal protection through the First Amendment guarantee of freedom of speech. In one case, the owner of the New York Yankees was sued for libel by a baseball umpire when a team news release called him a "scab" who "has had it in" for the Yankees. A lower court awarded damages, but the New York Supreme Court overturned the judgment, ruling that the comments in the new release constituted protected statements of opinion under the fair comment concept.

Don Sneed, Tim Wulfemeyer, and Harry Stonecipher, in a *Public Relations Review* article, say that a news release should be written to indicate clearly statements of opinion and statements of fact. They suggest that (1) opinion statements be accompanied by the facts upon which the opinions are based, (2) statements of opinion be clearly labeled as such, and (3) the context of the language surrounding the expression of opinion be reviewed for possible legal implications.

The Fair Comment Defense

Organizations can do much to ensure that their communications avoid materials that could lead to potential lawsuits. By the same token, organizations are somewhat limited in their ability to use legal measures to defend themselves against criticism.

Executives are often incensed when an environmental group includes their corporation on its annual "dirty dozen" polluters or similar lists. Executives are also unhappy when a broadcast consumer affairs reporter flatly calls the product a "rip-off."

A corporate reputation may be damaged and product sales may go down, but a defamation case is difficult to win because, as previously mentioned, the accuser must prove actual malice. Also operating is the concept of *fair comment and criticism*.

This defense is used by theater and music critics when they lambaste a play or concert. Fair comment also means that when companies and individuals voluntarily display their wares to the public for sale or consumption, they have no real recourse against criticism done with honest purpose and lack of malicious intent.

A utility company in Indiana, for example, once tried to sue a citizen who wrote a letter to a newspaper criticizing it for seeking a rate hike. The judge threw the suit out of court, stating that the rate increase was a "matter of public interest and concern" even if the letter writer didn't have all the facts straight.

Invasion of Privacy

An area of law that particularly applies to employees of an organization is *invasion of privacy*. Public relations staff must be particularly sensitive to the issue of privacy in at least four areas: (1) employee newsletters, (2) photo releases, (3) product publicity and advertising, and (4) media inquiries about employees.

Employee Newsletters

It is no longer true, if it ever was, that an organization has an unlimited right to publicize the activities of its employees. In fact, Morton J. Simon, a Philadelphia lawyer and author of *Public Relations Law*, wrote, "It should not be assumed that a person's status as an employee waives his right to privacy." Simon correctly points out that a company newsletter or magazine does not enjoy the same First Amendment protection that the news media enjoy when they claim "newsworthiness" and "public interest." A number of court cases, he says, show that company newsletters are considered commercial tools of trade.

This distinction does not impede the effectiveness of newsletters, but it does indicate editors should try to keep employee stories organization-oriented. Indeed, most lawsuits and complaints are generated by "personals columns" that may invade the privacy of employees. Although a mention that Joe Doaks honeymooned in Hawaii or that Mary Worth is now a great-grandmother may sound completely innocent, the individuals involved—for any number of reasons—may consider the information a violation of their privacy. The situation may be further compounded into possible defamation by "cutesy" editorial asides in poor taste.

In sum, one should avoid anything that might embarrass or subject an employee to ridicule by fellow employees. Here are some guidelines to remember when writing about employee activities:

- Keep the focus on organization-related activities.
- Have employees submit "personals" in writing.
- Double-check all information for accuracy.
- Ask: "Will this embarrass anyone or cause someone to be the butt of jokes?"
- Don't rely on secondhand information; confirm the facts with the person involved.
- Don't include racial or ethnic designations of employees in any articles.

Photo Releases

Ordinarily, a public relations practitioner doesn't need a signed release if a person gives "implied consent" by posing for a picture and is told how it will be used. This is particularly true for "news" photographs published in internal newsletters.

Public relations departments, however, should take the precaution of (1) filing all photographs, (2) dating them, and (3) giving the context of the situation. This precludes the use of old photos that could embarrass employees or subject them to ridicule. In other cases, it precludes using photographs of persons who are no longer employed or have died. This method also helps to make certain that a photo taken for the employee newsletter isn't used in an advertisement.

If a photo of an employee or customer is used in product publicity, sales brochures, or advertisements, the standard practice is to obtain a signed release. Here is a simplified release used by Hewlett-Packard Company:

I grant to Hewlett-Packard Company ("HP"), its representatives and employees the right to take photographs of me and my property in connection with the above identified subject and I authorize HP, its assigns and transferees to copyright, use, and publish the same in print and/or electronically.

I agree that HP may use such photographs of me with or without my name and for any lawful purpose, including for example, such purposes as publicity, illustration, and advertising.

Next we discuss the use of photographs and testimonials in an advertising context.

Product Publicity and Advertising

As already noted, an organization must have a signed release on file if it wants to use the photographs or comments of employees and other individuals in product publicity, sales brochures, and advertising. An added precaution is to give some financial compensation to make a more binding contract.

Chemical Bank of New York unfortunately learned this lesson the hard way. The bank used pictures of 39 employees in various advertisements designed to "humanize" the bank's image, but the employees maintained that no one had requested permission to use their photos in advertisements. Another problem was that the pictures had been taken up to five years before they began appearing in the series of advertisements.

An attorney for the employees, who sued for $600,000 in damages, said, "The bank took the individuality of these employees and used that individuality to make a profit." The judge agreed and ruled that the bank had violated New York's privacy law. The action is called *misappropriation of personality*, which is discussed later in this chapter. Jerry Della Femina, an advertising executive, succinctly makes the point: Get permission. "If I used my mother in an ad," he said, "I'd get her permission—and I almost trust her 100 percent."

Written permission also should be obtained if the employee's photograph is to appear in sales brochures or even in the corporate annual report. This rule also applies to other situations. A graduate of Lafayette College sued the college for using a photo of his mother and him at graduation ceremonies, without their permission, in a financial aid brochure.

Media Inquiries about Employees

Because press inquiries have the potential of invading an employee's right of privacy, public relations personnel should follow basic guidelines as to what information will be provided on the employee's behalf.

In general, employers should give a news reporter only basic information. This may include (1) confirmation that the person is an employee, (2) the person's title and job description, and (3) date of beginning employment, or, if applicable, date of termination.

Unless it is specified by law or permission is given by the employee, a public relations person should avoid providing information about an employee's (1) salary, (2) home address, (3) marital status, (4) number of children, (5) organizational memberships, and (6) job performance.

If a reporter does seek any of this information, because of the nature of the story, several methods may be followed.

First, a public relations person can volunteer to contact the employee and have the person speak directly with the reporter. What the employee chooses to tell the reporter is not then a company's responsibility. Second, many organizations do provide additional information to a reporter if it is included on an optional biographical sheet that the employee has filled out. In most cases, the form clearly states that the organization may use any of the information in answering press inquiries or writing its own news releases. A typical biographical form may have sections in which the employee can list his or her (1) honors and awards, (2) professional memberships, (3) marital status and names of any children, (4) previous employers, (5) educational background, and (6) hobbies or interests. This sheet should not be confused with the person's official employment application, which must remain confidential.

If an organization uses biographical sheets, it is important that they be dated and kept current. A sheet compiled by an employee five years previously may be hopelessly out of date. This is also true of *file photographs* taken at the time of a person's employment.

Copyright Law

Should a news release be copyrighted? How about a corporate annual report? Can a *New Yorker* cartoon be used in the company magazine without permission? What about reprinting an article from *Fortune* magazine and distributing it to the company's sales staff? Are government reports copyrighted? What constitutes copyright infringement?

These are some of the bothersome questions that a public relations professional should be able to answer. Knowledge of copyright law is important from two perspectives: (1) what organizational materials should be copyrighted and (2) how correctly to utilize the copyrighted materials of others.

Before going into these areas, however, it is important to know what copyright means. In very simple terms, *copyright* means protection of a creative work from unauthorized use. A section of the U.S. copyright law of 1978 states: "Copyright protection subsists . . . in the original works of authorship fixed in any tangible medium of expression now known or later developed." The word *authorship* is defined in seven categories: (1) literary works; (2) musical works; (3) dramatic works; (4) pantomimes and choreographic works; (5) pictorial, graphic, or sculptural works; (6) motion pictures; and (7) sound recordings. The word *fixed* means that the work is sufficiently permanent or stable to permit it to be perceived, reproduced, or otherwise communicated.

The shield of copyright protection was reduced somewhat in 1991 when the Supreme Court ruled unanimously that directories, computer databases, and other compilations of facts may be copied and republished unless they display "some minimum degree of creativity." The court stated, "Raw facts may be copied at will."

Thus, a copyright does not protect ideas, but only the specific ways in which those ideas are expressed. An idea for promoting a product, for example, cannot be copyrighted—but brochures, drawings, news features, animated cartoons, display booths, photographs, recordings, videotapes, corporate symbols, slogans, and the like that express a particular idea can be copyrighted.

Because much money, effort, time, and creative talent are spent on organizational materials, copyright protection is important. By copyrighting materials, a company can prevent competitors from capitalizing on its creative work or producing a facsimile brochure that tends to mislead the public. A manufacturer of personal computers would be in serious legal difficulties if it began distributing sales brochures that tended to look just like ones from Apple Computer. (The concept of trademark infringement [such as copying the Apple logo with slight changes] will be discussed in the section titled "Trademark Law.")

The law presumes that material produced in some tangible form is copyrighted from the moment it is created. This is particularly true if the material bears a copyright notice. One of the following methods may be employed:

- Using the letter "c" in a circle (©), followed by the word *copyright*.
- Citing the year of copyright and the name of the owner.

This presumption of copyright is often sufficient to discourage unauthorized use, and the writer or creator of the material has some legal protection if he or she can prove that the material was created before another person claims it.

A more formal step, providing full legal protection, is official registration of the copyrighted work within three months after creation. This is done by depositing two copies of the manuscript (it is not necessary that it has been published), recording, or artwork with the Copyright Office of the Library of Congress. Copyright registration forms are available from U.S. post offices. Registration is not a condition of copyright protection, but it is a prerequisite to an infringement action against unauthorized use by others.

Length of Copyright

The Copyright Term Extension Act, passed in 1998 and reaffirmed by the U.S. Supreme Court (*Eldred v. Ashcroft*) in 2003, protects original material for the life of the creator plus 70 years for individual works and 95 years from publication for copyrights held by corporations. The previous copyright legislation protected authors for their lifetime plus 50 years.

The impetus for a 20-year extension primarily came from the movie industry. Copyrights on the earliest version of Walt Disney's Mickey Mouse, for example, would have expired in 2003 if Congress had not passed the 1998 legislation. The extended time period was controversial. Publishers and media companies strongly supported the legislation, whereas libraries and consumers believed material should be more widely available for public use. As one academic told the *New York Times*, ". . . copyright is supposed to work for the public and not a small set of corporations."

Fair Use versus Infringement

Public relations people are in the business of gathering information from a variety of sources, so it is important to know where *fair use* ends and *infringement* begins.

Fair use means that part of a copyrighted article may be quoted directly, but the quoted material must be brief in relation to the length of the original work. It may be, for example, only one paragraph in a 750-word article and up to 300 words in a long article or book chapter. Complete attribution of the source must be given regardless of the length of the quotation. If the passage is quoted verbatim, quote marks must be used.

It is important to note, however, that the concept of fair use has distinct limitations if part of the copyrighted material is to be used in advertisements and promotional brochures. In this case, permission is required. It also is important for the original source to approve the context in which the quote is used. A quote out of context often runs into legal trouble if it implies endorsement of a product or service.

The copyright law does allow limited copying of a work for fair use such as criticism, comment, or research. However, in recent years, the courts have considerably

ON THE JOB
insights

Plagiarism versus Copyright Infringement

Copyright infringement and plagiarism differ. You may be guilty of copyright infringement even if you attribute the materials and give the source, but don't get permission from the author or publisher to reproduce the materials.

In the case of plagiarism, the author makes no attempt to attribute the information at all. As the guide for Hamilton College says, "Plagiarism is a form of fraud. You plagiarize if you present other writer's words or ideas as your own." Maurice Isserman, writing in the *Chronicle of Higher Education*, further explains, "Plagiarism substitutes someone else's prowess at explanation for your own efforts."

The World Wide Web has increased the problems of plagiarism because it is quite easy for anyone, from students to college presidents, to cut and paste entire paragraphs (or even pages) into a term paper or speech and claim it as their own creation. Of course, students also can purchase complete term papers online, but that loophole is rapidly shrinking as more sophisticated software programs, such as www.turnitin.com, can scan the entire Internet for other sources that use the same phrases used in a student's research paper.

John Barrie, founder of Turnitin, told the *Wall Street Journal* that ". . . 85 percent of the cases of plagiarism that we see are straight copies from the Internet—a student uses the Internet like a 1.5 billion-page cut-and-paste encyclopedia." Most universities have very strong rules about plagiarism, and it is not uncommon for students to receive an "F" in a course for plagiarism. In the business world, stealing someone else's words and expression of thought is called *theft of intellectual property* and lawsuits are filed.

Source: Dennis L. Wilcox. *Public Relations Writing and Media Techniques*, 5th ed. Boston: Allyn & Bacon, 2005, p. 77.

narrowed the concept of "fair use" when multiple copies of a copyrighted work are involved.

A landmark case was a successful lawsuit in 1991 by book publishers against Kinko's, a national chain of photocopying stores. The chain was charged with copyright infringement because it reproduced excerpts from books without permission and sold them in anthologies to college students. Although Kinko's argued "fair use" for educational purposes, the court rejected this defense. The court settlement cost Kinko's $500,000 in damages and almost $1.5 million in legal fees.

Even the unauthorized photocopying of newsletters and published articles can cost the organization large sums of money. Texaco, for example, lost a lawsuit filed by publishers of scientific journals, who claimed that the company violated the copyright law by permitting employees to photocopy articles for their files.

Organizations that have a single subscription to a newsletter and then circulate it via in-house e-mail also violate the law. Atlas Telecom paid a $100,000 settlement after admitting that it electronically distributed about a dozen telecommunications newsletters to its employees. According to the suit filed by Phillips Publishing, Inc., the company made hundreds of copies by reproducing the newsletters on the in-house database.

Such lawsuits can be avoided if an organization orders quantity reprints from the publisher and pays a licensing fee that permits it to make paper or electronic copies. Dow Jones, publisher of the *Wall Street Journal*, has a whole department (www.djreprints.com) that arranges reprints that can be used in print, e-mail, PDF, or Web link formats. The same concept applies to videotaping television shows or news programs for widespread distribution.

Government documents (city, county, state, and federal) are in the public domain and cannot be copyrighted. Public relations personnel, under the fair use doctrine, can freely use quotations and statistics from a government document, but care must be exercised to ensure that the material is in context and not misleading. The most common problem occurs when an organization uses a government report as a form of endorsement for its services or products. An airline, for example, might cite a government study showing that it provides the most service to customers, but neglect to state the basis of comparison or other factors.

Photography and Artwork

The copyright law makes it clear that freelance and commercial photographers retain ownership of their work. In other words, a customer who buys a copyrighted photo owns the item itself, but not the right to make additional copies. That right remains with the photographer unless transferred in writing.

In a further extension of this right, the duplication of copyrighted photos is also illegal. This was established in a 1990 U.S. Federal District Court case in which the Professional Photographers of America (PP of A) sued a nationwide photofinishing firm for ignoring copyright notices on pictures sent for additional copies.

Freelance photographers generally charge for a picture on the basis of its use. If it is used only once, perhaps for an employee newsletter, the fee is low. If, however, the company wants to use the picture in the corporate annual report or on the company calendar, the fee may be considerably higher. Consequently it is important for a public relations person to tell the photographer exactly how the picture will be used. Arrangements and fees then can be determined for (1) one-time use, (2) unlimited use, or (3) the payment of royalties every time the picture is used.

Computer manipulation of original artwork can also violate copyright. One photographer's picture of a racing yacht was used on a poster after the art director electronically changed the numbers on the sail and made the water a deeper blue. In another case, a photo distribution agency successfully sued *Newsday* for unauthorized use of a color image after the newspaper reconstructed the agency's picture using a computer scanner, then failed to credit the photographer. FPG International was awarded $20,000 in damages, ten times the initial licensing fee of $2000. In sum, slightly changing a copyrighted photo or a piece of artwork can be considered a violation of copyright if the intent is to capitalize on widespread recognition of the original art.

This was the case when the estate of the late children's author, Dr. Seuss, won a $1.5 million judgment against a Los Angeles T-shirt maker for infringement of copyright. The manufacturer had portrayed a parody of Dr. Seuss's Cat in the Hat character smoking marijuana and giving the peace sign. In another situation, the Rock and Roll Hall of Fame filed a copyright suit against a freelance photographer who snapped a picture of the unique building at sunset and sold posters of his work without paying a licensing fee.

The Rights of Freelance Writers

Although the rights of freelance photographers have been established for some years, it was only recently that freelance writers gained more control over the ownership of their work.

In the now famous Reid Case (*Community for Creative Nonviolence v. Reid*), the U.S. Supreme Court in 1989 ruled that writers retained ownership of their work and that purchasers of it simply gained a "license" to reproduce the copyrighted work.

Prior to this ruling, the common practice was to assume that commissioned articles were "work for hire" and the purchaser owned the copyright. In other words, a magazine could reproduce the article in any number of ways and even sell it to another publication without the writer's permission.

Under the new interpretation, ownership of a writer's work is subject to negotiation and contractual agreement. Writers may agree to assign all copyright rights to the work they have been hired to do or they may give permission only for a specific one-time use.

In a related matter, freelance writers are pressing for additional compensation if an organization puts their work on CD-ROM, online databases, or the Internet's World Wide Web. They won a major victory in 2001 when the Supreme Court (*New York Times v. Tasini*) ruled that publishers, by making articles accessible through electronic databases, infringed the copyrights of freelance contributors.

Public relations firms and corporate public relations departments are responsible for ensuring compliance with the copyright law. This means that all agreements with a freelance writer must be in writing, and the use of the material must be clearly stated. Ideally, public relations personnel should negotiate multiple rights and even complete ownership of the copyright.

Copyright Issues on the Internet

The emergence of the information superhighway, particularly the Internet and World Wide Web, has raised new issues about the protection of intellectual property. Two issues regarding copyright are: (1) the downloading of copyrighted material and (2) the unauthorized uploading of such material.

The Downloading of Material. In general, the same rules apply to cyberspace as to more earthbound methods of expressing and disseminating ideas. Original materials in digital form are still protected by copyright. The fair-use limits for materials found on the Internet are essentially the same as the fair use of materials disseminated by any other means.

Related to this is the use of news articles and features that are sent via e-mail or the Web to the clients of clipping services. An organization may use such clips to track its publicity efforts, but it can't distribute the article on its own Web site or intranet without permission and a royalty payment to the publication where the article appeared. One national clipping service, Burrelle's, has already made an agreement with more than 300 newspapers to have their customers pay a small royalty fee in exchange for being able to make photocopies of clippings and make greater use of them.

The Uploading of Material. In many cases, owners of copyrighted material have uploaded various kinds of information with the intention of making it freely available. Some examples are software, games, and even the entire text of *The Hitchhiker's Guide to the Galaxy*. The problem comes, however, when third parties upload copyrighted material without permission. Consequently, copyright holders are increasingly patrolling the Internet and World Wide Web to stop the unauthorized use of material. Some examples:

- Dutton Children's Books threatened a lawsuit against a New Mexico State University student for using Winnie the Pooh illustrations on his home page.
- Paramount Pictures sent warning notes to *Star Trek* fans against using the Internet to disseminate photos from the TV series.

- Elvis Presley Enterprises ordered the removal of sound clips of "Blue Suede Shoes" and "Hound Dog" from a home page that also displayed images from Graceland postcards.

The unauthorized use of copyrighted material on the Internet has led to calls for Congress to update the existing law to cover online information. One measure considered by the Senate would make it illegal to evade copyright protections built into electronically distributed material.

Copyright Guidelines

A number of points have been discussed about copyright. A public relations person should keep the following in mind:

- Ideas cannot be copyrighted, but the expression of those ideas can be.
- Major public relations materials (brochures, annual reports, videotapes, motion pictures, position papers, and the like) should be copyrighted, if only to prevent unauthorized use by competitors.
- Although there is a concept of *fair use*, any copyrighted material intended directly to advance the sales and profits of an organization should not be used unless permission is given.

ON THE JOB

global

In Europe, the Copyright Is Expiring on Elvis

The Recording Industry Association of America (RIAA) has launched a public relations and lobbying effort to convince European Union (EU) nations to extend the length of time that music can be copyrighted.

Copyright protection lasts only 50 years in Europe, compared with 95 years in the United States. That means that 1950s recordings by Elvis Presley and such jazz greats as Ella Fitzgerald will soon be in the public domain. This doesn't please American record companies; they believe that European recordings of these artists will enter the United States and the international market at cheaper prices, thus undercutting their profits.

If the American recording industry is unsuccessful in getting copyright terms extended in Europe, the next step is to convince U.S. Customs to seize such products and block them from the U.S. market.

Consumer and music lovers are less than enthusiastic. According to the *New York Times*, "They see many copyright protections as too lengthy, unfair to the public, and ultimately stifling to creativity."

- Copyrighted material should not be taken out of context, particularly if it implies endorsement of the organization's services or products.
- Quantity reprints of an article should be ordered from the publisher.
- Permission is required to use segments of television programs or motion pictures.
- Permission must be obtained to use segments of popular songs (written verses or sound recordings) from a recording company.
- Photographers and freelance writers retain the rights to their works. Permission and fees must be negotiated to use works for other purposes than originally agreed upon.
- Photographs of current celebrities or those who are now deceased cannot be used for promotion and publicity purposes without permission.
- Permission is required to reprint cartoon characters, such as Snoopy or Garfield. In addition, cartoons and other artwork or illustrations in a publication are copyrighted.

- Government documents are not copyrighted, but caution is necessary if the material is used in a way that implies endorsement of products or services.
- Private letters, or excerpts from them, cannot be published or used in sales and publicity materials without the permission of the letter writer.
- Original material posted on the Internet and the World Wide Web has copyright protection.
- The copyrighted material of others should not be posted on the Internet unless specific permission is granted.

Trademark Law

What do the names Coca-Cola, Marlboro, and IBM, the Olympic rings, and the logo of the Dallas Cowboys have in common? They are all registered trademarks protected by law.

A *trademark* is a word, symbol, or slogan, used singly or in combination, that identifies a product's origin. According to Susan L. Cohen, writing in *Editor & Publisher*'s annual trademark supplement, "It also serves as an indicator of quality, a kind of shorthand for consumers to use in recognizing goods in a complex marketplace." Research indicates, for example, that 53 percent of Americans say brand quality takes precedence over price considerations.

The concept of a trademark is nothing new. The ancient Egyptians carved marks into the stones of the pyramids, and the craftsmen of the Middle Ages used guild marks to identify the source and quality of products.

What is new, however, is the proliferation of trademarks and service marks in modern society. Coca-Cola may be the world's most recognized trademark, according to some studies, but it is only one of almost one million active trademarks registered with the federal Patent and Trademark Office. And, according to the International Trademark Association, the number keeps going up at a rapid rate.

The Protection of Trademarks

Trademarks are always capitalized and are never used as nouns. They are always used as adjectives modifying nouns. For example, the proper terms are *Kleenex tissues*, *Xerox copies*, and *Rollerblade skates*. A person who "uses a Kleenex," "makes a Xerox," or "goes Rollerblading" is violating trademark law.

In addition, organizations take the step of designating brand names and slogans with various marks. The registered trademark symbol is a superscript, small capital "R" in a circle—®. "Registered in U.S. Patent and Trademark Office" and "Reg. U.S. Pat. Off" may also be used. A "TM" in small capital letters indicates a trademark that isn't registered. It represents a company's common-law claim to a right of trademark or a trademark for which registration is pending.

A service mark is like a trademark, but it designates a service rather than a product, or is a logo. An "SM" in small capitals in a circle—(SM)—is the symbol for a registered service mark. If registration is pending, the "SM" should be used without the circle.

These symbols are used in advertising, product labeling, news releases, company brochures, and so on to let the public and competitors know that a name, slogan, or symbol is protected by law. See the ad on page 310 for an example of how organizations publicize their trademarks and service marks.

Public relations practitioners play an important role in protecting the trademarks of their employers. They safeguard trademarks and respect other organizational trademarks in the following ways:

● Ensure that company trademarks are capitalized and used properly in all organizational literature and graphics. Lax supervision can cause loss of trademark protection.

● Distribute trademark brochures to editors and reporters and place advertisements in trade publications, designating names to be capitalized.

● Educate employees as to what the organization's trademarks are and how to use them correctly.

● Monitor the mass media to make certain that trademarks are used correctly. If they are not, send a gentle reminder.

● Check publications to ensure that other organizations are not infringing on a registered trademark. If they are, the company legal department should protest with letters and threats of possible lawsuits.

ON THE JOB insights

Use the Logo, Pay the Fee

Sports logos are registered trademarks, and a licensing fee must be paid before anyone can use logos for commercial products and promotions.

Teams in the National Football League and the National Basketball Association earn more than $3 billion annually just selling licensed merchandise, and the sale of college and university trademarked goods is rapidly approaching that mark. Schools such as Notre Dame, Michigan, and Ohio State rake in more than $3 million a year in royalties from licensing their logos to be placed on everything from beer mugs to T-shirts.

The penalty for not paying a licensing fee is steep. The NFL, during Super Bowl week, typically confiscates about $1 million in bogus goods and files criminal charges against the offending vendors.

● Make sure the trademark is actually being used. A 1988 revision of the Trademark Act no longer permits an organization to hold a name in reserve.

● Ensure that the trademarks of other organizations are correctly used and properly noted.

● Avoid the use of trademarked symbols or cartoon figures in promotional materials without the explicit permission of the owner. In some cases, to be discussed, a licensing fee is required.

Organizations adamantly insist on the proper use of trademarks in order to avoid the problem of having a name or slogan become generic. Or, to put it another way, a brand name becomes a common noun through general public use. Some trade names that have become generic include *aspirin, thermos, cornflakes, nylon, cellophane,* and *yo-yo.* This means that any company can use these names to describe a product.

The Problem of Trademark Infringement

Today, when there are thousands of businesses and organizations, finding a trademark not already in use is extremely difficult. The task is even more frustrating if a company wants to use a trademark on an international level.

A good example is what happened to Nike at the 1992 Olympic Games in Barcelona. The athletic shoe manufacturer paid millions to be an official sponsor of

FedEx® Is Not Synonymous With Overnight Shipping.

That's why you can't FedEx or Federal Express your package. Neither FedEx® nor Federal Express® are nouns, verbs, adverbs or even participles. They are adjectives and identify our unique brand of shipping services. So if you want to send a package overnight, ask for FedEx® delivery services.

When you do, we think you'll know why we say "Why Fool Around With Anyone Else?"® After all, FedEx is "Absolutely, Positively the Best in the Business."® Help us protect our marks. Ask us before you use them, use them correctly, and, most of all, only ask for FedEx® delivery services.

FedEx.

Be absolutely sure.

www.fedex.com

© 1998 Federal Express Corporation

the games, and it planned to introduce a new line of clothes at the event. There was a snag, however. A Spanish high court ruled that the Beaverton, Oregon, firm's trademark infringed on the trademark of a Barcelona sock company that had registered "Nike" more than 60 years ago. The court barred Nike from selling or advertising its sports apparel in Spain, an action that cost the company about $20 million in marketing potential.

The complexity of finding a new name, coupled with the attempts of many to capitalize on an already known trade name, has spawned a number of lawsuits claiming trademark infringement. Here are some examples:

- *Entrepreneur* magazine was awarded $337,000 in court damages after filing a trademark infringement lawsuit against a public relations firm that changed its name to "EntrepreneurPR."

- Fox News filed a suit against satirist and author Al Franken because the title of his new book was *Lies and Lying Liars Who Tell Them: A Fair and Balanced Look at the Right*. Fox claimed that the phrase "fair and balanced" was trademarked.

- The widow of the man who said "Let's Roll" when he and others tried to overpower the hijackers of Flight 93 over Pennsylvania on September 11 petitioned the federal government to trademark the phrase. She wanted to license the phrase to fund a foundation to assist children who had lost a parent.

- Phi Beta Kappa, the academic honor society, filed a $5 million trademark infringement suit against Compaq Computer Corp. after the company launched a "Phi Beta Compaq" promotion targeted at college students.

ON THE JOB insights

Accenture: What's in a Name?

A name for a company or organization that isn't already trademarked is getting more difficult to find. As one consultant says, "There isn't a color, a fruit, an animal, or even a prehistoric one that isn't already trademarked by somebody."

Consequently, companies often select new names that sound like something made from leftover Scrabble tiles. A good example is *Accenture*, which is the new name of Arthur Andersen Consulting after a legal dispute with former partner Arthur Andersen, the accounting firm.

According to Jim Murphy, global director of marketing and communications, the company started with a slate of 5000 names. The list was then winnowed down to 500 that met the company's positioning goals. But after checking the list against trademark and other databases, including a Berlitz program designed to spot offensive or adverse translations in 50 countries, Andersen lost all but 29 names. From that list, Accenture, submitted by an employee in Oslo, emerged the winner.

The word, which doesn't exist in any dictionary, is supposed to connote an "accent on the future," according to Murphy. The downside of such coined names, however, is that they don't mean anything in themselves. Companies then have to spend considerable money to ensure that employees, customers, and the public identify the name with a particular company. In the case of Accenture, the company spent $175 million on an advertising and marketing communications campaign.

● MADD (Mothers Against Drunk Driving) filed a trademark suit against an organization calling itself DAMMADD, a nonprofit group established to spread antidrug messages. MADD said the similar name would confuse the public.

In all of these cases, organizations claimed that their registered trademarks were being improperly exploited for commercial or organizational purposes. Some guidelines used by courts to determine if there has been trademark infringement are as follows:

● Has the defendant used a name as a way of capitalizing on the reputation of another organization's trademark—and does the defendant benefit from the original organization's investment in popularizing its trademark?

● Is there an intent (real or otherwise) to create confusion in the public mind? Is there an intent to imply a connection between the defendant's product and the item identified by trademark?

● How similar are the two organizations? Are they providing the same kinds of products or services?

● Has the original organization actively protected the trademark by publicizing it and by actually continuing to use it in connection with its products or services?

● Is the trademark unique? A company with a trademark that merely describes a common product might be in trouble.

Misappropriation of Personality

A form of trademark infringement also can result from the unauthorized use of well-known entertainers, professional athletes, and other public figures in an organization's publicity and advertising materials. A photo of Tom Cruise may make a company's advertising campaign more interesting, but the courts call it "misappropriation of personality" if permission and licensing fees have not been negotiated.

Airbus Industrie got into trouble, for example, by featuring a photo of Sir Roger Bannister, famous for the four-minute mile, in one of its advertisements without seeking prior permission. As part of the settlement, the company had to run a full-page apology in *Fortune* and other magazines that had used the advertisement, as well as make a substantial donation to a charity approved by Sir Roger.

Deceased celebrities also are protected. To use a likeness or actual photo of a personality such as Elvis Presley, Marilyn Monroe, or even Princess Diana, the user must pay a licensing fee to an agent representing the family, studio, or estate of the deceased. The Presley estate, almost 30 years after his death, is still the "King" with about $40 million in income annually. The estate of Peanuts comic strip creator Charles Schulz collects about $30 million annually. NASCAR icon Dale Earnhardt is in a third-place tie with Beatle John Lennon at $20 million.

The legal doctrine is the *right of publicity*, which gives entertainers, athletes, and other celebrities the sole ability to cash in on their fame. The legal right is loosely akin to a trademark or copyright, and many states have made it a commercial asset that can be inherited by a celebrity's descendents. One California artist, for example, was sued by the heirs of the Three Stooges because he made a charcoal portrait of the famous acting team and reproduced it on T-shirts and lithographs.

Legal protection also extends to the use of "sound-alikes" or "look-alikes." Bette Midler won a $400,000 judgment against Young & Rubicam (later affirmed by the Supreme Court on appeal) after the advertising agency used another singer to do a "sound-alike" of her singing style in a rendition of the song "Do You Wanna Dance?" for a Ford commercial. The court ruled: "When a distinctive voice of a professional singer is widely known and is deliberately imitated in order to sell a product, the sellers have appropriated what is not theirs."

▌Regulations by Government Agencies

The promotion of products and services, whether through advertising, product publicity, or other techniques, is not protected by the First Amendment. Instead, the courts have traditionally ruled that such activities fall under the doctrine of *commercial speech*. This means that messages can be regulated by the state in the interest of public health, safety, and consumer protection.

Consequently, the states and the federal government have passed legislation that regulates commercial speech and even restricts it if standards of disclosure, truth, and accuracy are violated. One consequence was the banning of cigarette advertising on television in the 1960s. A more difficult legal question is whether government can completely ban the advertising or promotion of a legally sold product such as cigarettes or alcohol.

Public relations personnel involved in product publicity and the distribution of financial information should be aware of guidelines established by such government agencies as the Federal Trade Commission and the Securities and Exchange Commission.

The Federal Trade Commission

The Federal Trade Commission (FTC) has jurisdiction to determine that advertisements are not deceptive or misleading. Public relations personnel should also know that the commission has jurisdiction over product news releases and other forms of product publicity, such as videos and brochures.

In the eyes of the FTC, both advertisements and product publicity materials are vehicles of commercial trade—and therefore subject to regulation. In fact, Section 43(a) of the Lanham Act makes it clear that anyone, including public relations personnel, is subject to liability if that person participates in the making or dissemination of a false and misleading representation in any advertising or promotional material. This includes advertising and public relations firms, which also can be held liable for writing, producing, and distributing product publicity materials on behalf of clients.

An example of an FTC complaint is one filed against Campbell Soup Company for claiming that its soups were low in fat and cholesterol and thus helpful in fighting heart disease. The commission charged that the claim was deceptive because publicity and advertisements didn't disclose that the soups also were high in sodium, a condition that increases the risk of heart disease.

The Campbell Soup case raises an important aspect of FTC guidelines. Although a publicized fact may be accurate in itself, FTC staff also considers the context or "net impression received by the consumers." In Campbell's case, advertising copywriters and publicists ignored the information about high sodium, which placed an entirely new perspective on the health benefits of the soup.

Hollywood's abuse of endorsements and testimonials to publicize its films also has attracted the scrutiny of the FTC. It was discovered that Sony Pictures had concocted quotes from a fictitious movie critic to publicize four of its films. And Twentieth Century Fox admitted that it had hired actors to appear in "man in the street" commercials to portray unpaid moviegoers.

Excerpts in ads from regular reviewers also can be misleading and in violation of FTC guidelines. David Ansen, movie critic for *Newsweek*, was quoted that a film starring Chevy Chase and Goldie Hawn was "good fun." The context was much different. He told the *Wall Street Journal*, "I had written that though it was all intended as good fun, it's about as much fun as getting hit by a bus."

FTC investigators are always on the lookout for unsubstantiated claims and various forms of misleading or deceptive information. Some of the words in promotional materials that trigger FTC interest are: *authentic, certified, cure, custom-made, germ-free, natural, unbreakable, perfect, first-class, exclusive,* and *reliable.*

In recent years, the FTC also has established guidelines for "green" marketing and the use of "low-carb" in advertisements and publicity materials for food products. The following general guidelines, adapted from FTC regulations, should be taken into account when writing product publicity materials:

- Make sure the information is accurate and can be substantiated.
- Stick to the facts. Don't "hype" the product or service by using flowery, nonspecific adjectives and ambiguous claims.
- Make sure celebrities or others who endorse the product actually use it. They should not say anything about the product's properties that cannot be substantiated.
- Watch the language. Don't say "independent research study" when the research was done by the organization's staff.

- Provide proper context for statements and statistics attributed to government agencies. They don't endorse products.
- Describe tests and surveys in sufficient detail so the consumer understands what was tested under what conditions.
- Remember that a product is not "new" if only the packaging has been changed or the product is more than six months old.
- When comparing products or services with a competitor's, make certain you can substantiate your claims.
- Avoid misleading and deceptive product demonstrations.

Companies found in violation of FTC guidelines are usually given the opportunity to sign a *consent decree*. This means that the company admits no wrongdoing but agrees to change its advertising and publicity claims. Companies may also be fined by the FTC or ordered to engage in corrective advertising and publicity.

The Securities and Exchange Commission

The megamergers and the IPOs (initial public offerings) of many new companies in the 1990s made the Securities and Exchange Commission (SEC) a household name in the business world. This federal agency closely monitors the financial affairs of publicly traded companies and protects the interests of stockholders.

SEC guidelines on public disclosure and insider trading are particularly relevant to corporate public relations staff members who must meet the requirements. The distribution of misleading information or failure to make a timely disclosure of material information may be the basis of liability under the SEC code. A company may even be liable if, while it satisfies regulations by getting information out, it conveys crucial information in a vague way or buries it deep in the news release.

A good example is Enron, the Houston-based energy company that became a household word overnight when it became the largest corporate failure in U.S. history. The company was charged with a number of SEC violations, including the distribution of misleading news releases about its finances. According to Congressional testimony, the company issued a quarterly earnings news release that falsely led investors to believe that the company was "on track" to meet strong earnings growth in 2002. Three months later, the company was bankrupt.

The SEC has volumes of regulations, but the three concepts most pertinent to public relations personnel are as follows:

1. Full information must be given on anything that might materially affect the company's stock. This includes such things as (1) dividends or their deletion, (2) annual and quarterly earnings, (3) stock splits, (4) mergers or takeovers, (5) major management changes, (6) major product developments, (7) expansion plans, (8) change of business purpose, (9) defaults, (10) proxy materials, (11) disposition of major assets, (12) purchase of own stock, and (13) announcements of major contracts or orders.

2. Timely disclosure is essential. A company must act promptly (within minutes or a few hours) to dispel or confirm rumors that result in unusual market activity or market variations. The most common ways of dispensing such financial information are through use of electronic news release services, contact with the major international news services (Dow Jones Wire), and bulk faxing.

3. Insider trading is illegal. Company officials, including public relations staffs and outside counsel, cannot use inside information to buy and sell company stock. The landmark case on insider trading occurred in 1965, when Texas Gulf Sulphur executives used inside information about an ore strike in Canada to buy stock while at the same time issuing a news release downplaying rumors that a rich find had been made.

The courts are increasingly applying the *mosaic doctrine* to financial information. Maureen Rubin, an attorney and professor at California State University, Northridge, explains that a court may examine *all* information released by a company, including news releases, to determine whether, taken as a whole, they create an "overall misleading" impression. One such case was *Cytryn v. Cook* (1990), in which a U.S. District Court ruled that the proper test of a company's adequate financial disclosure was not the literal truth of each positive statement, but the overall misleading impression that it combined to create in the eyes of potential investors.

As a result of such cases, investor relations personnel must also avoid such practices as:

- Unrealistic sales and earnings reports
- Glowing descriptions of products in the experimental stage
- Announcements of possible mergers or takeovers that are only in the speculation stage
- Free trips for business reporters and offers of stock to financial analysts and editors of financial newsletters
- Omission of unfavorable news and developments
- Leaks of information to selected outsiders and financial columnists
- Dissemination of false rumors about a competitor's financial health

ON THE JOB
ethics
Investor Relations Group Adopts New Code

The National Investor Relations Institute (NIRI) has adopted a new code of ethics in the wake of corporate financial scandals such as Enron, Worldcom, and Tyco.

NIRI (www.niri.org) requires all its members to affirm the code in writing. Members sanctioned for violating laws or SEC regulations will be expelled from the organization. The 12-point code is:

- Maintain the highest legal and ethical standards.
- Avoid even the appearance of professional impropriety.
- Ensure full and fair disclosure.
- Provide fair access to corporate information.
- Serve the interests of shareholders.
- Keep track of company affairs and all investor relations (IR) laws and regulations.
- Keep confidential information confidential.
- Do not use confidential information for personal advantage.
- Exercise independent professional judgment.
- Avoid relationships that might affect ethical standing.
- Report fraudulent or illegal acts within the company.
- Represent oneself in a reputable and dignified manner.

In 1998, the SEC passed new regulations supporting the use of "plain English" in prospectuses and other financial documents. The new rules are supposed to make information understandable to the average investor by removing sentences littered with lawyerisms such as *aforementioned, hereby, therewith, whereas,* and *hereinafter.* According to SEC Chairman Arthur Levitt, the cover page, summary, and risk factor sections of prospectuses must be clear, concise, and understandable.

The SEC's booklet on "plain English" gives helpful writing hints such as (1) make sentences short; (2) use *we* and *our*; *you* and *your*; and (3) say it with an active verb. More information about SEC guidelines can be accessed at its Web site: www.sec.gov/.

Fair Disclosure Regulation.   Two years later, in 2000, the SEC issued another regulation regarding Fair Disclosure (known as Reg FD). Although regulations already existed regarding "material disclosure" of information that could affect the price of stock, the new regulation expanded the concept by requiring publicly traded companies to *broadly disseminate* "material" information via a news release, Webcast, or SEC filing.

According to the SEC, Reg FD ensures that all investors, not just brokerage firms and analysts, will receive financial information from a company at the same time. Schering-Plough, a drug maker, was fined $1 million by the SEC because the company disclosed "material nonpublic information" to analysts and portfolio managers without making the same information available to the public.

Sarbanes-Oxley Act.   The most recent legislation is the Sarbanes-Oxley Act, which was made law in 2002 as a result of the Enron and Worldcom financial scandals. The Enron scandal alone cost investors an estimated $90 billion.

Officially known as the *Public Company Accounting Reform and Investor Protection Act*, its purpose is to increase investor confidence in a company's accounting procedures. Chief executive officers (CEOs) and chief financial officers (CFOs) must now personally certify the accuracy of their financial reports and are subject to criminal proceedings if they are not accurate.

The law also forbids companies from giving personal loans to officers and directors, and it places more independent fiscal responsibility on boards of directors to ensure that the company is adhering to good corporate governance and accounting practices. One of the first executives to be charged under the Act was Richard Scrushy, former CEO of HealthSouth Corp. According to prosecutors, he was involved in a $2.7 billion accounting fraud at the company.

The jury is still out, however, as to whether the Sarbanes-Oxley Act will really ensure that the public will actually receive more detailed financial information from public companies. The Act is still being clarified and challenged in the courts, and attorneys have a powerful role in deciding what can and can't be released. Woody Wallace, head of an investor relations firm, told *O'Dwyer's PR Services Report*, "Most attorneys are conservative and are going to cut down what's being said. Less information and less useful information is being given out. News releases become cursory."

One fall-out of the Act, from a public relations standpoint, is the decision by communication conglomerates not to give a financial break-out of their different divisions, including public relations firms. Consequently, it has become practically impossible to say with any certainty what public relations firm is the largest in the world based on revenues. See the discussion on communications conglomerates in Chapter 4.

Other Regulatory Agencies

Although the FTC and the SEC are the major federal agencies concerned with the content of advertising and publicity materials, the Food and Drug Administration (FDA) and the Bureau of Alcohol, Tobacco and Firearms (BATF) have also established guidelines.

The Food and Drug Administration. The FDA oversees the advertising and promotion of prescription drugs, over-the-counter medicines, and cosmetics. Under the federal Food, Drug, and Cosmetic Act, any "person" (which includes advertising and public relations firms) who "causes the misbranding" of products through the dissemination of false and misleading information may be liable.

The FDA has specific guidelines for video, audio, and print news releases on health-care topics. First, the release must provide "fair balance" by telling consumers about the risks as well as the benefits of the drug or treatment. Second, the writer must be clear about the limitations of a particular drug or treatment, for example, that it may not help people with certain conditions. Third, a news release or media kit should be accompanied by supplementary product sheets or brochures that give full prescribing information.

Because prescription drugs have major FDA curbs on advertising and promotion, the drug companies try to sidestep the regulations by publicizing diseases. Eli Lilly & Co., the maker of Prozac, provides a good example. The company sponsors ads and distributes publicity about depression. And the Glaxo Institute for Digestive Health conducts information campaigns about the fact that stomach pains can be an indication of major problems. Of course, Glaxo also makes the ulcer drug Zantac.

Another public relations approach that has come under increased FDA scrutiny is the placement of celebrities on television talk shows who are being paid by the drug companies to mention the name of a particular drug while they talk about their recovery from cancer, a heart attack, or depression. Some programs, such as the *Today* show, have now banned such guests. Another promotions tool is the published book where the author is a health professional but the company's public relations staff has written most of the copy and, in many cases, the company has even subsidized the publishing of the book.

The Bureau of Alcohol, Tobacco, and Firearms. The Bureau of Alcohol, Tobacco, and Firearms (BATF) administers the Federal Alcohol Administration Act. Any advertising or publicity about products with alcohol must conform to various regulations regarding the risk and supposed benefits of such products.

Wineries, in particular, have run into problems by implying that there are health benefits associated with drinking wine. After intense lobbying by the $9 billion California wine industry, the BATF finally agreed to let wineries label bottles with such statements as "The proud people who made this wine encourage you to consult your family doctor about the health benefits of wine consumption." However, the agency still forbids wineries to use the somewhat famous quote, "As age enhances wine, wine enhances age."

"Food Slander" Laws. A recent development in state legislation is "food slander" laws. A dozen states have put "agricultural product disparagement" laws on their books, making it a crime to criticize or denigrate food with information that is not based on scientific fact.

The legislation, which resulted from the U.S. apple industry's losing almost $100 million because of the Alar scare, is designed to curtail activist groups that often use scare tactics and faulty information to disparage a particular food product. Millions of Americans learned about such laws when popular television celebrity Oprah Winfrey was sued by several Texas cattlemen for allegedly disparaging beef on her talk show. The trial, held in San Antonio, was a publicity bonanza for Oprah—and the jury acquitted her.

ON THE JOB insights

FCC Clamps Down on "Indecent" Broadcasting

The FCC, as a result of Janet Jackson's infamous "wardrobe malfunction" at the 2004 Super Bowl, has sent a strong message to broadcasters across the nation that "indecency" on the airwaves will no longer be permitted.

During the Super Bowl half-time show, Jackson was at the end of a duet with singer Justin Timberlake when he ripped off a piece of her black leather top, exposing her right breast. The FCC levied a $550,000 fine on CBS television (a division of Viacom) for airing the incident. The FCC, in another action, fined Clear Channel Communications, the largest radio station chain in the United States, $1.75 million over indecency complaints against Howard Stern and other radio personalities.

Public relations personnel also are feeling the heat as broadcasters express more caution booking talk show guests who discuss sexual and reproductive health.

One public relations firm, for example, reported that since the Super Bowl incident, two clients have had radio outlets cancel interviews. One was for a drug company that markets Zestra for female sexual dysfunction. Another client, a clinical psychologist, had her syndicated radio show dropped in three markets. Meanwhile, Victoria's Secret—wary of FCC wrath—decided to cancel its televised fashion show of its lingerie line.

The FCC's aggressive policy on indecency has some First Amendment experts concerned. Rodney Smolla, dean of the University of Richmond Law School, told the *New York Times*, "That one fleeting incident (Jackson) does not rise to the level of offensiveness that ought to empower the government to engage in such a punitive action."

In summary, public relations personnel have the responsibility to know, or at least be familiar with, all pertinent regulatory guidelines. A number of court cases have determined that you can be liable for disseminating false and misleading information on behalf of a client or employer. See the Insights Box on this page for FCC implications.

Corporate/Employee Free Speech

The First Amendment of the U.S. Constitution guarantees "freedom of speech," but exactly what speech is protected has been defined by the courts over the past 200 years, and is still being interpreted today. However, there is a well-established doctrine that commercial speech doesn't have the same First Amendment protection as other forms of speech.

Essentially, the government may regulate advertising that is false, misleading, or deceptive as well as advertising for unlawful goods and services. The courts also have ruled that product news releases, brochures, and other promotional vehicles intended to sell a product or service constitute commercial speech.

Another area, however, is what is termed *corporate free speech*. The courts, for the most part, have upheld the right of corporations and other organizations to express their views on public policy, proposed legislation, and a host of other issues that may be of societal or corporate concern. Organizations often do so through op-ed articles, letters to the editor, postings on their Web site, and even news releases.

Some landmark Supreme Court cases have helped establish the concept of corporate free speech. In 1978, for example, the Court struck down a Massachusetts law that prohibited corporations from publicizing their views on issues subject to the ballot box. Then, in 1980, the Court ruled that a New York Public Utilities Commission regulation prohibiting utilities from making statements of public policy and controversy was unconstitutional. Six years later, the Court ruled that the California Public Utilities Commission could not require PG&E to include messages from activist consumer groups in its mailings to customers. The utility argued that inclusion of such messages (called "bill stuffers") impaired the company's right to communicate its own messages.

Nike's Free Speech Battle

The Supreme Court again became involved with corporate free speech in 2003 when it was petitioned by Nike, the shoe and sports clothes manufacturer, to redress a California Supreme Court decision that had ruled that the company's efforts to explain its labor policies abroad was basically "garden variety commercial speech."

The case, *Nike v. Kasky*, raised the thorny question of how to deal with the blurred lines that often separate "free speech" and "commercial speech." Marc Kasky, an activist, had sued Nike, claiming that the company had made false and misleading statements that constituted unlawful and deceptive business practices. Nike, on the other hand, claimed that it had the right to express its views and defend itself against allegations by activist groups that it operated sweatshop factories in Asia and paid subpar wages.

The California Supreme Court disagreed. In its decision, it wrote "when a corporation, to maintain and increase its sales and profits, makes public statements defending labor practices and working conditions at factories where its products are made, those public statements are commercial speech that may be regulated to prevent consumer deception."

The U.S. Supreme Court, however, was less certain about the "commercial" nature of Nike's public relations campaign. Although it didn't make a decision and sent the case back to the California courts, Eugene Volokh, professor of law at UCLA, noted in a *Wall Street Journal* op-ed piece that Justice Stephen Breyer made an important point. According to Volokh, "Because the commercial message (buy our shoes) was mixed with a political message (our political opponents are wrong), and was presented outside a traditional advertising medium, it should have been treated as fully protected."

Nike, rather than face the California courts again, decided to settle the case with Kasky for a $1.5 million that would go to the Fair Labor Association to monitor American factories abroad, particularly in Asia. A number of groups that supported Nike's effort to defend corporate free speech, including PRSA and the Arthur W. Page Society, were somewhat disappointed that the conclusion of the case left many unanswered questions about the right of corporations to speak out on issues and even defend themselves against the charges of activist groups.

Within months of the Nike settlement, for example, People for the Ethical Treatment of Animals (PETA) sued KFC Corp., alleging that the company made false statements on its Web site and in news releases about its policies regarding the humane treatment of chickens in its operations. Is this an issue of commercial speech or corporate free speech? Stay tuned.

Employee Free Speech

A modern, progressive organization encourages employee comments and even criticisms. Many employee newspapers carry letters to the editor because they breed a healthy atmosphere of two-way communication and make company publications more credible.

Yet, at the same time, recent developments have indicated that not all is well for employee freedom of expression. A *Time* magazine essay by Barbara Ehrenreich, for example, gives startling examples of organizations denying free speech to employees. A grocery worker in Dallas was fired for wearing a Green Bay Packers T-shirt to work when the Dallas Cowboys were scheduled to play Green Bay in the conference playoffs. A worker at Caterpiller, Inc., was suspended for wearing a T-shirt titled "Defending the American Dream," a slogan of the union that had bitterly fought the company in a strike.

Employee freedom of expression and the issue of privacy have also been raised by court decisions that give employers the right to read employees' e-mail. Pillsbury, for example, fired a worker who posted an e-mail message to a colleague calling management "back-stabbing bastards." The employee sued, but the court sided with the company. In another case, Intel got a court injunction against a former employee who complained about the company in e-mails sent to thousands of employees. The

Does a corporation have the right of free speech? Nike took its case to the U.S. Supreme Court after the California court ruled that Nike's defense of its labor practices abroad was simply "commercial speech." Here, protesters unfurl banners opposing Nike's position.

Electronic Frontier Foundation, a group devoted to civil liberties in cyberspace, worried about violation of First Amendment rights. The company, however, contended that it wasn't a matter of free speech, but trespassing on company property.

Although employee privacy is still an issue, the trend line is for increased monitoring of employee e-mail by employers. Employers are concerned about being held liable if an employee posts a racial slur, engages in sexual harassment online, and even transmits sexually explicit jokes that would cause another employee to feel that the workplace was a "hostile" environment. In other words, you should assume that any e-mails you write at work are subject to monitoring and that you can be fired if you violate company policy.

Two other aspects of employee free speech are "whistle-blowing" and protection of an organization's trade secrets. State and federal laws generally protect the right of employees to "blow the whistle" if an organization is guilty of illegal activity.

It also is well established that an organization has a legal right to fire employees or sue former employees if they reveal proprietary information to the competition. Public relations firms, for example, usually have employees sign agreements that they will not divulge proprietary information about clients to outsiders or, if they leave the firm, to their new employers.

PR CASEBOOK

A Suggested Recipe for Martha Stewart: Litigation Public Relations

The practice of *litigation public relations* started in the 1990s. The O. J. Simpson murder trial gave the practice high visibility as both sides extensively used public relations to influence public perceptions—and even the jury pool—about the character of the defendant.

Since then, a number of public relations firms have started litigation practices to help both celebrities and organizations deal with criminal charges and class-action suits that can severely damage reputations and even the bottom line. In essence, litigation public relations is a form of reputation management.

As James Haggerty, author of *Winning Your Case with Pubic Relations*, writes "Communication is now central to the management of modern litigation. It can mean communicating to external audiences, such as the media, or to internal audiences, like employers, investors, shareholders, and others with a vested interest

in the organization." He continues, ". . . while you can have a victory in the courtroom of public opinion without a victory in the courtroom, your legal victory doesn't amount to much if, in the process, you sacrifice reputation, corporate character, and all of the other elements that make up an organization's goodwill in the marketplace."

Martha Stewart, the queen of home decorating and cooking, didn't win in the court of law or in the courtroom of public opinion. She was sentenced to five months in prison (plus five months home confinement) for lying to federal investigators about a stock sale and possible insider trading. On the courthouse steps after the conviction, Stewart told the press, "Whatever happened to me personally shouldn't have any

(continued)

PR CASEBOOK *(continued)*

effect whatsoever on the great company Martha Stewart Living Omnimedia."

Unfortunately, that wasn't the case. Stewart didn't realize that the whole business was based on her persona. As Steven Fink, a crisis communication consultant, noted, "People are buying her products because they have a positive impression of the public image of Martha Stewart. If that image becomes damaged, it can hurt her business in a serious way."

And it was serious. Although the revenues and stock price of her company declined during the pretrial period, total revenues dropped 33 percent in the three months following the conviction. The television program *Martha Stewart Living* lost half of its viewers after the verdict, and revenues from the program dropped 50 percent, causing the show to be suspended.

Public relations experts say that the basic concepts of litigation public relations practice could have saved Stewart, or at least resulted in a less painful outcome. Stewart, for example, stonewalled the media, even though there was intense public interest because of her celebrity status. Indeed, the public relations firm Hill & Knowlton found that 80 percent of Americans are willing to suspend judgment if an organization responds quickly to an accusation. Other studies have found that nearly three times as many people presumed an organization to be innocent when the company responded to all allegations, as opposed to saying "no comment."

Stewart was also faulted for not following any of the basic rules of crisis communications. According to *PRWeek*, Stewart "resisted making even the slightest apologetic gesture as she was

Martha Stewart reads a prepared statement after being convicted of lying to federal prosecutors about a stock sale based on insider information.

accused, tried, and convicted of Wall Street shenanigans." It also didn't help her reputation and image when she showed up for court with a $5,000 designer purse, which the media gleefully reported in full.

Liability for Sponsored Events

Public relations personnel often focus on the planning and logistics of an event; they must also take steps to protect the organization from liability and possible lawsuits.

Plant Tours and Open Houses

Plant tours should not be undertaken lightly. They require detailed planning by the public relations staff to guarantee the safety and comfort of visitors. Consideration must be given to such factors as (1) logistics, (2) possible work disruptions as groups pass through the plant, (3) safety, and (4) amount of staffing required.

A well-marked tour route is essential; it is equally important to have trained escort staff and tour guides. Guides should be well versed in company history and operations, and their comments should be somewhat standardized to make sure that key facts are conveyed. In addition, guides should be trained in first aid and thoroughly briefed on what to do in case of an accident or heart attack. At the beginning the guide should outline to the visitors what they will see, the amount of walking involved, the time required, and the number of stairs. This warning tells visitors with heart conditions or other physical handicaps what they can expect.

Many of the points about plant tours are applicable to open houses. The additional problem is having large numbers of people on the plant site at the same time. Such an event calls for special logistical planning by the public relations staff, possibly including the following measures: (1) arranging for extra liability insurance, (2) hiring off-duty police for security and traffic control, (3) arranging to have paramedics and an ambulance on site, and (4) making contractual agreements with vendors selling food or souvenirs.

Such precautions will generate goodwill and limit the company's liability. It should be noted, however, that a plaintiff can still collect if negligence on the part of the company can be proved.

Promotional Events

These events are planned primarily to promote product sales, increase organizational visibility, or raise money for charitable causes.

Events that attract crowds require the same kind of planning as does an open house. The public relations person should be concerned about traffic flow, adequate restroom facilities, signage, and security. Off-duty police officers are often hired to handle crowd control, protect celebrities or government officials, and make sure no disruptions occur.

Liability insurance is a necessity. Any public event sponsored by an organization should be insured against accidents that might result in lawsuits charging negligence. Organizations can purchase comprehensive insurance to cover a variety of events or a specific event.

The need for liability insurance also applies to charitable organizations if they sponsor a 10-K run, a bicycle race, or a hot-air balloon race. Participants should sign a release form that protects the organization against liability in case of a heart attack or an accident. An organization that sponsored a 5-K "fun run" had the participants sign a statement that stated in part, ". . . I assume all risk associated with running in this event, including, but not limited to, falls, contact with other participants, the effects of the weather, including high heat/or humidity, traffic, and other conditions of the road."

Promotional events that use public streets and parks also need permits from the appropriate city departments. A 10-K run or a parade, for example, requires permits from the police or the public safety department to block streets. Sponsors frequently hire off-duty police to control traffic.

A music store in one California city found out about these needs the hard way. It allowed a popular rock group to give an informal concert in front of the store as part of a promotion. Radio DJs spread the word and, as a result, a crowd of 8000 converged on the shopping center, causing a massive traffic jam. The city attorney filed charges against the store for creating a public disturbance and billed it $80,000 for police overtime pay to untangle the mess.

A food event, such as a chili cook-off or a German fest, requires a permit from the public health department and, if liquor is served, a permit from the state alcohol board. If the event is held inside a building not usually used for this purpose, a permit is often required from the fire inspector. In addition, a major deposit may be required as insurance that the organization will clean up a public space after the event.

▌Working with Lawyers

This chapter has outlined a number of areas in which the release of information (or the lack of release) raises legal issues for an organization. Public relations personnel must be aware of legal pitfalls, but they are not lawyers. By the same token, lawyers aren't experts in public relations and often have a poor understanding of how important the court of public opinion is in determining the reputation and credibility of an organization.

In today's business environment, with its high potential for litigation, it is essential for public relations professionals and lawyers to have cooperative relationships. Although much is written about the tug-of-war between public relations people and lawyers concerning the release of information, a survey by Kathy R. Fitzpatrick, a public relations professor now at the University of Florida, found that almost 85 percent of the public relations respondents said their relationship with legal counsel was either "excellent" or "good."

A number of steps can be taken by an organization to ensure that the public relations and legal staffs have a cordial, mutually supportive relationship:

- The public relations and legal staffs should report to the same top executive, who can listen to both sides and decide on a course of action.
- Public relations personnel should know basic legal concepts and regulatory guidelines in order to build trust and credibility with the legal department.
- Both functions should be represented on key committees.
- The organization should have a clearly defined statement of responsibilities for each staff and its relationship to the other. Neither should dominate.
- Periodic consultations should be held during which materials and programs are reviewed.
- The legal staff, as part of its duties, should brief public relations personnel on impending developments in litigation, so press inquiries can be answered in an appropriate manner.

SUMMARY

A Sampling of Legal Problems

There are a number of ways that a public relations practitioner may get caught up in a lawsuit or a case with a government regulatory agency. Practitioners may also be held legally liable if they provide advice or support the illegal activity of a client.

Libel and Defamation

There is now practically little difference between libel and slander; the two are often collectively referred to as *defamation*. The concept of defamation involves a false and malicious (or at least negligent) communication with an identifiable subject who is injured either financially or by loss of reputation or mental suffering. Libel suits can be avoided through the careful use of language. Some offensive communications will fall under the "fair comment" defense; an example of this would be a negative review by a theater critic.

Invasion of Privacy

Companies cannot assume when publishing newsletters that a person waives his or her right to privacy due to status as an employee. It is important to get written permission to publish photos or use employees in advertising materials, and to be cautious in releasing personal information about employees to the media.

Copyright Law

Copyright is the protection of creative work from unauthorized use. It is assumed that published works are copyrighted, and permission must be obtained to reprint such material. The "fair use" doctrine allows limited quotation, as in a book review. Unless a company has a specific contract with a freelance writer, photographer, or artist to produce work that will be exclusively owned by that company (a situation called "work for hire"), the freelancer owns his or her work. New copyright issues have been raised by the popularity of the Internet and the ease of downloading, uploading, and disseminating images and information.

Trademark Law

A *trademark* is a word, symbol, or slogan that identifies a product's origin. These can be registered with the U.S. Patent and Trademark Office. Trademarks are always capitalized and used as adjectives rather than nouns or verbs. Companies vigorously protect trademarks to prevent their becoming common nouns. One form of trademark infringement may be "misappropriation of personality," the use of a celebrity's name or image for advertising purposes without permission.

Regulations by Government Agencies

Commercial speech is regulated by the government in the interest of public health, safety, and consumer protection. Among the agencies involved in this regulation are the Federal Trade Commission, the Securities and Exchange Commission, the Food and Drug Administration, and the Bureau of Alcohol, Tobacco and Firearms.

Corporate/Employee Free Speech

Organizations, in general, have the right to express their opinions and views about a number of public issues. However, there is still some blurring of lines between what is considered "commercial speech" and "free speech," as illustrated by the Nike case. Employees are limited in expressing opinions within the corporate environment. E-mail, for example, is company property and subject to monitoring. Employees can be fired (or former employees sued) for revealing trade secrets. At the same time, "whistle-blowers" have protection against retaliation.

Liability for Sponsored Events

Plant tours, open houses, and other promotional events raise liability issues concerning safety and security. Liability insurance is a necessity. Permits may also be required for the use of public streets and parks and for serving food and liquor.

Working with Lawyers

Because of all the issues discussed in this chapter, a cooperative relationship must exist between public relations personnel and legal counsel. It helps if both groups report to the same top executive and both are represented on key committees. Public relations practitioners should also be aware of legal concepts and regulatory guidelines and receive briefings from the legal staff on impending developments.

Case Activity: **What Would You Do?**

Expresso Unlimited, a chain of coffee shops, has hired you as director of public relations and marketing. Some of your ideas include (1) a series of advertisements showing pictures and quotes from satisfied customers; (2) hiring a freelance photographer to build up a photo file for use in possible magazine articles, brochures, newsletters, and advertising; (3) reprinting and distributing various magazine articles that have been written about the company; (4) starting an employee newsletter with emphasis on employee features and "personals"; (5) including in the newsletter and advertisements cartoons about cof-

fee drinking from various publications, including the *New Yorker*; (6) citing a government study that rates the quality of coffee beans from around the world, and pointing out that Expresso Unlimited uses only the highest-quality beans; (7) writing a news release that quotes a survey showing that eight out of 10 serious coffee drinkers prefer Expresso Unlimited; and (8) creating a home page on the Internet that would include pictures of famous people drinking a cup of coffee.

Prepare a memo outlining the legal and regulatory factors that should be considered in implementing the above activities.

QUESTIONS for Review and Discussion

1. Why do public relations staff and firms need to know the legal aspects of creating and distributing messages?

2. How can a public relations person take precautions to avoid libel suits?

3. What is the concept of fair comment and criticism? Are there any limitations?

4. What precautions should a public relations person take to avoid invasion-of-privacy suits?

5. If an organization wants to use the photo or comments of an employee or a customer in an advertisement, what precautions should be taken?

6. When the media call about an employee, what kinds of information should the public relations person provide? What other approaches can be used?

7. What basic guidelines of copyright law should public relations professionals know about?

8. What rights do photographers and freelance writers have regarding ownership of their works?

9. How do public relations people help an organization protect its trademarks?

10. What is "misappropriation of personality"?

11. What should public relations people know about the regulations of the Federal Trade Commission?

12. What should public relations personnel know about the regulations of the Securities and Exchange Commission?

13. Review the Nike case about corporate free speech. Do you agree or disagree that organizations should have full First Amendment rights to answer charges from activist groups and present their opinions on various public issues? What about Nike? Do you agree with the California Supreme Court that Nike's defense of its labor practices abroad was simply "commercial" speech?

14. The casebook on Martha Stewart discusses litigation public relations. Do you think she could have done a better job of handling her reputation after being charged with lying to federal investigators about inside stock trading?

15. The FCC is clamping down on "indecency" on broadcast outlets. What is your opinion about this? Should government be involved in the content of broadcast programming?

16. What is the difference between plagiarism and copyright infringement?

17. Many companies contend that they have the right to read the e-mail of employees. What do you think? Is this a violation of privacy and employee free speech?

18. If an organization is sponsoring an open house or a promotional event, what legal aspects should be considered?

19. What should be the relationship between public relations staff and legal counsel in an organization?

SUGGESTED READINGS

Bunker, Matthew D., and Bolger, Bethany. "Protecting a Delicate Balance: Facts, Ideas, and Expression in Compilation Copyright Cases." *Journalism & Mass Communications Quarterly*, Vol. 80, No. 1, 2003, pp. 183–197.

Calabro, Sara. "Clippings and the Copyright Conundrum." *PRWeek*, July 15, 2002, p. 18.

Chabria, Anita. "Winning in the Court of Public Opinion." *PRWeek*, March 31, 2003, p. 18.

Chabria, Anita. "Stars in Scrapes: Litigation PR for Celebs." *PRWeek*, May 20, 2002, p. 18.

Clark, Cynthia. "What Every Public Company Must Know About Disclosing Information." *The Strategist*, Fall 2000, pp. 35–38.

Cordasco, Paul. "Experts Say Stewart Must Design New Crisis Strategy." *PRWeek*, June 24, 2002, p. 5.

Crawford, Alan Pell. "Off Court: Is Kobe Bryan Receiving the Right PR Counsel?" *Public Relations Tactics*, October 2003, pp. 6–7.

Doyne, Karen. "Litigation PR Vital to Winning in Court of Public Opinion." *PRWeek*, July 7, 2004, p. 2.

Forelle, Charles. "Caution: Your E-Mail Isn't Private." *Wall Street Journal*, July 14, 2004, p. D4.

Fraser, Jill Andresky. "Fighting for the Right to Communicate." *New York Times*, July 13, 2003, Section C, pp. 1, 10.

Gibson, Dirk C. "The Paradoxical Nature of Litigation Public Relations." *Public Relations Quarterly*, Spring 2003, pp. 32–34.

Glater, Jonathan D. "Stewart Likely to Influence Her Company Even From Jail." *New York Times*, July 17, 2004, pp. B1, B3.

Gorney, Carole. "One 'Strike Suit' and You're Out." *Public Relations Quarterly*, Fall 2003, pp. 36–38.

Greenhouse, Linda. "Nike Free Speech Case Is Unexpectedly Returned to California." *New York Times*, June 27, 2003, p. A15.

Haggerty, James F. *Winning Your Case with Public Relations*. New York: John Wiley & Sons, 2003.

Harmon, Amy. "A Corporate Victory, But One That Raises Public Consciousness: 20-Year Extension of Existing Copyright is Upheld." *New York Times*, January 16, 2003, pp. A22–23.

Hays, Constance L. "Stewart's Woes Hurt Company; Losses Expected Through 2004." *New York Times*, August 4, 2004, pp. C1, C3.

Hazley, Greg. "IROs Consider Impact of Sarbanes-Oxley at Two Years." *O'Dwyer's PR Services Report*, July 2004, pp. 1, 16–17.

Houston, Allen. "Ducking Beneath the FDA's Communications Barriers." *PRWeek*, February 25, 2002, p. 9.

Huff, Dianna. "Give Credit Where Credit Is Due: Proper Attribution for Communication." *Public Relations Tactics*, February 2003, p. 19.

Isserman, Marice. "Plagiarism: A Lie of the Mind." *Chronicle of Higher Education*, May 2, 2003, pp. B12–13.

Reber, Bryan, Cropp, Fritz., and Cameron, Glen. "Impossible Odds: Contributions of Legal Counsel and Public Relations Practitioners in a Bid for Conrail, Inc. by Norfolk Southern Corporation." *Journal of Public Relations Research*, Vol. 15, No. 1, 2003, pp. 1–25.

Weidlich, Thom. "PR Gavel-to-Gavel: As Courtroom Battles Become More Public, Litigation PR Becomes More Crucial." *PRWeek*, March 22, 2004, p. 17.

chapter **13**

New Technologies in Public Relations

Topics covered in this chapter include:

The Communications Explosion

The explosive growth of the Internet and the World Wide Web has created a form of mass communication unlike any other. In 1990, the Internet was used only by scientists to exchange information. Today, the Internet is a household word and a global communications tool for millions of people. According to a study commissioned by *pr reporter*, use of the new technology is the leading trend in public relations.

Internet users exchange messages around the world electronically. They "surf" the World Wide Web, tapping the masses of information and entertainment the interlocking system of computer networks offers, virtually unconstrained by time and space. Through the Internet's World Wide Web, thousands of companies, organizations, media, and individuals tell the world about themselves, sell their wares, and promote their ideas. By posting pages of printed words, graphics, photographs, and sounds, these people and organizations communicate with millions of "netizens" worldwide. Nielsen Media Research reported that 296 million people used the World Wide Web globally in the latter half of 2004, with 20 million of them making online purchases.

ON THE JOB

ethics

Who Is Concerned about the Digital Divide?

The following editorial in *Monde Diplomatique* expresses concern about the global digital divide. Read the statement and consider the questions presented.

The Internet became available to the public only a decade ago. In that short time, it has revolutionized political, economic, social, and cultural life to such an extent that we can now reasonably speak of the new Internet world order in telecommunications. Nothing is as it was before. For a large proportion of the world's people the speed and reliability of computer networks has changed their manner of communication, study, shopping, news, entertainment, political organization, cultural life, and work. The growth of Internet-based activities and e-mail has put the computer at the center of a network, relayed via a new generation of do-everything phones, that has transformed all areas of social activity.

But this remarkable transformation has largely been to the advantage of Western countries, already the beneficiaries of previous industrial revolutions. It is now exacerbating the digital gap between those who have an abundance of information technologies and the many more who would have none. Two figures give a sense of the inequality: 91 percent of the world's users of the Internet are drawn from only 19% of the world's population. The digital gap does as much to accentuate and aggravate the north-south divide as the traditional inequality between rich and poor—20 percent of the population of the rich countries own 85 percent of the world's wealth. If nothing is done cyber technologies will leave the inhabitants of the least advanced countries outside, especially in sub-Saharan Africa, where scarcely 1 percent of people have access, and those are mostly men.

Who is responsible for this digital divide? Should we really be concerned about the lack of Internet access in countries that have so many other basic infrastructure problems? Can the Internet be used as a development tool, offering developing countries a way to leapfrog forward in making progress toward filling basic needs?

Most importantly, what role can you envision for public relations professionals as part of the solution to the digital divide?

Despite the ubiquity of the Internet, a huge digital divide exists across the globe, which poses both a problem as well as a vast, as yet untapped, audience for public relations practitioners in both profit and nonprofit sectors.

The Internet is the most intriguing of the new electronic methods that are changing mass communications in general and providing public relations practice with innovative tools. According to the Middleberg/Ross Survey of journalists nationwide, the Internet is a rapidly growing means of receiving news releases, story ideas, and even audio and photo files from public relations sources.

Three familiar methods of communication—telephone, television, and the computer—are being blended together, forming new forms of transmission. A fundamental fact is that many emerging services are interactive; that is, they afford the two-way communication that is so vital in professional public relations. Instead of waiting for television networks and cable systems to provide specific programs, viewers can order pay-per-view movies and view them on their computers or move seamlessly between TV programming and high-speed Internet access on their television sets. News, music, movies, games, and Web content are now being delivered through the Internet to entertainment PCs and then transmitted via wireless systems to every room in the home. The home computer increasingly serves not only in its familiar roles as a workstation and instant messaging tool, but also as the family's information and entertainment portal.

The following are three key technologies that are contributing to this electronic outburst:

1. Fiber-optic cable. These cables are composed of strands of glass that are thinner than human hairs, which tremendously increases transmission volume and speed. They increasingly are being used in place of traditional copper cables. Verizon reports that one of its fiberglass cables can transmit a 500-page novel in slightly over two seconds.

2. Digital transmissions. Sounds and pictures are broken into electronic codes before they are transmitted and then once they meet their destination they are reconstructed back into their original form. Digitization will vastly improve TV picture quality, as demonstrated by high-definition television (HDTV), which is now increasingly common.

UNHCR Goodwill Ambassador Angelina Jolie sits and speaks with Sudanese women who have crossed the border into Tine, Chad, after fleeing fighting in the Darfur region of Sudan. The United Nations High Commission on Refugees effectively uses its Web site to show the activities of its high-profile ambassadors and give status reports from the field.

3. Wireless transmissions. In wireless networks, computers and mobile data devices are connected by short-range, high-speed data connections. Wireless networks typically operate in a range of 300 feet. However, cities recently have built wireless networks throughout downtown areas, turning commercial districts across America into large Internet cafés. Cell phones provide longer range wireless transmission, conveying not only voice, but also videoconferencing and television programming. Cellular signals now are delivering Internet and Web transmission at the same connection speed as cable, DSL, and institutional networks.

The enormous cost of development and construction has delayed general use of some electronic applications, but each year new ones reach consumers.

This chapter examines how recent developments and new technologies can be applied to accomplish public relations objectives. As you can see in Table 13.1, these new technologies have had an impact on the media, and consequently on public relations practice.

The Computer

The computer processor is no longer exclusive to personal computers. Many of the smart devices used by public relations professionals use computer processors. Personal organizers, calendars, as and contact lists reside on personal digital assistants (PDAs) and even on wristwatches. Computers enable the automation of office procedures so that tasks can be completed faster and more extensively than the old do-it-by-hand methods were capable of.

TABLE 13.1

Pros and Cons of New Media in Public Relations

TRADITIONAL MASS MEDIA	NEW MEDIA
Geographically constrained: Local or regional targets	Distance insensitive: Topic, need, or interest targeting worldwide
Hierarchical: Series of gatekeepers/editors	Flattened: One to many and many to many
Unidirectional: One-way dissemination	Interactive: Feedback, discussion, debate, and response to requests by person or machine
Space/time constraints: Limited pages and airtime	Fewer space/time constraints: Large, layered capacity for information
Professional communicators: Highly trained to professional standards	Nonprofessional: Anyone with limited training or professional values may participate
High access costs: Startup and production costs prohibitive	Low access costs: More affordable, but expensive computer programming talent required initially
General interest: Large audiences and broad coverage	Customized: Narrowcasts, even individually tailored
Linearity of content: News hierarchy	Nonlinearity of content: Hypertext links enable nonlinear navigation
Feedback: Slow, effortful, and limited	Feedback: E-mail and online chat are immediate and easy
Ad-driven: Big audiences and revenue	Diverse funding sources: Varied but limited revenue
Institution-bound: Corporate ownership	Decentralized: Grassroots efforts
Fixed format: Predictable in format, time and place	Flexible format: Emerging but fluid formats; multimedia
News, values, journalistic standards: Conventional	Formative standards: Currently obscure

Source: Adapted from *pr reporter*, May 17, 1999.

As a research tool, computers make an immense amount of information easily accessible through secondary analysis of data. E-mail and chat forums enhance environmental scanning and issues management. Three skills that are essential to success in public relations—project management, time billing, and digital presentation—all are made more efficient and flexible through the use of computers.

Most importantly, the computer should be viewed as the vehicle that can carry the practitioner into the maze of the Internet and World Wide Web. Communication and information resources abound in the online world, making life for public relations professionals more interesting and efficient.

The Internet

Created in the late 1960s by researchers who were searching for a way to link computers in separate cities, the Internet was initially an academic–government tool. It came into public use in the early 1990s; tie-ins developed between the American system and those in more than 150 other countries.

Internet use increased when graphics and sound were added, forming what came to be called the *World Wide Web*. Aware of the Web's commercial possibilities but not quite sure how to exploit them, tens of thousands of companies established sites on the Web. A Web site consists of one or more Web pages, the first of which is the home page. A person can visit a home page by typing its URL address, which is made up of letters, numbers, and punctuation marks, into a browser. An effective home page is a colorful mixture of text and graphics on which the sponsoring organization introduces itself.

The Internet has no official central control headquarters, so obtaining valid statistics on use of the global system is difficult. However, the number of *hits*, the number visitors to a site, can be determined. Because many hits are by "surfers" just searching to see what they can find, this figure is of limited commercial value. Figures for hits can be wildly inflated, because complex Web pages may generate hits for each major component of the page rather than counting only one hit per page. Furthermore, each time a user returns to a page during a visit, another hit is recorded. Several organizations, including the Audit Bureau of Circulation (ABC), are working on more sophisticated tracking methods that can count the number of unique visitors to a site.

The worldwide total of computer owners having access to the Internet, and using it, can only be estimated. A Nielsen Media Research 2004 study estimated that there were approximately 166 million Internet users in United States homes. The Nielsen figure for Internet use nearly tripled from its 1998 figure of 58 million.

In its sample of 6,000 households, Nielsen found Internet users to be well educated. Sixty percent were male, and 53 percent were between the ages of 16 and 34. These surveys depict a youthful, affluent, well-educated audience.

The Internet and Public Relations

The Internet gives public relations practitioners a multifaceted form of worldwide communication, primarily involving message exchange by e-mail, information delivery and persuasion through the Web, and extensive access to audiences for strategic research opportunities.

The following are the primary uses of the Internet by public relations professionals:

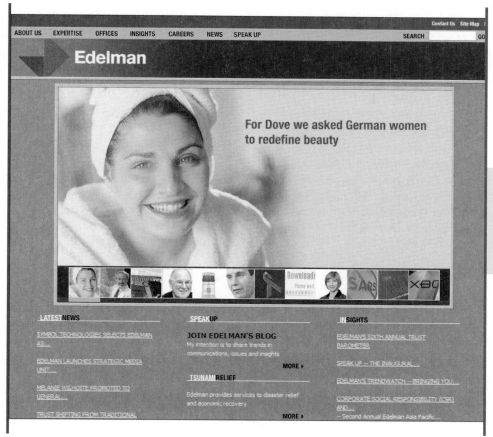

An example of how public relations firms use the Internet is the home page of Edelman Public Relations Worldwide. It offers a variety of information about clients.

- **E-mail distribution.** E-mail includes messages to individuals; newsletters to staff members; transmission of news releases, photos, and pitch letters to media offices; and dispatch and receipt of copy between public relations firms and clients, including fully formatted documents using software such as Adobe Acrobat. Most e-mail systems now accept hypertext e-mail that presents images in full color when the e-mail is opened. Professional Training Associates, a newsletter publisher, was able to send its direct mail postcard on the Internet to selected editors and reporters. The postcard announced a new Web site entitled Hard@Work with a whimsical shot of the publisher and editor perched on a rock in the middle of a stream.

- **World Wide Web sites.** These sites provide a way for organizations to tell Internet users what they do, to publicize projects, and to advocate policies. Edelman Public Relations Worldwide, for example, gives information about its clients. Ketchum offers recipes from its food-product clients.

- **Brochureware.** Although this term is used ironically by those who envision Web sites as a unique new channel, much of the content on Web sites is little more than an online version of the brochures and collateral materials that organizations provide to stakeholders. Public relations professionals should increasingly capitalize on the interactive and multimedia characteristics that distinguish Web communication from traditional print materials. Over time, interactivity and video clips will distinguish brochureware from its print predecessor, adding to the mix of communication tools available to the public relations professional.

- **Usenet discussion groups.** Individuals concerned with a certain issue discuss it by making comments and reading the responses of other participants. Sometimes this exchange is called a *newsgroup*. Usenet groups also are used for audience research, in which a participant requests opinions and facts. An estimated 10,000 such groups exist. One of the most popular sources of newsgroups is Google Groups, which is managed by the Web search engine Google.

- **Listservs.** PRFORUM and other listservs offer a similar interactive and dynamic opportunity for public relations professionals to query members of the discussion list. A participant must enroll with the list manager, thereby gaining access to the discussions. All messages submitted to the list appear in the participant's e-mail in-box, sometimes several score per day! To reduce e-mail traffic, a digest of the list can be specified so that only one e-mail summarizing the day's discussion is received.

Here are specific examples of how the Internet is used in public relations practice:

- Firms not only pitch stories to journalists via e-mail, but also rapidly respond to stories. Geoworks produces a smart cellular phone—a pager, an office organizer, a Web browser, and an e-mail tool all in one. Whenever its palm-sized computers were covered in a national magazine, Geoworks contacted the publication to tout its product as the next-generation device. Ensuing online dialogue with editors at *Newsweek*, *Business Week*, *ComputerWorld*, and *Time Digital* were crucial in raising awareness of smart phones.

- Organizations increasingly set up Web sites to serve informational needs of reporters, especially during a crisis or a breaking news situation. The Starr Report investigation of President Clinton's affair with Monica Lewinsky was released to the Web for wide and immediate dissemination. News organizations then made it available on their own Web sites, where an estimated 24.7 million people read parts of it in a matter of days.

- Xerox's public relations Web site offers answers to any question—any question at all. In response to an online question, the offbeat site reported its calculation that it would take 33,661 years to vacuum the state of Ohio! A Mention in *People* magazine and various TV news features resulted.

- The LifeSavers Web site, like many Web sites, offers free online games to attract users. Sweepstakes serve a similar role in attracting traffic to Web sites.

- Companies such as Boeing and Compaq have used Webcasting to increase coverage of important news conferences by broadcasting video footage over the Web via Medialink's Web site, NewStream.com.

- At least 400 health-care organizations and companies distribute medical information over their Web sites. Two examples include the American Medical Association, which provides information for physicians and patients about treatments, medical developments, and other health-care news, and the National Alliance of Breast Cancer Organizations (NABCO), which provides current information about breast cancer research and treatment, events, and links to other Web sites.

● The University of Wisconsin's Technology Enhancing Cancer Communication (TECC) (chess2.chsra.wisc.edu/tecc) offers support for cancer patients and their loved ones who provide care for them. Interactive technologies link people facing similar cancer challenges across distance and time and facilitate effective cancer communication between patient, partner/caregiver, and clinical teams. TECC explores how computers can be used to help those dealing with cancer or caring for loved ones with cancer.

● The governor of Hawaii used a Webcast to address critics and field questions from concerned citizens regarding a teachers' strike and lockout. At a minimal direct cost of $100, an enormous audience, estimated at 30,000, was reached. Facing a crisis in the schools, Governor Cayetano communicated directly to the audience, generating both advanced and follow-up coverage and ongoing access to the archived Webcast online.

Greenpeace, the activist environmental organization, uses its Web site to publicize its confrontations at sea with vessels whose work it opposes. Here, a Greenpeace ship tries to block passage of a Norwegian whaling vessel. The Web site carries news reports and background information from the Greenpeace point of view.

Key Aspects of the Internet

Public relations professionals should keep in mind the following important facts about the Internet:

● Its reach is worldwide. A message intended for local or regional use may draw reactions, good or bad, from unexpected places.

● The content of the Internet is virtually uncontrolled. Anyone can say or show anything without passing it through "gatekeepers," the editors and producers who approve the material that reaches the public through traditional media channels. Lack of editorial control permits unfettered freedom of speech, but it also permits distribution of unconfirmed, slanted, or even potentially libelous material. *Tactics*, which is published by PRSA, welcomes this freedom from editorial control. It asserts: "PR pros can now get messages out without passing them through the filter of editors and journalists. Traditional media gatekeepers have lost their power in today's print-and-click world."

● Issue tracking can be more thorough using the Internet and far more immediate. Services such as NewsEdge monitor Web-based news and wire services and alert users when relevant topics appear in Internet news sources. By monitoring the Internet, practitioners can keep track of what competitors, opponents, and the general audience are saying. Thus informed, practitioners can better shape their own tactics and messages as well as respond in real time to forestall erroneous or unbalanced stories

ON THE JOB global

The United Nations High Commission for Refugees Draws on the Web for Global Reach

The global digital divide does not cause the human tragedies that result in refugee camps. However, the digital revolution may be part of the solution by making the world small enough that we all become aware and involved with the plight of refugees.

The United Nations High Commissioner for Refugees (UNHCR.ch) Web site seeks to increase public awareness of the global refugee problem. The site includes maps, photographs, and print and video news about people who have abandoned their homes to escape war and persecution. A *Refugees Magazine* is available as well as UNHCR screensavers. Interviews with the Director of UNHCR can be viewed on demand.

International sponsors are helping local newspapers mount Web editions of their papers so that refugees can assess when conditions are favorable for a return to their homelands.

Spokes-persons provide testimonials and video from refugee camps. Angelina Jolie has been particularly active in the work of the UNHCR, taking time to appear in videos and to con-duct online chat sessions with interested persons around the world.

Source: Courtesy of UNHCR Public Information Section.

from gaining momentum without correction. A PR Newswire executive recalled how a story released by his service at 7:30 A.M. prompted an e-mail response by a public relations person. The result was a factually corrected release on PR Newswire by 7:35 A.M.

Internet Problems

In addition to its multiple benefits, the global spiderweb of interlocking computer networks also offers some challenges. The following should be kept in mind when planning Internet communication programs:

● The difficulty in finding desired information frustrates some users. Increasingly, search engines are prioritizing search results based on fee payments from companies and organizations, biasing search results.

ON THE JOB insights

Creating Winning Web Sites

A Web site can serve as a controlled, yet credible, tool for organizations to disseminate messages. National surveys indicate that audiences hold Web-based information in high regard. Internet information, according to one survey of over 1000 respondents by professors at the University of California at Santa Barbara, was as credible as TV, radio, and magazines, but less credible than newspapers. Researchers say that this high credibility perhaps explains why Web information is seldom double-checked with other sources by the audience.

Web sites also enable strategic targeting of messages to audiences. Responsible practitioners can get the word out to key publics using links to customized Web pages tailored to the particular public. However, according to Stuart Esrock and Greg Leichty, most corporate Web sites are used to service investors, customers, and, to a lesser extent, the media. Consequently, the communication potential of Web

sites has not yet been fully tapped.

To date, according to Candace White and colleagues at the University of Tennessee, most Web site planning is done by trial and error, with little formal research and evaluation. Practitioners report Web site development as a low priority on to-do lists because of skepticism about the site's effectiveness, inefficient evaluation methods, and lack of control over the site.

Opportunities for a broader range of publics should be developed as support for Web sites increases and public relations practitioners become more assertive in taking control of Web sites. Given the enormous and burgeoning audience for Web sites, as well as key target audiences, creating more effective Web sites will be essential for public relations departments.

Louis Falk of Florida International University offers some no-nonsense advice for Web site development:

- Make it fast. Be sure that a page loads in less than eight seconds.
- Use a functional, balanced design. Make sure that the site works on all major Web browsers, such as Internet Explorer and Netscape. Place the most important information on the left side of the page. Use standard colors that work consistently on many different browsers and machines. Offer an easy and logical interaction, making good use of internal search engines.
- Make sure there are no dead links.
- Include contact information.
- Identify your purpose(s). Public information differs dramatically from e-commerce, for instance.
- Keep it fresh. Not only should information be current, you also should check the site's performance on a regular basis.
- Register with major search engines. This ensures that you can be found.

- Controversial security problems and legal questions of copyright infringement, libel, invasion of privacy, and pornography remain unsolved.

- Time-consuming procedures for online transactions or product registrations can be terminated by an error message that the procedure was not successful, generating skepticism about the efficiency of the Web and its reliability as a communication tool.

- Malicious and irritating practices nag at online users. The Internet offers many opportunities for spammers to clutter e-mail channels with bogus or dubious offers.

Unsolicited advertising on the Web adds to this clutter, making the messages sent by public relations professionals less effective. Online users are perhaps most decisively impacted by those who program viruses to take down servers or disrupt personal computer systems.

In sum, the Internet is an evolving form of mass communication. Public relations tools are developed and then either scrapped or refined based on trial-and-error.

Other Computer Applications

Computers store, codify, analyze, and search out information at speeds far beyond human capabilities. They transmit information over long distances at fantastically

ON THE JOB insights

Getting Reporters to Use Your Web Site

According to the Nielsen Norman Group, professionals should conduct usability studies of their Web sites, especially to understand the problems and concerns of ordinary users and journalists. Nielsen Norman says that journalists frequently go to company Web sites as they start to work on a story. Reporters look to:

- Find a public relations contact.
- Check basic facts about a company.
- Discover a company's perspective on events.
- Check financial information.
- Download images to illustrate stories.

Typical steps taken by reporters include:

1. Getting to your site.
   - Tip: Submit the site to major search engines, such as Google.
   - Tip: Avoid Flash or Shockwave features that may not work or bog down the reporter's research.
2. Finding the news.
   - Tip: Don't lose reporters in the forest.
   - Tip: Clearly and prominently label information meant for reporters (e.g., Media; Press; News).
3. Looking for contact information.
   - Tip: Reporters in the Nielsen Norman Group study had a low success rate in finding the phone number for the public relations contact.
   - Tip: Put contact information on every page of your site, especially the phone number, to help journalists get answers quickly.
4. Researching a product, event, or person.
   - Tip: Dedicate an easy-to-find link to press releases.
   - Tip: Make releases searchable and sortable by topic or date.
   - Tip: Avoid pop-up windows for press releases—they imply skimpy information.
   - Tip: Link to third-party resources that provide credible supplements to the company's story.
5. Fact checking.
   - Tip: Provide fact sheets, executive biographies, financial data, and product information.
6. Looking at pictures.
   - Tip: Reporters like graphics, and they convey much about a company.
   - Tip: Don't overdo it; make sure the images are useful and not just "eye candy."

high speeds. The variety of tasks that computers can be used to accomplish make them powerful tools for public relations practice. Still more astounding is the anticipated development of the "thinking" computer, a machine designed to diagnose and solve problems in addition to calculating and processing data as present computers do. The highly publicized chess match in 1997 between Garry Kasparov and IBM Corporation's Deep Blue dramatically displayed the growing ability of computers to emulate human intelligence. Deep Blue won the match. The well-known physicist and thinker Stephen Hawking predicts that artificial intelligence will one day universally supercede human brainpower. The dazzling future aside, immediate application of the new technologies in public relations are well worth adopting right now. Promising new media tools are listed in Table 13.2.

Dictation and Voice Generation

Most computers being sold today have the memory and processing speed needed to recognize human speech. The software program Dragon Naturally Speaking not only recognizes the user's speech, but also improves its recognition accuracy by taking into account corrections the user makes in the dictated text on the computer screen. Over time, the program becomes more accurate in converting speech to word processing, presentation, Web, database, or spreadsheet content. Computer commands also may be spoken, including the command "Read Text," which prompts the computer to generate speech by reading the written text to the user. One of the important boons of this new technology may well be a reduction in painful repetitive motion syndrome injuries caused by hours of keyboarding.

Expert Systems

One modest form of artificial intelligence—expert system programming—has made its mark in the business world. Expert systems identify a limited domain of expertise and then emulate the decision making that an expert would undertake. In public relations, the expertise of a research expert is embodied in Publics PR Research Software™. The software not only streamlines the process of making a questionnaire, it also converts statistical results into plain language. (See Chapter 5 for details about research in public relations and the use of Publics PR Research Software™). Someday public relations professionals will use expert systems to assist with special-event planning, issue evaluation, and other domains of expertise in the field.

Public Relations Management Tools

Public relations professionals can use project-scheduling software such as Microsoft Project and MacProject to quickly create and modify Gantt charts, track resources, and monitor progress toward the completion of a project. (See Figure 13.1 for a sample Gantt chart.) Special software such as Timeslips streamlines the time-billing process and allows professionals to use the computer as a timer and recorder of billable hours. Software such as Spin Control and Vocus are used in public relations to manage the media relations process. Such programs help the public relations professional develop media contact databases, track mail and phone pitches to those contacts, and record news coverage obtained from the media relations effort.

TABLE 13.2

Some New Tools in Public Relations Practice. A wide range of technologies serve important functions of modern public relations and often are directed at particular audiences. Some of these technologies are just emerging, others are more commonly used.

NEW TECH TOOL	PR FUNCTION	TYPICAL AUDIENCE	TECHNIQUES/FEATURES
Internet	Media relations	Media contacts	Pitching stories and sending digital media kits
	Activism	Media	Evens the resource field for activist groups
	Crisis management	Media and internal audiences	Preemptive tool against investigative hatchet job
	Event or product promotion	Widespread, often teens or trendsetters	Guerrilla (subtle) and viral (self-generating) dissemination
Intranet	Internal communication	Employees and password-access outsiders	Enables confidential communication and rumor research
Online newswires, (e.g., Newstream.com)	Investor relations	Investors and financial media in 6000 online news-rooms	Submit to Business Wire and index with Yahoo! company news
Webcasting services such as Medialink	Meetings and media relations	Varied	Enables a large, geographically dispersed audience to participate online
Web searching	Issues tracking	Management	Search by client or industry name
Web site development	E-commerce and public information	Customers and constituents	Offer products and services
Online monitoring services, (e.g., Dialog NewsEdge, and Briefme.com)	Issues and crisis management	Practitioner receives news alerts	Enables monitoring of both slow-boil and breaking news about own organization
CD-ROM	Media relations	Media	Digital media kit or reporter's resource
	Employee communication	Employees	Interactive, audiovisual training and notification
Satellite and radio media tours	Publicity	Viewers and listeners	Overcomes distance barriers in media appearances
Web research	Audience analysis and message testing	Colleagues and clients	Online surveys, focus groups, secondary research, and usability studies
Media database software (e.g., prPowerBase)	Release distribution/ tracking	Media	Access and use Bacon's and other major data-bases
Research software (e.g., Publics, SPSS)	Formative and evaluative research	Client	Enables targeted audiences and tailored messages
Presentation software (e.g., Powerpoint)	Briefings	Varied	Multimedia features and last minute changes
Calendar software (e.g., Sidekick, Outlook)	Project and event coordination	Varied	Set up team meetings and recurring appointments
Project management software (e.g., Microsoft Project)	Production and campaign planning/tracking	Colleagues and clients	Enables control of complex projects
Time tracking and billing software (e.g., Timeslips)	Management	Colleagues and clients	Track time for productivity analysis and billing of services
Media management software (e.g., Vocus, Spinware)	Media relations	Media	Track media contacts and coverage, online press center
Creativity tools (e.g., Visio, Photoshop, Quark)	Materials production	Readers and viewers	Design and layout of materials
Netbusiness card	Firm visibility and marketing	Clients	Registered users appear in all major online Yellow Pages

FIGURE 13.1

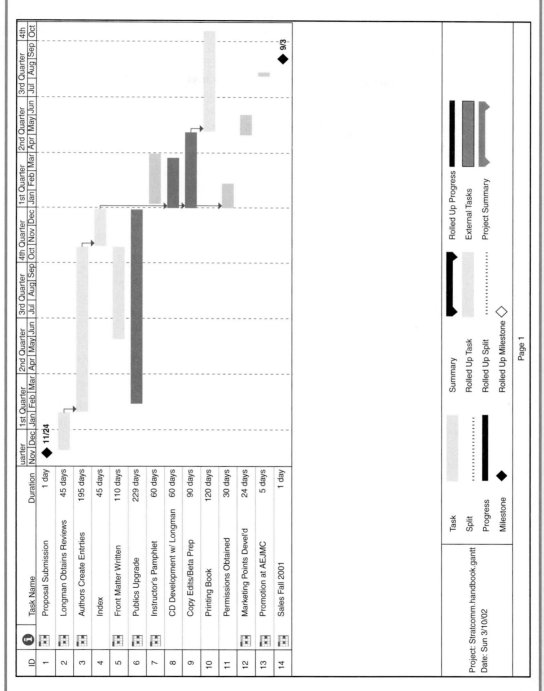

Microsoft Project Gantt Chart

Software such as Microsoft Project makes creation of Gantt charts easy and flexible. These charts provide a visual and linear direction of project tasks. For tracking progress, these charts can include deadlines and identify resources required for each task. The Gantt chart also can indicate percent complete as well as a comparison of the proposed timeline with the actual time each task took.

Processing of News Releases

Word processing programs are invaluable in creating news releases for different types of publications, including trade magazines, daily newspapers, and the business press. A draft document can be attached to e-mail for delivery to a client or supervisor. Changes made by others can be automatically highlighted in the text with the editor identified. Professionals can use mail merge features to customize or even localize releases to increase news value for individual editors in a distribution list.

However, when such batch-processing tools are used, care must be taken to ensure that the merge is done correctly. It can be irritating, and even insulting, to get a misaddressed message that appears to be personalized. In addition, unless care is taken, different versions of a document can be confused, leading to the distribution of an earlier draft. For example, a branch of the Centers for Disease Control and Prevention e-mailed an advisory to medical doctors that had comments and draft language embedded but hidden in the file. The hidden back-channel discussion of the draft was not deleted or locked, thus the physicians were able to view the comments. No harm was done because the comments were mostly text edits, but what if confidential deliberations had been included?

E-Mail

When a writer creates copy for a brochure, the edited text can be recorded on a disk for delivery to the printing company. Increasingly, the printing company will have suitable computer connections, enabling brochure copy to be transmitted electronically from the writer's computer into the printing company's computer or directly to a "smart" printer. No hard copy changes hands. New high-speed, high-quality customized printers such as HP's Indigo line of offset printers enable customized print jobs of magazine quality for annual reports or targeted, personalized messages that are orchestrated from the public relations office.

The frequent collaboration of public relations professionals with clients and colleagues has been greatly enhanced through the sharing of draft documents via e-mail. When compatible word processing, graphics, or desktop publishing software is used by both parties, documents attached to e-mail can be opened, edited, and returned, even when one person uses a Mac and the other is on a Windows machine. Even incompatible systems can communicate using software such as Adobe Acrobat to view documents and attach the equivalent of sticky notes to the document without actually being able to open and change the document.

Desktop Publishing

Computers can be used to create professional-looking newsletters and graphically illustrated material on a personal computer right in the office. This is known as *desktop publishing*.

Desktop publishing enables the public relations writer and editor to design and lay out reports, newsletters, brochures, and presentations by manipulating copy and graphics on a computer screen instead of a drawing board. It produces pages ready for offset printing, but often high-quality printers are used to print small batches of the materials in-house. For example, a professionally published media kit may include space for fact sheets or other inserts that are printed in-house. This "just-in-time" printing enables a sense of immediacy in content without sacrificing appearance.

Desktop publishing saves both money and time. Less than $5,000 will buy all the components necessary to produce high-quality newsletters and graphics in-house: a personal computer, a word-processing program, a graphics program, page-making software, and a magazine-quality laser printer. Producing materials in-house reduces the fuss and expense of involving a commercial printer. Apple Computer estimates that it takes 8 hours to produce a 16-page newsletter using desktop publishing, compared with 16 hours using traditional commercial printing methods.

Mailing Lists

Up-to-date mailing lists are vital in public relations work. Lists of names are typed into database programs such as Microsoft Works or ACT! contact management software and stored in computer memory. Changes of address or other alterations can be made by calling up a name and using a few keystrokes. When a mailing is to be made, the desired names on the master list can be activated and printed on adhesive labels or on individual envelopes.

The capability to select groups of names from the master list assists the practitioner in reaching target audiences. For example, when introducing its new models, Ford sought to generate ample publicity for more than 2000 of its dealers located in rural areas. As reported in *Public Relations Journal*, the automaker created a computer file on each dealer that included the address, phone number, and name of the local spokesperson. By combining this file with its standard news release, Ford created 9,600 customized news releases. Every release mentioned a local dealer by name and used local dealer data in the release. The releases also were sent to customers based on a carefully culled mailing list of potential customers in the dealer's territory.

Public relations departments and firms may compile their own computer lists of media contacts or purchase CD-ROM databases from press-directory companies, such as Bacon's MediaSource software, which provides postal addresses, e-mail addresses, and phone data for nearly 30,000 editors.

Online Conferences

Online conferences, which are essentially a series of typed messages exchanged among members of a group, are increasingly valuable in public relations work. Practitioners use their computers to "converse" with clients and suppliers or participate in forums on professional matters with their peers. The transcript of the exchange can be retained in computer memory or printed.

Because of the ubiquity of personal computers, online conferences are becoming commonplace. Mobile computing with laptop, mini-notebook, and palm-sized PDAs makes out-of-office conferences during business travel an important part of the business communication landscape. Free software such as Netmeeting is available for online conferencing. More sophisticated applications are available for those with more advanced needs.

Graphics

The use of computers to design eye-catching colored graphics—drawings, graphs, charts, and text—has emerged as a stellar new technology in public relations practice. Recent developments in computer software make such graphics possible.

Attractive graphics give visual impact to annual reports and employee publications, as well as to video programs and presentations. Imaginative visual effects may be obtained with only a modest investment of time and money. Representations of people, designs, and charts add visual zest that stimulates audiences. Increasingly, public relations departments and firms employ such graphics to dress up transparencies or digital presentations. (Presentation software is discussed in Chapter 16.)

Facsimile Transmission

An invaluable tool in public relations practice is facsimile transmission, commonly called the *fax*. Such frequently heard remarks as "I'll fax it to you" have added a new verb to the language. Public relations professionals can use a fax to send a news release, a draft of a client's newsletter, instructions from headquarters to a branch office, or any number of documents. By using broadcast fax, a sender can transmit a single document to hundreds of recipients simultaneously. A corporation, for example, can distribute a news release swiftly and equally to competing news media. In another application, a customer can call a major vendor such as PR Newswire or Business Wire via toll-free 800 number, request a piece of information, and receive it by fax within minutes.

A word of caution: Discretion should be used in faxing news releases to editors. Send only those you consider to be truly important and urgent. Editors complain, often quite sharply, about the amount of "junk fax" they receive. They say that the in-pouring of materials useless to them, including advertisements and irrelevant announcements, ties up their machines and may delay delivery of important news materials. Some states have enacted laws restricting distribution of unsolicited fax items.

Increasingly, the lines between fax and e-mail have blurred. It is now possible to use services that will convert an e-mail message into a broadcast fax that can be delivered to the physical fax machines of the target public. Similarly, incoming faxes to a professional's phone number can be received and forwarded as e-mail to the traveling public relations person.

Satellite Transmissions

Text messages and pictures can be flashed around the world in seconds using satellite transmission. Information travels through a ground "uplink" station to a transponder pad on a satellite. It is then bounced back to a receiving dish on the ground and sent to the destination computer. Enormous amounts of material can be transmitted at rates about 160 times faster than land lines, and at much lower cost.

The *Wall Street Journal*, *New York Times*, and *USA Today* use satellites to transmit entire page layouts to regional printing plants. The Associated Press, United Press International, and other news services transmit their stories and pictures by satellite. Television and radio networks deliver programs in the same manner.

News Release Delivery

More than a dozen American companies deliver news releases electronically to large newspapers and other major news media offices. The news releases are fed into computers at the receiving newsrooms and examined by editors.

The difference between news release delivery firms and the traditional news services such as the Associated Press is this: Newspapers, radio, and television stations pay large fees to receive the reports of the news services, which maintain staffs of editors and reporters to gather, analyze, select, and write the news in a neutral style. In contrast, the news release delivery companies are paid by creators of news releases to distribute the news releases to the media, who pay nothing to receive them. These delivery services are prepaid transmission belts, not selectors of material. However, they do enforce editing standards and occasionally reject releases as unsuitable.

One of the largest news release delivery companies is Business Wire. Using electronic circuits and satellite communications, the company can simultaneously reach more than 1,600 media points in the United States and Canada and more than 500 in Europe, Latin America, East Asia, and Australia. In addition, Business Wire provides rapid dissemination of financial news releases to more than 600 securities and investment firms worldwide. The company sends an average of 175 news releases daily for a roster of more than 9,000 clients.

Electronically delivered news releases have an advantage over the conventional variety. Releases transmitted by satellite tend to receive closer, faster attention from media editors than those arriving by mail.

Another large news release delivery company, PR Newswire, was the first to distribute its releases by satellite. PR Newswire's computers distribute releases and official statements from more than 7,500 organizations directly into newsroom computers. Each day, PR Newswire transmits approximately 150 such releases. PR Newswire releases are entered into several commercial databases.

Video and Audio News Release Distribution

Satellite transmission also makes the fast distribution of video news releases (VNRs) possible. The picture-and-voice releases are sent primarily to cable television networks, local cable systems, and local television stations. Nearly 30 companies produce and distribute hundreds of VNRs for clients. Only relatively few of the most newsworthy, technically superior VNRs succeed in obtaining airtime. (See Chapter 15 for a discussion of VNRs.) Successful VNRs usually feature video footage that would be difficult for a station to obtain, as demonstrated by the following examples:

- A VNR sponsored by OshKosh B'Gosh bib overalls quotes the winner of its Search for the Oldest Bib Overall contest, 89-year-old Claude Mehder, who owns a pair of circa-1901 bibs: "We'll keep having kids, as long as the bib overalls hold up."

- Ringling Brothers & Barnum & Bailey circus clowns helped *PC Computing* magazine conduct the Notebook Torture Test of laptop computers.

- "The Car of the Future," a VNR distributed by D. S. Simon Productions, included DVD video screens, on-board message systems, global positioning, and a home security monitor.

Voice-and-sound news releases for use on radio also are distributed by satellite.

Teleconferencing

The most spectacular use of satellite transmission for public relations purposes is *teleconferencing*, which is also called *videoconferencing*. A public relations professional can easily arrange a teleconference by employing a firm that specializes in this service. In the United States, some 20,000 sites are equipped to handle such events.

With teleconferencing, groups of conferees separated by thousands of miles can interact instantaneously with strong visual impact, saving time and transportation costs. In one five-year period, the Boeing Company used teleconferencing for 5,699 meetings and eliminated the need for more than 1.5 million miles of travel.

The most widely used form of teleconferencing blends one-way video and two-way audio. This one-way video technology, a form of direct broadcast satellite (DBS), broadcasts a live presentation to many locations simultaneously. DBS is the least expensive method because cameras, transmitters, and other expensive equipment are needed only at one end. The video signal can be received by small, relatively inexpensive antennas at locations around the world via satellite. Figure 13.2 shows, in schematic form, how satellite transmission works. Guests at receiving locations view the presentation on large screens. Regular telephone circuits back to the point of origin enable the guests to ask follow-up questions.

Here are examples of teleconferencing in operation:

● Ford Motor Company has installed a $10 million system connecting more than 200 Ford locations in North America. It provides customer and vendor relations as well as regular sales training events. Other companies have similar systems.

● A Midwestern magazine company incurred major costs for expensive executive travel on short notice to its parent company in New York, with as many as five flights a week. The costs for installation of a Picturetel system were recovered in a matter of months. The system's robotic camera can switch from a wide angle shot of all partic-

FIGURE 13.2

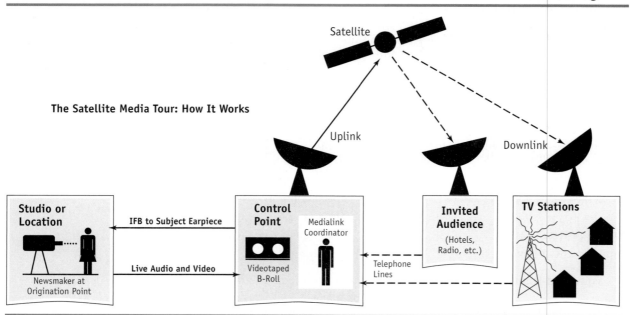

This diagram explains how a media satellite tour is conducted, enabling the person being interviewed to remain in one place while appearing on screens in other cities.

Source: MediaLink, Inc.

ipants at a large conference table to a full-screen shot of each speaker. The speaker's microphone activates the camera to "zero-in" on him or her while speaking, providing a fairly naturalistic meeting environment in all locations.

- The Whirlpool Corporation in the United States and an N. V. Philips division in the Netherlands needed to explain their new $2 billion joint-venture agreement. So they held an international teleconference for their respective stockholders and employees, the media, and financial analysts.

- Hill and Knowlton, on behalf of several government agencies, arranged a two-hour conference between Cairo, Egypt, and five U.S. cities that permitted several hundred U.S. investors to talk directly with high-ranking Egyptian officials about private investment in that nation.

- To introduce a newly developed hepatitis B vaccine, Merck Sharp & Dohme used a teleconference beamed to more than 400 locations where doctors, health-care workers, and reporters had gathered. After watching the presentation, the invited guests telephoned questions to a panel of experts.

A more economical system is the "slow-scan" conference. This provides for transmission of still pictures or slides over a telephone circuit between conference points, with voice transmission over a separate line.

To decide whether a teleconference will be cost-effective, a public relations practitioner should obtain quotes from vendors based on all of expenses involved and then compare those figures with the price of travel, lodging, and entertainment if all employees or invited guests were brought to a central conference location.

Those who use teleconferencing emphasize that it is most effective for reaching large audiences for such purposes as introducing a product, conducting a sales meetings, or announcing new corporate policies. However, teleconferencing does lack the personal warmth that comes from a handshake and a face-to-face conversation.

Webconferencing

The Web has become a less expensive alternative for videoconferencing. In its most basic form, Webconferencing is a "see-you-see-me" technology. Users with cameras and microphones mounted on their computers can engage in an Internet version of videophone. One of the authors of this text participated in a student's defense of his master's thesis using Microsoft Netshow. Audio was carried by telephone, and video was displayed on the computer screen via the Web. The 15-second delay in video feed and the student's preference for the comfort and support of a human presence suggest that such conferencing requires further development.

Increasingly, professionals are able to use the Web for interactive Webcasts that primarily serve for the dissemination of information. For example, a press conference might be Webcast to any and all who log in to the event online. The participants can ask questions of the news source during the conference by e-mail. Seminar-style events can attract a worldwide audience.

The Health Media Research Laboratory at the University of Michigan (www.healthmedia.umich.edu) regularly offers real-time Webcast seminars about cancer research. Past Webcasts are stored in an archive and can be viewed on demand. Discussion among participants takes place using AOL Instant Messenger. A recent

Webcast topic was "Fractional Factorial Designs," suggesting that the term *narrowcast* also may be appropriate, given that the topics are sometimes quite specialized.

Satellite Media Tours

Instead of having a celebrity—an actor or author, for example—crisscross the country on an expensive, time-consuming promotional tour, public relations sponsors increasingly use the so-called "satellite tour."

ON THE JOB insights

Building Relationships Online

Many definitions of public relations embrace the concept of *relationship management*, often emphasizing mutual benefit in the relationship between an organization and its publics. These definitions also take a longer-term perspective that stresses loyalty built upon trust and loyalty between parties. The unique features of new media, particularly the interactivity and decentralization of communication, afford public relations practitioners special opportunities to build beneficial relationships for the organization.

In a study funded by the Institute for Public Relations, Maria Len-Rios found that stronger relationships can result from more extensive use of an organization's Web site. Minor mistakes in content or online service are more likely to be forgiven, and loyal users will accept a more assertive program of e-mail offers and messages. These so-called "push" strategies include everything from requests for assistance with a charitable

cause to online sales offers to e-mail reminders for employees or members.

With precision public relations, practitioners narrowly target key publics. Online channels facilitate this narrow targeting through the creation of messages based on the each customer's individual characteristics. Provided permission is granted, e-mail and customized Web content can be tailored to the individual. As the relationship between an organization and an individual matures, more personalized or tailored messaging can be directed to that individual without violating the rules for appropriate online communication.

The interactivity of the Internet is particularly relevant to public relations. Building relationships through an interactive Web site will ultimately serve to improve the corporate image and align corporate policy with public opinion. This two-way symmetrical communication reflects change on the part of the organization to accommodate the public.

Some examples of such two-way communication include the following:

● Personalized satellite radio is available in luxury cars. With personalized satellite radio, music programming is tailored to personal tastes. Personalized news and current affairs will be offered in the near future, enabling drivers to save stories or forward stories to others.

● The natural spread of ideas, which is often called *viral marketing*, and tactics to spur social movements work well when push e-mail and tailored messages are directed to "e-fluentials," according to Burson-Marsteller. (See www.efluentials.com for more on e-fluentials.)

● Amazon.com offers each customer a personalized greeting and information on new books and products based on the customer's past activity on the Amazon Web site. For a regular and loyal user, this is likely to be viewed as a convenience, not an imposition.

With a satellite tour, the personality is stationed in a television studio, and TV reporters interview the personality by satellite from their home studios. Two-way television is used, permitting a visual dialogue. Each station's reporter is put through to the personality at a specified time; thus a series of interviews, 5 to 10 minutes each, can be done in sequence. Corporations also employ satellite media tours to promote their products or services, often using a well-known performer or other "name" figure as a spokesperson. See Figure 13.2.

Before his paralyzing spinal injury, actor Christopher Reeve set an endurance record by doing 45 consecutive interviews at one sitting. Tiresome mentally and physically, no doubt, but much faster and cheaper than visiting all those cities!

Other Tools

Numerous other electronic tools also are used regularly in public relations practice. New instruments based on digital transmission appear frequently.

Cellular Phones

Using cellular (cell) telephones, public relations professionals can be available anytime and at any place.

The public relations professional can even use a cellular telephone to conduct business while driving. A cellular system has interlocking low-power transmitters; as a motorist moves from one zone to another, calls from the car are switched by computer into the next zone, permitting continuous nonfading conversations. Interviews on talk radio shows by clients calling from a practitioner's moving car are one attention-getting device. But in one instance, a state representative was recorded on air as he rear-ended a car in stop-and-go traffic. Safety and etiquette are increasingly important objectives in public service announcements from cell phone companies. Safety considerations aside, all phones enable practitioners to be in touch no matter where they go in their busy days.

In health-care public relations, cellular phones are being used to provide treatment reminders and to organize activist and support groups. In addition, the nearly ubiquitous presence of cell phones in teen and young adult populations affords opportunities for clever public relations professionals to reach this important target audience. (See Chapter 7, page 190, for further discussion of cell phones and flash mob activity.)

Personal Digital Assistants

The almost ubiquitous Palm Pilot and smart cell phones such as Blackberry and Treo provide portable management of traditional information such as calendars and contacts. In addition, they also offer striking new business functions such as the electronic exchange of business cards by infrared beam between Palm Pilots. Many of these devices also offer Web browsing and Instant Internet (IM) messaging capabilities. Advanced wristwatches can download data from a personal computer, such as the day's meeting schedule or a database of reporters' telephone numbers.

Memory: The CD-R/RW, DVD-R/RW, and Flash Memory

The multimedia versions of the familiar music CD and the movie DVD offer an enormous capacity for message delivery in public relations; up to 300,000 pages of text, color pictures, and graphics can be stored on a single CD or DVD. CDs and DVDs with a "/RW" are rewritable and can be used to backup professional work. It only takes one computer crash for overly confident young professionals to realize the importance of backing up creative copy and irreplaceable records that a public relations client is expecting to use. Because of their high storage capacity, CDs and DVDs have become the common "coinage" in public relations firms for the transfer of Web pages, graphics, and entire publications among account or project team members.

Because materials can be delivered digitally to customers over the Internet or other wireless communication networks, some questions the utility of CDs and DVDs. However, many people prefer a tangible product over virtual information. Public relations practitioners should keep this human need for tangible communication products in mind when deciding how much information to provide exclusively in digital form. A "press disc," the CD/DVD version of a media kit, is being used, but reporters make little use of the novelty. A more efficient use of the disc technique is to distribute information to specific target audiences. For example, corporations may distribute their annual reports to stockholders on CD or DVD.

As an example of the CD's potential, Yale University Press issued a disc called Perseus for use in teaching Greek language and history. The disc has 25 volumes of Greek text with English translation, a 35,000-word Greek dictionary, and 6000 photos and drawings of architectural sites and artifacts. In Norway, a public health effort to enhance appropriate interaction and respect between boys and girls was modeled on a computer game that was distributed on CD. In the United States, alcohol, tobacco, and other drugs are discussed constructively by experts and former addicts in a television talk show format reminiscent of Sally Jesse Raphael's or Jerry Springer's. The difference is that these talk show segments appear on CD through a program sponsored by the Missouri Institute of Mental Health, enabling repeated viewing and convenient selection of segments.

Informational brochures can be placed on discs and mailed to target audiences. Buick, for example, mailed 20,000 discs to users of Apple personal computers to tell them about its new models. Recipients of the Buick disc were able to interact with the information presented. By pushing a few buttons, a user could load the trunk with luggage and ask questions about mileage, standard equipment, and how the Buick compared with other auto makes.

Even business cards have joined the digital age. Up to 600 megabytes of information can be placed on a small, circular CD that fits in the tray of the computer's CD-ROM drive. An agency can use a CD business card to present all collateral materials about the firm as well as sample campaigns, including video and audio clips, on one 25-megabyte business card (www.avo-card.com).

New technologies often have a limited lifespan. Increasingly, discs are being supplanted by flash memory sticks the size of a five-pack of gum that plug into the USB port of most modern computers. These memory sticks serve as portable, external hard drives that hold enormous amounts of data. Flash memory can be used to read and write large amounts of data for backups or for the delivery of very large files, such as multimedia presentations and photo layouts, to clients. Files can be viewed by a client or a colleague and then returned on the flash memory to the original machine.

Electronic Blackboards

Blackboards with chalk now belong to the past; companies are now using *whiteboards*. A person can write on a whiteboard with a liquid marker during a presentation, and the image on the whiteboard is then electronically scanned so that it can be saved or printed for future reference. The electronic whiteboard image also can be transmitted to Webconference participants in real-time or after a presentation is complete.

Blogs and Moblogs

The term *blog* is a contraction of two words, "Web" and "log." A blog is a regularly updated online diary that also features links to news items and stories on the Web. The individual running the site is called a *blogger*. This person typically is a pundit who wishes to express his or her views on the news. Some bloggers are professional journalists. A blog also serves as a public forum for active give-and-take with the blogger. *Moblogging* using cell phones with cameras is the latest rage. With moblogging, content is posted to the Internet from a mobile or portable device, such as a cellular phone or PDA. (See Chapter 15 for more information on blogs.)

A Peek at Future Technologies

Although it is unwise to predict the future in general, it is even more questionable in the fast-changing world of new media technologies. Nevertheless, it can be useful to anticipate what imminent technological advances may mean for public relations professionals.

- **Think digital, but not necessarily online.** Many public relations tools will involve specialized digital devices or media that are not online or that are used more frequently offline. For example, digital tablets and digital ink enable online content to be downloaded overnight so that the user can carry the lightweight device on a commuter train. Page loads are instantaneous because there is no download delay, and voice recognition/generation features enable commands and replies. News and other content can be read to the user by the tablet, making better use of professional travel time.

- **Forget Papyrus—and even drop paper.** As already noted, computer processing is not limited to traditional devices. Thin, lightweight tablets hardly larger than a yellow notepad can link to the Internet and carry the computing power of full-sized desktop computers. These devices recognize the user's handwriting and respond to touch commands on the screen, enabling notetaking and small group activity in public relations offices. An even more portable medium is reaching the consumer market. E-ink enables computer functions on a sheet of material the size and thickness of a typical plastic placemat at a dining table. Applications for public relations remain to be realized, but as a portable computer and a reading device, the potential communication angles should be very interesting.

● **Wireless broadband.** Cable and other high-capacity services such as satellite and DSL service often are collectively referred to as *broadband services*. Broadband enables online public relations professionals to meet the eight-second rule for loading time while offering broadcast-quality video and unlimited information stores to media, investors, and other publics. Cell and dish satellite companies have now broken the broadband barrier, meaning that wireless computers and cell devices will browse and communicate at speeds comparable to desktop machines on cable or DSL service today. These broadband speeds enable the Internet to offer a telephone service called VoIP (Voice over Internet Protocol) at low cost, especially for international calling.

● **Virtual presence.** Increased online capacity through broadband services will enable public relations professionals and Webmasters to create virtual environments and emulate the bricks-and-mortar presence of their organizations. Special boxes are becoming commercially available that will generate scents to accompany other elements of virtual reality to give users a sense of presence in a world created by the organization. Activist groups could convey pollution conditions. E-commerce sites could offer a restaurant aura (sounds, aroma, clientele, layout,

PR CASEBOOK

HP Leads in Video Communication

HP, formerly Hewlett-Packard, headquartered in Palo Alto, California, spends more than $20 million annually on video communications and produces some of the nation's most sophisticated business television.

The company began live interactive broadcasts in 1981, using a transmitter to reach more than 80 plant and sales sites nationwide. This enabled an executive to address many audiences simultaneously. By 1996, HP had 127 sites linked to its video communications network, including several in Canada, South America, and Europe.

HP also has 48 teleconference rooms at 44 locations in the United States, Europe, and Asia. These facilities allow participants to hold meetings with people in as many as eight locations. Two-way audio and video allow a truly interactive meeting format; participants can also share information, including files and graphics on personal computers.

HP is developing an interactive multimedia network so that employees eventually will be able to view live videos, including the company president's semiannual address, on their personal computers. "Until the majority of employees can view video on their PCs or workstations, I don't think business television is going to advance much," said Mary Anne Easley, manager of HP's employee communications.

To communicate with employees, HP also produces a high-quality in-house video magazine. Released four times a year at a cost of $50,000 an issue, it is formatted after television's entertainment and lifestyle programs. According to Easley, "Television is an effective medium for reaching the baby boomers, the production and clerical workers."

view) to help users decide where to make a reservation or what food suits their fancy for takeout.

● **Processing speed and memory capacity.** With continuing increases in computer chip capacity and speed, public relations professionals will enjoy digital tools in the future that are unimagined now. According to a National Public Radio program entitled *Talk of the Nation, Science Friday*, computer processors will be 25 times faster within five years. Quantum computing researchers are manipulating the spin of electrons in atoms to compute and record data at rates 1,000 times what we know today. Artificial intelligence to assist with crises, issues management, complex event management, and visual design will become commonplace. Multimedia and unusual hybrid media will meet public relations objectives such as on-demand information and virtual presence, which are currently constrained by machine limitations.

The future holds many changes and advances in communication tools and channels. However, each tool requires an "operator" with good managerial judgment and excellent people skills. In the midst of a new age of electronic wonders, most public relations triumphs will continue to hinge on human creativity.

SUMMARY

The Communications Explosion

In the 1990s, the Internet grew from a means of exchanging scientific information in a relatively small community to become a global communications tool for the masses, blending telephone, television, and the computer into an information superhighway. Three key factors that have contributed to the communication explosion: fiber-optic cable, the digital transmission of sound and pictures, and wireless technologies.

The Computer

The computer is not just a tool to handle office procedures; it is also the on-ramp to the Internet.

The Internet

One of the primary uses of the Internet is for communication, both in the form of e-mail and in information delivery and research opportunities. Its reach is worldwide, but keep in mind that Internet content is virtually uncontrolled. Users can become frustrated in trying to find information online. There are also problems with security and copyright infringement.

Other Computer Uses

Public relations practitioners use computers in the following tasks: dictation and voice generation, expert system programming, processing of news releases, e-mail, desktop publishing, mailing list generation, online conferencing, graphics production, and facsimile transmission. They also use computers as management tools.

Satellite Transmission

Major newspapers use satellites to transmit material to regional printing plants. A number of companies deliver news releases via satellite, including audio and video releases. Teleconferencing is a rapidly growing application of satellite transmission; approximately 20,000 U.S. sites are equipped to use this technology, saving companies time and money on business travel.

Other Tools

Other electronic tools include cell phones, personal digital assistants, CDs and DVDs, and electronic blackboards.

A Peek at Future Technologies

Future trends may include the use of offline digital devices, the growth of broadband and wireless broadband services, the development of "virtual presence" capabilities, and expanded processing speeds and memory capacity. All of these wonders will still require traditional managerial judgment and people skills.

Case Activity: **What Would You Do?**

Ashland Community Hospital is deeply involved in health education as part of its approach to preventive care. In the past, the hospital has distributed leaflets about various diseases and conducted community seminars on such topics as how to stop smoking, the importance of physical fitness, and how to detect early signs of cancer.

The hospital can use new technologies to expand its potential in health education. Write a proposal on how the hospital could use the Internet, the World Wide Web, e-mail, CDs and DVDs, and faxes to disseminate health-care information to the community.

QUESTIONS for Review and Discussion

1. What part of the Internet has home pages? What does the term *home page* mean?
2. What is the Internet, and what are some of its most promising uses in public relations?
3. Define the following terms: *broadband, virtual presence, brochureware, listservs, Webcasting*, and *artificial intelligence*.
4. How do you think public relations professionals should address the tangibility factor when pitching stories to reporters?
5. What is the difference between a news release delivery system such as Business Wire and a news service such as the Associated Press?
6. Teleconferencing is growing in popularity. Explain how it operates. How does it differ from Webconferencing? How do you think the two will merge as a result of broadband Internet service?
7. Authors frequently participate in satellite media tours. How do they work, and why do many authors prefer them to traditional book promotion tours?
8. What impact do you think the tailoring of messages to individual audience members will have on public relations? Will it make our work more difficult? Noticeably more effective? Less ethically sound?
9. As a public relations practitioner, how might you use online computer conference calls?
10. Do you think that new technologies will facilitate or hamper creativity in public relations?

SUGGESTED READINGS

Barkow, Tim. "Blogging for Business: Do You Really Want Your Employees to Have Their Own Blogs At Work?" *The Strategist*, Fall 2004, pp. 40–42.

Callison, Coy. "Media Relations and the Internet: How *Fortune* 500 Company Web Sites Assist Journalists in Newsgathering." *Public Relations Review*, Vol. 29, No. 1, 2003, pp. 29–41.

Cooley, Tracy. "Interactive Communication—Public Relations on the Web." *Public Relations Quarterly*, Summer 1999, pp. 41–42.

Coombs, W. Timothy. "The Internet as Potential Equalizer: New Leverage for Confronting Social Irresponsibility." *Public Relations Review*, Vol. 24, No. 3, 1998, pp. 289–304.

Frank, John N. "Blogs Offer New Way for PR Pros to Speak with Clients," *PR Week*, October 18, 204, p. 9.

Gordon, Andrew. "Wi-Fi Looks to Create Lasting Connection with the Public." *PRWeek*, May 5, 2003, p. 9.

Howard, Carole M. "Technology and Tabloids: How the New Media World Is Changing Our Jobs." *Public Relations Quarterly*, Spring 2000, pp. 8–12.

Ku, Gyotae, Kaid, Lynda Lee, and Pfau, Michael. "The Impact of Web Site Campaigning on Traditional News Media and Public Information Processing," *Journalism and Mass Communication Quarterly*, Vol. 80, Autumn 2003, pp. 528–547.

"Net Gains." *Tactics*, November 2002, pp. 1–30.

Porter, Lance V., and Sallot, Lynne M. "The Internet and Public Relations: Investigating Practitioners' Roles and World Wide Web Use." *Journalism and Mass Communication Quarterly*, Vol. 80, No. 3, 2003, pp. 603–622.

Porter, Lance V., Sallot, Lynne M., Cameron, Glen T., and Shamp, Scott. 'New Technologies and Public Relations: Exploring Practitioners' Use of Online Resources to Earn a Seat at the Management Table," *Journalism and Mass Communication Quarterly*, Vol. 78, Spring 2001, pp. 172–190.

"Turning off TV and Logging on: A New Study Reveals that the Millennial Generation Favors the Web." *pr reporter*, October 27, 2003, pp. 1–3.

Tyson, Ben, Sativa, Ross, Broderick, Steve, and Westover, Susan. "Getting Viewers to Your Web Site: A Study of Direct-mail CD-ROM Effectiveness." *Public Relations Quarterly*, Spring 2004, pp. 18–23.

Wickenden, David. "Tech Watch: High-tech Trends That Will Matter to PR Executives." *The Strategist*, Summer 2003, pp. 23–27.

chapter **14**

News Releases, Newsletters, and Brochures

The News Release

The *news release*, also called a *press release*, is the most commonly used public relations tactic. Basically, a news release is a simple document whose primary purpose is the dissemination of information to mass media such as newspapers, broadcast stations, and magazines.

Indeed, a great deal of the information that you read in your weekly or daily newspaper originates from a news release prepared by a publicist or public relations practitioner on behalf of a client or employer. Gary Putka, the Boston bureau chief of the *Wall Street Journal*, admits that "a good 50 percent" of the stories in the newspaper come from news releases. Another study, by Bennett & Company (Orlando), found that 75 percent of the responding journalists said they used public relations sources for their stories.

The media rely on news releases for several reasons. First, the reality of mass communications today is that reporters and editors spend most of their time processing information, not gathering it. Second, no media enterprise has enough staff to cover every single event in the community. Consequently, a lot of the more routine news in a newspaper is processed from information provided by public relations practitioners. As one editor of a major daily once said, public relations people are the newspaper's "unpaid reporters."

It must be remembered, however, that a news release is not paid advertising. News reporters and editors have no obligation to use any of the information from a news release in a news story. News releases are judged solely on newsworthiness, timeliness, interest to the readers, and other traditional news values. Consequently, it is important for any news release to be formatted correctly, well written, and contain accurate, timely information.

Planning a News Release

Before writing a news release, a number of questions should be answered to give the release direction and purpose. A planning worksheet should be used to answer the following questions:

- What is the key message? This should be expressed in one sentence.
- Who is the primary audience for the release? Is it for consumers who may buy a product or service? Or is it for purchasing agents in other companies? The answer to this question also affects whether the release is sent to a daily community newspaper or to a trade magazine.
- What does the target audience gain from the product or service? What are the potential benefits and rewards?
- What objective does the release serve? Is it to increase product sales, to enhance the organization's reputation, or to increase attendance at an event?

These planning questions are answered from a public relations perspective, but the next step is to think like a journalist and write a well-crafted news story that includes the traditional five Ws and H: who, what, when, where, why, and how. This is discussed further in the next several sections.

The Format of a News Release

News releases follow a standard, traditional format. You should use the following tips when crafting your own news releases. Other tips are given in the Insights box on page 359.

- Use standard 8.5-by-11 inch paper. It should be white or on the organization's letterhead.

- Identify the sender (contact) in the upper-left-hand corner of the page and provide the sender's name, address, and telephone number. Many releases also include a fax number and an e-mail address.

- After the contact information, write *For Immediate Release* if the material is intended for immediate publication, which is usually the case. Some practitioners discard the phrase because they say that all news releases are automatically assumed to be for immediate release.

- Leave 2 inches of space for editing convenience before starting the text.

- Provide a boldface headline that gives the key message of the release so the editor knows exactly what the release is about at a glance.

- Provide a dateline, for example: Minneapolis, MN: July 21, 2005. This indicates where the news release originated.

- Start the text with a clearly stated summary that contains the most important message you want to convey to the reader, even if he or she only reads the first paragraph. Lead paragraphs should be a maximum of three to five lines.

- Leave at least a 1.5-inch margin. Double-space the copy to give editors room to edit the material.

- Use standard 10 or 12 point standard type, such as Times Roman or Courier, because they are easy to read.

- Never split a paragraph from one page to the next. Place the word *more* at the bottom of each page.

- Place an identifying slug line and page number at the top of each page after the first one.

News releases that are prepared for Web news sites or e-mail have a somewhat different format. See the Insights box on page 360 for some guidelines.

The Content of a News Release

A news release, as already noted, is written like a news story. The lead paragraph is an integral and important part of the text, because it forms the apex of the journalistic "inverted pyramid" approach to writing. This means that the first paragraph succinctly summarizes the most important part of the story and succeeding paragraphs fill in the details in descending order of importance.

There are three reasons why you should use the inverted pyramid structure. First, if the editor or reporter doesn't find anything interesting in the first three or four lines of the news release, it won't be used. Second, editors cut stories from the bottom. In fact, Business Wire estimates that more than 90 percent of the news releases are

ON THE JOB insights

Rules for Writing a News Release

All news releases should be "news centered," according to Schubert Communications, a Pennsylvania public relations firm. Lisa Barbadora, director of public relations and marketing content for Schubert, gives these rules for writing news releases:

- Use short, succinct headlines and subheads to highlight main points and pique interest. They should not simply be a repeat of the information in the lead-in paragraph.
- Don't use generic words such as "the leading provider" or "world-class" to position your company. Be specific, such as "with annual revenues of."
- Don't describe products using phrases such as "unique" or "total solution." Use specific terms or examples to demonstrate the product's distinctiveness.
- Use descriptive and creative words to grab an editor's attention, but make sure they are accurate and not exaggerated.
- Don't highlight the name of your company or product in the headline of a news release if it is not highly recognized. If you are not a household name, focus on the news instead.

- Tell the news. Focus on how your announcement affects your industry and lead with that rather than overtly promoting your product or company.
- Critique your writing by asking yourself, "Who cares?" Why should readers be interested in this information?
- Don't throw the whole kitchen sink into a release. Better to break your news into several releases if material is lengthy.
- Don't use lame quotes. Write like someone is actually talking—eliminate the corporatese that editors love to ignore. Speak with pizzazz to increase your chances of being published.
- Target your writing. Create two different tailored releases that will go out to different types of media rather than a general release that isn't of great interest to either group.
- Look for creative ways to tie your announcement in with current news or trends.
- Write simply. Use contractions, write in active voice, be direct, avoid paired words such as "clear and simple," and incorporate common action-oriented phrases to generate excitement.

Sentences should be no longer than 34 words.

- Follow the *Associated Press Stylebook* and specific publications' editorial standards for dates, technical terms, abbreviations, punctuation, spellings, capitalization, and so on.
- Don't use metaphors unless they are used to paint a clearer picture for the reader.
- Don't overdo it. It's important to write colorfully, to focus on small specific details, to include descriptions of people, places, and events—but do not write poetry when you want press.
- Don't be formulaic in your news release writing. Not every release must start with the name of the company or product. Break out of the mold to attract media attention.
- Don't expect editors to print your entire release. Important information should be contained in the first two paragraphs.
- Make it clear how your announcement is relevant for the editors' readers.

Source: Jerry Walker. "18 Simple Rules for Writing a News Release." *O'Dwyer's PR Services Report,* November 2002, pp. 32–33.

rewritten in much shorter form than the original text. If the main details of the story are at the beginning, the release will still be understandable and informative even if most of the original text has been deleted.

A third reason for using the inverted pyramid is that readers don't always read the full story. Statistics show, for example, that the average reader spends less than

ON THE JOB insights

How to Write An Internet-Ready News Release

The format and content of news releases for distribution via e-mail and the Internet is somewhat different than the traditional 8.5-by-11, double-spaced format that is mailed or faxed to media outlets.

B. L. Ochman, writing in *The Strategist*, suggests that you should "think of the electronic news release as a teaser to get a reporter or editor to your Web site for additional information." He makes the following suggestions:

- Use a specific subject line that identifies exactly what the news release is about.
- Make your entire release a maximum of 200 words or less, in five short paragraphs. The idea is brevity so that reporters see the news release on one screen and don't have to scroll. If a journalist has hundreds of e-mails in his or her inbox, scrolling becomes a real chore.
- Write only two or three short sentences in each of the five paragraphs.
- Use bulleted points to convey key points.
- Above the headline or at the bottom of the release be sure to provide a contact name, phone number, e-mail address, and URL for additional information.
- Never send a release as an attachment. Journalists, because of possible virus infections, rarely open attachments.

Ochman concludes, "Write like you have 10 seconds to make a point. Because online, you do."

30 minutes a day reading a metropolitan daily newspaper. This means that they read a lot of headlines and first paragraphs, and not much else.

Here are some other guidelines for the content of a news release:

- **Use Associated Press (AP) style.** The vast majority of newspapers and broadcast stations use this stylebook as a guide for word usage, punctuation, and capitalization. A news release written in AP style makes the job of editors much easier and often makes a difference whether the release is used at all.

- **Be concise.** Edit the copy to remove excess words and "puff" words. Few news releases need to be more than two pages long. A reporter can obtain additional details by telephoning or e-mailing the source and checking for additional background information on the organization's Web site.

- **Avoid clichés and fancy phrases.** When editors get a release that uses terms such as *unique*, *revolutionary*, and *state-of-the-art*, they are likely to throw it away.

- **Avoid technical jargon.** Releases, for the most part, are written for general audiences unfamiliar with terms and jargon used within the organization. The objective is to write for understanding, not confusion.

- **Double-check all information.** Be absolutely certain that every fact and title in the release is correct and that every name is spelled properly. Check the copy for errors in grammar, punctuation, and sentence structure. Make sure trademarks are noted.

● **Eliminate boldface and capital letters.** Avoid boldfacing key words or sentences and don't place the name of the organization in all capital letters.

● **Include organization background.** A short paragraph at the end of the news release should give a thumbnail sketch of the organization. It may be a description of what the organization does or manufactures, how many employees it has, or whether it is a market leader in a particular industry.

● **Localize whenever possible.** Most studies show that news releases with a local angle get published more often than generic news releases giving a regional or national perspective. Airlines, for example, "localize" news releases about the total number passengers and revenues by breaking down such figures by specific cities and making that the lead paragraph for releases sent to journalists in those cities. Insurance companies also do "hometown" releases by mentioning local agents in the copy. The news release shown on page 362 is good example of the format and copy for a news release.

Publicity Photos

News releases are often accompanied by a photo. News releases about personnel often include a head-and-shoulder picture (often called a *mug shot*) of a person who has been hired as an executive or promoted in an organization. New product news releases often include a photo of the product in an attractive setting. See the publicity photo on page 363 for an example.

ON THE JOB ethics

What to Write, or Not Write

A common activity of public relations practitioners is to write news releases on behalf of a client or employer.

At times, the content and choice of words in a news release can be an ethical dilemma. Consider the following two scenarios:

● The president of a small business software company wants to get some publicity and visibility in the business press. He asks you to write a news release announcing that the company has recently received major contracts from large corporations such as General Electric, AT&T, Starbucks, and Exxon Mobil. The president then adds, "We only have a contract with AT&T right now, but we've been talking to the other companies, and it's a pretty sure thing that they will sign on." Given this information, would you go ahead and write the news release? Why or why not?

● A top-level executive has been fired by a company for manipulating accounts and claiming more sales for her division than could be documented. The media is calling about the executive's departure, so the president asks you to write a short news release that the executive has resigned "to pursue other business opportunities." Would you go ahead and write the news release? Why or why not?

FOR IMMEDIATE RELEASE

Contacts:
Mike Duggan, Golden Valley Microwave Foods
952-832-3439
-OR-
Bernice Neumann, Morgan&Myers
612-825-0050

ACT II INTRODUCES FIRST AND ONLY KETTLE CORN MICROWAVE POPCORN

MINNEAPOLIS, Minn. – July   – Sweet and salty, two classic flavor combinations, have long been paired in all-time favorite foods. Now, Golden Valley Microwave Foods (GVMF) has made microwave popcorn – one of America's favorite snacks – available in delicious slightly sweet, slightly salty ACT II® Kettle Corn.

An American tradition introduced by settlers in the 1700-1800s, kettle corn was first made outdoors by popping corn in large cast-iron kettles with rendered lard and sweeteners, such as molasses, honey or sugar. In the past decade, this tasty snack started being served again at outdoor gatherings, such as fairs, concerts, carnivals and flea markets, primarily in the Midwestern states.

-more-

GOLDEN VALLEY MICROWAVE FOODS • 7450 Metro Boulevard, Edina MN 55439 • Tel 800.328.6286 • Fax 952.835.9635

© ConAgra Brands, Inc. 2001. All Rights Reserved

-2-

"Kettle Corn doesn't have to be just for special occasions anymore," says Mike Duggan, Golden Valley Microwave Foods marketing manager. "We wanted to make this a fun flavor combination conveniently available to families whenever they want hot, fresh, great-tasting popcorn."

ACT II Kettle Corn is the first of its kind in a microwave form. The company spent eight years researching and developing an authentic kettle corn flavor. "We had to develop the process and source a natural sweetener that withstands high-temperature microwave heating without burning, and we succeeded," says Jim Montealegre, vice president of product development at GVMF.

ACT II Kettle Corn is available in a 3-, 5- and 6-pack carton and contains three 1-cup servings per bag. Suggested retail price ranges from $2.19 for a 3-pack to $2.99 for a 6-pack carton.

GVMF, based in Minneapolis, Minn., is the largest manufacturer of microwave popcorn in the world, selling its ACT II®, Orville Redenbacher's® and Healthy Choice® brands in 30 countries around the globe. Microwave popcorn, ready-to-eat sweet popcorn, popcorn balls, soft pretzels and snack mix are included in GVMF's product line. GVMF is the first and only microwave popcorn manufacturer to control all selecting of seed, growing, sorting and processing of corn, as well as bag manufacturing, used in its popcorn products.

XXXX

The news release is the workhorse of public relations. This is an example of a well-written and -formatted news release from Kettle Corn, which was prepared by Morgan & Myers public relations.

Studies show that more people "read" photographs than read articles. The Advertising Research Foundation found that three to four times as many people notice the average one-column photograph as read the average news story. In another study, Wayne Wanta of the University of Missouri found that articles accompanied by photographs are perceived as significantly more important than those without photographs.

Publicity photos, however, are not published if they are not of high resolution and if they don't appeal to media gatekeepers. Although professional photographers should always be hired to take the photos, public relations practitioners should supervise their work and select what photos are best suited for media use. Here are some additional suggestions:

Quality. Photos must have good contrast and sharp detail so that they reproduce in a variety of formats, including grainy newsprint. Digital photography is now the norm, and in many cases editors download digital photos from an organization's Web site. It is important, however, to understand that the beautiful photo on the computer screen may not come out the same way when it is printed, despite the claims of printer manufacturers. Most Web sites use images at 72 dpi (dots per inch) for fast downloading, but newspapers need photos at 150 to 200 dpi, and magazines need at least 300 dpi. Consequently, organizations usually have an online news or press room that provides high-resolution photos for journalists. Photos also are supplied to editors on CD and in 35-mm color slide format to ensure maximum reproduction quality.

Subject Matter. A variety of subjects can be used for publicity photos. Trade magazines, weekly newspapers, and organizational newsletters often use the standard "grip-and-grin" photo of a person receiving an award or a company president shaking hands with the mayor at a new store opening. This has been a staple of publicity photos for years, and there is no sign that they are going out of fashion despite being tired clichés. Another standard approach is the large group photograph, which is all right for the club newsletter, but almost never acceptable for a daily newspaper. A better approach is to take photos of people in groups of three or four people from the same city and send only that photo to editors in that specific city.

Composition. The best photos are uncluttered. Photo experts recommend (1) tight shots with minimum background, (2) an emphasis on detail, not whole scenes, (3) and limiting wasted space by reducing gaps between individuals or objects. At times, context also is important. A photo of a research scientist, for example, may have more interest if the photo shows the individual in a lab surrounded by technical equipment and high stacks of data printouts.

Action. Too many photos are static, with nothing happening except someone looking at the camera. It's better to show people doing something—talking, gesturing,

Media kits often include photos and color slides of the product. This is the color slide that accompanied the media kit for Kettle Corn, Act II.

laughing, running, or operating a machine. Action gives the photo interest and indicates to the reader that something is happening. Phil Douglis, a professional photographer, says, "Interactive exchanges are the most productive form of communication." Photojournalism is an ideal medium for visually expressing how people communicate interactively with each other.

Scale.   Another way to add interest is to use scale. Panasonic, for example, illustrated its new memory card (which is smaller than a person's hand) by having an executive hold the card while surrounded by a large stacks of printed material that could easily be stored in digital format on the card.

Camera Angle.   Interesting angles can make the subject of a photo more compelling. Some common methods are (1) shooting upward at a tall building to make it look even taller, (2) an aerial shot giving the viewer a chance to see something that he or she ordinarily couldn't, and (3) using a fish-eye lens to capture a 180-degree image.

Lighting.   Professional photographers use a variety of lighting techniques to ensure that the subject is portrayed, quite literally, in the best light. Product photos, for example, always have the light on the product and the background is usually dark or almost invisible. Background is important. If the executives at a banquet are all wearing dark suits, the photographer shouldn't line them up in front of a dark red curtain, because there will be no contrast. Also, outdoor shots require knowing where the sun is located so individuals are not squinting into the sun as the photo is taken.

Color.   In the past, most publicity photos were black and white for economic reasons. Today, with digital cameras and flash cards, almost all publicity photos are in color. Because of new printing technologies, many publications now use color on a regular basis. Daily newspapers, for example, regularly use color publicity photos in the food, business, sports, and travel sections. Publications have differing requirements. Some want photos that can be downloaded via Web sites; others want 35-mm slides, and still others want a color photograph that can be scanned.

Media Advisories and Fact Sheets

On occasion, the public relations staff will send a memo to reporters and editors about a news conference or upcoming event that they may wish to cover. Such memos also are used to let the media know about an interview opportunity with a visiting expert or alert them that a local person will be featured on a network television program. These *media advisories* also are referred to as *media alerts*. They may be sent with an accompanying news release or by themselves.

The most common format for media advisories to use is short, bulleted items rather than long paragraphs. A typical one-page advisory might contain the following elements: a one-line headline, a brief paragraph outlining the story idea, some of journalism's five Ws and H, and a short paragraph telling the reporter who to contact for more information or to make arrangements. The following is the text of a media advisory from Old Bay Seasonings.

MEDIA ALERT

ACT II® Microwave Popcorn Presents
Sundance "Minnesota style" at the Taste of Minnesota

WHAT: Beat the heat and check out some homegrown entertainment at the SMMASH Film Festival at the Taste of Minnesota, courtesy of ACT II® Microwave Popcorn. The SMMASH Film Festival features shorts and feature films...all from Minnesota independent filmmakers. It's a fun, entertaining way to stay cool. And you can see laugh-out-loud comedies, dramas and fast-paced action flicks shown daily in the air-conditioned theater tent. An all day pass is $4 for adults and $3 for children 12 and under. Shows run continuously Thursday afternoon, July 4, through Sunday, July 7.

WHY: While you're there, pick up free samples of ACT II Kettle Corn Microwave Popcorn at the old-fashioned ACT II sampling truck. Wesley "Pops" Ward, in his 1930 model A truck, will be serving great-tasting ACT II Kettle Corn throughout the weekend. With its sweet-salty taste sensation, Kettle Corn has become the fastest growing popcorn flavor on the market. Kettle Corn was first made outdoors by popping corn in large cast-iron kettles with rendered lard and sweeteners. Now, ACT II has made it available in a convenient microwave form. Stop by and see "Pops" for your free samples.

MEDIA OPPORTUNITIES: "Pops" is available for interviews and to deliver fresh-popped popcorn to your studio for a Taste of Minnesota preview.

WHEN AND WHERE: Taste of Minnesota, July 3-7

FOR MORE INFORMATION: Call Sara Sturm at 612-802-3668.

> Media alerts are a thumbnail sketch of the product and the special events surrounding its launch. As the name implies, it is an "alert" to the media in case they would like cover the announcement or event.

Media Alert

Who: Old Bay Seasoning, a unique blend of a dozen herbs and spices and a Chesapeake Bay cooking tradition for over 60 years, conducted a search for America's seafood lovers and Old Bay fans.
More than 1,600 people across the country entered the contest by briefly describing in 100 words or less why they are America's biggest seafood fanatics and Old Bay fans and providing their favorite unusual uses for Old Bay.

What: Ten lucky finalists from across the country were selected to vie for a $10,000 grand prize in the first-ever Old Bay Peel and Eat Shrimp Classic—a 10-minute, timed tournament to see who can peel and eat the most Old Bay-seasoned shrimp.

When: The contest will kick off Labor Day Weekend on Friday, August 30, from 11:30 A.M. to 12:30 P.M.

Where: Harborplace Amphitheater (outdoors)
200 East Pratt Street
Baltimore, Maryland

Special Guest: Tory McPhail, executive chef at Commander's Palace restaurant in New Orleans and rising star in the culinary industry, will be master of ceremonies for the event.

Contact: Amanda Hirschhorn, Hunter Public Relations
212/679.6660, ext. 239, or ahirschhorn@hunterpr.com
Event-day cell: 914/475.4074

SATELLITE FEED INFORMATION FOLLOWS
Friday, August 30
Feed Time: 3:30–3:45 P.M. ET (Fed in Rotation)
Coordinates: C-Band: Telstar 4 (C)/Transponder 11/AUDIO 6.2 & 6.8
DL FREQ: 3920 (V)

Fact sheets are another useful public relations tool. Fact sheets are often distributed to the media as part of a media kit or with a news release to give additional background information about the product, person, service, or event.

Fact sheets are usually one to two pages in length and serve as a "crib sheet" for journalists when they write a story. A fact sheet about an organization may use headings that provide (1) the organization's full name, (2) products or services offered, (3) its annual revenues, (4) the number of employees, (5) the names and one-

Fact sheets concentrate on the product or service's strengths and capabilities. Some give ingredients; others discuss how to prepare the product.

paragraph biographies of top executives, (6) the markets served, (7) position in the industry, and (8) any other pertinent details.

A variation on the fact sheet is the *FAQ* (Frequently Asked Questions). HP, for example, supplemented an Internet news release on its new ScanJet printer with a FAQ that answered typical consumer questions about the new product. A sample of a product information fact sheet is shown on page 366.

Media Kits

A *media kit*, which is sometimes referred to as a *press kit*, is usually prepared for major events and new product launches. Its purpose is to give editors and reporters a variety of information and resources that make it easier for the reporter to write about the topic.

The basic elements of a media kit are (1) the main news release; (2) a news feature about the development of the product or something similar; (3) fact sheets on the product, organization, or event; (4) background information; (5) photos and drawings with captions; (6) biographical material on the spokesperson or chief executives; and (7) some basic brochures. All information should be clearly identified; it's also important to prominently display contact information such as e-mail addresses, phone numbers, and Web site URLs.

The contents of a media kit are usually placed inside a custom-designed folder. The folder will vary based on the size of budget. Pillsbury designed a folder that was the shape of a large chocolate chip cookie with a bite taken out of it to launch its new Big DeLuxe Classics cookies. Other organizations, such as Cirque Du Soleil, just use a standard folder with its name emblazoned on it.

The typical media kit folder is 9 by 12 inches and has four surfaces: a cover, two inside pages (with pockets to hold news releases, etc.), and a back cover that gives the name and address of the organization. Another common feature is to have a slot on the inside page that holds a business card of the public relations contact person.

A good example of a well-designed media kit that fits the organization's products and personality was one done by Crayola to celebrate its 100th anniversary with a 25-city bus tour. The kit was a self-mailer that unfolded into a large round sheet 2 feet in diameter that featured artwork done with a rainbow of crayon colors. The kit also included a colorful news release (localized for each city) and two background articles on the history of the company. One piece of interesting trivia: "Since 1903, more than 120 billion crayons have been sold throughout the world. End-to-end they would circle the earth 200 times."

Compiling and producing a media kit is time consuming and expensive. It's not uncommon for press kits to cost $8 to $10 each by the time all of the materials have been produced. Much of the cost is in printing the kits. Consequently, Weber Shandwick has predicted the end of paper media kits. A poll by the firm of 1,500 media outlets in 2004 found that 70 percent of them prefer electronic communications. HP is part of the growing trend of those using online media kits. It issued a media kit online for a trade show instead of spending the money to print kits for editors covering the event. The cost savings was almost $20,000 over mailing printed kits to about 200 reporters.

Not every journalist, however, likes the digital approach. Daniel Cantelmo, writing in *Public Relations Quarterly*, quotes one senior editor for a high-technology magazine who said, "In 5 or 10 minutes, I can go through 25 printed press kits . . . and pick out exactly what I need. If I had to go through 25 CDs or online press kits, it would take hours. I don't have the time."

Pitch Letters

As previously noted, getting the attention of media gatekeepers is difficult because they receive literally hundreds of news releases and media kits every week.

Consequently, many public relations practitioners and publicists will write a short letter or note to the editor that tries to grab their attention. In the public relations industry, this is called a *pitch*. A generic pitch is shown below. It simply lets the editor know, in brief form, about the contents of the media kit. In many cases, the letter will be accompanied by a sample of the product.

Public relations people also use pitches—either mailed, e-mailed, or on the telephone—to ask editors to assign a reporter to a particular event, to pursue a feature angle on an issue or trend, or even to book a spokesperson on a forthcoming show.

A pitch letter outlines why a periodical or broadcast outlet should consider the information as a news article, photograph, or video feature.

ACT II

Kettle Corn
Old Fashioned
Sweet & Salty Popcorn

July

Dear Editor:

Gorp, chocolate covered nuts, salted nut rolls. The list of traditional sweet and salty foods that make for great flavor is long. Now, Golden Valley Microwave Foods is adding to that tradition with all-new ACT II® Kettle Corn, an early-American favorite style of popcorn available for the first time for microwave popping.

Although sweetened popcorn is a staple enjoyed from Europe to South America and Asia, Americans have only been able to find the old-fashioned slightly sweet, slightly salty popcorn – known as kettle corn – at local fairs, markets or other outdoor events mainly in the Midwest. A treat from pioneer days, kettle corn has traditionally been popped in large, black kettles with various oils, sweeteners and salt.

Enclosed you'll find further information on ACT II Kettle Corn Microwave Popcorn, along with a sample. Once you've tasted this first and only microwave kettle corn, we think you'll agree it's a delicious snack completely unique to the existing buttered and salted popcorn category.

We've also included a CD with media materials, photos and additional illustrated information about ACT II Kettle Corn.

Please call me at 612-825-0050 if you have any questions.

Sincerely,

Bernice Neumann
Bernice Neumann
Public Relations Counsel to Golden Valley Microwave Foods

GOLDEN VALLEY MICROWAVE FOODS • 7450 Metro Boulevard, Edina MN 55439 • Tel 800.328.6286 • Fax 952.835.9635

© ConAgra Brands, Inc. 2003. All Rights Reserved

ON THE JOB insights

Guidelines for Pitching Stories by E-Mail

Publicists frequently pitch story ideas by e-mail. In fact, many editors prefer this method compared to letters, faxes, or even phone calls.

However, it's important to remember some guidelines:

- Use a succinct subject line that tells the editor what you have to offer; don't try to be cute or gimmicky.
- Keep the message brief; one screen at the most.
- Don't include attachments unless the reporter is expecting you to do so. Many reporters, due to virus attacks, never open attachments unless they personally know the source.

- Don't send "blast" e-mails to large numbers of editors. E-mail systems are set up to filter messages with multiple recipients in the "To" and "BCC" fields, a sure sign of spam. If you do send an e-mail to multiple editors, break the list into small groups.
- Send tailored e-mail pitches to specific reporters and editors; the pitch should be relevant to their beats and publications.
- Personally check the names in your e-mail database to remove redundant recipients.
- Give editors the option of getting off your e-mail list;

it will make your list more targeted to those who are interested. By the same token, give editors the opportunity to sign-up for regular updates from your organization's Web site. If they cover your industry, they will appreciate it.

- Establish an e-mail relationship. As one reporter said, "The best e-mails come from people I know; I delete e-mails from PR people or agencies I don't recognize."

Source: Dennis L. Wilcox. *Public Relations Writing and Media Techniques*, 5th ed. Boston: Allyn & Bacon, 2005, p. 207.

Pitching is a fine art, however, and public relations personnel must first do some basic research about the publication or broadcast show that they want to contact. It's important to know the kinds of stories that a publication usually publishes or what kinds of guests appear on a particular talk show. Knowing a journalist's beat and the kinds of stories they have written in the past also is helpful.

The media expresses great interest in trends, so it's also a good idea to relate a particular product or service with something that is already identified as part of a particular fashion or lifestyle. Fineberg Publicity, a New York firm, convinced *Hard Copy* to do a 3-minute segment on its client Jockey International. The news hook was the "slit skirt" trend in the fashion industry and how women were buying stylish hosiery to complement their skirts. The segment showed celebrities wearing Jockey's hosiery products.

The best pitch letters show a lot of creativity and are successful in grabbing the editor's attention. *Ragan's Media Relations Report* gives some opening lines that generated media interest and resulting stories:

- "How many students does it take to change a light bulb?" (A pitch about a residence hall maintenance program operated by students on financial aid)

- "Would you like to replace your ex-husband with a plant?" (A pitch about a photographer who is expert at removing "exes" and other individuals out of old photos)

● "Our CEO ran 16 Boston Marathons . . . and now he thinks we can walk a mile around a river." (A pitch about a CEO leading employees on a daily walk instead of paying for expensive gym memberships or trainers)

See the Insights box on page 369 for information on pitching stories via e-mail.

Distributing Media Materials

News releases, photos, and media advisories are distributed via five major methods: (1) first-class mail, (2) fax, (3) e-mail, (4) electronic wire services, and (5) Web-based newsrooms. See the Insights box on page 371 for a comparison on the various methods.

Mail

A widely used distribution method, even in the Internet age, is still regular first-class mail or express shippers such as DHL or FedEx. Commonly called *snail mail* by the cyberspace community, some studies have shown that journalists still prefer this distribution method for unsolicited public relations materials.

Their preference, in part, is due to the exponential increase in e-mails that has engulfed almost everyone. According to one media survey by Jim Rink, an online newsletter publisher, one survey respondent said, "E-mail isn't as good as it was. Haven't you heard? SPAM is driving us crazy just like you." Another editor told Rink, "After 9/11, all I wanted was e-mail. Now all I want is fax. I get hundreds of e-mails weekly and I seldom read any but those from people I know."

In other words, the world still isn't a paperless society. Most organizations and public relations firms continue to print news releases and media kits even when they have companion electronic versions. The idea is to give editors and reporters whatever format they prefer.

Fax

Although facsimile machines have been declared artifacts of another age, the news of their death has been somewhat exaggerated. A fax is is as quick as a telephone call and has the advantage of providing information in both written and graphic form.

Ideally, the fax is used for late-breaking news developments or for sending the details of a hastily organized news conference without much lead time. The reality is that modern technology has made it possible to send faxes to every media outlet in the country within minutes. This is called *broadcast fax* or *bulk fax*. Presidential candidates, for example, are fond of faxing position papers and updated appearance schedules in this manner.

Editors, however, aren't particularly fond of bulk fax because it clogs up their machines in the same way that a mailbox gets overstuffed with junk mail. Fax, however, is still used when individuals want to get an actual copy of something instead of taking the time to download and print it from their computers. Also, in the age of e-mail, some public relations professionals say an editor will pay more attention to a single fax than a mailbox with 200 e-mails in it.

ON THE JOB insights

A Guide to Selecting Distribution Channels

Public relations materials such as news releases, media advisories, and media kits can be distributed a number of ways. Here are some general tips:

- **Mail.** A common method for distribution of routine materials to local and regional media. Mailing houses are effective for mailing media materials on a regional or national basis.
- **Fax.** Good for sending media advisories and alerts and late-breaking news. Not recommended for mass distribution of news releases.
- **Electronic wire services.** Best for distribution of financial news to large newspapers, Web news sites, and major broadcast outlets on a national or international basis when immediate dis-

closure is needed. Announcements of major new products also can be sent via electronic news wires such as PR Newswire or Business Wire.

- **Feature placement firms.** Good for reaching suburban newspapers and small weeklies. Best for feature-type material when you want to create awareness and visibility for a product or an organization through application stories, case studies, and consumer tips.
- **CD-ROM.** Best for background material, such as corporate profiles, executive bios, and product information sheets. Increasingly being used in place of printed media kits.
- **E-mail.** Good for suggesting story ideas to journalists, answering media queries, sending

news releases, and letting journalists know about a particular newsworthy item on the organization's Web site. Keep materials in the body of the e-mail, avoid attachments unless the journalist specifically requests them in that format.

- **Web sites.** An excellent place to post news releases and background material for possible reference by reporters and the public. An organization's online press or newsroom is a good place to post items, but there are other news sites on the Web where material can be posted and linked to the organization's Web site.

Source: Adapted from Dennis L. Wilcox. *Public Relations Writing & Media Techniques,* 5th ed. Boston: Allyn & Bacon, 2005, p. 286.

E-Mail

Despite the problem of e-mail, most surveys show that editors and reporters prefer to receive public relations materials via e-mail. Almost 60 percent of the journalists in Bennett & Co.'s 2004 media survey said they prefer to get information in such a manner. Seven out of 10 even said they read every e-mail they get except for obvious spam. And Vocus, a public relations measurement and evaluation firm, found that an even higher percentage of journalists prefer e-mail—almost 85 percent—over fax or regular mail.

The key to successful e-mail is having a good subject line. Kristen Stieffel, a news assistant for the Orlando (Florida) *Business Journal* says, "I look at the ones with good subject lines first." It's also highly recommended that you never send attachments to a journalist unless he or she specifically requests them. There are simply too many viruses going around for people to trust attachments. The alternative is to give the journalist links to Web-based material in the regular e-mail message.

In fact, Vocus concluded, "We suspect it (links) will quickly succeed attachments . . . in e-mail."

Here are some tips for e-mailing journalists with news releases and other materials. See the Insights box on page 369 for additional tips.

- Don't send HTML e-mail messages.
- Use extended headlines at the top of the news release that give the key message or point.
- Keep it short. Reporters hate to scroll through multiple screens.
- Use blind copy distribution. No reporter wants to know that they are part of a mass mailing.
- Continually update e-mail addresses.

An increasing problem is antispam software. Public relations professionals are finding that their news releases are being blocked as the software becomes more sophisticated.

Electronic News Services

Many organizations now use an electronic wire service to distribute news releases, photos, and advisories, which was discussed in Chapter 13. This is particularly true for corporate and financial information that must be released, according to SEC guidelines, to multiple media outlets at exactly the same time.

The two major newswires are Business Wire (www.businesswire.com) and PR Newswire (www.prnewswire.com). Each organization transmits more than 15,000 news releases monthly to daily newspapers, broadcast stations, and online news services. Another major distributor is US Newswire, a division of Medialink Worldwide, and Internet Wire, which exclusively uses Web portals.

No paper is involved; the release is automatically entered into the appropriate databases and computer queues, which can be accessed by editors and reporters throughout the world. They can then edit the release, write a headline, and then push another key to have it automatically set for publishing. Of course, they can easily click on the delete key, too.

Wire services are making the news release more sophisticated. Business Wire, for example, now has "smart" news releases that can be embedded with visuals and audio. A reporter also can click various hyperlinks to get more information and photographs or charts. National distribution of a "smart" release can cost $1,000, but a basic 400-word news release transmitted to all major media in the United States is about $600. If you want the entire planet to get the news release, it costs about $6,000.

Web Newsrooms

Most major organizations have a press room or a newsroom as part of their Web site. With a few clicks, a journalist can access everything from the organization's executive profiles to the most recent news releases. They also can download high-resolution photos and graphics and background materials, such as position papers and annual reports.

A company's online press room is accessed on a regular basis by reporters who cover a particular industry or group of companies. Sometimes the company will let reporters know via e-mail that a particular item is available on the company's site.

Because there are billions of Web pages, extra effort must be made to ensure that reporters are aware of the Web site and what's on it. A good online newsroom, according to surveys, should provide links to personnel in media relations who can answer questions from reporters in a timely manner.

In the 24/7 news cycle that exists today, it's important that a company keep its Web site up-to-date. If a major news development affects the organization, such as a plane crash for an airline, it's vital that information about the crash be updated hourly. Surveys have found that journalists go first to an organization's Web site for information in the case of a crisis. It's also important that the materials posted on a Web site are not just copies of the printed materials. They must be reformatted and offer short summaries, extensive links, and strong visual elements. All documents, however, should have a "printer-friendly" version.

ON THE JOB global

Introducing the $20 Bill to a Global Audience

More than 60 percent of all U.S. currency circulates outside the United States. This posed a challenge to the U.S. Bureau of Engraving and Printing when it introduced its newly designed $20 bill.

It was necessary to launch an international campaign to gain near-universal public awareness of the new colored notes so banks, tourism associations, and law-enforcement agencies around the world would recognize the new note as authentic. These same groups also needed to be informed of the security features of the new $20 bill that were designed to prevent counterfeiting.

Burson-Marsteller was engaged to conduct the campaign, and a dozen B-M offices around the world took the campaign to more than 50 nations. News releases, media kits, brochures, posters, and paid advertisements were distributed in 23 languages.

Media briefings, various public events, and seminars also were organized for banking and law-enforcement officials. An interactive Web site was built with an online press room, which included an interactive $20 bill highlighting the note's new features.

Media coverage occurred in more than 50 nations, including a six-minute piece on Russia's most popular news program. A panel of judges, organized by *PRWeek*, awarded the effort "Global Campaign of the Year" in 2004.

Newsletters and Magazines

Most organizations, whether it's the local Rotary Club or IBM, publish newsletters for their members, employees, retirees, and vendors and even for community opinion leaders. Subscription newsletters offer expert advice and inside information to individuals and organizations with specific interests in a particular topic or industry.

The typical newsletter is four to eight pages and printed on 8.5-by-11 paper. For the most part, newsletters emphasize short articles and have few graphic elements. A good example of a newsletter is *O'Dwyer's PR Newsletter*. It has a two-column format, and short articles are announced with boldface, underlined headlines one size larger than the text copy. In sum, newsletters are economical, easy to design, and can be used to convey information in a straightforward manner.

Newsletters for employees typically report personnel promotions, forthcoming events, policy announcements, news from field offices, the introduction of new products, productivity achievements by employee teams, opportunities to attend workshops and seminars, and the typical announcements from human resources. The objective is to make employees feel that they are being informed of company affairs.

An organizational newsletter aimed at an outside audience, members of the organization, or both, may contain items about political trends that could affect the organization, announcements of new programs, brief human interest stories, and features on community involvement. Many nonprofit groups have newsletters for their contributors to let them know how the organization is using their money and what programs are being funded. A newsletter is a brisk compilation of highlights and tidbits, not a place for contemplative essays or discussion.

The next step up from the newsletter is a newspaper, usually in tabloid format, that has a masthead, a number of photos, and the type of headlines that one would see in a regular weekly or daily newspaper. Many of these publications use extensive color throughout and can run up to 16 pages. *AT&T Now*, for example, is an eight-page tabloid that portrays a modern, up-to-date corporation. Jean Hurt, editor, describes the publication in the following way:

> In order to be an inviting employee-focused publication, we feature many names and faces. We bring AT&T's strategy to life by showing how AT&T people contribute to it. The look is contemporary and clean. Vibrant color and photography, particularly large frontpage photos, add interest and helps us compete against overflowing in boxes and commercial media. Liberal use of call-outs, headline decks, and sidebars serves the reader who prefers to scan. To better link our stories to the company's strategy, we accompany many stories with a small box containing a strategic summary.

A magazine is the apex of organizational publications. It is the most elaborate in terms of color, graphics, paper stock, and design. And it's always the most expensive to produce. Accenture's glossy magazine has an annual budget of $700,000. Boeing spends $500,000 on its quarterly *Aero* magazine. In general, magazines are written for specific audiences, which can include (1) employees and retirees, (2) stockholders and investors, (3) wholesalers of company products, and (4) consumers. See page 375 for the cover of Z, the magazine of the Cleveland Zoological Society.

The writing and designing of organizational periodicals is a multifaceted process, which space doesn't allow us to delve into here. However, the Insights box on page 376 gives some tips that are applicable for newsletters, newspapers, and magazines.

The Cleveland Zoological Society reaches its members and prospective contributors through a well-designed four-color magazine, simply titled "Z". (Design: Nesnadny + Schwartz: Cleveland + New York + Toronto)

Electronic Newsletters

Many organizations supplement their printed publications with electronic newsletters and magazines. In many instances, organizations are completely eliminating print publications. Electronic publications are known as *e-zines*, and their primary advantage is the instant dissemination of information to employees or members via a listserv.

Another major advantage of electronic newsletters, of course, is cost. An average print newsletter might cost up to 50 cents per individual copy, whereas an e-zine typically costs less than 5 cents per copy. Most rely on a simple format, which means text only, limited use of color, limited graphics, no photos, and no fancy design effects. This is because e-zines, which are sent via e-mail, are received on a variety of different e-mail systems around the world, many with limited graphics capabilities.

Electronic newsletters should be kept to three to five window panes at maximum. Individual news items should also be short, about 10 to 12 lines each. The writing style should be punchy and somewhat more informal than regular print publications. Most people don't like to scroll through a long newsletter. Most readers will only scan the newsletter for items of interest.

ON THE JOB insights

How to Create Newsletters and Brochures

Newsletters and brochures should be designed to convey information in an attractive, uncluttered way. Here are some guidelines:

Copy

- Less is better. Use short, punchy sentences. Keep paragraphs short.
- Use informative subheads to break up copy blocks.
- Use bullets to list key points.
- Summarize and repeat the two or three main points.
- Tell the complete story in headlines or pull-out quotes.
- Keep the reader in mind; what does he or she need to get out of the story?
- Use quotes from credible, outside sources.

Layout

- Don't try to fill every space; allow for plenty of white space.
- Organize layout from left to right and top to bottom. Most people read in this sequence.

- Avoid large blocks of reverse type (white on black background). It's difficult to read.
- Avoid photos and artwork as background screens for copy; it's also difficult to read.
- Facing pages should be composed as two-page spreads; that's how readers see them.
- Use graphics and photos to balance blocks of copy.
- Make photos and illustrations as large as possible. Whenever possible, use action-oriented photos.

Type

- The best type size for text is 10 or 11 point with 2 points of leading. If the audience is older people, increase the type size to 12 or 14 point.
- Use serif type for text. It is easier to read. Headlines can be set in sans serif type.
- Use a minimum number of fonts and type families. A three-ring circus of type is poor design and just confuses people.

- Use boldface sparingly. Use for subheads and for a few key words. Don't use it for an entire paragraph.
- Use italic type for emphasis sparingly, if at all.
- Avoid all caps in headlines. Capital and lowercase letters are more readable.

Color

- Use black ink for text. If you use a second color, apply it as a highlight to frame a story, a pull-quote (set in larger type), or an entire page.
- Headlines can use color, but the ink should be on the dark side rather than pastel.
- Avoid using extensive color on low-quality paper. If you have color, use coated stock (glossy) to get maximum color reproduction.

Source: Adapted from Dennis L. Wilcox. *Public Relations Writing & Media Techniques,* 5th ed. Boston: Allyn & Bacon, 2005, p. 352.

E-zines on Intranets

Many organizations, particularly large corporations, have established intranets for their employees. Essentially, an intranet works on the same principle as the Internet, but it is a private network within an organization for the exclusive use of employees and management. Intranets, because they are closed systems and the technical standards are set by the organization, are able to produce much more sophisticated electronic newsletters.

A good example of what is possible on an intranet is the online publication of HP, which is sent daily to 140,000 HP employees in 37 nations. *HPNow* is an attractive newsletter that includes color, graphics, photos, and links to thousands of archived pages that contain everything from past issues to news releases, speeches, organizational charts, position papers, and employee awards.

A typical issue of *HPNow* will have about three to eight stories, ranging in length from one paragraph to 2,000 words. Feature stories about HP products and how they are being used is a prominent feature of the publication. One article, complete with color photos, discussed the role of HP computers in the making of Dreamworks' animated film *Sinbad: Legend of the Seven Seas*.

Brochures

Writing brochures, like producing newsletters and magazines, requires the coordination of several elements. These include message content, type selection, graphics layout, and design. Public relations personnel, who are often charged with writing content, work with designers and printers to make the final product.

Brochures are often called *booklets*, *pamphlets*, or *leaflets*, depending on their size and content. A pamphlet or booklet, for example, is characterized by a booklike format and multiple pages. An example of a booklet is a corporate annual report.

A leaflet is often described as a single piece of paper printed on both sides and folded into three panels, giving it a 4-by-9-inch format. Handbills and flyers are printed on one side of a page and are often placed on bulletin boards. For the purposes of this section, however, the term *brochure* will be used for all of these formats.

Brochures are used primarily to give information about an organization, a product, or a service. Organizations mail them or hand them out to potential customers, place them in information racks, hand them out at conferences, and generally distribute them to anyone who wants basic information. Whenever an organization needs to explain something to a large number of people—employees, constituents, or customers—a brochure is a good way to do it.

The following are some basic questions to answer when planning a brochure:

- Who is the audience? What are its characteristics? Is it a particular demographic in terms of education, income, or ethnic background?

- What is the brochure supposed to accomplish? Is it to impress, entertain, sell, inform, or educate?

- What is the best format for getting the message across? Should it be a simple flier, a pocket-sized brochure, a cheaply printed leaflet, or a four-color brochure?

Factors such as budget, the number of copies needed, and the intended distribution method also must be considered. Whatever the format, the writer should keep it in mind as copy is developed. The most common mistake is to write more than the proposed format can accommodate. A second mistake is to cram everything in by reducing the type size or margins, making it difficult to read the text. In other words, less is best so that there is adequate room for white space and graphics.

The concept of good writing also applies to brochures. Short, declarative sentences are better than compound sentences. Short paragraphs are better than long ones. Major points should be placed in headlines, bulleted, or boldface. See the Insights box on page 376 for tips on how to write an effective brochure.

Annual Reports

The most expensive and time-consuming brochure prepared by an organization is the annual report. This is a fairly extensive print document complete with photos, charts, text, and color that is primarily produced for institutional and individual stockholders of a publicly held corporation.

Although many annual reports are fairly glitzy and strive to portray the organization as a well-run, successful company, much of the financial information provided is to satisfy the legal requirements of the SEC. The Sarbanes-Oxley Act (discussed in Chapter 12) has added even more requirements regarding accountability and the disclosure of information.

All of this legal and financial material, of course, is a dry accounting of what the company did in the previous year. Most public corporations tend to place all of this material at the back of the annual report and use the first half of the report to write about the company's success or strategy for the future in plain English. One major reason is that the annual report, given its cost, also doubles as a marketing tool that can help build stockholder loyalty, attract new investors, and even increase the company's customer base. As Bob Butter of Ketchum's global practice told *PRWeek*, "The annual report is still a company's most rounded capability presentation."

The theme of General Motors' 2003 annual report was "drive." After the CEO's letter to the stockholders, the report devoted almost 40 pages to its "great products" by showing lavish photos of GM's entire automobile line and the various markets for them. The next 40 pages carried all of the financial statistics in small type. Thus, the average stockholder got the highlights—and a review of today's models—and the stock analysts got the detailed financial data.

Public Relations Advertising

Traditionally, *advertising* is defined as purchased space or time that is used to sell goods or services. However, another form of advertising is used for public relations purposes. This form of advertising is sometimes called *corporate advertising* or *institutional advertising*. Such advertising is also paid space, but its primary purpose is to enhance public perceptions of the organization or to explain its viewpoint on a particular issue.

Such advertisements supplement regular public relations tactics such as news releases, op-ed articles, and even letters to the editor. Ads, however, can amplify the message and even receive greater visibility because organizations often purchase an entire page in a publication such as the *New York Times* or the *Wall Street Journal*.

Public relations advertising can be divided into four basic types: (1) general image building, (2) investor and financial relations, (3) advocacy, and (4) public service.

Image Building

Image-building advertising is intended primarily to strengthen a company's identity in the eyes of the public. Conglomerates whose divisions market unrelated products often use such advertising as a branding strategy.

Others use it to correct an unfavorable public impression. Wal-Mart, for example, used image-building advertisements to improve its corporate reputation after considerable negative media coverage regarding a class action suit for discriminating against women employees, charges by the federal government that the company hired illegal workers to clean stores, and local opposition to building new superstores. See the PR Casebook on page 108 in Chapter 4.

One full-page ad in the *Wall Street Journal*, for example, highlighted "Wal-Mart's Teacher of the Year Program" and its donation of $500,000 to the schools of state winners. The ad further states that Wal-Mart will contribute over $40 million to education in 2004. Corporate citizenship and reputation are very much on the minds of executives of the sixth largest corporation in the world.

Toyota, the Japanese automaker, regularly runs image advertisements in major U.S. magazines reaching opinion leaders to reinforce its contributions to the U.S. economy. Toyota's concern is the occasional calls by politicians and labor groups advocating more "protectionism" for American companies from foreign competition. Consequently, Toyota wants to reinforce its image as a good U.S. citizen. Here's the text of one Toyota ad:

> **Our blue-sky scenario**:
> **More U.S. manufacturing jobs**,
> **Cleaner**
> **U.S. manufacturing plants**.

Since 1986, Toyota has been building vehicles and creating manufacturing jobs in the U.S. Today, with our eight manufacturing plants, sales and marketing operations, research and design facilities, and through our dealers and suppliers, Toyota's U.S. operations account for more than 190,000 jobs! And with two new state of the art manufacturing facilities being built to strict environmental standards, we're continuing our commitment to responsible growth as an employer, and a neighbor.

Financial Relations

The second form of public relations advertising is aimed at stockholders and the financial community. A corporation often uses advertising to depict its financial strength and prospects to attract more investors.

On occasion, such advertising is done to counter negative news reports about a company's financial troubles or the fact that a top executive has been charged with improper accounting methods. Tyco, for example, used such ads to reassure investors that its new management was taking the proper steps after the former CEO was charged with financial fraud.

Advertising also is used extensively during proxy fights for control of companies or when a company is under attack from a competitor that has made an attractive offer to purchase shares from individual investors. PeopleSoft, for example, used extensive advertising to resist a takeover by Oracle Corporation. HP also used ads to assure stockholders that its purchase of Compaq was in their best interests.

Advocacy

The third, sometimes controversial, form of public relations advertising is advocacy. In such advertisements, corporations or associations try to influence public opinion—or even Congress—on a political or social issue. Only a small portion of public relations advertising by corporations is spent on advocacy, but many activist organizations, such as People for the Ethical Treatment of Animals (PETA), often take out ads encouraging citizen action on topics of public interest.

The Humane Society of the United States, for example, took out full-page ads in leading newspapers to protest Canada's decision to allow the harvesting of baby seals for their fur. The headline, in red and graphically bleeding, said, "O Canada, How Could You?" The ad gave information to readers on how to write their Congressional representative and also send letters to the prime minister of Canada.

Other forms of advocacy ads placed by special interest and political groups will be discussed in Chapter 18.

Public Service

Many nonprofit groups purchase advertising to inform and educate the public about a particular topic. In many instances, newspapers and magazines donate the space. The American Heart Association, for example, places ads that seek to educate people about the warning signs of a heart attack. It also places ads that warn people of the dangers of obesity and how being overweight can lead to heart attacks.

The Council on American-Islamic Relations (CAIR) engaged in an extensive education campaign after 9/11 to counter American stereotypes and prejudice about Islam. The series of ads, titled "I'm an American and I'm a Muslim," profiled Muslims who were professionals and solid citizens in their respective communities. The ads also tried to educate Americans about Islamic religious beliefs and practices. Its advertisements can be viewed at www.americanmuslims.info.

A public service campaign by the Texas Association Against Sexual Assault (TAASA) used traditional public relations tactics and advertising to create public awareness of sexual assault as a major problem. Each ad featured an actual survivor of sexual assault talking about her personal story. The campaign's goal was to raise awareness of sexual assault crisis services and to encourage public dialogue. See page 381 for an example of one advertisement that was used.

See the Insights box on page 379 for some basic elements in effective advertisements.

I was raped...
And at first I didn't tell anyone.
I was ashamed. I felt
so disposable.

A guy I met down at
Padre drugged and
raped me. At first,
I was in denial. But
the more I didn't talk
about it, the more it
was on my mind. Then,
I started talking about
it. And I haven't
stopped. Today, eight
months after, I have
good days and bad.
But more good than
bad.
I'm working on healing.
I'm talking.
my name is maggie.
I am a rape survivor.

TAASA
Texas Association Against Sexual Assault
Speak up. Speak out.
1·800·656·HOPE   taasa.org
Grant funded by Greg Abbott, Attorney General of Texas

The Texas Association Against Sexual Assault (TAASA) used traditional public relations techniques and advertising to create public awareness. Each ad, which also was used as posters, featured an actual survivor of a sexual assault, talking about her personal story.

PR CASEBOOK

It's Corny, but It Worked

Product publicity is one of the most difficult assignments in public relations because media gatekeepers are always sensitive about giving away "free advertising" to a company that's promoting a particular product.

Morgan & Myers, a public relations firm in Minneapolis, was able to surmount media skepticism with a creative media campaign for a relatively mundane product—microwave popcorn.

Golden Valley Microwave Foods, another Minnesota firm, wanted to introduce its new product, Act II Kettle Corn, that combined salt and a sweet taste in the same product. It already was the world's largest manufacturer of microwave popcorn, selling its Act II Orville Redenbacher's and Healthy Choice brands in 30 nations around the world.

Morgan & Myers came up with a media kit that attracted considerable media interest. Research showed that a large percentage of people eat microwave popcorn while watching rented videos at home, so the firm decided to package the media kit in a standard video case with the typical movie packaging.

The cover art on the case was a couple on a beach holding hands at sunset and the title, "When Sweet Met Salty." The subhead added, "Two unlikely opposites make one delicious couple." There was even the film reviewer comment, "This tasty romance had me craving more—Juliet Cruncher, Boston Popper." On the back cover, more reviews: "A delicious pair—Roger Corn, Los Angeles Grocery News."

The media kit was inside the video box. It contained (1) a pitch letter to editors, (2) a news release about the new product, (3) a fact sheet about the nutritional qualities of the product, (4)

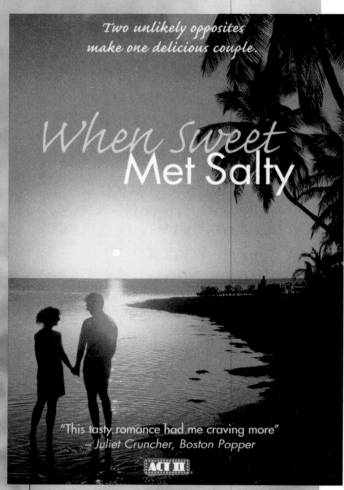

People often watch rented movies at home and eat popcorn, so Kettle Corn designed a media kit in the shape of a VHS movie box.

two 35-mm color slides showing a bowl of popcorn and the product package, (5) a media advisory about sponsorship of a civic event, "The Taste of Minnesota," where the company dispensed samples from a 1930 model A truck, and (6) a CD of all the media materials in digital form. These media materials are shown throughout this chapter.

The result: Nearly a third of the media in cities where Act II brands were strongest covered the story. Stories also appeared in major online and print media in 10 of the top major media markets, including *Newsday* and the *Chicago Tribune*. Virtually all news stories communicated two company messages: (1) Act II Kettle Corn was the first product of its kind on the market and (2) the distinctive sweet-salty flavor was the hallmark of kettle corn.

The campaign received the Bronze Anvil for Product Media Kits from the PRSA.

SUMMARY

The News Release

The news release is the most commonly used public relations tactic. News releases are sent to journalists and editors for possible use in the news columns, and they are the source for a large percentage of articles that are published. News releases must be accurate, informative, and written in journalistic style.

Publicity Photos

Publicity photos often accompany news releases to make a story more appealing. Photos must be high resolution and well composed. A photo can be made more interesting by manipulating the camera angle and lighting and by showing scale and action. Color photos are now commonly used in most publications.

Media Advisories and Fact Sheets

Advisories, or alerts, let journalists know about an upcoming event such as a news conference or photo or interview opportunities. Fact sheets give the 5 Ws and H of an event in outline form. Fact sheets also can be used to provide background on an executive, a product, or an organization.

Media Kits

A media kit, or press kit, is typically a folder containing news releases, photos, fact sheets, and features about a new product, an event, or other newsworthy projects undertaken by an organization. Many media kits are now produced in CD format to save costs.

Pitch Letters

Public relations personnel "pitch" journalists and editors with story ideas about their employer or client. Such pitches can be letters, e-mails, or even telephone calls. A good pitch is based on research and a creative idea that will appeal to the editor.

Distribution of Publicity Materials

Publicity materials can be distributed in five ways: (1) mail, (2) fax, (3) e-mail, (4) electronic wire services, and (5) Web pressrooms. Each has its advantages and disadvantages. Increasingly, publicity materials are distributed electronically.

Newsletters and Magazines

Newsletters are relatively economical to produce and are used to convey information in a relatively simple format. Many newsletters are now distributed via e-mail and listservs. Intranets allow organizations to distribute newsletters with highly sophisticated graphics on a daily basis. The second level of organizational publication is tabloid newspapers, which have more photos and graphics than newsletters do. The apex of organizational publishing is the four-color magazine.

Brochures

The objective of brochures is to inform and educate. Brochures come in all sizes and formats. For mass distribution, a relatively simple brochure or flier is the most economical. Annual reports for publicly owned corporations are mandated by the SEC, but most companies also use the annual report as a marketing tool.

Public Relations Advertising

Organizations may use paid space, or advertising, as part of their public relations outreach. Such advertising can be used for (1) image building and reputation enhancement, (2) financial relations, (3) advocacy, and (4) public service.

Case Activity: **What Would You Do?**

The Cleveland Repertory Theater will move into a new home next month. The $25 million building is part of the city's downtown redevelopment plan. The facility has state-of-the-art lighting and sound, seating for 750, and rooms for drama workshops. The architect is Skinner & Associates, and the contractor is BK Industries. Julie Andrews, star of stage and screen, will be the guest of honor at the official opening.

Write a general news release about the Repertory Theater and its planned grand opening. Second, write a pitch letter to the local media encouraging them to do feature stories about the new facility in advance of the opening. Third, write a media alert or advisory letting the press know that Julie Andrews will be available for interviews on a particular day. Fill in the appropriate quotations and information that you deem necessary.

QUESTIONS for Review and Discussion

1. What role do news releases play in the news process, and what ultimately appears in the newspaper or in the broadcast news show?

2. How should a news release be formatted? Why is the inverted pyramid structure used in news releases?

3. List at least six guidelines for writing a news release.

4. How does an e-mail news release differ from a standard news release?

5. Why is it a good idea to include a photograph with a news release? What six factors should be considered with regards to a publicity photo?

6. What's the difference between a media advisory and a fact sheet?

7. What's a media kit? What does a media kit typically contain?

8. Before pitching an item to a journalist or editor, why is it a good idea to first do some basic research on the individual, the publication, or the talk show?

9. Various methods can be used to deliver publicity materials to the media. Name the methods and compare their relative strengths and weaknesses. Some experts believe that e-mail is the ultimate distribution channel. Do you agree or disagree?

10. If you had a news release to distribute to daily newspapers in your region, what method would you use? Why?

11. What are the major advantages of electronic newsletters, or e-zines? Do you see any drawbacks?

12. Give some guidelines for writing and designing an effective newsletter or brochure.

13. There are four kinds of public relations advertising. Name them and give an example of each.

14. Wal-Mart, reacting to criticism of its policies and operations, has launched an image-reputation advertising campaign to give its viewpoint and to portray itself as a solid corporate citizen. Do you think such campaigns are effective? Why or why not?

SUGGESTED READINGS

Battenberg, Erik. "Design Guru Tells All: Tips for Publication Redesign." *Public Relations Tactics*, July 2002, pp. 1, 13.

Calabro, Sara. "Beyond the Wire: Enhancements in News Delivery." *PRWeek*, February 13, 2003, p. 18.

Cato, Sid. "The Legible Tangible Annual Report." *PRWeek*, April 22, 2001, p. 26.

Dysart, Joe. "E-mail Newsletters Dymystified." *Public Relations Tactics*, June 2003, p. 6.

Green, Sherri Deatherage. "All the News That's Fit to Download." *PRWeek*, April 26, 2004, p. 18.

Keppel, Don J. "So . . . . You Want a Brochure." *Public Relations Quarterly*, Summer 2003, pp. 43–44.

Hulin, Belinda. "What Do Editors Think? The Craft of Good Writing." *Public Relations Tactics*, February 2004, p. 19.

McGuire, Craig. "What a Difference a Yearly Report Makes." *PRWeek*, July 12, 2004, p. 18.

Oates, David B. "A Pitch Must Keep the Editor in Mind." *Public Relations Tactics*, December 2003, p. 13.

Pelham, Fran. "The Triple Crown of Public Relations: Pitch Letter, News Release, Feature Article." *Public Relations Quarterly*, Spring 2000, pp. 38–43.

Seitel, Fraser P. "A Good Lead Is the Key to Writing News Releases." *O'Dwyer's PR Services Report*, April 2004, pp. 37–38.

"Should You Keep the Media Enemies List? Fox News Does, but Our Experts Suggest Better Ways to Deal with Bad Coverage." *Ragan's Media Relations* Report, October 2004, pp. 1, 6.

Wilcox, Dennis L. *Public Relations Writing & Media Techniques*, 5th ed. Boston: Allyn & Bacon, 2005.

Wylie, Ann. "Clarify Complex Information with Metaphor." *Public Relations Tactics*, July 2004, p. 10.

Wylie, Ann. "Yes, You Can Make Your Press Release Creative." *Public Relations Tactics*, May 2004, p. 15.

Radio, Television, and the Web

Topics covered in this chapter include:

The Reach of Radio and Television

Broadcasting and its various forms, which now includes Webcasting, are important because they reach the vast majority of the American public on a daily basis. Each week, it is estimated that radio reaches 94 percent of Americans ages 12 and up, with a total audience of 223 million. A large percentage of this audience is reached in their cars; the average American now commutes nearly 50 minutes each workday.

Television also reaches a mass audience. The National Association of Broadcasters (NAB) says that local TV news attracts 150 million viewers. Network news reaches 30 million, and another 34 million are reached through regional and national cable shows.

Writing and preparing materials for broadcast and digital media, however, requires a special perspective. Instead of writing for the eye, a practitioner has to shift gears and think about adding audio and visual elements to the story. This chapter discusses the tactics used by public relations personnel, when they use radio, television, and the Web on behalf of their employers and clients.

Radio

News releases prepared for radio differ in several ways from releases prepared for print media. Although the basic identifying information is the same (letterhead, contact, subject), the standard practice is to write a radio release using all uppercase letters in a double-spaced format.

The length of the radio release should also be indicated. For example, "RADIO ANNOUNCEMENT: 30" or "RADIO ANNOUNCEMENT: 60." This indicates that the announcement will take 30 or 60 seconds to read.

The timing is vital, because broadcasters must fit their message into a rigid time frame that is measured down to the second. Most announcers read at a rate of 150 to 160 words per minute. Word lengths, of course, vary, so it's not feasible to set the timing based on the number of words in a message. Instead, the general practice is to use an approximate line count. With a word processor set for 60 spaces per line, the following standard can be applied:

2 lines = 10 seconds (about 25 words)

5 lines = 20 seconds (about 45 words)

8 lines = 30 seconds (about 65 words)

16 lines = 60 seconds (about 125 words)

The writing style of a radio release also differs. A news release for a newspaper uses standard English grammar and punctuation. Sentences often contain dependent and independent clauses. In a radio release, a more conversational style is used, and the emphasis is on strong, short sentences. This allows the announcer to breathe between thoughts and the listener to follow what is being said. An average sentence length of about 10 words is a good goal.

The following is an example of a 60-second news feature (153 words) distributed to radio stations by the North American Precis Syndicate for the National Automotive Parts Association (NAPA):

Car Care Corner

YOU CAN KEEP YOUR CAR, AND YOUR FAMILY ON THE ROAD TO SAFETY EVEN IN ROUGH WEATHER, IF YOU HEED A FEW HINTS. FIRST, HAVE YOUR BATTERY AND CHARGING SYSTEM TESTED BY A CERTIFIED TECHNICIAN. AN OLD BATTERY MAY FAIL IF IT HAS TO RUN LIGHTS, HEATER, DEFROSTER, DEFOGGER, AND WIPERS WHEN THE TEMPERATURE IS LOW. HAVE YOUR ANTIFREEZE CHANGED BY AN AUTOMOTIVE TECHNICIAN EVERY TWO YEARS. STEER CLEAR OF LOW TIRE INFLATION. A 30-DEGREE DROP IN TEMPERATURE CAN MAKE A FOUR TO FIVE POUND DIFFERENCE IN PRESSURE. LOW PRESSURE TIRES DON'T MEET THE ROAD PROPERLY OR SHED WATER EFFECTIVELY. CHECK TIRE WEAR. PUT A PENNY IN THE TREAD WITH LINCOLN'S HEAD DOWN. IF THE TOP OF HIS HEAD SHOWS, YOU NEED NEW TIRES. YOU CAN LEARN MORE FROM THE EXPERTS AT THE NATIONAL AUTOMOTIVE PARTS ASSOCIATION AT W-W-W—DOT—N-A-P-A—ON-LINE—DOT-COM.

Notice the spaces in the Web site address. This alerts the news announcer to read the URL slowly so people can remember it. The same rule is applied to telephone

ON THE JOB insights

Guidelines for Writing a Radio News Release

The following are tips from the Broadcast News Network, which writes and distributes news releases for a number of clients:

- Time is money in radio. Stories should be no longer than 60 seconds. Stories without actualities (soundbites) should be 30 seconds or less.
- The only way to time your story is to read it out loud, slowly.
- A long or overly commercial story is death. Rather than ed-

iting it, a busy radio newsperson will discard it.
- Convey your message with the smallest possible number of words and facts.
- A radio news release is not an advertisement; it is not a sales promotion piece. A radio news release is journalism—spoken.
- Announcers punctuate with their stories; not all sentences need verbs or subjects.
- Releases should be conversational. Use simple words and avoid legal-speak.

- After writing a radio news release, try to shorten every sentence.
- Listeners have short attention spans. Have something to say and say it right away.
- Never start a story with a name or a vital piece of information. While listeners are trying to figure out the person speaking and the subject matter, they don't pay attention to the specific information.

numbers, and oftentimes an address or telephone number is repeated a second time for listeners who are in the process of grabbing a pencil and pad.

Audio News Releases

Although broadcast-style news releases can be sent to radio stations for announcers to read, the most common and effective approach is to send the radio station a recording of the news announcement.

An *audio news release*, commonly called an *ANR*, can take two forms. One simple approach is for someone with a good radio voice to read the entire announcement; the person doing the reading may not be identified by name. This, in the trade, is called an *actuality*. The second approach is a bit more complicated, but still relatively easy to do. In this instance, an announcer is used, but a quote called a *soundbite* is included from a satisfied customer or a company spokesperson. This approach is better than a straight announcement because the message comes from a "real person" rather than a nameless announcer. This type of announcement is also more acceptable to stations; because the radio station's staff can elect to use the whole recorded announcement or take the role of announcer and just use the soundbite.

Format.   The preferred length for an ANR is one minute. However, shorter ones can be used. The audio recording should also be accompanied by a paper copy of the script. This enables the news director to judge the value of the tape without having to listen to it.

Here is a 60-second script for an ANR that includes a soundbite from a spokesperson. It was produced by Medialink for its client, Cigna Health Systems, and distributed to radio stations via satellite.

> **Worried at Work**
> **New Survey Shows American Workers Are Stressed Out**
> **But Can Take Simple Steps to Ease Workplace Tension**
>
> **SUGGESTED ANCHOR LEAD:** If you're feeling stressed out at work, you're not alone. A new survey shows economic uncertainty, dwindling retirement savings, and ongoing terrorist concerns have American workers increasingly stressed out. But as Roberta Facinelli explains, employees and employers alike can do things to counteract all this tension.
>
> **SCRIPT:** If you're like most American workers, you're facing increased stress on and off the job. In fact, according to a new nationwide study conducted by employee assistance experts at CIGNA Behavioral Health, almost half of employees surveyed have been tempted to quit their jobs over the past year, have quit, or are planning to soon, given the series of pressures they're facing. But according to CIGNA's Dr. Jodi Aronson Prohofsky, there are things you can do to ease workplace tension.
>
> **CUT (Aronson Prohofsky):** Simple changes in your lifestyle can help reduce stress. Exercising more often, volunteering, making time to read or engaging in a favorite hobby are all easy steps we can take. Many of us also take time out for reflection and meditation to deal with daily pressures.

SCRIPT: Employees often find workplace support programs a good place to start, so check with your employer. Many provide programs such as counseling services, flexible work schedules as well as nutrition and health programs—all of which can help reenergize stressed out workers to achieve a better work–life balance. I'm Roberta Facinelli.

SUGGESTED ANCHOR TAG: If you're interested in learning more about workplace stress reduction tips, visit www.cignabehavioral.com.

The Cigna script is an example of an ANR that gives information and tips to the listener in a conversational way. It contains helpful information about how to reduce stress and is not overly commercial. Cigna is mentioned in the context of the story, but primarily as a source of information. A station newsperson, no doubt, would find the subject current and newsworthy for the station's audience. Here's another ANR, which announces the results of a study. The 60-second "news release" was produced by West Glen Communications for the World Resources Institute. It was distributed in MP3 format by North American Network, Inc.

ANNOUNCER: A landmark report, released Thursday (July 10) calls for fundamental changes to how decisions are made—and who makes them—concerning the world's natural resources. The report—**World Resources: 2002–2004: Decisions for the Earth—Balance, Voice and Power**—stresses that these changes are urgently needed, in order to arrest the growing deterioration of the world's environment. **World Resources Institute** president Jonathan Lash. . . .

LASH: "Despite 10 years of resounding declarations and international environmental agreements, environmental problems are still getting worse in much of the world. The best way to change these trends is to inform people, empower them, and get them engaged."

ANNOUNCER: The report calls for the inclusion of the public in the decision-making process, strengthening the current loose international system of environmental governance; and better disclosure from business. It warns that nongovernmental organizations should adhere to the same standards of accountability and transparency they are asking from government and business.

Production and Delivery. Every ANR starts with a carefully written and accurately timed script. The next step is to record the words. When recording, it is imperative to control the quality of the sound. A few large organizations have complete recording studios, some hire radio station employees as consultants, but most organizations use a professional recording service.

Professional recording services have first-class equipment and skilled personnel. They can take a script, edit it, eliminate words or phrases that will not be understandable, record it at the proper sound levels, and produce a finished tape suitable for broadcasting.

Radio news stories and features can be produced in multiple copies on cassette or CD-ROM. The most common method, and the most economical, is to burn the recording to CD. In addition, the MP3 or iPod format for digital files is becoming increasingly popular.

Radio stations, like newspapers, have preferences about how they want to receive audio news releases. One survey by DWJ Television found that almost 75 percent of the radio news directors prefer to receive actualities by phone. This is particularly true for late-breaking news events in the station's service area. When a forest fire threatened vineyards in California's Napa Valley, a large winery contacted local stations and offered an ANR with a soundbite from the winery's president telling everyone that the grape harvest would not be affected. About 50 stations were called, and 40 accepted the ANR for broadcast use.

Organizations sending ANRs for national distribution usually use satellite or the World Wide Web.

Use of ANRs.   Producing ANRs is somewhat of a bargain compared with producing materials for television. Ford Motor Company, for example, spent $3,500 for national distribution of a news release on battery recycling as part of Earth Day activities. More than 600 radio stations picked up the ANR, and about 5 million people were reached. Despite their cost-effectiveness, an ANR should not be sent to every station. Stations have particular demographics. A release about the benefits of vitamin supplements for senior citizens isn't of much interest to a rock music station.

The use of ANRs is increasingly popular with radio stations. Thom Moon, director of operations at *Duncan's American Radio Quarterly*, told *PRWeek* that he thinks the major reason for this is the consolidation of ownership in radio broadcasting (Clear Channel now owns 1200 stations), which has resulted in cost-cutting and fewer news personnel.

Jack Trammell, president of VNR-1 Communications, echoed this thought. He told *pr reporter*, "They're telling us they're being forced to do more with less. As long as radio releases are well produced and stories don't appear to be blatant commercials, newsrooms are inclined to use them." Trammell conducted a survey of radio stations and found that 83 percent of them use radio news releases (RNRs). And 34 percent said such releases give them ideas for local stories. The news editors look for regional interest (34 percent), health information (23 percent), and financial news (11 percent). They also like technology stories, children's issues, politics, seasonal stories, and local interest issues.

Public Relations Tactics gives some additional tips from Trammell:

● **Topicality.** Stories may fail every other judgment criteria and still get airtime simply because they offer information on a hot topic. *Newsroom maxim:* News is about issues that matter to the majority of our listeners or viewers.

● **Timeliness.** Stories should be timed to correspond with annual seasons, governmental rulings, new laws, social trends, etc. *Newsroom maxim:* The favorite word in broadcasting is *now* followed by *today* and then *tomorrow*. The least favorite word is *yesterday*.

● **Localization.** Newsrooms emphasize local news. A national release should be relevant to a local audience. Reporters are always looking for the "local angle." *Newsroom maxim:* If it's not local, it's probably not news.

● **Humanization.** Show how real people are involved or affected. Impressive graphics and statistics mean nothing to audiences without a human angle. *Newsroom maxim:* People relate to people—and animals.

● **Visual appeal.** Successful stories provide vibrant, compelling soundbites or video footage that subtly promotes, but also illustrates and explains. *Newsroom maxim:* Say dog, see dog.

Additional tips about writing radio news releases are given in the Insights box on page 388.

Radio Public Service Announcements

Public relations personnel working for nonprofit organizations often prepare public service announcements (PSAs) for radio stations.

A *PSA* is defined by the FCC as an unpaid announcement that promotes the programs of government or voluntary agencies or that serves the public interest. In general, as part of their responsibility to serve the public interest, radio and TV stations provide airtime to charitable and civic organizations to make the public aware of and educate them about such topics as heart disease, mental illness, and AIDs.

According to DWJ Television, a video producer, PSAs give various government and nonprofit organizations an opportunity to use the same channels of communication as major advertisers, but at only a fraction of the cost. DWJ further states, "It is not unusual for a television campaign, produced and distributed on a budget of $25,000 to $40,000, to get airtime that would have cost $1 [million] to $5 million or more for paid advertising."

Profit-making organizations do not qualify for PSAs despite their claims of "public service," but sometimes an informational campaign by a trade group qualifies. For example, the Aluminum Association received airtime on a number of stations by producing a PSA about how to recycle aluminum cans. Before the announcement was released, the association received an average of 453 calls a month. Five months after the PSA began appearing, the association had received 9,500 calls at its toll-free number. The PSA was used in 46 states, and 244 stations reported 16,464 broadcasts of the announcement.

Format and Production.   Radio PSAs, like radio news releases, are written in uppercase and double-spaced. Their length can be 60, 30, 20, 15, or 10 seconds. And, unlike radio news releases, the standard practice is to submit multiple PSAs on the same subject in various lengths.

The idea is to give the station flexibility in using a PSA of a particular length to fill a specific time slot. DWJ Television explains: "Some stations air PSAs in a way that relates length to time of play, for example, placing one length in their early news shows and another in the late news shows. Supplying both lengths allows a campaign to be heard by those who only watch one of these shows."

Not all PSAs, however, are incorporated into a radio news show. PSAs, like advertisements, may be used during breaks in regular entertainment programming. Radio news releases, however, are confined to being read during a regular news program.

PSAs can be delivered in the same way as radio news releases. Scripts can simply be mailed to the station for reading by announcers. Another popular approach is to mail stations a cassette or CD with announcements of varying lengths. Once a recording is made, it also can be transmitted via telephone.

Here is a basic PSA produced by the American Red Cross, which shows how the same topic can be treated in various lengths:

20 seconds

Ever give a gift that didn't go over real big? One that ended up in the closet the second you left the room? There is a gift that's guaranteed to be well received. Because it will save someone's life. The gift is blood, and it's desperately needed. Please give blood. There's a life to be saved right now. Call the American Red Cross at 1-800-GIVE LIFE.

60 seconds

We want you to give a gift to somebody, but it's not a gift you buy. We want you to give a gift, but not necessarily to someone you know. Some of you will be happy to do it. Some of you may be hesitant. But the person who receives your gift will consider it so precious, they'll carry it with them the rest of their life. The gift is blood and, every day in America, thousands of people desperately need it. Every day, we wonder if there will be enough for them. Some days, we barely make it. To those of you who give blood regularly, the American Red Cross and the many people whose lives you've saved would like to thank you. Those of you who haven't given recently, please help us again There's a life to be saved right now. To find out how convenient it is to give blood, call the American Red Cross today at 1-800-GIVE-LIFE. That's 1-800-GIVE-LIFE.

Another PSA script, showing sound and music, is shown in the Insights box on page 394.

Use of Radio PSAs. Almost any topic or issue can be the subject of a PSA. Stations, however, seem to be more receptive to particular topics. A survey of radio station public affairs directors by West Glen Communications, a producer of PSAs, found that local community issues and events were most likely to receive airtime, followed by children's issues. The respondents also expressed a preference for PSAs involving health and safety, service organizations, breast cancer, and other cancers.

The majority of respondents also prefer PSAs that include a local phone number rather than a national toll-free number. Because of this preference, many national groups, including the American Cancer Society, have a policy of distributing scripts to chapters that can be "localized" before they are sent to radio stations.

Other studies have shown that an organization needs to provide helpful information in a PSA and not make a direct pitch for donations. Radio stations tend to shun PSAs that ask people for money. A more subtle approach is to tell people about the organization and give them a phone number or a Web site to get more information— and perhaps make a donation once they know about the organization.

Radio Media Tours

Another public relations tactic for radio is the *radio media tour (RMT)*. Essentially, a spokesperson conducts a series of around-the-country, one-on-one interviews with radio announcers from a central location. A public relations practitioner (often called

ON THE JOB insights

Adding Music and Sound to a PSA

You can make your radio PSA more interesting if you take the time to incorporate music and other sounds (SFX) into the speaker's script (VO). The Santa Clara County (California) Network for a Hate Free Community distributed this PSA in a CD format to radio stations in the area.

Don't Teach Hate (60 Seconds)

MUSIC   MUSIC BOX VERSION OF "WHEELS ON THE BUS"

SFX: BABY TALK, CHILDREN LAUGHING

VO: **AT SIX WEEKS BABIES LEARN TO SMILE**.

SFX: BABY COOING

VO: **BY SIX MONTHS THEY WILL RESPOND TO DIFFERENT COLORS**.

SFX: BABY LAUGHING

VO: **AT SIXTEEN MONTHS, THEY DEVELOP A SENSE OF SELF**.

SFX: BABY SAYS "MINE!"

VO: **AT WHAT AGE DO THEY LEARN TO HATE?**

SFX: (PAUSE—MUSIC STOPS)

SFX: HORN HONKS, BRAKES SLAM.

ANGRY MAN'S VOICE: JEEZ, FREAKIN' FOREIGNERS, TOO DAMN STUPID TO OPERATE A CAR. YOU OKAY, BACK THERE, SPORT?

(MUSIC UP)

BABY'S VOICE: "M OKAY DADDY.

VO: **THEY LEARN TO HATE WHEN YOU TEACH THEM. YOUR CHILDREN ARE LISTENING AND THEY'RE LEARNING FROM YOU. INSULTS AND SLURS BASED ON RACE, RELIGION, DISABILITY, GENDER OR SEXUAL ORIENTATION TEACH CHILDREN IT'S OKAY TO HATE. HATE IS THE ENEMY IN SANTA CLARA COUNTY AND YOU ARE ON THE FRONT LINE.**

To report a hate crime or to receive services, call the Santa Clara County Network for a Hate Free Community at (408) 792-2304.

a *publicist* in such a situation) prebooks telephone interviews with DJs, news directors, or talk show hosts around the country, and the personality simply gives interviews over the phone that can be broadcast live or recorded for later use.

A major selling point of the RMT is its relatively low cost and the convenience of giving numerous short interviews from one central location. David Thalberg, vice president of Ruder/Finn, told *Ragan's Media Relations Report*, "You don't have to go to a station and put on a suit. Your client can do the interview over the phone, seated in his or her office, with all the supplementary material he or she needs to come across as authoritative and informed."

Laurence Mosowitz, president of Medialink, echos this aspect of convenience. He told *PRWeek*, "It is such an easy, flexible medium. We can interview a star in bed at his hotel and broadcast it to the country. Radio is delicious."

A major multinational pharmaceutical concern, Schering-Plough, used an RMT to point out that most smokers in the United States fail to recognize the warning signs of chronic bronchitis. Of course, the company makes a drug for such a condition. The RMT was picked up by 88 stations with an audience of more than 2.8 million. The RMT was part of a campaign that also used a *satellite media tour (SMT)* for television stations. SMTs are discussed in the next section.

Television

There are four approaches for getting an organization's news and viewpoints on local television. The first approach is to simply send the same news release that the local print media receive. If the news director thinks the topic is newsworthy, the item may become a brief 10-second mention by the announcer on a news program. A news release may also prompt the assignment editor to consider visual treatment of the subject and assign the topic to a reporter and a camera crew for follow-up.

A second approach is a media alert or advisory informing the assignment editor about a particular event or occasion that would lend itself to video coverage. Media alerts, which were discussed in the last chapter, can be sent via e-mail, fax, or even regular mail.

The third approach is to phone or e-mail the assignment editor and make a pitch to have the station do a particular story. The art of making a pitch to a television news editor is to emphasize the visual aspects of the story.

The fourth approach is to produce a *video news release (VNR)* that, like an ANR, is formatted for immediate use with a minimum of effort by station personnel. The VNR also has the advantage of being used by numerous stations on a regional, national, or even global basis.

Video News Releases

An estimated 5000 VNRs are produced annually in the United States. Large organizations seeking enhanced recognition for their names, products, services, and causes are the primary clients for VNRs. The production of VNRs can be more easily justified if there is potential for national distribution and multiple pickups by television stations and cable systems.

A typical 90-second VNR, says one producer, costs a minimum of $20,000 to $50,000 for production and distribution. Costs vary, however, depending on the number of location shots, special effects, the use of celebrities, and the number of staff required to produce a high-quality tape that meets broadcast standards.

Because of the cost, a public relations department or firm must carefully analyze the news potential of the information and consider whether the topic lends itself to a fast-paced, action-oriented visual presentation. A VNR should not be produced if there's nothing but talking heads, charts, and graphs. Another aspect to consider is whether the topic will still be current by the time the video is produced. On average, it takes four to six weeks to script, produce, and distribute a high-quality VNR. In a crisis situation or for a fast-breaking news event, however, a VNR can be produced in a matter of hours or days. The VNR for Segway in the Casebook on pages 413 and 414, for example, was produced in 10 days by Burson-Marsteller.

Another example of a fast response with a VNR is Pepsi. Within a week of news reports that syringes and other sharp objects had been found in cans of Diet Pepsi, the soft-drink company produced and distributed a VNR showing that the insertion of foreign objects into cans on their high-speed bottling lines was virtually impossible. This VNR, because of its timely nature and high public interest, reached a total of 186 million viewers and helped avoid a massive sales decline of Pepsi products.

When some customers claimed they had found syringes in Pepsi cans, the company distributed a video news release (VNR) showing that the intrusion into its high-speed bottling process was virtually impossible. The claim proved to be a hoax.

Format. Writing a script for a VNR is a bit more complicated than writing one for an ANR because the writer has to visualize the scene, much like a playwright or screenwriter. Adam Shell, in *Public Relations Tactics*, describes the required skills:

> Producing a VNR requires expert interviewing skills, speedy video editing, creative eye for visuals, and political savvy. The job of the VNR producer is not unlike that of a broadcast journalist. The instincts are the same. Engaging soundbites are a result of clever questioning. Good pictures come from creative camera work. A concise, newsworthy VNR comes from good writing and editing. Deadlines have to be met, too. And then there's all the tiny details and decisions that have to be made on the spot. Not to mention figuring out subtle ways to make sure the client's signage appears on the video without turning off the news directors.

Perhaps the best way to illustrate some of Shell's comments is to show a typical VNR script. See pages 397 to 399 for a script prepared by Medialink for Beringer Vineyards.

Production. Although public relations writers can easily handle the job of writing radio news releases and doing basic announcements for local TV stations, the production of a VNR is another matter. The entire process is highly technical, requiring trained professionals and sophisticated equipment.

Consequently, public relations departments and firms usually outsource production to a firm specializing in scripting and producing VNRs. Public relations personnel, however, usually serve as liaison and give the producer an outline of what the VNR is supposed to accomplish. The public relations person also will work with the producer to line up location shots, props, and the individuals who will be featured.

Medialink, a major producer and distributor of VNRs, gives some tips about the production of VNRs that best meet the needs of TV news directors:

● Give TV news directors maximum flexibility in editing the tape using their own anchors or announcers. This can be done by producing the VNR on split audio

VISUAL	**AUDIO**

Medialink

FADE IN:

Suggested Anchor Lead-in:

Despite the economy and world events, things are going "GRAPE" in California's wine country. The "CRUSH," officially underway in the heart of wine country, is the most exciting time of year. Grapes generate (help generate) billions of dollars in travel, tourism, jobs and sales. Especially in the Napa Valley where wine makers consistently create some of the world's finest wine. The buzz this year? A later than usual harvest may produce even higher quality wines.

As Mother nature places the finishing touches on this year's grape harvest, wine lovers are out in force, pursuing their passion in restaurants, hotels and wine tasting rooms. If the bottom line is good taste, Elizabeth Anderson uncorks some vintage secrets.

NAT SOT (:04 approx)

NARRATION

Coming to a glass near you...

Pour Nouveau-Beringer

The grapes of California's crush.

Crush, picking-harvest

92% of America's wine is produced in California...some of the world's best in Napa Valley.

Wine, grapes

Napa beauty shot

Beringer's Nouveau, the first wine of the 2002 vintage, will beat all California wines to market. Of the Golden State's 847 wineries, this landmark is the oldest in Napa Valley...bottling award-winning magic for 125 years.

Wine picking, crush-harvest.

Nouveau, Beringer beauty shots, famous

NAT SOT Beringer Winemaker

Exteriors, wine is poured.

"The grapes are ready...just the right sugar content."

See Beringer name of famous real estate

Historical video (from tv cmxl)

B-roll to complement what he says

Continuously show various vineyards – St. Clements, Stags Leap

Barrels, caves

Dissolve to: Beringer and awards See 4

The script of a video news release requires thinking about the visuals at the same time that you write copy and plan for interview excerpts. This two-column format, showing visual and audio components, shows how a script is written.

Medialink

VISUAL	AUDIO
winery of the year awards -- better than saying it -- articles, visuals, awards, Beringer Winemaker walks and tastes grapes in vineyards	**NARRATION** Beringer's legendary winemaker knows the secret to good taste. **SOT - Winemaker** "Making perfect wine means growing, harvesting and crushing perfect grapes at the right time in the best climate, using unique barrels & caves and land that, naturally, have the ideal temperature for storing/aging wine. Ingredients that cant be duplicated! Of California's wine country, Napa is a small region.but produces the best and most critically acclaimed wines. Due to a later than usual harvest this year, the wines are expected to be <u>even better</u>. Just some reasons why we consistently capture top winery awards over our traditional European competitors."
ON CAMERA B-roll to compliment what he says Continuously show various Vineyards-various, St. Clements, Stags Leap Barrels, caves Napa region visual. Beauty shots grapes, and wine. Sunrise, sunset Workers in field. Awards, articles or Beringer & industry Tourism: wining, dining, purchasing Lots of Nat Sot (natural sound) Harvest, Tourists, restaurant type activity Wine-sipping, etc. dissolve to:	
	NAT SOT :03 (harvest-crush-machinery) **NARRATION** The crush proves good things come in small packages: grapes are the state's 3rd leading crop.providing 145-thousand jobs and a \$33 billion dollar bottom line. NAT SOT (cheers!) If California were a nation, it would be the 4th leading wine-producing country behind Italy, France and Spain. Even in a tough economy,
Crush activity. Grapes splash into camera Agricultural activity Regional shots, tourists, perhaps purchasing wine. Wining, dining. Tourism, tourists in wine room Crowds toast, hear Japanese tourists toast	

(continued)

Medialink

VISUAL	AUDIO
in their language	This all American industry is wining, dining and growing!
Shopping and buying wine	
Scenery, tourism, wine tasting, etc.	**SOT: Napa Valley Wine Association Expert**
ON CAMERA *See this person in her own vineyard, as talks*	"Sales go up despite a volatile stock market or the economy. More people are cocooning.staying home…and what is better to enjoy at home than a good wine? Loyal consumers still spend for their favorite brand. Wine remains one of life's pleasures that is still affordable, you have a fabulous tourist destination…and a lot of history and art...all in one glass…it's magical"
Begin **Montage** of beauty shots	**NAT SOT (:01)**
Recapping what we've seen, visually	**NARRATION**
Cave gates open, see rare wines	It's a complex recipe of earth, light, air, hidden caves, historical vineyards and oak barrels of TLC…
Gate has Beringer Logo on it.	
Tourists mill thru barrels and caves, dissolves	**NAT SOT (glasses clink-toast) :02**
To caves, vineyards, barrels, etc.	**NARRATION**
Dissolve to:	The easy part….
Conclude with sunset, beauty shots	**NAT SOT (couple pours, sips Nouveau)**
Tasting and purchasing wine, closeup	**NARRATION**
Couple toasts, Pour wine. Beauty shot	..is up to you.
Wide shot winery, sunset, happy ending visual	**ELIZABETH ANDERSON REPORTING**
	SUGGESTED ANCHOR TAG
	This year's California harvest shows more Chardonnay grapes being crushed and bottled than anything else…followed by Cabernet, Zinfandel, Merlot, Chenin Blanc, Syrah-Shiraz and Sauvignon Blanc.
	Beringer's finest costs about $125.00. But, you can pay as little as $8-dollars and still have a 4-star experience.
	To find out more, click onto www.Beringer.com

(continued)

(the announcer track on one audio channel and the natural sound of the VNR on another). This way, the news director has the option of "stripping" the announcer's voice and inserting the voice of a local reporter or announcer.

● Produce the VNR with news footage in mind. Keep soundbites short and to the point. Avoid commercial-like shots with sophisticated effects.

● Never superimpose your own written information on the actual videotape. TV news departments usually generate their own written notes in their own typeface and style.

● Never use a stand-up reporter. Stations do not want a reporter who is not on their own staff appearing in their newscast.

● Provide TV stations with a local angle. This can be done by sending supplemental facts and figures that reflect the local situation. This can be added to the VNR when it is edited for broadcast.

● Good graphics, including animation, are a plus. Stations are attracted to artwork that shows things in a clear, concise manner.

Delivery.   The VNR package should also include two or three minutes of B-roll, or background pictures, for use by the TV news producer in repackaging the story. Typical B-roll includes additional interviews, soundbites, and file footage. A Nielsen Media Research survey of 130 TV news directors, for example, found that 70 percent wanted a VNR with B-roll attached.

An advisory will accompany the VNR package or will be sent to news directors before the actual satellite transmission of the video to the station. The advisory, in printed form, should contain the basics: the key elements of the story, background and description of the visuals, editorial and technical contacts, satellite coordinates, and date/time of the transmission. Many stations prefer to receive this advisory by fax instead of e-mail or wire service. A fax is on printed paper and can be passed around the newsroom so many staffers can see it.

Satellite distribution is the most cost-effective way of distributing VNRs on a national or even global scale. In addition, it is the preferred method of most news directors. Virtually every television station in the country has at least one satellite receiving dish. The old method was analog transmission, but an increasing number of stations are now receiving digital transmissions via satellite.

Katie Sweeney, writing in *Public Relations Tactics*, explains the advantages of digital transmission: ". . . TV producers don't have to downlink a VNR at a scheduled time from a satellite feed. Instead the VNR file is sent directly to an assignment editor's desktop where the editor can preview it and decide whether to download at any time. Editors are able to select content, drag and drop files to other station systems, such as editing suites and play-to-air servers."

VNRs and other publicity material can also be distributed via Web-based systems, which will be discussed in the section on Webcasting.

On occasion, VNRs are not time sensitive in that the subject matter stays current for several months. Such VNRs are known as *evergreens*, because they are always in season. A VNR on research regarding AIDs, for example, could be held by a news editor for use in an eventual series, or a VNR from the U.S. Forest Service on how to prevent forest fires could be held in reserve until summer, when the danger of fire is highest. In these cases, organizations often mail the station a videotape or a DVD of the VNR.

Mail distribution also is used to send *stock footage*, standard video shots of a company's production line, headquarters, or other activities that a station can store until the company is in the news. Then, as the anchor gives the current news, the viewers see the stock footage on the screen.

Use of VNRs. Larry Moskowitz, president of Medialink, says every TV station in the United States uses VNRs in their newscasts. He told a radio show talk host, "We determined prima facie and scientifically and electronically that every TV station in America has used and probably uses regularly this material from corporations and organizations that we provide as VNRs, or B-roll." West Glen Communications estimates that 90 percent of the stations use VNRs.

These optimistic statistics, however, are tempered by the reality that TV stations today receive so many VNRs that they are overwhelmed. Consequently, the competition is intense, and unless the VNR meets multiple criteria, it won't be used. Even if it is used, public relations departments and firm must be realistic about audience reach. A well-done VNR, according to surveys, usually gets 40 to 50 station airings with an audience of 2 to 3 million people. In other words, for every VNR that gets millions of viewers, there are hundreds that don't. See the Insights box on this page for a list of the top 10 VNRs in a recent year.

Television Public Service Announcements. Television stations, like radio stations, use PSAs on behalf of governmental agencies, community organizations, and charitable groups. In fact, a survey by News Broadcast Network found that the typical TV station runs an average of 137 PSAs per week as part of its commitment to public service.

Many of the guidelines for radio PSAs, which were discussed previously, apply to television PSAs. They must be short, to the point, and professionally produced. Television is different, however, in that both audio

ON THE JOB insights

VNRs Reach Millions of People

Here's a list of the top 10 VNRs that, according to Nielsen Media Research, were used by television stations in a recent year:

- **Insurance Institute for Highway Safety (IIHS):** The crashworthiness of large pick-up trucks (213 million viewers, 1,855 airings)
- **British Airways:** Improvements to the Concorde (191 million viewers, 214 airings)
- **Buena Vista film studio:** Pearl Harbor world premiere (190 million viewers, 204 airings)
- **Insurance Institute for Highway Safety (IIHS):** SUV bumper crash test (157 million viewers, 1,332 airings)
- **Motorola:** The role of mobile phones (146 million viewers, 92 airings)
- **Insurance Institute for Highway Safety (IIHS):**

Crash-test results of Dodge Grand Caravan/ Hyundai Elantra (139 million viewers, 1,309 airings)
- **Ericsson:** Consumer-oriented technology products (130 million viewers, 181 airings)
- **European Space Agency:** The first European astronaut (121.6 million viewers, 298 airings)
- **Taco Bell:** The reentry of 15-year-old space station Mir as part of a product promotion (121 million viewers, 1,615 airings)
- **Novartis:** FDA approval of Gleevec oral therapy drug (120 million viewers, 1,062 airings)

Overall, the top 10 VNRs reached a total global audience of more than 1.5 billion viewers in the United States, Canada, Europe, Asia, and Australia.

and visual elements must be present. Even a simple PSA, consisting of the announcer reading text, is accompanied by photo or artwork that is shown on the screen at the same time.

The next step up is to have a spokesperson, such as a celebrity, talk directly into the camera for 30 seconds. The Anxiety Disorder Coalition, for example, used entertainer Donny Osmond to deliver its message. Here is the 30-second script for Osmond's appearance:

> **Donny Osmond on Camera:** A FEW YEARS AGO I COULDN'T HAVE WALKED ON THIS STAGE WITHOUT FEELING LIKE I WAS DYING INSIDE. THIS WASN'T ONLY FEAR OF PERFORMING. CERTAIN SIMPLE ACTIVITIES, SUCH AS GOING TO THE MALL OR INTERACTING WITH STRANGERS, WOULD PARALYZE ME WITH FEAR.
>
> I'M TALKING ABOUT A MEDICAL CONDITION CALLED SOCIAL ANXIETY DISORDER. WHEN THE FEAR OF BEING EMBARRASSED OR HUMILIATED IN FRONT OF OTHER PEOPLE CONTROLS YOUR LIFE.
>
> OVER 10 MILLION PEOPLE HAVE THIS DISORDER. I GOT HELP. YOU CAN TOO.
>
> **Voice-Over Narrator (Below information is featured as a template):** IF YOU THINK YOU HAVE SOCIAL ANXIETY DISORDER CONTACT THE SOCIAL ANXIETY DISORDER COALITION
>
> - A public service message
> - Social Anxiety Disorder Coalition
> - 1-800-934-6276
> - www.allergictopeople.com

In the trade, the Osmond PSA is known as a *talking head*. This means that the format is relatively simple; it involves just one person speaking to the camera. There are no other visual cues such as other scenes or action. A more sophisticated and more complex approach is to involve action and a number of scenes to give the PSA more movement and visual appeal.

When there are a number of different elements, the script begins to look like a page from the manuscript of a play. In film and video production, it is often called a *storyboard*. Its purpose is to provide dialog and to describe the scenes and visual aspects so the camera crew knows the general outline of the scene. A good example is a VNR storyboard that was created for the American Cancer Society. The VNR was aimed at preventing teenage smoking. The writer, Jeff Goldsmith, created a parody using the motif of a television game show, "Cancer for Cash." One scene shows three showgirls spinning a coffin on stage to select questions for contestants. The person who got the right answer got "cancer cash" for chemotherapy treatments.

Satellite Media Tours

The television equivalent to the radio media tour is the *satellite media tour (SMT)*. Essentially, an SMT is a series of prebooked, one-on-one interviews from a fixed location (usually a television studio) via satellite with a series of television journalists or talk show hosts. (See also Chapter 13.)

The SMT concept started several decades ago when companies began to put their CEOs in front of television cameras. The public relations staff would line up reporters in advance to interview the spokesperson via satellite feed during allocated timeframes of one to five minutes. This way, journalists throughout the country could personally interview a CEO in New York even if they were based in San Francisco. For busy CEOs, the satellite was a time-efficient way to give interviews.

Today, the SMT is a staple of the public relations and television industry. In fact, a survey by West Glen Communications found that nearly 85 percent of the nation's television stations participate in satellite tours.

The easiest way to do an SMT is to simply make the spokesperson available for an interview at a designated time. Celebrities are always popular, but an organization also can use articulate experts. In general, the spokesperson sits in a chair or at a desk in front of a television camera. Viewers usually see the local news anchor asking questions and the spokesperson on a large screen, via satellite, answering them in much the same way that anchors talk to reporters at the scene of an event.

Another popular approach to SMTs is to get out of the television studio and do them on location. When the National Pork Producers Council wanted to promote outdoor winter grilling, its public relations staff hired a team from Broadcast News Network to fire up an outdoor grill in Aspen, Colorado, and put a celebrity chef in a parka to give interviews, via satellite, while he cooked several pork recipes. In another example, the Hawaii Tourism Board targeted television stations in New England on a cold winter day with a SMT originating from Hawaii's sunny and warm beaches.

ON THE JOB insights

Guidelines for a Successful SMT

Anecdotal evidence indicates that four out of five pitched satellite media tours don't get aired. You can increase the odds if you follow these "do's" and "don'ts" compiled by *PRWeek*:

Do

- Include a relevant angle for the stations in every market you pitch.
- Use an interesting, visually appealing background or set. It often makes the difference between your SMT getting on the air or not.
- Get stations involved by sending them items that will help them perform and promote the interview.

- Respect producers' wishes when they tell you they will get back to you. Incessant follow-up will only annoy those who you are trying to convince.
- Localize your SMT. If local audiences aren't going to be interested, neither are the producers airing the story.
- Be clear in your pitch. Provide producers with the who, what, when, and why right away.
- Use credible, knowledgeable spokespersons who project confidence and are personable.

Don't

- Let the SMT become a commercial. If producers think there is

the possibility of too many product mentions, they won't book it.
- Be dishonest with producers about the content of your SMT.
- Pitch your SMT to more than one producer at a station.
- Be conservative with amount of talent. A boring medical SMT will pack more punch if you present a patient along with the doctor.
- Surprise the producer. Newscasts are planned to the minute and unexpected events (spokesperson cancels) will not be appreciated.

Some additional guidelines for SMTs are provided in the Insights box on page 403.

News Feeds.   A variation on the SMT is a news feed that provides video and soundbites of an event to TV stations across the country via satellite. The news feed may be live from the event as it is taking place (real time) or it could be video shot at the event, edited, and then made available as a package.

In either case, the sponsoring organization hires a production firm to record the event. Major fashion shows, which take place in New York or Europe, often arrange for video feeds to media outlets around the world. Major auctions also sent video feeds to media outlets and even gatherings of interested buyers. DWJ Television, for example, was hired by Christie's to cover the auction of 56 outfits worn by women at Academy Award ceremonies. Stations could air the entire auction or simply make a video clip for use in later newscasts.

Personal Appearances

Radio and television stations increasingly operate on round-the-clock schedules. They require vast amounts of programming to fill the time available.

Thus far, this chapter has concentrated on how to prepare and generate timely material for newscasts. This section focuses on how to get spokespersons on talk and magazine shows. In these cases, your contact is no longer the news department, but the directors and producers of such programs. The most valuable communication tools in reaching these people are the telephone and the persuasive pitch litter (discussed in Chapter 14).

Before contacting directors and producers, however, it is necessary for the public relations staff to do their homework. They must be totally familiar with a show's format and content, as well as the type of audience that it reaches. Media directories are available, such as *Bacon's*, that give key information about specific programs, such as the names and addresses of producers, the program format, audience demographics, and the purpose of the show.

A second approach, and one that is highly recommended, is to actually watch the program and study the format. In the case of a talk or interview show, what is the style of the moderator or host? What kinds of topics are discussed? How important is the personality or prominence of the guest? How long is the show or a segment? Does the show lend itself to product demonstrations or other visual aids? The answers to such questions will help determine whether the show is appropriate for your spokesperson and how to tailor a pitch letter to achieve maximum results.

Television talk shows and interviews are a proven public relations tactic for increasing the visibility of a personality and the products they may be endorsing. Here Queen Latifah, the queen of hip hop and an actress, gives an interview to Katie Couric.

Talk Shows

Radio and television talk shows have been a staple of broadcasting for many years. KABC in Los Angeles started the trend in 1960, when it became the first radio station in the country to convert to an all-news-and-talk format. Today, more than 1,110 radio stations have adopted the format. Stations that play music also may include talk shows as part of their programming. In fact, it is estimated that there are now more than 4,000 radio talk shows in the United States.

The same growth applies to television. Phil Donahue began his show in 1967. Today, there are more than 20 nationally syndicated talk shows and a countless number of locally produced talk shows. For the past decade, the number one syndicated daytime talk show has been the *Oprah Winfrey Show*, attracting abut 8 million viewers on a daily basis. On the network level, three shows are the Holy Grail for publicists: NBC's *Today*, ABC's *Good Morning America*, and CBS's *Early Show*. Collectively, these three shows draw about 14 million viewers between 7 and 9 A.M. every weekday. As *PRWeek* says, "There's simply no better way to hit millions of consumers in one shot."

The advantage of talk shows is the opportunity to have viewers see and hear the organization's spokesperson without the filter of journalists and editors interpreting and deciding what is newsworthy. Another advantage is to be on the program longer than the traditional 30-second soundbite in a news program.

Most public relations practitioners never book a spokesperson on the *Today* show or *Oprah*, but there are other countless opportunities at the local and state level. When thinking about booking a spokesperson on a talk show, here's a checklist of questions to consider:

- Is the topic newsworthy? Is there a new angle on something already in the news?
- Is the topic timely? Is it tied to some lifestyle or cultural trend?
- Is the information useful to viewers? How-to and consumer tips are popular.
- Does the spokesperson have viewer appeal? A celebrity may be acceptable, but there must be a natural tie-in with the organization and the topic to be discussed.

ON THE JOB insights

The Ideal Talk Show Guest

What constitutes a killer TV guest? Senior producer for *Your World with Cavuto*, Gresham Strigel, shared his thoughts with *Bulldog Reporter*, a media placement newsletter:

- Guests should be personable and approachable when producers conduct preinterviews on the phone. They are forthright but not aggressive. "If you're wishy-washy, non-committed, or stilted, you're not going much further."

- Guests should have strong opinions. "We don't call certain people back because they have been trained not to say anything. The stronger your position is, and the higher up it is, the more media attention you're going to get. Nobody likes guests who play it safe."

- Guests should be passionate about the subject. "We don't want people who are robotic—who just spit out facts. If you convey passion about what you're talking about, you jump off the screen."

- Guests should be able to debate without getting personal or mean-spirited. "Smile. . . . Audiences like to see someone who is comfortable on-screen—someone who is happy to be there."

- Guests should have engaging, outgoing personalities. "Talking heads and ivory-tower types don't do well on television. They're better suited for print, where their personality—or lack of it—can't turn audiences off."

- Can the spokesperson stay on track and give succinct, concise statements. The spokesperson must stay focused and make sure that the key messages are mentioned.
- Can the spokesperson refrain from getting too commercial? Talk show hosts don't' want guests who sound like an advertisement.

See the Insights box on page 405 for more information on what makes an ideal talk show guest.

Magazine Shows

The term *magazine* refers to a television program format that is based on a variety of video segments in much the same way that print magazines have a variety of articles. These shows may have a guest related to the feature that's being shown, but the main focus is on a video story that may run from 3 to 10 minutes. At the network level, CBS's *60 Minutes* is an example of a magazine program.

Many human-interest magazine shows are produced at the local level. A sampling of magazine shows in one large city featured such subjects as a one-pound baby who survived, a treatment for anorexia nervosa, a couple who started a successful cookie company, remedies for back pain, tips on dog training, a black-belt karate expert, blue-collar job stress, and the work habits of a successful author.

Most, if not all, of these features came about as the result of someone making a pitch to the show's producers. The objective of the segments, at least from the perspective of the people featured, is exposure and the generation of new business. The tips on dog-training, for example, featured a local breeder who also operated a dog obedience school. The karate expert ran a martial arts academy, and even the story of the one-pound baby was placed by a local hospital touting its infant care specialty.

Booking a Guest

The contact for a talk show may the executive producer or assistant producer of the show. If it is a network or nationally syndicated show, the contact person may have the title of *talent coordinator* or *talent executive*. Whatever the title, these people are known in the broadcasting industry as *bookers* because they are responsible for booking a constant supply of timely guests for the show.

One common approach in placing a guest is to place a phone call to the booker briefly outlining the qualifications of the proposed speaker and why this person would be a timely guest. Publicists also can write a brief one-page letter or send an e-mail telling the booker the story angle, why it's relevant to the show's audience, and why the proposed speaker is qualified to talk on the subject. In many cases, the booker will ask for video clips of the spokesperson on previous TV shows or newspaper clips relating to press interviews.

In all cases, it's important to be honest about the experience and personality of the spokesperson. A major complaint of producers is that the guests often bear no resemblance to how they were described in the initial contact. Barbara Hoffman, producer of *Doctor to Doctor*, told *O'Dwyer's PR Newsletter* that the best pitches come from publicists whose "clients are always exactly what they say they are, always prepared, interesting, on time, and always have something unusual or cutting edge to offer my program."

In recent years, there has been some controversy over guests who are invited because they are celebrities and have large audience appeal. However, once they get on

How to Place a Client on a TV Talk Show

Television stations are looking for interesting, articulate guests for their talk shows. The larger the station, the more stringent are its requirements for accepting a guest. This summary of needs and procedures for *AM/San Francisco*, the morning show on KGO-TV, the ABC network outlet in San Francisco, is typical of those for metropolitan stations. The information is from an article published in *Bulldog*, a West Coast public relations newsletter.

The station wants guests "who will provide information that will help our viewers to save money and save time, helpful hints around the house, consumer-type things." The station also uses guests from the business community who can comment on money, taxes, the stock market, and similar topics.

KGO-TV defines the audience for this show as primarily non-working women, 18 to 49, married, with at least one child. The show also attracts working viewers before they leave for their jobs.

Segments on the one-hour show run from six to ten minutes. The usual pattern is to open with a celebrity-entertainer, then offer two segments on consumer topics. Segments 4, 5, and 6 cover "more serious subjects."

The production staff will normally consider for appearance only those who have appeared on television previously. Usually it asks to see a video clip of a prior TV appearance; an effective clip is an important way to gain acceptance.

"TV is a visual medium and a lot of our audience isn't just sit-ting there watching. They're folding clothes or ironing, so we need a voice that will grab their attention."

The public relations practitioner should submit a brief written query to the show's producer—"a one-page letter getting straight to the basics: whom you're offering, what their experience is, exactly what their topic would be, what shows they've been on previously, a bio (biographical statement) and all other information available on the person, as well as clippings, copies of articles on the person or topic."

Staff members try to answer queries in about a week, perhaps sooner. The show is booked at least a week in advance but sometimes has last-minute openings.

the show, it turns out that they are endorsers of various products. See the Ethics box on page 408.

In general, talk shows book guests three to four weeks in advance. Unless a topic or a person is extremely timely or controversial, it is rare or a person to be booked on one or two day's notice. Public relations strategists must keep this in mind as part of overall campaign planning.

Product Placements

Television's dramatic and comedy shows, as well as the film industry, are good vehicles for promoting a company's products and services. It is not a coincidence that the hero of a detective series drives a Dodge Viper or that the heroine is seen boarding a United Airlines flight.

Should Guests on TV Talk Shows Reveal Their Sponsors?

Actress Lauren Bacall, appearing on NBC's *Today* show, talked about a dear friend who had gone blind from an eye disease and urged the audience to see their doctors to be tested for it. She also mentioned a drug, Visudyne, that was a new treatment for the disease.

Meanwhile, over at ABC's *Good Morning America* show, actress Kathleen Turner was telling Diane Sawyer about her battle with rheumatoid arthritis and mentioned that a drug, *Enbrel*, helped ease the pain. A month later, Olympic gold medal skater Peggy Fleming appeared on the show to talk about cho-

lesterol and heart disease. Near the beginning of the interview, Fleming said, "My doctor has put me on *Lipitor* and my cholesterol has dropped considerably."

What the viewing audience didn't know was that each of these celebrities was being paid a hefty fee by a drug company to mention its product in prime time. Indeed, even the talk show hosts apparently didn't know until the *New York Times* wrote an investigative piece on drug companies using "stealth marketing" tactics to get product mentions on regular news and talk shows.

This raises a dilemma for public relations personnel who

often book guests on various radio and television talk shows. Should you tell the show's producer up-front that a celebrity is under contract as an endorser of a particular product? If you do, it may mean that your spokesperson won't be booked, because programs such as NBC's *Today* show tends to shy away from what is called "stealth marketing."

What are your responsibilities? What is the responsibility of the talk show hosts? Should the public know that Peggy Fleming is appearing as an endorser of a product?

Such product placements, often called *plugs*, are often negotiated by product publicists and talent agencies. This is really nothing new. *IPRA Frontline* reports, "In the early 1900s, Henry Ford had an affinity for Hollywood and perhaps it is no coincidence that his Model T's were the predominant vehicle appearing in the first motion pictures of the era."

Product placements, however, came of age with the movie *ET* in the early 1980s. The story goes that M&M Candies made a classic marketing mistake by not allowing the film to use M&Ms as the prominently displayed trail of candy that the young hero used to lure his big-eyed friend home. Instead, Hershey's Reese's Pieces jumped at the chance, and the rest is history. Sales of Reese's Pieces skyrocketed, and even today, more than 20 years after the film's debut, the candy and *ET* remain forever linked in popular culture and the minds of a whole generation of *ET* fans.

The placement of Reese's Pieces in *ET*, according to marketing experts, was one of the most famous product-placement scenes of all time. And it spawned a whole new industry of product placements in television shows and movies. Clothing manufacturers and retailers are particularly active in product placements because studies show that today's youth gets most of their fashion ideas from watching television shows. This is why American Eagle Outfitters provided the entire wardrobe for the cast of *Dawson's Creek*, and *Buffy the Vampire Slayer* wore jeans from the Gap. It also explains why Tom Cruise wore Ray-Bans in *Risky Business*, James Bond drives a BMW, and the characters in *Swordfish* drank Heineken beer.

The high point for retailing, in recent years, was the series *Sex and the City*. According to the *Wall Street Journal*, "By incorporating brands, and often specific products, into its plotline, the show touched off runs on Oscar de la Renta cocktail dresses, Fendi handbags, and countless other fashion trophies." When the lead character Carrie Bradshaw had her silver leather Manolo Blahnik pumps stolen at a party, viewers rushed to stores to get their own pair (price $630).

Sex and the City is no longer on the air, but retailers are looking for the next winning series to display their goods. K-Mart has selected some possibilities. Actors on shows such as *One Tree Hill* and *Summerland* will wear K-Mart's back-to-school lines in multiple episodes. Other retailers, such as Donna Karan, are dressing stars for guest appearances on shows. Jennifer Lopez, for example, was outfitted for a guest spot on the season premiere of NBC's *Will & Grace*.

Automakers are particularly active in product placements. Perhaps the most successful product placement in recent years was Pontiac's decision to make a deal with Oprah Winfrey for her first show of the season. Everyone in the studio audience—all 267 of them—received a free Pontiac G6. It cost General Motors almost $8 million, but the automaker reached an estimated 8 to 9 million viewers and reaped a flood of media publicity throughout the United States and the world for its new model. Comparatively speaking, GM thought it was a good deal, advertising in national markets would have cost even more. And it would not have been as credible as Oprah saying to her nationwide audience that Pontiac was a great car.

ON THE JOB

global

Product Placement in China

Product placements are common in American television programs but in China the sponsoring company may even produce the shows. Chinese broadcasters are strapped for cash, so they often accept entertainment programs produced and branded by the companies themselves.

One example is a television show, *Mommy & Baby—Healthy World,* that is broadcast in three major Chinese cities. According to the *Wall Street Journal*, "Cameras follow the day-to-day practical problems of raising kids under the age of three, including nutrition. The program is partially paid for by H. J. Heinz Co., which features its baby food on the show."

Another program is *Lycra My Show*, which is somewhat based on *American Idol*. Contestants sing while wearing stretchy Lycra-based clothing, vying for money and a recording contract. A division of Koch Industries, which makes Lycra fabric, produces the show and makes it available for free to Chinese television stations.

In another example, Ford Motor Co. produced a *Survivor*-like show entitled *Ford Maverick Beyond Infinity*. Other sponsors that paid for the scripting and production of the show included Nike and Nestle. The plot line was summarized by the *Wall Street Journal*: "In it, 12 contestants on a tropical island hunted for treasure in a Ford Maverick sport-utility vehicle, leapt into rafts while wearing Nike clothing, and cooled off with Nestle drinks. The winner took home a Ford Maverick."

Tim Leckey, Ford's marketing director in China, said it best: "We really built the show around the product."

Even *Spider-Man* is not immune to the forces of product placement. Cingular Wireless teamed up with Columbia Pictures to promote the blockbuster. A Cingular billboard briefly appeared in an action scene, but that was only the beginning. The company then went on to promote the film and its cell phone business by (1) sending two *Spider-Man*–branded Dodge Vipers on an 80-stop road tour promoting a Cingular sweepstakes to win the sports car, (2) creating a *Spider-Man* faceplate for its phones, and (3) setting up a corporate Web site where customers could download such things as a *Spider-Man* screensaver.

Cingular thought the promotional tie-in with *Spider-Man* was worthwhile because it reached young people, who are a big market for cell phones. It also generated the product-branding concept that Cingular was a "cool" company.

Although product placements and tie-ins on a high-profile television series or a major film can cost millions of dollars, not all product placements are in that league. A low-profile item such as a can of soda or a bag of chips in a scene may cost virtually nothing except for providing the actors and camera crew an ample supply of the product on a daily basis. There also is the practice of "in-kind" funding. A hotel, for example, may get its name or facilities in a television series or film by providing free room and board to the actors and the camera crew.

Another opportunity for product exposure on television is on game shows. *The Price is Right*, for example, uses a variety of products as prizes to contestants. In one episode, for example, the prize was a tent, a camp table and chairs, and lanterns. It was a great, low-cost product placement for Coleman for less than $200.

Public relations specialists should always be on the alert to opportunities for publicity on television programs and upcoming movies. If the company's service or product lends itself to a particular program, the normal procedure is to contact the show's producers directly or through an agent who specializes in matching company products with the show's needs. At the national level, the services of a product placement firm in Hollywood or New York is helpful. At last count, almost 40 agencies were engaged in the booming industry of product placements.

Issues Placement

A logical extension of product placements is convincing popular television programs to write an issue or cause into their plotlines. Writers for issue-oriented shows such as *The West Wing*, *ER*, and *Law & Order* are constantly bombarded with requests from a variety of nonprofit and special-interest groups.

The National Campaign to Prevent Teen Pregnancy, for example, worked very hard to get the issue of teen pregnancy on *Dawson's Creek* because it reached so many young people. The result was a scene in which Dawson's mom talked to her son's girlfriend, Joey, about ways to prevent pregnancy. Many social and health organizations also lobby the producers of daytime soap operas to write scripts where the major characters deal with cancer, diabetes, drug abuse, alcoholism, and an assortment of other problems.

The idea is to educate the public about a social issue or a health problem in an entertaining way. Someone once said, "It's like hiding the aspirin in the ice cream." Even the federal government works with popular television programs to write scripts that deal with the dangers and prevention of drug abuse. All of this has not escaped the notice of the drug companies; they are now exploring the opportunities for getting their products mentioned in plotlines, too.

The flip side of asking scriptwriters to include material is asking them to give a more balanced portrayal of an issue. The health-care industry, for example, is concerned about balance in such programs as *ER*. The popular program deals with a variety of health issues and, in many cases, health maintenance organizations (HMOs) are portrayed in an unfavorable light. Even the American Bar Association gets upset about the portrayal of lawyers in some series. Consequently, these organizations often meet with the program's scriptwriters to educate them about the facts so the program is more balanced.

Ultimately, however, the programs are designed as entertainment. Scriptwriters, like newspaper editors, make their own evaluations and judgments.

Other Forms of Placement

Another form of product placement is agreements with radio stations to promote a product or event as part of their programming. The most common example is a concert promoter giving DJs 10 tickets to a "hot" concert that are then awarded as prizes to listeners who answer a question or call within 30 seconds.

A nonprofit group sponsoring a fund-raising festival also may make arrangements for a radio station (or television station) to co-sponsor an event as part of the station's own promotional activities. This means that the station will actively promote the festival on the air through PSAs and DJ chatter between songs. The arrangement also may call for a popular DJ to broadcast live from the festival and give away T-shirts with the station's logo on them. This, too, is good promotion for the festival and the radio station, because it attracts people to the event.

The station's director of promotions or marketing often is in charge of deciding what civic events to sponsor with other groups. The station will usually agree to a certain number of promotional spots in exchange for being listed in the organization's news releases, programs, print advertising, and event banners as a sponsor of the event. Such terms are spelled out in a standard contract, which is often supplied by the radio or television station.

Stations will not necessarily promote or co-sponsor every event. They must be convinced that their involvement will benefit the station in terms of greater public exposure, increased audience, and improved market position.

The Web

This chapter has emphasized radio and television, but it would be incomplete if the Internet was not mentioned as a major vehicle for distributing information and also reaching millions of people.

One important development has been the advent of Web-based news sites. There are more than 6,000 news sites, and the number grows each day. In addition, according to West Glen Communications, "more than 50 percent of the 110 million users of the Internet in the United States use this medium as a source of news and information."

MSNBC.com, for example, reaches 4 million viewers a day, which no daily newspaper in the United States can match. Dean Wright, editor-in-chief of MSNBC.com told *Jack O'Dwyer's Newsletter*, "No one would seriously suggest that the daily newspaper is irrelevant. But the Web is something that can't be ignored. The message I have for PR pros is, if you want to reach out to a highly desirable demographic—people at work—then you must include the Web in your plans."

Elizabeth Shepard, editor-in-chief of Epicurious.com and Concierge.com, agrees. She says Epicurious.com, the longest-running and largest food site on the Internet, gets 20 million page views per month. She told *Jack O'Dwyer's Newsletter*, "People contact me about new restaurant openings or special tasting menus, new wines that are launching in the U.S., or special distribution of wines in certain areas." Needless to say, such a Web site is an excellent publicity opportunity for restaurants and wineries.

Many Web sites, of course, are extensions of a particular newspaper, magazine, radio or television station, or even television network. That means that the materials used by these traditional media may also wind up on their Web sites. Articles from *Gourmet*, *Bon Appetit*, and *Parade*, for example, can be found on Epicurious.com, but most of these sites also have editors who are looking for original material. Public relations practitioners should not neglect such sites in today's world.

Weblogs

Weblogs, or *blogs*, have become an integral part of the Internet. Essentially, blogs are regularly updated online personal journals with links to items of interest on the Web. The Pew Internet and American Life Project found that more than 2 million Americans have their own blogs.

Most bloggers are amateurs, but many are professional journalists who like to express their opinions, observations, and criticisms about almost everything. And, although the mass majority of bloggers are obscure, others have risen in prominence and have a large following. Ana Marie Cox, for example, gets 430,000 page views per week at her site, www.wonkette.com. For the first time, both the Democrats and the Republicans issued press credentials to some of these bloggers to cover their conventions. See Chapter 18 for further discussion of the impact of bloggers on political campaigns.

Increasingly, a number of public relations practitioners are becoming bloggers on behalf of their employers and clients because, as one professional says, "They (blogs) let businesses take their message right to the public without the TV network news or the local newspaper having to act as a mouthpiece." Jason Kottke, a San Francisco Web designer and blogger, told *PRWeek*:

> A clever Weblog can combine the information dissemination of a traditional Web site with the communication you get with direct mail, e-mail, or an e-mail newsletter. The frequent updates, along with looser writing style adopted by many Webloggers gives your customers the impression that you're having a conversation with them instead of just shoving information at them in a press release form.

Public relations personnel also are starting to pitch Weblogs. One public relations firm didn't think a client's minor software upgrade was worth a news release, but staff did send an e-mail to some bloggers covering the industry and got a favorable response. The Heritage Foundation, a conservative think tank, also took the time to e-mail 175 political bloggers and found that most of them would be interested in receiving information from the organization.

Another aspect of blogs, which causes headaches for public relations staffs, is what the writers may say about a company or its products. As *Ragan's Media Relations Report* says, "A prominent blogger who trashes a product, service, or company can do serious damage to sales or public image. Bloggers also frequently post links to mainstream or other news articles—making the reach of offending news coverage that much greater."

Consequently, it is recommended that public relations personnel monitor Weblogs that reach large numbers of consumers or that cover a particular industry. Oftentimes, the information being disseminated is untrue or distorted, and it's necessary for the organization to set the record straight. At other times, a blog site may be an excellent opportunity to place positive information about the organization.

Organizational Webcasts

The previous chapter indicated that public relations materials, such as news releases, media kits, fact sheets, brochures, and so on, were commonly posted on an organization's Web site. Many organizations also operate online pressrooms or newsrooms to provide information for journalists who need photos, executive profiles, or the most recent annual report.

Now, most organizations also are posting SMTs, news feeds, and online news conferences on the Internet to reach an ever-expanding audience though continuous audio and video, which is called *Webcasting*.

Webcasts also can be used for live events such as news conferences and new product introductions that are made available in real time to online journalists, consumers, employees, or other key audiences. Such access makes it easier for journalists to cover the organization and get the information they need. Marc Wein, president of Murray Hill Studios in New York, told *Public Relations Tactics*, "We did one press conference where almost nobody showed up; we did a live stream onto the Web and we had dozens of reporters watching it."

Six Flags Magic Mountain in Valencia, California, for example, produced a VNR about a new ride, but it also digitized the video B-roll of the actual ride and distributed it via its Web site. Visitors to the site could experience the ride from their own PC screen in full motion and full sound.

In another application, Orbis Broadcast Group produced a health-care VNR for television stations that included information on how viewers could find additional information at a Web site. When viewers went to the Web site, they were able to take part in chat sessions with physicians, attend virtual press events, and find other consumer-friendly health information provided by leading health-care organizations. Indeed, one advantage of the Internet is the opportunity for consumers to get more information about a product and even engage in interactive discussion with company representatives about it.

Sometimes, a Webcast is used in conjunction with a telephone conference call. XM Satellite Radio, for example, sent out a media advisory about a conference call to announce and discuss its third quarter financial results. The company provided a call-in number, but also stated, "The conference call also can be accessed via a live Webcast on the company's Web site, located at www.exradio.com."

PR CASEBOOK

VNR Introduces New Transport Vehicle to the World

The Segway Human Transporter, called the "world's first self-balancing, electric-powered personal transportation machine," had its first public preview in a video news release.

Burson-Marsteller public relations was charged with creating a VNR that would help position the new form of personal transportation as a new

(continued)

PR CASEBOOK *(continued)*

productivity tool. The team was given only 10 days to produce the VNR and keep a high level of secrecy about the product. There was already "buzz" about the device, but most people didn't really know what "it" was.

According to *PRWeek*, "Explaining how the machine worked and how it could positively impact productivity, the environment, and urban transportation were important parts of the VNR, as well as showing real people using the device to give audiences a sense of how safe and easy its operation is." The B-M team developed a script that gave insights into the technology behind the vehicle and also showed it going up hills, through water, and on footpaths.

The VNR was sent by National Satellite, a distribution firm, on launch day to television stations throughout the United States. Broadcast news reports about the new device reached more than 100 million people, and an even larger number of people around the world were reached via print media and television.

Police in Boston were among the first to test the Segway Human Transporter after a video news release announced the invention to the world.

SUMMARY

The Reach of Radio and TV

In today's society, radio and television reach the vast majority of people on a daily basis.

Radio News Releases

These releases, unlike those for print media, must be written for the ear. A popular format is the audio news release (ANR) that includes an announcer and a quote (soundbite) from a spokesperson. Radio news releases should be no longer than 60 seconds.

Public Services Announcements

Both radio and television stations accept public service announcements (PSHs) from nonprofit organizations that wish to inform and educate the public about health issues or upcoming civic events. PSAs are like advertisements, but stations don't charge to air them. Television PSAs require visual aids.

Broadcast Media Tours

A radio media tour (RMT) and a television satellite media tour (SMT) happen when an organization's spokesperson is interviewed from a central location by journalists across the country. Each journalist is able to conduct a one-on-one interview for several minutes.

Video News Releases

The video news release (VNR) is produced in a format that television stations can easily use or edit based on their needs. VNRs are relatively expensive to produce, but they have great potential for reaching large audiences.

News Feeds

With a news feed, an organization arranges for coverage of a particular event, and television stations across the country can watch it in "real time" or receive an edited version of it for later use.

Personal Appearances

Public relations personnel often book spokespersons on radio and television talk shows. The guest must have a good personality, be knowledgeable, and give short, concise answers.

Product Placements

Producers are increasingly making deals with companies to feature their products on television shows or movies. Nonprofit organizations also lobby to have scripts mention key health messages and deal with various social issues.

Web Sites and Streaming Media

Public relations personnel should not overlook Web news sites for placement of publicity. In addition, the popularity of Weblogs, or blogs, means that public relations personnel should also harness them as a tactic for reaching an audience. Organizations are increasingly using Webcasts to transmit news conferences and interact with journalists.

Case Activity: **What Would You Do?**

Lysol has a new antibacterial kitchen cleanser on the market. This is not exactly earthshaking news. You work for a pubic relations firm that is given the assignment of coming up with a video news release (VNR) that would be newsworthy enough to get on the evening news. Come up with an angle and then develop a storyboard outlining the visual and audio elements. Use the a two-column format: the visual description on the left and the audio portion on the right. See pages 397 to 399 for an example.

QUESTIONS for Review and Discussion

1. Why should public relations personnel consider radio and television as major tools in reaching the public?
2. Radio news releases must be tightly written. What's the general guideline for the number of lines and words in a 30-second news release? What other guidelines should be kept in mind when writing a radio news release?
3. How does an audio news release differ from a standard radio news release?
4. Review the audio news release on page 389 from Cigna Health Care Systems. What aspects of this release illustrate good guidelines for writing an effective release?
5. What is a public service announcement (PSA)? How does it differ from a standard radio news release?
6. What is the advantage of a radio media tour (RMT) or a satellite media tour (SMT) to the organization and journalists? Are there any disadvantages?
7. What are some guidelines for a successful SMT?
8. List four ways that an organization can get its news and viewpoints on local television.
9. What are the format and characteristics of a video news release (VNR)? What is a B-roll?
10. What's a news feed, and how is it used in public relations?
11. What makes an ideal radio or television talk show guest/spokesperson?
12. What three television talk shows are the Holy Grail of public relations?
13. How do you book a guest on a radio or television talk/magazine show?

14. Companies increasingly are working with television programs and film studios to get their products featured as part of a program or movie. What do you think of this trend?

15. How can a public relations person work with radio and television stations on joint promotions?

16. How is the Web used in public relations?

17. A new online trend is Weblogs, or blogs. Why should public relations personnel pay attention to these sites?

SUGGESTED READINGS

Calabro, Sara. "Pitching a VNR: Winning over Television's Gatekeepers." *PRWeek*, January 19, 2004, p. 18.

Callison, Coy. "Media Relations and the Internet: How *Fortune* 500 Company Web Sites Assist Journalists in News Gathering." *Public Relations Review*, Vol. 29, No. 1, 2003, pp. 29–41.

Chabria, Anita. "Broadcast News: TV Producers Have Better and Faster Access to VNRs than Ever Before." *PRWeek*, May 31, 2004, p. 13.

Chabria, Anita. "PR Firms Vie for Hollywood Product Placement Power." *PRWeek*, May 13, 2002, p. 9.

Chabria, Anita. "Getting a Product in Front of the Cameras." *PRWeek*, May 6, 2002, p. 18.

Eisenstadt, David. "How to Make Video News Releases Work." *Public Relations Quarterly*, Winter 2002, pp. 24–25.

Eskridge, Amy Goldwert. "Getting Your Best Results from a Video News Release." *Public Relations Tactics*, June 2004, p. 27.

"Finding The Right News Desk: How to Pitch Stories—and Sources!—to the Evergrowing National Public Radio." *Ragan's Media Relations Report*, September 2004, p. 5.

Fowler, Geoffrey A. "Product Placement Now Star on Chinese TV." *Wall Street Journal*, June 2, 2004, pp. B1, B3.

Hachigian, David, and Hallahan, Kirk. "Perceptions of Public Relations Web Sites by Computer Industry Journalists." *Public Relations Review*, Vol. 29, No. 1, 2003, pp. 43–62.

Hill, Bob. "A Guided Tour: Tips for SMT Spokespeople." *Public Relations Tactics*, July 2003, pp. 15, 17.

Klam, Matthew. "The Bloggers on the Bus." *New York Times Magazine*, September 26, 2004, pp. 42–49, 115, 123.

Lipton, Lauren. "After 'Sex' Fashion World Looks for a New TV Showcase." *Wall Street Journal*, September 17, 2004, pp. B1, B7.

Quenqua, Douglas. "PSAs: Tugging at Heartstrings and Purse Strings." *PRWeek*, June 14, 2004, p. 18.

Quenqua, Douglas. "How to Walk the Talk Shows." *PRWeek*, March 15, 2004, p. 18.

Quenqua, Douglas. "Production, Subject, Audience: Getting a PSA on the Air." *PRWeek*, March 3, 2003, p. 18.

Shortman, Melanie. "Get on a Morning Show, and You'll Rise and Shine." *PRWeek*, February 17, 2003, p. 18.

Sweeney, Katie. "Ahead of Schedule: When It Comes to SMTs, Pitch Early." *Public Relations Tactics*, July 2004, p. 14.

Sweeney, Katie. "Broadcast PR Executives: Controversy Aside, Stations Stand by VNRs." *Public Relations Tactics*, June 2004, p. 22.

Trammell, Jack. "Five Rules for Television and Radio Placements." *Public Relations Tactics*, June 2003, p. 21.

Walker, Jerry. "Bookers Are Looking for Guests Who Fit the News." *O'Dwyer's PR Services Report*, September 2003, pp. 32–33.

Walker, Jerry. "Ten Tips for Making a Good Impression in a TV Interview." *O'Dwyer's PR Services Report*, July 2003, p. 32.

Walker, Jerry. "Getting a Story Through a Busy TV Newsroom." *O'Dwyer's PR Services Report*, May 2003, pp. 31, 33.

Wallace, Michelle. "Budgeting for a Creative Satellite Media Tour." *Public Relations Tactics*, July 2004, p. 16.

chapter 16

Speechwriting, Presentations, and Media Interviews

Topics covered in this chapter include:

The Art of Speechwriting

Work in public relations requires excellent knowledge of interpersonal communications, and one form of this is speechwriting. Other forms of face-to-face communications include giving speeches and presentations, conducting one-on-one media interviews, organizing news conferences, and even hosting journalists on a press tour. At some point in a public relations career, you will be asked to do all of these activities, which are the topic of this tactics chapter.

Public relations practitioners frequently are called on to write a speech for their employers or clients. As speechwriters, their role is a hidden one. They labor silently to produce the words that may sparkle like champagne when poured forth by their employers from the lecterns of conventions, civic banquets, and annual meetings.

In the White House, the wraps of anonymity usually are drawn around the writers who churn out speeches and statements for the President of the United States. A president utters a memorable phrase and gets the credit, but a high-level speechwriter probably created it. There is nothing disreputable about this. Presidents, as well as CEOs of corporations, have more urgent tasks than to think up catchy phrases. The speechwriter finds personal satisfaction in creating competent speeches for someone else.

Most large corporations employ speechwriters, some of whom receive annual salaries in the six figures. Smaller organizations often use professional freelance writers who command anywhere from $1,000 to $10,000 for a speech. Still other organizations simply have speeches written in-house by their own public relations staff, which often has other duties in addition to speechwriting.

Research Is the First Step

Speechwriting doesn't take place in a vacuum. If you are given a speechwriting assignment, several preliminary steps must be taken before a speech outline can even be started. The first step is to research the intended audience of the speech. Who? What? Where? When? How many people? What time of day? Purpose of the meeting? Length of speech? Purpose of the talk? Other speakers on the program? A speechwriter finds answers to these questions by talking with the organizers of the event or meeting. Don't accept vague answers; keep asking follow-up questions until you have a complete picture.

A good description of the event and the audience will help to determine the tone, structure, and content of the speech so that the speech is relevant to the audience. A good example of defining an audience is when an EDS corporate executive was asked to give a keynote address for a meeting of the Association of American Chambers of Commerce of Latin America in Lima, Peru. Beth Pedison, executive speechwriter for EDS, analyzed the intended audience in the following way:

> Intended Audience: 400 top Latin American and Caribbean business executives, government leaders, and Chamber representatives. Because the audience came from diverse industries, countries, and company sizes, their familiarity with information technology varied widely. We didn't want to talk down to those who were technologically savvy, or talk over the heads of those who were not technologically proficient. English was the business language of the conference and the speech, although most everyone in the audience spoke English as a second language. Therefore, we needed

to keep sentence structure simple, and avoid the use of colloquialisms, contractions, or U.S.-centric language.

The second research step is to know everything about the executive who's going to give the speech. A good speechwriter will take the time to determine the speaker's speech pattern by listening to how he or she talks to other groups and subordinates. The purpose is to see how the speaker's mind works, what words or phrases are favored, and what kind of opinions are expressed. In addition to listening, it's also a good idea to go over material that the executive has written or, if written by others, that the executive or client admires in terms of style and method of presentation.

Another part of this research is to have lengthy conversations with the speaker before writing a rough draft of the talk. In an informal setting, you and the speaker should discuss the speech in terms of the audience being addressed, the objective, the theme, the kind of facts and statistics that should be gathered, and the major points that need to be included. In this way, the speechwriter is better able to think like the speaker and write a speech that fits the person's beliefs and speech pattern.

This is how Marie L. Lerch, director of public relations and communication for Booz Allen & Hamilton, described her work with the company's chairman for a diversity awards speech to company employees:

> The central message, "Do the Right Thing," has been Mr. Stasior's core theme throughout his tenure as chairman. I worked with him to adapt the theme to the issue of diversity; researched quotes and other materials that would add color and emphasis to the message; and interviewed him to flesh out his ideas and words on the subject. With notes and research in hand, I developed a first draft of the speech, which Mr. Stasior and I revised together in its final form.

Objectives and Approach

Preparing a speech takes a great deal of energy and time on the part of the speechwriter and the speaker. Therefore, it's important to determine what the speech is supposed to accomplish. In other words, what information and opinions should the audience have when the speech is concluded?

Everything that goes into a speech should be pertinent to the key objectives of the speech. Material that does not help to attain the objectives or communicate key message points should not be used. Whether the objective is to inform, persuade, activate, or commemorate, that objective should be uppermost in the speechwriter's mind.

A good example of setting objectives was done by Melissa Brown, a freelance speechwriter, who was commissioned to write a speech for the president of the Grocery Manufacturers of America (GMA), who was going to speak at the International Food and Lifestyles Media Conference in Cincinnati. The topic of the speech was "The Changing Challenges Facing the Food Industry."

The objectives of the speech were as follows:

● Give food writers useful, research-based information on the lifestyles of American consumers, thus positioning GMA as a good source of statistics/information.

● Neutralize misinformation presented by opponents of biotechnologically developed food products, presenting the industry's side of the story and exposing the lack of credentials of a major voice in the opposition.

Speechwriters are in demand and well paid. This advertisement from Saudi Aramco is an example of opportunities in the field.

● Provide information on the good work the industry has accomplished in addressing environmental issues, in particular, packaging and solid waste.

● Demonstrate to GMA board that the association is speaking out on the issues that affect their businesses.

● Frame the arguments other food industry spokespeople can use in other opportunities within their companies and with the press.

The approach might be described as the tone of the speech. A friendly audience may appreciate a one-sided talk, with no attempt to present both sides of an issue. For example, a politician at a fund-raising dinner of supporters does not bother to give the opposition's views. Also, an executive talking to the company's sales force does not need to give the pros and cons of competing products.

Many speaking engagements, however, take place before neutral audiences such as a civic club (Lions, Rotary, Kiwanis) and any other number of civic groups where the audience may have mixed views or even a lack of knowledge about a particular subject. The Lifestyles Media Conference, mentioned earlier, is such a speaking engagement. Some of the people in the audience will be strong supporters or opponents of foods created through biotechnology.

In such a case, it is wise to take a more objective approach and give an overview of the various viewpoints. The speech can still advocate a particular position, but the audience will appreciate the fact that you have included other points of view. From the standpoint of persuasion, a speaker also will have more control over how the opposition view is expressed, instead of an audience member bringing it up.

Hostile or unfriendly audiences present the greatest challenge. They are already predisposed against what you say, and they tend to reject anything that does not square with their opinions. Remember the old saying: "Don't confuse me with the facts—my mind is already made up." The best approach in this situation is for the speaker to find some common ground with the audience. This technique lets the audience know that the speaker shares or at least understands some of their concerns.

ON THE JOB

global

A Chinese Approach to Speechwriting

An important speech takes a lot of preparation and polishing, but President Jiang Zemin's opening speech to the Communist Party's 16th Congress was an extraordinary effort. More than 900 people labored in a year-long effort to compose the speech, which ran 70 pages.

Preparation for the speech started with meetings in 16 provinces to talk about what should be in the speech. A large number of Chinese citizens were canvassed, and a first draft of the speech was prepared for comment by President Jiang and other officials of the Communist Party. About six months later, a team of writers worked for eight days to polish the "masterpiece."

The speech, which took more than two hours to deliver, apparently was a big hit. More than 1.1 million copies of the speech were sold in Beijing alone, according to the Xinhua News Agency.

Writing the Speech

After determining the objectives and approach, the next step is to write an outline of the speech. Such an outline has three main parts: the opening, the body, and the closing.

The opening is the part of the speech that must get the audience's attention, establish empathy and a relationship, and point toward a conclusion. A good approach is to tell the audience what the topic is, why it is important to them, and the direction you plan to take in addressing it.

The body of the speech presents the evidence that leads to the conclusion. The outline should list all of the key points. In this section, the speechwriter will list quotes from acknowledged experts in the field, facts and figures, and examples that support the speaker's theme or point of view. The conclusion summarizes the evidence, pointing out what it means to the audience.

The outline should be discussed with the speaker to ensure that the approach is acceptable and that all of the necessary facts, statistics, and quotes are assembled. Oftentimes, the speechwriter may have to do some additional research or track down some obscure fact that the speaker wants to use.

Once the outline is approved, the speechwriter writes a first draft of the speech. The speechwriter should keep in mind the time constraints on the speech. It's no use writing a 45-minute speech if the request by the host organization is for a 20-minute speech. Some guidelines on the length of speeches will be given shortly.

A speech is built in blocks that are joined by transitions. The following pattern for assembling the blocks provides an all-purpose organizational structure on which most speeches can be built:

Beginning

1. Introduction (establish contact with the audience).
2. Statement of the main purpose of the speech.

Middle

3. Development of the theme with examples, facts, and anecdotes. Enumeration of individual points is valuable here. It gives a sense of structure and controlled use of time.
4. Statement of secondary theme, if any.
5. Enunciation of the main point that the speaker has been building up to. This main point is the heart of the speech.
6. A pause at this plateau, with an anecdote or two. This is the soft place where the audience absorbs the point just made.

End

7. Restatement of the theme in summary form.
8. A brief, brisk conclusion.

Word choice, which is based on the nature of the audience, is an important part of the first draft. See the Insights box on page 423 for some guidelines on writing copy for the ear.

The speaker should use this draft to add new thoughts, cross out copy that doesn't seem to fit, and rewrite sentences to reflect his or her particular vocabulary and speaking style.

Experienced speechwriters caution that you should not feel dejected if the first, second, or even third draft comes back in tatters. It is only through this process that the speech becomes the natural expression of the speaker's personality. This is the ideal process. The most successful speakers take the time to work with their speechwriters. Unfortunately, too many executives fail to understand this.

A report prepared by Burson-Marsteller offers reasons why business people have trouble explaining themselves to the public. The report noted:

> All too often the chief executive expects a speech to appear magically on his desk without any contribution on this part. He feels too busy to give the speech the attention it deserves. In the end, he becomes the victim of his own neglect. He stumbles through a speech which, from start to finish, sounds contrived. And then he wonders why nobody listened to what he said.

Coaching the Speaker

In addition to writing a speech, a speechwriter often serves as a coach for the speaker. Whether the speech is memorized (rare) or read, a coach helps the speaker rehearse and polish the delivery so that he or she becomes totally familiar with it. The tone of

ON THE JOB insights

Speechwriting for the Ear: Some Guidelines

The words used in the text of a speech can make a major difference in how well the audience can follow the speech and easily understand it. Here are some guidelines for selecting the right words:

● **Use personal pronouns.** "You" and "we" make the talk more conversational and lets the listeners know that the speaker is talking to them.

● **Avoid jargon.** Every field has its own vocabulary of specialized words. Don't use words and acronyms that are unfamiliar to your audience. You may know what "ROI" means, but many people in audience may not.

● **Use simple words.** Don't say "print media" when you mean "newspapers." Don't say "possess" when "have" means the same thing.

● **Use round numbers.** Don't say "253,520,000 Web sites"; say "more than 250 million Web sites."

● **Use contractions.** Instead of "do not," say "don't." Say

"won't" instead of "would not." It makes the speech more conversational.

● **Avoid empty phrases.** Don't say "In spite of the fact" when "since" or "because" works just as well.

● **Use active verbs.** Say "I think" instead of "It is my conviction that . . ."

● **Don't dilute expressions of opinion.** It blunts the crispness of your talk if you use waffling terms such as "Of course, it's only my opinion but . . ." or "It seems to me . . . ."

● **Avoid modifiers.** Words such as "very" or "most" should be deleted.

● **Use direct quotes.** Identify the name or source first, and then give a direct quote. For example, "John Baskin, a reporter for the *New York Times*, wrote . . . ."

● **Vary sentence length.** In general, short sentences are best. However, occasionally break up a series of short sentences with some longer ones.

● **Use questions.** Such an approach often gets the audience more involved. "Does anyone here know the average family income in the United States?" You can also ask rhetorical questions: "What would you do in such a situation?"

● **Make comparisons and contrasts.** "An extra 1 percent in sales tax will provide enough money to build three new branch libraries."

● **Create patterns of thought.** It's all right to restate and rephrase to create a particular pattern of emphasis. Senator Hillary Clinton once used this phrasing in one of her speeches: "If women are healthy and educated, their families will flourish. If women are free from violence, their families with flourish. If women have a right to work . . . their families will flourish."

Source: Dennis L. Wilcox. *Public Relations Writing and Media Techniques*, 5th ed. Boston: Allyn & Bacon, 2005, p. 470.

voice, emphasis given to certain words or phrases, pauses, gestures, and rate of delivery are all important. Nonverbal communication is an essential part of the speech, and the Insights box on page 424 gives some guidelines for the speaker to come across as friendly, assured, and self-confident.

Some speakers prefer to have certain phrases underlined and to have detailed cues in the script, such as "pause," "look at the audience," or "make point with arm raised." Others don't want such cues; it's a matter of preference.

ON THE JOB insights

Nonverbal Communication Says a Lot

An individual speaking at a conference, a news conference, or even in a one-to-one interview with a journalist communicates a lot through his or her body language. Veteran speaker Jack Pyle offers the SPEAK method as an approach to nonverbal communication. The following is adapted from his remarks to *PR Reporter*.

- **S = Smile.** It's one of your best communication tools; it makes a good first impression and helps others want to hear what you have to say.
- **P = Posture.** Stand straight, and don't slouch or lean on the podium. President Bush was faulted in the first 2004 Presidential debate with John Kerry because he kept leaning on the podium, signaling to the audience that he wasn't as self-confident as his words indicated.
- **E = Eye Contact.** A person who is believable and honest "looks you straight in the eye." Don't stare, but look at someone in the audience for about three seconds before moving on.
- **A = Animation.** Show your interest in the subject with energy and animation. Be enthusiastic. "A" also is for attitude. Make sure you feel good about yourself and what you are saying. A good attitude, in today's public skepticism of corporate CEOs, is one of humility. Martha Stewart, charged with lying to federal investigators about insider trading, didn't learn this lesson until after she was convicted.
- **K = Kinetics (motion).** Use your arms to make gestures that support your words. Use your hand to emphasize a point; occasionally move to the side of the podium as if you are personally talking to someone in the audience. However, motion doesn't mean rocking back and forth on your feet as you talk, adjusting your hair, or fiddling with your tie.

Format is also a matter of personal preference. Some people prefer to have the speech double-spaced; others want triple spacing. A few like to have the speech in all capital letters, but the standard practice is caps and lowercase with heads and subheads in boldface type. A speech is often printed in large type, 14 to 20 points, so the speaker can easily read it, even in a dim light.

The speaker should be sufficiently familiar with the note cards or prepared text to permit abridgment on brief notice. Such advance thinking is particularly important for a speaker at a luncheon meeting. All too often, the meal is served late or the group takes an excessive amount of time discussing internal matters or making general announcements, leaving a speaker far less time than originally planned.

The same thing can happen at an evening banquet. For example, the awards ceremony may take longer than expected, and the speaker is introduced at 9:15 P.M., three hours after everyone has sat down to dinner. In this instance, the most applause is for the speaker who realizes the time and makes a brief speech.

Giving a Speech or Presentation

Writing a speech focuses almost exclusively on content. Giving a speech or presentation is all about delivery. Public relations practitioners in the course of their daily work may not give many formal speeches to large audiences, but they do give any number of presentations to their employers and clients about proposed new programs, progress on current programs, or the results of a particular campaign.

Much that has already been said about writing a speech also is applicable to giving a speech or presentation. You still need to know the audience and objective of the speech. Is it to inform, persuade, celebrate, amuse, or entertain? An informative speech might tell the audience how something was done. A persuasive speech attempts to motivate the audience into doing something—approving the new plan, volunteering to serve on a task force, or writing their local legislator. A celebratory speech is designed to honor some person or event. If it's a retirement party, you can be somewhat amusing and offer some platitudes that no doubt will be well received.

Appealing to the Ear

The average speech or presentation has only one brief exposure—the few minutes during which the speaker is presenting it. There is no chance to go back, no time to let it slowly digest, no opportunity for clarification. The message must be clearly understood at the time it is given.

Public relations personnel are usually accomplished writers, but they must realize that speaking is quite another form of communication. As Louis Nizer, a writer, once said, "The words may be the same, but the grammar, rhetoric, and phrasing are different. It is a different mode of expression—a different language."

With a speech, you have to build up to a major point and prepare the audience for what is coming. The lead of a news release attempts to say everything in about 15 or 20 words right at the beginning. If a speaker were to use the same form as a news release, most of the audience probably would not hear the main point of the speech. When a speaker begins to talk, the audience is still settling down. Therefore, the first words of a speech often are devoted to setting the stage thanking the host, making a humorous comment, or saying how nice it is to be there. Here's the opening of the EDS speech for the Association of American Chambers of Commerce in Latin America:

> Hello. I am glad to be with you at this important event. I am enthusiastic about the event's theme, "The Transformation of the Americas," as well as the topic for this panel, "Opportunities Created by Advances in Information Technology," because I truly believe we are in a major transformation, and tremendous opportunities abound.

People's minds wander during a speech. As your speech progresses, it's a good idea to restate and summarize the key points. One platitude of the speaking circuit, and a valid one, is to "tell them what you are going to tell them, tell it to them, and then tell them what you have told them." In this way, an audience is given a series of guideposts as they listen to the presentation.

Some concepts used by writers are, of course, transferable to speaking. The words used should be clear, concise, short, and definite. Use words that specify, explain, and paint pictures for the audience. In addition, avoid delivering a speech in a monotone voice. This puts audiences to sleep.

Keeping the Audience in Mind

It has already been noted that the first step in speechwriting is determining the composition of the audience. This also is true if you are the speaker. A talk before a professional group can be more relevant if you prepare for it by doing some preliminary research.

Talk to some members of that particular profession. Get an idea of the issues or problems they face. Another approach is to go online to the site of the organization, whether it's local or international, and see what is posted. Some speakers may even visit the local library and look through some issues of the organization's national magazine. Of course, the organization's contact who invited you should be consulted about the group and what they are expecting from your talk.

Your familiarity with the organization can pay dividends in terms of making relevant references to the group within the context of the talk. This can help you choose examples, quotes, and stories that are meaningful—and appreciated.

Audiences usually remember only a small part of what they hear. The speaker therefore must make sure they hear things that stick in their minds. A vague generality has little or no chance of being understood or remembered. A speaker can issue the vague call for more transparency and financial accountability in corporations, but the audience will better remember the point if he or she is more specific, for example, calling for new federal regulations that would severely penalize corporations for failing to write annual reports that a sixth grader could understand.

In most cases, the person who is asked to speak is perceived to be an expert on a given subject. Consequently, the audience wants the benefit of that person's thoughts, analysis, and even opinions on a particular situation or issue. They don't want platitudes or statements that are vague and self-evident.

Here are some tips about keeping the audience in mind:

- **Know your listeners.** Think about such demographics as age, income, education, occupation, and gender.
- **Use their language.** Use terms and expressions that are familiar to the audience.
- **Use visuals.** Audiences remember better if information is presented in visual form, such as charts or bulleted slides.
- **Use humor carefully.** Avoid side comments and jokes that may offend. The safest humor is a story that a speaker tells about himself or herself.
- **Watch your facts.** Be absolutely certain that the information is accurate.
- **Focus on the benefit.** Any speech must tell listeners what they will gain from the ideas presented.

Length of the Presentation

With regard to the length of a presentation, the axiom "less is best" is a good one. Most speeches and presentations, except those given at an academic conference or technical seminar, should be 20 to 30 minutes in length. A 20-minute speech is about 2,500 to 3,000 words, or about 10 pages double-spaced. The general rule is that a speaker can read about 150 to 160 words per minute.

If there is only one major speaker, a luncheon speech at a civic club usually is 20 to 30 minutes. If there are several speakers and business is conducted, a guest speaker often may speak for only 15 to 20 minutes. Many organizations that meet for breakfast or lunch have strict rules on ending a meeting at a specific time, and a speaker going beyond that time does so at his or her peril.

Evening talks at banquets also require brevity. A keynote speaker, as already noted, may be only part of a long program that includes a number of speakers and awards. The audience is tired, so the best advice is to talk for no more than 15 or 20 minutes.

Eye Contact and Gestures

Don't read a speech with your eyes glued to the lectern. It is important to look frequently at the audience and establish eye contact, which is another reason for being totally familiar with your text or note cards. Experts recommend that a speaker should look at specific people in the audience for several seconds before moving on to another part of the audience. Eye contact, according to research studies, is a major factor that establishes a speaker's rapport and credibility with an audience.

Speakers should be animated and use gestures to get their points across. Here, U.S. Senator Hillary Clinton speaks to an audience at the John F. Kennedy Library and Museum upon receiving the Distinguished American Award.

Gestures also play a major role in establishing credibility. Gestures, however, should agree or complement the vocal message to be effective. Many speakers, for example, extend their arms and hands when making a particular point. See the Insights box on page 424 for additional guidelines.

Nervous gestures, however, are distracting. Don't play with your hair, fiddle with a pen, fondle your necklace or tie, pull on your ears, or keep moving your leg or foot. Posture also is a gesture. Don't hunch over the podium; stand up straight. Pay attention to your facial expression; smile at your audience, express enthusiasm, and show that you are deeply interested in the subject. Audiences pick up on nonverbal cues and assess the speaker accordingly.

Visual Aids

A banquet speaker, making an after-dinner speech, usually delivers his or her message without visual aids. Many speeches and presentations, however, benefit from the use of visual aids to present information in a memorable way. Consider the following research findings:

- Sight accounts for 83 percent of what we learn.
- When a visual is combined with a voice, retention increases by 50 percent.
- Color increases a viewer's tendency to act on information by 26 percent.
- Use of video increases retention by 50 percent and accelerates buying decisions by 72 percent.
- The time required to present a concept can be reduced by up to 40 percent with visuals.

ON THE JOB insights

Visual Aids Improve Meeting Results

Speakers who use visual aids such as slides, film-strips, and overhead transparencies not only keep their audiences more interested but also accomplish greater results. A study sponsored by the Wharton School of Business at the University of Pennsylvania showed the following percentages:

	WITH VISUALS	WITHOUT VISUALS
Speaker's goal achieved	67%	33%
Group consensus reached	79%	58%
Information retained	50%	10%
Average meeting length	19 minutes	28 minutes

The effectiveness of visual aids is also elaborated on in the Insights box at left, which shows how a speaker's effectiveness is enhanced by visual aids.

It is important to understand the advantages and disadvantages of each visual aid technique to determine what is most effective for a given situation. If the presentation is at a workshop or seminar where the objective is to inform and educate an audience, a PowerPoint presentation may be the best approach. If, on the other hand, the workshop has the objective of generating ideas and audience discussion, perhaps an easel with a blank pad of paper is the only visual aid required.

A major speech for a large convention, however, may be more effective if one uses 35-mm slides and video clips. This was the case when Hector Ruiz, president of AMD, addressed the annual meeting of high-technology manufacturers in Las Vegas. He used three short videos in his talk to illustrate how AMD partnered with other companies to solve their particular problems and, along the way, create new products.

PowerPoint.   The leading presentation software is Microsoft's PowerPoint. *USA Today* business writer Kevin Maney said it best when he wrote, "PowerPoint users are inheriting the earth. The software's computer-generated, graphic-artsy presentation slides are everywhere—meetings, speeches, sales pitches, Web sites. They're becoming an essential to getting through the business day as coffee and Post-It notes."

In fact, PowerPoint presentations have become so common that one study flatly claimed that it was ". . . a way of life, considering that more than 90 percent of computer-based presentation visuals in the United States are created using it." Not everyone is happy with this situation. Many public relations professionals say the program has been overused to the point that audiences have begun to groan when the someone fires up the LCD projector with yet another PowerPoint presentation.

PowerPoint, however, is a very versatile software program from the standpoint of preparing information that can be used in a variety of ways. Here are some of the ways it can be used:

● **Use your computer monitor.** A desktop or laptop computer is the ideal way to show the presentation to one or two individuals. The laptop or notebook presentation is popular on media tours and when talking one-to-one with a journalist or financial analyst.

● **Harness your laptop to a computer projector.** If you are reaching a larger audience, technology has now advanced so you can show a PowerPoint presentation on a large screen in a meeting hall.

- **Post PowerPoint presentations on the Web.** You can post an entire slide presentation to the organization's Web site or intranet.

- **Make overhead transparencies.** A PowerPoint presentation can be downloaded and printed on clear plastic sheets, called transparencies. Some speakers, for example, carry a set of transparencies just in case the computer projector (LCD) malfunctions. Also, a speaker should not always count on an LCD projector being available.

- **Print pages.** "Hard" copies of a presentation can be distributed to members of the audience. The software allows the creator to place thumbnails of each slide on the left column of a printout and give a place for individuals to take notes on the right side of the page.

- **Create 35-mm slides.** A PowerPoint presentation can also be converted to 35-mm slides and then shown using a slide projector and a carousel slide tray. This approach is a good backup in case the organization or meeting room doesn't have an LCD projector. Using a slide projector also means that a speaker doesn't have to bring a laptop computer or worry about connections between the LCD projector and the laptop, which can be tricky at times.

- **Create CDs and DVDs.** Many organizations put PowerPoint presentations on CDs or, increasingly, on DVDs, so they can be easily sent to media reporters, customers, and field personnel, who can then view them at a convenient time.

Whatever the medium, some design rules about the composition of a PowerPoint slide should be kept in mind.

One key rule is to keep it simple. If the slide is too cluttered with text, borders, and even clip art, it cuts down on readability and retention. Peter Nolan, writing in *Public Relations Tactics*, says, "The last thing any presenter wants is to have the audience reading a heavy text slide rather than paying attention to what is being said. Presentation slides should support the speaker with a few key words or easily understood graphics."

A good solution to Nolan's concern is the 4 by 4 rule. Use no more than four bullets and no more than four or five words for each bullet. Others, such as Cornelius Pratt, formerly of Michigan State University, recommend a "triple-seven" rule: no more than seven bullets, no more than seven words per bullet, and no more than seven lines per bulleted slide. This is not to say that every slide should look exactly the same. Transitional slides, those bridging from one topic or major point to another, may consist of only one or two words or perhaps a photo or piece of clip art. In general, the axiom holds—less is better.

In terms of type size, the standard rule is 24- to 28-point type for all words. Anything smaller will be difficult to see from the back of the room. There should also be about a 2-inch margin around any copy; this ensures that any text will fit the configuration of a slide projector and a 35-mm slide, if that medium is used. PowerPoint has text boxes that supply the right amount of space around the text.

Color also is an important consideration. PowerPoint has hundreds of colors available on its palette, but that doesn't mean you should use all of them. Multiple colors for the background and text only distract the audience and give the impression of an incoherent presentation. Maney, from *USA Today*, says ". . . people spend too much time messing with the PowerPoint and not enough time messing with the message."

In other words, keep it simple. Use clear, bold fonts for colors that contrast with the background. According to research, a dark blue background conveys a corporate approach. Green works well when feedback is desired, and reds motivate the audience to action. Yellows and purples are not recommended for most business presentations. In general, black is the best color for text, but remember the contrast rule. Black type on a dark blue or red background won't be readable. Other experts recommend earth tones and middle-range colors for a slide's background so there is a maximum contrast between the text (black or another dark color) and the background.

Slide Presentations.   PowerPoint presentations, as previously mentioned, can be converted to 35-mm slides. This format is often used for presentations in school classrooms and at civic club meetings where an LCD projector may not be readily available. The carousel projector may not be high-tech, but it is still found in more meeting rooms and classrooms than the more expensive LCD projector. This is rapidly changing, however.

A 35-mm slide presentation, like a PowerPoint presentation, needs a script that is coordinated with the slides. Speakers using a slide presentation often write their speeches in a two-column format, with the slide number or description on the left side and the text on the right side, in much the same manner that a video news release (VNR) is formatted (see page 397). This allows the speaker to coordinate his or her slides with what is being said. There's nothing worse than a slide showing one thing and the speaker talking about something else.

The timing of the slides in a presentation varies. It's possible to make a good presentation with just a few slides. In fact, Pratt recommends one PowerPoint or 35-mm slide with text every five minutes. Others, however, say that a 35-mm slide presentation with a lot of photos could have about 100 slides changed at the rate of 4 or 5 per minute. The general guideline is that a slide should be on the screen long enough for the audience to digest and understand it. Photos, of course, take less time than text.

Transparencies.   The traditional workhorse in the seminar or workshop is the overhead projector. Organizations still use transparencies—often created using PowerPoint software—in training sessions and other situations where a high-tech approach is not really needed. An overhead projector is much cheaper than equipping multiple rooms with LCD projectors. Transparencies also are relatively inexpensive and can be made on a photocopy machine at the last minute. Color transparencies, however, are about as expensive as making color 35-mm slides.

The same rules apply to formatting and text size. Use 24- to 28-point type, keep the text to four or five lines per page, and use a 2-inch margin. One common problem with transparencies is that speakers often turn their back on the audience while they read the text on the screen.

Charts and Graphs.   These also can be formatted in PowerPoint and enlarged onto large poster boards or projected onto the screen. Common charts are pie charts or bar graphs. The main rule is to keep them relatively simple so they can be readily understood by the audience.

Flip Charts.   Another visual aid is the flip-chart, information on poster boards or a large-page tablet mounted on an easel. This format is used in small group presentations. The speaker uses the flip-chart as an integral part of his or her presentation as new pages are flipped or new posters are exposed to the audience. As previously mentioned, meetings designed to solicit audience ideas and feedback use a blank pad on the easel to display ideas. A more sophisticated approach is the "smart" whiteboard, which allows anything written on it to be electronically transferred to a printer or even to computers in front of everyone in the group.

Speaker Training and Placement

Giving speeches and presentations is an important part of an organization's outreach to its key publics. A talk by an executive is an effective medium for building relationships through face-to-face interaction. It adds a human dimension to any organization, and it also offers the chance for interaction between a speaker and the audience.

Speeches, therefore, should be an integral part of an organization's overall public relations program. Indeed, public relations personnel are often involved in training speakers and seeking appropriate forums where key publics can be reached.

Executive Training

Today, the public is demanding more disclosure and accountability from organizations, which is forcing many executives to mount the speaker's platform.

Ned Scharff, a longtime speech writer at Merrill Lynch & Co., says it best in an article for *The Strategist*: "If the . . . CEO is to excel as a leader, he or she cannot avoid giving speeches. People have a deep-seated need to see and hear their leaders actively expressing vision and conviction. The more trying the circumstances, the greater the need."

According to *PRWeek*, today's CEOs are public figures, and the era of corporate scandals has made it particularly important for them to explain how they operate. Reporter Douglas Quenqua sums it up: "Humility is a running theme these days. With self-obsessed CEOs like Martha Stewart and Ken Lay getting so much attention, it's important for the good guys to assure the audience of their humanity."

As a consequence, more executives are taking courses designed to improve their public speaking skills. Cincinnati Gas & Electric, for example, holds seminars of this kind for both executives and middle managers. Other companies also have rushed into formal speech training for executives so they can represent the organization at various conferences and seminars. An articulate CEO can do much to increase the visibility of the organization and position it as a leader in the industry.

Outside consultants specializing in speech training are often hired to work with executive on how to give speeches, because this is almost becoming a prerequisite for anyone seeking the top job in an organization. In the past, a brilliant engineer or research scientist could become a CEO but, today, that person would also need to be an excellent speaker.

Media Training

In one survey of executives, *pr reporter* found that over half spend 10 hours or more each month meeting with outside groups. In addition, the majority average 20 speeches a year, about two-thirds spend time on press conferences, and another third appear on television talk shows.

This aspect of conducting news conferences and having to deal with multiple one-on-one requests from print and broadcast for interviews has also made media training a top priority of many organizations. And it's not only for CEOs. Increasingly, plant and store managers are being given media training because local media will call them before calling corporate headquarters in some distant city.

Many consultants, often former print and broadcast journalists, offer media training. However, most organizations rely on their own in-house public relations department or their outside public relations firm to provide such training.

The idea is that executives and middle managers don't know much about how the mass media operates and how to conduct a media interview. In many cases, it is the responsibility of the public relations professional to tell them such things as how to answer a question in 15 seconds or less. Media interviews are discussed further later in this chapter.

Public relations practitioners often train executives to do media interviews by playing the role of a reporter in a mock interview. They start by asking some basic questions so the executive can get comfortable; then they will start asking more complex and controversial questions to give the executive some experience in handling such inquiries. At times, executives become very agitated about such questions, but it's better to do this in a mock interview than in a real one. Another common approach is to videotape the executive answering questions so that he or she can hear the tone of their voice and view the kind of nonverbal communication they are using.

Media training can be divided into two parts: what to say and how to say it. Public relations personnel are most effective in helping executives crystallize what they want to say. Another consideration is what to say that will advance organizational objectives. Media trainers tell executives to be concise and to keep on message—to make sure that one or two key points get through to the audience.

How to say it is another matter. Print journalists often summarize and synthesize a whole conversation. Broadcast journalists, on the other hand, often edit a videotape and take a particular statement that may or may not be in context. Media training helps executives understand the difference and deal with it.

Another aspect of media training is to educate executives how news is produced and processed. Few executives, for example, realize that a reporter's story is often edited and changed by a newspaper's copy desk or that the headline is written by someone else other than the reporter. Executives also have trouble understanding why a 20-minute interview videotaped by a camera crew winds up as a 20-second story on the air.

Speaker Bureaus

Executives and local plant managers aren't the only ones who give speeches and presentations. Many organizations also effectively use technical experts, middle managers, and even rank-and-file employees on a systematic basis to extend the organization's outreach to potential customers, the industry, and the community.

In every organization, there are individuals who are capable of giving speeches and presentations. In many cases, it is part of their job description. Technical staff, for example, are often asked by professional groups to share their research or talk about the development of a particular product. In other situations, a community group may want a general overview about how the company is dealing with a sluggish economy.

One way of organizing an organization's outreach (whether it's IBM or the American Cancer Society) is to set up a speaker's bureau. This is more than just a list of employees who are willing to speak. It is also a center that trains speakers; produces supporting audiovisual aids, such as PowerPoint presentations and videos; and even develops key messages about the organization, product, or service that should be included in the presentation.

Ideally, a speaker's bureau will have a list of employees who are experts on a variety of subjects. A person in finance may be an expert on worker's compensation, and an engineer in product development may have expertise with lasers. Such expertise is the focus of the presentation, and speakers should avoid giving a sales pitch. One expert says, "A presentation that turns out to be a sales pitch will ensure low evaluations by the audience, and a one-way ticket home. . . ." In other words, the corporate logo is in the background, just as it is in a satellite media conference (SMT) or even a video news release (VNR).

An organization usually publicizes the existence of a speaker's bureau by preparing a simple pamphlet or brochure and sending it to various clubs and organizations in the community that regularly use speakers. Another method is to place advertisements about the speaker's bureau in the local newspaper.

The public relations department also fields calls from various organizations that need a speaker on a particular topic. At other times, the public relations staff is more proactive and will call an influential organization to offer the services of a speaker on a particular topic. One of the most difficult jobs in any club is that of program director, and they often welcome such suggestions.

Once a speaker has been booked, the manager of the speaker's bureau usually handles all the logistical details. He or she briefs the speaker on (1) the size and composition of the audience, (2) the location, (3) the availability of audiovisual equipment, (4) the projected length of the presentation, (5) directions to the meeting, and (6) the primary organizational contacts.

Placement of the organization's top executives, however, tends to be more strategic. Top executives often get more requests for speeches than they can ever fulfill, so the problem is in selecting a few of the invitations that are extended.

The criteria, at this point, becomes somewhat pragmatic and cold-hearted. Public relations staff are charged with screening the invitations on the basis of such factors as the venue, the nature of the group, the size of the audience, and whether the audience is an important public to the organization. If most or all of these factors are positive, the executive will most likely consent to give a speech or presentation.

Media requests for interviews are treated in much the same way. Busy executives consent to media interviews only if the publication is influential, has high circulation, and reaches key audiences. A business executive, for example, rarely turns down an interview with a reporter from the *Wall Street Journal, Fortune, Forbes, The Economist*, or the *Financial Times*. By the same token, a university president rarely turns down an interview request from the *Chronicle of Higher Education*.

Steve Albertini, executive vice president of Tierney Communications in Philadelphia, points out the importance of such publications from the standpoint of executives actually being coached for an upcoming interview. He told *PRWeek*, "For those who need to prepare for a scheduled interview in two weeks for, say, *The Wall Street Journal*, we'll be working with them every day for a full week. We might also give them a course in PR101. . . . "

On the other hand, there are numerous publications that don't have the status of the *Wall Street Journal* or that aren't particularly high on an organization's strategic communications list. Saying "no" to requests for one-on-one interviews is discussed in the section on media interviews.

At other times, the public relations staff actively seeks speaking and media opportunities for the chief executive. If the chief executive wants to become a leader in the industry, for example, the public relations staff actively seeks out speech opportunities before prestigious audiences and "pitches" publications such as *Fortune* to do a feature story on the executive's leadership qualities.

A good example of how strategic executive speech placement works is what Ronald J. McCall, owner of his own executive communication firm, did for the chief executive of Duke Energy, a $15 billion gas and electric utility. He told *Speechwriter's Newsletter*:

> The company was perceived as a local utility, and we wanted more of a national presence, so I placed the chief executive on the *Business Week* symposium for chief executive officers. That was the first time he was able to tell the Duke Energy story, and he did in front of a very influential audience of other chief executive officers from across the country. Every one of them needed some kind of energy, whether it be gas or electricity. Every one of them was a potential customer.

Another example of strategic thinking is United Parcel Service (UPS). Several years ago, the company organized an executive communications program that actively promoted its top executives as business leaders through speeches at national and regional business and trade events. The idea, says Steve Soltis, head of the UPS team, is to use senior management as a component of brand building.

Telephone Hotlines. Somewhat related to the organization's speakers bureau is a telephone hotline service operated by a trade association or company to provide quick answers, particularly to the media. Such a facility generally offers a toll-free telephone service using the 800 prefix. One advantage of a telephone hotline is talking with a person immediately. E-mail queries on the organization's Web site often go days without being answered.

The following advertisement by the Edison Electric Institute Information Service in *Editor & Publisher*, the newspaper trade journal, illustrates how a hotline functions:

You Don't Need a Press Conference to Get the Energy Story

Let's have a conference right now.
    And it won't cost you a dime.
    One of our experts is ready to help you with your network feature, or editorial.
    Ask for facts, background, and the national perspective on electric energy.
    Ask about energy sources, economics, and the environment.
    Because energy is one of the crucial issues in American life today, there's someone on the hotline 24 hours a day, 7 days a week.
    Just think. By using the phone, you'll be saving energy while writing about it.
    Call toll-free 800-424-8897.

Publicity Opportunities

The number of people a speech or presentation reaches can be substantially increased through publicity.

Before the Event. Whenever anyone from your organization speaks in public, the public relations staff must make sure that the appropriate media are notified in advance. This often takes the form of a media advisory, which was discussed in Chapter 14.

An advisory is simply a short note or memo, via letter or e-mail, alerting a media outlet that an organizational representative will speaking on a particular topic on a certain date at a particular time and location. In a brief sentence or two, a public relations staffer will say why the talk is important and offer a good news angle. It may be tied to a particular issue or trend in society.

If it's a major policy speech by the CEO, an advance text is often sent to the media and selected reporters covering that particular beat. See the PR Casebook on page 446 about a speech that gained widespread coverage in such a way. An advance text, however, should have an embargo date. In other words, the media is requested to not use the story until after the speech has been given. There are two reasons for this. First, news stories about the speech may reduce attendance at the event. Second, accidents happen, and the speech may be cancelled for some reason. The media would be embarrassed covering a speech that was never given.

If the speech is a major one, it's also possible to arrange with a production company to do a Webcast of the speech so reporters across the country can listen to it in real time. This was discussed in Chapter 15.

ON THE JOB insights

The Speech as News Release

The audience reach of a speech is multiplied many times when a news release is distributed that summarizes the speaker's key message. A speech news release follows many of the same structural guidelines outlined in Chapter 14, but there are some specific concepts that you should keep in mind.

"The key to writing stories about speeches is to summarize the speech or to present one or two key points in the lead sentence," says Douglas Starr, a professor of journalism and public relations at Texas A&M University.

In an article for *PR Tactics*, Starr says a speech news release should follow a particular format. He says, "Answers to the questions—Who, Said What, to Whom—must be in the lead of every speech story. Answers to the questions—Where, When, How, Why—may be placed in the second paragraph."

The most common mistake inexperienced writers make is to tell readers that a *speaker spoke about a topic* instead of saying what the *speaker said about the topic*. An example of the first approach is "Susan Jones, president of XYZ corporation, spoke about environmental regulations." A better approach would be, "Susan Jones, president of XYZ Corporation, says rigid environmental regulations are strangling the economy." See the difference?

The second sentence or paragraph of a speech news release usually describes the event where the speech was given, the location, the attendance, and the rea-

son for the meeting. It is unnecessary, however, to give the title of a person's speech or even the theme of the convention or meeting. They are meaningless to the reader.

The third and subsequent paragraphs may contain speaker quotes, additional facts or figures, and other relevant information that helps provide context for the speech. When attributing quotes, "said" is the preferred verb. However, some writers vary this by using the terms "stated," or "added." Starr suggests you stay away from such attribution terms as "discussed," "addressed," and "spoke," because they don't say anything.

Source: Dennis L. Wilcox. Public Relations Writing and Media Techniques, 5th ed. Boston: Allyn & Bacon, 2005, p. 493.

After the Event.   After a major speech has been given, the work of the public relations staff is just beginning. Public relations practitioners prepare audio, video, and print news releases about the speech for distribution to appropriate media. Television stations, in particular, appreciate a short video clip that can be used on the next newscast. See the Insights box on page 435 about how to write a news release about a speech.

A number of other tactics are possible. One is the conversion of the speech into an op-ed article for newspapers and magazines. Another is the speech reprint, packaging the speech (with some editing) into a brochure that can be mailed to customers, employees, and opinion leaders in a particular industry. Excerpts can be posted, with video clips, on the organization's Web site.

Another possibility is submitting the speech to the publication *Vital Speeches of the Day*. Some organizations even make arrangements for the speech to be printed as part of the *Congressional Record*.

Media Interviews

Another widely used spoken method of publicizing an individual or a cause is the interview, which may appear in print form in newspapers and magazines or on television and radio. Satellite Media Tours (SMTs) are a popular new method, which was discussed in the last chapter. The ability of the person being interviewed to communicate easily is essential to success. Although required to stay in the background, with fingers crossed that all goes well, a public relations specialist can do much to prepare the interviewee.

Andrew D. Gilman, president of CommCore in New York City, emphasizes the need for preparation. He says, "I would no more think of putting a client on a witness stand or through a deposition without thorough and adequate presentation than I would ask a client to be interviewed by a skillful and well-prepared journalist without a similar thorough and adequate preparation."

Purpose and Objective

In all interviews, the person being questioned should say something that will inform or entertain the audience. The practitioner should prepare the interviewee to meet this need. An adroit interviewer attempts to develop a theme in the conversation—to draw out comments that make a discernible point or illuminate the character of the person being interviewed. The latter can help the interviewer—and his or her own cause as well—by being ready to volunteer specific information, personal data, or opinions about the cause under discussion as soon as the conversational opportunity arises.

In setting up an interview, the public relations person should obtain from the interviewer an understanding as to its purpose. Armed with this information, the practitioner can assemble facts and data for the client to use in the discussion. The practitioner also can aid the client by providing tips about the interviewer's style.

Some interviewers on the radio talk shows that have proliferated in recent years ask "cream puff" questions, while others bore in, trying to upset the guest into unplanned admissions or embarrassment. Thus, it is especially important to be well acquainted with the interviewer's style, whether it be Larry King before a national audience of millions or a local broadcaster. Short, direct answers delivered without hesitation help a guest project an image of strength and credibility.

Print Differs from Broadcast

A significant difference exists between interviews in print and those on radio and television. In a print interview, the information and character impressions the public receives about the interviewee have been filtered through the mind of the writer. The person interviewed is interpreted by the reporter, not projected directly to the audience. On radio and television, however, listeners hear the interviewee's voice without intervention by a third party. During a television interview, where personality has the strongest impact of all, the speaker is both seen and heard. Because of the intimacy of television, a person with a weak message who projects charm or authority may influence an audience more than one with a strong message who does not project well. A charismatic speaker with a strong message can have enormous impact. See Chapter 15 for more information on radio and television talk shows.

Know When to Say No

When an organization or individual is advocating a particular cause or policy, opportunities to give newspaper interviews are welcomed, indeed sought after. Situations arise, however, when the better part of public relations wisdom is to reject a request for an interview, either print or electronic. Such rejection need not imply that an organization has a sinister secret or fails to understand the need for public contact.

For example, a corporation may be planning a fundamental operational change involving an increase in production at some plants and the closing of another, outdated facility. Details are incomplete, and company employees have not been told. A reporter, either suspecting a change or by sheer chance, requests an interview with the company's chief executive officer.

Normally, the interview request would be welcomed, to give the executive public exposure and an opportunity to enunciate company philosophy. At this moment, however, public relations advisers fear that the reporter's questions might uncover the changes prematurely, or at least force the executive into evasive answers that might hurt the firm's credibility. So the interview request is declined, or delayed until a later date, as politely as possible. The next week, when all is in place, the chief executive announces the changes at a news conference. *Avoiding trouble is a hidden but vital part of a public relations adviser's role.* At a later time, the public relations representative might make a special effort to do the would-be interviewer a favor on a story.

An alternative approach would be for the chief executive officer to grant the interview, with the understanding that only topics specified in advance would be discussed. Very rarely is such an approach acceptable, however, because reporters usually resent any restrictions and try to uncover the reasons for them.

The Print Interview

An interview with a newspaper reporter may last about an hour, perhaps at lunch or over coffee in an informal setting. The result of this person-to-person talk may be a published story of perhaps 400 to 600 words. The interviewer weaves bits from the conversation together in direct and indirect quotation form, works in background material, and perhaps injects personal observations about the interviewee. The latter has no control over what is published, beyond the self-control he or she exercises in answering the questions. Neither the person being interviewed nor a public relations representative should ask to approve an interview story before it is published. Such requests are rebuffed automatically as a form of censorship.

Magazine interviews usually explore the subject in greater depth than those in newspapers, because the writer may have more space available. Most magazine interviews have the same format as those in newspapers. Others appear in question-and-answer form. These require prolonged taped questioning of the interviewee by one or more writers and editors. During in-depth interviews, the person interviewed must guard against saying something that can be taken out of context.

Radio and Television Interviews

The possibilities for public relations people to have their clients interviewed on the air are immense. The current popularity of talk shows, both on local stations and syndicated satellite networks, provides many opportunities for on-air appearances in which the guest expresses opinions and answers call-in questions. (See Chapter 15.) A successful radio or television broadcast interview appearance has three principal requirements:

1. **Preparation**. Guests should know what they want to say.
2. **Concise speech.** Guests should answer questions and make statements precisely and briefly. They shouldn't hold forth in excessive detail or drag in extraneous material. Responses should be kept to 30 seconds or less, because seconds count on the air. The interviewer must conduct the program under severe time restrictions.
3. **Relaxation.** "Mike fright" is a common ailment for which no automatic cure exists. It will diminish, however, if the guest concentrates on talking to the interviewer in a casual person-to-person manner, forgetting the audience as much as possible. Guests should speak up firmly; the control room can cut down their volume if necessary.

A public relations adviser can help an interview guest on all of these points. Answers to anticipated questions may be worked out and polished during a mock interview in which the practitioner plays the role of broadcaster. A tape recording or videotape of a practice session will help the prospective guest to correct weaknesses.

All too often, the hosts on talk shows know little about their guests for the day's broadcast. The public relations adviser can overcome this difficulty by sending the host in advance a fact sheet summarizing the important information and listing questions the broadcaster might wish to ask. On network shows such as David Letterman's, nationally syndicated talk shows such as Oprah Winfrey's, and local programs on metropolitan stations, support staffs do the preliminary work with guests. Interviewers on hundreds of smaller local television and radio stations, however, lack such staffs. They may go on the air almost "cold" unless provided with volunteered information.

News Conferences

At a news conference, communication is two-way. The person speaking for a company or a cause submits to questioning by reporters, usually after a brief opening statement. A news conference makes possible quick, widespread dissemination of the sponsor's

One spoken tactic that has the potential of reaching millions of people is the appearance on a national talk show. Here, Gov. Arnold Schwarzenegger of California shares a story with Jay Leno on the *Late Night Show*.

information and opinions through the news media. It avoids the time-consuming task of presenting the information to the news outlets individually and ensures that the intensely competitive newspapers and electronic media hear the news simultaneously. From a public relations point of view, these are the principal advantages of the news conference. Against these important pluses must be weighed the fact that the person holding the conference is open to severe and potentially antagonistic questioning.

In public relations strategy, the news conference can be either an offensive or a defensive device, depending on the client's need.

Most news conferences—or press conferences, as they frequently are called—are *positive* in intent; they are affirmative actions to project the host's plans or point of view. A corporation may hold a news conference to unveil a new product whose manufacture will create many new jobs, or a civic leader may do so to reveal the goals and plans for a countywide charity fund drive she will head. Such news conferences should be carefully planned and scheduled well in advance under the most favorable circumstances.

Public relations specialists also must deal frequently with unanticipated, controversial situations. A business firm, an association, or a politician becomes embroiled in difficulty that is at best embarrassing, possibly incriminating. Press and public demand an explanation. A bare-bones printed statement is not enough to satisfy the clamor and may draw greater press scrutiny of the stonewalling organization. A well-prepared spokesperson may be able to achieve a measure of understanding and sympathy by issuing a carefully composed printed statement when the news conference opens.

No matter how trying the circumstances, the person holding the news conference should create an atmosphere of cooperation and project a sincere intent to be helpful. The worst thing he or she can do is to appear resentful of the questioning. The person never should succumb to a display of bad temper. A good posture is to admit that the situation is bad and that the organization is doing everything in its power to

News conferences are an opportunity to talk with many reporters at the same time. Some news conferences are somewhat formal and take place in a meeting room. However, many are informal, such as this one in which former President Bill Clinton and Sen. Hillary Clinton speak to reporters after meeting with local Buddhist leaders and relief volunteers gathering supplies for tsunami victims in Sri Lanka.

correct it, the approach described by Professor Timothy Coombs at Wayne State University as the "mortification" strategy. (Further discussion of crisis public relations appears in Chapter 10.)

Rarely, an organization or public person caught in an embarrassing situation foolishly attempts to quiet public concern by holding a news conference that really isn't a news conference. The host reads a brief, inadequate statement, then refuses to answer questions from reporters. This practice alienates the press.

Two more types of news conferences are held. One is spontaneous, arising out of a news event: the winner of a Nobel Prize meets the press to explain the award-winning work or a runner who has just set a world's record breathlessly describes his feelings. The other type is the regularly scheduled conference held by a public official at stated times, even when there is nothing special to announce. Usually this is called a briefing—the daily State Department briefing, for example.

Planning and Conducting a News Conference

First comes the question, "Should we hold a news conference or not?" Frequently the answer should be "No!" The essential element of a news conference is *news*. If reporters and camera crews summoned to a conference hear propaganda instead of facts or information of minor interest to a limited group, they go away disgusted. Their valuable time has been wasted—and it *is* valuable. If editors send reporters to a conference that has been called merely to satisfy the host's sense of self-importance, they resent the fact. If the material involved fails to meet the criteria of significant news, a wise public relations representative will distribute it through a press release.

Every news outlet that might be interested in the material should be invited to a news conference. An ignored media outlet may become an enemy, like a person who isn't asked to a party. The invitation should describe the general nature of the material to be discussed so an editor will know what type of reporter to assign.

What hour is best? This depends upon the local media situation. If the city has only an afternoon newspaper, 9:30 or 10 A.M. is good, because this gives a reporter time to write a story before a midday deadline. If the city's newspaper publishes in the morning, 2 P.M. is a suitable hour.

Another prime goal of news conference sponsors is the early evening newscasts on local television stations, or even network TV newscasts if the information is important enough. A conference at 2 P.M. is about the latest that a television crew can cover and still get the material processed at a comfortable pace for inclusion in a dinner-hour show. This time period can be shortened a little in an emergency.

A warning: A public relations representative in a city with only an afternoon newspaper who schedules a news conference after that paper's deadline, yet in time for the news to appear on the early evening television newscasts, makes a grave blunder. Newspaper editors resent such favoritism to television and have long memories. Knowledge of, and sensitivity to, local news media deadlines are necessary.

Here are two pieces of advice from longtime public relations specialists to persons who hold news conferences:

1. The speaker should never attempt to talk off-the-record at a news conference. If the information is so secret that it should not be published, then the speaker shouldn't tell it to reporters. Many editors forbid their reporters to honor off-the-record statements, because too often the person making them is merely attempting to prevent publication of material that is legitimate news but might be embarrassing. Any statement made before a group will not stay secret long, anyway.

2. The speaker should never lie! If he or she is pushed into a corner and believes that answering a specific question would be unwise, it is far better to say, "No comment" in some form than to answer falsely. A person caught in a lie to the media suffers a critical loss of credibility.

Preparing the Location

At a news conference, public relations representatives resemble producers of a movie or television show. They are responsible for briefing the spokesperson, making arrangements, and ensuring that the conference runs smoothly. They stay in the background, however.

Bulldog Reporter, a West Coast public relations newsletter, suggests the following checklist for a practitioner asked to organize a news conference. The time factors given are normal for such events as new product introductions, but conferences concerning spot news developments for the daily press and electronic media often are called on notice of a few days or even a few hours.

- Select a convenient location, one that is fairly easy for news representatives to reach with minimal travel time.
- Set the date and time. Times between midmorning and midafternoon are good. Friday afternoons are deadly, as are days before holidays.
- When possible, issue an invitation to a news conference about six to eight weeks ahead of time, but one month is acceptable. The invitation should include the purpose of the conference, names of spokespersons, and why the event has significant news value. Of course, the date, time, and location must be provided.

- Distribute a media release about the upcoming news conference when appropriate. This depends on the importance of the event.

- Write a statement for the spokesperson to give at the conference and make sure that he or she understands and rehearses it. In addition, rehearse the entire conference.

- Try to anticipate questions so the spokesperson can readily answer difficult queries. Problem/solution rehearsals prepare the spokesperson.

- Prepare printed materials for distribution at the conference. These should include a brief fact sheet with names and titles of participants, a basic news release, and basic support materials. This is sometimes called a media kit.

- Prepare visual materials as necessary. These may include slides, transparencies, posters, or even a short videotape.

- Make advance arrangements for the room. Be sure that there are enough chairs and leave a center aisle for photographers. If a lectern is used, make certain that it is large enough to accommodate multiple microphones.

- Arrive 30 to 60 minutes early to double-check arrangements. Test the microphones, arrange name tags for invited guests, and distribute literature.

Some organizations provide coffee and sweet rolls for their media guests as a courtesy. Others find this gesture unnecessary because most of the newspeople are in a hurry. Liquor should not be served at a regular news conference. Such socializing should be reserved for the press party, discussed in the next section.

At some news conferences, still photographers are given two or three minutes to take their pictures before questioning begins. Some photographers complain that, thus restricted, they cannot obtain candid shots. If free shooting is permitted, as usually is the best practice, the physical arrangements should give the photographers operating space without allowing them to obstruct the view of reporters.

A practitioner should take particular care to arrange the room in such a way that the electronic equipment does not impede the print reporters. Some find it good policy for the speaker to remain after the news conference ends and make brief on-camera statements for individual TV stations, if their reporters request this attention. Such statements should not go beyond anything the speaker has said to the entire body of reporters.

A final problem in managing a news conference is knowing when to end it. The public relations representative serving as backstage watchdog should avoid cutting off the questioning prematurely. To do so creates antagonism from the reporters. Letting a conference run down like a tired clock is almost as bad. A moment comes when reporters run out of fresh questions. A speaker may not recognize this. If not, the practitioner may step forward and say something like, "I'm sorry, but I know some of you have deadlines to make. So we have time for just two more questions."

The Press Party and the Media Tour

In the typical news conference, the purpose is to transmit information and opinion from the organization to the news media in a businesslike, time-efficient manner. Often, however, a corporation, an association, or a political figure wishes to deliver a message or build rapport with the media on a more personal basis; then a social setting is desirable. Thus is born the press party or the press trip.

The Press Party

This gathering may be a luncheon, a dinner, or a reception. Whatever form the party takes, standard practice is for the host to rise at the end of the socializing period and make the "pitch." This may be a hard-news announcement, a brief policy statement followed by a question-and-answer period, or merely a soft-sell thank-you to the guests for coming and giving the host an opportunity to know them better. Guests usually are given press packets of information, either when they arrive or as they leave. Parties giving the press a preview of an art exhibit, a new headquarters building, and so forth are widely used.

The press party is a softening-up process, and both sides know it.

The advantages of a press party to its host can be substantial under the proper circumstances. During chitchat over food or drink, officials of the host organization become acquainted with media people who write, edit, or broadcast material about them. Although the benefit from the host's point of view is difficult to measure immediately, the party opens the channels of communication.

Also, if the host has an important policy position to present, the assumption—not necessarily correct—is that editors and reporters will be more receptive after a social hour. The host who expects that food and drink will buy favorable press coverage may receive an unpleasant surprise. Conscientious reporters and editors will not be swayed by a free drink and a plate of prime rib followed by baked Alaska. In their view, they have already given something to the host by setting aside a part of their day for the party. They accept invitations to press parties because they wish to develop potential news contacts within the host's organization and to learn more about its officials.

The Media Tour

There are three kinds of media tours. The most common is a trip, often disparagingly called a "junket," during which editors and reporters are invited to inspect a company's manufacturing facilities in several cities, ride an inaugural flight of a new air route, or watch previews of the television network programs for the fall season in Hollywood or New York. The host usually picks up the tab for transporting, feeding, and housing the reporters.

A variation of the media tour is the familiarization trip. "Fam trips," as they are called, are offered to travel writers and editors by the tourism industry (see Chapter 22). Convention and visitor bureaus, as well as major resorts, pay all expenses in the hope that the writers will report favorably on their experiences. Travel articles in magazines and newspapers usually result from a reporter's "fam trip."

In the third kind of media tour, widely used in high-technology industries, the organization's executives travel to key cities to talk with selected editors; for example, top Apple Computer executives toured the East Coast to talk with key magazine editors and demonstrate the capabilities of the new Apple iMac computer. Depending on editors' preferences, the executives may visit a publication and give a background briefing to key editors, or a hotel conference room may be set up so that the traveling executives may talk with editors from several publications at the same time.

The Ethics of Who Pays for What. In recent years, severe soul-searching by media members, as well as by professional public relations personnel who feel it is unethical to offer lavish travel and gifts, has led to increased self-regulation by both groups as to when a press tour or "junket" is appropriate and how much should be spent.

The policies of major dailies forbid employees to accept any gifts, housing, or transportation; the newspapers pay all costs associated with a press tour on which a staff member is sent. In contrast, some smaller dailies, weeklies, and trade magazines accept offers for an expense-paid trip. Their managers maintain that they don't have the resources of large dailies to reimburse an organization for expenses and such trips are legitimate for covering a newsworthy activity.

Some newspapers with policies forbidding acceptance of travel and gifts don't extend the restrictions to all departments. Reporters in the "hard news" area, for example, cannot accept gifts or travel, but such policy may not be enforced for reporters who write "soft news" for sports, travel, and lifestyle sections. Few newspapers, for example, pay for the press box seats provided for reporters covering a professional football game, nor does the travel editor usually pay the full rate for rooms at beach resorts that are the focus of travel articles.

ON THE JOB ethics

Press Party at Disney World Criticized

Disney World in Florida threw a press party to celebrate its 15th anniversary, and more than 10,000 journalists showed up.

The park offered to pay the entire expense of any invited journalist who wanted to come, but it was also aware that many media outlets had policies about their news staff accepting such offers. Therefore, Disney public relations staffers sent invitations outlining three options:

1. Disney World and its travel-promotion partners would pay all of the journalist's travel, lodging, and food costs.
2. Disney World would pay $150 daily to a visiting journalist, and his or her employer could reimburse the journalist for anything over that amount.
3. A journalist's employer could pay all of his or her expenses.

The *New York Times*, however, editorialized that the journalists who accepted the free trip "debased" journalism and gave the public impression that the entire press was "on the take." The *St. Petersburg Times* called the party "junket journalism" and also castigated Disney World for trying to "buy the press." Smaller newspapers and broadcasting station were less outraged. They said their journalists could not attend such an event if Disney had not offered to pay all or part of the expenses.

Disney World did receive a large amount of favorable news stories about the park as a result of the anniversary celebration, except for the media-ethics dispute. The total cost was about $7.5 million to host all the journalists, according to *Editor & Publisher*.

Did Disney and its public relations staff do anything wrong in terms of inviting the journalists? Do you think Disney should be criticized for trying to "buy the press"? Why or why not? Is this a public relations ethics concern, or primarily one of ethics for the mass media?

Given the mixed and often confusing policies of various media, the public relations professional must use common sense and discretion. He or she, first of all, should not violate the PRSA code of ethics, which forbids lavish gifts and free trips that have nothing to do with covering a legitimate news event. Second, the public relations person should be sensitive to the policies of news outlets and should design events to stay within them. A wise alternative is to offer a reporter the option of reimbursing the company for travel and hotel expenses associated with a press tour.

In terms of gift-giving, the sensible approach is a token of remembrance such as a pen, note pad, or a company paperweight. Some large newspapers will not permit even these token gifts. (Ethics are discussed extensively in Chapter 3.)

Organizing a Press Party or Media Tour

The key to a successful event is detailed organization. Every step of the process should be checked out meticulously.

In planning the press event, the practitioner has to consider a variety of details. Menus for a luncheon or dinner should be chosen carefully. Do any of the guests have dietary restrictions? Has the exact hour of serving been arranged with the restaurant or caterer, to allow sufficient time for the program? The usual check on microphone and physical facilities is essential.

Even such a seemingly trivial item as a name tag requires the practitioner's careful attention. Name tags prepared in advance are lined up on a check-in table at the entrance to the room. A host or hostess hands the tags to the arriving guests. A guest who can be welcomed by name, without having to state it, feels subtly flattered. Almost inevitably, though, some name tags will be unclaimed because individuals who accepted fail to show up. In a perfect world, absentees would telephone to cancel their acceptances, but public relations life doesn't work that way. Occasionally, an invited person who failed to answer the invitation will arrive unexpectedly; blank name tags should be kept available for such a situation.

Fouled-up transportation is perhaps the worst grief for a person conducting a press tour. For example, buses that failed to arrive at the departure point on time to carry press covering the Centennial Olympics in Atlanta marred the opening days of the Games and dampened coverage by some reporters throughout this highly successful, vast special event. Some guests may be prima donnas who will be dissatisfied with almost any hotel room assigned to them. None of the tour guests should be allowed to feel that others are receiving favored treatment. Maintaining a firm tour schedule is essential. At each stop, the host should round up the strays a few minutes before the departure time.

As much as possible, the public relations representative should "walk through" the entire route to confirm arrangements and look for possibly embarrassing hidden troubles. When North American Aviation introduced a new jet fighter to the national press at the Palmdale, California, airport in the Mojave desert, it asked the pilot to impress the guests by diving and creating a sonic boom. He did so—and pieces of glass went flying through the reception area from windows broken by the impact of the boom. The pilot climbed to do it again, but the hosts stopped him in time by yelling into the radio, "Call it off!"

PR CASEBOOK
Speech Receives Widespread Coverage

A speech with a theme that connects with an audience's core values and provides an inspirational message is always well received. This was the kind of speech that Kay Coles James, director of the U.S. Office of Personnel Management, gave to employees of the Defense Information Systems Agency.

The theme, "They Said It Couldn't Be Done," had the objective of raising morale, maintaining professionalism, and motivating employees during a particularly critical time of global conflict. The Defense Information Systems Agency is a major provider of communications and computer capabilities to U.S. forces in Iraq, Afghanistan, and other locations around the globe.

James, who was invited to speak at the agency's Executive Speaker Forum, reminded the audience that nothing is ever impossible, and American history is filled with amazing feats accomplished by everyday people. According to *Public Relations Tactics*, "The speech recognized the important contributions audience members made in turning political promises into results for U.S. taxpayers. It then developed the theme 'They Said It Couldn't Be Done' by including personalized references to the Korean War memorial and a quotation from former President Ronald Reagan to support the idea that it is never impossible to overcome challenges."

The speech also positioned the U.S. Office of Personnel Management as a leader in managing the "human capital" to meet the needs of the federal government.

Although the media were not permitted to attend the speech, it generated extensive media coverage anyway, thanks to speech transcripts and news releases sent to all media by agency public relations personnel. The speech was also reprinted in full in *Vital Speeches of the Day* and *Executive Speeches*.

The PRSA awarded the speech and the post-speech publicity efforts a Bronze Anvil for 2004.

SUMMARY

The Art of Speechwriting
This is a systematic process that requires research into the prospective audience and a thorough understanding of the speaker's beliefs and how he or she expresses them. The objectives and key message points must be decided upon. First an outline is done and then a draft of the speech is written.

Writing a Speech
The writing style and word choice must be designed for the ear. Writing should be conversational, concise, and clear. Simple sentences are preferred, and words should paint pictures in the minds of the audience. All speeches have a beginning, a middle, and an end.

Giving a Speech or Presentation
Unlike journalistic writing, in which the most important point is in the lead paragraph, a speech builds up to a main point. Before speaking before a group, it's wise to find out as much as you can about the group and its interests. Nonverbal communication is an important part of any presentation. A speaker

should be enthusiastic, maintain eye contact with the audience, smile, and use gestures appropriately. Most speeches should be between 20 and 30 minutes long.

Visual Aids Help a Speech

People retain more information if they can hear and see it at the same time. The most common presentation software is PowerPoint, which can be used in a variety of ways. The major point is to keep slides simple and uncluttered. Other visual aids can include 35-mm slides, transparencies, charts and graphs, and flip-charts.

Speaker Training

Public relations personnel often train executives to give effective speeches and presentations. Such appearances give the organization a human face and help build relationships. Another area is media training. Executives and middle managers must know how the media operates and how to give succinct, short answers.

Speaker Bureaus

Many organizations operate speaker bureaus in which employees share their expertise with community groups free of charge. Operating a speaker's bureau requires public relations staff to train speakers, provide audiovisual materials, and handle the logistics of booking them for appearances. A variation of the speaker's bureau is a telephone hotline for media inquiries.

Publicity Opportunities for Speakers

The audience for a speech can be expanded through publicity, such as news releases, media advisories, speech reprints, op-ed articles, and video clips of the speech on the organization's Web site. The speech also can be Webcast to journalists in real time or delayed for later viewing.

Media Interviews

A face-to-face interview with a print or broadcast journalist is a good way to communicate an organization's perspective. Before being interviewed, however, the individual should have a clear idea of what the journalist needs and how key messages of the organization can be effectively communicated. Public relations personnel often brief and prepare executives for various interviews.

News Conferences

A news conference is a way that an organization can distribute information to multiple journalists at the same time. It is a format for journalists to ask questions. News conferences should only be held when there is news that requires elaboration and clarification.

Press Parties and Media Tours

These activities are designed to build a relationship with journalists and to offer them the opportunity to visit plant sites or other locations. Media tours should have news value and not be just a "junket" or "vacation" for journalists.

Case Activity: **What Would You Do?**

Speechwriting is a highly refined skill. The president of a local company has hired you to write a 10-minute speech that he plans to present at the monthly meeting of the American Management Association. This group, consisting of corporate managers, wants to hear the president's views on the pros and cons of outsourcing various corporate functions, such as accounting, customer service, and management information systems (MIS), to locations such as India, where labor costs are cheaper. The president is a busy man, but he does tell you that he thinks outsourcing is an excellent way to keep American business and industry competitive. Taking the audience into consideration, do some research and draft a speech for the president. You should aim to write a speech that is five pages, doubled-spaced.

QUESTIONS for Review and Discussion

1. What preliminary steps should be taken before writing a draft of a speech for an executive in the organization?

2. Why is it important to establish the objective of and approach to a speech before writing it?

3. What are the eight aspects of organization for an effective speech?

4. Why should an executive work with a speech-writer on drafting and formatting a particular speech or presentation?

5. How does writing a speech differ from writing a news release or even a brochure?

6. Give at least five tips about the use of words in a speech.

7. Every speaker engages in nonverbal communication. What is nonverbal communication? Can you give some examples?

8. Why is it necessary to know the demographics and interests of your audience before you speak? How do you find this information?

9. How long is a typical speech? How long is the text of a 20-minute speech?

10. What gestures should you avoid when giving a speech?

11. Is there any evidence that visual aids improve the effectiveness of a presentation?

12. Identify at least three ways that PowerPoint software can be used.

13. What are some general guidelines for using PowerPoint slides?

14. Why do executives and middle managers need media training?

15. How does a speaker's bureau operate? What's a telephone hotline for journalists?

16. What can you do before and after a speech is given to generate media publicity and expand the audience for the speech?

17. What are the benefits of one-on-one media interviews? Are there any pitfalls?

18. Do public relations practitioners always have to honor a media request for an interview with the CEO? Why or why not?

19. What are the logistics of organizing a news conference?

20. How do press parties and media tours differ?

21. Should organizations pick up the tab for journalists who go on a media tour? What about giving journalists gifts?

SUGGESTED READINGS

Adams, Bill. "Media Training Is Not Enough When Preparing Executives for the Press." *Public Relations Tactics*, May 2003, p. 18.

Adams, Bill. "Ask the Professor: Points about PowerPoint." *Public Relations Tactics*, February 2003, p. 2.

Burnett, James. "Poynter Study Finds Increased Media Reliance on Spokespeople." *PRWeek*, March 25, 2002, p. 1.

Detz, Joan. "Humor in Presentations: What Works, What Doesn't, and Why." *Public Relations Tactics*, February 2004, p. 29.

Green, Sherri Deatherage. "Preparing Second-Tier Executives for the Spotlight." *PRWeek*, November 10, 2003.

Green, Sherri Deatherage. "Speaking Terms: Picking a CEO's Platform." *PRWeek*, October 6, 2003, p. 20.

Howard, Carole. "When a Reporter Calls." *Public Relations Tactics*, December 2002, p. 10.

Ketchner, Kathy. "Preparing for Better Presentations." *Public Relations Tactics*, February 2004, p. 27.

Markman, Steve. "Winning Techniques to Make Presentations More Compelling." *Public Relations Tactics*, May 2002, p. 17.

McLoughlin, Barry. "The Truth About Media Training." *Public Relations Tactics*, December 2002, p. 12.

Praeger, Jane. "Ten Tips to Make Your Presentation Compelling." *Public Relations Tactics*, May 2004, p. 17.

Pratt, Cornelius B. "The Misuse of PowerPoint." *Public Relations Quarterly*, Fall 2003, pp. 20–23.

Quenqua, Douglas. "A New Kind of Speech for a New King of CEO." *PRWeek*, April 5, 2004, p. 18.

Stewart, Joan. "Demystifying Speakers Bureaus." *Public Relations Tactics*, April 2001, p. 10.

Trickett, Eleanor. "Building Relationships with Reporters." *PRWeek*, January 14, 2002, p. 22.

Walker, Jerry. "Media Coach Puts Clients in Reporter's Shoes." *O'Dwyer's PR Services* Report, February 2003, p. 28.

Wallace, Michele. "The Red Light Is On—Is Your Spokesperson Ready? *Public Relations Tactics*, July 2002, p. 17.

chapter 17

Corporations

Topics covered in this chapter include:

Today's Modern Corporation

Today, giant corporations have operations and customers around the world. International conglomerates control subsidiary companies that often produce a grab bag of seemingly unrelated products under the same corporate banner. These companies deal with a number of governments at many levels. Their operations affect the environment, control the employment of thousands, and have an impact on the financial and social well-being of millions.

The large size of these corporations, however, also brings remoteness. A corporation has a "face" in terms of its products, logo, and brand being readily visible in advertising and billboards from Azerbaijan to Zimbabwe and all the nations in between. However, the average consumer really can't really comprehend organizations such as Wal-Mart, with $256 billion in worldwide sales, or MobilExxon, with $246 billion in global sales. These figures boggle the mind, and they represent more than the combined gross national product (GNP) of many nations.

As a result, the public is distrustful of the power, influence, and credibility of such giant corporations and business in general. When U.S. gasoline prices rise rapidly, for example, suspicion spreads that the oil companies have conspired to gouge the public, a distrust that the oil companies never fully allay. Major corporate financial scandals and the misdeeds of corporate executives also take their toll.

For example, fewer than 3 in 10 Americans (27 percent) feel that most large U.S. corporations are trustworthy, according to a recent Roper survey. And a Gallup poll reveals that business leaders and stockbrokers have joined used car dealers in the category of "least trusted" individuals in American society. Gallup polls also indicate that 82 percent of the public believes that the top executives of larger corporations receive outrageous salaries in the millions of dollars and, at the same time, improperly use corporate funds to fund lavish lifestyles.

Public perceptions of greed and corporate misdeeds are reinforced by stories in the media. Hundreds of stories were written about celebrity CEO Martha Stewart's indictment, trial, and conviction for lying to federal investigators about a stock sale, but other executives from such corporations as Enron, WorldCom, Adelphia, and Tyco were also in the news for falsifying financial records or raiding the corporate treasury. By early 2004, a total of 34 criminal indictments had been filed, and another 20 investigations were underway involving other major corporations with household names.

The Role of Public Relations

The extensive negative publicity about corporations and business in general over the past several years has made it imperative that companies make a special effort to regain public credibility and trust. Thus, the concept of *corporate social responsibility (CSR)* is now high on the priority list of executives and their public relations staffs who are charged with improving the reputation and citizenship of their employers.

Indeed, the public relations profession has taken steps to outline a plan of action for rebuilding public trust in business. A coalition of 19 U.S.-based organizations—including the Council of Public Relations Firms, the International Association of Business Communicators, and the National Investor Relations Institute—published a white paper in 2003 titled *Restoring Trust in Business: Models for Action*.

"These are people who deal with trust issues all the time," says James Murphy, global managing director of communications for Accenture, and chair of the coalition.

"Therefore, we're in a good position to address them." The 10-page white paper asked American businesses and their leaders to act in three main areas: (1) adopt ethical principles, (2) pursue transparency and disclosure, and (3) make trust a fundamental precept of corporate governance. Copies of the report were sent to *Fortune* 500 CEOs and to the 50,000 public relations professionals represented by member groups in the coalition.

The importance of public relations in CSR is explained by Jack Bergen, senior vice president of marketing and communications for Siemens Corporation. He told *PRWeek*, "We are the eyes and ears of an organization. The best way to be socially responsible is to have your eyes and ears trained on all the stakeholders, to know what they want and need from the company. These are classic public affairs issues and the idea that they should be handled by anyone else would show a lack of understanding."

A number of strategies and tactics can be used to implement CSR, which involves corporate performance as well as effective communications. One of the more important ones is the role of the public relations executive in counseling the CEO.

The public relations executive serves as a link between the chief executive and the realities of the marketplace and the organization, according to Mark Schumann, global communications practice leader with Tower Perrin. He told an international IABC conference that CEOs are often "disconnected" and surrounded by other executives who simply agree with whatever the CEO says. Schumann told *PRWeek*, ". . . everyone sucks up and lies to them." Schumann believes corporate public relations professionals should be the ". . . playwright and director, but we also need to be the toughest critics" to ensure that the CEO comes across as concerned and involved with employees and customers.

Corporations seek a better reputation for a variety of reasons. First, responsible business practices ward off increased government regulation. As a result of the major financial scandals such as Enron, the U.S. Congress passed additional laws regarding accounting practices and disclosure (see discussion about the Sarbanes-Oxley Act in Chapter 12). Second, there is the matter of employee morale; companies with good policies and a good reputation tend to have less employee turnover. Corporate reputation also affects the bottom line. A survey of executives by the Center for Corporate Citizenship with the Hitachi Foundation, for example, found that 82 percent of the respondents believe that good corporate citizenship contributes to meeting the organization's financial objectives. In addition, 53 percent say corporate citizenship is important to their customers.

Being a good corporate citizen is an admirable goal, but corporations also face a number of pressures and counterpressures when making decisions and forming policies. General Electric, the world's largest corporation, with a market value of about $340 billion, once outlined four key factors that have to be considered at all times when making a decision:

- **Political.** How do government regulations and other pressures affect the decision?
- **Technological.** Do we have the engineering knowledge to accomplish the goal?
- **Social.** What is our responsibility to society?
- **Economic.** Will we make a profit?

The following sections discuss various facets of today's modern corporation and kinds of activities that require the expertise and counsel of public relations professionals.

Media Relations

Reporting by the media is a major source of public information and perceptions about the business world and individual companies. In recent years, the news hasn't been all that favorable.

Major financial scandals such as Enron, WorldCom, Healthsouth, and Tyco haven't helped the overall reputation of business, nor has the extensive of coverage of criminal trials for CEOs such as Martha Stewart. Negative coverage can cause a corporation's reputation to plummet. Wal-Mart, once ranked number one in corporate reputation, saw its position drop to seventh in the space of six months after coverage regarding the hiring of illegal immigrants and the filing of a class-action suit that claimed that it discriminated against female employees.

As a result, corporate executives are somewhat defensive about how journalists cover business, because they feel that too much emphasis has been given to corporate misdeeds. One survey, by Jericho Communications, found that almost half of the respondents agreed with the statement that a "CEO must view the media as an enemy." Another 60 percent said an executive can best avoid controversy by "limiting exposure to the media" and through "secrecy and tighter control of information."

Many corporate executives take this approach because they have several continuing complaints about media coverage. These include inaccuracy, incomplete coverage, inadequate research and preparation for interviews, and antibusiness bias. One survey by the American Press Institute, for example, found about a third of the CEOs polled were dissatisfied with the business news they found in their local newspapers.

Business editors and reporters state in response that often they cannot publish or broadcast thorough, evenhanded stories about business because many company executives, uncooperative and wary, erect barriers against them. Writers complain about their inability to obtain direct access to decision-making executives and being restricted to using news releases that don't contain the information they need. Journalists assert, too, that some business leaders don't understand the concept of objectivity and assume that any story involving unfavorable news about their company is intentionally bad.

Journalists also say it's a major mistake for corporate executives to slash public relations and communications during times of financial scandal and economic downturn. A survey of journalists conducted by Middleberg Euro RSCG, a public relations firm, and the Columbia University Graduate School of Journalism, found that journalists also believe corporations should focus on delivering more fact-driven messages. Don Middleberg, director of the survey, told *PRWeek*, "You (executives) should communicate factually, frequently, and consistently. Use this time wisely, say the journalists, to position yourself."

Public relations practitioners serving businesses stand in the middle. They must interpret their companies and clients to the media, while showing their chief executive and other high officials how open, friendly media relations can serve their interests. One major interest that executives have is corporate reputation, and this is often tarnished or enhanced by the type of media coverage that an organization receives.

One survey by Hill & Knowlton, for example, found that Canadian CEOs believe that print and broadcast media criticism is the biggest threat to their company's reputation; even ahead of such things as disasters and allegations by the government about employee or product safety.

At the same time, surveys show that the media is probably the most effective way for an organization to get its message across and to achieve business goals. A *PRWeek* survey of CEOs, for example, found that more than 80 percent of the respondents said conducting media interviews was the most effective for the company to spread its message, followed by attending or speaking at industry conferences and tradeshows. In third place was meeting with key industry and financial analysts; fourth place was "authoring op-eds, bylined articles, or letters-to-the editor." Media and speaker training for executives was discussed in Chapter 16.

There will continue to be complaints from the both corporate executives and journalists about the quality of American business reporting. The survey by the American Press Institute, for example, found that both camps gave the quality of business reporting low grades. Only 10 percent of CEOs thought local coverage of their company was "excellent," and only 14 percent of the business editors thought their reporting staffs were "excellent."

One major problem faced by newspapers is the lack of qualified reporters. Dr. William Winter, president of the American Press Institute, told *PRWeek*, "There's a general recognition that there is a small number of people coming out of college who are prepared to be good business journalists." On the other hand, there seems to be an abundance of young people who want to be sports writers.

Public relations professionals, realizing that business reporters often don't have adequate business preparation, spend a great deal of time and energy providing background and briefing reporters on the business operations of their clients and employers. It's one way of ensuring that coverage will be more accurate and thorough.

Customer Relations

The day when a business could operate successfully on the Latin precept of *caveat emptor*—"Let the buyer beware"—is long gone. In today's society, sellers are expected to deliver goods and services of safe, acceptable quality on honest terms. Consumers' rights are protected by the federal government, and federal and state agencies enforce those rights. The Federal Trade Commission (FTC) regulates truth in advertising, the National Highway Traffic Safety Administration sets standards for automakers, and the Consumer Product Safety Commission examines the safety of other manufactured goods.

Customer service, in many respects, is the front line of public relations. A single incident, or a series of incidents, can severely damage a company's reputation and erode public trust in its products and services. See the PR Casebook on page 454 about Eddie Bauer for an example. Customer satisfaction is important because of word-of-mouth. A person who has a bad experience, surveys indicate, shares his or her story with an average of 17 people, whereas a person with a good experience will tell an average of 11 people. The rapid growth of the Internet and Weblogs, however, has considerably changed the math. Today, a dissatisfied customer is capable of informing thousands, or even millions, of people in just one posting.

Traditionally, customer service has been separate from the communications or public relations function in a company. Bob Seltzer, a leader in Ruder Finn's marketing practice, told *PRWeek*, "I defy anyone to explain the wisdom of this. How a company talks to its customers is among, if not the, most critical communications it has." Rande Swann, director of public relations for the Regional Airport Authority of

PR CASEBOOK

Eddie Bauer's Blunder

The Eddie Bauer, Inc., clothing chain, caught in a racial discrimination crisis, responded so slowly and clumsily that it compounded its problem. Two black teenage youths were shopping at an Eddie Bauer store in Maryland. As they left, police officers moonlighting as security guards accused one youth of shoplifting the shirt he was wearing. He told them he had purchased the shirt on a previous visit to the store and didn't have with him the sales receipt they demanded. The officers ordered him to take off the shirt and leave it until he brought in the receipt. He returned with the receipt the next day and was given the shirt. A company spokesperson later called the incident "minor" and implied that the company had done the young man a favor by returning it.

Angered at her son's treatment, the youth's mother phoned the Eddie Bauer corporate headquarters to complain. She said she was told someone would call her back. When weeks passed without a return call, she told the story to the *Washington Post*, which published it.

In response to public criticism and a threatened lawsuit, Eddie Bauer hired Hill and Knowlton, the public relations firm, to help. With Hill and Knowlton's guidance, the company president issued a belated apology and went to Washington, where he conferred with NAACP officials. He promised a sensitivity training program for employees. The company donated truckloads of clothing to homeless shelters.

These gestures were insufficient to placate critics. Other black customers told stories of discrimination. The young man's mother pointed out that while the company president was in Washington he spoke with NAACP officials but didn't apologize to the two young men or see them or their families.

Even Bauer's act of hiring Hill and Knowlton drew criticism. *Washington Post* columnist Jonathan Yardley wrote, "Taking on a high-octane public relations firm is *prima facie* evidence of guilt."

The company's delay in response and perceived failure to recognize the personal feelings of the individuals involved made a bad situation even worse.

Louisville, Kentucky, agrees. He says, "Our reputation is probably based more on how we serve our customers than any other single thing. If we don't have a reputation for great service, we don't have travelers."

Increasingly, however, corporations are realizing that customer relations serves as a telltale public relations barometer. Many public relations departments now regularly monitor customer feedback in a variety of ways to determine what policies and communications strategies need to be revised. One common method is to monitor customer queries to the organization's Web site. Indeed, most companies have a link for "contacting us" on its Web site. Another method is the content analysis of phone calls to the customer service center.

Small companies can easily monitor the nature of customer comments and also respond in a timely manner. It gets more difficult, however, for a large company. Ford

Motor Company, for example, receives about 7500 phone calls to its national customer service center every day. New software technologies can help.

AllDorm, a California company, offers an example. It specializes in providing products and services to college students nationwide. When it was first started, AllDorm was able to provide one-on-one communication with its customers. As the company grew larger and more successful, however, it began to lose its personal touch. Consequently, it hired a firm to design a software program that would automatically send a postorder survey form to a customer asking about his or her purchasing experience. The system also has triggers built into it to immediately flag dissatisfied customers so customer service representatives can phone them. AllDorm also has put in place a system where useful information from customers is forwarded to marketing and the public relations department.

This sharing of information is valuable from the standpoint of getting public relations professionals involved in active listening so they can strategize on what steps a company should take to ensure a good reputation among customers. As Andy Hopson, CEO of Burson-Marsteller's northeast region, told *PRWeek*, "Ignoring complaints can ultimately damage a company's reputation."

Public relations professionals also pay attention to consumer surveys. One such mechanism is the American Customer Satisfaction Index, which is the definitive benchmark of how buyers feel about what business is selling to them. The index, which has been tracking customer satisfaction for 200 companies in 40 industries for over a decade, has found that a company offering the lowest prices may not necessarily get the highest satisfaction rating. Wal-Mart, for example, only scores 75 out of 100 points, compared with the national average of 74.4 for all companies.

The company with the highest customer satisfaction score for a retailer (88 points), two years in a row, has been the Internet giant Amazon.com. Low prices and a wide selection play a part, but the real difference is customer service. Bill Price, a former vice president of global customer service at Amazon, told the *New York Times* that the company has been able to provide a variety of features and services that make it more friendly, more reliable, and easier to use. He says, "Our job was to listen to customers and invent for customers."

Reaching Diverse Markets

The United States is becoming more diverse every year, which is now being recognized by corporate marketing and communications departments. Reaching such diverse audiences was covered in Chapter 11, but it's worthwhile to summarize some key aspects.

According to the U.S. Census Bureau, the U.S. population is now 12 percent African American; 13 percent Latino; and 4 percent Asian and Pacific Islander. As these groups continue to expand and become more affluent, they will constitute a larger share of the consumer marketplace. By 2007, for example, it's estimated that buying power among Hispanics will increase 315 percent. The increase among Asians will be 287 percent, and among African Americans 170 percent.

According to Gina Amaro, director of multicultural and international markets for PR Newswire, "Companies that focus solely on one audience when creating products are missing an enormous opportunity. Furthermore, companies that do not incorporate a multicultural marketing and PR campaign to communicate these products and services to their many niche audiences will miss even larger opportunities."

Many public relations firms have set up specialty practices for multicultural marketing and communications. Edelman Worldwide, for example, has a diversity practice that assists companies. One client, Unilever, hired Edelman to organize a Hispanic marketing communications campaign for six of its personal care products, including Dove Soap.

Companies also have set up departments to reach minority audiences. Wells Fargo Bank, for example, organized an Emerging Markets division to help increase home ownership among minority families. Part of this initiative is a Hispanic Customer Service Center in Las Cruces, New Mexico, which provides specialized services to Spanish-speaking homebuyers in 16 states. In addition to translating brochures and other information into Spanish, bilingual customer service representatives are available to answer e-mail and telephone inquiries.

Yahoo! also has recognized the potential of the Hispanic market. It began Yahoo! en Español, which is now the top online destination for U.S. Hispanics. Special features, such as music, news, and various promotions, are designed exclusively for this audience. Gina Amaro of PR Newswire agrees with this approach. She says that it is vitally important to build relationships with niche audiences by communicating to them in their language and culture.

Consumer Activism

A dissatisfied customer can often be mollified by prompt and courteous attention to his or her complaint or even an offer by the company to replace the item or provide some discount coupons toward future purchases. A more serious and complex threat to corporate reputation, which can also affect sales, are consumer activists who demand changes in corporate policies.

Tyson Foods, a major American producer of meat and poultry products, was accused of inhumane treatment of animals by various animal rights groups, such as the People for the Ethical Treatment of Animals (PETA). The corporate response was to establish an office of animal well-being to assure retailers and consumers that it takes humane animal handling seriously.

Ed Nicholson, Tyson's director of media and community relations, told *PRWeek*, "The people from PETA are not going to be satisfied unless we go out of business, but there are consumers less radical than PETA who are still concerned about animal-handling practices." The new wellness office, headed by a veterinarian, will oversee audits of animal-handling practices and make them available to customers on request.

KFC also has been targeted by PETA and other animal rights groups, whose efforts have received extensive media publicity. The charges of inhumane animal treatment and how chickens are slaughtered can and do affect consumer buying decisions, especially when activists are outside a franchise wearing T-shirts that say "KFC Tortures Animals." In such a situation, the public relations staff has the difficult job of defending the company against what it believes are unfounded allegations and to also, at the same time, assure the public that KFC's policies do provide for the humane slaughter of its chickens.

Consequently, when it came to light that a KFC subcontractor was mistreating chickens, the company immediately called the abuse by workers appalling and told the subcontractor to clean up its act—or lose its contract. In this instance, because of a quick response, the media was able to include KFC's response in the story about the abuses, which were documented on videotape.

Corporations face a variety of challenges today from advocacy groups quite adept at generating media coverage for their particular cause. Here, the People for the Ethical Treatment of Animals (PETA) demonstrate outside a Kentucky Fried Chicken restaurant in Hong Kong to protest what they claim is the restaurant chain's cruel treatment of chickens.

Coca-Cola also has its problems with its reputation among its customers. Some activist groups charged the giant bottler with contributing to childhood obesity by selling its products in schools. Karl Bjorhus, director of health and nutrition communications for the bottler, told *PRWeek*, "We have been listening and trying to understand what people's concerns are."

As a result, the company issued a series of initiatives designed to improve its image among parents and educators. The company announced new *Guidelines for School–Beverage Partnerships*. Included was a measure that allowed local school officials to opt for Coke vending machines carrying a variety of Coke nonsoda products and providing devices preventing elementary school students from buying from soft drink machines during school hours.

Another activist group had other concerns. One campaign, Stop Killer Coke, claimed that Coca-Cola was using paramilitary thugs in Colombia to intimidate workers and prevent unionization. The company said the charges were "false and outrageous," but that didn't stop the campaign's organizers from spreading the word to colleges, high schools, and unions. As a result, at least six colleges booted Coke beverages off their campuses, and several food co-ops decided to stop selling Coke products. In such a situation, even false allegations can affect the sales of a product. For a related problem, see the Ethics box on page 458.

In today's climate of media attention to such health-related topics such as obesity, every food product company is suspect. McDonald's was the subject of a movie documentary, *Super Size Me*, in which the producer decided to eat three meals a day at McDonald's for several months. He of course details how all the "junk food" made him overweight and prone to major health problems.

In this case, McDonald's reaction was aggressive. Walt Riker, vice president of corporate communications, told *PRWeek*, "We're responding aggressively because the film is a gross misrepresentation of what McDonald's is about. The scam in the movie

ON THE JOB ethics

Standing on Principle, or Bowing to Consumer Pressure?

Procter & Gamble has a problem. Two influential conservative groups have called for a boycott of Crest toothpaste and Tide detergent. The boycott was called because the company posted a statement on its intranet telling employees that it opposes a proposed statute in Cincinnati, its headquarters, that would preclude protecting gays and lesbians from discrimination.

The leaders of the two groups, Focus on the Family and the American Family Association, contend that P&G is implicitly supporting same-sex marriage. "For Procter & Gamble to align itself with radical groups committed to redefining marriage in our country is an affront to its customers," says Dr. James C. Dodson, head of Focus on the Family. He has called for the boycott on his syndicated radio program, which claims to reach 9 million listeners a week.

P&G believes the two conservative Christian groups are distorting the issue by relating the issue of same-sex marriage with proposed legislation that exempts gays and lesbians from discrimination laws. However, the company has to consider what impact a boycott would have on sales. This poses an ethical dilemma. Should the company stand by its beliefs in this matter, or should it retract its opposition to the proposed statute and avoid being boycotted?

is that he has given the impression of that he only ate three basic meals day, but the reality is that he stuffed himself with 5,000 to 7,000 calories, which is two or three times the recommended amount."

According to *PRWeek*, "McDonald's has been engaging the media in interviews and the company has made its global nutritionist, Cathy Kapica, available." Kapica appeared on CNN and CNBC, and gave a number of newspaper interviews about the film producer's "extreme behavior." The company also distributed a VNR and an ANR giving its views on smart choices in diet and exercise. It also sent briefing materials to its 2,700 franchises so they could talk to local media in an informed way.

Ford Motor Company also faced reputation and trust problems with consumers after Bluewater, an environmental group, took out full-page ads in various newspapers accusing the automaker of continuing to make "America's worst gas guzzlers." The ads went on to say, "Don't buy Bill Ford's Environmental Promises. Don't Buy His Cars."

Even Caterpillar, a maker of heavy earth-moving equipment, isn't immune to activist groups who question the company's sale of bulldozers to Israel. The Stop Cat Coalition says the company is supporting the demolition of Palestinian houses in the West Bank and Gaza. It wants the company to stop selling bulldozers to Israel, but the company says it won't change its sales policy.

Benjamin Cordant, who works in the public affairs department at Caterpillar, says that Caterpillar has publicly stated its position and has communicated with employees and stockholders about its decision. The company's stance is that it has no right or means to oversee how its equipment is used around the world. One factor influencing the company decision, no doubt, is how many customers would decide not to buy a Caterpillar product because of its sales to Israel.

At the strategic level, a company weighs the potential impact of the charges or allegations on potential customer reaction and possible effect on sales before deciding on a course of action. Activist consumer groups are a major challenge to the public relations staff of an organization. Do you accommodate? Do you stonewall? Do you change policy? A discussion of issues management is in Chapter 10, but here are some general guidelines from Douglas Quenqua, which appeared in *PRWeek*, on how to be proactive.

Do

- Work with groups who are more interested in solutions than getting publicity.
- Offer transparency. Activists who feel you're not open aren't likely to keep dealing with you.
- Turn their suggestions into action. Activist want results.

Don't

- Get emotional when dealing with advocacy groups.
- Agree to work with anyone making threats.
- Expect immediate results. Working with adversaries takes patience—establishing trust takes time.

Consumer Boycotts

The boycott—a refusal to buy the products or services of an offending company—has a long history and is a widely used publicity tool of the consumer movement.

PETA, for example, announced that consumers should boycott Safeway until it improved conditions for farm animals. The key aspect of theater for this protest was Safeway's annual stockholders meeting in which activists would unfurl a banner saying, "Safeway means animal cruelty." It was, as *PRWeek* says, "all the makings of a PR person's worst nightmare."

Safeway headed off a boycott by negotiating. Just days before the annual meeting, the company's public affairs staff began working with PETA and quickly announced new standards for monitoring conditions with meat suppliers. Instead of a protest, PETA supporters showed up at the annual meeting with a large "Thank You" sign for entering stockholders. In addition, PETA ended its 20-state boycott of the chain. The director of public affairs for Safeway said the boycott didn't have any effect on sales, but PETA took a different tact. Its director told *PRWeek*, "It's just a truism that you don't want your corporation targeted by activists. My hunch is the timing of the call (from Safeway public affairs) was not purely coincidental."

The success of consumer boycotts is mixed. Various activist groups have boycotted Procter & Gamble for years without much effect because the company makes so many products under their own brand names that consumers can't keep track of what P&G makes.

On the other hand, a single product name is more vulnerable. Back in 1995, Shell Oil Company decided to sink an aging oil platform in the Atlantic Ocean; environmental activists violently objected. Sales dropped by 70 percent in some European nations, prompting the company's decision to dispose of the oil platform in another way. During the 1980s, Barclays Bank continued to do business in South Africa during apartheid, but suffered a 10 percent drop in the bank's share of the student market within two years.

More recently, activists conducted a successful boycott against Triumph, a British underwear company that operated a plant in Burma under that country's military dictatorship. The Burma campaign reached the public with a poster showing a woman wearing a barbed wire bra. The slogan was, "Support breasts, not dictators." Triumph was inundated with consumer complaints and, within 8 days, closed its factory in Burma. "The fact that it was about bras helped," said the activist group director. "We knew it would appeal to the media."

Activists point out that a boycott doesn't have to be 100 percent effective in order to change corporate policies. Even a 5 percent drop in sales will often cause corporations to rethink their policies and mode of operations. Nike got serious about sweatshop conditions abroad only after activist groups caused its stock and sales to drop. Nike was losing market position, so it decided to formulate new policies for its subcontractors abroad and become active in a global alliance of manufacturers to monitor working conditions in overseas factories.

Employee Relations

Customers are a primary public for any profit-making organization, but so are employees. They, in many ways, are the front line of any effective public relations program. A company's reputation, for example, is often enhanced or damaged by how rank-and-file employees feel about their employer. One Internet survey of consumers by Golin/Harris International, for example, found that 70 percent of the respondents believed that the number one criterion for good corporate citizenship was treating its employees well.

Employees have been called the organization's "ambassadors" because they represent the company within a large circle of family, relatives, and friends. If morale is low or if employees feel the company is not treating them fairly, it's reflected in their comments to others. On the other hand, enthusiastic employees can do much to enhance an organization's reputation within a community as a good place to work. This, in turn, generates more job applicants and also enhances employee-retention rates.

Consequently, the public relations department, often working with the human resources department, concentrates on communicating with employees just as vigorously as it does on delivering the corporate story to the outside world. A workplace that respects its management, has pride in its products, and believes it is being treated fairly is a key factor in corporate success.

Surveys indicate, however, that the success of communication efforts varies widely among organizations. According to a survey of 1,000 U.S. workers by Towers Perrin, 20 percent believe their organization does not tell them the truth. About half of the respondents say their company generally tells employees the truth, and about the same percentage believe that their employers try too hard to "spin" the truth. Another finding: Almost half believe they get more reliable information from their direct supervisors than they do from senior executives.

The extensive media coverage of corporate scandals also has taken its toll in terms of employee perceptions. A Fleischman-Hillard survey of workers, for example, found that 80 percent believe that greed is driving corporate scandals. The majority also agreed that corporations care more about stock value than customers' needs. On the plus side, however, more than 70 percent of the respondents thought the information they received from their employer was "adequate" to "very comprehensive."

Director, Employee Communications

Join Citrix, a cutting-edge team that is setting new benchmarks for success and a company that has earned a reputation as a market leader!

In this position, you will provide senior-level direction and leadership for the development and implementation of strategic employee and executive communications programs. The selected candidate will possess a Bachelor's degree or equivalent foreign education in English, Journalism, Communications or PR. (In lieu of degree in stated field, we will accept degree in any field together with 2 years experience developing employee & executive communications programs). At least 4 years related experience or 4 years senior-level leadership experience in developing & implementing strategic employee & executive communication programs which involves working with senior execs. in a high-tech Fortune 500 company, and must have included writing speeches, managing content of company Web site and leading change management communications programs. (Job Code: DEC41)

We offer excellent compensation and an outstanding benefits package. Forward resume by e-mail to citrixrecruiting@citrix.com or by mail to Recruiting, Citrix Systems, Inc., 851 W. Cypress Creek Rd., Ft. Lauderdale, FL 33309. Reference job code in subject line of e-mail or in written response. EEO/AA Employer

---

www.citrix.com

Employee communication is a major part of effective public relations for a large corporation. This ad from Citrix Corporation outlines some of the duties.

The value of credible and trustworthy communications cannot be underestimated. Mark Schumann of Towers Perrin told *Public Relations Tactics*, "Regardless of the topic, an organization will find it difficult to motivate, engage, and retain their most talented employees if their messages are not believed." Don Etling of Fleishman-Hillard told *PRWeek*, "We look at internal communications as something that affects performance, whether you have two or 200 employees. Companies that do a good job of explaining their values, not just to their partners, investors, and clients, but also to their employees, seem to enjoy better results. . . . Companies really need to look at this as a performance issue."

Public relations professionals, however, will tell organizations that effective employee relations is more than just a string of well-written and informative messages. A survey by Meta Group, for example, found that the majority of information technology (IT) companies admitted that they had an employee morale problem due to lack of job growth and curtailed budgets. At the same time, however, only about 10 percent of the companies polled saw employee communications as an answer. The top three solutions, according to *PRWeek*, were (1) employee recognition, (2) skill-development opportunities, and (3) career development. Communications ranked ninth, behind events, annual action plans, challenging work, and professional development.

In other words, public relations staffs have to do more than make sure the quarterly employee newsletter is produced. They also have an obligation to counsel management about programs, policies, and actions that build employee loyalty, support, and productivity.

A good example of successful corporate policies that build employee loyalty is the annual survey by *Working Mother* magazine that compiles a list of the 100 best companies for working mothers. An analysis of these companies, compared with other organizations, shows the following:

- 100 percent of the 100 best companies offer flextime, versus 55 percent companies nationwide.
- 99 percent of the 100 best offer an employee assistance programs, versus 67 percent nationwide.
- 98 percent of the 100 best offer elder-care resource and referral services, versus 20 percent nationwide.
- 96 percent of the 100 best offer child-care resource and referral services, versus 18 percent nationwide.
- 94 percent of the 100 best offer compressed workweeks, versus 31 percent nationwide.
- 93 percent of the 100 best offer job-sharing, versus 22 percent nationwide.

Many employee issues must be addressed by the company, and public relations professionals often are involved in counseling not only what policies should be created but how they should be implemented and communicated. One such issue is health and medical benefits. Company information about benefits should be written in plain English instead of legalese so employees thoroughly understand what is covered. If there is a change in a health plan, the company must spend time and effort, often through small-group meetings, to explain the changes and why they are necessary.

Another issue is sexual harassment. This worries both employees and management for both legal and ethical reasons. The U.S. Supreme Court ruled in *Monitor Savings Bank v. Vinson* (1986) that a company may be held liable in sexual harassment suits even if management is unaware of the problem and has a general policy condemning any form of verbal or nonverbal behavior that causes employees to feel "uncomfortable" or consider the workplace a "hostile environment."

Organizations, to protect themselves from liability and the unfavorable publicity of a lawsuit, not only have to have a policy, they must also clearly communicate the policy to employees and conduct workshops to ensure that everyone thoroughly understands what might be considered sexual harassment. What about off-color jokes at the water cooler or via e-mail? What about a *Playboy* calendar in someone's cubicle? What about a co-worker constantly asking you for a date?

Layoffs and Outsourcing

A national economic downturn usually means that many people lose their jobs. Immediately after the 9/11 terrorist attack on the United States, for example, more than 400,000 people lost their jobs, and the airline and travel industries were particularly hard hit.

Layoffs present a major public relations challenge to an organization. Julie Hood, an editor of *PRWeek*, says it best: "The way in which a company handles job reductions can have a significant impact on its reputation, its share price, and its ongoing ability to recruit and maintain good staff. And that presents a major challenge for communication departments."

Although human resource (HR) departments are most involved in layoffs, it's also a situation where the expertise of the public relations department is harnessed to ensure employee understanding and support. One cardinal rule is that a layoff is never announced to the media before employees are first informed. Another cardinal rule is that employees should be informed in person by their immediate supervisor—the traditional "pink slip" or an e-mail message is unacceptable. Employees who are being retained should also be called in by their immediate supervisor to let them know their status.

The rumor mill works overtime when there is uncertainty among employees about their job security, so it's also important for the company to publicly announce the layoffs and the impact as quickly as possible. Companies should be very forthright and upfront about layoffs; this is not the time to issue vague statements and "maybes" that just fuel the rumor mill.

Companies that are interested in their reputation and employee trust also make every effort to cushion the layoff by implementing various programs. Merrill Lynch, for example, laid off 6,000 employees by giving them the option of "voluntary separation" in exchange for one year's pay and a percentage of their annual bonus. Other companies offer out-placement services, the use of office space, and other programs. Such programs do much to retain employee goodwill even as workers are being laid off.

A more contentious issue, which has become an emotional and political football in recent years, is the matter of outsourcing white-collar jobs to such nations as India. The practice is commonly called *offshoring*, and many American companies are now using lower-paid professionals in India and other Asian nation to do everything from customer service to software engineering and accounting.

Prior to this, labor unions and human rights groups had raised the issue of sweatshop labor in which women and children were being exploited in Third World factories. This time, however, *offshoring* is being framed by the media as a middle-class job drain that's taking a toll on educated workers. Jim Martinez of GCI public relations says the issue is the "perfect storm" generated by a number of political and economic factors coming together at the same time.

The increasing practice of offshoring presents major internal communication challenges for public relations departments. How do you explain the corporate policy? How do you overcome employee suspicion that their jobs are vulnerable because a software engineer in India works for a fraction of what U.S. workers are paid?

Companies and various business associations have tried to show that offshoring doesn't really cause job losses in the United States or that outsourcing makes the company more competitive and actually creates more U.S. jobs. The American Electronics Association (AEA) issued a report saying that offshoring is just the reality of the global economy, and it's unfair to blame it as the main cause of job losses. It remains to be seen whether U.S. employees are convinced.

Minorities in the Workforce

As discussed earlier, the United States is becoming more diverse. This brings intensified problems of language and cultural differences to the workplace. Traditionally, senior executives have been white males, although there has been some advancement of females and minorities in the executive suite.

The greatest change, of course, has been in the composition of rank-and-file employees. As more minorities join the workforce, often coming from different cultures and religious faiths, an employer must be sensitive to their needs. English as a second language is one hurdle; public relations staffs must be sure that employee communications are written in plain English and that basic words are used to communicate key messages.

Even menu selections in the employee cafeteria must be considered. Asians are used to eating rice instead of mashed potatoes and gravy. There is also the need to expand offerings for vegetarians, to make sure that pork alternatives are available, and that there are plenty of fresh fruits for people on health diets. Religious beliefs must be respected and accommodated. Devout Muslims pray to Mecca five times a day, and many organizations have provided space for prayer. Jews, on the other hand, have several Holy Days that require certain dietary restrictions and attendance at the synagogue.

In today's world, companies must embrace diversity and also actively recruit ethnic minorities and people of color. A failure to do so can cause major public relations problems for an organization. If a large minority group in the community believes a company fails to hire enough of its members, the result may be a product boycott, rallies at corporate headquarters, and even lawsuits—which usually are given extensive coverage in the media. Such situations should never arise if the company has good policies in place and it remains sensitive to employee concerns.

When it fails to do so, the cost in money and a corporate reputation can be great. Texaco, Inc., provides a notorious example. After lingering in federal court for more than two years, a suit against the oil company by 1,300 employees charging racial discrimination was blown wide open by disclosure of tapes recorded secretly at meetings of high company executives. The executives were heard using racial slurs against employees and discussing the destruction of documents the employees might use in their suit. Eleven days later, Texaco agreed to pay $176 million to settle the case—the largest settlement ever in a racial discrimination suit.

Employee Volunteerism

Many companies, as part of their corporate citizenship outreach, have programs that allow employees to volunteer for charitable work on company time. Citizens Financial Corp., for example, provides the business expertise of its staff to nonprofits. Liberty Mutual Group, a Boston insurance firm, supplies hundreds of workers each year who volunteer for an all-day United Way drive to fix up food pantries, halfway houses, and other nonprofit facilities.

Timberland Company, a major manufacturer of hiking boots and other outdoor gear, is generally considered the ideal model. It gives workers one week a year with pay to work for local charities. It also offers four paid sabbaticals each year to workers who agree to work full-time for up to six months at a nonprofit. In addition, the company shuts down one day each year, at the estimated loss of $2 million in sales, so its 5,400 employees can take part in various company-sponsored philanthropic projects.

According to the *New York Times*, "One of Timberland's most notable cleanup projects was at an elementary school close to the World Trade Center on September 11. As smoke and debris from the disaster spread across the city, a team of 60 Timberland volunteers from New Hampshire and Massachusetts continued to fix up the school's playground until the work was completed late that evening."

Timberland's executives say doing good is good business. Offering employees a chance to help local charities on company time enables the company to attract and retain good talent. "People like to feel good about where they work and what they do," says Jeffrey Swartz, Timberland's CEO. As a result, Timberland is consistently ranked by *Fortune* magazine as one of the 100 best companies to work for in America.

Investor Relations

Another major component of keeping a company's health and wealth is communicating with shareholders and prospective investors. Investor relations (IR) is at the center of that process.

The goal of investor relations is to combine the disciplines of communications and finance to accurately portray a company's prospects from an investment standpoint. Some key audiences are financial analysts, individual and institutional investors, shareholders, prospective shareholders, and the financial media. Increasingly, employees are an important public, too, because they have stock options and 401 plans.

Individuals who specialize in investor or financial relations, according to salary surveys, are the highest-paid professionals in the public relations field. One reason for this is that they must be very knowledgeable about finance and a myriad of regulations set down by the SEC on initial stock offerings (IPOs), mergers, accounting requirements, the contents of quarterly financial reports, and public disclosure of information. A company going public for the first time, for example, is required by the SEC to observe a "quiet time" when company executives are not allowed to talk about the offering to analysts or the financial press to avoid "hyping" the stock.

Mergers also require the expertise of investor relations experts in order to satisfy SEC rules and also to keep the various publics informed. Investor relations could have been better, the experts say, when HP merged with Compaq Computer. On the day that the $20 billion deal was announced, both companies saw significant drops in the value of their stock. Lou Thompson, president of the National Investor Relations Institute (NIRI), said that both companies failed to convince skeptical market analysts that the merger was a good idea before going public with the announcement.

Market skepticism, however, was just the start of HP's problems. Walter Hewlett, son of the cofounder of the company, immediately denounced the merger and led a stockholder protest that gained national headlines. The family of cofounder David Packard also weighed in against the deal. There was an intense proxy fight that involved mass mailings to stockholders, full-page ads in the *Wall Street Journal*, and impassioned speeches at the annual meeting. The fight over the merger, which was ultimately approved, cost each side millions of dollars. In the bitter fight, most experts agreed that HP suffered damage to its reputation and brand.

In another situation, Google's IPO had to be delayed because CEO and founder Marc Benioff made some comments about the stock offering in a major magazine interview during the SEC's mandated "quiet period." The foul-up gave Google a rocky start in terms of positioning the stock and building a good impression among Wall Street analysts.

Investor relations staff primarily communicate with institutional investors, individual investors, stockbrokers, and financial analysts. They are also sources of information for the financial press such as the *Wall Street Journal*, *Barron's*, and the *Financial Times*. In their jobs, they make many presentations, conduct field trips for analysts and portfolio managers, analyze stockholder demographics, oversee corporate annual reports, and prepare materials for potential investors.

Marketing Communications

Many companies use the tools and tactics of public relations to support the marketing and sales objectives of their business. This is called *marketing communications* or *marketing public relations*.

Thomas L. Harris, author of *A Marketer's Guide to Public Relations*, defines marketing public relations (MPR) as "The process of planning, executing, and evaluating programs that encourage purchase and consumer satisfaction through credible communication of information and impressions that identify companies and their products with the needs, wants, concerns, and interests of consumers."

In many cases, marketing public relations is coordinated with a company's messages in advertising, marketing, direct mail, and promotion. This has led to the concept of *integrated marketing communications (IMC)* in which companies manage all sources of information about a product or service in order to ensure maximum message penetration. This concept was first discussed in Chapter 1 as a major concept in today's modern public relations practice.

In an integrated program, for example, public relations activities are often geared to obtaining early awareness and credibility for a product. Publicity in the form of news stories builds credibility, excitement in the marketplace, and consumer anticipation. These messages make audiences more receptive to advertising and promotions about the product in the later phases of the campaign. Indeed, there is a growing body of support that public relations is the foundation stone for branding and positioning a product or service.

The redesigned Volkswagen Beetle was introduced to American consumers in such a way. Volkswagen won early support of key auto trade and business media by inviting them to participate in background sessions on the car during the preproduction stage. The resulting stories started to build "buzz," or word-of-mouth talk, about the new model. The car was introduced using video news releases and interactive satellite feeds that resulted in 800 individual TV segments, including appearances on *Today* and *Good Morning America*. Such media coverage provided a powerful third-party endorsement that was then merchandised with clever advertising taglines such as "Less flower. More power." Toyota, in the introduction of its new hybrid cars, followed the same format several years later.

*Pfizer Inc discovers, develops, manufactures and markets leading prescription medicines for humans and animals, and many of the world's best-known over-the-counter brands. As we continue to grow our respected and highly successful Consumer Healthcare business, we have a unique opportunity for a **Manager, Marketing Communications** in our **Morris Plains, N.J.** office.*

MANAGER, MARKETING COMMUNICATIONS

Your primary responsibilities will involve program development and execution of public relations programming for our U.S. based healthcare brands. In addition, you will provide strategic direction for global PR programming; oversee media relations and all relevant monitoring; take charge of agency and vendor management; and coordinate both budget and event management. Further, you will organize and execute presentations at large-scale meetings.

Successful candidates will have a Bachelor's degree and 7-10 years of experience in consumer packaged goods/healthcare/pharmaceutical public relations (agency experience a plus). Demonstrated client side experience is preferred.

We offer a competitive salary and comprehensive benefits. For immediate consideration, please submit your resume with salary requirements to the Pfizer Web site at **www.pfizer.com**, submitting on **Job Req #04Mar0427950**. (Only those with salary requirements will be considered. No phone calls, please.) Although we appreciate your interest in our company, we will only be able to respond to those individuals in whom we have further interest. We are an equal opportunity employer.

Marketing communications is a popular area of public relations work. This ad from Pfizer outlines some of the duties.

The objectives of marketing communications, often called *marcom* in industry jargon, are accomplished in several ways.

Product Publicity

The cost and clutter of advertising have mounted dramatically, and companies have found that creative product publicity is a cost-effective way of reaching potential customers. Even mundane household products, if presented properly, can be newsworthy and catch media attention.

Clorox, for example, generated many news articles and broadcast mentions for its Combat cockroach killer by sponsoring a contest to find America's five worst cockroach-infested homes. And Dove Deodorant sponsored a Most Beautiful Underarms pageant at Grand Central Station in New York. Miss Florida won the crown. The contest received airtime on *Today*, *Fox & Friends*, and mention on the news shows of 400 television stations.

A company also can generate product publicity by sponsoring a poll. The ClorTrimeton Allergy Index has measured pollen counts since 1984. Polls, in order to get media attention, can be somewhat frivolous and even unscientific. *Food & Wine* magazine, along with America Online, did such a survey and announced to the world that the supermarket checkout line is the most popular choice for where to meet a mate. It also found that whipped cream is the sexiest food, but that chocolate mousse is better than sex.

Product publicity can be generated in other ways. Old Bay seafood seasoning sponsors a shrimp-eating contest; Briggs Stratton, which makes lawnmowers, compiles an annual top ten list of beautiful lawns; Hershey's chocolate made the *Guinness Record Book* by making the world's largest candy Kiss, which weighed several tons.

Product Placement.   A product that appears as part of a movie or television program is a form of product placement. This was discussed in Chapter 15, so only a brief mention will be made here. Essentially, a brand is built by exposure in multiple films and television shows. The Corvette that the actors drive to the airport, the United flight that takes them to a destination, the Hilton they stay in, and the Grey Goose vodka martini they order in the bar are all examples of product placement.

Increasingly, product placements are the result of fees paid to film studios and television producers. At times, there is a trade-off; the Gap, for example, volunteers to provide the entire wardrobe for a television show, which reduces the cost of production for the producer and also gives the clothing firm high visibility.

On occasion, the filmmaker has a story line that requires a specific product. Tom Hanks, for example, played a FedEx man stranded on a deserted island in *Cast Away*. *Where the Heart Is* was a tale of a pregnant teen living in an Oklahoma Wal-Mart. Both corporations gave their permission for portrayal of its product. In another situation, the movie *Harold and Kumar Go to White Castle* gave the White Castle chain national visibility. The film producers originally wrote the screenplay for Krispy Kreme doughnuts, but that company refused permission, because the two characters in the movie smoke marijuana and are somewhat slovenly characters. That didn't bother White Castle.

Product placement opportunities also are available on local and national game shows that give products to the winners.

Cause-Related Marketing

Companies in highly competitive fields, where there is little differentiation between products or services, often strive to stand out and enhance their reputation for CSR by engaging in cause-related marketing. In essence, this means that a profit-making company collaborates with a nonprofit organization to advance its cause and, at the same time, increase sales. A good example is Dannon yogurt brand, which tells customers that 1.5 percent of its sales go to support the National Wildlife Federation.

Companies supporting worthy causes have good customer support. One study, by Cone/Roper, found that 79 percent of Americans feel companies have a responsibility to support causes as part of its corporate citizenship. More important, 81 percent said they were likely to switch brands, when price and quality were equal, to support the cause.

American Express was not the first company to do cause-related marketing, but its success in raising money to restore the aging Statue of Liberty and Ellis Island in 1984 set a new benchmark for effectiveness. The company spent $6 million publicizing the fact that one penny of every dollar spent on its credit cards would go to the restoration. American Express raised $1.7 million for the cause. It also saw the use of its cards jump 28 percent, and applications for new cards increased 17 percent. In addition, it was an excellent branding strategy—the easy association in the public's mind between American Express and an American icon.

Sometimes, a corporation will organize its own cause. Bristol-Myers Squibb, for example, organized a bicycle Tour of Hope to raise funds for cancer research and to help cancer survivors be more proactive in their care. Spectrum Science Public Relations was engaged to organize, promote, and publicize the cross-country tour. Cycling clubs and cancer advocacy groups were contacted to generate supporters for local rides, and a nationwide search was conducted to find avid cyclists who had a strong connection to cancer, either through relatives or their work.

Twenty-six cyclists were ultimately selected. They received two months of personal training and were given custom-made Trek racing bikes, the same model used by Lance Armstrong, six-time champion of the Tour de France. The tour started in Los Angeles and finished in Washington, D.C. John Seng, Spectrum president, told *PRWeek*, "It wasn't just about driving awareness, but motivating people to show their care and concern." More than $1.3 million was raised, and 40,000 Cancer Promises were signed to find a cure for cancer, and almost 2,000 riders participated in the Tour of Hope.

Selecting a charity or a cause event to support involves strategic thinking. A chain of pet care stores, for example, would be better served by sponsoring projects with the Humane Society of America than contributing a percentage of its sales to the American Cancer Society. By the same token, a company like Bristol-Myers Squibb that makes drugs to treat cancer would find such a relationship a good fit. Here are some tips for conducting cause-related marketing:

- Look for a cause related to your products or services or that exemplifies a product quality.
- Consider causes that appeal to your primary customers.
- Choose a charity that doesn't already have multiple sponsors.
- Choose a local organization if the purpose is to build brand awareness for local franchises.
- Don't use cause-related efforts as a tactic to salvage image after a major scandal; it usually backfires.
- Understand that association with a cause or nonprofit is a long-term commitment.
- Realize that additional budget must be spent to create public awareness and build brand recognition with the cause.

Corporate Sponsorships

A form of cause-related marketing is corporate sponsorship of various activities and events such as concerts, art exhibits, races, and scientific expeditions. The ultimate corporate sponsorship is the Olympics, which is discussed in the Insights box on page 470.

Companies spend about $10 billion annually sponsoring activities ranging from the Indianapolis 500, the Kentucky Derby, the Academy Awards, PGA golf tournaments, and even the road show of Britney Spears or Madonna. Many of these events,

Olympic Torch Visits Six Continents

The 2004 Olympics marked the first time that the Olympic Torch went around the world—traveling 78,000 kilometers in 78 days—before a runner made the final lap and ignited the cauldron at the opening ceremonies in Athens before a live audience of 72,000 and a global TV audience of 4 billion.

Almost 4000 torchbearers carried the flame to previous host cities and, for the first time, the flame visited Africa and Latin America. An estimated 260 million people saw the flame during the relay, which made Coca Cola and Samsung Electronics who paid hefty undisclosed fees to the Athens 2004 Organizing Committee, very happy corporate sponsors.

Gabriel Kahn, a reporter for the *Wall Street Journal*, summarized what the two corporate sponsors received in return: "The sponsors . . . turn each stop along the relay into a golden marketing opportunity. Both Samsung and Coke get to choose some of the relay runners for each city. Their corporate logos emblazon all sorts of torch-related paraphernalia. And as the relay entourage

winds it way through each city, Coke and Samsung trucks leave behind a stream of pennants, pins, and sodas."

Both Coca Cola and Samsung also were official sponsors of the Olympic games, which runs about $40 million per sponsor. Samsung, for example, integrated its brand presence into interactive experiences, bus wraps, airport luggage carts, and other signage. Both sponsors also operated extensive hospitality centers for athletes and visiting dignitaries.

Elli Panagiotopoulou Giokeza, writing in IPRA's *Frontline*, explains why corporate sponsors are attracted to the Olympics: "The sponsorship of the Olympic Games is a great communication tool, which not only extends the corporate visibility of the companies involved, but also provides them with the possibility to increase their relationship with the consumer and their respective trade audiences."

Another reason is given by Josh McCall in *PRWeek*: "The Olympics continue to be among the most prominent platforms for branding on the planet." One

Corporations sponsor a number of special events for public relations, marketing, and image-building purposes. Here, Olympic Ambassador Spiros Lambridis holds the Olympic flame on arrival at Beijing in the Olympic Torch relay that visited 34 cities on six continents before arriving in Athens. The relay was underwritten and sponsored by Coca-Cola and Samsung.

study, for example, showed that half of U.S. consumers thought Olympic sponsors were industry leaders.

unlike causes, are money-making operations in their own right, but a large part of the underwriting often comes from sponsorships provided by other corporations.

The popularity of sponsored events is due to several reasons. These events (1) enhance the reputation and image of the sponsoring company through association, (2) give product brands high visibility among key purchasing publics, (3) provide a focal point for marketing efforts and sales campaigns, and (4) generate publicity and media coverage.

Sponsorships can be more effective than advertising. Visa International, for example, spends about $200,000 annually sponsoring the USA-Visa Decathlon Team, or about the price of a 30-second prime time TV commercial. Speedo, the swimwear manufacturer, sponsors the U.S. Olympic swim team, but also gets its name before millions of television viewers, because most of the swimmers from other nations also wear Speedo swim caps and suits. In Sydney, about 70 percent of the Gold medalists in swimming wore Speedo gear. This translates to brand dominance in sales.

Local stadiums and concert halls almost everywhere now have corporate names. An obscure technology company, 3COM, got reams of national publicity when Candlestick Park in San Francisco became 3COM park. Naming rights to the new baseball stadium in San Francisco went to SBC, the telephone company. In Philadelphia, Lincoln Financial Group—not exactly a household name—snapped up naming rights for the new stadium for the Eagles pro football team. The company's reasoning: Its name becomes recognized as a major brand by those attending Eagle games and the 10 to 12 million fans that watch home games on television.

ON THE JOB insights

Selection Criteria for Corporate Sponsorships

Corporations are inundated with requests from organizations to sponsor everything from rock concerts to museum exhibits and sporting events. Consequently, each corporation selects sponsorships that best support its marketing and public relations objectives. A company considering a sponsorship should ask these questions:

- Can the company afford to fulfill the obligation? The sponsorship fee is just the starting point. Count on doubling it to have an adequate total event budget.
- Is the event or organization compatible with the company's values and mission statement?

- Does the event reach the corporation's target audience?
- Is there enough time before the event to maximize the company's use of the sponsorship?
- Are the event organizers experienced and professional?
- Is the event newsworthy enough to provide the company with opportunities for publicity?
- Will the event be televised?
- Will the sales force support the event and use it to leverage sales?
- Does the event give the company a chance to develop new contacts and business opportunities?

- Can the company live with the event on a long-term basis while its value builds?
- Is there an opportunity for employee involvement? Corporate sponsorships can be used to build employee morale and teamwork.
- Is the event compatible with the "personality" of the company's products?
- Can the company reduce the cash outlay and enhance the marketing appeal by trading off products and in-kind services?
- Will management support the event? If the answer is yes to the previous questions, the likelihood of management support of the sponsorship is fairly high.

Naming rights, however, are not forever, and the fortunes of high-flying corporations can change. Enron got great visibility for putting its name on the stadium of the Houston Astros, but its collapse into financial scandal caused the team to quickly disassociate itself from its corporate partner. Today, Minute Maid has its name emblazoned in stadium lights.

The demographic characteristics of potential customers determine, for the most part, what events a company will sponsor. Manufacturers of luxury products usually sponsor events that draw the interest of affluent consumers. That's why Lexus, a luxury car, sponsors polo championships. Tennis also has fairly affluent demographics, so Volvo sponsors tennis tournaments. General Motors GMC division, however, is interested in selling pickup trucks, so it sponsors a 15-city Country-Western tour. See the Insights box on page 471 for more guidelines on corporate sponsorships.

On occasion, a company will sponsor an event for the primary purpose of enhancing its reputation among opinion leaders and influential decision makers. Atofina Chemicals, for example, usually sponsors events that advance science education. However, it did agree to sponsor an exhibit of Degas' ballet-themed works at the Philadelphia Art Museum to highlight the company's history as a Paris-based corporation. One objective was to increase employee pride. The company's 1,200 employees in Philadelphia and their families were invited to an exclusive showing at the museum before the exhibit was open to the public. In addition, the company used the exhibit and museum as a centerpiece for entertaining customers and their significant others. It also organized events for and donations of products to the Philadelphia High School for the Creative and Performing Arts.

Environmental Relations

Another aspect of CSR that is coming to the forefront in the first decade of the 21st century is increased corporate concern for the environment and the maintenance of sustainable resources.

The 1990s saw major clashes and confrontations between corporations and activist nongovernmental organizations (commonly referred to as NGOs) about a host of environmental and human rights issues. The trend line in the 21st century, however, is for more cooperation and partnerships among former adversaries. Many companies, such as Shell, are now issuing annual corporate responsibility reports and working with environmental groups to clean up the environment, preserve wilderness areas, and even replace exploited natural resources.

Home Depot is a good case study. Between 1997 and 1999, the giant chain of homebuilding supplies was the target of environmentalists who picketed hundreds of Home Depot stores. They were concerned that the company, the world's largest retailer of lumber, was causing the massive destruction of forests around the world by not ensuring that its supplies didn't come from endangered forests. The protests received extensive media coverage and the company, quite frankly, was worried about a consumer backlash and sliding sales.

The company correctly perceived the potential problem as an issue that needed to be addressed (see discussion of issues management in Chapter 10). As a first step, the company agreed to stop using products from endangered forests and backed up its decision by slashing its imports from Indonesia, where loggers were practically clear-cutting tropical forests, by 90 percent. It also pressured Canada to declare logging off-limits in the Great Bear Rainforest in British Columbia. In another effort, it mediated an agreement between timber companies and environmentalists in Chile to preserve natural forests and establish guidelines for the sustainable farming of new trees.

The partnership between Home Depot and environmental groups is a win-win situation. The company gets credit for being environmentally concerned, which results in less negative publicity and more customer loyalty. The environmental groups, in turn, have more power to accomplish their objectives. Randy Hayes, president of the Rainforest Action Network, told the *Wall Street Journal*, "If you've got Home Depot carrying your water, you're going to get a lot farther than as just an environmental group."

Other large corporations around the world are forging alliances with various NGOs to preserve the environment, promote human rights, and provide social/medical services. The following are some examples of long-term CSR programs:

● The Royal Dutch/Shell Group has set the abolishment of child labor as its goal. Shell companies in 112 nations have procedures in place to prevent the use of child labor.

● Unilever, the food and consumer products company, is helping to restore a dying river estuary in the Philippines. The campaign is one of several programs by the company's global Water Sustainability Initiative.

● Volvo Corporation is working with the UN High Commissioner for Human Rights on a project addressing discrimination in the workplace.

● LM Ericsson, a Swedish telecommunications company, has a program to provide and maintain mobile communications equipment and expertise for humanitarian relief operations.

● Merck, the pharmaceutical giant, is a partner with the Bill and Melinda Gates Foundation on a five-year AIDS project in Botswana and is selling its drugs at cost in developing nations.

Corporate Philanthropy

Another manifestation of CSR is corporate philanthropy. This, in essence, is the donation of funds, products, and services to various causes. The range is everything from providing uniforms and equipment to a local Little League baseball team to a multi-million dollar donation to a university for upgrading its programs in science and engineering. In many cases, the organization's public relations department handles corporate charitable giving as part of its responsibilities.

In a recent year, American corporations and their foundations gave more than $12 billion to a variety of causes. Although there is a common perception that corporate philanthropy provides the lion's share of donations, the actual percentage is very small. Of the $241 billion total given in 2002, only 5.1 percent was from corporations. The largest amount of money given, 76.3 percent, was given by individuals. See Chapter 20 on nonprofits for more information on fund-raising.

Corporations, of course, have long used philanthropy to demonstrate community goodwill and to polish their reputations as a good citizen. There's also evidence that corporate giving is good for business and retaining customers. As previously noted, the Hill & Knowlton survey found that 79 percent of Americans claim to take corporate citizenship into consideration when purchasing products. At the same time, 76 percent of the respondents believe that companies participate in philanthropic activities to get favorable publicity, whereas only 24 percent believe corporations are truly committed to the causes they support.

Getting good publicity, no doubt, is a factor, but companies should not believe that this is the ultimate objective. Cone/Roper, a survey organization, says companies should be very careful about bragging about their good deeds, because the public will be skeptical about the motivation. Instead, companies should concentrate on the people they help, and the programs they showcase should be more than "window dressing." The research firm further states, "Never do it for publicity. Do it for building your business, your brand equity, and your stakeholder relations."

It also should be noted that companies don't give to anything and everything. A series of small grants to a wide variety of causes doesn't really help any particular charity, and it dilutes the impact of the contributions. Home Banc Mortgage Corporation, for example, used to give $300,000 annually in small grants to a variety of causes, but it eventually decided that the available funds could have more impact (and visibility) if only one or two causes were heavily funded. Consequently, the company now gives most of its charitable funds to Habitat for Humanity, a nonprofit that builds homes for low-income families.

In Home Banc's case, funding Habitat for Humanity is a strategic decision to funnel contributions into a cause directly related to home ownership, which is the business of the mortgage company. HP also is strategic in deciding where to place its charitable contributions. It expends considerable money on a scholarship program and summer jobs for minority and female engineering and computer science majors. Another major initiative is gifts of its computers, medical equipment, and test equipment to institutions of higher learning. The company's giving philosophy is clearly stated: "HP giving to colleges and universities meets university needs for products while attracting higher skilled workers to the industries we support."

Strategic philanthropy is defined by Paul Davis Jones and Cary Raymond of IDPR Group as "the long-term socially responsible contribution of dollars, volunteers, products, and expertise to a cause aligned with the strategic business goals of an organization." Such giving, they say, can reap a number of benefits for the corporation, including:

- Strengthened reputation and brand recognition
- Increased media opportunities
- Improved community and government relations
- Facilitation of employee recruitment and retention
- Enhanced marketing
- Access to research and development
- Increased corporate profitability

Corporate philanthropy, despite its potential benefits, does have its limitations. A large grant by a corporation, for example, cannot offset a major financial scandal or the negative publicity of a class-action suit for discrimination of female employees. Philanthropy, as Phillip Morris found out, also can't erase public concern about the promotion and marketing of tobacco products. Wal-Mart, faced with community opposition to "big-box" stores, probably won't change the opponent's minds by giving several million dollars to local schools.

ON THE JOB insights

The Value of Corporate Philanthropy

Corporate philanthropy is viewed favorably by employees, customers, and shareholders, according to a survey conducted by the Council on Foundations (COF) and the Walker Information Group. The following is a summary of the major findings:

Employees

One-third to two-thirds agree that (1) a good giving record is a main reason for remaining with an employer, (2) corporate generosity is one of the factors that differentiates a company, and (3) a company that does good deeds gains their admiration.

Customers

One-third say they would select a company on its giving record.

Shareholders

One-third attest to the effect of corporate philanthropy programs on their investment decisions and specifically say corporate generosity (1) affects the bottom line, (2) positively affects stock performance, and (3) affects where to invest.

Type of Program

Stakeholders rate companies highest for higher visibility efforts, such as providing sponsorship support for worthwhile nonprofit events and causes and having employee volunteers. Fewer stakeholders rate companies positively for contributing cash or donating in-kind products and services.

Recommendations

Based on the results, the following recommendations are made:

- Set out a strategic plan for corporate philanthropy that is both focused and consistent with your overall corporate goals.
- Take stock of and quantify what the company does in the area of corporate philanthropy.
- Realize that of all a company's stakeholder groups, the employees are likely to know best the company and what it does in philanthropy.
- Ensure that the CEO and other senior leaders are aware of the significant role they play in how stakeholders form perceptions of a company's philanthropic programs.
- Ensure that an effective and realistic external communications effort is a key element of our philanthropic program.
- Develop and conduct a process to reassess the way the philanthropy function is delivered.

Source: PRWeek, May 5, 2003, p. 15.

Another downside to corporate philanthropy is when special interest groups object to the cause that's being funded. Pro-life groups, for example, often target companies that give grants to Planned Parenthood and ask their supporters to boycott the company's products. Bank of America was caught in a controversy when it decided to stop funding the Boy Scouts of America because of the group's refusal to admit gays. Although gay activists were pleased by the action, a storm of protest arose from other bank customers who supported the Boy Scouts. Many canceled their accounts and encouraged others to do the same.

According to Paul Holmes, a columnist for *PRWeek*, there's even a Washington, D.C. group called the Capital Research Center that seeks to "end the liberal bias in corporate philanthropy." It objects to company donations to "anti-business" charities such as the National Wildlife Federation.

All this leaves corporations somewhat in a quandary about what charities are "safe" and which ones might raise controversy and protests at annual stockholder meetings. There's also the consideration of what special groups are most influential or have the ability to cause headaches for the corporation through boycotts, pickets, and demonstrations. In bottom-line terms, the corporation also thinks about what decision would be best in terms of keeping its overall customer base. Pro-life groups had originally forced Dayton-Hudson Corporation, a department store chain, to cancel its contributions to Planned Parenthood, but the company reversed its decision after hundreds of irate customers sent in cut-up credit cards.

Despite the possible downsides and controversies, corporate philanthropy is a good tool for enhancing reputation, building relationships with key audiences, and increasing employee and customer loyalty. It also serves the public interest in many ways. See the Insights box on page 475 about the value of corporate philanthropy.

SUMMARY

Today's Modern Corporation

Today, giant corporations have operations and customers around the globe. The public is often distrustful of these large entities because of their perceived wealth and power. Corporate financial scandals in recent years have further eroded public trust.

The Role of Public Relations

Corporations must make special efforts to win back public credibility and trust, and the concept of *corporate social responsibility (CSR)* is high on the list of priorities. Public relations professionals are on the frontline in this effort, counseling companies to be more transparent in their operations, to adopt ethical principles of conduct, and to improve corporate governance.

Media Relations

The public's perception of business comes primarily from the mass media. Consequently, it is important for organizations to effectively tell their story and build a rapport with business editors and reporters by being accessible, open, and honest about company operations and policies.

Customer Relations

Customer service, in many ways, is the frontline of public relations. Customer satisfaction is important for building loyalty and telling others about the product or the reputation of the company. Public relations professionals solicit customer feedback as often as possible and act to satisfy customers' needs for communication and service.

Reaching a Diverse Market

The U.S. population is becoming more diverse, and companies are now establishing communication programs, as well as marketing strategies, to serve this growing audience.

Consumer Activism

In today's society, any number of special interest groups exert pressure on corporations to be socially responsible. Companies cannot avoid activist groups; they must engage in dialogue to work out differences. Oftentimes, the public relations staff is the mediator. Consumer boycotts also require public relations expertise to deal effectively with a group's demands.

Employee Relations

Emloyees are the "ambassadors" of a company and are the primary source of information about the company to their friends and relatives. Employee morale is important, and a good communications program—coupled with enlightened company policies—does much to maintain high productivity and employee retention.

Layoffs and Outsourcing

The cardinal rule, from a public relations standpoint, is to first talk to employees in person before announcing a layoff to the public. Many companies ease the impact of a layoff by providing a severance package. Off-shoring is a rising concern of American workers, and companies must be sensitive to possible criticism.

Minorities in the Workplace

The American workforce is becoming increasingly diverse. Companies must take this into consideration when planning employee communication campaigns.

Employee Volunteerism

Many companies provide opportunities for employees to volunteer for charitable work on company time. This increases employee morale and loyalty.

Investor Relations

Public relations professionals who work in investor relations must be knowledgeable about communications and finance. It's the highest paying field in public relations, but the practitioner must have extensive knowledge of government regulations.

Marketing Communications

Increasingly, companies take an integrated approach to campaigns. Public relations, marketing, and adver-tising staffs work together to complement each other's expertise. Product publicity and product placement are part of marketing communications. Cause-related marketing involves partnerships with nonprofit organizations to promote a particular cause. Another aspect of marketing communications is corporate sponsorships.

Environmental Relations

A new trend line is for corporations and activist organizations to have a dialogue and engage in collaborative efforts to change situations that damage the environment or violate human rights.

Corporate Philanthropy

Companies give about $12 billion a year to worthy causes. It's important to select a charity that is complementary to the organization's business and customer profile. In general, corporate philanthropy is part of an organization's commitment to be socially responsible.

Case Activity: **What Would You Do?**

McDonald's is under attack from several quarters. Government studies say that obesity among adults and children is a major problem, and fast-food chains such as McDonald's are singled out as a major contributor to obesity. In the United Kingdom, for example, 8.5 percent of 6-year-olds and 15 percent of 15-year-olds are obese.

Adding to McDonald's problem is a film entitled *Super Size Me*, in which the producer spends a month eating only McDonald's food. The film tracks his weight gain and declining state of health, plus his failed attempts to engage McDonald's executives in dialogue. The film, to say the least, is less than favorable in its portrayal of McDonald's. There's also a growing lobby advocating the banning of marketing to children. One activist leader says, "McDonald's could engineer a huge PR coup if it voluntarily ceased to promote its food directly to children."

What should McDonald's do? It has already made changes in its menu to offer more salads and fruits, plus it has curbed its "supersize" meal option. Should it respond aggressively to refuting *Super Size Me*, or would that just supply more publicity for the film? What kind of media relations is needed in this situation? What kind of communications should be done with customers, employees, and stockholders? How should the company deal with the food activists? Should the response be more cause-related marketing or corporate sponsorships of events? What about strategies in corporate philanthropy?

QUESTIONS for Review and Discussion

1. What are the characteristics of today's modern corporation? Why is there so much public suspicion and distrust? Is there any evidence to support the public's perceptions?

2. What is the concept of corporate social responsibility (CSR), and why is it important to today's corporations? What is the role of public relations professionals in this concept?

3. General Electric says that a corporation must consider four factors when making any decision. What are they?

4. Corporate executives indicate that they are wary of the media. What reasons do they give? Do you think their concerns are valid? Journalists also are critical of business executives. What are their complaints?

5. Why is it important for corporate executives to have a good relationship with the mass media?

6. Traditionally, customer relations and public relations have been separate corporate functions. Do you think the two functions should be merged? Why or why not?

7. Why is it important for companies to consider diversity in their marketing and public relations strategies?

8. Consumer activists are very vocal about the misdeeds of corporations. How should a company react to charges and allegations from activist groups such as PETA? What factors would go into your decision making?

9. If an activist group has called for the boycott of a particular company's products, would you be inclined to stop buying the product? Why or why not? Under what circumstances would you join a boycott against a company?

10. Why is employee relations so important to a company's image and reputation?

11. What employee policies do *Fortune's* 100 best companies have that distinguish them from other corporations?

12. How should a company tell its employees about a layoff?

13. How can a company benefit from meeting the needs of a diverse workforce?

14. Many companies give workers time off with pay to volunteer on local charitable projects. Would you be more inclined to work for such a company? Why or why not?

15. Give some examples of product publicity and product placement.

16. What is cause-related marketing? Give some examples. What guidelines should be considered when partnering with a cause?

17. Give four reasons why corporate sponsorship of concerts, festivals, and even the Olympics is considered a good marketing and public relations strategy.

18. Corporations, throughout the 1990s, had frequent clashes with environmental and human rights groups. Today, there seems to be more cooperation and collaboration. Why do you think this has occurred?

19. Corporate philanthropy is now very strategic; companies support organizations and causes that have a direct relationship to their business. Do you think all this makes corporate philanthropy too self-serving? Why or why not?

SUGGESTED READINGS

Amaro, Gina. "Multicultural Efforts to Require Company-Wide Involvement." *PRWeek*, February 9, 2004, p. 7.

Bloom, Jonah. "Corporate Social Responsibility: Conscientious Objectives." *PRWeek*, May 13, 2002, pp. 12–13.

Calabro, Sara. "Surveys Finds Lack of Trust in Internal Communications." *PRWeek*, January 12, 2004, p. 2.

Carlton, Jim. "Once Targeted by Protesters, Home Depot Plays Green Role." *Wall Street Journal*, August 6, 2004, pp. A1, A6.

Creamer, Matthew. "Offshoring Reputation." *PRWeek*, April 5, 2004, p. 13.

Creamer, Matthew. "Survey Points to Low Quality of U.S. Business Journalism." *PRWeek*, March 10, 2003, p. 3.

Frank, John, and Gordon, Andrew. "Employee Comms Hurt by Scandals, Surveys Reveal." *PRWeek*, September 30, 2003, p. 3.

Genova, Jane. "CSR Programs Yield Bottom Line Payoffs." *O'Dwyer's PR Services Report*, June 2003, pp. 1, 23, 25.

Hood, Julia. "CEO Survey Reveals Reputation Concerns." *PRWeek*, November 10, 2003, pp. 1, 15–22.

Kahn, Gabriel. "How Olympic Torch Made 100-Mile Trip Through Six Continents." *Wall Street Journal*, July 19, 2004, pp. A1, A6.

Kinnick, Katherine N. "How Corporate America Grieves: Response to September 11 in Public Relations Advertising." *Public Relations Review*, Vol. 29, No. 4, 2003, pp. 443–459.

Krautter, Kimberly. "Give and Take: Corporate Philanthropy." *PRWeek*, May 5, 2003, p. 15.

Makovsky, Kenneth D. "What Price Credibility?" *The Strategist*, Fall 2003, pp. 3–7.

McCall, Josh. "Marketing Opportunities for 2004 Olympics Proved Solid." *PRWeek*, August 30, 2004, p. 9.

McCauley, Kevin. "Coke's Image Under Attack." *O'Dwyer's PR Services Report*, June 2004, pp. 1, 8, 10–11.

McGuire, Craig. "Hearing the Customer Out." *PRWeek*, February 23, 2004, p. 23.

McNeil, Donald. "At Last, a Company Takes PETA Seriously." *New York Times*, July 25, 2004, Section 4, p. 4.

O'Brien, Keith. "Financial Communications in the Public Eye." *PRWeek*, June 20, 2004, p. 28.

Park, Dong-Jin, and Berger, Bruce K. "The Presentation of CEOs in the Press, 1900–2000: Increasing Salience, Positive Valence, and a Focus on Competency and Personal Dimensions of Image." *Journal of Public Relations Research*, Vol. 16, No. 1, 2004, pp. 93–125.

Pereira, Joseph. "Doing Good and Doing Well at Timberland." *New York Times*, September 9, 2003, pp. B1, B10.

Quenqua, Douglas. "Finding the Right Cause to Support." *PRWeek*, October 27, 2003, p. 20.

Quenqua, Douglas. "The Proactive Approach to Averting Protests." *PRWeek*, January 6, 2003, p. 18.

Rhody, Ron. "Standing Upright in Perilous Times: The CEO, The Board, and Us." *Public Relations Quarterly*, Spring 2004, pp. 2–6.

Shortman, Melanie. "Artful Communication: Companies Are Getting Maximum ROI Out of Their Sponsorship Dollars." *PRWeek*, January 12, 2004, p. 21.

Taylor, William. "Companies Find They Can't Buy Love With Bargains." *New York Times*, August 8, 2004, Business Section A, p. 5.

chapter **18**

Politics and Government

Topics covered in this chapter include:

Government Relations

A specialized component of corporate communications is government relations. This activity is so important that many companies, particularly in highly regulated industries, have separate departments of government relations. The reason is simple. The actions of governmental bodies at the local, state, and federal level have a major impact on how a business operates.

Government relations specialists, often called *public affairs specialists*, have a number of functions: They gather information, disseminate management's views, cooperate with government on projects of mutual benefit, and motivate employees to participate in the political process.

As the eyes and ears of a business or industry, practitioners spend much time gathering and processing information. They monitor the activities of many legislative bodies and regulatory agencies to keep track of issues coming up for debate and possible vote. Such intelligence gathering enables a corporation or an industry to plan ahead and, if necessary, adjust policies or provide information that may influence the nature of government decision making.

Monitoring government takes many forms. Probably the most active presence in Washington, D.C., and many state capitals is the trade association that represents a particular industry. A Boston University survey showed that 67 percent of the responding companies monitored government activity in Washington through their trade associations. Second on the list were frequent trips to Washington by senior public affairs officers and corporate executives; 58 percent of the respondents said they engaged in this activity. Almost 45 percent of the responding firms reported that they also had a company office in the nation's capital.

Government relations specialists spend a great amount of time disseminating information about the company's position to a variety of key publics. Spoken tactics may include an informal office visit to a government official or testimony at a public hearing. In addition, public affairs people are often called upon to give a speech or write one for a senior executive.

Written tactics may include writing letters and op-ed articles, preparing position papers, producing newsletters, and placing advocacy advertising. Although legislators are a primary audience, the Foundation for Public Affairs reports that nine of 10 companies also communicate with employees on public policy issues, whereas another 40 percent communicate with retirees, customers, and other publics such as taxpayers and government employees.

The importance of effective governmental relations to the economic well-being of a company is best summarized by a *New York Times* writer:

> Public relations executives can rightly point out that, with the cacophony of interests clamoring for attention in Washington, there is a role for professional advice on how to insure that one's message is heard. With the expanding role of Congress and the increasing complexity of government, this probably is true now more than ever. There are undoubtedly times that public relations firms can help journalists, politicians and clients.

Corporations are also actively engaged in lobbying and making campaign contributions, which are discussed next.

ON THE JOB insights

Skills Needed for Work in Public Affairs

Work in public affairs, including governmental relations, is a specialty area of public relations that requires certain skills and abilities. The following list is adapted from an article by Doug Pinkham, president of the Public Affairs Council in Washington, D.C., in the organization's newsletter:

● **Knowledge of how public relations and public affairs supports business goals.** You need to measure and evaluate your programs, not on the basis of clips or bills lobbied, but whether you have improved the reputation of the company among key stakeholders.

● **A knack for discerning which opponents to take seriously.** In the Internet age, anyone can be an activist and set up a Web site. A search on Google, for example, will reveal 1.3 million hits for the word "boycott." You need the ability to evaluate which activist groups are credible, and those that aren't. In too many cases, corporations have caused more media attention by refuting charges that few people took seriously in the first place.

● **Ability to integrate all communications functions.** You need to coordinate the efforts of multiple corporate departments during a crisis situation.

● **Understanding how to control key messages.** The development of key messages, representing all divisions and companies of the corporate parent, should be centralized at company headquarters. If message development is decentralized, consumers may get mixed messages.

● **Ability to have influence without being too partisan.** Build relationships with both Democrats and Republicans; don't favor one party over another.

● **Talent for synthesizing, filtering, and validating information.** Today's problem is information overload. You need the ability to extract the nuggets of relevant information and position your department as the one that can make sense out of all the noise.

● **Aptitude for information technology.** Elections, legislative battles, and even reputations are now being won and lost because

of the Internet. Every public policy or public relations campaign needs an on-line strategy. You need to be Web-savvy to build networks of supporters, communicate with thought-leaders, keep employees informed, and get your message to key audiences.

● **Global perspective.** American companies need to learn more about other countries where they manufacture or market their products and services. You need to build relationships with local communities and entire nations so that everyone benefits from economic growth.

● **Sustain strong personal relationships.** Public relations is not a direct-mail business. Success demands a commitment to individual service and personal integrity. You also need to develop a reputation for intelligence and credibility. Reporters, political leaders, and other stakeholders are deluged with news and opinion; they rely on those individuals who they respect on a personal level.

Source: Public Relations Quarterly, Spring 2004, p. 15.

Lobbying

Lobbying is closely aligned with governmental relations or public affairs, and the distinction between the two often blurs. This is because most campaigns to influence impending legislation have multiple levels. One level is informing and convincing the public about the correctness of the organization's viewpoint, which the public affairs specialist does.

Lobbying, on the other hand, is a more specific activity. *Webster's New World Dictionary* defines a *lobbyist* as "a person . . . who tries to influence the voting on legislation or the decisions of government administrators." In other words, a lobbyist directs his or her energies to the defeat, passage, or amendment of proposed legislation and regulatory agency policies.

A good example of how a public information campaign and a lobbying effort work in tandem was a $20 million campaign by Canada's lumber exporters. They sought the repeal of a 27 percent American import tariff on lumber coming into the United States.

The tariff was imposed by Congress after American lumber companies conducted a vigorous lobbying campaign that convinced lawmakers that their Canadian counterparts benefit from unfair government subsidies. The result, they claimed, was the sale of Canadian lumber in the United States at uncompetitive prices.

The Forest Products Association of Canada (FPAC) retained several U.S. public relations firms to inform the buying public that the price of lumber would substantially increase because of the tariff. In the meantime, the organization also hired several public affairs and lobbying firms in Washington, D.C., to present its case to various members of Congress for repeal of the tax.

Lobbyists can be found at the local, state, and federal levels of government. California, for example, has about 900 registered lobbyists who represent more than 1600 special-interest groups. The interests represented in Sacramento include large corporations, business and trade groups, unions, environmental groups, local governments, nonprofit groups, school districts, and members of various professional groups.

The number and variety of special interests multiply at the federal level. One directory of Washington lobbyists lists 20,000 individuals and organizations. The interests represented include virtually the entire spectrum of U.S. business, educational, religious, local, national, and international pursuits.

The diversity of those groups can be illustrated with the debate about managed health care and patient rights. Opposing new regulations are (1) insurance companies, (2) HMO trade groups, (3) the United States Chamber of Commerce, (4) the National Federation of Independent Business, and (5) the American Association of Health Plans. Groups supporting patient rights include (1) a broad coalition of consumer groups, (2) the American Medical Association, and (3) the Trial Lawyers of America.

The groups opposed to patient rights legislation are concerned about higher costs to employers, increased government control of health care delivery systems, and more litigation and lawsuits. As a result, the health industry has spent millions of dollars to lobby against any legislation.

The Nature of Lobbying

Although the public perceives that only big business lobbies, a variety of special interests do it. *Fortune* magazine, for example, ranked the top 25 lobbying groups in Washington in terms of influence, and the American Association of Retired Persons (AARP) was first on the list. The next four rankings, in descending order, were (1) the American Israel Public Affairs Committee, (2) the National Federation of Independent Business, (3) the National Rifle Association, and (4) the AFL-CIO.

ON THE JOB insights

Lobbyists Get into Food Fight

The food business in the United States is a $500 billion industry, and what foods get listed on the U.S. government's food guidelines is the subject of much lobbying by various producers and groups.

The guidelines, issued every five years by the Department of Health and Human Services and the Agriculture Department (USDA), form the basis for school lunches and other federal nutrition programs. They also tell the general public what foods should be in a healthy diet. The recommendations are usually summarized and portrayed in a colorful graphic in the shape of a pyramid that is widely publicized and promoted.

Any changes in the guidelines, of course, can swing food companies' sales by millions of dollars. That's why the U.S. Potato Board is lobbying hard to stay in the pyramid, as the lowly spud is all but blacklisted by

low-carbohydrate diets. At the same time, the National Diary Council is arguing for an increase in the recommended number of dairy product servings, and the baked-goods industry is defending its current prominent place in the recommendations. Its major concern, however, is the trend of low-carb diets that place more emphasis on whole-grain products instead of ones made with enriched white flour.

The parade continues. The executive director of USDA's Center for Nutrition Policy, the group responsible for the pyramid overhaul, receives a daily stream of food groups to press their case. In a single day, the director met with such diverse groups as the National Cattlemen's Beef Association, the Chocolate Manufacturer's Association, and the California Walnut Commission.

Potato lobbyists, in the meantime, kept in close contact with their political allies, including Senator Larry Craig, an Idaho Republican, and other members of the Congressional Potato Caucus. This group is made up of legislators who come from states where potato farming is big business, and they are concerned about a major blow to a state's economy if the potato is shunned by the American consumer.

Competing lobbying efforts often cancel each other out. All this leaves legislators and regulatory personnel the responsibility to weigh the pros and cons of an issue before voting. Indeed, *Time* magazine notes that lobbyists representing all sides of an issue "do serve a useful purpose by showing busy legislators the virtues and pitfalls of complex legislation." A classic conflict is the debate between saving jobs and improving the environment. A coalition of environmental groups constantly lobbies Congress for tougher legislation to clean up industrial pollution or protect endangered species. Simultaneously, local communities and unions often argue that the proposed legislation would mean the loss of jobs and economic chaos.

Environmental groups argue the "public interest;" so do opposing groups. Is it in the "public interest," they ask, to throw thousands of people out of work or to legislate so many restrictions on the manufacture of a product that it becomes more expensive to the average consumer? The answer, quite often, depends on whether the person is a steel worker, a logger, a consumer, or a member of the World Wildlife Federation.

The Problem of Influence Peddling

Although a case can be made for lobbying as a legitimate activity, deep public suspicion exists about former legislators and officials who capitalize on their connections and charge large fees for doing what is commonly described as *influence peddling*.

Indeed, the roster of registered lobbyists in Washington includes a virtual "who's who" of former legislators and government officials from both Democratic and Republican parties. A good example is Powell Tate, a major public affairs firm in Washington, D.C. The president is Sheila Tate, who served as Nancy Reagan's press secretary and the former President Bush's transition press secretary. Tate's partner is Jody Powell, the former press secretary of President Carter. Together, they know on a first-name basis key Republican and Democratic lawmakers as well as the major journalists covering the Capitol.

The Ethics in Government Act forbids government officials from actively lobbying their former agencies for one year after leaving office. Critics say that it has had little or no impact. A good case study is the U.S. Department of Homeland Security. When Tom Ridge became director of the White House Office of Homeland Security after the 9/11 attack, he brought together a number of trusted aides to help set up the office. Then, when he became the first Secretary of Homeland Security in President Bush's cabinet, many of his senior aides left government and started new careers as lobbyists for companies seeking contracts with the department, which has a $40 billion budget to spend.

Rebecca L. Halkias, who was Ridge's legislative director in the White House, told the *New York Times*, "My one year is up, so I can lobby him and lobby the White House and lobby the Hill." In the same story, reporter Philip Shenon wrote that Blank Rome Government Relations, the lobbying arm of a large Philadelphia law firm, was particularly well connected to Ridge because the firm had hired three former senior aides from the Department of Homeland Security. "Homeland Security appears to be viewed by lobbying firms as a huge honey pot," said Fred Wertheimer, president of a nonprofit group that advocates restrictions on corporate lobbying.

Unlike federal agency personnel, members of Congress can become lobbyists immediately after leaving office. A good example is former Representative J. C. Watts (R-OK) who announced the formation of a group of lobbying and public affairs firms exactly one day after leaving office. High-ranking members of Watts' congressional staff moved with him to his new offices to begin their careers as lobbyists of their former colleagues.

Even congressional staff members who know intimately the structure and operations of key committees begin second careers as lobbyists. Ann Eppard, an administrative assistant for 22 years to Congressman Bud Shuster, a Republican from Pennsylvania, set up shop after he became chair of the House Transportation Committee. In short order, she had clients such as Federal Express and the American Road and Transportation Builders Association, which had vital interests before the committee.

Such connections, and the "cashing in" on them, give the press and public the uneasy feeling that influence peddling is alive and well in the nation's capitol. It also gives credence to the cliché, "It's not what you know, but who you know."

ON THE JOB insights

Advocates Outgunned in Lobbying Showdown

Gun control advocates lobbied hard for renewal of the federal ban on the manufacture and import of semiautomatic assault weapons but, in the end, they were outgunned by the firepower of the National Rifle Association.

On the surface, it seemed that the gun control advocates had all the firepower. Public opinion polls showed that two-thirds of Americans supported the ban, major law enforcement agencies backed it, and four former Presidents (both Democratic and Republican) had worked to get the law passed in the first place. In addition, there was an army of gun control advocates throughout the country lobbying their elected Congressional representatives. A group called the Brady Campaign to Prevent Gun Violence also placed a series of provocative full-page ads in major daily newspapers to put pressure on President Bush to support the ban.

So, what went wrong? The answer, most observers agree, was the formidable lobbying power of the National Rifle Association with its 4 million members. It

made killing the ban a high priority because the organization claimed it was not effective in preventing crimes with semiautomatic assault weapons. NRA official Kelly Hobbs told the press, "Why keep bad policy on the books? This law has affected law-biding gun owners. That's the only group it's impacted."

Although President Bush publicly said he would sign the bill for extension if it came to his desk, critics said he did nothing to encourage the Republican majority in the House of Representatives to bring the bill to a vote. House Majority Leader Tom DeLay (R-Texas) strongly opposed the extension, and he controls what bills come up for a vote, so President Bush was fairly safe in having it both ways—public support for ban but not being put in a position to sign it.

The NRA's influence may have been a deciding factor. It announced that it would not announce whether it was supporting Bush in the reelection campaign until after the bill expired. Once the bill was certain to expire, the NRA launched a series of TV ads against John Kerry, the Democratic candidate.

So, on September 13, at midnight, the ban on semiautomatic assault weapons expired without a single shot (vote) fired by the U.S. House of Representatives on the issue.

A Lobbying Reform Bill

Politicians of both parties have regularly decried the influence of lobbyists, but reform has taken a half-century. At least 10 times since the first loophole-riddled lobbying regulations were passed in 1946, efforts to update the law failed to get past the legislative obstacles.

In 1995, however, Congress did pass a measure designed to reform lobbying, and President Clinton signed it. Part of the impetus, no doubt, was the impact of polls indicating that the public believed lobbyists had runaway influence in Washington.

One key provision was an expanded definition of who is considered to be a "lobbyist." The new law defines a lobbyist as "someone hired to influence lawmakers, government officials or their aides, and who spends at least 20 percent of his or her time representing any client in a six-month period."

Another key provision requires lobbyists to register with Congress and disclose their clients, the issue areas in which lobbying is being done, and roughly how much is being paid for it. Violators face civil fines of up to $50,000.

The tougher restrictions on lobbyists also apply to eating and drinking. Under the new law, lobbyist-paid lavish lunches and drawn-out dinners are forbidden. Receptions at which finger food is served are allowed. Lobbyists call this the *toothpick rule*. The law also prohibits a lobbyist from buying a meal for a lawmaker unless at least 25 people from an organization attend. That is considered a "widely attended event" at which a lobbyist could not monopolize a lawmaker's time.

New rules also exist for gifts and travel. Senators, their aides, and other Senate officers are barred from accepting gifts worth more than $50 and from accepting privately paid travel to "recreational events." Similar rules about gift giving govern the executive branch of government.

Although there are still loopholes, individuals and organizations violating the law face stiff fines. One case concerns Michael Espy, former Agriculture Secretary in the Clinton Administration. Although he was eventually acquitted of criminal activity in accepting $33,000 in gifts and travel from companies he regulated, some of the companies were not so fortunate. In civil actions, the Smith Barney brokerage firm was fined $1 million for giving Espy a $2,200 Super Bowl ticket, while Robert Mondavi Corp. had to pay $120,000 for giving him six $31 bottles of wine and a $207 dinner at a Washington restaurant.

One area exempted from the lobby reform bill was financial disclosures for so-called "grassroots" lobbying. In many respects, it is the fastest growing area in the political persuasion business.

Grassroots Lobbying

Grassroots lobbying is now an $800 million industry, according to *Campaigns and Elections*, a bimonthly magazine for "political professionals." What makes it so attractive to various groups is that there are virtually no rules or regulations.

The tools of such lobbying are advocacy advertising, toll-free phone lines, bulk faxing, Web sites, and computerized direct mail aimed at generating phone calls and letters from the public to Congress, the White House, and governmental regulatory agencies.

One major firm, Bonner & Associates, has a highly sophisticated communications system that includes banks of telephones and computers that can call or send letters to thousands of citizens within hours. For example, the American Bankers Association hired Bonner to kill a Congressional bill that would lower credit card interest rates. The firm orchestrated 10,000 phone calls from citizens and community leaders to 10 members of the House Banking Committee. The bill died in committee.

Grassroots lobbying also involves coalition building. The basic idea is to get individuals and groups with no financial interest in an issue to speak on the sponsor's behalf. The premise is that letters and phone calls from private citizens are

ON THE JOB

insights

Guidelines for Grassroots Lobbying

Legitimate coalitions of companies, associations, and citizens are effective grassroots tools, but "misleading front groups and sneak attacks are recipes for trouble," says Jay Lawrence, senior vice president of Fleishman-Hillard public relations.

Lawrence gives these tips for effective grassroots lobbying in *O'Dwyer's PR Services Report:*

- **Target the effort.** Few campaigns need to reach every congressman or state legislator.
- **Go after "persuadables."** Narrow the audience by concentrating on fence-sitters.
- **Build coalitions on economic self-interest.** Go after individuals and organizations who would be financially affected.

- **Think politically.** Find people who know legislative decision-makers or have some connection with them.
- **Letters are best.** Personal letters are the most effective—far better than postcards, mailgrams, and petitions. The best letters are short and simple.
- **Make it easy.** Provide sample drafts of letters, as well as pens, paper, and even stamps.
- **Arrange meetings.** The best single communication is a meeting in the official's home district with a group of interested constituents.
- **Avoid stealth tactics.** If you can't say up front whose interest you are promoting and why, it is a good idea to take another look at the effort.

more influential than arguments from vested interests.

A good example comes from another Bonner campaign. In this case, Congress was considering an auto pollution bill opposed by car manufacturers. The auto companies sought opposition to the bill from beyond the auto industry. Key legislators soon began hearing from disabled and elderly people who were convinced the bill would force the industry to build cars too small to hold walkers and wheelchairs and from Little League parents worried that fuel-efficient station wagons would not accommodate a whole team. The bill was defeated.

Although public involvement in legislative issues is admirable, critics say grassroots lobbying, with its orchestration of public feedback, often slips into the category of unethical behavior.

Another problem involves doing grassroots lobbying under the cover of front groups (see Chapter 3). This is called *stealth lobbying*, because the public isn't told what vested interests are behind a particular campaign.

In one example, APCO Associates organized the Mississippians for a Fair Legal System (M-Fair) to solicit public support for tort reform. What the public didn't know was that the sponsoring organization, the American Tort Reform Association, included large tobacco and chemical companies, which wanted legislation limiting liability for dangerous or defective products.

Such "grassroots" campaigns make public interest groups wonder if they really shouldn't be called "Astroturf" campaigns, since the "grass" is artificial. Michael Pertschuk, codirector of the Advocacy Institute in Washington, D.C., told *O'Dwyer's PR Services Report*, "Astroturf groups are usually founded with corporate seed money that is funneled through PR firms." An example is the group National Smokers Alliance, organized by Burson-Marsteller with seed money from Philip Morris.

Election Campaigns

Public affairs activities and lobbying, either in the halls of Congress or at the grassroots level, are year-round activities. During election years, either at the Congressional or presidential level, an army of fund-raisers, political strategists, speechwriters, and communications consultants are mobilized to help candidates win elections.

The high cost of running for office in the United States has made fund-raising virtually a full-time, year-round job for every incumbent and aspirant to office. In fact, American-style campaigning is the most expensive in the world. According to *The Economist*, a colossal $4 billion was spent on the 2004 congressional and presidential races—a third more than was spent in the 2000 election. Of that amount, paid advertising by the two major presidential candidates topped $600 million. This was despite the advent of the McCain-Feingold Campaign Finance Act that was passed in 2002, which will be discussed shortly.

It's difficult to comprehend such large figures, but the *New York Times*, in an analysis of costs associated with the 2004 presidential campaign, gives some insight into where all the money goes. Some typical costs based on interviews with political consultants, vendors, and campaign experts are as follows:

DESCRIPTION OF ACTIVITY	COST
An average full day of campaigning, including the cost of travel, renting halls, preparing stages, and advance work	$100,000
One week of television advertisements that the average voter could be expected to see five times	$525,000 New York $210,000 Dallas
	$105,000 Minneapolis
	$10,000 Butte, Montana
Salary of one advance person, first year out of college, per month	$3,000 (not including expense account)
Direct mail fund-raising appeal to 100,000 potential donors	$50,000
One hour of travel on Air Force One	$40,000
5000 two-color bumper stickers	$588
5000 yard signs with wire frame	$2,134
2500 round two-color buttons	$499
One 4 × 10 foot two-color banner	$200

Given these costs, presidential candidates and their staffs expend a considerable amount of time and energy doing fund-raising. John Kerry, for example, raised more than $225 million through August of 2004, which made him the best-financed challenger in campaign history, according to the *New York Times*. George Bush, in contrast, had already raised $228 million through June for the November election, which was twice as much as he raised in 2000. In addition, each candidate received $75 million in federal funds after being nominated by their respective parties. See the Insights box on page 490 about the cost of the national party conventions.

Candidates retain professionals to organize fund-raising activities. A standard activity in Washington, D.C., and other major cities across the country is the luncheon, reception, or dinner on behalf of a candidate. The *Wall Street Journal*, for example, reported that 14 such events were held on a single day in October, raising $650,000 for Congressional incumbents.

At the presidential level, the stakes increase. President Bush collected $4 million at a $2,000 per person dinner in Manhattan. His running mate, Dick Cheney, managed to collect more than $1.6 million on the same day at separate events in Virginia and Massachusetts.

Attending such events are individual donors and lobbyists for various organizations. Although a chicken dinner or a cheese platter with crackers and champagne are

ON THE JOB insights

Getting Nominated in United States Is an Expensive Proposition

The Republican convention in New York City that nominated President Bush for a second term was an expensive proposition. According to the *New York Times*, "The four-day Republican National Convention cost more than $154 million to stage. . . . making the 19 hours of speeches and two years of planning the most expensive such event in the nation's history."

The G.O.P., in a detailed 2300-page filing with the Federal Election Commission (FEC), reported that the New York host committee spent $81.6 million and the city spent about $58 million on police and other services, most of which is reimbursed by the federal government. In addition, the U.S. government gives each political party a $15 million subsidy to help stage the convention.

Some costs for the convention included (1) $301,460 for limousine services, (2) $281,000 to build the circular stage where Bush gave his acceptance speech, (3) $1.4 million to the fund-raising firm, (4) $11 million to a Texas firm for remodeling Madison Square Garden, (5) $750,000 for Broadway play tickets,

Presidential nominating conventions are big business. The 2004 Republican National Convention cost about $154 million to stage. Here, candidates President Bush and Vice President Cheney, with their wives, greet the audience on an custom-built circular stage that cost $281,000.

(6) $207,000 for balloons that dropped from the ceiling after the president's speech, (7) $6,192 spent at the Stage Door Deli, and even (8) $2,269 for bowling at Chelsea Piers.

The Democratic Convention in Boston nominating John Kerry was a less lavish affair; it only cost about $100 million, which included about $35 million for police and city services.

Federal law puts restrictions on campaign spending, but the nominating conventions remain a major vehicle for corporations to give unlimited cash contributions through city host committees. The New York committee, for example, received $1.15 million from Goldman Sachs, $1.1 million from Merrill Lynch, and $2.45 million worth of computer equipment and services from IBM.

not exactly worth $2,000 a person in literal terms, the idea is to show support of the candidate and to have contact with him or her. No business is actually discussed, but the occasion gives both individuals and lobbyists for special interests an opportunity to show the "flag" and perhaps influence legislation or personnel appointments at a later date after the election—if the candidate wins.

Professional fund-raisers recruit lobbyists to hawk tickets, decide whom to invite, design and mail invitations, employ people to make follow-up calls, rent the room, hire the caterer, make name tags, tell the candidate who came and who didn't, and hound attendees to make good on their pledges.

Some consultants specialize in direct mail and telemarketing. They are assisted by firms that specialize in computer databases and mailing lists. Aristotle Publishers, for example, claims to have records on 128 million registered voters. A candidate can get a tailored list of prospects using any number of demographic variables, including party affiliation, voting record, contribution record, age, geographic location, and opinions on various issues.

Other firms handle mass mailings on behalf of candidates. Kiplinger Computer and Mailing Services, for example, is capable of running envelopes at 10,000 per hour and printing personalized letters at 120 pages per minute.

The latest tool for fund-raising and reaching supporters is the Internet. One use of the Internet is for research. The *Wall Street Journal*, for example, reported that a Kerry support organization in Concord, New Hampshire, was able to track down Democratic women voters, aged 18 to 30, who were interested in abortion rights. Within seconds, the computer was able to generate the names of 812 local women and also give a street map marking their addresses. Members of Planned Parenthood and other Kerry supporters followed up with a door-to-visits on behalf of the presidential candidate.

Although the Internet was first used for fund-raising and building grass-roots support during the 2000 presidential election, its effectiveness wasn't proven until the 2004 election. Former Vermont governor Howard Dean, an early leader in the Democratic primaries, used the Internet to build a grassroots network and raise money. Douglas Quenqua, a reporter of *PRWeek*, does a good job of describing the Dean campaign. He wrote, "Dean established and motivated a huge network of supporters—not to mention raised an unprecedented amount of money in small increments—through interactive, Web-based messaging, blogs, constant e-mail communications, and prodigious use of Meetup.com, the Web site that allows people to find one another based first on common interest, then geography."

Although Dean eventually lost to John Kerry in the primaries, he and his campaign consultants, including some very savvy Web designers, set the standard. The Kerry organization, for example, went on to establish its own Web presence for fund-raising and raised more than $75 million after the primaries.

Experts say that the Internet's major value is in organizing people and getting them in contact with each other in a very cost-efficient way. Ultimately, however, winning elections still requires a great amount of one-on-one contact. Mark Macarato, co-chair in Nashville for Dean, told *PRWeek*, "When you don't have money for mailings and fund-raisers and you're outside the Democratic power structure, the net is just a wonderful tool to get things rolling. The Internet is a very efficient way to connect people, replacing the inefficient tool of a phone call. What is changed is the ability to organize quickly and efficiently." Macarato continued, "But you need old-fashioned shoe-leather campaigning to take it from there."

Dean volunteers, for example, visited various cities to talk with online supporters at meetings, socials, and workshops to help organize door-to-door campaigns on behalf of their candidate.

Other groups of consultants and technicians also are employed by candidates in election campaigns. They are writers of position papers, speechwriters, graphic artists, computer experts, Webmasters, media strategists, advertising experts, radio and television producers, public affairs experts, pollsters, and public relations specialists. A highly visible and critical job is done by advance people who spend many hours organizing events, arranging every detail, and making sure there's a cheering crowd—with signs—when the candidate arrives. On a single day, for example, a presidential candidate may give five to seven talks at rallies in multiple states.

Campaign Finance Reform

The high cost of political campaigning and the heavy reliance of candidates on the large donations by individuals, corporations, labor unions, and other special interest groups led to the passing of the McCain-Feingold Act in 2002 that set limits on contributions.

Essentially, the legislation, which was reaffirmed in 2003 by the U.S. Supreme Court, divided contributions into three areas:

● **Soft Money.** National political parties are prohibited from accepting large, unlimited contributions from corporations, unions, and individuals. State and local party committees can accept up to $10,000 from individuals for get-out-the-vote and voter registration efforts in federal elections, as long as those efforts do not refer to any clearly identified federal candidate and all the money is raised locally.

● **Hard Money.** Individuals can now give a total of $95,000 in each two-year election cycle to all federal candidates, political parties, and political action committees (PACs) combined. That includes maximum contributions of $2,000 per election directly to a candidate and $25,000 to a political party per year.

● **Issue Advertising.** Advertising in support of a specific candidate must be paid for only with regulated hard money. Ads that fall into this category cannot be broadcast within 30 days of a primary or 60 days of a general election.

John McCain, U.S. Senator from Arizona, uses Congressional hearings to generate publicity and public support for many of his pet projects, including campaign finance reform.

527s Become a Major Issue

Although McCain-Feingold drastically reduced the amount of "soft" money given to candidates and political parties, it had some unintended effects. One effect was the migration of soft money to other "independent" partisan organizations.

These organizations are called 527s, which refers to Section 527 of the Internal Revenue Code, which allows them to retain nonprofit status while running partisan ads as long as they are not directly coordinated with the national political parties or candidates they support.

The Democratic Party was the first to benefit from a 527 group. One early group, formed during the Clinton administration, was MoveOn.org, a liberal online group,

First Arsenic Now Mercury

GEORGE BUSH'S EPA AND THE POLITICS OF POLLUTION

America learned this week that tuna, and many other fish, can contain harmful levels of toxic mercury. Forty-five states already post warnings of mercury contamination in their lakes and streams. So why is President Bush trying to weaken controls on mercury pollution?

It's déjà vu all over again. Early in his presidency, George Bush tried to allow more arsenic in drinking water. Now, he wants the EPA to let coal-fired power plants treat their mercury pollution as "non-hazardous" even though mercury threatens pregnant women and children. The Bush administration's

ploy would allow coal-fired power plants to put more mercury into the air, where it rains down on lakes and oceans, is swallowed by fish, and could wind up on your plate. Exposure to mercury can cause learning disabilities and neurological damage in kids and the developing fetus.

Guess who is praising this scheme? Coal power companies, who are big mercury polluters and big political contributors, too.

The Mercury Money Trail

The big mercury polluters and their trade associations are aggressive political players in Washington. Their

executives and PACs are also generous political donors. It's no surprise that the Bush administration is following the industry's script for weakening mercury regulations.

Last time around, President Bush had to back down on arsenic in the face of a massive outcry from people across the political spectrum.

Let's make history repeat itself.

Tell President Bush to get serious about reducing mercury pollution. Our kids deserve no less. Let the Bush administration and the EPA hear your voice about its proposed mercury rule. Go to www.nrdc.org

NRDC
THE EARTH'S BEST DEFENSE

MoveOn.ORG
Democracy in Action.

YES, I want to join the Natural Resources Defense Council and help thwart President Bush's plan to weaken controls on toxic mercury. Here is my tax-deductible gift of $_____.

NAME
ADDRESS
CITY   STATE   ZIP

Advocacy groups, known as 527s under the Campaign Reform Act, were active in the 2004 presidential campaign. Although not affiliated with either major political party, their support was evident. Here, the National Resource Defense Council and the MoveOn.org take President Bush to task for trying to weaken controls on mercury pollution.

that originally raised money and support for President Clinton's defense when he was impeached by the U.S. House of Representatives and then acquitted by the U.S. Senate.

Another group, America Coming Together (ACT) was a liberal, pro-Democratic group organized in 2004 to do advocacy advertising and voter mobilization work. Although not directly affiliated with the Democratic Party, members of this group knocked on 21 million doors, placed 39 million phone calls, mailed 72 million pieces of literature, and placed a number of ads attacking George W. Bush's policies. In one quarter, ACT raised $24 million for its activities.

Media Fund, another pro-Democratic group, raised and spent more than $45 million by September on attack ads. One ad, for example, carried this copy: "During the past three years, it's true that George W. Bush has created more jobs. Unfortunately, they were created in places like China." Another 527 group, Real Voices, ran ads that showed families of servicemen killed in Iraq and raised questions about Bush's handling of the war.

It didn't take the Republican Party long to figure out that third-party partisan groups were also an opportunity to launch attack ads against John Kerry without having to take responsibility for the content. The first major 527 was Swift Boat Veterans for Truth, later named the Swift Vets and POWs for Truth. In short order, the group raised $15 million for ads on television and in newspapers. One television ad, for example, showed a series of veterans questioning Kerry's service medals in Vietnam and his participation in the Paris peace talks. The last veteran flatly states, "John Kerry cannot be trusted."

Other partisan Republican groups were the Club for Growth and the Progress for America Voter Fund. As the election wound down to the final weeks, the latter group spent about $30 million on attack ads. One ad flashed photos of Osama bin Laden and other terrorists and asked, "Would you trust Kerry up against these fanatic killers? President Bush didn't start this war . . . but he will finish it."

Another side effect of such advertising was the media news coverage they generated. The allegations of the Swift Boat Veterans, for example, became a major campaign issue, and the media devoted countless news stories to the group and its charges. Advocacy groups know that shrill ads grab media attention and stories. A group only has to place attack ads on a few small stations and cable outlets at a minimum cost, and the resulting news media stories will carry the message to a national audience.

It has been estimated that third-party partisan groups spent about $400 million in the 2004 presidential campaign trying to influence voters. Such expenditures raised new concerns about the influx of major amounts of unregulated money into the political process. There was also the major question as to how "independent" these 527 organizations were from the major political parties. The Swift Boat Veterans group, according to a report in the *New York Times*, showed ". . . a web of connections to the Bush family, high-profile Texas political figures, and President Bush's chief political aide."

"This has become the primary issue in this year's (2004) election," says Fred Wertheimer, president of Democracy 21, a group advocating restrictions on 527s. In fact, the Federal Election Commission (FEC) is considering reforms for the 2006 election cycle. One suggestion before the FEC is to restrict partisan groups that are formed exclusively for advocating the election of one candidate, but to allow most major nonprofits to escape restrictions if political work is only part of their activities. In other words, such organizations as the World Wildlife Fund (WWF) would be exempt even if the group criticized the president for his environmental policies.

The issue of advocacy, however, concerns issues of free speech and First Amendment rights, so a spirited debate no doubt will be the order of the day. The McCain-Feingold Act went all the way to the Supreme Court because various groups believed restrictions on contributions abridged their freedom of speech.

Public Affairs in Government

Since the time of the ancient Egyptians 5,000 years ago, governments have always engaged in what is known in the 21st century as public information, public relations, and public affairs.

The Rosetta Stone, discovered by Napoleon's troops and used by scholars as the key to understanding Egyptian hieroglyphics, turned out to be a publicity release for the reign of Ptolemy V. Julius Caesar was known in his day as a master of staged events in which his army's entrances into Rome after successful battles were highly orchestrated.

There has always been a need for government communications, if for no other reason than to inform citizens of the services available and the manner in which they may be used. In a democracy, public information is crucial if citizens are to make intelligent judgments about the policies and activities of their elected representatives. Through information it is hoped that citizens will have the necessary background to participate fully in the formation of government policies.

The objectives of government information efforts have been summarized by William Ragan, former director of public affairs for the United States Civil Service Commission:

1. Inform the public about the public's business. In other words, communicate the work of government agencies.

2. Improve the effectiveness of agency operations through appropriate public information techniques. In other words, explain agency programs so that citizens understand and can take actions necessary to benefit from them.

3. Provide feedback to government administrators so that programs and policies can be modified, amended, or continued.

4. Advise management on how best to communicate a decision or a program to the widest number of citizens.

5. Serve as an ombudsman. Represent the public and listen to its representatives. Make sure that individual problems of the taxpayer are satisfactorily solved.

6. Educate administrators and bureaucrats about the role of the mass media and how to work with media representatives.

"Public Information" versus "Public Relations"

Although many of the objectives described by Ragan would be considered appropriate goals in almost any field of public relations, in government such activities are never referred to as "public relations." Instead, various euphemisms are used. The most common titles are (1) public information officer, (2) director of public affairs, (3) press secretary, (4) administrative aide, and (5) government program analyst.

In addition, government agencies do not have departments of public relations. Instead, the FBI has an External Affairs Division; the Interstate Commerce Commission has an Office of Communications and Consumer Affairs; and the Environmental Protection Agency has an Office of Public Awareness. The military services usually have Offices of Public Affairs.

Such euphemisms serve to reconcile two essentially contradictory facts: (1) The government needs to inform its citizens and (2) it is against the law to use appropriated money for the employment of "publicity experts."

As early as 1913, Congress saw a potential danger in executive branch agencies' spending taxpayer dollars to sway the American public to support programs of various administrations. Consequently, the Gillett Amendment (Section 3107 of Title V of the United States Code) was passed: It stated, "Appropriated funds may not be used to pay a publicity expert unless specifically appropriated for that purpose." The law was reinforced in 1919 with prohibition of the use of any appropriations for services, messages, or publications designed to influence a member of Congress. Another law that year required executive agencies to utilize the U.S. Government Printing Office so that publications could be more closely monitored than in the past. Restrictions also prohibit executive departments from mailing any material to the public without a specific request.

Congress was clearly attempting to limit the authority of the executive branch to spend taxpayer money on public relations efforts to gain support for pet projects of the president. Some presidents chafed at this, but others thought it was entirely proper that the government should not be in the business of propagandizing the taxpayers. President Eisenhower, for example, ordered all executive branch agencies to dispense with field office information activity. The only problem was the great number of public and press requests for information. Consequently, information offices lost their titles but continued their dissemination functions under such titles as "technical liaison officers" for the Corps of Engineers and "assistant to the director" in the Bureau of Reclamation.

In 1972, alarmed by Richard Nixon's expansion of the White House communications staff, Congress reaffirmed prior legislation by stating that no part of any appropriation bill could be used for publicity or propaganda purposes designed to support or defeat legislation before Congress.

Although most citizens would agree that government should not use tax money to persuade the public of the merits or demerits of a particular bill or program, there is a thin line between merely providing information and using information as a lobbying tool.

If a public affairs officer for the Pentagon testifies about the number of surface-to-air missiles deployed by North Korea, does this constitute information or an attempt to influence congressional appropriations? Or, to use another example, is a speech by the Surgeon General about the dangers of passive smoking only information or support of legislation that would ban cigarette smoking from all federal buildings?

While ascertaining the difference between "public relations" and "public information" may be an interesting semantic game, the fact remains that the terms *public relations* and *publicity* are seldom used by a government agency.

Scope of Federal Government Information

The U.S. government is said to be the world's premier collector of information. It also is maintained, without much disagreement, that the government is one of the world's greatest disseminators of information.

Ascertaining the exact size of the government's "public relations" effort, however, is like trying to guess the number of jelly beans in a large jar. One of the major difficulties is forming a standard definition of what constitutes "public affairs" activity.

The General Accounting Office (GAO) once estimated that probably $2.3 billion was spent each year by federal agencies and the White House on "public relations" activity. Others, often critics of government public relations, have estimated that between 10,000 and 12,000 federal employees are involved in what might be called "public relations" work. It is said, for example, that the Department of Defense has about 1,000 people working in public affairs/information jobs.

Such figures, however, give a false impression of government agencies in general. At the Commerce Department, for example, there are 25 public affairs people out of 36,000 employees. The Immigration and Naturalization Service has eight public affairs officers in a staff of 24,000. The Customs Department has 15 public affairs officers in a staff of 18,000. *O'Dwyer's PR Services Report* says, "That translates to 1/10 of one percent of its workforce. . . ."

Advertising is another governmental activity. Federal agencies spend several hundred million dollars a year on public service advertising, primarily to promote military recruitment, government health services, and the U.S. Postal Service. The following sections discuss the public affairs efforts of federal agencies, Congress, and the White House.

ON THE JOB
global

Danish Post Office Races to a New Image

After 350 years as the Royal Danish Mail, the national postal service had been privatized and had become Post Denmark. The public, however, still perceived it as out of touch and bureaucratic.

Post Denmark wanted to position itself in the public mind as a modern, dynamic organization with a new logo, so it sponsored a Round Denmark bicycle race under the auspices of the Danish Cycle Union.

The race covered 860 kilometers through 30 cities. Sixteen teams from 14 countries competed, and the race was watched on the roadside by more than 1.2 million spectators. Besides press briefings and regular news releases, TV spots extolled the post office during the five-day event.

About 77 percent of the population saw or read about the race, and all of the Post's 1,254 offices conducted special promotions. Awareness of Post Denmark as a new, dynamic entity increased dramatically, and the logo became widely recognized.

Government Agencies. Public affairs officers (PAOs) and public information specialists engage in tasks common to the public relations department of corporation. They typically answer press and public inquiries, write news releases, work on newsletters, prepare speeches for top officials, oversee the production of brochures, and plan special events. Senior-level public affairs specialists also try to counsel top management about communications strategies and how the agency should respond to a crisis situation.

One of the largest public affairs operations in the federal government is operated by the U.S. Department of Defense, which is the cabinet-level agency that oversees the armed forces. Its operations vary from the mundane to the exotic. One of the longest-running public relations efforts has been the preparation and distribution of "hometown" releases by the military. The Fleet Home Town News Center, established during World War II, sends approximately a million news releases annually about the promotions and transfers of U.S. Navy, Marine Corps, and Coast Guard personnel to their hometown media.

A more exotic assignment for a military public affairs officer is to give background briefings and escort journalists who want to cover military operations on a battlefield. A large number of PAOs were assigned as escorts when the military initiated the policy of "embedding" journalists within military units during the invasion of Iraq.

Another recent assignment for PAOs was former President Ronald Reagan's state funeral. They were responsible for setting up the media centers, accrediting the journalists, and coordinating the logistics of the various ceremonies in California and Washington, D.C.

The Pentagon (a common name for the Defense Department) also engages in recruitment drives. One recent campaign was directed to the parents of young men and women after research showed that only 11 percent of adults surveyed would recommend the military to their children The ad campaign, with a $1.7 million budget, featured soldiers telling about the job skills and qualities of character that they gained by joining the military.

Another major operation of the Pentagon is assisting Hollywood with the production of movies. More than 20 public information specialists are assigned as liaisons with the film and television industry. They review scripts and proposals, advise producers on military procedures, and decide how much assistance, if any, a film or TV show portraying the military should receive.

The film *Black Hawk Down*, for example, received military assistance by providing boot-camp training to the actors, technical advisors, eight choppers, and more than 100 soldiers—a package worth about $2 million. The movie *Pearl Harbor* also got considerable help, including the use of an aircraft carrier. Not all films portraying the military, however, get assistance. The Pentagon turned down a request from the producers of *Broken Arrow* because it featured John Travolta as a deluded Air Force pilot who steals two nuclear missiles with ease.

In recent years, the Pentagon and its PAOs have been on the firing line, so to speak, because of American military operations in Afghanistan and Iraq. See the PR Casebook on page 499 to read about some controversial issues and how the military responded.

Other federal agencies also conduct campaigns to inform citizens. In many cases, a public relations firm is selected through a bidding process to execute the campaign. Some recent examples of campaigns are as follows:

● The U.S. Census Bureau retained Burson-Marsteller to inform American citizens abroad about the importance of being included in the census.

● The American Battle Monuments Commission, an agency of the executive branch, retained Burson-Marsteller to coordinate the opening and press coverage of the new World War II memorial on the Washington Mall.

● The Centers for Disease Control and Prevention (CDC) launched a campaign, with the assistance of Ogilvy PR Worldwide, to inform Americans about who was most vulnerable to getting influenza and who should get the flu vaccine.

● The Department of Commerce retained Edelman Worldwide to launch a campaign to lure more foreign visitors to the United States.

● The National Endowment for the Arts (NEA) retained Edelman's Washington office to coordinate promotion and public relations for a national tour bringing Shakespeare productions to local communities.

PR CASEBOOK

Pentagon Gets Flak in the War on Terrorism

Pentagon public affairs officers (PAOs) have a difficult tightrope to walk. On one hand, they are committed to providing access and information. On the other hand, the security and safety of troops in a combat area comes before disclosure of information. It's a tough balancing act that isn't always successful.

The return of U.S. soldiers' bodies to bases in America from Iraq, for example, erupted into a full-scale controversy after the Pentagon barred journalists from covering the unloading of flag-draped coffins from cargo planes. Critics said this was a blatant attempt by the Pentagon and the Bush Administration to insulate the public from the realties of war and play down the rising insurgency. As Ken Auletta in the *New Yorker* commented, "Americans get impatient and images of returning coffins would weaken the administration's case." The Pentagon, in turn, responded that showing such images would only help the terrorists erode America's commitment to liberate Iraq.

Some months later, the Pentagon was again embroiled in a controversy over the release of photos graphically showing the abuse of Iraqi prisoners by U.S. soldiers at Abu Ghraib prison outside Baghdad. The photos shocked the world, and there was evidence that even more photos were available that showed Iraqi prisoners being threatened with dogs, Iraqi women being forced to bare their breasts, and Iraqi men being forced to perform various sexual acts such as masturbation and oral sex.

The Pentagon and the Administration again stonewalled the release of such photos, saying their release would violate privacy concerns and undermine later prosecutions. There was also the argument that release of more photos would only inflame passions in Iraq and around the Arab world and put U.S. soldiers at risk.

Public relations experts in crisis management, however, generally agreed that it would have been better to release all the photos at once for one big media story instead of having them dribble out over a period of months, which would result in multiple stories. The basic recommendation from the experts: Get the information out as soon as possible, and also immediately tell the public what corrective action is being taken.

Even Pentagon PAOs agree. Major Martha Brooks Scott trains future PAOs and told *PRWeek*, "We learn the best thing to do as a PAO is to advise your primary to get the word out early, good or bad. When you leave time for people to speculate, they go in either direction, so if you are going to come out with bad news, do it early."

However, PAOs work for commanding officers, and it isn't always that simple. Lt. John Oliveira, a PAO for 16 years, resigned from the Navy because he didn't believe in "spinning" a war he didn't agree with. He told *PRWeek*, "Anybody in the PR field, no matter where you work, you have to have some kind of faith, have to believe in what you're doing to have credibility as a PR professional."

The Pentagon also got into another damage-control mode some months after the prison-abuse controversy. In this instance, it was a choreographed letter-writing campaign by an Army commander in Iraq who asked each of his soldiers to sign and send home a letter to the local newspaper extolling U.S. accomplishments in rebuilding Iraq. The Gannett News Service exposed the letter campaign after identical letters showed up in at least 12 different newspapers across the United States.

Army officials, when first confronted with this questionable letter-writing campaign,

(continued)

PR CASEBOOK *(continued)*

defended it. According to *PRWeek*, an Army officer said, "We do not see anything was done wrong in this situation. Soldiers and commanders have the right to speak their minds as far as putting forth good Army stories because they are tired of the negative reports in the press."

The Pentagon, after receiving widespread criticism, amended its attitude several days later. It announced that commanders in Iraq had been warned to stop providing form letters for their soldiers to sign and mail back to their hometown newspapers.

● The Federal Trade Commission (FTC) launched a campaign to inform Americans about Internet privacy and security. An animated turtle mascot, Dewie, was part of the campaign.

● The Department of Housing and Urban Development (HUD) conducted a campaign encouraging home ownership among minorities.

● The National Highway Traffic Safety Administration (NHTSA) conducted a campaign during National Child Safety Week to inform parents about the importance of child safety seats.

Government entities, such as the United States Postal Service, gain visibility through a variety of public relations activities. Lance Armstrong, six-time winner of the Tour de France, is sponsored by the postal service. Sporting events, in particular, are densely populated by sponsor logos that appear on billboards, programs, and even the clothing of the contestants.

- The White House Office of National Drug Control Policy invested $100 million in campaign to convince 14- to 16-year-olds not to smoke marijuana.

- The U.S. Bureau of Engraving and Printing retained Burson-Marsteller to promote and publicize the new $20 and $50 dollar bills on a global basis.

ON THE JOB ethics

Payments to Commentator Raise Ethical Concerns

A common public relations tactic is to place spokespersons on radio and television talk shows to mention an organization's products or services. In such cases, however, ethical practice in public relations (and journalism) is for public disclosure of the organization sponsoring the spokesperson.

The U.S. Office of Education and its public relations firm, Ketchum, got into hot water when it was revealed that the conservative commentator, Armstrong Williams, actively promoted President Bush's No Child Left Behind Act without letting the public know that he was paid $240,000 by Ketchum on behalf of the government.

Williams who has a syndicated television show and newspaper column, originally claimed that the payment was for advertising, but the *New York Times* reported that the contract also stipulated that "Mr. Williams is to regularly comment on the N.C.L.B. during the course of his broadcasts" and "Secretary Paige and other department officials shall have the option of appearing from time to time as studio guests." In addition, "Mr.

Williams shall utilize his long-term working relationships with America's Black Forum—An African-American news program—to encourage the producers to periodically address the No Child Left Behind Act."

The revelation, first reported by *USA Today*, caused a storm of criticism from legislators in both political parties as well as public relations professionals. Democratic congressman George Miller called the payments "a very dangerous practice that deceives the public" by concealing the role of taxpayer dollars in promoting partisan policies. "Are they funding propaganda?" he asked.

Judith T. Phair, president of the Public Relations Society of America (PRSA) also was critical. She said, on the organization's Web site, "Any paid endorsement that is not fully disclosed as such and is presented as objective news coverage is a violation of the group's code of ethics, which requires that public relations professionals engage in open, honest communications and fully disclose sponsors or financial interests involved in any paid communications activities."

Paul Holmes, publisher of a public relations industry publication, the *Holmes Report*, told the *New York Times*, "There are absolutely no circumstances under which this can be an acceptable practice. It's a colossal error in judgment. It's wrong on so many levels, I don't know where to begin. This undermines the very value public relations purports to bring to the communication sphere, credibility."

Cathy Cripps, president of the Council of Public Relations Firms, agreed that "public relations needs to express total accuracy and truthfulness," but added, "it was the spokesperson's responsibility to disclose the affiliation" rather than Ketchum's. Representatives of Ketchum made no comment and referred reporters to the U.S. Department of Education.

New York Times columnist Stuart Elliott noted, however, that the Web site of Ketchum's parent company, Omnicom Group (www.omnicomgroup.com) includes a corporate code of ethics that "could be read to proscribe the payments Ketchum made to Mr. Williams."

(continued)

ON THE JOB **ethics,** *continued*

The section on unethical or illegal practices, he wrote, gives examples such as "improper inducements that are not consistent with customary business practice" along with taking unfair advantage "of anyone through manipulation, concealment, misrepresentation of material facts or any other unfair practice."

As a result of the furor over the admission that Mr. Armstrong failed to tell his readers and listeners that he was a paid spokesperson for the No Child Left Behind Act, the Federal Communications Commission (FCC) launched an investigation to determine if FCC rules about "payola" and sponsorship provisions were violated. Meanwhile, several weeks after the controversy broke, Ketchum issued a state-

ment regretting its "lapse of judgment" in handling the account.

The Armstrong affair was not the first time that Ketchum, a major public relations firm, has been under fire for its work on behalf of government agencies. Earlier, in 2004, Ketchum produced a video news release (VNR) for the Department of Health and Human Services to inform the public about the benefits of the new Medicare Bill signed by President Bush.

Critics complained that the VNR violated federal law that prohibits the use of federal money for "publicity or propaganda purposes" not authorized by Congress. One scene, for example, includes President Bush receiving a standing ovation as he signed the Medicare Bill. The major complaint was that the

source of the VNR was not properly identified as a government agency. The department and Ketchum, however, claimed that the VNR was properly identified and, if television stations chose to leave out the attribution, that was their problem.

However, the General Accounting Office (GAO) ruled that the Bush Administration did violate federal law by producing and disseminating the VNR that portrayed the new Medicare law as a boon to the elderly. In its ruling, the GAO dismissed the argument that the TV stations knew the source of the VNR. The intended audience, it said, was not news directors but viewers and the "video release did not alert viewers that the Centers for Medicare and Medicad Services was the source."

The information campaigns just described are fairly common and routine in most federal agencies. At times, however, public affairs staffs can find themselves on the frontline of a crisis or a controversy that involves handling hundreds of press calls in a single day. See the Insights box on page 482.

Public affairs staff in the U.S. Department of Justice, for example, had to deal with numerous inquiries and critics regarding the USA PATRIOT Act. Civil liberties advocates have publicly attacked the measure, and organizations such as the American Civil Liberties Union (ACLU) have launched campaigns to have the Act rescinded. Consequently, Attorney General John Ashcroft and department spokespeople have spent considerable time and energy defending the Act and, as one public affairs staffer said, "setting the record straight."

The U.S. Transportation Security Administration (TSA) is a relatively new agency that is responsible for all security at airports and on planes. It was formed after the 9/11 attack, and it didn't have much time to organize a public affairs staff before it had to start its work. As a consequence, the agency's mission of informing and educating the public got off to a somewhat rocky start. The public affairs staff was given an unused conference room in the Department of Transportation to start its work, with only one or two staffers attempting to handle hundreds of public and media calls.

The Department of Homeland Security, which was formed from the merging of 22 different agencies, also had growing pains. One problem was cohesion; it took time to get public affairs staffs from so many agencies to operate as a unit. There were also problems in message formulation. Dennis Murphy, director of public affairs for border and transportation security, told *PRWeek*, "We want to get the word out quickly . . . but operations folks want to make sure we're not saying too much." An ongoing public information problem is the color system for security alerts; most Americans still don't understand it.

Two U.S. Department of State activities, public diplomacy and the Voice of America (VOA), are discussed in the next chapter. These tools are used to build relationships with other nations and their citizens.

Congressional Efforts.   The House of Representatives and the Senate are great disseminators of information. Members regularly produce a barrage of news releases, newsletters, recordings, brochures, taped radio interviews, and videotapes—all designed to inform voters back home about Congress.

Critics complain that most materials are self-promotional and have little value. The franking privilege (free postage) is singled out for the most criticism. The late Senator John Heinz, a Republican from Pennsylvania, once distributed 15 million pieces of mail, financed by taxpayers, during one election year. Obviously, the franking privilege is a real advantage for an incumbent.

All members of Congress also employ a press secretary. According to Edward Downes of Boston University, "Capitol Hill's press secretaries play a significant role in the shaping of America's messages and consequent public policies. In their role as proxy for individual members, the press secretaries act as gatekeepers, determining what information to share with, and hold from, the media; thus, they have command over news shared with the citizenry."

White House Efforts.   At the apex of government public relations efforts is the White House. The president receives more media attention than all the federal agencies and Congress combined. It is duly reported when the president visits a neighborhood school, tours a housing development, meets a head of state, or even chokes on a pretzel while watching a football game.

All presidents have taken advantage of the intense media interest to implement public relations strategies that would improve their popularity, generate support for programs, and explain embarrassing policy decisions. And each president has had his own communication style.

Ronald Reagan, by most accounts, was considered the master communicator. He was extremely effective on television and could read a teleprompter with perfect inflection. He understood the importance of using symbolism and giving simple, down-to-earth speeches that often ended with "God bless you." Reagan's approach was the use of the carefully packaged sound bite and staged event. Terrance Hunt, an Associated Press reporter who covered the Reagan years, says the former president's funeral in 2004 recalled the high style and stagecraft of his presidency. "Presidential appearances were arranged like movie scenes with Reagan in the starring role. There was a heavy emphasis on staging and lighting," says Hunt.

George H. W. Bush (senior) was no Ronald Reagan as a public speaker, but he did project enthusiasm for his job and had a friendly, but formal, working relationship with the White House press corps. Bill Clinton, on the other hand, was more populist in his communication style. He was at home with today's information technology, experts say, and made effective use of television talk shows. Clinton was most effective when he talked one-on-one with an interviewer or a member of the audience.

George W. Bush's style is more like Ronald Reagan's "down-home" style. He is plainspoken, uses short declarative sentences, is self-effacing in speeches to groups across the nation, and does a very good job of staying "on message." He comes across as sincerely committed to his beliefs. During the 2004 presidential campaign, polls indicated that many voters thought Bush came across as a more likable person than John Kerry. See the earlier section on the 2004 presidential campaign.

President Bush also has adopted Reagan's approach to stagecraft and symbolism. A team of television and video experts makes sure every Bush appearance is well choreographed for maximum visual effect. The attention to detail ranges from having audience members behind Bush being asked to take off their ties so they look more like ordinary taxpayers who would benefit from his tax cut to arranging the television angle at Mount Rushmore so Bush's head would be aligned with the four former presidents carved in granite on the mountain. For the anniversary of the 9/11 terrorist attack, the White House rented three barges of giant Musco lights to illuminate the Statue of Liberty in the background while President Bush gave his speech. According to the *New York Times*, "It was the ultimate patriotic backdrop for Mr. Bush who spoke from Ellis Island."

The staged event that got the most press, and criticism, was Bush's appearance on the aircraft carrier Abraham Lincoln where he announced the end of major combat in Iraq. The White House staff planned his arrival in a flight suit and his early evening speech so that the setting sun cast a golden glow on his face. In addition, ship crew members were arranged in coordinated shirt colors over Bush's right shoulder while the banner "Mission Accomplished" was positioned to capture the President in a single shot. Michael Deaver, the master communications strategist for Ronald Reagan, was impressed. He told the *New York Times*, "They understand they have to build a set, whether it's an aircraft carrier or the Rose Garden or the South Lawn. They understand what's around the head is just as important as the head."

The photo op is a major public relations tool for the White House. Here, President Bush poses with sailors and pilots aboard the USS Abraham Lincoln off the California coast after landing in a small jet. He used the occasion, somewhat prematurely, to declare that major combat in Iraq was finished.

The Bush administration's concept of stagecraft also manifested itself in tight control over information and limited media access, except when it could be totally controlled. Bush, for example, gave substantially fewer press conferences, interviews, and other media events than either Bill Clinton or George H. W. Bush in their first two years. According to Ken Auletta, a respected chronicler of the communications industry, Bush was wary of the press and thought journalists as a whole were too liberal to do a decent job of objectively covering the White House. Auletta's article in the *New Yorker* was titled, "Fortress Bush: How the White House Keeps the Press Under Control" (January 19, 2004).

Another aspect of Bush's communications style was his insistence that everyone in the Administration stay on message. Michael Deaver, previously mentioned, told Auletta, "This is the most disciplined White House in history." Thanks to e-mail, everyone in the Administration speaks with one voice, partly because everyone gets the daily "talking point" every morning when they come to work. Although "staying on message" is generally considered a good strategy in public relations, critics say Bush "stayed on message" even if the evidence or facts didn't substantiate the message. Critics say, for example, that Bush insisted Saddam Hussein was a threat to the United States even though no weapons of mass destruction were found. Bush also said Saddam Hussein harbored terrorists, but no evidence was found to substantiate that either. In the 2004 presidential election, facts didn't seem to matter as much as voter's perceptions of each candidate's trustworthiness and likeability.

All presidents, of course, have assistance in their constant quest to be popular, sell their policies, and be perceived as effective leaders. On every White House staff are experts in communications strategy, media relations, speech writing, and staging the perfect event. In addition, advance people plan every presidential appearance and trip in meticulous detail. They confirm that the person who heads the receiving line is politically correct and that the sound system works. They make arrangements for the press, organize the cheering crowds, select the people in the front rows, select the best symbolic photo opportunity, decide where the television cameras will be positioned, and plan the president's entrance and exit to the last second. The Secret Service, responsible for protecting the president, also does a detailed analysis of the site and the guests. Nothing is left to chance.

The top public relations person in the White House is the Director of Communications. In the first two years of the Bush administration, that individual was Karen Hughes, who also became a special counselor to the president. Her job was to advise the president on communications strategy, and she is generally acknowledged as the architect of the "compassionate" side of Bush's basic conservatism. It was her decision, for example, to have President Bush visit a local mosque to show support for Muslims just days after the 9/11 terrorist attack. The event was a symbolic attempt to assure Muslims in America and around the world that the "war on terrorism" was not a war on Islam.

Hughes also helped Bush set the tone for his speeches. For example, she was instrumental in formulating Bush's speech to the joint session of Congress about America's planned reaction to terrorist attack. Some aides pressed for a bellicose declaration of war on terrorists, but Hughes intervened and shaped the "reassurance theme" that he ultimately used to great effect. In fact, many analysts said it was one of President Bush's best speeches.

Hughes left her powerful position in 2003 because her husband and children wanted to move back to Texas, but she remained close to the President as a frequent advisor and loyalist. Tucker Eskew, former head of the White House Office of Global

Communications, told *PRWeek* that Hughes served a unique set of purposes in the Bush message machine: "She's a message crafter, master of ceremonies, and mother-confessor all rolled into one," he said.

The most visible person, on a daily basis, is the president's press secretary, who has the high-pressure duty of briefing reporters on a daily basis. The chief spokesperson for President Bush's first two years of office was Ari Fleischer, who also worked on the Bush presidential campaign in 2000.

Fleischer says the role of press secretary ". . . is to faithfully articulate what the president thinks and why he thinks it. That's what a press secretary ultimately does for a living. A substantial part of it is trying to help the press, but never forgetting that you represent and work for the president." Indeed, he had a reputation among journalists for his fierce loyalty to the President that sometimes got in the way of effective media relations.

Fleischer resigned in 2003 to write and lecture, and Scott McClellan, a Texan, became press secretary. When Fleischer resigned, he quipped to the press, "I want to do something more relaxing—like dismantle live nuclear weapons." He also told the *New York Times*, in a final interview, "One of the hardest parts of this job is walking the tightrope that exists between the White House and the press corps. Because I'm also the advocate for the press, even though the press will be loath to admit it. My job is to push to get clarity. But particularly, during a time of war, I knew there were some questions that the press had that the White House would not answer."

Despite the pressure-cooker environment of being grilled by a roomful of aggressive, competitive reporters every day—often on live television—the job of press secretary to the president has its rewards. Former press secretary Marlin Fitzwater, who served George Bush senior and Ronald Reagan, says, "It's the greatest job in the world and worth taking no matter how much trouble your President is in. Now, you may die in the job, it may ruin your life and reputation. But it still will have been the greatest experience in your life." Most former press secretaries also give the advice, "keep a sense of humor."

State Information Services

Every state provides public information services. In California, the most populous state, there are about 175 public information officers (PIOs) in about 70 state agencies. On a daily basis, PIOs provide routine information to the public and the press on the policies, programs, and activities of the various state agencies.

State agencies also conduct a variety of public information and education campaigns, often with the assistance of public relations firms that have been selected through a bidding process. A state agency, for example, will issue a request for proposal (RFP) and award a contract on the basis of presentations from competing firms.

One program area is health and safety. Most states, in recent years, have spent considerable money convincing people not to smoke. The funds, from the national tobacco settlement and state-imposed cigarette taxes, have provided somewhat of a windfall in available funds. California, for example, generates about $120 million annually from tobacco taxes, and about 10 percent of that is devoted to antismoking advertising and public relations. It's somewhat ironic, however, that as smoking decreases, the amount of taxes collected also decreases, and there is less money for such campaigns.

The California Department of Health Services (DHS) also runs various campaigns on a variety of health issues, such as encouraging immunization shots for children, screening for breast cancer, and preventing teen pregnancy. The California Highway Patrol (CHP) also conducts safety campaigns. One recent campaign was an effort to increase seat-belt use and decrease drunk driving accidents among African Americans. Statistical data indicated that this audience was less likely to use seat belts and more likely to die in an alcohol-rated crash. According to the CHP, leaders in the African-American community supported the campaign and didn't find it to be discriminatory.

Governmental agencies promote health and safety in a number of public information campaigns. This poster by California Department of Health Services advocates breast exams for women over 40.

ON THE JOB

ethics

Fake News or Information?

Video news releases are a standard public relations tactic, but the use of them by the Bush Administration has stirred major controversy and criticism. The *New York Times* has called VNRs distributed by government agencies "fake news," and is concerned that the public is not being told that a particular video clip or narration originated from a government agency.

Public relations executives, including government agency officials, contend that all government-produced VNRs are clearly identified as to the source. "Talk to the television stations that ran it without attribution," says William A. Pierce, spokesman for the Department of Health and Human Services. He is further quoted in the *New York Times,* "This is not our problem. We can't be held responsible for their actions." Rick Rice, a California governmental agency official, points out that VNRs are just like printed news releases and, ultimately, a journalist decides what to use—and even attribute.

What do you think? First, is it a legitimate information function of governmental agencies to produce VNRs? Second, if government-produced VNRs are aired, who has the ultimate responsibility to ensure that the public knows the source of the news item?

In Virginia, the Department of Health launched a campaign to reduce the number of instances of statutory rape and other forms of sexual coercion. The campaign had the slogan "Isn't She a Little Young" with the tagline "Sex with a minor. Don't go There." The health department used billboards and sent 255,000 postcards, posters, coasters, and napkins to bars and restaurants in the state.

Other state campaigns have targeted litter. The Texas Department of Transportation conducted an antilitter campaign with the slogan "Don't Mess With Texas." Research showed that most of the litter on the highways was from people under the age of 24. Therefore, the campaign was pitched to this audience through videos and high school assembly programs. In California, the slogan was "Don't Trash California." Ogilvy PR Worldwide received a $6.5 million contract to conduct a multicultural, statewide effort in English, Spanish, and Asian languages. Radio spots and billboards were used to reach the driving public.

States also promote tourism through advertising and public relations campaigns. Tourism and conventions are the second largest industry in Wisconsin, so the Department of Tourism concentrates on branding Wisconsin as a destination for cheese lovers (350 types of cheese are produced here) and beer drinkers ("Beer Capital of the U.S."). The Illinois Department of Commerce and Economic Opportunity also is interested in tourism and recently awarded a $6.5 million contract to Edelman Worldwide to develop it. Pennsylvania spends between $8 million and $12 million annually promoting tourism.

Another area is economic development. Delaware, a small state with less than 800,000 people, hired a public relations firm to conduct a $600,000 campaign to attract business investment. The public relations firm used the slogan "It's good being first," referring to Delaware being the first state to adopt the U.S. Constitution. The public relations firm admitted it was a difficult assignment. The firm's president told *PRWeek*, "As opposed to having a bad image, Delaware simply has no image at all."

Meanwhile, down in Florida, the Department of Citrus tapped Golin/Harris International to reemphasize the role of orange juice in breakfasts. The citrus industry is a $9 billion business in Florida and employs 90,000 workers. Consequently, the state wants to position orange juice as an essential part of breakfast for the American family. The slogan: "The best start under the sun."

City Information Services

Cities employ information specialists to disseminate news and information from numerous municipal departments. Such agencies may include the airport, transit district, redevelopment office, parks and recreation, convention and visitors bureau, police and fire, city council, and the mayor's office.

The information flow occurs in many ways, but all have the objective of informing citizens and helping them take full advantage of opportunities. The city council holds neighborhood meetings; an airport commission sets up an exhibit showing the growth needs of the airport; the recreation department promotes summer swimming lessons; and the city's human rights commission sponsors a festival promoting multiculturalism.

Cities also promote themselves to attract new business. *PRWeek* reports "The competition for cities and wider regions to attract businesses is as intense as ever, experts say, with an estimated 12,000 economic development organizations vying for the roughly 500 annual corporate moves/expansions that involve 250 or more jobs each."

Bob Marcusse, President of the Kansas City Area Development Council, told *PRWeek*, "The stakes are so high because success means millions of dollars in taxes, it means wealth creation, it means jobs. It is the lifeblood of the community."

Consequently, many cities pump millions of dollars into attracting new business through a variety of communication tools that include elaborate brochures, placement of favorable "success" stories in the nation's press, direct mail, telemarketing, trade fairs, special events, and meetings with business executives.

Cities also promote themselves in an effort to increase tourism, which is further discussed in Chapter 22. An example of city information efforts is the campaign by the Panama City (Florida) Convention and Visitors Bureau to position itself as a prime destination for college students during spring break. According to *PRWeek*, the bureau spent about $300,000 promoting the city through posters, news releases, brochures, advertising, and special events to let students know that they were welcome. Indeed, the "spring breakers," as they are called, pumped about $135 million into the local economy.

Improving the image of a city is also an objective. Gary, Indiana, long a city in decline because of steel mill closings, bid $1.2 million to play host to the Miss U.S.A. beauty pageant. It was hoped that the pageant, televised nationally, would bring recognition and some degree of prestige to the city. The mayor told a *New York Times* reporter that the pageant "has the ability to build local pride in the city and the psychology of the public in a positive way. If you don't have that, nothing else you do is going to work."

Although beauty pageants are a good "hook" for creating national visibility and tourism for a city, extensive information efforts are also needed when a natural disaster strikes. When Des Moines, Iowa, was flooded several years ago and the city's water supply became contaminated, the city conducted an aggressive information campaign to keep the public informed of flood developments and hold anxiety to a minimum.

A public relations career in local government has its rewards. Ed Skyler, the press secretary of New York City Mayor Michael Bloomberg, told *PRWeek*:

> There are a lot of excellent PR people who are drawn to the public sector because of the wide range of issues that they can deal with, from public safety to healthcare to the economy and economic development to housing, labor relations and union issues. Part of it is the pace and part of it is the exposure to different communities. It's good

training for any industry; there are few industries that you don't come into contact with while working in government.

Criticism of Government Information Efforts

Although the need for government to inform citizens and publicize programs is accepted in principle, many critics still express skepticism about the activity.

Taxpayer groups, for example, often oppose the employment of information and public affairs officers as costly and unnecessary. When the U.S. Department of Homeland Security public affairs office posted a job position for a Hollywood liaison, taxpayer groups protested. "It's probably an unnecessary position in that the existing PR department should be able to handle Hollywood's requests," said Pete Sepp, director of communications for the National Taxpayers Union.

Budget hawks in Congress also worry about cost and intent. Brad Sherman (R-CA) told the *Los Angeles Daily News,* "There's a growing tendency to spend money to make government look good. It's hard for me to think this is the best possible use of taxpayer's dollars." Congressional lawmakers were even more critical of a proposal to spend $10 million over a five-year period to boost the image of AmeriCorps as an effective volunteer service organization. House Majority Whip Roy Blount (R-MO) said, "AmeriCorps should be spending its taxpayer funds to help the needy. The good they can do for Americans in need with their $10 million PR budget will be its own positive message."

Others, including journalists, criticize public information activities because legislators are notorious for sending reams of useless news releases that often just promote themselves. Such abuse, coupled with snide news stories about the cost of maintaining government "public relations" experts, rankle dedicated public information officers (PIOs) at the various state and federal agencies who work very hard to keep the public informed with a daily diet of announcements and news stories. One PIO for a California agency said, "I'd like to see the press find out what's going on in state government without us."

Indeed, a major source of media hostility seems to stem from the fact that reporters are heavily dependent on handouts. In one study, almost 90 percent of a state government's news releases were used by daily and weekly newspapers. The textbook *Media: An Introductory Analysis of American Mass Communications* by Sandman, Rubin, and Sachsman puts it succinctly: "If a newspaper were to quit relying on news releases, but continued covering the news it now covers, it would need at least two or three times more reporters."

News releases, however, are only one aspect of helping the media do their job. The city of Homestead, Florida, spent $70,000 on facilities and staff just to handle the deluge of reporters who descended on the city in the aftermath of Hurricane Andrew. And cities across the country also spent considerable amounts of money providing news facilities for visiting reporters when presidential candidates George Bush or John Kerry came to town.

Public information efforts also are justified in terms of cost efficiency. The U.S. Department of Agriculture public affairs office receives several hundred inquiries a year. Two-thirds of the requests can be answered with a simple pamphlet, brochure, or a link on its Web site.

There is also the argument about how much the public saves through preventive public relations. The taxpayers of California spend about $7 billion annually to deal with the associated costs of teenage pregnancy, so $5.7 million spent on a successful education campaign could save the state considerably more in reduced welfare costs.

Michigan's $100,000 expenditure to educate citizens about recycling aerosol cans does much to reduce the costs of opening more landfills.

An Associated Press reporter acknowledged in a story that government information does have value. He wrote:

> While some of the money and manpower goes for self-promotion, by far the greater amount is committed to an indispensable function of a democratic government—informing the people.
>
> What good would it serve for the Consumer Product Safety Commission to recall a faulty kerosene heater and not go to the expense of alerting the public to its action? An informed citizenry needs the government to distribute its economic statistics, announce its antitrust suits, tell about the health of the president, give crop forecasts.

SUMMARY

Corporate Public Affairs

A major component of corporate communications is public affairs, which primarily deals with governmental relations at the local, state, national, and even international levels. Public affairs specialists build relationships with civil servants and elected officials and also monitor governmental actions that may affect the employer or client. Trade groups, primarily based in state capitals or Washington, D.C., have public affairs specialists representing various professions and industries.

Lobbying

A public affairs specialist primarily provides information about the organization's viewpoint to the public and government entities. A lobbyist has a more specialized function to directly work for the defeat, passage, or amendment of proposed legislation and regulatory agency policies. In recent years, there has been public concern about "influence peddling" in terms of former legislators and other officials becoming lobbyists and "cashing in" on their knowledge and connections. To curb abuse, several laws have been passed to regulate lobbyists.

Election Campaigns

The cost of running for office in the United States is the highest in the world. An army of specialists, including public relations experts, are retained by major candidates to organize and raise money for election campaigns. In recent years, the Internet has played an important role in raising money, generating high visibility for candidates, and increasing the number of registered voters.

Campaign Finance Reform

The large amount of "soft money" given to candidates was curtailed by the McCain-Feingold Act, and individuals and groups have restrictions on how much can be given to candidates, state parties, and national parties. However, 527 groups are a loophole in this law. These partisan organizations, which have no official connection to the candidate or the political party, were a major force in the 2004 presidential elections in terms of placing numerous "attack" ads.

Public Affairs in Government

Governments, since the ancient Egyptians, have always engaged in campaigns to inform, motivate, and even persuade the public. In the United States, Congress forbids federal agencies from "persuading" the public, so the emphasis is on "public information" efforts. All agencies of the federal government employ public affairs officers and public information specialists. Members of Congress also engage in extensive "information" efforts to reach their constituents.

The White House

The apex of all government information and public relations efforts is the White House; the president's every move and action is chronicled by the mass media. Presidents throughout history have used this media attention to lead the nation, convince the public to support administration policies, and get reelected. The White House press secretary probably has the most stressful and demanding job in terms of dealing with the press on a daily basis.

State Information Services

Various states employ public information officers to tell the public about the activities and policies of various agencies. In addition, agencies conduct a number of campaigns to inform the public about health and safety issues. Another initiative is to promote the state as a tourist destination.

City Information Services

All major cities employ public information specialists to tell citizens about city services and promote economic development.

Criticism of Government Information Services

Although taxpayer groups and journalists often criticize expenditures for information efforts, an informed public is the core of a democracy. In addition, preventive information campaigns often save government millions of dollars a year by reducing litter, teen pregnancy, and smoking.

Case Activity: **What Would You Do?**

The city council of Lakewood (population 150,000), in cooperation with a citizens' commission, has decided that there is a need to improve citizen participation in the city's curbside recycling program. Such a program is environmentally sound, and there are other reasons to increase participation. The city's only landfill is rapidly filling up, and there are new state mandates for recycling.

Recycling is still a relatively new concept for the majority of Lakewood households—only 45 percent of them are separating their trash for recycling. The percentage is even lower among residents in the middle- to lower-income brackets. The objective is to get 80 percent of the households to use the curbside recycling program.

What kind of public information would you recommend to accomplish this objective? Develop a list of program strategies and communication tactics.

QUESTIONS for Review and Discussion

1. What is the difference between someone working in corporate public affairs (governmental relations) and a lobbyist?

2. What skills are needed for work in corporate public affairs?

3. The public, in general, has low esteem for lobbyists. Do you think the perception is justified? Why or why not?

4. Lobbyists for the food industry are very involved in trying to influence federal guidelines for good nutrition. What's at stake for them and the industries they represent?

5. Many lobbyists are former legislators and government officials. Do you think they exercise undue influence in the shaping of legislation? Why or why not?

6. Gun control groups used full-page ads in major newspapers to rally public support for continuing the ban on semiautomatic assault weapons. Review the ad on page 486. Do you think the ad was effective? Why or why not?

7. What were the major points of the lobbying reform act? Do you think the law has curtailed excessive "influence-peddling"? Why or why not?

8. Name some guidelines for ethical grassroots lobbying.

9. The issue has been raised about the use of "front groups" in grassroots lobbying efforts. Do you think the public has a right to know what special interests are funding many of these efforts?

10. Summarize the major parts of the McCain-Feingold Act. Do you think this law has effectively curtailed unregulated large gifts to candidates and parties?

11. Fund-raisers play a crucial role in elections. Would you like to be a political fund-raiser? Why or why not?

12. How did Howard Dean use the Internet in the Democratic primaries? Do you think the Internet will play an even more important role in the 2006 elections?

13. The major issue of the 2004 presidential election was the activities of 527s. Explain what these groups are and how they operated during the election. What's your opinion of 527s? Should the Federal Election Commission (FEC) ban them? Why or why not?

14. Why do government agencies engage in "public information" efforts instead of "public relations" activities? Are there any laws involved? If so, what are they?

15. The Pentagon was criticized for stonewalling information regarding abuse of Iraqi prisoners. Do you think the criticism was justified? Why or why not? What about commanders asking soldiers to sign form letters supporting the war and sending them to their hometown newspapers?

16. Federal agencies engage in any number of public information campaigns. What is your opinion on this? Are these campaigns just a waste of taxpayer dollars, or are they legitimate and necessary?

17. Ketchum, as part of its contract with the U.S. Office of Education, arranged for the commentator Armstrong Williams to receive $240,000 to promote the No Child Left Behind Act. Was it the responsibility of Williams to disclose this payment, or was it the obligation of Ketchum? Do you think Ketchum violated The Council of Public Relations Firms' code of ethics?

18. George W. Bush and John Kerry have very different communication styles. Do you think these "styles" were a deciding factor in the 2004 presidential election?

19. The office of White House Press Secretary is one of the most demanding jobs in communications. Why is it so demanding, and would you ever aspire to hold this job? Why or why not?

SUGGESTED READINGS

Auletta, Ken. "Fortress Bush: How the White House Keeps the Press Under Control." *New Yorker*, January 19, 2004, pp. 53–65.

Barstow, David, and Stein, Robin. "Under Bush, a New Age of Prepackaged TV News." *New York Times,* March 13, 2005, www.nytimes.com/2005/03/13/politics.

Belzer, Wendy M. "How to Get a Job on Capitol Hill." *Public Relations Tactics*, April 2004, p. 25.

Birstine, Leigh Anne. "The Makings of a Public Affairs Officer." *Public Relations Tactics*, October 2002, p. 15.

Bumiller, Elisabeth. "Relaxing and Reflecting, Fleischer Loosens Up." *New York Times*, July 14, 2003, p. A15.

Bumiller, Elisabeth. "Keepers of Bush Image Lift Stagecraft to New Heights." *New York Times*, May 16, 2003, pp. A1, A20.

Calmes, Joann. "Explosive Images: Crisis Veterans Offer Advice to White House on Release of Iraqi Prison-Abuse Photos." *Wall Street Journal*, May 13, 2004, pp. B1, B6.

Gourevitch, Philip. "Bushspeak: The President's Vernacular Style." *New Yorker*, September 13, 2004, pp. 36–43.

Greenhouse, Linda. "Justices in a 5-to-4 Decision, Back Campaign Finance Law that Curbs Contributions." *New York Times*, December 11, 2003, pp. A1, A24.

Griffo, Paul. "Legitimate News Releases or Propaganda? Debtating the Ethics of VNRs." *Public Relations Tactics*, June 2004, p. 20.

Hazley, Greg. "PR Is Favorite Target of Statehouse Cuts." *O'Dwyer's PR Services Report*, June 2004, pp. 13, 30.

Judge, Clark S. "PR Lessons from the Pentagon." *Wall Street Journal*, April 1, 2003, p. A24.

Lee, Mordecai. "The First Federal Information Service, 1920–1933: At US Bureau of Efficiency!" *Public Relations Review*, Vol. 29, No. 4, 2003, pp. 415–425.

Pear, Robert. "Ruling Says White House's Medicare Videos Were Illegal." *New York Times*, May 20, 2004, p. A21.

Pinkham, Doug. "What It Takes in Public Affairs and Public Relations." *Public Relations Quarterly*, Spring 2004, p. 15.

Quenqua, Douglas. "Lessons from the Campaign Trail: Public Affairs Tactics Often Mirror Those Used on the Political Stage." *PRWeek*, September 20, 2004, pp. 14–15.

Quenqua, Douglas. "NSA Reaches Out to Media to Gain Friendlier Image." *PRWeek*, May 10, 2004, p. 12.

Quenqua, Douglas. "A Lesson in Public Affairs: Military PAOs are Trained, Not Born." *PRWeek*, February 9, 2004, p. 15.

Quenqua, Douglas. "Is Ban on Coffin Coverage a Legitimate Wartime Tactic?" *PRWeek*, January 26, 2004, p. 9.

Rutenberg, Jim. "Scary Ads Take Campaign to a Grim New Level: Both Candidates Play to Voters' Anxieties as Race Nears End." *New York Times*, October 17, 2004, pp. A1, A20.

Schlesinger, Jacob M. "Kerry Fails to Stick to the Script: Loquacious Candidate's Message Gets Muddled as Speeches Ramble." *Wall Street Journal*, September 21, 2004, p. A4.

Slackman, Michael. "GOP Convention Costs $154 Million, Most of it Donated." *New York Times*, October 16, 2004, p. A26.

Souley, Boubacar, and Wicks, Robert H. "Going Negative: Candidate Usage of Internet Web Sites During the 2000 Presidential Campaign." *Journalism & Mass Communications Quarterly*, Vol. 80, No. 1, 2003, pp. 128–144.

Worth, Robert F. "Cash Collectors for Kerry Race Run the Gamut." *New York Times*, August 16, 2004, pp. A1, 10.

Wright, Mark. "PR Goes to War: An Inside Look at the U.S. Army's Public Affairs Detachments." *The Strategist*, Winter 2002, pp. 30–33.

Zamiska, Nicholas. "Food-Pyramid Frenzy: Lobbyists Fight to Defend Sugar, Potatoes and Bread in Recommended U.S. Diet." *Wall Street Journal*, July 29, 2004, pp. B1, B2.

Zernike, Kate, and Rutenberg, Jim. "Friendly Fire: The Birth of an Anti-Kerry Ad." *New York Times*, August 20, 2004, pp. A1, A16.

chapter 19

International
Public Relations

Topics covered in this chapter include:

What Is International Public Relations?

International public relations may be defined as the planned and organized effort of a company, institution, or government to establish mutually beneficial relations with the publics of other nations. These publics, in turn, may be defined as the various groups of people who are affected by, or who can affect, the operations of a particular firm, institution, or government.

International public relations may also be viewed from the standpoint of its practice in individual countries. Although public relations is commonly regarded as a concept developed in the United States at the beginning of the 20th century, some of its elements, such as countering unfavorable public attitudes by means of disclosure of operations through publicity and annual reports, were practiced by railroad companies and at least one shareholding corporation in Germany as far back as the mid-19th century, to mention only one such country. (See Chapter 2.)

Even so, it is largely American techniques that have been adapted to national and regional public relations practices throughout the world, including many totalitarian nations. Today, although in some languages there is no term comparable to *public relations*, the practice has spread to most countries, especially those with industrial bases and large urban populations. This is primarily the result of worldwide technological, social, economic, and political changes and the growing understanding that public relations is an essential component of advertising, marketing, and diplomacy.

International Corporate Public Relations

In this section, we explore the new age of global marketing and point out that differences in language, laws, and cultural mores must be overcome when companies conduct business in foreign countries. We also discuss how U.S. public relations firms represent foreign interests in this country as well as U.S. corporations in other parts of the world. Aspects of public relations practice in some other countries are delineated.

The New Age of Global Marketing

For decades, hundreds of corporations based in the United States have been engaged in international business operations, including marketing, advertising, and public relations. These activities swelled to unprecedented proportions during the 1990s, largely because of new communications technologies, development of 24-hour financial markets almost worldwide, the lowering of trade barriers, the growth of sophisticated foreign competition in traditionally "American" markets, and the shrinking cultural differences that are bringing the "global village" ever closer to reality.

Today almost one-third of all U.S. corporate profits are generated through international business. In the case of Coca-Cola, probably the best-known brand name in the world, international sales account for 70 percent of the company's revenues.

At the same time, overseas investors are moving into American industry. It is not uncommon for 15 to 20 percent of a U.S. company's stock to be held abroad. The United Kingdom, for example, has a direct foreign investment in the United States exceeding $122 billion, followed by Japan and the Netherlands with nearly half that sum each, according to the U.S. Department of Commerce.

Public relations is an essential ingredient in the global megamarketing mix being created. The 15 largest public relations organizations now generate between 30 and 40 percent of their fees outside the United States. Because of fax machines, e-mail, on-line services, and the Internet, boutique firms are challenging the big agencies for international business. (See Chapter 4.)

Fueling the new age of global marketing are satellite television, computer networks, electronic mail, fax, fiber optics, cellular telephone systems, and emerg-

ON THE JOB insights

Corporate Communications on a Global Scale

Bayer, a German pharmaceuticals and chemicals company, is a global conglomerate that manufactures over 10,000 products. However, it is best known around the world for its Bayer aspirin brand that is sold in practically every country. Bayer employs more than 120,000 people worldwide and has subsidiaries in many nations.

The scope of its global operations also means that it has an extensive communications and public relations operation. Almost 200 communications professionals work at Bayer headquarters, and there are another 150 staffers around the globe. The staff in Germany generates more than 500 news releases annually to international media, holds about 50 news conferences a year, and participates in about 150 trade fairs worldwide.

Bayer also has regional operations in corporate communications. One center is in Singapore to serve about 15 Asia-Pacific nations of diverse cultures, languages, and heritages. Bayer's

objective is to substantially increase market share in the region by 2010, and company executives say corporate communications has a key role to play in strategically positioning the company in the region. Some initiatives have included the "Bayer Young Environmental Project" in Southeast Asia, the *Healthy Living* radio show in China, and educational programs in Japan on biotechnology.

A major global activity is employee communications. Bayer uses an interactive Intranet publication called Bayer News Channel (BNC) and the Intranet-based BNC-TV for employees. In addition, the company produces a variety of newspapers, brochures, and magazines for employees and outside stakeholders with a total circulation of more than 10 million copies.

Twice a year, the corporate communications heads of Bayer's largest markets have a meeting to discuss communication issues, develop strategies, and share ideas. New communications

staffers from around the world are trained through a one-week seminar at corporate headquarters.

The worldwide communications staff also exchanges ideas and programs on a daily basis through e-mail, telephone news conferences, and Webcasts. A successful community relations program in Singapore or Mexico City, for example, may be adapted and used in other markets around the world.

Bayer manages the complexity of its global communications through an integrated approach. According to IPRA's *Frontline,* "Aligning different communications disciplines increases efficiency and contributes to a focused message to the company's customers and clients." Heiner Springer, head of global corporate communications, says, "If we want to be successful as a company, what really matters are good products, good people, and a good reputation. Because, ultimately, a good reputation is our license to operate."

ing technologies such as integrated services digital networks (ISDN), which enable users to send voice, data, graphics, and video over existing copper cables. For example, Hill and Knowlton has its own satellite transmission facilities, and the General Electric Company has formed an international telecommunications network, enabling employees to communicate worldwide using voice, video, and computer data simply by dialing seven digits on a telephone. Using three satellite systems, Cable News Network (CNN) is viewed by more than 200 million people in more than 140 countries. A number of newspapers and magazines are reaching millions with international editions. *Reader's Digest*, to cite one example, distributes about 11.5 million copies abroad—44 national editions in more than a dozen languages.

Differences in language, laws, and cultural mores among countries (to be discussed shortly) pose serious problems. There also is a need for both managers and employees to learn to think and act in global terms as quickly as possible. Already, Burson-Marsteller, with offices in many countries, has been spending more than $1 million a year on training tapes and traveling teams of trainers and seminars to foster a uniform approach to client projects.

Much of the new business jousting takes place on West European terrain, where a recently unified European Union (EU) attracts enormous attention. Although hampered by recession in recent years, public relations expenditures have increased significantly. The growth has been precipitated in part by expansion of commercial television resulting from widespread privatization, the desire of viewers for more varied programming, satellite technology, and slowly developing EU business patterns. Satellite TV reaches well over 30 million people, mostly through cable systems; direct transmission of programming to homes by high-powered satellites bypassed conventional networks, local stations, and cable systems. On the print side, the business press has been growing about 20 percent every year, and there are about 15,000 trade publications in Western Europe.

Although the EU promoted the phrase "a single Europe," corporations and public relations firms still face the complex task of communicating effectively to 400 million people in 25 countries speaking multiple languages. See the Insights box on page 517 about Bayer's global communication effort.

Trade is now a global enterprise, but not everyone is happy about it. Here, protestors demonstrate against the World Trade Organization (WTO) and its policies. Today, as never before, international organizations and corporations must pay attention to public opinion on a global basis.

ON THE JOB

ethics

Got a News Release?
Please Include Cash

Paying a reporter or an editor to publish or broadcast a news release has long been a common practice in many parts of the world, especially in emerging nations where salaries are low.

In Russia, the practice of paying for placement is called *zakazukhi* (bought articles), and the International Public Relations Association (IPRA) has announced the formation of an international committee to eliminate the practice. According to IPRA president Alasdair Sutherland, "The credibility of any publication can only be based on its independent objectivity. As long as the practice of illicit paid-for-editorial continues in any marketplace, the local public can never have confidence in what they read."

The issue of *zakazukhi* in Russia was brought into the open when a public relations firm in Moscow, Promaco, issued a fictitious news release to see how much various publications would

charge to publish it as a news item. According to the *Economist*, "Of the 21 publications tested, one published the news release for free (but without checking its accuracy). Four asked for more information, and did not run stories. Three said they would run the article as an advertisement. But 13 papers and magazines offered to run it as an article, for fees ranging from around $135 at *Tribuna*, a paper backed by Gazprom, the national gas company, to more than $2,000 in the official government newspaper, *Rossiskaya Gazeta*. . . ."

IPRA President Alasdair Sutherland, who is an executive at Manning, Selvage & Lee public relations, said "IPRA has long been aware of this unethical practice in a number of marketplaces around the world, especially in some where the concept of a free press is comparatively 'new.' . . . We urge both Russian and international public relations

clients not to support this illegal practice in the future. According to our code, no IPRA member is permitted to use such methods."

Russian editors were less than embarrassed. According to the *Economist*, "The editor of *Noviye Izvestiya* said it made no difference to readers whether articles were paid or not." Another editor suggested that public relations firms were really to blame. When the newspaper wants to run the news release as an advertisement, the public relations firms just take their business elsewhere.

What do you think? If you were doing public relations for an American or European firm in Moscow, would you go along with the local custom of *zakazukhi?* Or would you refuse to pay the media for using your news release? How about the common practice in China of giving reporters "transportation" money for attending a news conference?

Language and Cultural Differences

Companies operating in other nations are confronted with essentially the same public relations challenges as those in the United States. The objective is to create and maintain mutually beneficial relationships, but the task is more complex on an international and intercultural level.

Public relations practitioners need to recognize cultural differences, adapt to local customs, and understand the finer points of verbal and nonverbal communication in individual nations. Experts in intercultural communication point out that many cultures, particularly non-Western ones, are "high-context" communication societies. This means that the meaning of the spoken word is often implicit and based on the environmental context and the relationship rather than on explicit, categorical statements. The communication style of Asian and Arab nations, for example, are "high context."

This is in contrast with the European and American communication styles, which are considered "low context." Great emphasis is placed on exact words, and the receiver is expected to derive most of the meaning from the written or verbalized statements, not from nonverbal behavior cues. Legal documents produced in the West are the ultimate in explicit wording.

The concept of low- and high-context communication styles is manifested in several ways. Americans, for example, tend to be very direct (and often blunt) in their communication style. In high-context cultures, Americans often are perceived as verbose, opinionated, and very focused on getting to the point as soon as possible. They also are clock watchers, get upset if meetings don't start on time, and carry day planners as if they were bibles.

The communication style in a high-context culture is quite different. Group harmony is more important than take-charge individualistic traits, a social relationship must be built before business is conducted, a handshake takes the place of a legal contract, and being on time to a meeting isn't all that important. One aspect of high-context Asian cultures is "loss of face." Individuals don't want to offend, so a person will never say "no" outright. A Japanese executive, for example, will suck air through his or her teeth and exclaim, "Sa! That will be very difficult" when they really mean "no."

Language, of course, is another challenge. The following are some examples of the type of language problems that have been encountered:

● A British executive staying at a hotel in New York was embarrassed because he asked the front desk for a "rubber," which is an eraser in England. The hotel staff thought he wanted a condom.

● A producer of calzones, which are cheese and meat-filled turnovers, had a major marketing problem in Spain because in Spanish *calzone* means "underwear."

● The Milk Processor Association found that the catchy phase "Got Milk?" didn't translate too well into Spanish. The literal translation was "Are You Lactating?"

● A business executive took the time to memorize the names of the Chinese executives he was going to visit in Singapore, but didn't realize that the surname comes first in Chinese. So he essentially called his contacts by their first name, which they thought was too friendly and informal for a first meeting.

● The "thumbs up" gesture in the United States means "well done" or "good job." In other cultures, it can be considered offensive and should be avoided. Also, the thumb-and-forefinger "OK" sign is an obscene gesture in many cultures.

Cultural differences provide additional pitfalls, as shown by the following examples:

● In the United States, white signifies purity; in most Asian nations, white is the color of death.

ON THE JOB global

In China, Green Hats are a No-No

China, with its more than a billion citizens, is a major market for companies around the world. By the same token, China's economic and industrial capacity makes it a major player on the world stage.

Doing business in China, however, requires a degree of cultural sensitivity in public relations. A Washington State agriculture official, for example, thought it was a great idea to hand out bright green baseball caps at every stop without noticing that none of the men put them on, and all the women giggled. That's because a green hat is the Chinese symbol of a cuckold.

A Canadian also caused a problem when he told his Chinese guests that his product was successful in Japan and, since all Asian cultures are simi-

lar, he was sure the product would be a hit in China. What he failed to understand was that resentment of Japan runs very high in China, which was bombed and occupied by Japan during World War II.

One also doesn't discuss Taiwan as being a nation, because the Chinese believe it is simply a breakaway province from the mainland. Don't give clocks or umbrellas as gifts. It signals that the receiver will have bad luck. Also, don't give gifts wrapped in white ribbon, which is the symbol of death; it's better to use red ribbon, which is the symbol of good luck. Even champagne toasts have their protocol; lower the rim of your glass when clicking a toast as a way of honoring your guest.

In media relations, an outright bribe can cause a Chinese re-

porter to "lose face," but a red envelope containing money "thanking" them for coming to your news conference or event is considered standard operating procedure. The "gift" is for taking the time to interview your client or employer, not an incentive for them to write a story.

As in any other country, public relations professionals should strive to localize news releases and information. In China, that means mentioning local business partners or customers. It also pays to include the names of local government or Communist party dignitaries in media materials and to invite them to news conferences and special events. All media materials should be translated into basic Chinese, although most Chinese journalists can now read English.

- In China, tables at a banquet are never numbered. The Chinese think such tables appear to rank guests or that certain numbers are unlucky. It's better to direct a guest to the "primrose" or "hollyhock" table.

- German and Swiss executives think a person is uncouth if he or she uses first names, particularly at public events.

- The proper etiquette for drinking in Korea is to fill your neighbor's glass as well as your own.

- In Thailand, patting a child on the head is seen as a grave offense because the head is considered sacred. Also, it's offensive to show the soles of your feet to another person in Thailand and other Asian nations.

- In Latin America, a greeting often includes physical contact by hugging the individual or grabbing them by the arm.

● News releases in Malaysia should be distributed in four languages to avoid alienating any segment of the press.

● Gift-giving is common in Asian cultures. Executives, meeting for the first time, will exchange gifts as a way of building a social relationship.

All of these illustrations indicate that Americans and others not only must learn the customs of the country in which they are working, but they also should rely on native professionals to guide them. Media materials and advertising must be translated, and the best approach is to employ native speakers who have extensive experience in translating ad copy and public relations materials. See the FedEx news releases below.

Representing Foreign Corporations in the United States

Industries in other countries frequently employ American public relations firms to advance their needs in this country. Carl Levin, vice president and senior consultant, Burson-Marsteller, Washington, D.C., tells why:

● To hold off protectionist moves threatening their company or industry
● To defeat legislation affecting the sale of a client's product
● To support expansion of the client's markets in the United States
● To provide ongoing information on political, sociological, and commercial developments in the United States that could bear on the client's business inter-

International public relations requires the translation of news releases into several languages. Here, the first part of this FedEx announcement is in English. Also shown is the same announcement in Thai. (MDK consulting/Bangkok)

ests, not only here but worldwide. In the well-organized foreign company, this information is factored into day-to-day policy decisions as well as periodic strategic plans.

A fifth reason might be crisis communications. Bridgestone, a Japanese company, found itself on the defensive when its American company, Firestone, had to recall millions of tires for safety reasons. Japanese management, unfamiliar with American expectations of open communications, stumbled badly in the initial stages of the recall because the Japanese CEO didn't issue an apology or offer to fix the problem. Only after Bridgestone hired an American public relations firm did the company combat Ford Motor Company's assertions that the tire company was completely at fault. See Chapter 1 for the background on this.

Representing U.S. Corporations in Other Nations

Many U.S. corporations are global in scope in terms of employees, products, manufacturing plants, and distribution centers. In fact, the top five global giants in descending order of market value are all American: General Electric, ExxonMobil, Microsoft, Pfizer, and Citigroup.

Public relations professionals who work for these giants, as well as a host of other American companies, are automatically in the field of international public relations, because their work involves many nations. Many of these corporations also retain global public relations firms such as Burson-Marsteller and Hill & Knowlton to provide services from offices in major cities around the world. The global scope of public relations firms was discussed in Chapter 4.

American companies, at the start of the 21st century and in the aftermath of the 9/11 terrorist attack in 2001, face a number of challenges abroad in terms of competing with other large corporations headquartered in other nations, dealing with sustainable development, being boycotted by nations that disagree with

ON THE JOB

global

Israel Worried about Its Image

The Israeli–Palestinian conflict has produced any number of news stories and photos showing Israeli soldiers, tanks, helicopters, and guided missiles being used against a relatively unarmed Palestinian population. As Israeli's minister of information, Nachman Shai, says, "We looked like Goliath and they looked like David."

This has caused some concern for the Israeli government, particularly as it affects opinion in the United States, because it is important to have the continuing support of the American population and the government. That support is in danger if public opinion shifts to increased sympathy for the Palestinian cause.

The Palestinians are also beginning to realize how decisive the battle for public opinion is, and various Arab groups, such as the Arab-American Anti-Discrimination Committee (ADC), have stepped up publicity efforts to inform Americans about the Palestinian side of the conflict. The group has taken full-page ads in daily newspapers across the country and written op-ed articles.

Israel has also been active, encouraging the Jewish community in the United States to be more proactive in explaining the Israeli side of the conflict. In addition, a New York public relations firm has been hired to place Israel's representatives in various media outlets. According to Steve Rubenstein, from Rubenstein Associates, "We felt people were missing the whole truth and that if we could show a fuller picture visually, it would be easier to make the Israeli case."

American foreign policy, and being good corporate citizens at the local and national level.

David Drobis, a former senior partner and chair of Ketchum, outlined some of these challenges in a talk to the International Communications Consultancy Organization (ICCO). According to Drobis, one major challenge is to better communicate the economic advantages of globalization to the world's people. The *Economist*, for example, has called globalization a massive communications failure because the public and private sectors have done such a poor job communicating the benefits, being transparent about their activities, and building important alliances.

Drobis believes that public relations professionals are the best-suited group to explain the benefits of globalization. These benefits must be communicated to three key groups. The first group is the companies themselves. Companies must realize that international capitalism has a bad connotation in many parts of the world because it's perceived as nothing more than "a byword for oppression, exploitation, and injustice by rapacious multinationals."

Companies, Drobis says, have done little to correct this view despite the efforts of a few highly responsible companies who have outstanding programs. He continues, "companies must take into consideration a broad group of stakeholders as they pursue their business goals globally. And by doing so, there are tangible and intangible business benefits. In this way, good corporate citizenship is not a cost of doing business, but rather a driver of business success. What's good for the soul is also good for business."

Studies show, says Drobis, "that companies that pursue initiatives—be they related to the environment, labor standards, or human rights—are rewarded with improved business success in a number of areas, including shareholder value, revenue, operational efficiencies, higher employee morale and productivity, and corporate reputation."

The second group that must be informed of the benefits of globalization is nongovernment organizations (NGOs). Although many NGOs are outright hostile to all private enterprise, American companies must realize that NGOs can become an important seal of approval and brands. Indeed, major mainstream NGOs such as the World Wildlife Federation and Greenpeace are working with corporations on sustainable development programs. The *Financial Times* notes, "A new type of relationship is emerging between companies and NGOs, where NGOs act as certification bodies, vertifying and, in many cases, permitting the use of their logos, showing that products and services are being produced in a socially responsible and environmentally friendly ways."

The third group is international institutions such as World Trade Organization (WTO), the World Bank, the International Monetary Fund (IMF), or even the United Nations. Drobis says these organizations are unfairly criticized as being undemocratic, but fairly criticized for being nontransparent. An article in *Foreign Affairs* puts it this way: "To outsiders, even within the same government, these institutions can look like closed and secretive clubs. Increased transparency is essential. International organizations can provide more access to their deliberations, even after the fact."

Drobis, in giving advice to American companies doing business abroad, concludes that the era of "relationship building" is over. Instead, he says, the 21st century is one of "confidence building" in the international arena so various publics not only trust corporations to do the right thing, but believe globalization is a benefit to hundreds of millions of poor people around the globe.

International Government Public Relations

In this section, we explore how and why the governments of most nations seek to influence the opinions and actions of governments and people in other countries. Many employ U.S. public relations firms for this purpose.

Influencing Other Countries

The governments of virtually every country have one or more departments involved in communicating with other nations. Much effort and millions of dollars are spent on the tourism industry, attracting visitors whose expenditures aid their hosts' economies. Even larger sums are devoted to lobbying efforts to obtain favorable legislation for a country's products; for example, Costa Rica urged the U.S. Congress to let its sugar into the nation at favorable rates, and the Department of State threatened to enact trade sanctions against countries such as Korea and China that persisted in "pirating" U.S. products such as computers and books without payment.

Many countries send shortwave broadcasts worldwide to foster their national interests and prestige, keep in touch with nationals abroad, disseminate news, and influence the internal affairs of other nations.

Information Efforts by the United States. The American government is the major disseminator of information around the world. This is called *public diplomacy*, because it is an open communication process primarily intended to present American society in all its complexity so citizens and governments of other nations can understand the context of U.S. actions and policies. Another function is to promote the American values of democracy, free trade, and open communication around the world.

The United States Information Agency (USIA), created in 1953 by President Dwight Eisenhower, was the primary agency involved in shaping America's image abroad. USIA, in many ways, was the direct descendant of George Creel's Committee on Public Information (CPI) during World War I and Elmer Davis's Office of War Information, in World War II (see Chapter 2).

Following World War II, the new threat, of course, was the outbreak of the Cold War with the Soviet Union and the Communist bloc nations in Eastern Europe. The Cold War was a war of words on both sides to win the "hearts and minds" of governments and their citizens around the world. Some USIA activities included (1) the stationing of public affairs officers (PAOs) at every American embassy to work with local media, (2) publication of books and magazines, (3) distribution of American films and TV programs, (4) sponsorship of tours by American dance and musical groups, (5) art shows, (6) student and faculty exchange programs such as the Fulbright program, and (7) sponsorship of lecture tours by American authors and intellectuals.

At the height of the Cold War, USIA had a budget of about $900 million and 12,000 employees. When the Soviet Union imploded in the early 1990s, the fortunes of the USIA began to fall as Congress and other critics decided that the United States didn't need such a large public profile in the world. As a result, the agency was abolished in 1999 and most of its functions were transferred to the U.S. Department of State under an undersecretary of state for public affairs and diplomacy. The staff was cut 40 percent and funding for projects decreased sharply.

PR CASEBOOK

American "Public Diplomacy" Is Criticized

Perhaps the easiest part of the War on Terrorism was the toppling of the Taliban regime in Afghanistan and the removal of Saddam Hussein's government in Baghdad. Most experts agree, however, that the toughest part will be winning the war of worldwide public opinion.

The U.S. government is now engaged in a war of ideas. As the *Economist* points out, "It has to persuade America, its allies and Muslims around the world that its fight is against terror, not Islam." Many experts are less optimistic about winning this part of the war. One Arab expert told the Associated Press, "The U.S. point of view is not unknown to the Arab people, they just don't buy it." According to the *New York Times*, "Many Muslims say American policy favors Israelis over Palestinians and needs to be altered before sentiments will change."

John Paluszek, senior counsel of Ketchum, puts it more bluntly. He wrote in *PRWeek*, "It's the policy, stupid." He continues, "It is policy—and related action—that matters most in successful PR. Recent opinion polls tell us that it's current American foreign policy, not traditional American values, that is unacceptable to many people in the Middle East." Indeed an Advisory Group on Diplomacy for the Arab and Muslim World appointed by Congress concluded, "much of the resentment toward America stems from our policies" and "In this time of peril, public diplomacy is absurdly and dangerously underfunded."

Although funding is a major problem, critics also say that the limited monies available have been poorly spent. One project that received considerable criticism was a multimillion dollar

American public diplomacy abroad has taken a severe beating since the invasion of Iraq. Here, Turkish protestors carry signs protesting the visit of President Bush to attend a meeting of NATO in Ankara.

advertising campaign initiated by Charlotte Beers, a former CEO of two major advertising agencies. She was named Undersecretary of Public Diplomacy and Public Affairs in 2001. Almost immediately she decided on using advertising as a major tool to win "hearts and minds." Her idea was a series of television commercials with the theme "shared values" that would show Muslim men and women leading happy and productive lives in a religion-tolerant America. As one critic dryly noted, "It was like this was the 1930s and the government was running commercials showing happy blacks in America."

Although the ads were used in Indonesia, the world's largest Muslim nation, most television stations in the Middle East refused to accept the ads because they were considered nothing but "propaganda." Also, of the Muslims featured in

PR CASEBOOK *(continued)*

the ads, none of them were Arabs. After about five weeks, the State Department suspended the advertising program, and Charlotte Beers, barely 18 months into her job, resigned for "health reasons."

Jennifer Aaker, an associate professor of marketing at Stanford University's School of Business, told the *New York Times*, "One of the reasons that the effort failed was because of the underlying product—our policies were not perceived as pro-Middle East. We failed to understand the media, the culture, even the language of the region. It is difficult to garner favorable perceptions of the American brand in that context."

Meanwhile, global opinion polls have offered less than good news. In early 2004, the Pew Global Attitudes Survey found widespread skepticism of America's motives for the Iraq war. A majority of respondents in Jordan, Morocco, and Turkey said they believed that suicide bombings in Iraq against Americans and other Westerners were justified. In Pakistan, 65 percent of the population have a favorable view of Osama Bin

Laden; and 75 percent of the French respondents supported "an independent European foreign policy" as opposed to one aligned with American foreign policy.

New U.S. restrictions on foreign exchange students also have taken their toll. Harold Pachios, a member of the U.S. Advisory Commission on Public Diplomacy, told *PRWeek*, "Exchanges are a key historical component of public diplomacy. Now there is an endless number of Fulbright Scholarship recipients who can't arrive in time to take up their studies, and there are endless stories of important people over here on some mission or another to learn about the U.S. and can't get here. The message is: You're not wanted here." In 2004, for example, the number of international students in the U.S. dropped 30 percent from the previous year.

U.S. Secretary of State Colin Powell sees a brighter day for public diplomacy. He told NBC's Tom Brokaw, "I think we'll close the gap as we move forward. Iraq was a very difficult issue for many nations and for people in many nations, but we did the right thing."

The 9/11 terrorist attack on the United States created a new impetus to "sell" America and the U.S. decision to invade Afghanistan and Iraq. Once again, the cry was to "win the hearts and minds" of the world's people and to gain public, as well as international support, for U.S. actions. The effort, however, was somewhat diffused and confused because the Pentagon and the White House undertook public diplomacy efforts rather than the U.S. State Department. See the PR Casebook on the previous page about U.S. efforts in public diplomacy.

The 9/11 Commission, in its 2004 final report, called for centralization of U.S. diplomacy efforts, a more robust and targeted program, and a drastic increase in funding of diplomatic exchanges and campaigns. Currently, the budget for the State Department's public diplomacy programs worldwide is $685 million (2004), a small increase from pre-9/11 levels. Comparatively, says *PRWeek*, the budget for the Department of Homeland Security is more than $30 billion.

Broadcast Efforts.   The Voice of America (VOA), created in 1948, was part of USIA for several decades. When USIA was dismantled and moved to the State Department, VOA was placed under the control of an independent federal agency, the Broadcasting Board of Governors (BOG). The idea was to have a firewall between the agency and the administration to ensure that VOA would continue to be an objective news service with credibility around the world. Article One of the VOA, for example, states that it should be a "reliable and authoritative source of news" and the news should be "accurate, objective, and comprehensive."

Its core work has traditionally been broadcasting news, sports, and entertainment around the world via shortwave. This is still done to a large extent, but VOA has also established AM and FM radio transmitters throughout the world to reach an even broader audience. In addition, the agency supplies many radio and television stations throughout the world with various news, music, and talk programs free of charge. The VOA also offers audio streaming on World Wide Web. The worldwide audience for VOA is difficult to judge, given all the methods of distribution, but estimates are several hundred million listeners.

VOA is the major voice of the United States abroad, but the government isn't always happy with its strict adherence to journalistic standards and objectivity. Consequently, the government also operates other radio and television services that are more proactive in advancing U.S. interests and foreign policy. *Radio Free Europe* was started in 1949 to reach the nations of Eastern Europe under the thumb of the Soviet Union. *Radio Liberty* was also started, under CIA funding, to broadcast directly to the citizens of the Soviet Union. The Soviet response during the Cold War was to jam these broadcasts because they were American "propaganda." Although both services still exist, they have significantly fewer staff and do less broadcasting.

More recently, Congress has set up radio and television services focusing on Iraq and the Middle East. *Radio Sawa*, for example, injects news tidbits written from an American perspective into a heavy rotation of American and Middle Eastern pop music. A similar radio service aimed at Iranian youth is *Radio Farda*. On the television side, the U.S. government has started *Al Hurra* that, according to the *New York Times*, is "a slickly produced Arab-language news and entertainment network that will be beamed by satellite from a Washington suburb to the Middle East." It is the American government's answer to the popular pan-Arab television service, Al Jazeera.

It should be noted that the VOA, including such services as *Radio Sawa*, are not directed at U.S. citizens. By design, under the United States Information and Educational Exchange Act of 1948, Congress prohibits the government from directing its public diplomacy efforts toward its own citizens. There were Congressional fears of the government propagandizing its own citizens.

ON THE JOB

global

Modifying Attitudes in South Africa

As a way to protest apartheid, some residents of Durban, South Africa, refused to pay taxes. With the coming of democracy, however, the Inner West City Council asked a marketing and public relations firm, Langa Shangase, Vulindleia, to devise an attitude modification campaign. The objective: to bring more than 17,500 homeowners to an understanding of how cities are financed and to expand the base of taxpayers.

The African concept of "ubuntu" was adopted to convey the benefits of developing a sense of communal belonging. "One City, One Tax Base" was a theme. Because of low literacy levels, campaign leaders focused on radio and face-to-face community meetings for message delivery.

Three months of research and development of trainers was followed by six months of implementation, during which the council received monthly feedback on key issues. In all, 22,600 people attended 630 community meetings. Leaders hailed not only the increase in tax payments but also the spirit of consultation and tolerance that pervaded the community.

The International Public Relations Association gave the campaign a Golden World Award for Excellence in Public Relations.

U.S. Firms Working for Foreign Governments

For fees ranging upward of $1 million per year, several hundred American public relations firms work in this country for other nations. In recent years, for example, Hill and Knowlton has represented Indonesia and Morocco; Burson-Marsteller has represented Argentina, Costa Rica, Hungary, and Russia (the latter mainly in trade fairs); and Ruder, Finn & Rotman has represented El Salvador, Israel, and Japan. Especially active in representing other nations is Doremus & Company, whose clients have included Egypt, Iran, Jordan, the Philippines, Saudi Arabia, and Tunisia.

In many cases, the objective is to influence U.S. foreign policy, generate tourism, create favorable public opinion about the country, or encourage trade. Table 19.1 shows a sampling of accounts reported by *O'Dwyer's Newsletter*.

The Countries' Goals.   What do these countries seek to accomplish? Burson-Marsteller's Carl Levin says that they pursue several goals, including:

- To advance political objectives
- To be counseled on the United States' probable reaction to the client government's projected action
- To advance the country's commercial interests—for example, sales in the United States, increased U.S. private investment, and tourism
- To assist in communications in English
- To counsel and help win understanding and support on a specific issue undermining the client's standing in the United States and the world community
- To help modify laws and regulations inhibiting the client's activities in the United States

Under the Foreign Agents Registration Act of 1938, all legal, political, fundraising, public relations, and lobbying consultants hired by foreign governments to work in the United States must register with the Department of Justice. They are required to file reports with the Attorney General listing all activities on behalf of a foreign principal, compensation received, and expenses incurred.

Action Programs.   Normally hired by an embassy after open bidding for the account, the firm first gathers detailed information about the client country, including

TABLE 19.1

Recent Accounts Handled by U.S. Firms		
CLIENT	**PUBLIC RELATIONS FIRM**	**CONTRACT**
Mexico Tourism Board	Burson-Marsteller	$4,500,000
Rwanda	Jefferson Waterman	$300,000
Ukraine	Barbour Griffith & Rogers	$720,000
Germany	Powell Tate/Weber-Shandwick	$660,000
Hong Kong	Burson-Marsteller	$500,000

past media coverage. Attitudes toward the country are ascertained both informally and through surveys.

The action program decided on will likely include the establishment of a national information bureau to provide facts and published statements of favorable opinion about the country. Appointments are made with key media people and other influential citizens, including educators, business leaders, and government officials. These people are often invited to visit the client country on expense-paid trips, although some news media people decline on ethical grounds. (Ethical questions will be discussed in more detail shortly.)

Gradually, through expert and persistent methods of persuasion and the expenditure of what may run into millions of dollars, critical public attitudes may be changed or reinforced. Success is difficult to judge.

Public relations firms have played a major role in the worldwide sales of state-owned enterprises (a process known as privatization) during the last decade. More than 2,700 such enterprises were transferred into private hands in more than 95 countries in a five-year period, according to the International Finance Corporation. Tens of thousands of companies were privatized in Eastern Europe. For example, Burson-Marsteller designed and implemented public education campaigns in Russia, Kazakstan, and Ukraine in support of market reform and privatization.

Problems and Rewards.   The toughest problems confronting the firm are often as follows:

- Deciding to represent a country, such as Zimbabwe or China, whose human rights violations may reflect adversely on the agency itself
- Persuading the heads of such a nation to alter some of its practices so that the favorable public image sought may reflect reality
- Convincing officials of a client country, which may totally control the flow of news internally, that the American press is independent from government control and that they should never expect coverage that is 100 percent favorable
- Deciding whether to represent a nation such as Belarus, in which the autocratic head the state, Aleksandr Lukashenko, has drastically reduced civil liberties and crushed any opposition.

Why, then, do these firms work for other governments? Perhaps even those that are unpopular? Said Burson-Marsteller's Carl Levin: "I do not think it is overreaching to state that in helping friendly foreign clients we also advance our national interests. And we help in ways that our government cannot." Black, Manafort, Stone & Kelly felt the same way, but dropped a $950,000 contract with an agency close to the Philippines president when President Reagan called on Marcos to resign. At the same time, Qorvis Communications represents Saudi Arabia (see the Insights box on page 531) and has earned about $20 million for its efforts. The account, however, has not been without controversy. Several senior officers of Qorvis resigned, according to newspaper reports, because they were uncomfortable working on the Saudi account.

Intervention Tactics.   Placing full-page advertisements in major papers such as *The Washington Post* and the *New York Times* is almost invariably the first action taken by agents of foreign governments in seeking to influence American public opinion during a crisis. Surveys have shown that a high percentage of the nation's lawmakers

ON THE JOB insights

Desert Kingdom Steps Up PR Efforts

Saudi Arabia has a public relations problem. Osama bin Laden was born there, 15 of the 19 hijackers that flew planes into the World Trade Center and the Pentagon were Saudi citizens, and it was only one of three nations that recognized the Taliban as the government of Afghanistan before U.S. forces toppled the regime.

All of this has caused the American media, government officials, and even the public to question the Saudi commitment to the War on Terrorism, let alone being a solid ally of the United States. American officials, for example, criticized the Saudi government for not fully cooperating in rounding up suspected terrorists within their own nation or providing information about the hijackers right after 9/11.

Consequently, the Saudi government has spent millions in the past several years on lobbying, advertising, and public relations in the United States to convince the American public of its "steadfast commitment" to fighting terrorism and being a strong ally of the U.S. for more than 60 years. Qorvis Communications, a Washington D.C. public relations and public affairs firm, has done the bulk of the Saudi government's outreach. In 2003, for example, the Saudi's paid the firm about $20 million for such efforts.

These efforts have included a number of activities such as handling all media inquiries, preparing news releases and media kits, and writing op-ed pieces to highlight the Kingdom's commitment to the war on terrorism. The firm

also prepares radio and print ads and writes letters on behalf of Saudi Arabia to members of Congress and White House officials. Qorvis also arranged for Adel Al-Jubeir, Saudi foreign advisor, to be interviewed on major television news and talk shows in the United States.

In a more recent effort, Qorvis placed radio ads in 19 U.S. cities after the 9/11 Commission reported that there was no evidence that the Saudi government supported Al-Qaeda. The ad campaign, according to Prince Saud Al-Faisal, the Kingdom's Minister of Foreign Affairs, was to "put to rest the false accusations that have cast fear and doubt over Saudi Arabia. For too long, Saudi Arabia stood morbidly accused of funding and support in terrorism."

and administrators read the *Post* before or soon after arriving in their offices. The *Times*, in particular, is read by opinion leaders throughout the country, and the advertisements gain important visibility, influencing editorial writers and others. Members of Congress often use these political statements in addresses to their colleagues and obtain permission to insert their remarks in the *Congressional Record*. The advertisements are generally followed by personal visits and telephone calls by foreign government agency people and their key supporters. Arrangements are made to place representatives on broadcast network and cable programs. Press conferences are arranged, and newsletters are hastily dispatched to media, government, and other leaders.

Some examples of recent campaigns include:

● The Republic of Kazakhstan placed full-paged ads in major American newspapers after its national elections to reinforce public perceptions that it was a democracy.

The ad's headline: "Today, Kazakhstan has another asset besides oil, gas and minerals. Democracy."

- The Armenian National Committee of America (ANCA) launched a major public relations and lobbying effort to have the U.S. government take Armenia off the list of nations that were considered a terrorist risk under new guidelines. Members of Congress were lobbied, and Armenian-Americans bombarded the White House with e-mail and faxes. Armenia was removed from the list.

- Hong Kong launched an extensive tourism and promotion campaign to attract tourists back to the city after the SARS outbreak that killed almost 300 people. Tourism dropped almost 70 percent in one year.

- Croatia, often perceived in a negative light because of the fighting in the 1990s between Serbs and Croats, launched a public relations and advertising effort to let investors and potential tourists know that it was a "normal country, a market economy, a democratic society, and a Mediterranean country."

- Zimbabwe's opposition group, Movement for Democratic Change (MDC), launched a global public relations and lobbying effort to gain wide international support for fresh elections and human rights reform in that nation.

- The American Jewish Committee, plus other Jewish groups, launched a $1 million television advertising campaign in the United States to "show Americans a side of Israel beyond the bloody conflict that dominates the news media while reinforcing its image as a democratic nation."

The Rise of NGOs

Hundreds of nongovernmental organizations (NGOs) depend on international support for their programs and causes. Such organizations as Greenpeace, Amnesty International, Doctors Without Borders, Oxfam, and a large number of groups opposed to globalization have been effective in getting their message out via the World Wide Web, e-mail, and demonstrations.

One study by StrategyOne, the research arm of Edelman Worldwide, showed that media coverage of such organizations more than doubled over a four-year period, and NGOs were perceived by the public to be more credible than the news media or corporations when it came to issues such as labor, health, and the environment.

Thought leaders, for example, trust NGOs more than government or corporations because they consider their motivation to be based on "morals" rather than "profit." Public Affairs Council president Doug Pinkham said the StrategyOne report should be taken as a "wake-up call" by large corporations that have failed to embrace greater social responsibility and transparency. Pinkham told *PRWeek*, "The next five to ten years will be challenging for companies that operate on a world stage with the rise of technologically enabled activism."

Indeed, there is increasing evidence that giant corporations are cooperating with activist NGOs to form more socially responsible policies. Citigroup, for example, adopted new policies to reduce habitat loss and climate change after the Rainforest Action Network (RAN) urged customers to cut up their Citicards and plastered the Internet with nasty jibes against named executives. NGOs and their influence were discussed in Chapter 17.

Public Relations Development in Other Nations

On a global basic, public relations as an occupation and a career has achieved its highest development in the industrialized nations of the world—the United States, Canada, Western Europe, and parts of Asia. It emerges more readily in nations that have multiparty political systems, considerable private ownership of business and industry, large-scale urbanization, and relatively high per capita income levels, which also impacts literacy and educational opportunities.

China has experienced explosive growth in public relations as it has become industrialized and embraced a relatively free market economy. As discussed in Chapter 1, the growth of public relations activity in China has been tremendous in the past decade. Public relations revenues for the past several years have experienced double-digit gains, and China is now the second largest market in Asia after Japan. The United States and other European nations began exporting their public relations expertise to the People's Republic of China during the mid-1980s. Hill & Knowlton, active in Asia for more than 30 years, began its Beijing operation in a hotel room with three U.S. expatriates and a locally hired employee. Today, almost every global public relations firm has a Beijing office to represent U.S. and European companies in the Chinese market.

Other nations, to varying degrees, also have developed larger and more sophisticated public relations industries within the past decade. Here are some thumbnail sketches from around the globe:

- **Thailand.** This nation has a great deal of foreign investment and is becoming an assembly center for automobiles. It's the primary hub in Southeast Asia for international tourism, and a number of public relations firms, advertising firms, and corporations have well-qualified staffs to handle media relations, product publicity, and special event promotion. However, it lacks a cohesive national organization of public relations practitioners that promotes professional development.

- **Japan.** Business and industry are still in the stage of perceiving public relations as primarily media relations. Public relations firms and corporate communications departments work very closely with the more than 400-plus reporters' clubs that filter and process all information for more than 150 newsgathering organizations. See page 534 for an ad by a Japanese public relations firm.

- **Australia, Singapore, and Hong Kong.** These are relatively mature public relations markets, offering a variety of services ranging from financial relations to media relations and special event promotions. More attention is given to overall strategic planning and integrating communications for overall corporate objectives.

- **Russian Federation and Former Republics.** The rise of a market economy and private enterprise has spurred the development of public relations activity, but the continuing stagnation of the Russian economy has stunted its development. The press and journalists are still very dependent on supplemental income, and news articles can still be "bought" without much effort.

- **Middle East.** The Middle East comprises 22 nations and more than 300 million people. In general, the public relations industry is relatively immature,

Public Relations:
The more chaotic the world,
the more essential our skills become.

Public relations is now an international enterprise and every country has its own industry. This ad is for a Japanese public relations firm.

Inoue Public Relations is a Japanese PR agency staffed by highly creative, bilingual professionals. We have over 33 years experience assisting overseas firms in communicating their messages and visions to a Japanese audience.

Inoue Public Relations is the first and only Asian recipient of IPRA's Golden World Award Grand Prize.

Our clients range from Fortune 500 market leaders to ambitious high-tech start-ups. With in-depth experience in all areas of communications, Inoue Public Relations can show you how best to take advantage of the many opportunities that lay ahead in Japan.

If you're looking for a top-rate public relations consultancy in Japan, look no further. Contact:

Inoue Public Relations
Since 1970

Homepage: www.inoue-pr.com
Email: info@inoue-pr.com or inouetak@inoue-pr.com

Shinjuku-gyoenmae Annex 6F
4-34, Yotsuya, Shinjuku-ku, Tokyo 160-0004, Japan

Tel (81) 3 5269-2301 Fax (81) 3 5269-2305

IPRA **FRONTLINE** 39

unstructured, and lacking in trained personnel. There is government-censored media and fear of transparent communications. Dubai, which is in the United Arab Emirates, in recent years has positioned itself as a major business center and has attracted many international companies. In such a situation, it's expected that public relations services will expand.

● **Africa.** South Africa is a relatively mature market with a long tradition of public relations education, professional development for practitioners, and large corporations with international outreach. Nigeria, the most populous nation in Africa, has made strides in developing its public relations industry.

● **Mexico.** Traditionally, small public relations firms dominated the market and provided primarily product publicity. With the North American Free Trade Agreement, international firms have established operations with more sophisticated approaches to strategic communications.

● **India.** The Indian market, with more than 1 billion people, is a major market for products, services, and public relations expertise. There are at least 1000 large and small public relations firms serving the subcontinent, but training and educating qualified practitioners continues to be a major problem.

● **Brazil.** This is the largest economy in South America, and there are about 1000 public relations firms in the country, primarily in the São Paulo area. To date, few global public relations firms have established a presence, primarily because Brazilian corporations still spend a disproportionate amount of their budgets on advertising campaigns. Issues management, public affairs, internal communications, and marketing communications are still somewhat undeveloped fields.

Opportunities in International Work

The 1990s, according to many experts, represented a new golden age of global marketing and public relations. The opening of the European Market, coupled with economic and social reforms in East European countries and the former Soviet Union hastened the reality of a global economy.

All of these developments led Jerry Dalton, past president of the PRSA, to say: "I think more and more American firms are going to become part of those overseas markets, and I expect a lot of Americans in public relations will be living overseas." Indeed, Dalton believes that the fastest-growing career field for practitioners is international public relations. He adds: "Students who can communicate well and are fluent in a foreign language may be able to write their own ticket." But the coming of the "global village," as Marshall McLuhan once described it, still means that there will be a multiplicity of languages, customs, and values that public relations professionals will have to understand.

Many transnational corporations, putting an increased emphasis on international customer relations, are hiring "corporate protocol" officers to be responsible for doing everything from booking hotels, planning banquets, and hiring limousines, to scheduling plant tours, arranging security, and selecting gifts for foreign officials and major customers. They even brief company executives on current events, advise on the correct protocol for greeting royalty, and "hand out sheet music for sing-alongs at Korean banquets," according to a *New York Times* article.

Its author, Paul Finney, says: "Corporations tend to fill their protocol jobs with people who have backgrounds in public relations, marketing, [and] meeting planning and who have a knowledge of the industry." Although knowledge of foreign languages is a plus, it is not a prerequisite. One protocol officer is quoted as saying, "At AT&T, we're dealing with over 100 countries. You can rent language skills—interpreters, translators—if you need them."

COMMUNICATIONS MANAGER, AMERICAS

Cathay Pacific Airways, Asia's premier international airline, is now seeking candidates to fill the position based in Los Angeles.

Responsibilities:
- Effectively communicate and generate goodwill with key organizations to positively affect their behavior, especially toward purchasing our company's products and services.
- Maintain and develop key media relationships. Coordinate interviews between influential media contacts and company's key personnel.
- Act as the company's spokesperson. Create and distribute press releases.
- Increase visibility of our company in N. America through special events and activities.
- Maintain good internal staff communications. Handle crisis communications effectively.
- Effectively keep our company's name in front of key publics through innovative and concentrated community support opportunities.
- Support the company's N. America Marketing & Sales initiatives.

Requirements:
- Minimum 5 years experience in Public Relations with important projects involved.
- Ability to communicate effectively at all levels with superior oral and written skills.
- College degree with strong PC knowledge.
- Superior independent work capability.
- Excellent decision-making, problem-solving, time management and organization skills. Must be detailed oriented.

We offer a unique package of benefits including attractive salary plus profit sharing; company sponsored insurance, travel benefits, pension & 401k option.

Forward resume immed to Personnel & Administration Manager via Fax 1-310-615-0042 or email: usa#personnel@cathaypacific.com.

There are a number of employment opportunities in international public relations. Here, Hong Kong–based Cathay Pacific seeks a communications manager for North America.

Gavin Anderson, chairman of Gavin Anderson & Company, which has several offices abroad, is an expert in international public relations. He writes:

Practitioners of either global or international public relations are cultural interpreters. They must understand the business and general culture of both their clients (or employers) and the country or countries in which they hope to do business. Whether as an outside or inhouse consultant, the first task is to tell a U.S. company going abroad (or a foreign party coming to the United States) how to get things done. How does the market work? What are the business habits? What is the infrastructure? The consultant also needs to understand how things work in the host country, to recognize what will need translation and adaptation . . .

The field needs practitioners with an interest in and knowledge of foreign cultures on top of top-notch public relations skills. They need a good sense of working environments, and while they may not have answers for every country, they should know what questions to ask and where to get the information needed. They need to know where the potential dangers are, so as to not replenish the business bloopers book.

The decision to seek an international career should be made during the early academic years, so that a student can take multiple courses in international relations, global marketing techniques, the basics of strategic public relations planning, foreign languages, social and economic geography, and cross-cultural communication. Graduate study is an asset. Many students serve internships with international corporations as a desirable starting point.

Taking the U.S. Foreign Service Officers' examination is the first requirement for international government careers. Foreign service work with the innumerable federal agencies often requires a substantial period of government, mass media, or public relations service in this country before foreign assignments are made.

SUMMARY

What Is International Public Relations?

Public relations now takes place on a global scale, with relationships being built with the publics of all nations. Although some elements of public relations were being practiced in Europe over a hundred years ago, American techniques are those most commonly adapted to use throughout the world.

International Corporate Public Relations

In the new age of global marketing, public relations firms represent foreign interests in the United States as well as the interests of American corporations around the world. This means that the practitioner must deal with issues of language and cultural differences, including subtle differences in customs and etiquette and even ethical dilemmas involving bribery.

International Government Public Relations

Most governments seek to influence the international policies of other countries as well as the opinions and actions of the public. These communications can range from promoting tourism to attempts to influence trade policies. The U.S. government refers to its international information effort as "public diplomacy," the attempt to enhance understanding of our culture and promote our foreign policy objectives. The Voice of America radio broadcasts are part of this program. There are also U.S. public relations firms working for foreign governments, helping them advance their political objectives and commercial interests, counseling them on probable U.S. reactions to their proposed actions, and assisting in communications in English.

The Rise of NGOs

Among nongovernmental organizations depending on international support for their causes are Greenpeace, Amnesty International, Doctors Without Borders, Oxfam, and the International Red Cross. Such organizations are widely believed to be more credible than the news media on such issues as labor, health, and the environment, partly because they are perceived to lack the self-interest ascribed to governments and corporations.

Foreign Public Relations Organizations

Public relations practitioners have formed organizations wherever their work has flourished, hoping to exchange information, maintain and improve professional and ethical standards, and aid in the development of their work.

Opportunities in International Work

As global marketing and communications have expanded in recent years, so too have opportunities for international public relations work. Fluency in foreign language is a valued skill but not a prerequisite; also important are backgrounds in international relations, global marketing techniques, social and economic geography, and cross-cultural communication.

Case Activity: **What Would You Do?**

The killer waves of the tsunami that hit 11 nations around the Indian Ocean in late December 2004 did more than kill an estimated 155,000 people, including more than 6,000 foreign tourists. It also caused significant damage to the thriving tourism industry of such nations as Thailand, Indonesia, Sri Lanka, and the Maldives. In Thailand alone, the Phuket Tourist Association estimated that the falloff of tourism during the high season of January and February cost the local economy about $500 million.

Hotels and beaches, once crowded, are now deserted. International news coverage focused on the death and destruction but, in most cases, didn't mention the fact that most hotels and tourist attractions remained intact. In Phuket, for example, only 5,000 of

Phuket Island's 35,000 rooms were lost. Reconstruction work has proceeded rapidly, but tourist officials still worry that it will take years to restore tourism to its pre-tsunami levels.

About 100 tourism officials, government ministers, and travel association representatives from the affected nations met in Thailand and declared, "Our aim is to ensure that the tourism sector emerges from this disaster stronger and more resilient than before." What would you recommend for an integrated international public relations, marketing, and promotion campaign to restore the area's reputation as a tourist mecca?

QUESTIONS for Review and Discussion

1. What is meant by international public relations? What are some of the reasons for its growth in recent decades?

2. How does public relations fit into the mix of global marketing operations?

3. What are some of the difficulties that a corporation is likely to encounter when it conducts business in another country?

4. What objectives do foreign nations seek to accomplish by hiring U.S. public relations firms to represent them in America?

5. Describe the efforts of the U.S. government to win the "hearts and minds" of citizens in other nations.

6. The U.S. government conducted an extensive program of "public diplomacy" as part of the War on Terrorism. Do you think it was effective? Why or why not? What suggestions do you have for U.S. public diplomacy efforts?

7. What is the Russian practice of *zakazukhi?* Why does the IPRA consider it a bad practice?

8. Why is Israel worried about its image in the United States and other nations?

9. International public relations requires knowledge of a nation's history and political sensitivities. What kinds of things should you know if you were going to practice public relations in the People's Republic of China?

10. What kinds of ethical dilemmas do public relations firms face when they are asked to do work for a particular nation?

11. What does the abbreviation "NGO" mean? How has the new information technology enabled NGOs to expand their influence?

12. What opportunities exist for someone who wants to specialize in international public relations as a career?

SUGGESTED READINGS

Badler, Dick. "10 Rules for Building a Successful Global Corporate Communications Organization." *The Strategist*, Winter 2004, pp. 18–21.

DeLange, Rob. "Public Affairs Practitioners in the Netherlands: A Profile Study." *Public Relations Review*, Vol. 26, No. 1, 2000, pp. 15–29.

Drobis, David R. "The New Global Imperative for Public Relations." *O'Dwyer's PR Services Report*, January 2002, pp. 8, 26–28.

Dyson, Tim. "Global PR: A World of Difference." *IPRA Frontline*, June 2003, pp. 23–26.

Freitag, Alan R. "Ascending Cultural Competence Potential: An Assessment and Profile of U.S. Public Relations Practitioners' Preparation for International Assignments." *Journal of Public Relations Research*, Vol. 14, No. 3, 2002, pp. 207–227.

Gorman, Carol Kinsey. "Cross-Cultural Business Practices." *Communication World*, February–March 2002, pp. 22–24.

Holtzhausen, Derina R., and Peterson, Barbara, K. "Exploding the Myth of the Symmetrical/Asymmetrical Dichotomy: Public Relations Models in the New South Africa." *Journal of Public Relations Research*, Vol. 15, No. 4, 2003, pp. 305–341.

Hood, Julia. "U.S. Companies Need to Be Locally Minded Overseas." *PRWeek*, February 23, 2003, p. 9.

Kelly, William, Masumoto, Tomoko, and Gibson, Dirk. "Kisha Kurabu and Koho: Japanese Media Relations and Public Relations." *Public Relations Review*, Vol. 28, No. 3, No. 3, pp. 265–281.

Marqis, Christopher. "Efforts to Promote U.S. Falls Short, Critics Say." *New York Times*, December 29, 2003, p. A6.

Mateas, Margo M. "Spotlight on Diversity: Managing Diversity in Virtual Teams across the Globe." *Public Relations Tactics*, Vol. 11, No. 8, 2004, p. 20.

Paluszek, John. "How Do We Fit Into The World?" *The Strategist*, Winter 2004, pp. 6–11.

Rendon, Jim. "When Nations Need a Little Marketing." *New York Times*, November 23, 2003, Business section, p. 5.

Stateman, Alison. "From Canada to Bosnia: The Life of a Foreign Service Officer." *Public Relations Tactics*, June 2003, p. 12.

"Living with the Enemy: Non-governmental Organizations and Business." *Economist*, August 9, 2003, pp. 49–50.

Taylor, Maureen. "Exploring Public Relations in Croatia Through Relational Communication and Media Richness Theories." *Public Relations Review*, Vol. 30, No. 2, 2004, pp. 145–160.

Watson, David R., and Sallot, Lynne M. "Public Relations Practice in Japan: An Exploratory Study." *Public Relations Review*, Vol. 27, No. 4, 2001, pp. 389–402.

Zhang, Juyan, and Benoit, William L. "Message Strategies of Saudi Arabia's Image Restoration Campaign after 9/11." *Public Relations Review*, Vol. 30, No. 2, pp. 161–167.

chapter 20

Nonprofit Organizations

Topics covered in this chapter include:

The Role of Public Relations

A broad area of public relations work, and the source of many jobs, is the nonprofit organization. The range of nonprofit institutions is astounding, from small city historical societies to gigantic international foundations that disperse million-dollar grants.

The crucial point about nonprofit organizations is that they are tax exempt. The federal government grants them this status because they enhance the well-being of their members, as with trade associations, or enhance the human condition in some way, as with environmental work or medical research. Many nonprofit organizations could not survive if they were taxed, because they face the unending public relations task of raising money to pay their expenses and finance their projects.

Basic Needs of Nonprofits

Mothers Against Drunk Driving (MADD) seems to have little in common with the American Red Cross or the National Academy of songwriters, yet all three engage in the same types of tasks in order to succeed:

- All three create communication campaigns and programs such as special events, Internet Web sites, brochures, and radio and television appearances that stimulate public interest in organizational goals and invite public participation.
- They develop a strong staff to handle the work. Recruiting volunteers and keeping them enthusiastic are essential.
- These organizations establish a realistic fund-raising goal and a plan to attain it.

The significance of these factors will become evident as we examine the various types of nonprofit organizations. For convenience, such organizations can be grouped roughly as membership groups, advocacy agencies, or social organizations.

Membership Organizations

A membership organization consists of people with a common interest, in either business or social life. The purpose of a membership organization is mutual help and self-improvement. These organizations often use the strength of their common bond to improve community welfare, endorse legislation, and support socially valuable causes.

Trade Associations

At last count, there were about 6,000 trade and professional associations in the United States. Because federal laws and regulations often can affect the fortunes of an entire industry, about one-third of these groups are based in the Washington, D.C., area. There, association staffs can monitor congressional activity, lobby for or against legislation, communicate late-breaking developments to the membership, and see government officials on a regular basis.

The membership of a trade association usually consists of manufacturers, wholesalers, retailers, or distributors in the same field. Memberships are held by corporate entities, not individuals. The following are a few examples of trade associations:

- Electronic Industries Association
- National Soft Drink Association
- National Association of Home Builders

Although individual members may be direct rivals in the marketplace, they work together to promote the entire industry, generate public support, and share information of general interest to the entire membership.

By representing its entire industry, an association often is more effective as a news source than is an individual company. When a news situation develops involving a particular field, reporters often turn to the spokesperson of its association for comment.

Labor Unions

Since the mid-1970s, labor unions in the United States have suffered serious losses in membership, and consequently in political clout. The United Auto Workers, for example, saw membership fall from 1.5 million in 1979 to approximately 700,000 in 2004. The perception of unions as money hungry, inflexible, lacking in concern for the public interest, and at times arrogant created a severe image problem. Media coverage often showed union members in negative, adversarial positions that sometimes inconvenienced the public.

Today, total union membership amounts to less than 15 percent of all American workers, with the figure dropping to about 10 percent in the private sector.

Nevertheless, labor unions still are very much a part of the American scene, from players in the National Basketball Association to UPS employees scurrying with deliveries in our communities. The union movement is relying on public relations tools to regain strength and influence. Unions must seek to build their memberships, protect members' job security, and improve their public images.

In every national political campaign, unions spend millions of dollars in support of candidates they regard as friendly. Some of this money goes directly to candidates, but significant amounts are devoted to "issue ads" that do not explicitly endorse an individual. This questionable practice enables support of candidates beyond individual campaign spending limits; probusiness organizations counter with their own issue ads. Significant sums of union money also are spent on lobbying efforts. In one six-month period, the AFL-CIO spent $1.4 million on lobbying.

Like corporations, union managements employ public relations when communicating with their internal audiences. They must keep their memberships informed about what they receive in return for their dues, including social and recreational programs and the representation to company management that the union leadership supplies.

Professional Associations

Members of a profession or skilled craft organize for mutual benefit. In many ways, their goals resemble those of labor unions in that they seek improved earning power, better working conditions, and public acceptance of their role in society. Because professional organizations do not engage in collective bargaining between employers and employees as labor unions do, they instead place their major emphasis on setting standards for professional performance, establishing codes of ethics, determining requirements for admission to the field, and encouraging members to upgrade skills through continuing education. In some cases, professional organizations have quasi-legal power to license and censure members. In most cases, however, professional groups use the techniques of peer pressure and persuasion to police their membership.

In general, professional associations are national in scope with district, state, or local chapters. Many scientific and scholarly associations, however, are international, with chapters in many nations. Organizations such as the Public Relations Society of America (PRSA) and the International Association of Business Communicators (IABC) are classified as professional associations.

Public relations specialists for professional organizations use the same techniques as their colleagues in other branches of practice. And like their counterparts in trade groups and labor unions, many professional associations maintain a Washington office or one in the state capital and employ lobbyists to advocate positions. One of the most politically active groups is the American Medical Association (AMA).

The lobbying power exercised in Washington by major professional associations is especially evident in the efforts of the AMA. With 220,000 physician members, the AMA has developed a grassroots effort to apply both public and backstage pressures to shape medical liability reform, also called "tort reform," in Congress to the association's advantage. The AMA argues that medical liability settlements are excessive. The AMA provides a Physician Action Kit, expert testimony to Congress, talking points for members to use when speaking about medical liability reform, and a paper confronting the myths of medical liability reform in addition to sponsoring letter-writing campaigns.

Public relations activity on behalf of individual professionals is a relatively new development. Traditionally, lawyers and medical doctors did not advertise or seek to publicize themselves in any way. The taboo arose in part from the rules and regulations of the professional societies. Until recently, many medical societies prohibited their members from hiring public relations firms. The Supreme Court, in several cases, however, said that such regulations infringed on free speech. And the Federal Trade Commission ruled in 1980 that the American Medical Association couldn't tell its members not to advertise.

Many attorneys and physicians still feel uncomfortable about advertising their services, but competition for clients and patients is breaking down the traditional taboos. A survey by *Attorneys Marketing Report*, for example, shows the majority of lawyers using Yellow Pages advertising. In descending order of frequency, they also use (1) entertainment of clients, (2) brochures, (3) seminars, and (4) newsletters. With the rise of general practitioners promoting their services for elective procedures such as laser removal of hair or dark blemishes as a supplemental revenue stream, the competitive market will most likely mean even more public relations activity for professionals.

The *Wall Street Journal* observed another trend: "Medical associations are also hiring public relations firms to publicize new or controversial techniques. 'Fat suctioning' was the focus of a press briefing publicized by Doremus & Co. for the American Society of Plastic and Reconstructive Surgeons."

ON THE JOB

insights

Web-Based Techniques for Grassroots Campaigns

Advocacy groups often operate on limited budgets and volunteer efforts. Here are some of the ways that the Web can be a powerful tool to leverage limited resources in public relations:

- Facilitate communication among members through online notices, instant messaging, and chat rooms.
- Educate the general audience about an issue and the advocacy group's stance.
- Generate letters to officials by providing downloadable text, mail and e-mail addresses, and fax numbers.
- Provide an automated method in five mouse clicks for sending a form letter to officials.
- Solicit feedback, volunteer support, and campaign ideas.
- Identify frequent questions to refine message strategies for greater clarity.
- Conduct content analysis of questions, comments, and chat transcripts for strategic plan refinement.

Chambers of Commerce

A *chamber* is an association of businesspersons, often joined by professionals, who work to improve their city's commercial climate and to publicize its attractions. State chambers of commerce and, nationally, the Chamber of Commerce of the United States provide guidance to local chambers and speak for business interests before state legislatures and the federal government.

Often, the chamber of commerce is the public relations arm of city government. The chamber staff often produces the brochures and maps sent to individuals who seek information about visiting the city or who are considering moving to the area. Chambers also conduct polls and compile statistics about the economic health of the city, including data on major industries, employment rates, availability of schools and hospitals, housing costs, and so on. Attracting conventions and new businesses to the city also is an important part of chamber work.

Chambers of commerce play the role of community booster: They spotlight the unique characteristics of a city and sing its praises to anyone who will listen. Chambers often coin a slogan for a city, such as "Furniture Capital of Indiana." Chambers tend to be boosters of business growth.

Advocacy Groups

The environment holds a high place on the public agenda, primarily because of vigorous campaigns by environmental organizations. By promoting recycling, eliminating toxic waste sites, purifying the air and water, and preserving natural resources, such organizations strongly influence our collective conscience. Organizations that fight for social causes also achieve significant impact, both positive and negative.

Some of these organizations work relatively quietly through lobbying, litigation, and public education. Others are stridently confrontational.

Environmental Groups

Greenpeace, an organization that operates in 30 countries, including the United States, with 5 million members, is perhaps the best known of the confrontational groups. Television viewers are familiar with the daredevil efforts of some members in small boats to stop nuclear warships and other vessels they regard as harmful to the public.

Recently contributions to Greenpeace have declined; so has the group's political influence. In total membership, Greenpeace is second to the much less flamboyant National Wildlife Foundation, followed by the Sierra Club and the Nature Conservancy.

The principal ways that environmental organizations work to achieve their goals are lobbying, litigation, mass demonstrations, boycotts, and reconciliation.

Other Activist Groups

The work of major organizations that receive frequent national attention is illustrative of intense efforts by relatively less prominent associations as well. The National Rifle Association influences Congress and state legislatures through lobbying and campaign contributions. The American Tobacco Institute fights hard to defeat laws limiting smoking by adults. The Christian Coalition fights abortion with public statements, mailings, and telephone calls, and works through the right wing of the Republican Party. Christian church denominations sometimes adopt an activist role. The Southern Baptist Convention mounted a boycott of Disney corporation and all of its subsidiaries in protest of sex and violence in Disney entertainment productions. The boycott was also motivated by "gay days" at Disney's theme parks.

ON THE JOB

global

Environmental Issues Prompt Planetary Perspective

Because environmental issues often have global implications, groups such as Greenpeace enjoy global membership and operate in many countries. Although most ecosystems span national boundaries, and pollution of the environment respects no border, some issues are naturally defined as truly global concerns. Greenpeace took on Atlantic Richfield for its oil exploration in the Arctic National Wildlife Refuge.

A Greenpeace advocacy advertisement in the *New York Times* depicted an offshore oil rig, citing it as a threat to life in the refuge. The ad maintained that the "real problem" was global warming, pointing out that exploration for new oil reserves postpones the shift from fossil fuels to renewable energy sources. The ad ended on a global note: "If you plan to live on this planet for the foreseeable future, it's your fight, too."

Methods of Operation

The principal ways in which advocacy groups work to achieve their goals include:

● **Lobbying.** Much of this is done at state and local government levels, because environmental problems often can be resolved there. For example, approximately 150 organizations campaigned for laws to forbid smoking in public places and to restrict the sale of tobacco. The campaign has had numerous successes.

● **Litigation.** Through litigation, organizations file suits seeking court rulings favorable to their projects or attempting to block unfavorable projects. The Sierra Club did so in a years-long action that resulted in a decision by the U.S. Fish and Wildlife Service declaring the northern spotted owl a threatened species. The American Horse Council contends against changes in insurance laws that would discourage many horse enthusiasts who would not be covered in the event of a horse-related accident.

● **Mass demonstrations.** Designed to demonstrate public support for a cause and in some cases to harass the operators of projects to which the groups object, mass demonstrations require intricate public relations organizational work. Organizers must obtain permits, inform the media, and arrange transportation, housing, programs, and crowd control. A mass demonstration of farmers dependent upon irrigation water from drought-threatened rivers in Klamath Falls, Oregon, culminated with the arrival on a truck trailer of a gigantic metal pail, the symbol of the grassroots movement.

● **Boycotts.** "Hit them in the pocketbook" is the principle underlying use of the boycott to achieve a goal. Some boycotts achieve easily identifiable results. Others stay in effect for years with little evident success. One environmental success story occurred when the Rainforest Action Network boycotted Burger King for buying Central American beef raised in cleared rain forests. The fast-food chain agreed to stop such purchases. See Chapter 17 for more information on consumer boycotts and their effectiveness.

● **Reconciliation.** Some environmental organizations find good results by cooperating with corporations to solve pollution problems. The Environmental Defense Fund joined a task force with McDonald's to deal with the fast-food chain's solid waste problem, leading to a company decision to phase out its polystyrene packaging.

ON THE JOB ethics

Working within the System or Selling Out?

Since the 1950s, Americans have joined in events organized by the environmental group Keep America Beautiful (KAB) to clean up neighborhoods and towns. Many also may recall the evocative image of the Native American chief who cries over the abuse of our land. The ad continues to appear as a classic public service announcement.

But the group has its detractors. According to *O'Dwyer's PR Services Report*, KAB includes among its major donors both Anheuser-Busch and Coca-Cola, "whose bottles and cans most clutter parks and waterfronts in

the first place." KAB's antigraffiti campaign is sponsored by the Sherwin-Williams paint company. Competing environmental groups say KAB was formed to oppose bottle bill legislation to require recycling of beverage containers, with KAB favoring individual responsibility and community initiative over mandatory recycling.

KAB responds that there is nothing wrong with corporations acting in their own enlightened self-interest by supporting the quiet, constructive work of environmental groups. A KAB spokesperson dismisses the crit-

ics this way: ". . . if you're not jumping off a smokestack or lying in front of a bulldozer, then you're part of a crooked establishment."

Where do you stand regarding KAB?

Should KAB take sponsorship money from companies that could be part of the problem in the first place?

Do you think a proactive approach that minimizes protest is the way to go for environmental groups?

How would the contingency theory covered in Chapter 10 apply to developing your stance if you were KAB?

Fund-Raising

Direct mail fund-raising and publicity campaigns are basic tools of advocacy groups. Raising money to conduct their programs is an unending and costly problem for them. In the 1990s, Greenpeace sent out 4.5 million pieces of mail a month for this purpose. With so many groups in the field, competition for donations is intense. Some professional fund-raisers believe that as a whole, the groups depend too much on direct mail and should place more emphasis on face-to-face solicitation. Ironically, while some environmental groups advocate preservation of forests, they also create mountains of waste paper by sending millions of "junk mail" letters to raise funds for their organization.

Social Issue Organizations

Several other widely known organizations are similar to the environmental groups in structure, but with social and behavioral goals. They use public relations methods such as those just described.

Mothers Against Drunk Driving (MADD) is one such group. The antiabortion Right to Life movement and the prochoice National Organization for Women (NOW), bitter enemies, frequently clash in rival public demonstrations. Animal rights groups such as People for the Ethical Treatment of Animals (PETA) at times resort to extreme confrontational tactics such as raiding animal research laboratories and seeking to shame the wearers of fur. The group's campaign against the dairy industry takes a different tack—humor and parody—on the Web site at www.milksucks.com.

Other groups, such as the American Family Association, pressure advertisers to drop sponsorship of television shows that they consider contrary to family values. As a result of massive letter campaigns by this group, Coca-Cola and Procter & Gamble decided to cancel commercials on objectionable programs. Members of the AFA also pressured Pepsi into canceling its Madonna ads after seeing the star's video clip for her song "Like a Prayer." Kansas Action for Children, a child advocacy group in Topeka, Kansas, provides an exhaustive databook as well as a report card to assess child well-being in the state. The grades and the data influence policy and legislation concerning children and teens.

Social Organizations

The term "social" includes social service, health, cultural, philanthropic, and religious groups serving the public in their various ways. Because communication is essential for their success, they require active, creative public relations programs.

Because these organizations are not profit oriented, the practice of public relations on their behalf differs somewhat from that in the business world. Traditionally, nonprofit social agencies have been seen as the "good guys" of society—high-minded, compassionate organizations whose members work to help people achieve a better life. Recently, that perception has changed in some cases.

Numerous agencies have been caught by the recent American urge to scrutinize all aspects of the government and social establishment. Famous organizations usually regarded as sacrosanct have found themselves in trouble. The Girl Scouts of America was accused of having such heavy overhead expense for its annual national cookie sale that the girls themselves received little direct benefit. The Boy Scouts of America ran into difficulty for barring homosexuals from membership. Nevertheless, a national survey of 2,553 U.S. citizens by the D.C.-based Independent Sector found high confidence in

Mothers Against Drunk Driving (MADD) urges people who have been drinking to call a friend or a cab to take them home. This poster, with its succinct headline, delivers the message in a graphic manner.

the efficiency and effectiveness of charitable organizations.

For many nonprofit groups, obtaining operating funds is a necessity that dominates much of their effort. Without generous contributions from companies and individuals whose money is earned in the marketplace, nonprofit organizations could not exist. As an indication of the scope of philanthropy in the United States, and of the money needed to keep voluntary service agencies operating, American contributions to charity were $240.72 billion in 2003, according to the American Association of Fund-Raising Counsel (see Figure 20.1). Additional funds are donated to specialized nonprofit organizations that do not fall under the "charity" mantle, and still more are contributed by federal, state, and local governments. Competition among nonprofit agencies for their share of donations is intense.

In general terms, nonprofit social organizations are of two types: services, typified nationally by the Visiting Nurse Association and the Boys Clubs of America; and causes, whose advocacy role is exemplified by the National Safety Council and the National Association for the Advancement of Colored People (NAACP). Organizations frequently have dual roles, both service and advocacy.

Categories of Social Agencies

For purposes of identification, nonprofit social organizations and their functions may be grouped into seven categories:

1. Social service agencies. These organizations serve the social needs of individuals and families in many forms. Among prominent national organizations of this type are Goodwill Industries, the American Red Cross, the Boy Scouts and Girl Scouts of America, and the YMCA. Local chapters carry out national programs. Ser-

FIGURE 20.1

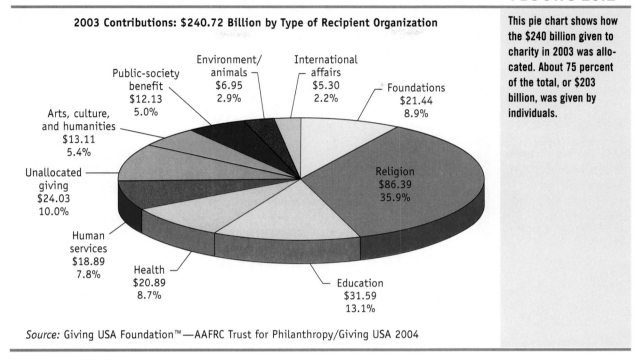

2003 Contributions: $240.72 Billion by Type of Recipient Organization

Public-society benefit $12.13 5.0%

Environment/ animals $6.95 2.9%

International affairs $5.30 2.2%

Foundations $21.44 8.9%

Arts, culture, and humanities $13.11 5.4%

Unallocated giving $24.03 10.0%

Religion $86.39 35.9%

Human services $18.89 7.8%

Health $20.89 8.7%

Education $31.59 13.1%

Source: Giving USA Foundation™—AAFRC Trust for Philanthropy/Giving USA 2004

This pie chart shows how the $240 billion given to charity in 2003 was allocated. About 75 percent of the total, or $203 billion, was given by individuals.

vice clubs such as the Rotary, the Kiwanis, the Lions, and the Exchange Club also raise significant amounts of money for charitable projects.

2. Health agencies. Many health agencies combat a specific illness through education, research, and treatment, whereas others deliver generalized health services in communities. Typical national organizations include the American Heart Association, the American Cancer Society, and the National Multiple Sclerosis Society.

3. Hospitals. Public relations work for hospitals is a large and expanding field. The role of hospitals has taken on new dimensions. In addition to caring for ill and injured patients, hospitals conduct preventive health programs and provide other health-related social services that go well beyond the traditional institutional concept. Hospitals may be tax-supported institutions, nonprofit organizations, or profit-making corporations.

4. Religious organizations. The mission of organized religion, as perceived by many faiths today, includes much more than holding weekly worship services and underwriting parochial schools. Churches distribute charity, conduct personal guidance programs, provide leadership on moral and ethical issues in their communities, and operate social centers where diverse groups gather. Some denominations operate retirement homes and nursing facilities for the elderly. At times, religious organizations assume political roles to further their goals. The nondenominational Salvation Army provides the needy with shelter, food, and clothing. It has a vigorous public relations program to earn its place at the top of the fund-raising ranks.

A recent study by the Brookings Institution, titled "Fiscal Capacity of the Voluntary Sector," stated in this regard: "Because religion occupies a stable, central role in

Stop Disease
SOAP
Alto a las enfermedades
막으십시오 질병을
Ngừa Bệnh
病気撲滅
Pigilan ang Sakit
防止疾病
California Department of Health Services, Division of Communicable Disease Control
IMM-780 (12/03)

Health agencies, in order to reach everyone, often distribute posters and information in several languages. They also use simple symbols to communicate with individuals who are illiterate.

American life, religious institutions will be looked to as a backup finance and delivery mechanism by other subsectors . . . particularly . . . in the human service field."

5. Welfare agencies. Most continuing welfare payments to persons in need are made by government agencies, using tax-generated funds. Public information officers of these agencies have the important functions of making certain that those entitled to the services know about them and improving public understanding of how the services function.

6. Cultural organizations. Development of interest and participation in the cultural aspects of life falls heavily into the hands of nonprofit organizations. So, in many instances, does the operation of libraries; musical organizations, such as symphony orchestras; and museums of art, history, and natural science. Such institutions frequently receive at least part of their income from government sources; many are operated by governments. Even government-operated cultural institutions depend on privately supported organizations such as Friends of the Museum to raise supplementary funds.

7. Foundations. The hundreds of tax-free foundations in the United States constitute about 9 percent of total charitable giving. Money to establish a foundation is provided by a wealthy individual or family, a group of contributors, an organization, or a corporation. The foundation's capital is invested, and earnings from the investments are distributed as grants to qualified applicants.

The public knows about such mammoth national organizations as the Ford Foundation, the Rockefeller Foundation, and the Annenberg Foundation. Many are probably not aware, however, of many smaller foundations, some of them extremely

The Advertising Council often produces ads as a public service for national groups such as the American Cancer Society. This ad raises public awareness of colon cancer.

important in their specialized fields, that distribute funds for research, education, public performances, displays, and similar purposes.

Giving away money constructively is more difficult than most people realize. Again, public relations representation has a significant role. The requirements of a foundation must be made known to potential applicants for grants. Inquiries must be handled and announcements of grants made.

This summary shows the many diverse, personally satisfying opportunities that are available to public relations practitioners in the social agency fields.

Public Relations Goals

Every voluntary agency should establish a set of public relations goals. When doing so, its management should heed the advice of its public relations staff members, for they are trained to sense public moods and ultimately are responsible for achieving the goals. Emphasis on goals will vary, depending on the purpose of each organization. In general, however, nonprofit organizations should design their public relations to achieve the following objectives:

- Develop public awareness of the organization's purpose and activities.
- Induce individuals to use the services the organization provides.
- Create educational materials—especially important for health-oriented agencies.
- Recruit and train volunteer workers.
- Obtain funds to operate the organization.

The sections that follow discuss ways in which each of these goals can be pursued.

Public Awareness. The news media provide well-organized channels for stimulating public interest in nonprofit organizations and are receptive to newsworthy

Social service agencies often provide the logistics and the volunteers when there is a community disaster. Here, a rescue worker works in a bucket line in New York to remove rubble from ground zero at the World Trade Center.

material from them. Newspapers usually publish advance stories about meetings, training sessions, and similar routine activities. Beyond that, much depends upon the ingenuity of the public relations practitioner in proposing feature articles and photographs. Television and radio stations will broadcast important news items about organizations and are receptive to feature stories and guest appearances by organization representatives. Stories about activities are best told in terms of individuals, rather than in high-flown abstractions. Practitioners should look for unusual or appealing personal stories, such as a retired teacher helping Asian refugee children to learn English.

Creation of events that make news and attract crowds is another way to increase public awareness. Such activities might include an open house in a new hospital wing or a concert by members of the local symphony orchestra for an audience of blind children.

Novelty stunts sometimes draw attention to a cause greater than their intrinsic value seems to justify. For example, a bed race around the parking lot of a shopping center by teams of students at the local university who are conducting a campus fund drive for the March of Dimes could be fun. It would draw almost certain local television coverage and raise money, too.

Very serious, dramatic messages also can be widely dispersed by staging an event made for television coverage. A North Carolina sheriff was saddened and frustrated by the number of unwanted animals put to death in his county animal shelter. He arranged for telecast of the euthanasia death of a 35-pound collie mix during his local public affairs show, *Sheriff's Beat*. Response was tremendous in the area, with adoptions up 300 percent and markedly increased spaying/neutering by local veterinarians. The story garnered national coverage as well, raising awareness across the nation of the need to control dog and cat reproduction.

Publication and distribution of brochures explaining an organization's objectives, operation of a speaker's bureau, showings of films provided by general headquarters of national nonprofit organizations, and periodic news bulletins distributed to opinion leaders are quiet but effective ways of telling an organization's story.

Use of Services.   Closely tied to creation of public awareness is the problem of inducing individuals and families to use an organization's services. Free medical examinations, free clothing and food to the urgently needy, family counseling, nursing service for shut-ins, cultural programs at museums and libraries, offers of scholarships—all of these and many other services provided by nonprofit organizations cannot achieve their full value unless potential users know about them.

Because of shyness or embarrassment, persons who would benefit from available services sometimes hesitate to use them. Written and spoken material designed to attract these persons should emphasize the ease of participation and, in matters of health, family, and financial aid, the privacy of the consultations. The American Cancer Society's widely publicized warning list of cancer danger signals is an example of this approach.

Creation of Educational Materials.   Public relations representatives of nonprofit organizations spend a substantial portion of their time preparing written and audiovisual materials. These are basic to almost any organization's program.

The quickest way to inform a person about an organization is to hand out a brochure. Brochures provide a first impression. They should be visually appealing and contain basic information, simply written. The writer should answer a reader's obvious questions: What does the organization do? What are its facilities? What services does it offer me? How do I go about participating in its activities and services? The brochure should contain a concise history of the organization and attractive illustrations. When appropriate, it may include a membership application form or a coupon to accompany a donation. Videotapes also are very effective as introductory tools.

Organizations may design logos, or symbols, that help them keep their activities in the public eye. Another basic piece of printed material is a news bulletin, usually monthly or quarterly, mailed to members, the news media, and perhaps to a carefully composed list of other interested parties. This bulletin may range from a single duplicated sheet to an elaborately printed magazine. A source of public relations support for national philanthropic organizations is the Advertising Council. This is a not-for-profit association of advertising professionals who volunteer their creative and technical skills for organizations. The council handles more than 30 public service campaigns a year for nonsectarian, nonpartisan organizations, chosen from 300 to 500 annual requests. Newspapers and radio and television stations publish or broadcast free of charge the advertisements the Council sends them.

One of the best ways to tell an organization's story succinctly and impressively is with an audiovisual package. This may be a slide show or a video, usually lasting about 20 minutes, to be shown to community audiences and/or on a continuing basis in the organization's building.

Volunteer Workers.   A corps of volunteer workers is essential to the success of almost every philanthropic enterprise. Far more work needs to be done than a necessarily small professional staff can accomplish. Recruiting and training volunteers and maintaining their enthusiasm so they will be dependable long-term workers are important public relations functions. Organizations usually have a chairperson of volunteers, who works with the public relations (often called community relations) director.

The statistics are impressive. One in five American adults volunteers time for charitable causes, according to a Bureau of Labor Statistics survey. The median weekly time volunteers contribute is slightly more than four hours. Yet the demand for more volunteers is intense.

What motivates people to volunteer? The sense of making a personal contribution to society is a primary factor. Volunteer work can fill a void in the life of an individual who no longer has business or family responsibilities. It also provides social contacts. Why does a former business leader living in a retirement community join a squad of former corporate executives who patrol its streets and public places each Monday, picking up wastepaper? The answer is twofold: pride in making a contribution to local well-being and satisfaction in having a structured activity that partially replaces a former business routine. For the same reasons, the retired executive spends another day each week as a hospital volunteer. These motives are basic to such volunteerism.

Social prestige plays a role, too. Appearing as a model in a fashion show that raises funds for scholarships carries a social cachet. So does selling tickets for a debutante ball, the profits from which go to the American Cancer Society. Serving as a docent, or guide, at a historical museum also attracts individuals who enjoy being seen in a prestigious setting. Yet persons who do well at these valuable jobs might be unwilling

Massive rallies often are held by non-profit groups to call the nation's attention to a particular issue or problem. Here, actors Camryn Manheim, Cybill Shepherd, Whoopi Goldberg, and Ashley Judd lend their celebrity status to an abortion-rights rally in Washington, D.C.

to stuff envelopes for a charity solicitation or spend hours in a back room sorting and mending used clothing for resale in a community thrift shop—jobs that are equally important. Such tasks can be assigned to those volunteers who enjoy working inconspicuously and dread meeting the public. Religious commitment is another powerful motivating force for volunteers.

Retirees Make Excellent Volunteers. Retired men and women, who are increasing in number, form an excellent source of volunteers. The Retired Senior Volunteers Program (RSVP) operates 750 projects nationwide, staffing them from its membership of 365,000. The largest organization of seniors, the American Association of Retired Persons (AARP), directs its members into volunteer work through its AARP Volunteer Talent Bank.

How to Recruit Volunteers. Recruiters of volunteers should make clear to potential workers what the proposed jobs entail and, if possible, offer a selection of tasks suitable to differing tastes. A volunteer who has been fast-talked into undertaking an assignment he or she dislikes will probably quit after a short time.

The public relations practitioner can help in recruiting by providing information resources to explain the organization's purpose, to show the essential role its volunteers play, and to stress the sense of achievement and social satisfaction that volunteers find in their work. Testimony from successful, satisfied volunteers is an excellent recruiting tool.

Like all persons, volunteers enjoy recognition, and they should receive it. Certificates of commendation and luncheons at which their work is praised are just two ways of expressing appreciation. Hospital auxiliaries in particular keep charts showing how many hours of service each volunteer has contributed. Service pins or similar tokens are awarded for certain high totals of hours worked. Every organization that uses volunteers should be sure to say, "Thank you!"

Former President Jimmy Carter and his wife, Rosalyn, generate a great deal of publicity and public support for the organization Habitat for Humanity. Here, they work on the construction of a home in Greater Miami, Florida, where 14 homes and a day care center were being built by the organization.

Fund-Raising

At board meetings of voluntary agencies, large and small, from coast to coast, the most frequently asked question is "Where will we get the money?" Discussion of ways to maintain present programs and to add new ones revolves around that inevitable query.

Finding ways to pay the bills is a critical problem for virtually all nonprofit organizations, even those that receive government grants to finance part of their work. Fund-raising has been elevated to a highly developed art and science.

Although the largest, most publicized donations are made by corporations and foundations, the total of individual contributions far exceeds combined corporate and foundation giving, amounting to about 75 percent, about \$203 billion, in annual U.S. philanthropic donations. Depending on their needs, voluntary organizations may try to catch minnows—hundreds of small contributions—or angle for the huge marlin— large gifts from big-money sources. Some national organizations raise massive sums. The Salvation Army, Catholic Charities USA, and the United Jewish Appeal are among the largest recipients.

Public relations representatives may participate directly in fund-raising by organizing and conducting solicitation programs or they may serve as consultants to specialized development departments of their organizations. Organizations often employ professional firms to conduct their campaigns on a fee basis. In that case, the organization's public relations representatives usually have a liaison function.

Fund-raising on a major scale requires high-level planning and organization. An organizational chart for a typical fund-raising campaign is shown in Figure 20.2.

The Risks of Fund-Raising. Fund-raising involves risks as well as benefits. Adherence to high ethical standards of solicitation and close control of money-raising costs, so that expenses constitute only a reasonable percentage of the funds collected,

FIGURE 20.2

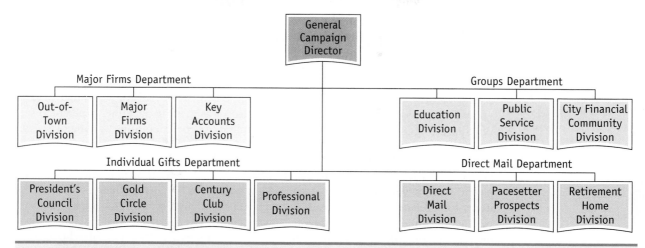

Organizational Chart for Communitywide Fund Drive

This chart shows the basic structure of a fund drive. Specialized groups should be added in each division as necessary to meet local organizational and geographical needs.

are essential if an organization is to maintain public credibility. Numerous groups have suffered severe damage to their reputations from disclosures that only a small portion of the money they raised was applied to the cause they advocated, with the rest consumed by solicitation expenses and administrative overhead.

Fund-raising and administrative costs fluctuate widely among organizations, depending on circumstances, and it is difficult to establish absolute percentage standards for acceptable costs. New organizations, for example, have special start-up expenses. In general, an organization is in trouble if its fund-raising costs are more than 25 percent of what it takes in or if fund-raising and "administrative overhead" exceed 40 to 50 percent.

Some examples among respected national organizations include the following: The American Cancer Society applies 78.2 cents of every dollar it raises to its anti-cancer work; solicitation costs are 12.1 cents and administrative overhead 9.7 cents. The American Heart Association applies 75 cents to its work, with 14 cents for solicitation and 11 cents for administration. The National Charities Information Bureau sets a standard that 70 percent of funds raised by a charity should go into programs.

Motivations for Giving. An understanding of what motivates individuals and companies to give money is important to anyone involved in fund-raising. An intrinsic desire to share a portion of one's resources, however small, with the needy and others served by philanthropic agencies is a primary factor—the inherent generosity possessed in some degree by almost everyone. Another urge, also very human, if less laudable, is ego satisfaction. Those who are motivated by it range from donors to large institutions who insist that the buildings they give be named for them, down to the individuals who are influenced to help a cause by the knowledge that their names will be published in a list of contributors. Peer pressure is a third factor; saying "no" to a request from a friend is difficult. The cliché about "keeping up with the Joneses" applies here, openly or subtly.

Although many companies truly desire to contribute a share of their profits to the community well-being, they also are aware that news of their generosity improves their images as good corporate citizens. Individuals and corporations alike may receive income tax deductions from their donations, a fact that is less of a motivating factor in many instances than the cynical believe.

Independent Sector commissioned the Gallup Poll to do a survey on volunteerism and giving. The survey found that 53 percent of those responding cited "assisting those who are less fortunate" as their personal motive for volunteering and giving. The second most frequently cited reason was gaining a feeling of personal satisfaction; religion was third. Only 6 percent cited tax considerations as a major reason for giving.

Fund-raisers know that although many contributors desire nothing more than the personal satisfaction of giving, others like to receive something tangible—a plastic poppy from a veterans' organization, for example. This fact influences the sale of items for philanthropic purposes. When a neighbor high school girl rings the doorbell, selling candy to raise funds for a stricken classmate, multiple forces are at work—instinctive generosity, peer pressure (not to be known in the neighborhood as a tightwad), and the desire to receive something for the money given. Even when householders are on a strict diet, they almost always will accept the candy in return for their contribution rather than merely give the money.

In a unique fund-raising drive, the University of California, Berkeley, Museum of Paleontology requested donations toward any bone in the dinosaur's skeleton—from the skull for $5,000 to toes and claws for $500. Contributions helped the museum to display the skeleton in its new Valley Life Sciences Building.

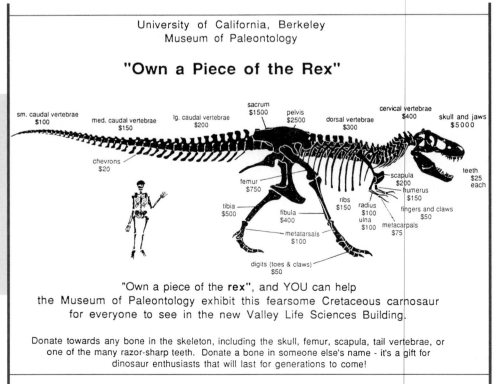

University of California, Berkeley
Museum of Paleontology

"Own a Piece of the Rex"

sm. caudal vertebrae $100
med. caudal vertebrae $150
lg. caudal vertebrae $200
sacrum $1500
pelvis $2500
dorsal vertebrae $300
cervical vertebrae $400
skull and jaws $5000
chevrons $20
femur $750
scapula $200
humerus $150
teeth $25 each
tibia $500
fibula $400
ribs $150
radius $100
ulna $100
fingers and claws $50
metacarpals $75
metatarsals $100
digits (toes & claws) $50

"Own a piece of the **rex**", and YOU can help
the Museum of Paleontology exhibit this fearsome Cretaceous carnosaur
for everyone to see in the new Valley Life Sciences Building.

Donate towards any bone in the skeleton, including the skull, femur, scapula, tail vertebrae, or
one of the many razor-sharp teeth. Donate a bone in someone else's name - it's a gift for
dinosaur enthusiasts that will last for generations to come!

insights

Writing a "Case for Support"

Charitable organizations requesting major funds from wealthy individuals, foundations, and corporations usually prepare a "case for support." The following is an outline of what should be contained in such a document.

Background of the Organization

The background information should include the organization's founding date, its purpose and objectives, what distinguishes the organization from similar organizations, and the evolution (development) of objectives and services.

Current Status of Organization's Services

The number of paid and volunteer staff, facilities, the number of clients served annually, current budget, a breakdown of how that budget is allocated, and geographical areas served should be included here.

Need for Organization's Services

The report should present factual and statistical evidence, the availability of similar services, evidence showing the seriousness of the problem, and the uniqueness of the program.

Sources of Current Funding

Public donations, foundations and corporations, and government funding should be listed.

Administration of the Organization

The report should discuss the background of the executive director and qualifications of key staff and the board of directors (including names and titles).

Tax Status of Organization

The tax status of the organization should be stated.

Community Support

Letters from satisfied clients, letters from community leaders, and favorable media coverage of programs will demonstrate community support.

Current Needs of the Organization

Specific programs, specific staffing, financial costs, the amount of financial support needed, and sources of possible funding should be discussed.

Benefits to the Community from the New or Expanded Program

The report should persuasively present the proposed benefits to the community.

Request for Specific Amount of Funds

This portion will explain the need for the donor's participation and benefits to the donor.

The Competitive Factor. The soliciting organization also should analyze the competition it faces from other fund-raising efforts. The competitive factor is important. The public becomes resentful and uncooperative if approached too frequently for contributions. This is why the United Way of America exists: to consolidate solicitations of numerous important local service agencies into a single unified annual campaign.

The voluntary United Way management in a community, with professional guidance, announces a campaign goal. The money collected in the drive is distributed among participating agencies according to a percentage formula determined by the United Way budget committee.

Types of Fund-Raising.   Philanthropic organizations raise funds in several ways:

- Corporate and foundation donations
- Structured capital campaigns
- Direct mail
- Sponsorship of events
- Telephone solicitations
- Use of telephone numbers with "800" and "900" area codes for contributors
- Commercial enterprises

Corporate and Foundation Donations.   Organizations seeking donations from major corporations normally should do so through the local corporate offices or sales outlets. Some corporations give local offices a free hand to make donations up to a certain amount. Even when the decisions are made at corporate headquarters, local recommendation is important. Requests to foundations generally should be made to the main office, which will send application forms.

Corporations make donations estimated at more than $9 billion a year to all causes, of which roughly 40 percent goes to education. Much of this is distributed in large sums for major projects, but an increasing amount is going to smaller local programs. A directory, the *Guide to Corporate Giving*, published by the American Council for the Arts in New York, describes the contribution programs of 711 leading corporations. Corporations often fix the amount they will contribute each year as a certain percentage of pretax profits. This ranges from less than 1 percent to more than 2.5 percent.

Increasingly, corporations make donations on a matching basis with gifts by their employees. The matching most commonly is done on a dollar-for-dollar basis; if an employee gives $1 to a philanthropic cause, the employer does the same. Some corporations match at a two-to-one rate or higher.

Corporations make contributions to charities in less direct ways, too, some of them quite self-serving. (The practice of cause-related marketing is explained in Chapter 17.) When applying for a charitable donation, an applicant should submit a "case for support" letter that covers the following elements: background of the organization, current status of organization's services, need for organization's services, sources of current funding, administration of the organization, community support, current needs of organization, benefits to the community of the donation, and request for specific amount of funds.

Structured Capital Campaigns.   The effort to raise major amounts of money for a new wing of a hospital, for an engineering building on a campus, or even for the reconstruction and renovation of San Francisco's famed cable car system is often called a *capital* campaign.

In a capital campaign, emphasis is placed on substantial gifts from corporations and individuals. One key concept of a capital campaign, is that 90 percent of the total amount raised will come from only 10 percent of the contributors. In a $10 million campaign to add a wing to an art museum, for example, it is not unusual that the lead gift will be $1 or $2 million.

Capital campaigns require considerable expertise and, for this reason, many organizations retain professional fund-raising counsel. A number of U.S. firms offer these services; the most reputable ones belong to the American Association of Fund-Raising Counsel.

ON THE JOB global

AIDS Campaign Targets Youth in Tanzania

Youth aged 15–19 are just 20 percent of the Tanzanian population, but they account for 60 percent of the new HIV infections in the country. Among sexually active boys in this age group, more than 70 percent have never used a condom.

The Tanzania AIDS Commission, with the help of the Johns Hopkins University Center for Communication programs, decided that a multi-media campaign was needed to help youth understand the risks associated with HIV/AIDS and to help them learn ways to protect themselves.

The centerpiece of the campaign was a brochure with the key messages; 100,000 were distributed through the schools and various youth organizations. Other campaign materials included T-shirts and baseball caps to publicize the campaign during community events, posters to promote events, and voluntary counseling and referral slips distributed during football matches.

The AIDS commission also worked with the Dar es Salaam Football Association to create a youth football league. Matches were played over a period of eight weeks in high-density neighborhoods and key campaign messages were promoted to the crowd. Musical performances by groups and artists popular with the young were given before the matches, at half-time, and after the games to capture youth attention and reinforce AIDS messages.

More than 40,000 attended the football matches, with another 40,000 going to various road shows performed by musical groups. Results from exit interviews showed a high level of recall for campaign messages among attendees and a positive association between message exposure and a commitment to safe sex. More than 60 articles about the campaign—and its key messages—appeared in the Tanzanian media.

The campaign received a Golden Globe award from the International Public Relations Association (IPRA) for its effectiveness.

Traditionally, professional fund-raisers were paid by organizations for their work either in salary or by a negotiated fee. In a controversial decision, however, the National Society of Fund-Raising Executives changed its code of ethics in 1989 to permit its members to accept commissions based on the amount of money they raise.

The preparation for a capital campaign, whether managed by a professional counseling firm or by the institution's own development staff, is almost as important as the campaign itself. The Insights box describes the steps to be taken in organizing and conducting a capital campaign.

A fund campaign usually is organized along quasi-military lines, with division leaders and team captains.

Donors often are recognized by the size of their gifts, and terms such as *patron* or *founder* are used. Major donors may be given the opportunity to have rooms or public places in the building named after them. Hospitals, for example, prepare "memorial" brochures that show floor plans and the cost of endowing certain facilities.

Direct Mail.   Although direct mail can be an expensive form of solicitation because of the costs of developing or renting mailing lists, preparing the printed materials, and mailing them, it is increasingly competitive with advertising costs directed at similarly

ON THE JOB insights

Steps in Running a Capital Campaign

Robert B. Sharp, a California professional consultant, recommends the following steps in running a capital campaign.

Conduct a Feasibility Study

Commission an objective review of the cause behind the proposed campaign. This should . . . provide a monetary goal for the campaign, as well as a "gift model"—a chart breaking down the goal into individual gift amounts and indicating how many of each are needed. The review should also lead to the development of a clear "case statement."

Get the Board's Approval and Support of the Feasibility Study

The board should take steps to carry out the recommendations. (This often results in delays.) . . .

Enlist Volunteer Leadership

Choose a campaign chairman and a volunteer chairman. These volunteers will carry the campaign through the private phase to achieve a major portion of the goal before soliciting the general public.

Begin Soliciting Gifts

Using the feasibility study's gift model and suggested campaign phases, begin solicitation of prospects, moving from attempts to get larger gifts to efforts to obtain lesser ones.

Stop for a Midpoint Evaluation

This evaluation, taking place well into the campaign, should make needed adjustments in the drive's time line, financial goal, or strategy. It is here that the campaign is usually announced to the public through the media. Announcement of the campaign should be

made only when the goal is assured.

Determine Closing Strategies

Decide what changes need to be made to meet or exceed the original goal. Also, determine when and how to begin general public solicitation.

Honor Volunteer Leadership

Plan special events and permanent recognition.

Perform "Administrative Wrap-up"

Because many large gifts may be divided into pledge payments, set up procedures to process these and to encourage timely payments. Review what the campaign has achieved and then consider the campaign's implications for future fund-raising efforts.

Source: Condensed from *Chronicle of Philanthropy,* February 2, 1990.

targeted audiences. An organization can reduce costs by conducting an effective local, limited direct mail campaign on its own if it develops an up-to-date mailing list of "good" names known to be potential donors and can provide enough volunteers to stuff and address the solicitation envelopes. Regional and national organizations, and some large local ones, either employ direct mail specialists or rent carefully chosen mailing lists from list brokers.

The old days when direct mailing pieces came addressed to "Occupant" are largely gone, thanks to the wonders of computerized mailing lists. Now the letters arrive individually addressed. Inside, the appeal letter may bear a personalized salutation and include personal allusions within the text.

The abundance and diversity of mailing lists for rent are impressive. One company offers more than 8,000 different mailing lists. A common rental price is $40 per thousand names. Other lists cost more, depending on their special value. *Direct*

ON THE JOB ethics

Public Relations Faces Tough Calls on Health-Care Issues

Doctors and nurses joined forces in the Ad Hoc Committee to Defend Health Care, an activist group opposed to purportedly excessive profits of hospitals. Their Boston Tea Party reenactment, covered in *O'Dwyer's PR Services Report*, won publicity for their claim that $125 billion in corporate health-care revenues could be better spent on research and improved patient care. Decrying rushed hospital stays, denial of services, and wasteful bureaucracy, the activists tossed annual reports of for-profit hospitals and HMOs into Boston Harbor.

The other side in the dispute responded that so-called "jungle capitalism" bankrolls research to develop lifesaving techniques and provides a stable health care system best able to serve patients. One could add that competition and profit is what drives innovation and excellence throughout the American system.

Which side in this fight would you most want to help with your developing public relations knowledge and skills?

Would you turn down a good job offer from the opposing side for this issue?

Do you think that you could change the organization's stance with your public relations counsel? In other words, could you take a job with the opposition to shape it up enough to live with yourself every payday?

Mail List Rates and Data, updated bimonthly by Standard Rate & Data Service, Inc., is a basic reference book for direct mail lists. The best lists contain donors to similar causes. Direct Media List Management Group, for example, offered a list of almost 1.5 million "aware" women who have contributed to at least one of 27 causes.

Recently, however, the *Chronicle of Philanthropy* has reported a sharp decline in direct mail contributions received by several large national organizations, such as the Disabled American Veterans and National Easter Seals. The publication asserts, "Americans have become increasingly fed up with direct-mail appeals from charities."

Direct e-mail campaigns also can be arranged at reasonable costs with companies that compile e-mail addresses similar to print mail lists. Such targeting greatly increases the predictable percentage of successful contacts from the mailing. A response of 1 percent on a mailing usually is regarded as satisfactory; 2 percent is excellent.

Take the following steps to make a profitable return on direct mail investments:

1. Make use of an attention-getting headline.
2. Follow with an inspirational lead-in on why and how a donation will benefit clients of the charitable agency.
3. Give a clear definition of the charitable agency's purpose and objectives.
4. Humanize the cause by giving an example of a child or family that benefited.
5. Include testimonials and endorsements from credible individuals.
6. Ask for specific action and provide an easy method for the recipient to respond. Self-addressed stamped envelopes and pledge cards often are included.
7. Close with a postscript that gives the strongest reason for reader response.

One marketing research firm enhanced direct-mail precision by identifying 34 human factors such as age, gender, education, and levels of economic well-being. It fed these factors into computers along with a list of 36,000 Zip code markets and produced 40 neighborhood types. An organization interested in reaching one of these types—the supereducated top income level, for example—could use suitable mailing lists broken down to postal area routes.

Attractive, informative mailing pieces that stimulate recipients to donate are keys to successful solicitation. The classic direct-mail format consists of a mailing envelope, letter, brochure, and response device, often with a postage-paid return envelope.

Sponsorship of Events.   The range of events a philanthropic organization can sponsor to raise funds is limited only by the imagination of its members.

Participation contests are a popular method. Walkathons and jogathons appeal to the current American emphasis on using the legs for exercise. Nationally, the March of Dimes holds an annual 32-kilometer WalkAmerica in 1,100 cities on the same day. Local organizations do the same in their own communities. Bikeathons are popular, too. The money-raising device is the same in all such events: Each entrant signs up sponsors who promise to pay a specified amount to the fund for each mile or kilometer the entrant walks, jogs, runs, or cycles.

Staging of parties, charity balls, concerts, and similar events in which tickets are sold is another widely used approach. Often, however, big parties create more publicity than profit, with 25 to 50 percent of the money raised going to expenses. Other methods include sponsorship of a motion-picture opening, a theater night, or a sporting event. Barbecues flourish as money-raisers in western cities. Seeking to attract donors from the under-30 age group, some organizations use the "fun" approach by raffling off such items as Madonna's sequined brassiere (for $2500) and a T-shirt by artist Felix Gonzalez-Torres with the message "Nobody Owns Me" (for $50).

Sale of a product, in which the organization keeps a portion of the selling price, ranges from the church baked-goods stand, which yields almost 100 percent profit because members contribute homemade products, to the massive national Girl Scout cookie sale, which grosses about $375 million annually. A key to success in all charity-fund sales is abundant publicity in the local news media.

Direct solicitation of funds over television by telethons is used primarily in large cities. A television station sets aside a block of airtime for the telethon sponsored by a philanthropic organization. Best known of the national telethons is the one conducted annually by comedian Jerry Lewis for muscular dystrophy. Another high-profile event was the celebrity telethon for aid to victims of the terrorist attacks on the World Trade Center and Pentagon in September 2001.

Telephone Solicitations.   Solicitation of donations by telephone is a relatively inexpensive way to seek funds but is of uncertain effectiveness. Many groups hold down their cost of solicitation by using a WATS (Wide Area Telephone Service) line that provides unlimited calls for a flat fee, without individual toll charges. Some people resent receiving telephone solicitations. If the recipient of the call is unfamiliar with the cause, it must be explained clearly and concisely—which is not always easy for a volunteer solicitor to do. The problem of converting verbal promises by telephone into confirmed written pledges also arises. The normal method is for the sponsoring organization to send a filled-in pledge form to the donor for signature.

Use of "800" or "900" Telephone Numbers.   Toll-free telephone numbers with area codes of 800, permitting callers to phone an organization long distance without cost to themselves, have been in use for years. A 900 code has been added by the telephone companies that requires users to pay a fee for each call placed. The phone company takes a service charge from this fee, and the remainder goes to the party being called.

Charitable organizations increasingly are using 900 numbers in fund-raising. Although the callers must pay for their calls, they have the convenience of making a pledge without having to read solicitation material and write a response. Public television station WNET in New York used a 900 number in an annual pledge drive and received $235,000 in contributions through it.

Commercial Enterprises.   Rather than depending entirely on contributions, some nonprofit organizations go into business on their own or make tie-ins with commercial firms from which they earn a profit. Use of this approach is growing, but it entails risks that must be carefully assessed.

Three types of commercial money-raising are the most common:

1. License the use of an organization's name to endorse a product and receive payment for each item sold.
2. Share profits with a corporation to receive a share of its profits from sales of a special product, such as Newman's Own salad dressing.
3. Operate a business that generates revenue for the organization.

Advocates describe commercial involvement by nonprofit organizations as creating wealth, not receiving it, but the risks for an organization are obvious. Entrepreneurship requires good business management, not always available in charitable organizations. Businesses can lose money as well as make it. Ill-advised lending of an organization's name to a shoddy product or a high-pressure telemarketing scheme can damage a charity's reputation.

Any nonprofit organization contemplating operation of a business should check the tax laws, which require that the enterprise be "substantially related" to the purpose of the nonprofit group.

PR CASEBOOK

A Lesson in Fund-Raising

The Old Globe Theater in San Diego's Balboa Park is an integral part of the city's cultural life. It attracts about 300,000 playgoers a year to its 325 evening performances and has a splendid professional reputation.

The theater's board of directors knew that it needed rehearsal space, refurbishing, and a concession area. They also wanted to pay off debt incurred from rebuilding part of the theater damaged by fire and to acquire a $2 million endowment and reserve fund.

The board decided to conduct a $10 million capital fund campaign. An article in the *Chronicle of Philanthropy* tells how they did so successfully despite severe obstacles.

(continued)

PR CASEBOOK *(continued)*

First, the directors conducted a feasibility study. This showed that San Diego's community leaders did not regard the theater's financial needs as compelling; it also showed that the theater's volunteer leadership lacked members who could make large personal contributions and solicit major campaign gifts.

After a delay caused in part by the death of the theater's campaign consultant, Robert B. Sharp took the job, and the campaign was revitalized. New volunteer leaders were recruited. Several events then occurred:

- A four-color brochure was published to be given to donor prospects.
- A few donors made large gifts as a nucleus of the drive.
- At cocktail parties, board members and major donors heard a presentation about the campaign. They were asked to pick names of people they knew from a list of 20,000 season ticket holders. This provided a list for solicitation.
- A precise goal was set for each prospect—2 to 5 percent of the donor's estimated "adjusted gross worth." The campaign hired a researcher to examine various credit and public records to determine what these goals should be.

With this list, the campaign reached full speed. The cochair made a challenge gift of $500,000 that required the theater to raise $1.5 million within seven months.

Prospective donors were invited to dinner and a play and then taken backstage and given a slide presentation before seeing the play. The campaign used slides rather than a videotape because they enabled the speaker to pause during the presentation for questions.

Solicitors went after the largest gifts first, then moved step-by-step to the smaller prospects. They had a gift model showing the various sizes of gifts sought, from a high of $1 million down to $1,000, and the number of prospects for each size (three for $1 million, 1500 for $1000). Actual donors in each category proved to be about one-third of the category's prospects.

So far, everything had been done on a personal basis without major publicity. A total of $8.5 million was raised from individuals, corporations, and foundations.

Then the campaign went public with a media blitz to solicit gifts under $10,000 from the general public. The final phase involved sending direct mail pieces to theater constituents who had not contributed.

Large donors were recognized by having their family coats of arms incorporated in the design of the new facilities, and they received framed versions of the coats of arms. An importing company donated research to find coats of arms for families lacking them.

A crucial part of this successful campaign was the identification of potential large donors and the analysis of how much each might donate, so that solicitors could make their calls with specific money targets in mind.

| Hospital Public Relations

The public relations staff of a hospital has two primary roles: (1) to strengthen and maintain the public's perception of the institution as a place where medical skill, compassion, and efficiency are paramount and (2) to help market the hospital's proliferating array of services. Many hospitals have sought to redefine themselves as community health centers. Basically, hospitals, like hotels, must have high room-occupancy rates to succeed financially. They supplement this fundamental source of income by creating and marketing supplementary services, an area that offers a challenge to public relations people.

Typical of these supplementary services are alcoholism rehabilitation, childbirth and parenting education, hospices for the terminally ill, pastoral care, and physician referral services.

Hospital Audiences

Because hospitals sell a product (improved health), parallels exist between their public relations objectives and those of other corporations. They focus on diverse audiences, external and internal; involve themselves in public affairs and legislation because they operate under a mass of government regulations; and stress consumer relations. In the case of hospitals, this involves keeping patients and their families satisfied, as well as seeking new clients. Hospitals produce publications for external and internal audiences. They have an additional function that other corporate public relations practitioners don't need to handle—the development and nurturing of volunteer organizations.

Hospital public relations programs have four basic audiences: patients, medical and administrative staffs, news media, and the community as a whole. The four audiences overlap, but each needs a special focus. Careful scrutiny can identify significant subaudiences within these four—for example, the elderly; women who have babies or soon will give birth; victims of heart disease, cancer, and stroke who need support groups after hospitalization; potential financial donors to the hospital; and community opinion leaders whose goodwill helps to build the institution's reputation. Each group can be cultivated by public relations techniques discussed in this textbook.

A Sampling of Public Relations Efforts

The reputations of some hospitals have been damaged by the public's perception of them as cold institutions that don't care enough about individual patients. Complaints by patients about poor food and brusque nurses add to the problem.

Here are a few examples of methods hospitals use to project a positive image:

- Sponsorship of community health fairs, offering free screenings to detect symptoms of certain diseases and low-cost comprehensive blood tests.
- A "direct line" telephone system within the hospital on which patients and visitors can register complaints and suggestions 24 hours a day.
- Bingo games on a closed-circuit television system, for which patients pay a small fee and win cash prizes. This brightens the patients' day.

SUMMARY

The Role of Public Relations

Nonprofit organizations have been given tax-exempt status because their primary goal is to enhance the well-being of their members or the human condition. Fund-raising is a major public relations task in these groups.

Basic Needs of Nonprofits

Although there is a broad range of nonprofit organizations, they all create communications campaigns and programs, require a staff (including volunteers) to handle their work, and are involved in fund-raising.

Membership Organizations

A membership organization is made up of people with a common interest, either business or social. Such groups include trade associations, labor unions, professional associations, and chambers of commerce.

Advocacy Groups

Advocacy groups work for social causes such as the environment, civil rights, gun ownership, or the prochoice movement. Their efforts include lobbying, litigation, mass demonstrations, boycotts, reconciliation, and public education. As with other nonprofits, fund-raising is an unending issue with these groups.

Social Organizations

Social service groups, health agencies, hospitals, religious organizations, welfare agencies, cultural groups, and foundations all fall into the category of social organizations. Their public relations goals include developing public awareness, getting individuals to use their services, creating educational materials, recruiting volunteers, and fund-raising. Fund-raising can take the form of corporate and foundation donations, structured capital campaigns, direct mail, sponsorship of events, telephone solicitations, the use of toll-free numbers, and commercial enterprises.

Case Activity: **What Would You Do?**

The Vision Council of America is a trade group representing the optical industry. Its three core membership groups are ophthalmologists, opticians, and optometrists.

The group decides to launch a consumer education program after research reveals a reluctance to take children for eye exams because parents rely on free in-school screenings. Additional research shows that 80 percent of learning before age 12 is accomplished through vision, yet traditional in-school vision screenings miss between 70 and 80 percent of children's vision problems.

Your public relations firm is retained to conduct a national consumer education program emphasizing the importance of annual eye exams for children. What would you suggest? Program elements that you should consider include key publics, message themes, time of year, strategies, and innovative communication tactics, especially new technologies such as CD-ROM and the Web.

QUESTIONS for Review and Discussion

1. Trade associations, like other membership organizations, often have headquarters in Washington, D.C., or a state capital. Why?
2. What has caused the recent intensified scrutiny of nonprofit organizations?
3. Name the seven categories of social agencies.
4. What challenges do labor unions face today?
5. What are the differences and similarities among trade groups, labor unions, and professional associations?
6. What motivates people to serve as volunteer workers?
7. Describe four commonly used types of fund-raising.
8. Chambers of commerce often are described as the public relations arm of city government. Why?
9. Identify four methods advocacy groups use to further their causes.
10. What two principal roles does a hospital public relations staff fulfill?

SUGGESTED READINGS

Feen, Diane. "Doctors Use PR to Create Media Buzz." *O'Dwyer's PR Services Report*, October 2000, pp. 14–18.

Feen, Diane. "Push to 'Brand' Spurs Healthcare PR Growth." *O'Dwyer's PR Services Report*, October 2002, pp. 1, 10, 38.

Frank, John N. "Survey: Corporations Seek PR Benefits from Nonprofit Partnerships." *PR Week*, October 25, 2003, pp. 1, 17–24.

Kelly, Kathleen S. *Effective Fund-Raising Management*. Mahwah, NJ: Lawrence Erlbaum, 1998.

Kinnick, Katherine N., Krugman, Dean M., and Cameron, Glen T. "Compassion Fatigue: Communication and Burnout toward Social Problems." *Journalism and Mass Communication Quarterly*, Vol. 73, No. 3, Autumn 1996, pp. 687–707.

Lilienthal, Steve. "The Cause and Effect: What Makes Non-profits 'Hot' or 'Cold.' " *PR Week*, July 19, 1999, p. 23.

Londner, Robin. "Global Activists Not So Green About PR Tactics." *PRWeek*, July 30, 2001, p. 10.

Simmons, Donna. "Use of the Staged Event in Successful Community Activism." *Public Relations Quarterly*, Spring 2003, pp. 35–39.

Ward, David. "Media Maintains Its Interest in Art: Many Opportunities Exist for Media Coverage of Art, but PR Pros Must Overcome the Intense Competition and a Lack of Attention Paid to Unknown Artists." *PR Week*, August 23, 2004, p. 11.

Weidlich, Thom. "New York Transit Museum Displays Early PR Work." *PR Week*, August 23, 2004, p. 5.

chapter 21

Education

Topics covered in this chapter include:

Colleges and Universities

Higher education is big business in the United States. California, the most populous state, with 35 million residents, spends $17 billion annually on four-year public colleges and universities. Another $6 billion is spent on two-year community colleges.

It's also a business that has millions of customers—students. In the United States, almost 16 million students are enrolled at more than 4000 college and universities. Almost every one of these institutions has personnel working in such activities as public relations, marketing communications, and fund-raising. See page 572 for a typical job description.

Development and Public Relations Offices

The president (or chancellor) is the chief public relations officer of a college or university; he or she sets policy and is responsible for all operations, under the guidance of the institution's governing board.

In large universities, the vice president for development and university relations (that person may have some other title) supervises the office of development, which includes a division for alumni relations, and also the office of public relations; these functions are combined in smaller institutions. Development and alumni personnel seek to enhance the prestige and financial support of the institution. Among other activities, they conduct meetings and seminars, publish newsletters and magazines, and arrange tours. Their primary responsibilities are to build alumni loyalty and generate funding from private sources.

The public relations director, generally aided by one or more chief assistants, supervises the information news service, publications, and special events. Depending on the size of the institution, perhaps a dozen or more employees will carry out these functions, including writing, photography, graphic design, broadcasting, and computer networking.

Figure 21.1 shows the organization of a public relations staff at a typical university.

In addition, scores of specialists at a large university perform diverse information activities in agricultural, medical, engineering, extension, continuing education, and other such units, including sports.

News Bureau

The most visible aspect of a university public relations program is its news bureau. Among other activities, an active bureau produces hundreds of news releases, photographs, and special columns and articles for the print media. It prepares programs of news and features about faculty activities and personalities for stations. It provides assistance and information for reporters, editors, and broadcasters affiliated with the state, regional, and national media. The staff responds to hundreds of telephone calls from members of the news media and the public seeking information.

Serving the Publics

To carry out their complex functions, top development and public relations specialists must be a part of the management team of the college or university. At some institutions this is not so, and the public relations program suffers. Ideally, these

Vice President for Public Relations and Marketing

St. Bonaventure University invites nominations and applications for the position of Vice President for Public Relations and Marketing. The University's chief communications professional, the Vice President reports directly to the University President and is a member of the senior administrative staff.

The official spokesperson for the University, the Vice President provides executive leadership for all public relations and marketing programs for the University, including promoting its image to alumni, benefactors, friends, current and future students, and all others. The Vice President will also lead the communications and marketing effort for both the University's 150th anniversary in 2008 and the multi-year capital campaign in conjunction with this celebration.

The Vice President for Public Relations and Marketing provides executive oversight for all official University publications, advertisements and publicity, including the official University Web page and the use of its logo. The Vice President is a member of the President's Cabinet and participates in overall planning and direction of institutional affairs.

The University seeks a seasoned communications and marketing professional to lead an independent and motivated full-time staff of five, assisted by part-time assistants and student interns from the Russell J. Jandoli School of Journalism and Mass Communication at the University, whose graduates have won five Pulitzer Prizes.

St. Bonaventure is the nation's first Franciscan university, with approximately 3,000 undergraduate, graduate and continuing education students. Home of the internationally recognized Franciscan Institute, the University serves as the summer home of the National Shakespeare Company and competes in the Atlantic 10 Conference. The campus, spread over 500 acres in a valley surrounded by the Allegheny Mountains, lies between the welcoming communities of Olean and Allegany, which total about 25,000 residents. Shops, restaurants and theaters are nearby, while summer and winter resorts with swimming, golfing, boating, hiking and excellent skiing are just minutes away. For a more in-depth view, visit our Web site at **www.sbu.edu.**

Requirements: Seven years of progressively responsible experience in the public relations, communications and/or marketing fields. Previous experience in higher education is preferred. Master's degree/public relations accreditation is preferred, but not as much as experience.

Compensation will be competitive and commensurate with experience. Candidate review will begin immediately and continue until suitable candidates are identified. Those interested may send a cover letter, résumé and three references to search committee chair **Suzanne Wilcox English, Director of Media Relations, St. Bonaventure University, 224 Hopkins Hall, St. Bonaventure, NY 14778, or fax to (716) 375-2380. EOE.**

This position announcement in the *Chronicle of Higher Education* describes the duties and responsibilities of a communications executive at a private university.

FIGURE 21.1

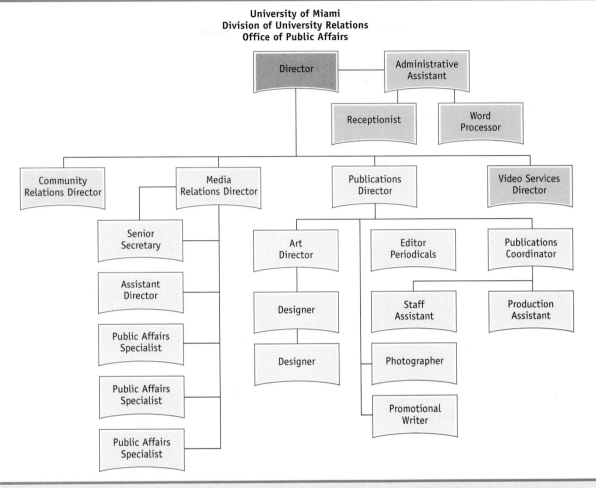

Organizational chart of the University of Miami's public affairs office, showing the division of responsibility for the various areas of operation.

leaders should attend all top-level meetings involving the president and other administrators, learning the whys and wherefores of decisions made and lending counsel. Only then can they satisfactorily develop action programs and respond to questions from the publics those programs concern. They are indeed the arms and voice of the administration.

Faculty and Staff.   As noted in previous chapters, every sound public relations program begins with the internal constituency. Able college presidents involve their faculty in decision making to the fullest extent possible, given the complexities of running a major institution. It is a maxim that the employees of a company or institution serve as its major public relations representatives because they come into contact with so many people. Good morale, a necessity, is achieved in large measure through communication.

College administrators communicate with their faculty and staff members through e-mail and internal newsletters and newspapers; journals describing research, service, and other accomplishments (which also are sent to outside constituencies); periodic meetings at which policies are explained and questions answered; and in numerous other ways.

Faculty and staff members who fully understand the college's philosophy, operations, and needs generally will respond with heightened performance. For example, when the University of Georgia sought to obtain $2.5 million in contributions from its faculty members as part of an $80 million bicentennial enrichment campaign, they responded with a generous outpouring of nearly $6 million—a signal to outside contributors that helped ensure the success of the program.

Students. Because of their large numbers and the many families that they represent, students make up the largest public relations arm—for good or bad—that a university has. The quality of the teaching they receive is the greatest determinant of their allegiance to the institution. However, a sound administrative attitude toward students, involving them as much as possible in decisions that affect their campus lives, is extremely important. So are other forms of communication, achieved through support of student publications and broadcast stations and numerous other ways. When, upon graduation, they are asked to join the university's alumni association, chances are good that, if they are pleased with their collegiate experience, many will support the university in its future undertakings. A public relations effort directed at students is thus essential.

Alumni and Other Donors. The loyalty and financial support of alumni are crucial to the ongoing operations of a college or university. Alumni are considered the major foundation of any fund-raising effort because of their immediate association with the institution. Donors who are not alumni also are cultivated for major gifts based on their interest in a particular field or discipline.

Indeed, fund-raising has increased dramatically at most public and private universities in recent years as costs have risen and allocations from state legislatures and federal agencies have dramatically declined. Total nongovernmental financial support for higher education was $31.6 billion in 2002, according to Giving U.S.A., an annual tally of charitable contributions published by the A.A.F.R.C. Trust for Philanthropy, a unit of the American Association of Fundraising Counsel. This amount represents 13 percent of the total charitable giving in the United States, which was $241 billion. See page 549 in Chapter 20 for a breakdown.

In addition to annual operating fund campaigns, universities are increasingly conducting long-range capital campaigns for large amounts of money. As 2004 closed, more than 20 American universities were in the process of raising $1 billion or more. New York University, for example, embarked on a seven-year $2.5 billion campaign, and the University of Virginia began a multiyear $3 billion campaign. In 2002, the University of Southern California completed a $2.85 billion campaign after nine years of fund-raising.

Such large amounts, coupled with annual alumni campaigns, has caused a major demand for experienced fund-raisers. The median annual salary of a chief development officer at a university offering doctoral degrees is now $166,000, according to the annual survey by the *Chronicle of Higher Education*. In contrast, the median salary of a chief public relations officer is $113,000 at doctoral institutions. Salaries at four-year institutions are somewhat lower.

Colleges and universities raise money for a variety of purposes. This may include such projects as recruiting new faculty, buying equipment, building student residence halls, providing scholarships, remodeling classrooms, and upgrading campus computer networks. New York University, for example, is planning to add 125 new faculty to its 625-member arts and sciences faculty over a five-year period. Money also will be spent on laboratories, offices, and housing for the new professors.

Many institutions employ students to participate in fund-raising phonothons. At the University of Michigan students called 970,000 alumni and raised $8.3 million during a nine-month period. Computerized dialing systems are often used.

At most institutions, letters are mailed to specific graduating classes over the names of members who have agreed to be class agents for that purpose.

Year-by-year contributions are sought, as are bequests and annuities. In return, the colleges publish honor rolls listing donors, invite contributors to join honorary clubs (the President's Club, for example), and name rooms and buildings for the largest

ON THE JOB ethics

Professors as Paid Spokespersons

The *Wall Street Journal* poses an interesting question: "If a professor takes money from a company and then argues in the media for a position the company favors, is he an independent expert—or a paid shill?"

Professors are usually perceived by the public and the media as knowledgeable, objective, and highly credible so they often are used by public relations firms and their clients to speak on behalf of a particular viewpoint. Nucor, a U.S. steel company, for example, hired Peter Morici, a business professor at the University of Maryland, to argue in favor of steel tariffs put in place by the Bush administration. He was quoted in scores of newspaper articles and wrote

two dozen op-ed pieces for various publications.

Morici, through his research, was already a supporter of steel tariffs, but as the *Wall Street Journal* noted, "In the vast majority of cases, his role as a paid consultant to Nucor wasn't disclosed." He was identified only as a professor at the University of Maryland. Morici defended his work for Nucor. He told the newspaper that working for Nucor "gave me an opportunity to do more to get my message and research out."

A number of academics, including Morici, argue there is nothing wrong being paid by public relations firms and special interest groups if their opinions match the viewpoint of the employer. They,

for example, must spend time doing interviews and writing op-ed pieces so why shouldn't they be paid? At the same time, however, public relations executives admit that the experts often don't disclose their consulting relationships when contacted by the media.

What do you think? Do academics have an obligation to tell reporters and talk show hosts that they are being paid by a special interest to express their views on a particular issue? Or is the burden of disclosure the sole responsibility of the media as part of its obligation to its readers and viewers? Do you think such disclosure would dilute the effectiveness of the spokesperson?

ON THE JOB
ethics

Doctoring Photos to Show Diversity

It was a great photo for the cover of the new University of Wisconsin admissions brochure. It showed a group of happy and cheering students at a football game. The photo, however, was not exactly accurate; it had been doctored.

The original picture contained no black faces, but university officials desperately wanted their admissions materials to reflect a diverse student body. So, using photo-design software, the director of university publications and the director of undergraduate admissions simply asked their staff to add one.

Meanwhile, at the University of Idaho, the school's Web site showed another group of smiling students with two faces—one black and one Asian—that had been digitally pasted onto white bodies.

The digital manipulation of photographs to show di-

versity raises some ethical questions. The implicit message of a photograph is that it shows something that actually occurred. So, in the interest of political correctness and diversity, should photos be changed?

One defense is that the photograph isn't really a fake; it's entirely reasonable that a crowd at a football game would include blacks and Asians. Another argument is that doctoring a photo is artistic license. If a technician airbrushes a student picking his nose out of a photo, no one seems to mind. Others, however, say it's wrong to lie about who was in a particular photograph.

What do you think? If you were the director of publications for a university, would you use digital techniques to alter a photo for the purpose of showing diversity in the student body?

givers. Recently, even admission to the university can be a reward. In an odd twist on the fund-raising and recruitment functions of university public relations, donors to Yonsei University in South Korea can guarantee a student admission to the private institution for a cool $1.5 million contribution. More typically, educational events and tours to foreign countries are arranged to build and sustain alumni interest. Class reunions are said to be the most powerful instruments in getting alumni to give.

Universities often use matching grants to make a donor's contribution go further—and thus make giving more attractive. For instance, a donor in Dallas who wanted to remain anonymous contributed $8 million toward the establishment of faculty enrichment chairs at the University of Texas at Austin. The sum was matched by foundations, and the entire $16 million, in turn, was matched by the university, making possible the establishment of 32 new chairs. Such support is essential in order for good universities to become great universities.

Influential alumni and other important friends of colleges and universities also are encouraged, through personal contact and correspondence, to provide political clout with legislative bodies and boards of regents in support of the institutions' financial and other objectives. Such support also is important in the recruitment of students with outstanding academic, athletic, or other achievements.

Government. State and federal governments often hold the vital key to whether universities receive sufficient monies to maintain facilities, faculty, and programs. Most large institutions have someone who regularly monitors the state legislature on appropriations and issues ranging from laboratory experiments on animals to standardized tests and taxes. Their work includes (1) competing with other state institutions for money, (2) defending proposed increases in higher-education budgets and protecting against cuts, (3) establishing an institution's identity in the minds of legislators, and (4) responding to lawmakers' requests for favors. Said Robert Dickens, coordinator of government relations for the University of Nevada at Reno: "When I say I'm a lobbyist, some people look at me as if I need a shower. It's a new business with the universities, and some people think it's a dirty business. But nothing's dirtier than not having resources." See the Insights box below for a citizen lobbying campaign by the University of Maryland.

The declining federal support for higher education also has led to an increase in the number of government relations experts representing universities in Washington, D.C. Their work complements that of the American Council on Education, the National Association of Land-Grant Universities, and the Association of American Universities. They not only lobby members of Congress regarding legislation that

ON THE JOB insights

Citizen Lobbyists Help the University of Maryland

Many different interests, including higher education, compete when it comes to state legislative appropriations, and lobbying is a time-honored tradition.

The University of Maryland system, faced with potential budget cuts from the legislature, organized students, alumni, and parents into an aggressive lobbying group to fight any cuts. Using $20,000 raised through private donations, the university's public relations and governmental relations staff organized a crash course for more than 100 individuals to learn about the legislative process and how to present the system's case to legislators.

Armed with background and convincing arguments, individuals used a variety of communication tools to reach legislators, including personal visits, phone calls, e-mails, letters, and even approaching them at social gatherings. The "citizen lobbyists" also were encouraged

to talk with other alumni about the University of Maryland's needs and to write letters to the editors in newspapers across the state.

According to an article in the *Chronicle of Higher Education*, the tactics worked. After a preliminary budget hearing at the state capitol, the university put out an e-mail "action alert" to volunteers, who sent legislators 400 e-mail messages within 30 minutes. As a consequence, the State Senate proposed only a $2 million cut in higher education funds, compared with a $37 million cut proposed by the House.

Other universities, such as Penn State and the University of Wisconsin, also are mobilizing their alumni to lobby on behalf of the university. The rallying cry, made by the president of the University of Maryland system, is "Higher education has lots of friends, but too few advocates."

State legislatures and universities have a major public relations challenge as tuition keeps going up. Here, college students in California stage a protest against higher fees outside a restaurant owned by Gov. Arnold Schwarzenegger in Santa Monica.

might have an adverse or favorable effect on their clients but also seek information from federal agencies about new programs and uncommitted funds.

The Community.   As in the case of industry, a college or university must maintain a good relationship with the members of the community in which it is situated. The greatest supporters that an institution may have are the people within its immediate sphere of influence, many of whom mingle with its faculty, staff members, and students. Tax dollars also are an immense benefit, although the fact that university property is tax exempt may impose a strain unless the institution voluntarily agrees to some form of compensation for services such as fire and police protection.

In order to bridge the town–gown gap, faculty and staff members are encouraged to achieve community visibility through work with civic and other organizations. Business groups often take the lead. The Chamber of Commerce in Lawrence, Kansas, for example, for many years sponsored an annual barbecue, including various other activities, to give faculty and townspeople an opportunity to get to know each other better.

Prospective Students.   Suffering from declining revenues, increased costs of operation, and a dwindling pool of prospective students occasioned by lower birthrates, many colleges have turned to highly competitive recruiting methods. Some, in the "hard-sell" classification, use extensive advertising in print and broadcast media and on billboards. Other colleges and universities have replaced their catalogues and brochures with four-color, slick materials that use bright graphics and catchy headlines to lure students. Most, if not all, now use the Web.

Various other recruiting devices are used. Vanderbilt University sent personalized videotapes to about 40 highly coveted high school seniors. The College of the Atlantic took prospective students on a 90-foot sailing yacht party. Stanford University was host to 750 high school students who stayed overnight in dormitory rooms, visited classes, attended a musical program, and participated in a campus scavenger hunt. Brown University each spring sponsors a party for up to 250 prospects on an Amtrak train traveling between Washington and Providence, Rhode Island. As competition for students has increased, so have the costs of recruiting them. Expenditures on admissions and recruitment have run about $700,000 or more for private universities and in excess of $600,000 for public universities. This high level of activity creates many opportunities for employment in public relations and development.

The purchase of mailing lists is a common tool of student recruitment. Each of approximately 900 colleges annually buys from 10,000 to 15,000 names and addresses of high school students who have taken College Board Examinations. The most sought-after prospects are National Merit Scholarship winners, and it is not uncommon for competing universities to shower a prospect with such lures as free tuition for four years, a private dorm room, guarantees of priority registration, and so on. See the PR Casebook on page 584 to read about a special event that was used to attract students.

Other Publics.   Examples of other groups requiring special attention are shown in Figure 21.2.

Support for Advancement Officers

Most public relations, alumni, and development leaders—known as *advancement officers*—enjoy the many services of the Council for Advancement and Support

FIGURE 21.2

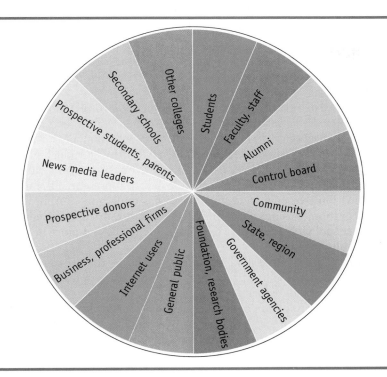

This wheel shows the variety of publics with which college public relations offices endeavor to maintain communication and feedback.

of Education (CASE), with headquarters in Washington, D.C. The aims of CASE are described as building public understanding, stepping up the level of alumni involvement and support, strengthening communication with internal and external audiences, improving government relations, and increasing private financial support. Among CASE's current objectives are (1) helping leaders at historically black institutions advance in their careers, (2) publicizing a code of ethics, (3) developing gift and expenditure reporting standards, (4) improving the communication of university research to the public, and (5) studying the impact of new technologies.

Representing more than 2,400 institutional members, CASE serves nationally as a principal public affairs arm for education, monitoring federal rights legislation and regulations and working with the American Council on Education and other associations on education-related issues. The organization provides district conferences and institutes, evaluation and critique services, a certification program, awards, reference materials, and placement opportunities. Thousands each summer attend its four-day assembly, replete with workshops.

Elementary and Secondary Schools

The strategic planning and skillful execution of public relations programs have materially strengthened many of the nation's elementary and secondary school systems during recent decades.

Response to Contemporary Issues

Should public tax money be used so that parents disaffected with the public schools can send their children to private, often religion-supported schools.

Should standard courses and programs be offered in non-English languages to accommodate significant numbers of first generation immigrants and children of illegal aliens working in the United States?

Many weighty questions such as these examples confronted the nation and its educational systems as the new century dawned. In fact, education has become one of the crucial planks in political platforms for candidates. Many of these issues are part of two decades of widespread debate spawned by the National Commission on Excellence in Education. Citing "a nation at risk," the commission called for massive educational reform. The resulting nationwide debate represented the most searching public examination that education in America has undergone during the last several decades: integration, busing, accountability, book censorship, sex education, discipline, crime, school violence, and drugs—all these issues and more have commanded continuing public attention.

The 18-member commission proposed increasing requirements in five major areas: content, standards and expectations, time, teaching, and leadership and financial support—all deemed inadequate.

News of the commission's recommendations reached the offices of thousands of school superintendents almost immediately over the Education U.S.A. Newsline and Information Network, an electronic news and advisory service of the National School Public Relations Association (NSPRA). When local media people called shortly thereafter, many of the more alert superintendents and their communication coordinators were prepared to offer reactions.

Governors and business leaders began holding annual two-day National Education Summits to plan school advancement. Corporations throughout the country and smaller businesses formed alliances with schools. Many were year-by-year "Adopt-a-School" arrangements, but some extended for 10 years or longer.

Thousands of schools established projects in buying and selling to educate children on the principles of free enterprise. In many classrooms, however, corporate logos and learning went hand in hand. A report by Consumers Union found that many of America's 43 million school-age children were being bombarded by a growing number of blatantly commercial messages. According to the Center for Commercial-Free Public Education, schools have signed exclusive promotional deals with companies selling soft drinks, sneakers, and telecommunications equipment. Among them was a 10-year contract that the Colorado Springs schools signed with the Coca-Cola Company for $9 million. Pepsi paid $2.1 million to the Jefferson County school district in Colorado. Many found such exclusive contracts troubling because they limit student choice and can require educational institutions to toe the line. At one school, a boy was even suspended for a day for wearing a Pepsi shirt on Coke day.

Overall, however, the partnership with business strengthened the schools. According to the Council on Aid to Education, corporations donate well over $50 million each year to K–12 (kindergarten through 12th grade) schools.

In order to increase public awareness of changing attitudes and their own needs, the largest, most progressive public school systems and independent private schools, as well as thousands of smaller ones, have long maintained public relations programs.

But the necessity for sound community relations—at the heart of both management and public relations—was more evident as the new century approached than ever before. If funds were not available or the system too small to warrant a full-fledged public relations program, then a sole information specialist was employed, full- or part-time. School public relations had come into its own.

Reaching the Publics

The primary publics of a school system are teachers, children, parents, staff, and the community. As in all public relations, research, planning, action, and evaluation comprise the essential steps with which to reach these publics. On the desks of information directors, communication coordinators, and school–community relations specialists (or whatever the title may be, and it varies widely) are booklets prepared by national and state offices detailing hundreds of ways in which they may carry out their mission. Perhaps the best way to describe school public relations in its major aspects is to examine some of the outstanding communication programs in elementary and secondary school public relations.

Building Community Support. When almost one-third of the elementary schools in the Fort Worth Independent School District tested low in pupils' reading skills, the superintendent asked the public for help. Business leaders, librarians, and teachers, coordinated by the schools' community relations division, developed a year-long awareness campaign with the theme, "Reading Takes You Places."

Communication plans included news releases, bilingual fliers to parents and community leaders, and TV and cable messages, with personal contacts before each activity. Newspapers, the city transportation authority, and advertising companies provided free advertising.

Business firms supported such activities as book donations to libraries and a Reading Rodeo attended by more than 700 children in 69 schools. Community groups such as the Dallas Mavericks and museums also participated. The Reading Summit involving sponsorship by the Governors Business Council drew broad media coverage.

By year's end, only three schools failed to meet state expectations, and a 91-percent improvement rate was recorded in the number of low-performance schools.

Beating the Odds at the Polls. Supporters of the Everett (Washington) School District faced a difficult problem: winning a tax levy election that required turning out 40 percent of the voters who voted in the last major election and getting 60 percent of them to vote "yes." The almost 50 percent of voters receiving a permanent absentee ballot were traditionally very negative toward tax measures, and 70 percent of households in the district had no school-age children.

Discarding traditional communication methods, the citizens' committee planned a highly focused campaign. It sought to identify likely "yes" voters and to aim all signs, mailings, brochures, and personal contact at them.

Two campaigns were waged: one for absentee voters and one for election-day voters. About 20 people devoted 25 evenings to phoning targeted voters, getting out mailings, and writing personal messages. On election day, poll watchers looked for "yes" walk-ins; those who had not voted by 4 P.M. were called and reminded to vote.

The levy passed with an almost 64 percent "yes" vote. All project goals were met or exceeded. The committee analyzed every aspect of the election, including the database of 12,000 district supporters, and began a continuing campaign aimed at turning "maybe" voters to "yes" voters in the next election.

Crisis Communication. For emergencies such as earthquakes, sudden loss of utilities, severe storms, hazardous material spills, explosions, fires, tornadoes, school shootings, plane crashes, bomb threats—for all such crises, a communication plan should be in readiness. See also the Global box on page 583 about how a school handled sexual abuse allegations.

Such plan components were dwarfed by the tragic shooting of 12 students and a teacher at Columbine High School in Colorado. Winner of a Silver Anvil Award from the Public Relations Society of America, the school system's public relations professionals were thrust into the spotlight as the voice of the community as well as the organization. The team managed speculation and rumor flamed by 750 media outlets worldwide; helped the community deal with the unforgettable experience and the heart-rending images; and restored calm and confidence to the school system and thereby to the community.

Public relations executive for the school district, Rick Kaufman, drew upon his emergency medical technician experience to help victims at the site, then organized a crisis communication team to handle the onslaught of coverage and inquiries. Symbolic of the eloquence of the communication efforts and the perspective provided by the communication team is this quote by Marilyn Saltzman, manager of communication services: ". . . Columbine is a beautiful flower that blooms in the mountains of Colorado . . . I would hate for it to be a synonym for 'massacre.' " While effectively managing the immediate crisis, the communication department has helped to heal a community and move forward.

Marketing of Public Schools. A pioneer in public opinion surveying in education, William J. Banach, administrative director at the Macomb Intermediate School District in Mount Clemens, Michigan, developed a two-year plan designed to discover what the public wants in its schools. The plan also sought ways to respond to those desires and to educate citizens about actions the school could and could not take. Banach based the campaign on what he termed "the 90-7-3 concept of school communication":

> Ninety percent of the school's image is who we are and what we do 24 hours a day. How school people think, act, and appear and what they say are key factors in marketing. This is why staff training is an integral part of a marketing program—to help people understand their communication roles and how important they are.
>
> Seven percent of the marketing effort is listening—tuning in to find out what people like, don't like, want, don't want. Anything we do to know more about our "customers" is worth doing.
>
> Three percent of marketing is outbound communication—publications, posters, news releases, and other visible and tangible items.

In successive phases, the marketing plan at Mount Clemens was targeted at (1) elementary parents, with a focus on reading, writing, and arithmetic; (2) secondary

ON THE JOB global

Australian School Rebuilds Its Tarnished Reputation

The Anglican Church Grammar School in Brisbane, Australia, faced with a series of sexual abuse claims, had a major public relations problem on its hands. Extensive media coverage had caused considerable anxiety among past and current parents, as well as the entire community.

The school, known as "Churchie," engaged Rowland Communications Group to work with the school's board of directors and headmaster on communication strategies that would reassure the community that the school was taking the charges seriously and were putting strict policies in effect to prevent future cases. They developed a policy of "victim-first" communication and put a priority on first informing the immediate

school community of parents, students, and alumni.

To assess the situation, Rowland first audited every Australian media story about sexual abuse claims by past and current students in other schools. The firm also identified key opinion leaders in Brisbane who could be effective spokespersons for the school.

Communication tools to key audiences included (1) regular staff updates, (2) letters to parents, (3) student briefings via assemblies, (4) teachers, (5) newsletter articles and a Web site, and (6) media advisories. Meetings also were held with the editors of the daily newspaper, the *Courier Journal*, which had prominently displayed sexual abuse allegations against current and former staff for sev-

eral months. After the headmaster met with the editor and explained the proactive steps "Churchie" was taking, fairer and more supportive stories appeared.

All media coverage, once the communications program started, portrayed key messages about the school's efforts to deal with the alleged victims and the new policies in place. The headmaster received hundreds of supportive calls, e-mails, and letters. No students on "Churchie's" waiting list withdrew, and the school reclaimed much of its traditional reputation as an outstanding institution.

As a result, the IPRA gave the school and Rowland a Golden Globe award for conducting an outstanding crisis recovery program.

students and their parents, emphasizing "the basics and beyond" and beginning with specific objectives based on survey results and meetings with student leaders; and (3) citizens without children in school.

Arrangements were made for teachers to apply "No. 1 apple" stickers to outstanding student papers, and all classroom papers were sent home each Friday. Posters welcoming visitors were placed at each school. The slogan "Your public schools . . . There's no better place to learn" was displayed on billboards, calendars, bookmarks, bumper stickers, T-shirt transfers, and thank-you cards.

A survey made a year after the campaign began revealed enhanced public confidence in the schools. The Macomb Plan, as it is called, has attracted national attention.

PR CASEBOOK
West Point Celebrates Its 200th Anniversary

An anniversary is always a good vehicle to increase visibility and public awareness of an organization. The U.S. Military Academy at West Point seized such an opportunity when it came time to celebrate its bicentennial. It was also an opportunity to reverse a trend in lower student enrollments.

The public affairs office at West Point, with a budget of $300,000, decided that the mass media would be the best way to spread the message about the proud tradition of West Point and its long history. As a first step, the public affairs staff prepared a series of media materials. This included (1) a 22-minute bicentennial video, (2) a PSA, (3) a 70-page bicentennial pictorial history, (4) a VNR, (5) a media kit, (6) posters, and (7) even reproductions of archival black-and-white photos from the academy's past.

A number of newspapers and magazine used features about the history of the Academy and covered various anniversary events throughout the year. In addition, the Smithsonian Museum of American History held a special exhibit based on the academy's history, which also generated many news stories.

A major initiative was "pitching" the Academy's story to major broadcast programs. The History Channel, the Discovery Channel, and PBS all ran programs about the West Point bicentennial, and the National Geographic Channel even produced and ran a series of 14 half-hour shows based on West Point. The Turner Classic Movies ran a "West Point-themed movie" for four Mondays in a row.

The media coverage not only increased the visibility of the Academy, but enrollments actually went up. The enrollment for the Class of 2006 increased 7 percent, and the Class of 2007 experienced a 13 percent increase in students.

PRWeek named the West Point program the "Public Sector Campaign of the Year in 2003." As one judge remarked, "It just goes to show what can happen when you make the most of a milestone. They took that anniversary, and got every inch of mileage there was to be had."

SUMMARY

Colleges and Universities

Public relations at colleges and universities involves both development, or fund-raising, and enhancing the prestige of the institution. The office of development and public relations may conduct meetings, publish newsletters, and arrange tours. The audiences for communications will include alumni, students, prospective students, faculty and staff, government, and the general public.

Elementary and Secondary Schools

Public education has received increasing attention in recent years from the media, especially during political campaigns. Issues include school vouchers, curriculum standards, bilingual education, integration, book censorship, sex education, and school violence. Public relations practitioners working with the schools must address all these areas, reaching such publics as teachers, children, parents, staff, and the community. Goals will include building community support for programs and encouraging financial support through taxes. Schools also must have communications plans in readiness for crisis situations, whether these involve earthquakes, power loss, severe weather, fires, bomb threats, or school violence.

Case Activity: What Would You Do?

Southwestern University has a public relations problem. The campus administration, taking the route of many other universities, has signed a contract with Carl's Jr. to open a fast-food franchise on campus. The decision was based on competitive bidding, and campus administrators made the decision that Carl's Jr. was the best choice to answer the needs of hungry students. Remodeling of a space in the student union has already begun to accommodate the new franchise when, much to everyone's surprise, the student/faculty gay and lesbian association of the university publicly denounces the contract.

Representatives of the organization say the university should not let Carl's Jr. operate on campus because the founder of the company, Carl Karcher, is antigay. About 20 years ago, they say, he gave a political donation to a state senator who introduced a bill in the state legislature that would have banned homosexual teachers from the classroom. The bill, however, was never passed. Although Karcher is no longer actively involved in the management of the restaurant chain, the gay and lesbian association says the university should honor its commitment to diversity and equality by denying the franchise. The university president is caught in a bind, since he has been most vocal about campus climate and expressing zero tolerance about any form of "hate" speech.

If you were the vice president of public relations for the university, what would you recommend? Should the university cancel the contract to satisfy the gay/lesbian association? What about the numerous university students who are looking forward to having the fast-food franchise on campus? What steps would you recommend to resolve the issue?

QUESTIONS for Review and Discussion

1. Who is the chief public relations officer on a college or university campus? Why?

2. A college news bureau is involved in a vast array of day-to-day public relations operations. Name five or six of these functions.

3. With what primary public does a sound university public relations program begin? Why? List eight other constituencies that must be addressed in such a program.

4. In what ways may powerful alumni and other friends provide support for an institution of higher learning? What is the role of the development office in gaining this support? What is CASE, and what support does it provide for public relations and alumni officers?

5. The National Commission on Excellence in Education called for massive educational reform. How did school officials respond?

6. What strategic plan did a citizens committee of the Everett (Washington) School District employ to win its bond-issue election?

7. Do you agree with the marketing concept used by public relations people in the Macomb Intermediate School District in Mount Clemens, Michigan? Describe the key points of this plan in explaining your answer.

8. What public relations problems may be evident when a community turns down a bond issue to improve school financing? What public relations actions do you consider important in building and maintaining strong support of schools?

SUGGESTED READINGS

Brainard, Jeffrey. "Lobbying to Bring Home the Bacon: In Pursuit of Earmarks and to Influence Policy, Higher Education Has Become a Major Player on Capitol Hill." *Chronicle of Higher Education*, October 22, 2004, pp. A26–A36.

Cotton, Raymond D. "Friends or Foes? The Press and College Presidents." *Chronicle of Higher Education*, September 12, 2003, pp. C2–3.

Deutsch, Claudia H. "A Much-Loved Concept Gets a Few New Twists: Corporate Matching Funds." *New York Times*, November 17, 2003, p. A6.

Drozdowski, Mark J. "The Fund Raiser: Certifiable." *Chronicle of Higher Education*, July 16, 2004, p. C3.

Potter, Will. "Citizen Lobbyists." *Chronicle of Higher Education*, April 25, 2003, pp. A24–25.

Ross, John. "Colleges Should Stop Counting Their National News Clips." *Chronicle of Higher Education*, February 21, 2003.

Schroeder, Michael. "Some Professors Take Payments to Express Views." *Wall Street Journal*, December 10, 2004, pp. B1, B3.

Steinberg, Jacques. "A Mill Town Spins Out College Images." *New York Times*, December 18, 2002.

Strom, Stephanie. "Gifts to Charity in 2002 Stayed Unexpectedly High." *New York Times*, June 23, 2003, p. A14.

Strout, Erin. "It's $300 Million, but Don't Call It a Gift." *Chronicle of Higher Education*, May 28, 2004, pp. A24–26.

chapter **22**

Entertainment, Sports, and Travel

Topics covered in this chapter include:

Fascination with Celebrity

A dominant factor in today's mass media is the publicizing and glorification of celebrities. Sports heroes and television personalities in particular, along with radio talk-show hosts, members of the British royal family, movie stars, high-profile criminals, and some politicians, are written about, photographed, and discussed almost incessantly.

In some cases, such celebrity results from natural public curiosity about an individual's achievements or position in life. Frequently, however, it is carefully nurtured by publicists for the client's ego satisfaction or commercial gain.

The publicity buildup of individuals is outside the mainstream of public relations work, and some professional practitioners are embarrassed by the exaggerations and tactics used by promoters of so-called "beautiful people." Nevertheless, all students of public relations should know how the personal publicity trade operates. At some point, knowledge of personal publicity techniques may be useful.

Enduring Celebrity: When the Good and Beautiful Die Young

Diana, Princess of Wales, was a worldwide celebrity as the divorced wife of Prince Charles, heir to the British throne. Her svelte, gracious manner and high-fashion clothing, plus public interest in the collapse of her once-romantic marriage, created huge media attention. She appeared on the cover of *People Weekly* 41 times in a 16-year period and became known to headline writers as "Princess Di."

Princess Diana's death in a dramatic, high-speed race to elude press photographers captured world attention. Diana joined a tragic list of celebrities taken all too young from their lives of fame and adulation, including people such as James Dean, Elvis, John Lennon, and John F. Kennedy and his brother Robert. According to Irving Rein, author of *High Visibility*, celebrities exist in one-sided, idealized relationships in which the celebrity demands nothing of us. And, unlike our family and workmates, we get to pick our celebrity idols.

In death, this ideal, though distant, relationship is severed, and the youthful image is frozen in time. The tragedy and the timeless glamor galvanize us into a mass audience. Princess Diana's funeral was viewed by an estimated 2.5 billion people around the world. An estimated 152,000 visitors to her burial shrine on the family estate paid $24 each to see her childhood home, view family movies in a remodeled stable, and gaze at her island mausoleum. Even in death, both adulation and revenue can follow from celebrity.

The Mystique of Personality

Why is the public so eager to read about and watch personalities it regards as celebrities? What drives individuals to seek such attention?

The abundance of mass media outlets today and their intense competition for audiences draws on the natural instinct of humans to know about each other's lives. Appearances on talk shows, fawning TV interviews, sympathetic magazine articles, online chat sessions, and ghost-written books contribute to the buildup.

Christine Kelly of *Sassy* magazine writes bluntly, "No-talents become celebrities all the time," a fact that she attributes largely to television. "Once TV started, the whole celeb-creation and worship careened out of control . . . TV gives the false impression that celebrities are talking right to you, and you feel like they're your friends."

Here are some of the motivating factors in the cult of personality.

Fame

Some individuals draw public attention due to their accomplishments or positions. The President of the United States is automatically a celebrity. So is the Pope.

Notoriety

Even people who commit major crimes or are involved unfavorably in spectacular trials are treated as celebrities. Barbara Goldsmith commented on this fact in the *New York Times:*

> The line between fame and notoriety has been erased. Today we are faced with a vast confusing jumble of celebrities: the talented and the untalented, heroes and villains, people of accomplishment and those who have accomplished nothing at all, the criteria of their celebrity being that their images encapsulate some form of the American dream, that they give enough of an appearance of leadership, heroism, wealth, success, danger, glamour and excitement to feed our fantasies. We no longer demand reality, only that which is real-seeming.

> Goldsmith adds, "The public appetite for celebrity and pseudo-event has grown to Pantagruelian proportions, and for the first time in history, the machinery of communications is able to keep up with these demands, even to outrun them, creating new needs we never knew existed. To one extent or another, all the branches of the media have become complicitous to this pursuit. . . . "

Self-Glorification

Donald Trump, a New York real-estate high roller with an insatiable desire for publicity, is a striking example of the urge for self-glorification. He put his name on the buildings and casinos he bought and has a personal press agent in addition to the Trump Organization's aggressive public relations department. He has even telephoned reporters with stories about himself. Most recently, Trump is the star of the television show *The Apprentice*, even as he fends off bankruptcy proceedings against one of his properties. Love him or loathe him, "The Donald," as he is sometimes called, is the consummate newsmaker and celebrity. He is also a remarkable survivor of personal and business crises and scandals. In 2004, Donald Trump was a keynote speaker at the Public Relations Society of America International Conference, which is a tribute to his resilience and ability to survive, even prosper, in the limelight and media spotlight.

Repair of a Bad Image

Public relations counselors who specialize in handling individuals sometimes work to create a positive image for a prominent person who has been cast in an unfavorable light by news stories.

Kathie Lee Gifford, the perky TV personality, suffered a severe blow to her reputation when it was revealed that some of her "Kathie Lee" line of clothing sold by Wal-Mart was made by Honduran child labor and in New York sweatshops.

Gifford hired Howard Rubenstein, a counselor with 50 years in the profession, to help her. She proclaimed her dismay and lack of knowledge that her name was being used in such practices and then sent her husband with a large amount of cash to pay some of the mistreated workers. Under Rubenstein's guidance, she sought to reverse her role from apparent offender to righteous crusader against such mistreatment of workers.

The counselor arranged for Gifford to meet the U.S. Secretary of Labor and arrange a conference of national retailers and manufacturers on working conditions. She also held a news conference with Governor George Pataki of New York and another at the New York Fashion Cafe. She also met with several unions. She proclaimed her new role as an anti-sweatshop activist in a letter in *USA Today* and a television interview with Larry King.

The climax of Kathie Lee's campaign came when she stood beside President Clinton in the White House Rose Garden as he signed an agreement with 10 manufacturers who promised to put labels on their products stating that they had not been made in sweatshops. The combination of constructive actions and celebrity publicity can send a compelling message.

Desire for Money

Personal publicity can build on itself. A publicist may arrange for an obscure film actress to attend a party as the guest of a well-known performer and then issue a news release about the couple. Another party and another news release follow. Soon, the news releases refer to the actress as a celebrity. Presto, she is one. No one officially proclaims who has celebrity status, but once a critical mass of coverage occurs, that celebrity's value in the marketplace rises. Contracts and sales of everything from books to movies to television series, as well as endorsements and appearance fees, are suddenly under negotiation by members of the celebrity's entourage.

Once established as a star, companies such as Celebrity Connection provide unique services. Celebrity Connection's Web site www.celebconn.com describes the company as "a unique global firm dedicated to creating relationships between you, your clients, and the celebrity community and finding you the right celebrity for your cause. We provide services ranging from celebrity acquisition and coordination to total event management."

Indicative of the commercialization of personality is the success of companies that keep databases on well-known persons and offer daily bulletins on their comings and goings. The databases also have the names of managers, lawyers, and publicists who represent celebrities. The daily bulletins tip off the media about availability of prominent people for a television talk show or a feature interview. These services help business, industry, and charities locate celebrities who might serve as a spokesperson or a charity chairperson or add glamor to a major event.

Psychological Explanations

Psychologists offer varied explanations of why the public becomes impressed—*fascinated* might be the more accurate word—by highly publicized individuals. In pretelevision days, the publicity departments of the motion picture studios promoted their male and female stars as glamour figures who lived in a special world of privilege and wealth. Dreaming of achieving such glory for themselves, young people with and without talent came to Hollywood to crash the magical gates, almost always in vain. Thousands more back home spun fantasies about being Rita Hayworth or Cary Grant. They cherished machine-autographed pictures of their favorites and read with relish inflated stories about the stars in fan magazines, visualizing themselves in the glamor figures' places.

In the earlier days of personality buildup, wish-fulfillment was a compelling force. It still is. Exposure on television in the intimacy of the family living room, however, makes personalities seem much closer to admiring viewers today than the remote gods and goddesses were in the glory days of the major motion picture studios. Such is the power of television, in fact, that reporters and news anchors who talk on camera about the activities of celebrities attain celebrity status themselves.

Many ordinary people leading routine lives yearn for heroes. Professional and big-time college sports provide personalities for hero worship. Publicists emphasize the performances of certain players, and television game announcers often build up the stars' roles out of proportion to their achievements; this emphasis creates hero figures for youthful sports enthusiasts to emulate. Similar exaggerated treatment is applied to entertainers and politicians. Syndicated gossip columnist Liz Smith once tried to explain the American cult of personality by saying, "Maybe it's because we all want someone to look up to or spit on, and we don't have royalty."

In addition to admiration for individual performers, members of the public develop a vicarious sense of belonging that creates support for athletic teams. Sports publicists exploit this feeling in numerous ways. A winning baseball team becomes "our" team in conversations among patrons of a bar. To signify their loyalty, children and adults alike wear baseball caps bearing the insignia of their favorite major league teams. It isn't surprising that alumni of a university gnaw their fingernails while watching their school basketball team in a tight game, but the same intensity of support is found among fans who have no direct tie to the school.

Still another factor is the desire for entertainment most people feel. Reading fan magazines, watching a favorite star being interviewed, or lining up in front of a box office hours before it opens to be sure of getting a ticket—these are ways to bring variety and a little excitement into the daily routine of life.

A public relations practitioner assigned to build up the public image of an individual should analyze the ways in which these psychological factors can be applied. Because the client's cooperation is vital in promotional work, a wise publicist explains this background and tells the client why various actions are planned.

The Practitioner's Responsibility

Handling publicity for an individual carries special responsibilities. Often the client turns to the publicist for personal advice, especially when trouble arises.

Damage Control

A practitioner handling an individual client is responsible for protecting the client from bad publicity as well as generating positive news. When the client appears in a bad light because of misbehavior or an irresponsible public statement, the publicist

ON THE JOB ethics

A Difficult Sports Secret

You are a sports information officer for a university whose high-scoring basketball team hopes to win the national championship. One late evening in the locker room you overhear two top players talking about how they shaved points in two recent games by intentionally missing free throws. Your team won the games, but by a smaller margin than the Las Vegas "odds-makers" had predicted. Gamblers rewarded them with gifts of expensive sports cars, kept hidden at an off-campus location. You hear that the players are planning to shave points again in the early rounds of the tournament for hefty cash payments.

If you keep the cheating secret, the university might win the national title and obtain generous contributions from enthusiastic alumni. If you report your information to an academic or police authority and a public gambling scandal occurs, the school will suffer disqualification, shame, and financial loss. You will be vilified by many in the university community for "blowing the whistle" when the outcome of games was never put in jeopardy by these players. You consider a constructive approach, because your team did win the previous games. You could tell the players that you know about their scheme and demand that they play competitively from now on or you will report them to the NCAA.

If you don't report the circumstantial evidence you have, will you be guilty of unethical behavior?

What about criminal charges against you for aiding and abetting a criminal act?

If you do report the previous incident, what sort of crisis management approach would you develop?

must try to minimize the harm done to the client's public image. To use a naval term, the objective is damage control.

Politicians who say something controversial in public, and then later wish they hadn't, try to squirm out of the predicament by claiming they were misquoted. This is a foolish defense unless the politician can prove conclusively that he or she was indeed quoted incorrectly. Reporters resent accusations of inaccuracy and may hold a grudge against the accuser. If the accused reporter has the politician's statement on tape, the politician appears even worse. A better defense is for the politician to explain what he or she intended and to express regret for the slip of the tongue.

A similar approach is recommended for Hollywood celebrities who are caught in scandalous acts or unfounded rumor mills. Experts suggest immediate response so that the momentum of subsequent stories is minimized. A brief, honest statement of regret for bad behavior or denial of rumors works well. Television's mass audience enjoys celebrity news. TV lends itself to a short statement that makes a perfect 20-second sound bite to fit in a brief story. Then the celebrity needs to disappear from sight and take care of personal matters.

Ethical Problems for Publicists

Personal misconduct by a client, or the appearance of misconduct, strains a practitioner's ingenuity and at times his or her ethical principles. Some practitioners will lie outright to protect a client, a dishonest practice that looks even worse if the media show the statement to be a lie. On occasion, a practitioner acting in good faith may be victimized because the client has lied.

Issuing a prepared statement to explain the client's conduct, while leaving reporters and their editors dissatisfied, is regarded as safer than having the client call a news conference, unless the client is a victim of circumstances and is best served by talking fully and openly. The decision about holding a news conference also is influenced by how articulate and self-controlled the client is. Under questioning, a person may say something that compounds the problem. (Defensive news conferences are discussed further in Chapter 16.)

Conducting a Personality Campaign

A campaign to generate public awareness of an individual should be planned just as meticulously as any other public relations project. Practitioners conducting such campaigns follow a standard step-by-step process.

Interview the Client

The client should answer a detailed personal questionnaire. The practitioner should be a dogged, probing interviewer, digging for interesting and possibly newsworthy facts about the person's life, activities, and beliefs. When talking about themselves, individuals frequently fail to realize that certain elements of their experiences have publicity value under the right circumstances.

Perhaps, for example, the client is a little-known actress who has won a role as a midwestern farmer's young wife in a motion picture. During her get-acquainted talks with the publicist, she happens to mention in passing that while growing up in a small town she belonged to the 4-H Club. The feature angle can be the realism she brings to the movie role: When she was a member of the youth organization, she actually did the farm jobs she will perform in the film.

Not only must practitioners draw out such details from their clients, they must also have the ingenuity to develop these facts as story angles. When the actress is placed as a guest on a television talk show, the publicist should prompt her in advance to recall incidents from her 4-H experience. Two or three humorous anecdotes about mishaps with pigs and chickens, tossed into the TV interview, give it verve.

Prepare a Biography of the Client

The basic biography should be limited to four typed pages, perhaps fewer. News and feature angles should be placed high in the "bio," as it is termed, so an editor or producer can find them quickly. The biography, a portrait and other photographs of the client, and, if possible, additional personal background items should be assembled in a media kit for extensive distribution. Usually the kit is a cardboard folder with inside pockets.

Plan a Marketing Strategy

The practitioner should determine precisely what is to be sold. Is the purpose only to increase public awareness of the individual, or is it to publicize the client's product, such as a new television series, motion picture, or book? Next, the practitioner should decide which audiences are the most important to reach. For instance, an interview with a romantic operatic tenor on a rock-'n'-roll radio station would be inadvisable. But an appearance by the singer on a public television station's talk show would be right on target. A politician trying to project herself as a representative of minority groups should be scheduled to speak before audiences in minority neighborhoods and placed on radio stations whose demographic reports show that they attract minority listeners.

Conduct the Campaign

In most cases, the best course is to project the client on multiple media simultaneously. Radio and television appearances create public awareness and often make newspaper feature stories easier to obtain. The process works in reverse as well. Using telephone calls and "pitch" letters to editors and program directors, the publicist should propose print and on-air interviews with the client. Every such approach should include a news or feature angle for the interviewer to develop. Because magazine articles require longer to reach print, the publicist should begin efforts to obtain them as early as feasible.

An interview in an important magazine—a rising female movie star in *Cosmopolitan* or *Ladies' Home Journal*, for example—has major impact among women readers. Backstage maneuvering often takes place before such an interview appears. Agents for entertainers on their way up eagerly seek to obtain such an interview. When a personality is "hot" or at the top of the ladder, however, magazine editors compete for the privilege of publishing the interview. The star's agent plays them off against each other, perhaps offering exclusivity but demanding such rewards as a cover picture of the star, the right to choose the interviewer (friendly, of course), and even approval of the article. Editors of some magazines yield to publicists' demands. Other publications refuse to do so.

News Releases. News releases are an important publicity tool, but the practitioner should avoid too much puffery. *Bulldog Reporter*, a West Coast public relations newsletter, once gave a "fireplug" award to a press agent who wrote a release about a Frank Sinatra concert in the Dominican Republic. The release said, in part:

> The Sinatra concert represented the first time a legendary star has ever performed for a subscription pay television service. The historical event, in a balmy night that could only rival, not surpass, the audience's decibel level for enthusiasm, should overshadow any in-person star appearance ever offered on subscription television. The Sinatra and Santana/Heart doubleheaders may well be recorded as pay TV milestones.

Photographs. Photographs of the client should be submitted to the print media as often as justifiable. Media kits usually include the standard head-and-shoulders portrait, often called a "mug shot." Photographs of the client doing something interesting or appearing in a newsworthy group may be published merely with a caption, without an accompanying story. The practitioner and the photographer should be inventive, putting the client into unusual situations. The justification for a successful submission may be thin if the picture is not colorful and/or timely. If the client seeks national attention, such pictures should be submitted to the news services so that, if newsworthy, they will be distributed to hundreds of newspapers. (Requirements for photographs are discussed in Chapter 15.)

Sharply increased awareness among editors of women's concern about sexual exploitation has largely eliminated "cheesecake" pictures—photographs of nubile young women in which the news angle often is as skimpy as their attire—from newspaper pages. At one time such pictures were published frequently as editors tried to spice up their pages. Such photos, blatantly contrived and perhaps in bad taste—

Publicity, often calling "getting ink," is important in the entertainment business. The publicist for the Harlem Globetrotters got extensive media coverage by having the team present Pope John Paul II with a basketball while they were playing exhibition games in Italy.

such as the one of a smiling man pointing to the replica of a check painted on the bare stomach of a belly dancer—occasionally show up in print today. The caption of the photo of the belly dancer's stomach read: "Julian Caruso, an entertainment manager, arrived in court in Stafford, England, yesterday to pay a parking fine. He didn't want to pay the fine, the equivalent of $17, because, he said, Stafford lacks adequate parking. To emphasize his displeasure, he presented the court a check written on the stomach of a belly dancer, Sandrina. Court officials took a look at her—real name, Sandra Audley—and decided they couldn't handle the check in that form."

Stunts like this are a throwback to old-time gimmick press agentry, yet sometimes they succeed. The picture was distributed by the Associated Press and published large size in at least one metropolitan newspaper.

Cheesecake photographs still are printed in the trade press, even though they are seldom seen in daily newspapers in America. Certain British and Australian newspapers, however, continue to publish large photos of skimpily clad young women, who are often topless.

Public Appearances. Another way to intensify awareness of individual clients is to arrange for them to appear frequently in public places. Commercial organizations at times invite celebrities of various types or pay them fees to dress up dinner meetings, conventions, and even store openings. A major savings and loan association employed a group of early-day television performers to appear at openings of branch offices. Each day for a week for two hours an entertainer stood in a guest booth, signing autographs and chatting with visitors, who received a paperback book of pictures recalling television's pioneer period. Refreshments were served. A company photographer took pictures of the celebrity talking to guests. Visitors who appeared in the pictures received copies as souvenirs. These appearances benefited the sponsor by attracting crowds and helped the entertainers stay in the public eye.

Awards. A much-used device, and a successful one, is to have a client receive an award. The practitioner should be alert for news of awards to be given and nominate the client for appropriate ones. Follow-up communications with persuasive material from the practitioner may convince the sponsor to make the award to the client. In some instances, the idea of an award is proposed to an organization by a practitioner, whose client then conveniently is declared the first recipient. The entertainment business generates immense amounts of publicity for individuals and shows with its Oscar and Emmy awards. Winning an Academy Award greatly strengthens a performer's career.

Psychologists believe that televised awards ceremonies give viewers a sense of structure in life. This return to normalcy partly explains why the Emmy awards ceremony was rescheduled twice after the September 11 attack on the World Trade Center and Pentagon so that "the show could go on."

Nicknames and Labels.   Creating catchy nicknames for clients, especially sports and entertainment figures, helps the practitioner get their names into print. Celebrity worshipers like to call their heroes and heroines by nicknames, as though they have personal relationships with them. Thus, we see and hear familiarities for professional basketball players such as "Air Jordan" and "Sir Charles" Barkley and "Old Blue Eyes" and "The Boss" for entertainers.

A questionable variation of the nickname consists of adding a descriptive word to the name of the person being publicized to create a desirable image or career association. Sometimes this is done to provide a respectable veneer for a person of dubious background. In the Palm Springs resort area, to cite one instance, a socially active figure named Ray Ryan hired a practitioner whose task was to build up the image of Ryan as a well-to-do oilman. In every news release about Ryan and every telegram inviting social, business, and media individuals to Ryan's elaborate parties, the practitioner referred to his client as "oilman Ray Ryan." Publications in the area consistently printed "oilman Ray Ryan," generating the effect the publicist desired. Actually, Ryan also was involved in big-time professional gambling—an involvement apparently responsible for the fact that when he turned the ignition key of his automobile one day, a bomb planted in the car killed him.

Record the Results

Those who employ practitioners want tangible results in return for their fees. The practitioner also needs to compile and analyze the results of a personality campaign to determine the effectiveness of the various methods used. Tearsheets, photographs, copies of news releases, and, when possible, videotape clips of the client's public appearances should be given to the client. Clipping services help the practitioner assemble this material. At the end of the campaign, or at intervals in a long-term program, summaries of what has been accomplished should be submitted to the client.

Promoting an Entertainment Event

Attracting attendance at an event—anything from a theatrical performance to a fundraising fashion show or a street carnival—requires a well-planned publicity campaign.

Publicity to Stimulate Ticket Sales

The primary goal of any campaign for an entertainment event is to sell tickets. An advance publicity buildup informs listeners, readers, and viewers that an event will occur and stimulates their desire to attend. Rarely, except for community events publicized in smaller cities, do newspaper stories and broadcasts about an entertainment event include detailed information on ticket prices and availability. Those facts usually are deemed too commercial by editors and should be announced in paid advertising. However, some newspapers may include prices, times, and so on in tabular listings of scheduled entertainments. Performance dates usually are included in publicity stories.

Stories about a forthcoming theatrical event, motion picture, rock concert, book, or similar commercial activity should concentrate on the personalities, style, popularity of the activity or product. Every time the product or show is mentioned, public awareness grows. Thus, astute practitioners search for fresh news angles to produce as many stories as possible. The promotion of Harry Potter is a good example.

An Example: Publicizing a Play

The methods for publicizing a new play are the same whether the work will be performed on Broadway by professionals or in the local municipal auditorium by a little-theater group.

Stories include an announcement that the play will be presented, followed by releases reporting the casting of lead characters, the beginning of rehearsals, and the opening date. Feature stories, or "readers," discuss the play's theme and background, with quotations from the playwright and director inserted to emphasize an important point. In interviews, the play's star can tell why he or she finds the role significant or amusing.

Photographs of show scenes, taken in costume during rehearsal, should be distributed to the media to give potential customers a preview. As a reminder, a brief "opening tonight" story may be distributed. If a newspaper lists theatrical events in tabular

Books, before publication, often have extensive promotion and publicity that create "buzz." Here, young customers line up at a New England book fair to get the latest Harry Potter book, "Harry Potter and the Order of the Phoenix."

form, the practitioner might submit an entry about the show. In some instances, publicity also can be generated through use of e-mail and the World Wide Web.

The "Drip-Drip-Drip" Technique

Motion picture studios, television production firms, and networks apply the principle of "drip-drip-drip" publicity when a show is being shot. In other words, there is a steady output of information about the production. A public relations specialist, called a unit man or woman, is assigned to a film during production and turns out a flow of stories for the general and trade press and plays host to media visitors to the set. The television networks mail out daily news bulletins about their shows to media television editors. They assemble the editors annually to preview new programs and interview their stars. The heaviest barrage of publicity is released shortly before the show openings.

As an example of the uncertainty and high stakes surrounding television programming, the national television networks—ABC, CBS, NBC, Fox, UPN, and WB—offer dozens of pilot programs, most of which lack staying power. Other such pilots may survive near-death experiences the way *Seinfeld* did in 1989 when ratings were dismal. A year later, the comedy series reappeared to begin a rise in popularity that culminated in the hype surrounding the final episode. An audience estimated at 80 million generated advertising revenues of $1.6 million for a 30-second spot. The publicity and suspense surrounding the final episode were so great that Jerry Seinfeld declared, "I'm sick of myself." The comedian's discomfort probably was relieved somewhat by his $1 million salary per episode.

A much-publicized device is to have a star unveil his or her star in the cement of the Hollywood Walk of Fame, just before the star's new film appears. Videotaped recordings of the event turn up on TV stations across the country.

One danger of excessive promotion of an event, however, is that audience expectation may become too high, so that the performance proves to be a disappointment. A skilled practitioner will stay away from "hype" that can lead to a sense of anticlimax.

A Look at the Movie Industry

Motion picture public relations departments use market research and demographics and psychographics to define the target audiences they seek to reach. Most motion picture publicity is aimed at 18- to 24-year-olds, where the largest audience lies. Seventy-five percent of the film audience is under age 39, although increased attendance by older moviegoers has become evident recently.

Professional entertainment publicity work is concentrated in New York and Los Angeles, the former as the nation's theatrical center and the latter as the motion picture center. (American television production is divided primarily between these two cities, with the larger portion in Los Angeles.)

A typical Los Angeles–area public relations firm specializing in personalities and entertainment has two staffs: one staff of "planters," who deliver to media offices publicity stories about individual clients and the projects in which they are engaged, and another staff of "bookers," whose job is to place clients on talk shows and in other public appearances. Some publicity stories are for general release; others are prepared especially for a single media outlet such as a syndicated Hollywood columnist or a

ON THE JOB insights

Celebrity Publicists Have It Easy—Not!

Many aspiring public relations students believe that it would be fun and glamorous to work in entertainment public relations. And, in fact, the glamor and glitz, as well as the fascination of the personalities, do exist. But being a publicist to the stars can have its drawbacks, a truism that dates back to the ancient Mayan civilization. Mayan rulers of independent municipalities vied for loyalty primarily through events and publicity to achieve celebrity status for themselves. According to an article in *Antiquity*, scribes who failed to raise the celebrity status of their rulers could have fingernails removed and fingers broken.

Nothing quite so dire takes place in modern celebrity public relations. The challenges have more to do with a hectic pace, late hours, and the demands of magazines such as *People* and *GQ* for exclusive interviews. The paparazzi with their invasive cameras and tabloids with their scurrilous headlines both seek to do damage to your celebrity client—simply to sell newspapers and tabloids. Your job as a celebrity publicist is to manage these forces effectively for your client.

Perhaps the biggest challenge, though, is to deal with wrongdoing on the part of a celebrity. Whether this behavior is a lark such as Britney Spears' short and impulsive marriage in Las Vegas to a childhood friend or murder charges against a client, the publicist will face some hectic days. Anita Chabria of *PRWeek* offers the following do's and do not's of litigation PR for celebs:

DO'S	DONT'S
Do make sure that your statements are accurate. The press will pick up on even innocent mistakes as potential lies.	Don't keep quiet. Give an attorney respect, but don't fear giving an opinion if he or she is hamming it up too much in court or in front of the cameras.
Do get written approval of all statements before releasing them.	Don't avoid giving details. If it's in the public record, it's fair game.
Do ask the attorney to speak directly to media. It ensures that statements are worded correctly.	Don't talk too much. Keep brief and to the point, without adding details of your own.

major newspaper. The latter type is marked "exclusive," permitting the publication or station that uses it to claim credit for "breaking" the story.

Another device is to provide supplies of tickets for a new movie or show to radio stations, whose disc jockeys award them to listeners as prizes in on-the-air contests. In the process, these announcers mention the name of the show dozens of times. Glamorous premieres and trips for media guests to distant points so that they can watch the filming or attend an opening are used occasionally, too.

For such services to individual or corporate entertainment clients, major Hollywood publicists charge at least $3,000 a month, with a three-month minimum. The major studios and networks have their own public relations staffs.

Entertainment firms also may specialize in arranging product placement in movies and television programs. Usually the movie or television producers trade visible placement of a product in the show in exchange for free use of the item in the film.

For example, Ford Motor Company provided the Explorer sport utility vehicle that was destroyed by a dinosaur in the movie *Jurassic Park*. The vehicle was then marketed with Mattel Toys as the *Jurassic Park* Explorer.

The fast-food industry also provides excellent opportunities for market-based public relations involving giveaways of film characters with meals. Movies such as *The Lion King* received huge boosts in visibility and ticket sales. Characters from a film can provide a key incentive to young customers in the highly competitive takeout business, providing a large but transitory advantage in the so-called "burger wars."

Sports Publicity

The sports mania flourishing in the United States and in various forms around the world is stimulated by intense public relations efforts. Programs at both the big-time college and professional levels seek to arouse public interest in teams and players, sell tickets to games, and publicize the corporate sponsors who subsidize many events. Increasingly, too, sports publicists work with marketing specialists to promote the sale of booster souvenirs and clothing, a lucrative sideline for teams.

Sports publicists use the normal tools of public relations—media kits, statistics, interviews, television appearances, and the like—to distribute information. But dealing with facts is only part of their role. They also try to stir emotions. For college publicists, this means creating enthusiasm among alumni and making the school glamorous and exciting in order to recruit high school students. Publicists for professional teams work to make them appear to be hometown representatives of civic pride, not merely athletes playing for high salaries.

Sometimes these efforts succeed spectacularly, if the team is a winner. When a team is an inept loser, however, the sports publicist's life turns grim. He or she must find ways to soothe public displeasure and, through methods such as having players

Sports figures and their teams receive considerable publicity by appearing on various sports and game shows. Here, Diane Taurasi *(right)* of the Phoenix Mercurys (National Basketball Association) appears on ESPN after receiving the Rookie of the Year award.

conduct clinics at playgrounds and make sympathetic visits to hospitals, create a mood of patient hopefulness: "Wait 'til next year!"

Emerging sports increasingly compete for prominence and fan loyalty against more established sports. Soccer is widely popular among youth in America, leading to hopes among its promoters that the professional game will make inroads in the U.S. sports market. The Professional Golf Association (PGA) bought an 11-page advertising supplement in *Business Week* magazine to promote the professional golfer as a great athlete, philanthropic leader, and consummate professional in the face of rigorous travel and performance pressures.

Because the public yearns for heroes, publicists focus on building up the images of star players, sometimes to excess. They know that stars sell tickets. The 1998 baseball season featured record-breaking home-run performances by both Mark McGwire and Sammy Sosa. The home-run race may not have been the sole attraction that saved baseball from doldrums that many traced to the baseball strike and shortened season several years earlier. Nevertheless, the two sluggers are credited with bringing baseball "all the way back" as America's sport. By contrast, media treatment of McGwire's successor as home-run king reflects the principle in public relations that building positive relationships over time leads to success. Less attention and adulation was accorded Barry Bonds in 2001 when he broke McGwire's record, partly because of Bonds's diffidence toward the media over the years.

Because sports in America is big business, with $150 billion in gross annual revenues, an unseemly side frequently crops up in sports coverage. The impasse between players and owners in the National Hockey League (NHL) was only the latest instance that caused fans to lose patience with both the wealthy owners and the highly paid players. Intractable positions by both sides threaten the future of the professional league.

Public relations plays a critical role in sports, far beyond the promotion of celebrities. Two important areas are sports crisis management and sponsorship management. According to John Eckel of Hill and Knowlton Sports, professional communicators must deal with the media focus on issues ranging from player strikes to high ticket and concession costs to boorish athletes who deny that they are role models, even while they benefit from their visibility as role models. Jay Rosenstein of Cohn & Wolfe attributes much of sports crisis public relations to the "human factor in the sports world, where egos are otherworldly, behavior is reminiscent of the entertainment world, and media focus is unrelenting."

Management of sports sponsorships has become systematic and deliberate. For example, Edelman Event and Sponsorship Marketing uses its "M.U.S.T.S.ystem" to evaluate sponsorships. The acronym means:

Media appeal

User friendliness

Sales appeal

Thematic applications

Special event potential

The advertising agency DDB Needham studied the effectiveness of a very high profile sponsorship, the Summer Olympics. The agency found that the Olympic Games require a huge commitment of $40 million per sponsor, plus extensive costs in marketing that sponsorship to the company's benefit in sales and goodwill. Only about

ON THE JOB

global

Beijing Garners Sports and Travel Prize

The selection of Beijing as the venue for the 2008 Olympic Games was both a sports and travel coup for the Chinese government. The *Beijing Morning Post* trumpeted the selection with the headline, "Smiles Everywhere, Joy Ignites." And indeed, China has received the opportunity to manage what Richard Yarbrough calls "one of the world's largest bullhorns" for displaying a city and country's achievements and character.

However, the hosting of the Games in Beijing is not without conflict, and some of the conflict management techniques described in Chapter 10 may have to be applied to travel and sports public relations surrounding the Games. The following are prominent issues that the Olympic organizers must address:

- Taiwan has expressed fear that the Games will fuel Chinese na-

tionalism, leading to stronger moves to reincorporate the island nation into China.
- The Dalai Lama and his Tibetan government in exile have heralded the Games coming to China, provided that it is a stimulus for societal change and freedom.
- The United States has urged China to show a "modern" face to the world, which it appears to be striving to accomplish.
- Amnesty International has remained neutral about the Games, urging China to improve its human rights record.
- Perhaps a sore loser, French officials argue that awarding the Games to China flouts freedom and violates human rights, much like giving the 1936 Games to Nazi Germany.
- In Germany, the interior minister opines that the Games will spur China's democratic development.

- Sponsors look on with concern that their enormous corporate contributions to the Games in China will not besmirch their companies.
- Environmental activists look with interest at one of the three themes of the Olympics offered by Beijing: A Green Olympics that showcases environmental concerns for the globe and showcases the billions spent on environmental reform in China.

The Chinese government, in collaboration with its public relations firm Weber Shandwick Worldwide, has begun to address these issues proactively. A combination of effective communication and constructive behavior may enable "Smiles Everywhere, Joy Ignites" to be the headline once again at the close of the 2008 Olympic Games.

half of sponsors successfully linked their names to the Games. The agency recommends an integrated plan that uses the sponsorship as the focal point but includes many opportunities for coverage. Perhaps the best example was the daily auctioning of custom-made, numbered Hanes T-shirts for 500 consecutive days before the 1996 Olympics. The Olympic sponsor donated the million-dollar proceeds to children in war-ravaged Sarajevo, a former Olympic city.

Travel Promotion

With money in their pockets, people want to go places and see things. Stimulating that desire and then turning it into the purchase of tickets and reservations is the goal of the travel industry. Public relations has an essential role in the process, not only in attracting visitors to destinations but in keeping them happy once they arrive.

Like entertainment and sports, travel draws from the public's recreation dollars. Often its promoters intertwine their projects with those of entertainment and sports entrepreneurs.

Phases of Travel Promotion

Traditionally, the practice of travel public relations has involved three steps:

1. Stimulating the public's desire to visit a place
2. Arranging for the travelers to reach it
3. Making certain that visitors are comfortable, well treated, and entertained when they get there

Recently, terrorism has focused emphasis on a crucial new element—protecting the travelers' safety.

Stimulation is accomplished through travel articles in magazines and newspapers, alluring brochures distributed by travel agents and by direct mail, travel films, and videos, and presentations on the World Wide Web. Solicitation of associations and companies to hold conventions in a given place encourages travel by groups.

Some publications have their own travel writers; others purchase freelance articles and pictures. Well-done articles by public relations practitioners about travel destinations often are published, too, if written in an informational manner without resorting to blatant salesmanship and purple prose. Aware of public resistance to such exaggeration, *Condé Nast Traveler* magazine carries the slogan "Truth in Travel" on its cover. In fact, *O'Dwyer's PR Services Report* warns that "PR overkill" results from indiscriminate distribution of news releases, nagging follow-up calls to editors about releases, ignorance about the publication being pitched with a story, and excessive handling of writers on arranged trips so that the writer finds it difficult to get a complete picture of the travel destination.

Arrangements for travel are made through travel agencies or by direct booking at airlines, airports, and railroad and bus stations. Complicated tours and cruises are arranged most frequently by travel agencies, which charge customers retail prices for accommodations and receive a 10 percent commission from the travel supplier. Wholesalers create package tours that are sold by travel agencies.

To promote sales, the 38,000 U.S. travel agencies distribute literature, sponsor travel fairs, and encourage group travel by showing destination films at invitational meetings. Cities and states operate convention and travel departments to encourage tourism. A widely used method of promoting travel is the familiarization trip, commonly called a "fam trip," in which travel writers and/or travel salespeople are invited to a resort, theme park, or other destination for an inspection visit. In the past, fam trips often were loosely structured mass junkets. Today they are smaller and more focused.

Good treatment of travelers is a critical phase of travel promotion. If a couple spends a large sum on a trip, then encounters poor accommodations, rude hotel clerks, misplaced luggage, and inferior sightseeing arrangements, they come home angry. And they will tell their friends vehemently how bad the trip was.

Even the best arrangements go awry at times. Planes are late, tour members miss the bus, and bad weather riles tempers. This is where the personal touch means so much. An attentive, cheerful tour director or hotel manager can soothe guests, and a "make-good" gesture such as a free drink or meal does wonders. Careful training of travel personnel is essential. Many travelers, especially in foreign countries, are uneasy in strange surroundings and depend more on others than they would at home.

Fear of Terrorism

The tragic events of September 11 in New York, Washington, D.C., and Pennsylvania created an upsurge of fear and uncertainty about traveling. The Travel Industry Association of America estimates that the impact two months after the terrorist attacks was $43 billion in lost revenue and the disappearance of 527,000 tourism-related jobs. President George W. Bush taped two public service announcements to encourage

ON THE JOB ethics

How Many "Freebies" to Accept?

Creation of newspaper and magazine stories about travel destinations, which are essential in tourism promotion, poses a problem for writers and public relations people. Who should pay the writer's expenses in researching these stories?

Some large newspapers forbid their travel writers to accept free or discounted hotel rooms, meals, and travel tickets. They believe that such subsidies may cause writers to slant their articles too favorably, perhaps subconsciously.

Many smaller publications and most freelance writers cannot afford such an expensive rule, however, and following it would prevent them from preparing travel articles. One freelance travel writer, Jeff Miller, took the publishing industry to task in *Editor & Publisher* magazine for paying $150 per newspaper story and $500 to 1000 per magazine

story while banning writers from taking subsidized trips. Travel writers claim the hypocritical policy makes the publications look good, but that it is regularly ignored by travel writers who simply cannot make a living without subsidized trips. The writers contend that pride in their professional objectivity keeps them from being influenced by their hosts' "freebies." Some point to critical articles they have written on subsidized trips.

For the public relations director of a resort, cruise, or other travel attraction, the situation presents two problems: (1) How much hospitality can be given to the press before the "freebies" become a form of bribery? and (2) How does the director screen requests from self-described travel writers who request free housing or travel?

The Society of American Travel Writers (SATW) sets the following guideline:

Free or reduced-rate transportation and other travel expenses must be offered and accepted only with the mutual understanding that reportorial research is involved and any resultant story will be reported with the same standards of journalistic accuracy as that of comparable coverage and criticism in theater, business and finance, music, sports, and other news sections that provide the public with objective and helpful information.

What do you think of the SATW guidelines? Are they specific enough to guide you in your public relations position for a gorgeous Caribbean resort?

What of the "no sponsored trips" policy at some newspapers and magazines?

Do you believe that heavily discounted trips tend to buy writer loyalty in the same way that free trips do?

travel on behalf of the industry. Nevertheless, Americans were shocked to realize how vulnerable their country was to terrorism.

Security measures were strengthened at airports and aboard airplanes, causing travelers inconvenience and delay. Even so, security experts emphasize the impossibility of a 100 percent guarantee against terrorist attacks.

Travel Business on the Internet Takes Off

Airline tickets, hotel accommodations, and travel packages can be readily shopped for and then booked on the World Wide Web. Consumers have found the convenience and the discounted Internet specials to be highly attractive, resulting in a major increase in online travel transactions. Web sites such as Travelocity.com not only offer complete airline booking services but also provide e-mail notification to members of fare changes for itineraries selected by the online user. Airlines and hotels find that last-minute inventory of seats or rooms can be sold effectively online. Because of such online commerce, hotels, resorts, and cruise lines can afford to mount extensive Web sites that provide outstanding information to consumers and journalists alike.

Appeals to Target Audiences

Travel promoters identify target audiences, creating special appeals and trips for them. Great Britain's skillfully designed publicity in the United States is a successful example. Its basic appeal is an invitation to visit the country's historic places and pageants. It also offers London theatrical tours, golf expeditions to famous courses in Scotland, genealogical research parties for those seeking family roots, and tours of the cathedrals. Special tours can be arranged for other purposes as well.

There's always something new in the travel industry. Here, Queen Mary 2 makes its way past the Statue of Liberty in New York on its maiden voyage from England. A public relations firm handled the logistics of media coverage. Media were interested because the luxury cruise ship is the largest, longest, tallest, and most expensive ($800 million) ship ever built.

Packaging. *Packaging* is a key word in travel public relations. Cruises for family reunions or school groups, family skiing vacations, university alumni study groups, archaeological expeditions, even trips to remote Tibet are just a few of the so-called niche travel packages that are offered. A package usually consists of a prepaid arrangement for transportation, housing, most meals, and entertainment, with a professional escort to handle the details. Supplementary side trips often are offered for extra fees.

Appeals to Seniors. The largest special travel audience of all is older citizens. Retired persons have time to travel, and many have ample money to do so. Hotels, motels, and airlines frequently offer discounts to attract them. As a means of keeping old-school loyalties alive, many colleges conduct alumni tours, heavily attended by senior citizens.

A large percentage of cruise passengers, especially on longer voyages, are retirees. Alert travel promoters design trips with them in mind, including such niceties as pairing compatible widows to share cabins and arranging trips ashore that require little walking. Shipboard entertainment and recreational activities with appeal to older persons—nostalgic music for dancing rather than current hits, for example—are important, too.

Times of Crisis

Public relations in travel requires crisis management, just as in corporate work. Crises come in many forms, from those of dangerous magnitude to the small but embarrassing varieties.

The spate of attacks against Florida tourists in the early 1990s led to one of the highest-stake crisis management efforts of all time. A multibillion dollar source of revenue, Florida tourism suffered a deluge of damaging international publicity when nine foreign tourists were killed in separate incidents, mostly during robberies. Some victims were exchange students, whereas others were tourists gunned down only a few days after their arrival from abroad. Attempting to limit the damage, the Florida Division of Tourism sent faxes to 28,000 travel agents in North America, England, and Europe describing steps taken to help travelers and providing an 800 number for inquiries. Travel to Florida from Europe that winter decreased almost 50 percent from normal. Florida's strenuous public relations efforts to repair the damage to its tourism have paid off with a rebound in rates of tourism to Florida.

On a different level, the luxurious liner *Queen Elizabeth II* departed on a high-priced cruise before refurbishing was completed. Many passengers had unpleasant trips because some of the facilities were in disrepair, leading to one news report describing the ship as a floating construction project. Others had their reservations cancelled because their cabins were not completed. After bad international publicity and a class-action suit by some passengers, the Cunard cruise line offered a settlement. It gave full refunds of cruise fares plus a travel credit for a future cruise.

Sometimes a crisis results from a fluke. The supersonic Concorde flew to Tucson, Arizona, to pick up about 100 tourists who had paid up to $12,000 each for a flight to England, five days in London, and a return cruise. As the Concorde was being pulled out from the gate, a tow bar broke and a flying piece of debris punctured two tires on the plane. Because the Concorde carried only one spare, a second tire had to be flown out from New York. During the anticipated wait of several hours, passengers were entertained by an impromptu champagne breakfast on the taxi strip. Then airline officials realized that because of the Tucson delay, the Concorde could not make its necessary refueling stop in New York without violating that city's noise curfew law. The flight had to be postponed until the next day. Passengers who had expected to fly across the Atlantic at twice the speed of sound spent the night instead in a Tucson hotel and lost a day of their London visit.

Travel firms need to make certain that they provide equal facilities and service to all races and that their facilities are free from environmental pollution, as witness a cruise ship that had to pay a heavy fine after an environmentally aware passenger videotaped its crew members tossing debris overboard.

PR CASEBOOK

Viral Marketing—Word-of-Mouth Communication Updated

Long before the rise of the Internet, professional communicators recognized the value of favorable recommendations and "buzz" about a product or service. For public relations programs, the primary objective was often to enhance or maintain the reputation of a company or celebrity. Today, spreading the word can generate greater traffic to a Web site, where both marketing and public relations objectives can be met. The primary purpose of viral marketing is to stimulate impulse purchases or downloads, but increasingly pass-it-on techniques on the Web serve public relations objectives in reputation management and message dissemination. Generating excitement about the release of a musician's latest CD or the opening of a movie are two common uses of viral marketing in the entertainment business.

Viral marketing has adopted a new terminology and some special techniques that take advantage of new technology to stimulate a natural inclination to tell others about a good deal, a good service, or a good group. For example, Hotmail began to offer free e-mail in 1997, including a message on each e-mail: "get your free, private e-mail." Within a year and a half, Hotmail garnered 12 million subscribers for a total investment of half million dollars.

Viral marketing firms devise ways to stimulate the natural spread of recommendations through financial incentives called *cohort communication*. Going beyond the relatively natural spread of information through tactics similar to Hotmail's inviting message, viral marketing specialists orchestrate dissemination of favorable reviews. Software systems track referrals to a Web site or recommendations sent to friends, chalking up cash or merchandise credits for the sender. Recommending a CD to friends can earn the recommender credit or free downloads of music tracks, for example.

Detractors worry that viral marketing is easily recognized as commercial manipulation, except among hard-core enthusiasts. Others say that it is deceptive and unethical to facilitate or reward what should be a natural process of trusted friends exchanging tips and links about great deals or great Web sites. For example, the music industry recruits fans to log onto chat rooms and fan Web sites to hype a band's new album. Some liken this to the questionable old practice of payola in the radio industry—payment to disk jockeys for air time.

Viral marketing companies argue that the technique will work only when the idea, the movement, or the product earns genuine support

(continued)

PR CASEBOOK *(continued)*

from the marketplace. Then, Netizens take advantage of the convenience of the Web to forward what they like to others. Jupiter Communications found that over half of online users visit sites based on a recommendation and nearly all have forwarded a recommendation to another friend. Public relations professionals will need to make careful and ethical decisions to decide how best to use the Web to spread a message.

To explore viral marketing on your own and to consider how to adapt the techniques to your own public relations activities on campus, visit some of the Web sites of the following viral marketing companies:

- Caffeine Online Marketing Solutions at www.getcaffeinated.com
- Viralon Corporation at www.viralon.com
- EmailFactory.com at www.emailfactory.com

SUMMARY

Fascination with Celebrity

Today's mass media focus on the publicizing and glorification of celebrities in the fields of sports and entertainment and even high-profile criminals, some politicians, and members of the British royal family. Although the publicity buildup of individuals is not in the mainstream of public relations work, students in the field should learn how the personal publicity trade operates.

Enduring Celebrity: When the Good and Beautiful Die Young

Lady Diana Spencer achieved celebrity status through her marriage to Charles, Prince of Wales and heir to the British throne. The public was obsessed with her clothing, her public appearances, her eating disorder, and the failure of her marriage. Her early death has frozen her youthful image in time, and visitors to her family estate have paid to view the site of her burial.

The Mystique of Personality

Celebrities are motivated by fame (or notoriety), self-glorification, the attempt at positive image creation, and the desire for monetary gain. The public is impressed because of wish fulfillment, hero worship, a vicarious sense of belonging, and a desire for entertainment.

The Practitioner's Responsibility

A big factor for the public relations practitioner handling a personality will be damage control from misbehavior or an irresponsible public statement. This may strain the practitioner's ethical principles; it is never wise to lie to protect a client.

Conducting a Personality Campaign

A practitioner planning a campaign to generate public awareness of an individual must interview the client, prepare a biography, plan a marketing strategy, and conduct the campaign through news releases, photographs, and public appearances.

Promoting an Entertainment Event

Publicity campaigns to promote events may include publicity to stimulate ticket sales. The "drip-drip-drip" technique involves a steady output of information as the event is being planned. The motion picture industry defines target audiences.

Sports Publicity

Sports publicists promote both big-time college and professional teams. This effort becomes more difficult when the team isn't winning. Emerging sports must compete for prominence and fan loyalty with more established sports. Some publicity focuses on building images of star players. Publicity efforts will also include both sports crisis and sponsorship management.

Travel Promotion

Travel promotion will involve encouraging the public's desire to visit a place, arranging for them to reach it, making sure they enjoy their trip, and protecting their safety. Campaigns may include a familiarization trip to increase travel agents' awareness.

Case Activity: **What Would You Do?**

Martha Stewart, homemaking and lifestyle guru and media magnate, was convicted of lying to investigators during an insider trading stock sale case. Stewart opted to drop all legal appeals to serve her sentence without delay. The celebrity entered Alderson Federal Prison Camp, a minimum security prison near her 90-year-old mother and her own estate in Westbury, Connecticut, in October, expressing the hope that she would be released in time for spring planting in her garden.

Your celebrity public relations firm has been hired to develop a strategic communication plan for Martha's attempt to recapture the limelight and public support for her media and endorsement empire.

The overall goal should be to focus attention on Martha's many talents and her plucky response to her legal troubles, not on her legal problems themselves.

The firm is instructed to use traditional celebrity promotion tactics but also to capitalize on new technologies. You have suggested that a crisis communication plan also be implemented in the event of any further, although unforseen, developments on the legal front or any further erosion of the financial picture for Stewart's business enterprises. What would be your three main objectives, and what strategies would you showcase to achieve them? For your crisis communication plan, how would you handle further charges against Stewart regarding financial dealings if they were to arise?

QUESTIONS for Review and Discussion

1. Why do public relations students need to understand how the personal publicity trade functions, even if they do not plan to handle theatrical or sports clients?
2. Which of the five motivating factors in the cult of personality (fame, notoriety, self-glorification, repair of bad image, desire for money) make the most sense to you and why?
3. Name two psychological factors underlying the American obsession with celebrities.
4. When politicians say something they wish they hadn't and it is published, they often claim that they were misquoted. Why is this poor policy?
5. What is the first step in preparing a campaign to increase the public's awareness of an individual client?
6. What is a "bio"? What should it contain?
7. "Cheesecake" photographs once were commonplace in American newspapers, but few are published now. Why is this so?
8. What does Edelman's MUSTS acronym stand for? In your opinion, why is each element important?
9. Why do practitioners put emphasis on certain players on sports teams?
10. What are the basic phases of travel promotion?

SUGGESTED READINGS

Anderson, William B. "Crafting the National Pastime's Image: The History of Major-League, Baseball Public Relations." *Journalism and Communication Monographs*, Vol. 5, No. 1, 2003, pp. 1–43.

"Access Hollywood: Pat Kingsley Rewrites the Rules of Celebrity PR." *PR Tactics*, July 1999, pp. 26–27.
Chabria, Anita. "Stars in Scrapes: Litigation PR for Celebs." *PRWeek*, May 20, 2002, p. 18.

Chabria, Anita. "Travel Takes Off Again: Travel Has Picked Up in 2004, But the Industry Still Has Numerous Challenges to Overcome," *PR Week*, October 18, 2004, p. 17.

Giffard, C. Anthony, and Rivenburgh, Nancy K. "News Agencies, National Images, and Global Media Events." *Journalism and Mass Communication Quarterly*, Vol. 77, Spring 2000, pp. 8–21.

Hardin, Robin, and McClung, Steven. "Collegiate Sports Information: A Profile of the Profession." *Public Relations Quarterly*, Summer 2002, pp. 35–39.

Hindman, Elizabeth B. "The Princess and the Paparazzi: Blame, Responsibility, and the Media's Role in the Death of Diana." *Journalism and Mass Communication Quarterly*, Vol. 80, Autumn 2003, pp. 666–668.

Malinkina, Olga V., and McLead, Douglas M. "From Afghanistan to Chechnya: News Coverage by Izvestia and the *New York Times*." *Journalism and Mass Communication Quarterly*, Vol. 77, Spring 2000, pp. 37–49.

Sonmez, Sevil F., Apostolopoulos, Yiorgos, and Tarlow, Peter. "Tourism in Crisis: Managing Effects of Terrorism." *Journal of Travel Research*, Vol. 38, August 1999, pp. 13–18.

Tilson, Donn J. "Public Relations and Hollywood: A Fistful of Publicity." *Public Relations Quarterly*, Spring 2003, pp. 10–13.

Directory of Useful Web Sites

Public relations requires research and facts. Here's a sampling of sites on the Internet where you can find information.

General Information

www.highbeam.com: Provides full-text articles from multiple sources, including newspapers, newswires, magazines, etc.

www.newsindex.com: Offers access to hundreds of articles.

www.writersdigest.com/101sites/: "Best Web Sites for Writers," from dictionaries to general reference tools and writer's organizations.

www.bartleby.com/people/Strunk-W.html: Strunk & White's *The Elements of Style* online.

www.pollingreport.com: Compilation of findings from surveys regarding trends in public opinion.

www.thomas.loc.gov: Site of the Library of Congress and the starting point for legislative and Congressional information.

www.infoplease.com: Online almanacs on various topics from business to history and sports.

www.biography.com: Backgrounds on current and historical figures.

www.acronymfinder.com: Definitions of acronyms, abbreviations, and initialisms.

www.howstuffworks.com: Descriptions, diagrams, and photos that show how devices work.

www.statistics.com: Statistics from government agencies and other sources on a range of subjects.

www.ipl.org: The Internet Public Library; a University of Michigan site that gives links to all kinds of sources, from dictionaries to writing guides to newspapers.

resourceshelf.freepint.com: A favorite among reference librarians.

www.salary.com: Salaries in all fields, including public relations.

Public Relations

www.about.com: Provides multiple guide sites. Public relations site offers articles, directories, forums, etc.

www.pr-education.org: An aggregation of PR-related sites and services.

www.prplace.com: Lists Internet addresses and hot links to PR organizations and how-to information in the public relations field.

www.prcentral.com: Good source of case studies, also offers a news release library.

www.businesswire.com: News releases by company and industry.

www.prnewswire.com: News releases by company and industry.

www.workinpr.com: Job announcements, trends in employment, etc.

www.tsnn.com: The Trade Show News Network.

Organizations

www.prfirms.org: Council of Public Relations Firms

www.iabc.com: International Association of Business Communicators (IABC)

www.prsa.org: Public Relations Society of America (PRSA)

www.ipra.org: International Public Relations Association (IPRA)

www.pac.org: Public Affairs Council

www.niri.org: National Investor Relations Institute (NIRI)

www.instituteforpr.com: Institute of Public Relations (IPR)

www.ifea.com: International Festivals and Events Association (IFEA)

Publications

www.odwyerpr.com: O'Dwyer's PR/Marketing Communications Web site

www.prandmarketing.com: *PR News*

www.prexec.com: Ragan's newsletters and public relations resources

www.prsa.org/magazines.tactics: *Public Relations Tactics*

www.prsa.org/magazines.Strategist: *The Strategist*

www.prweekus.com: *PRWeek*

www.iabc.com/cw: *Communication World*

www.combriefings.com: *Communication Briefings*

Bibliography of Selected Books, Directories, and Periodicals

■ General Books

Bobbitt, Randy, and Sullivan, Ruth. *Developing the Public Relations Campaign: A Team-Based Approach.* Boston: Allyn and Bacon, 2005.

Caywood, Clarke, editor. *The Handbook of Strategic Public Relations and Integrated Communications.* New York: McGraw-Hill, 1997.

Cottle, Simon. *News, Public Relations, and Power.* Thousand Oaks, CA: Sage Publications, 2003.

Cutlip, Scott M., Center, Allen H., and Broom, Glen M. *Effective Public Relations,* 8th ed. Upper Saddle River, NJ: Prentice Hall, 2000.

Dilenschneider, Robert L., editor. *Dartnell's Public Relations Handbook,* 4th ed. Chicago: Dartnell, 1996.

Dozier, David M., with Grunig, James, and Grunig, Larissa. *Manager's Guide to Excellence in Public Relations and Communication Management.* Mahwah, NJ: Lawrence Erlbaum, 1995.

Elwood, William N. *Public Relations Inquiry as Rhetorical Criticism: Case Studies of Corporate Discourse and Social Influence.* Westport, CT: Praeger, 1995.

Grunig, James E., editor. *Excellence in Public Relations and Communication Management.* Hillsdale, NJ: Lawrence Erlbaum, 1991.

Grunig, Larissa A., Grunig, James E., and Dozier, David M. *Excellent Public Relations and Effective Organizations.* Mahwah, NJ: Lawrence Erlbaum, 2002.

Guth, David W., and Marsh, Charles. *Public Relations: A Values-Driven Approach.* Boston, 2d ed. Allyn and Bacon, 2003.

Harris, Thomas L. *Value-Added Public Relations.* Lincolnwood, IL: NTC Contemporary Books, 1998.

Heath, Robert L., editor. *Encyclopedia of Pubic Relations.* Thousand Oaks, CA: Sage Publications, 2004.

Heath, Robert L., editor. *Handbook of Public Relations.* Thousand Oaks, CA: Sage Publications, 2001.

Kendall, Robert. *Public Relations Campaign Strategies: Planning for Implementation,* 2d ed. New York: HarperCollins, 1996.

Lattimore, Dan, Baskin, Otis, Heiman, Suzette T., Toth, Elizabeth, and VanLeuven, James K. *Public Relations: The Profession and the Practice.* New York: McGraw-Hill, 2004.

Matera, Fran R., and Artique, Ray J. *Public Relations Campaigns and Techniques: Building Bridges to the 21st Century.* Boston: Allyn and Bacon, 2000.

McElreath, Mark. *Managing Systematic and Ethical Public Relations Campaigns,* 2d ed. Madison, WI: Brown & Benchmark, 1997.

Mickey, Thomas J. *Deconstructing Public Relations: Public Relations Criticism.* Mahwah, NJ: Lawrence Erlbaum, 2003.

Newsom, Doug, Turk, Judy Vanslyke, and Kruckeberg, Dean. *This Is PR: The Realities of Public Relations,* 8th ed. Belmont, CA: Thomson/Wadsworth, 2004.

Seitel, Fraser P. *The Practice of Public Relations,* 9th ed. Upper Saddle River, NJ: Prentice Hall, 2004.

Smith, Ronald D. *Strategic Planning for Public Relations,* 2d ed. Mahwah, NJ: Lawrence Erlbaum, 2005.

Theaker, Alison. *The Public Relations Handbook.* New York: Routledge, 2001.

Toth, Elizabeth L., and Heath, Robert L., editors. *Rhetorical and Critical Approaches to Public Relations.* Hillsdale, NJ: Lawrence Erlbaum, 1991.

Wilcox, Dennis L., and Cameron, Glen T. *Public Relations: Strategies and Tactics,* 8th ed. Boston: Allyn and Bacon, 2006.

Wilson, Laurie J. *Strategic Program Planning for Effective Public Relations Campaigns.* Dubuque, IA: Kendall-Hunt, 2000.

■ Special Interest Books

Business/Management

Austin, Erica W., and Pinkleton, Bruce E. *Strategic Public Relations Management.* Mahwah, NJ: Lawrence Erlbaum, 2001.

Ferguson, Sherry D. *Communication Planning: An Integrated Approach.* Thousand Oaks, CA: Sage Publications, 1999.

Ledingham, John A., and Bruning, Stephen D. *Public Relations as Relationship Management.* Mahwah: Lawrence Erlbaum, 1999.

Saffir, Leonard. *Power Public Relations: How to Master the New PR,* 2d ed. Lincolnwood, IL: NTC/Contemporary Publishing, 2001.

Careers

Helitzer, Melvin. *The Dream Job: Sports Publicity, Promotion, and Public Relations.* Athens, OH: University Sports Press, 1992.

Mogel, Leonard. *Making It in Public Relations: An Insider's Guide to Career Opportunities,* 2d ed. Mahwah, NJ: Lawrence Erlbaum, 2002.

Ross, Billy I., and Johnson, Keith F., editors. *Where Shall I Go to Study Advertising and Public Relations?* Lubbock, TX: Advertising Education Publications, 2004. (Pamphlet listing college and university programs.)

Sequin, James, editor. *Business Communications: The Real World and Your Career.* Belmont, CA: Southwestern College Publishing, 2000.

Case Studies

Center, Allen, and Jackson, Patrick. *Public Relations Practices: Managerial Case Studies and Problems,* 6th ed. Upper Saddle River, NJ: Prentice Hall, 2002.

Hendrix, Jerry A. *Public Relations Cases,* 6th ed. Belmont, CA: Thomson/Wadsworth, 2004.

Lamb, Lawrence F., and McKee, Kathy Brittain. *Applied Public Relations: Cases in Stakeholder Management.* Mahwah, NJ: Lawrence Erlbaum, 2004.

Matera, Fran R., and Artique, Ray J. *Public Relations Campaigns and Techniques: Building Bridges to the 21st Century.* Boston: Allyn and Bacon, 2000.

Moss, Danny, and DeSanto, Barbara. *Public Relations Cases: International Perspectives.* New York: Routledge, 2001.

Peterson, Gary L. *Communicating in Organizations: A Casebook.* Needham Heights, MA: Allyn and Bacon, 2000.

Communication/Persuasion

Bryant, Jennings, and Zillmann, Dolf. *Media Effects: Advances in Theory and Research.* Hillsdale, NJ: Lawrence Erlbaum, 1994.

Combs, James E., and Nimmo, Dan. *The New Propaganda: The Dictatorship of Palaver in Contemporary Politics.* New York: Longman, 1993.

DeFleur, Melvin L., and Dennis, Everette E. *Understanding Mass Communication.* Boston: Houghton Mifflin, 2001.

Jowett, Garth S., and O'Donnell, Victoria. *Propaganda and Persuasion.* 3d ed. Thousand Oaks, CA: Sage Publications, 1999.

Larson, Charles U. *Persuasion: Reception and Responsibility,* 10th ed. Belmont, CA: Thomson/Wadsworth, 2004.

Samovar, Larry, and Porter, Richard. *Intercultural Communication: A Reader,* 9th ed. Belmont, CA: Wadsworth, 2002.

Severin, Werner, and Tankard, James. *Communication Theories: Origins, Methods, Uses,* 5th ed. New York: Longman, 2000.

Simons, Herbert W., Morreale, Joanne, and Gronbeck, Bruce. *Persuasion in Society.* Thousand Oaks, CA: Sage Publications, 2000.

Crisis Communications

Adamson, Jim. *The Denny's Story: How a Company in Crisis Resurrected Its Good Name.* New York: John Wiley & Sons, 2001.

Coombs, W. Timothy. *Ongoing Crisis Communication: Planning, Managing, and Responding.* Thousand Oaks, CA: Sage Publications, 1999.

Fearn-Banks, Kathleen. *Crisis Communications: A Casebook Approach,* 2d ed. Mahwah, NJ: Lawrence Erlbaum, 2002.

Lerbinger, Otto. *The Crisis Manager: Facing Risk and Responsibility.* Mahwah, NJ: Lawrence Erlbaum, 1997.

Millar, Dan P., and Heath, Robert L., editors. *A Rhetorical Approach to Crisis Communications.* Mahwah, NJ: Lawrence Erlbaum, 2004.

Mitroff, Ian I. *Managing Crises Before They Happen.* New York: AMACOM, 2001.

Ogizek, Michel, and Guilery, Jean-Michel. *Communicating in Crisis: A Theoretical and Practical Guide to Crisis Management.* New York: Aldine De Gruyter Publishers, 1999.

Cultural Diversity/Gender

Banks, Stephen P. *Multicultural Public Relations: A Social Interpretive Approach.* Thousand Oaks, CA: Sage Publications, 1995.

Biagi, Shirley, and Kern-Foxworth, Marilyn. *Facing Differences: Race, Gender, and Mass Media.* Thousand Oaks, CA: Pine Forge Press, 1997.

Grunig, Larissa A., Toth, Elizabeth L., and Hon, Linda C. *Women in Public Relations: How Gender Influences Practice.* New York: Guilford Publications, 2001.

Desktop Publishing/Design

Kostelnick, Charles, and Roberts, David D. *Designing Visual Language: Strategies for Professional Communicators.* Boston: Allyn and Bacon, 1998.

Morton, Linda P. *Public Relations Publications: Designing for Target Audiences.* Norman, OK: Sultan Communication Books, 2001.

Education

Bagin, Don and Gallagher, Donald. *The School and Community Relations,* 8th ed. Boston: Allyn and Bacon, 2002.

Kowalski, Theodore J. *Public Relations in Schools.* Upper Saddle River, NJ: Prentice Hall, 2000.

Employee Relations

D'Aprix, Roger. *Communicating for Change: Connecting the Workplace with the Marketplace.* San Francisco: Jossey-Bass, 1996.

Holtz, Shel. *Intranets: The Communicator's Guide to Content, Design, and Management.* Chicago: Lawrence Ragan Communications, 1997.

Jablin, Fred M., and Putnam, Linda, editors. *The New Handbook of Organizational Communication.* Thousand Oaks, CA: Sage Publications, 2000.

Peterson, Gary L. *Communicating in Organizations*, 2d ed. Boston: Allyn and Bacon, 2000.

Spicer, Christopher. *Organizational Public Relations: A Political Perspective.* Mahwah, NJ: Lawrence Erlbaum, 1997.

Ethics

Day, Louis A. *Ethics in Media Communications: Cases and Controversies.* Belmont, CA: Wadsworth, 1997.

McElreath, Mark P. *Managing Systematic and Ethical Public Relations.* Dubuque, IA: Brown and Benchmark, 1997.

Seib, Philip, and Fitzpatrick, Kathy. *Public Relations Ethics.* Belmont, CA: Thomson/Wadsworth, 1995.

Stauber, John, and Rampton, Sheldon. Toxic Sludge Is Good for You: Damn Lies and the Public Relations Industry. Monroe, ME: Common Courage Press, 1995. (Critical analysis of public relations.)

Financial/Investor Relations

Higgins, Richard B. *Best Practices in Global Investor Relations.* Westport, CT: Greenwood, 2000.

Marcus, Bruce W., and Lee, Wallace Sherwood. *New Dimensions in Investor Relations: Competing for Capital in the 21st Century.* New York: John Wiley & Sons, 1998.

Trautmann, Ted, and Hamilton, James. *Informal Corporate Disclosure Under Federal Securities Law: Press Releases, Analyst Calls, and Other Communications.* Riverwoods, IL: CCH Incorporated, 2001.

Fund-Raising/Development

Ciconte, Barbara K., and Jacob, Jeanne G. *Fund Raising Basics: A Complete Guide.* Gaithersburg, MD: Aspen Publications, 1997.

Kelly, Kathleen S. *Effective Fund-Raising Management.* Mahwah, NJ: Lawrence Erlbaum, 1996.

Rosso, Henry. *Achieving Excellence in Fund-Raising.* San Francisco: Jossey-Bass, 1991.

Government/Public Affairs

Fitzwater, Marlin. *Call the Briefing! Reagan & Bush, Sam & Helen; a Decade with Presidents and the Press.* New York: New York Times Books, 1995.

Kurtz, Howard. *Spin Cycle: How the White House and the Media Manipulate the News.* New York: Touchstone, 1998.

Lewis, Michael. *Trail Fever: Spin Doctors, Rented Strangers, and Thumb Wrestling on the Road to the White House.* New York: Vintage Books, 1998.

Rollins, Ed, and DeFrank, Tom. *Bare Knuckles and Back Rooms.* New York: Broadway Books, 1996.

Walsh, Kenneth T. *Feeding the Beast: The White House Versus the Press.* New York: Random House, 1996.

History

Cutlip, Scott M. *Public Relations History: From the Seventeenth to the Twentieth Century.* Hillsdale, NJ: Lawrence Erlbaum, 1995.

Cutlip, Scott M. *The Unseen Power: Public Relations. A History.* Hillsdale, NJ: Lawrence Erlbaum, 1994.

Ewen, Stuart. *PR! A Social History of Spin.* New York: Basic Books, 1996.

Griese, Noel. *Arthur W. Page: Publisher, Public Relations Pioneer, Patriot.* Atlanta: Anvil Publishers, 2001.

Miller, Karen S. *The Voice of Business: Hill & Knowlton and Post-War Public Relations.* Chapel Hill: University of North Carolina Press, 1999.

Tye, Larry. *The Father of Spin: Edward L. Bernays and the Birth of Public Relations.* New York: Crown, 1998.

International

Grunig, Larissa A., and Grunig, James E. *Excellent Public Relations and Effective Organizations: A Study of Communication Management in Three Countries.* Mahwah, NJ: Lawrence Erlbaum, 2002.

Hall, Bradford J. *Among Cultures: The Challenge of Communication*, 2d ed. Belmont, CA: Thomson/Wadsworth, 2005.

Jandt, Fred E. *Intercultural Communication: An Introduction.* Thousand Oaks, CA: Sage Publications, 1998.

Samovar, Larry A., and Porter, Richard E. *Intercultural Communication: A Reader*, 10th ed. Belmont, CA: Thomson/Wadsworth, 2003.

Internet/World Wide Web

Albarran, Alan B., and Goff, David H. *Understanding the Web: Social, Political, and Economic Dimensions of the Internet.* Ames, IA: Iowa State University Press, 2000.

Alexander, Janet E., and Tate, Marsha Ann. *Web Wisdom: How to Evaluate and Create Information Quality on the Web.* Mahwah, NJ: Lawrence Erlbaum, 1999.

Holtz, Shel. *Public Relations on the Internet: Winning Strategies to Inform and Influence the Media, the Investment Community, the Government, the Public, and More!* New York: AMACOM, 1999.

McGuire, Mary, Stilborne, Linda, McAdams, Melinda, and Hyatt, Laurel. *The Internet Handbook for Writers, Researchers, and Journalists.* New York: Guilford Publications, 2000.

Middleburg, Don. *Winning PR in the Wired World.* New York: McGraw-Hill, 2001.

Sterne, Jim, and Priore, Anthony. *E-Mail Marketing: Using E-Mail to Reach Your Target Audience and Build Customer Relationships.* New York: John Wiley & Sons, 2001.

Witmer, Diane F. *Spinning the Web: A Handbook for Public Relations on the Internet.* Boston: Allyn and Bacon: 2000.

Issues Management

Heath, Robert L. *Strategic Issues Management: Organizations and Public Policy Challenges*, 2d ed. Thousand Oaks, CA: Sage Publications, 1997.

Law

Gower, Karla K. *Legal and Ethical Restraints on Public Relations.* Prospect Heights, IL: Waveland Press, 2003.

Haggerty, James F. *Winning Your Case with Public Relations.* New York: John Wiley & Sons, 2003.

Middleton, Kent, and Chamberlin, Bill. *Law of Public Communication*, 5th ed. Boston: Allyn and Bacon, 2005.

Moore, Roy L., Farrar, Ronald T., and Collins, Erik L. *Advertising and Public Relations Law.* Mahwah, NJ: Lawrence Erlbaum, 1998.

Roschwalb, Susanne A., and Stack, Richard A. *Litigation Public Relations: Courting Public Opinion.* Washington, D.C.: Fred B. Rothman, 1995.

Marketing

Duncan, Tom. *Principles of Advertising and IMC*, 2nd ed. New York: McGraw-Hill, 2004.

Gronstedt, Anders. *The Customer Century: Lessons from World Class Companies in Integrated Marketing and Communications.* New York: Routledge, 2000.

Henry, Rene A. *Marketing Public Relations: The HOWS That Make It Work.* Ames, IA: Iowa State University Press, 2000.

Murphy, John H., and Cunningham, Isabella. *Marketing Communications Management.* Lincolnwood, IL: NTC Contemporary Books, 1999.

Schreiber, Alfred. *Multicultural Marketing.* Lincolnwood, IL: NTC/Contemporary Publishing, 2000.

Schultz, Don E., and Barnes, Beth E. *Strategic Brand Communications Campaigns.* Lincolnwood, IL: NTC Contemporary Books, 1999.

Media/Press Relations

Hart, Hal. *Successful Spokespersons Are Made, Not Born.* Bloomington, IN: First Books Library, 2001.

Howard, Carole M., and Mathews, Wilima K. *On Deadline: Managing Media Relations*, 3d ed. Prospect Heights, IL: Waveland Press, 2002.

Strick, Michael. *Spin: How to Turn the Power of the Press to Your Advantage.* Washington, D.C.: Regnery Publishing, 1998.

Wallack, Katie, Woodruff, Katie, and Diaz, Iris. *News for a Change: An Advocate's Guide to Working with the Media.* Thousand Oaks, CA: Sage Publications, 1999.

Nonprofit Groups/Health Agencies

Berkowitz, Eric N., Pol, Louis G., and Thomas, Richard K. *Healthcare Marketing Research: Tools and Techniques for Understanding and Analyzing Today's Healthcare Environment.* New York: McGraw-Hill, 1997.

Rice, Ronald E., and Atkin, Charles K. *Public Information Campaigns*, 3d ed. Thousand Oaks, CA: Sage Publications, 2001.

Rungard, John. *Marketing and Public Relations Handbook for Museums, Galleries, and Heritage Attractions.* Blue Ridge Summit, PA: Rowman & Littlefield, 2000.

Publicity/Promotion

See also "Writing in Public Relations" section.

Levine, Michael. *Guerilla PR: How to Wage an Effective Publicity Campaign Without Going Broke.* New York: Harper Business, 1994.

Yale, David. *Publicity & Media Relations Checklist.* Lincolnwood, IL: NTC Business, 1995.

Research Methods

Berger, Arthur Asa. *Media and Communication Research Methods: An Introduction to Qualitative and Quantitative Research Approaches.* Thousand Oaks, CA: Sage Publications, 2000.

Ferguson, Sherry D. *Researching the Public Opinion Environment: Theories and Methods.* Thousand Oaks, CA: Sage Publications, 2000.

Fern, Edward F. *Advanced Focus Group Research.* Thousand Oaks, CA: Sage Publications, 2001.

Frey, Lawrence R., Botan, Carl H., and Kreps, Gary L. *Investigating Communication: An Introduction to Research Methods,* 2d ed. Boston: Allyn and Bacon, 2000.

Gubrium, Jaber E., and Holstein, James A. *Handbook of Interview Research.* Thousand Oaks, CA: Sage Publications, 2001.

Gunter, Barrie. *Media Research Methods: Measuring Audiences, Reactions, Impact.* Thousand Oaks, CA: Sage Publications, 2000.

Stacks, Don W. *Primer of Public Relations Research.* New York: The Guilford Press, 2002.

Special Events

Allen, Judy. *The Business of Event Planning: Behind-the-Scenes Secrets of Successful Special Events.* Etobicoke, Ontario: John Wiley & Sons, 2002.

Boehme, Ann J. *Planning Successful Meetings & Events.* New York: AMACOM, 1999.

Coons, Patricia C. Gala: *The Special Event Planner for Professionals and Volunteers.* Herndon, VA: Capital Books, 1999.

Goldblatt, Jeff. *Special Events: The Art and Science of Celebration.* New York: Van Nostrand Reinhold, 1997.

Jasso, Gayle. *Special Events from A to Z.* Thousand Oaks, CA: Sage Publications, 1996.

Speeches/Presentations

Beebe, Steven A., and Beebe, Susan. *Public Speaking: An Audience-Centered Approach,* 4th ed. Boston: Allyn and Bacon, 2000.

Brody, Marjorie. *Speaking Your Way to the Top: Making Powerful Business Presentations.* Boston: Allyn and Bacon, 1998.

Daly, John A., and Engleberg, Isa. *Presentations in Everyday Life.* Boston: Houghton Mifflin, 2001.

DiSanza, James, and Legge, Nancy. *Business and Professional Communication: Plans, Processes, and Performance.* Boston: Allyn and Bacon, 2000.

Fujishin, Randy. *The Natural Speaker,* 3d ed. Boston: Allyn and Bacon, 2000.

Writing in Public Relations

Bivins, Thomas H. *Public Relations Writing: The Essentials of Style and Format,* 4th ed. Lincolnwood, IL: NTC Contemporary Books, 1999.

Carstarphen, Meta G., and Wells, Richard A. *Writing PR: A Multimedia Approach.* Boston: Allyn and Bacon, 2004.

Diggs-Brown, Barbara, and Glou, Jodi L. G. *The PR Style Guide: Formats for Public Relations Practice.* Belmont, CA: Thomson/Wadsworth, 2004.

Newsom, Doug, and Haynes, Jim. *Public Relations Writing: Form and Style,* 7th ed. Belmont, CA: Thomson/Wadsworth, 2005.

Treadwell, Donald, and Treadwell, Jill B. *Public Relations Writing: Principles in Practice.* Thousand Oaks, CA: Sage Publications, 2004.

Whitaker, W. Richard, Ramsey, Janet E., and Smith, Ronald D. *Media Writing: Print, Broadcast, and Public Relations,* 2d ed. Mahwah, NJ: Lawrence Erlbaum, 2005.

Wilcox, Dennis L. *Public Relations Writing and Media Techniques,* 5th edition. Boston: Allyn and Bacon, 2005.

Zappala, Joseph M., and Carden, Ann R. *Public Relations Worktext.* Mahwah, NJ: Lawrence Erlbaum, 2004.

■ Directories

Directories are valuable tools for public relations personnel who need to com-municate with a variety of specialized audiences. The following is a selected list of the leading national and international directories.

Media Directories

All-In-One Media Directory. Gebbie Press, Box 1000, New Paltz, NY 12561.

American College Media Directory. Vineberg Communications, 6120 Grand Central Parkway, Forest Hills, NY 11375.

Bacon's Media Directories: Newspaper/Magazines, Radio/TV/ Cable, Media Calendar, Business Media, International Media Directory, New York Publicity Outlets, Metro California Outlets, Computer & High-Tech Media, and Medical & Health Media. Bacon Information, Inc., 332 S. Michigan Avenue, Chicago, IL 60604.

Broadcasting Cable Yearbook. Broadcasting & Cable Magazine, PO Box 7820, Torrance, CA 90504.

Burrelle's Media Directories: Newspapers and Related Media, Magazines and Newsletters, Radio, Television, and Cable. Burrelle's Media Directory, 75 E. Northfield Rd., Livingston, NJ 07039.

Cable & Station Coverage Atlas. Warren Publications, 2115 Ward Court NW, Washington, D.C. 20037.

College Media Directory. Oxbridge Communications, 150 Fifth Avenue, Suite 302, New York, NY 10011.

Editor & Publisher International Yearbook. Editor & Publisher, 11 W. 19th St., New York, NY 10011-4234.

Gale's Directory of Publications. Gale Group, PO Box 9187, Farmington Hills, MI 48333.

Hispanic American Information Directory. Gale Group, 27500 Drake Road, Farmington Hills, MI 48331-335.

Hudson's Washington News Media Directory. Hudson Associates, PO Box 311, Rhinebeck, NY 12572.

Literary Marketplace. R. R. Bowker Company, 245 W. 17th St., New York, NY 10011.

MediaMap. MediaMap, 130 The Great Road, Bedford, MA 01730.

National Directory of Community Newspapers. American Newspaper Representatives, 1700 W. Beaver Road, Suite 340, Troy, MI 48084.

National Directory of Magazines. Oxbridge Communications, 150 Fifth Avenue, Suite 302, New York, NY 10011.

North American Senior Media Directory. Gem Publishing Group, 250 E. Riverview Circle, Reno, NV 89509.

Publicists Guide to Senior Media. Promo Works, 4165 E. Thousand Oaks Blvd., Suite 335, Westlake Village, CA 91362.

Standard Rate and Data Services: Business Publications, Community Publications, Newspapers, and Spot Radio. SRDS, 3004 Glenview Rd., Wilmette, IL 60091.

The Top 200+ TV New Talk and Magazine Shows. Bradley Communications, PO Box 1206, Lansdowne, PA 19050.

U.S. All Media E-mail Directory. Direct Contact Media Services, PO Box 6726, Kennewick, WA 99336.

International Media Directories

Asia Pacific Media Guide. Asian News Service, 633 West 5th Street, Suite 2020, Los Angeles, CA 90071.

Benn's Media. Benn's Business Information Services, Riverbank House, Angelhare, Tonbridge, Kent TN9 1SE, United Kingdom.

Central American Media Directory. Florida International University School of Journalism, North Miami Campus, 3000 N.E. 151st Street, Miami, FL 33181.

Dun's Europe. Dun & Bradstreet Information Services, 3 Sylvan Way, Persipanny, NJ 07054.

European Media Yearbook: Western and Eastern Europe. CIT Publications, 3 Colleton Crescent, Exeter/Devon EX2 4DG, England.

Hollis PR Annual and Hollis Europe. Harlequin House, 7 High Street, Teddington, England TW11 8EL.

Urlichs International Directory. Reed Elsevier, 121 Chanlon Road, New Providence, NJ 07974.

Willing's Press Guide. Harlequin House, 7 High Street, Teddington, England TW11 8EL.

World Radio/TV Handbook. BPI Communications, 1695 Oak Street, Lakewood, NJ 08701.

Other Selected Directories

Awards, Honors, and Prizes. Gale Research, PO Box 9187, Farmington Hills, MI 48333.

Broadcast Interview Source. BIS, Inc., 2233 Wisconsin Avenue, Washington, D.C. 20007.

Business Organizations, Agencies, and Publications Directory. Gale Research, PO Box 9187, Farmington Hills, MI 48333.

Celebrity Source: Prime Time Television and Cast Directory. The Celebrity Source, 8033 Sunset Blvd., Suite 1108, Los Angeles, CA 90046.

Congressional Yellow Book. Leadership Directories, 1301 Pennsylvania Avenue NW, Suite 925, Washington, D.C. 20004.

Corporate Directory of Technology Companies. CorpTech, 12 Alfred Street, Suite 200, Woburn, MA 01801–9998.

Directory of Online Databases. Online Information Services, 152 Main Road, Long Hanborough, Oxford OX7 2JY, England.

Hudson's Subscription Newsletter Directory. Hudson Associates, PO Box 311, Rhinebeck, NY 12572.

National Directory of Mailing Lists. Oxbridge Communications, 150 Fifth Avenue, New York, NY 10011.

National PR Pitch Book. Infocom Group, 5900 Hollis Street, Suite R2, Emeryville, CA 94608-2008.

O'Dwyer's Directory of Corporate Communications; Directory of PR Executives; Directory of PR Firms. O'Dwyer's 271 Madison Avenue, New York, NY 10016.

Professional Freelance Writer's Directory. National Writer's Association, 1450 South Havana Street, Suite 424, Aurora, CO 80012.

The Society of American Travel Writer's Directory. Society of American Travel, 4101 Lake Boone Trail, Suite 201, Raleigh, NC 27607.

The Sourcebook of Multicultural Experts. Multicultural Marketing Resources, 332 Bleeker Street, Suite G41, New York, NY 10014.

Yearbook of Experts, Authorities, and Spokespersons. Broadcast Interview Source, 2233 Wisconsin Avenue NW, Suite 301, Washington, D.C. 20007.

■ Periodicals

CASE Currents. Council for the Advancement and Support of Education, 11 Dupont Circle, Washington, DC. 20036. Monthly.

Communication Briefings. 700 Black Horse Pike, Suite 110, Blackwood, NJ 08012. Monthly.

Communication World. International Association of Business Communicators (IABC), One Hallidie Plaza, Suite 600, San Francisco, CA 94102. Monthly.

International Public Relations Review. International Public Relations Association (IPRA). Cardinal House, 7 Woseley Road, East Molesey, Surrey KT8 9EL, United Kingdom. Quarterly.

Investor Relations Update. National Investor Relations Institute (NIRI), 8045 Leesburg Pike, Suite 600, Vienna, VA 22182. Monthly.

Jack O'Dwyer's PR Newsletter. O'Dwyer's, 271 Madison Ave., New York, NY 10016. Weekly.

Journal of Public Relations Research. Lawrence Erlbaum, 10 Industrial Ave., Mahwah, NJ 07430. Quarterly.

O'Dwyer's PR Services Report. O'Dwyer's, 271 Madison Ave., New York, NY 10016. Monthly.

pr reporter. Box 600, Exeter, NH 03833. Weekly.

PRWeek. 220 Fifth Avenue, New York, NY 10001. Weekly.

Public Relations News. 1201 Seven Locks Road, Potomac, MD 20854-3394. Weekly.

Public Relations Quarterly. 44 W. Market St., Rhinebeck, NY 12572. Quarterly.

Public Relations Review. JAI Press, 100 Prospect St., PO Box 811, Stamford, CT 06904-0811. Quarterly.

Public Relations Strategist. Public Relations Society of America (PRSA), 33 Irving Place, New York, NY 10003-2376. Quarterly.

Public Relations Tactics. Public Relations Society of America (PRSA), 33 Irving Place, New York, NY 10003-2376. Monthly.

Ragan Report. 212 West Superior St., Suite 200, Chicago, IL 60605. Weekly.

Special Events Report. 213 W. Institute Pl., Chicago, IL 60605. Biweekly.

Index

THE BAREFOOT BOOK OF

TRICKSTER TALES

Barefoot Collections
an imprint of
Barefoot Books
41 Schermerhorn Street, Suite 145
Brooklyn, New York
NY 11201-4845

Graphic design by Design / Section
Color reproduction by Grafiscan, Italy
Printed and bound in Hong Kong by South Sea International Press

ISBN 1 902283 08 2

Library of Congress Cataloging-in-Publication Data is available on request

1 3 5 7 9 8 6 4 2

THE BAREFOOT BOOK OF

TRICKSTER TALES

Retold by Richard Walker

Illustrated by Claudio Muñoz

BAREFOOT BOOKS

Contents

Foreword

In this anthology, you will travel the world and share some of my favorite trickster stories. Tricksters are those engaging characters who use all kinds of cunning tactics to overcome the seemingly insurmountable odds that are always stacked against them. You may well recognize some of the tricksters in these pages – Brer Rabbit, for instance – while others will not be quite so familiar. Some of the characters are human, some are animals, and in one story – "Turtle Goes on the Warpath" – even inanimate objects take on a life of their own.

Different peoples have different tricksters and I've tried to include a rich variety in my ragbag of rogues. I have chosen tales that I enjoy telling out loud and, although they come from different lands and peoples, you will hear my voice in all of them. Possibly you will find here and there just a hint of how they might have originally sounded, but I have chosen to tell them in my own way. For this is part of the magic of stories: many of them have traveled thousands of miles to settle comfortably into the repertoire of a storyteller in quite another land.

So I bid you welcome to the treasure store that I have selected for you. I hope you will enjoy reading this book quietly to yourself and, at other times, sharing the stories out loud with your family and friends. Above all, I hope that you find these stories entertaining and that you will get as much pleasure from them as they have given to me.

Richard Walker

Jack and the Wizard

ENGLISH

Jack had been out adventuring and was pleased to be on his way home to his wife, Mary. The problem was that he had no money and was starving hungry, so when he saw a tree loaded with hazelnuts it seeemed only right that he should "borrow" a few to see him on his way.

A few minutes later, he was walking along cracking the shells and enjoying the wonderful sweet flavor of the nuts when he came across one that was hollow. He looked and saw that a small grub

8

had bored its way
through the shell, eaten all
the goodness inside it and left by
the same hole.

"Mmm," he thought, "that might be useful."

So he put the empty hazelnut shell in his top
pocket and continued on down the road, munching
away. After a while, though, things stopped being so
good, because he had a hole in his tooth and it was
beginning to fill up. First it was just uncomfortable, then it
began to throb a little and soon it became a furiously raging
toothache that he didn't like at all. As if that wasn't bad
enough, it started to rain and he was getting wet through.

Jack knocked on the first door he came to. It opened and
there stood a great giant of a blacksmith
with brawny, muscular arms, a big
leather apron and a scowling face.
"What do you want?" he said.
"Just to come in and shelter
from the rain."
"Well you can't, so
shove off!" And with

that the door was slammed in Jack's face.

He continued on along the road out of the village and then he saw a path leading toward a rocky cliff-face. He followed the path and found a cave where at least he could take shelter from the rain.

Jack sat down on a stone at the back of the cave. What with being soaked to the skin and having an awful toothache, he was just about as miserable as he could ever remember being.

Then he realized that he wasn't alone.

He knew that if he just peeked over his shoulder, he'd see someone lurking in the darkness behind him. He didn't want to look, but you know how it can be: his brain was telling him to stay just as he was, but his head and eyes were determined to look, whatever his brain had to say about it.

He turned around, and there in the darkness he saw a man with a tall pointy hat, a long flowing cloak and a dense white beard. It was a wizard and one Jack knew to be very tricky indeed.

"Hello, Jack," he said. "I'm really pleased to see you here. I've got a job for you."

"What's that?"

"Under this cave is the place where I carry out my experiments, and it's getting very dirty. I can't find anybody to clean it for me so I've decided that you can be my servant."

"Oh no!" said Jack. "I'll be no servant of yours."

"You will," said the wizard, "if you want to get rid of your toothache. I can do two sorts of magic: one, and you'll have toothache for the rest of your life; the other, and it will go away forever – but only if you come with me. Now which is it to be?"

Jack thought for a second or two then said, "I'll come along with you for a while if you get rid of my toothache, but I won't be your servant. Instead I'll be your storyteller. How about that?"

It was the wizard's turn to think. It had been many long years since anybody had told him stories, and memories of bedtime tales and story time at wizards' school came flooding back to him. It would be really nice to hear some more.

"Very well," he said and Jack's toothache disappeared. "Now you must come with me, and if I enjoy the stories, all well and good. But if I don't, then you'll be my servant, whatever you say." And he set off down the dark spiral passage at the back of the cave with Jack following closely behind.

They went deep underground until they came to where the wizard did his magic. Jack saw bottles of bright, bubbling, colored liquids all around the place, joined up by a wild maze of tubing, and there was a big brass dome with lightning flashing from it. Strange boxes were piled higgledy-piggledy all around, even stranger shapes hung from the ceiling, and everything was dusty and covered in cobwebs. There were things going bang and things going fizz … and just two chairs in the middle of it all. The wizard sat on one and pointed to the other, but although Jack loved telling stories, he'd no intention of staying there any longer than he could possibly avoid.

"Before I tell you a tale," he said hesitantly, "how about showing me some magic?"

"Very well," replied the wizard, thinking that he might enjoy showing off a little. "What would you like me to do?"

"Can you do the trick where you change into different animals?"

"Easy," said the wizard, and with a twist of his ears and the puffing out of his cheeks there was a flash as he changed into a goat.

"Not bad, but a goat's quite small, isn't it? It's probably quite easy.

How about something bigger?"

Somehow the wizard, in the shape of a goat, managed to twist his ears and puff out his cheeks. There was another flash and there stood an elephant, which lumbered around smashing all the magical equipment.

"I bet you can't do something even bigger …" said Jack, "… something like a dinosaur?!"

Once again there was a flash and the cave was filled with the enormous bulk of a Tyrannosaurus Rex, its head pressed against the ceiling, which began to crumble under the pressure.

"Very good," said Jack quickly. "Obviously big things must be easy. But how about a mouse?"

It was quite a relief to see the wizard shrink down to a tiny mouse that scurried around doing no damage at all. Jack noticed that every time the wizard changed from whatever form he was in before, he somehow managed to twist his ears and puff out his cheeks.

"I know," said Jack, reaching into his pocket and removing the thing he had placed there right at the beginning of his adventure. "Can you change into something small enough to fit into this nut shell?"

"Easy peasy," said the wizard and changed into an ant.

"Prove that you're small enough," said Jack, putting the nut on the ground. The ant confidently walked into it, but as soon as it did, Jack took a large fistful of mud from the floor and crammed it in behind, pushing the creature against the side so that it could not move at all and certainly couldn't twist its ears or puff out its cheeks. Jack got more mud and pushed the nut into the middle of it, then holding it firmly he ran out of the wizard's cave, up the spiral passage and out through the top cave. He ran down the path and, as he did so, he felt the ball of mud getting harder and harder as the wizard, in the shape of an ant, tried to move around to work his magic.

Jack ran to the door that he'd knocked on during the rainstorm and once again it was opened by the bad-tempered blacksmith.

"What do you want now?"

"I just wondered," said Jack, "whether you could break this ball of mud on your anvil?"

"Give it here," said the blacksmith and tried to crush it with his great strong hands, but it was as hard as iron.

They went into the workshop and the smith placed the mud ball on his anvil. He took a small hammer and swung it as hard as he could, but it just bounced off the ball, slipped from his hand and clattered on to the floor.

He took a bigger hammer, but once again it didn't even leave a mark on the ball, so he tried a chisel which bent and a pickaxe which split as it hit the mud ball. There was only one thing left and that was his grandad's hammer. This blacksmith was a giant of a man but his grandad had been almost twice his size and he'd left him his great hammer. It was so heavy that he'd never managed to lift it, but this time he was determined not only to lift it but to smash the mud ball with it.

He dragged it from the corner and over to the anvil, got his enormous shoulder under it and with all his strength began to heave it off the ground. Jack took one look and decided the best thing for him to do was to hide. He burrowed deep into a corner behind a pile of boxes.

It was all the blacksmith could manage to allow his grandad's hammer to drop on to the ball of mud, but it was enough. First a flake or two fell off and then a crack appeared that went deep into the mud, through the nut shell, through the mud in the shell and right to where the wizard was trapped. A thick red smoke began to pour from the crack and swirl round and round in the room until it settled into the shape of the wizard, who had the worst headache he had ever had in his life and was very angry indeed.

"Where's Jack?!!!" he roared, but couldn't see him hiding in the corner. What he did see was the giant of a blacksmith who was using a hammer almost as big as himself.

"Now, you're what I want for a servant," said the wizard and flicked his fingers. The blacksmith started to protest but the two of them vanished before he could utter a word.

Jack came out from hiding and had a look around the blacksmith's place to see if he could find anything to "borrow" to help him on his journey (note I say "borrow," because Jack was never a thief). He found some food and a horse to ride and so he returned home in style.

Mary ran to greet him and asked what had happened.

"Well, if I told you, Mary," said Jack, "you'd probably never believe me."

And do you know … she never did.

The Spirits in the Leather Bag

KAMPUCHEAN

There was once a prince who loved stories. He had an old faithful servant and every night, when he went to bed, the servant would come to tell him a story. It started when he was quite young and carried on until he was old enough to marry.

I'm afraid that the prince was jealous of his stories and never told them to anybody else. When he was young, his friends would come up to him and say, "You must know some wonderful tales. Please tell us some." But the prince would just walk away.

When each tale was told to him, the spirit of that story would go into a leather bag that hung behind his bedroom door. There it had to stay until its story was told again, but, as I say, the prince never passed on any of the wonderful tales he heard.

Needless to say, the bag became very crowded and the spirits grew angry. Although they belonged to stories that were intended to give pleasure, it was hot and uncomfortable in the bag and they whispered together, very quietly so that they couldn't be heard outside, as they plotted revenge on the prince.

Eventually the time came when the prince was old enough to marry and a wedding was arranged with a beautiful princess. It was going to be a splendid occasion, the best that anybody could remember, and everybody would be there to celebrate the special day.

The night before the wedding, although by now he was fully grown, the prince still called the old and faithful servant to him and asked for a story, and afterward, when the old man had gone, the spirit joined the others in the leather bag.

The prince awoke in the morning and went to get ready for his wedding day. Meanwhile, in the leather bag, the spirits schemed.

"I know," said one, "we must get our revenge today and spoil the occasion. On his way to the temple, the prince is bound to be hot and thirsty. When he passes the river, he will want a drink and, just to make sure, I will make myself into a hollow gourd. When he passes me, he will call out to have me filled with water so that he can quench his thirst, but when he raises me to his lips, I will change into a sword and attack him."

"That's a good idea," said another, "but he will also pass the strawberry field and, just in case your plan doesn't work, I will make myself into a tempting strawberry that he will be bound to ask for. When he eats me, I will change into a wasp and sting his throat."

"Nice," said another, "but should your plans fail, I have another one. I know that at important events such as this they put a sack of rice for the prince to stand on as he alights from his carriage. I will become sharp pieces of broken glass and hide in the sack so that,

when he steps on me, his feet will be cut to shreds."

Finally, a dark, slippery spirit spoke from deep down in the bag. "Your plans are good, my friends, but I have another one. I will become a poisonous snake and hide in his bed. If he manages to overcome all your traps, I will wait until he and his new wife fall asleep and then I will bite him."

As they prepared to put their plans into action, the spirits grew so excited that they forgot to whisper quietly but instead began to shout to each other.

The old servant heard the racket they were making as he passed the door. He stopped to listen and then understood not only their plans, but also the desperation which had caused them to seek revenge. Somehow he had

21

to get the prince to tell the stories, but first he had to save the royal wedding day.

As the oldest retainer to the prince – and his storyteller – he was asked to travel in the royal coach with his master and all the important guests. So he was there when they passed the river and the prince saw the gourd.

"I'm so hot and thirsty. Will someone please get me a drink of water?" the prince said.

"Certainly not!" said the old man. "Why, it would make you sweat and spoil the look of your wedding clothes. In any event, we haven't time to stop."

The important guests were shocked that the old man had spoken in that way and even more surprised when the prince replied, "So be it," and they went on their way.

A little further along, they passed the strawberry fields and the prince couldn't help but notice one large, succulent, juicy strawberry that stood out from all the rest. "Please let us stop," he said, "just for a moment, so that I can eat that splendid strawberry."

22

"Certainly not!" said the old man. "Why, you would mess your fingers and spoil your clothes. Anyway, as I have said before, we have no time to waste on this journey!"

Once again, everybody was shocked at the way the old man spoke to the prince, but he just said, "You have been my servant and friend all my life. I cannot remember any time when you have been wrong before and so you must be right now." And they continued on their way to the temple.

Eventually, the coach stopped in the courtyard and the customary sack of rice was placed for the prince to step on to. Everybody gathered around to watch, but then the old servant pushed past him and caused his master to stumble as he got down from the coach, and to miss the sack of rice altogether.

The guests were furious, but the prince just said, "He has been my servant for as long as I can remember and I cannot be angry with him on this special day. He must be getting old, that's all."

With that the prince stepped into the temple and the wedding began.

Much later, after all the celebrations and feasting, the prince and his new wife were escorted to their bedchamber. As they reached their door, however, the old servant pushed past them and barged into the room. He had a drawn sword and hacked with it at their bed.

"What are you doing?" said the prince. "I have forgiven you much today but this I do not understand. Speak now!"

The old servant did not say a word but instead drew back the bed covers and showed the body of an enormous snake that had been cut into many pieces by his sword.

"How did you know, my old friend?" said the prince.

The servant explained everything to the prince and then warned him that the story spirits included many tricksters who, in their desperation to be released, had plotted to use their subterfuge against him.

"Apart from one of them," he said, "they meant no real harm – just to spoil your day and teach you a lesson. But now, master, you must learn from them. Stories can only live when they are told, not when their spirits are fastened up in a leather bag."

I'm pleased to say that the prince did learn his lesson. From that day on, he told many stories and, as a result, the spirits were able to wander freely again.

The Frail Old Woman

BENGALI

There was once a frail old woman, so thin the skin hung in folds from her ancient bones. All of her family had grown up and moved away to start lives of their own and she now lived alone, apart from her two faithful dogs. I'm afraid that she didn't look after herself very well and certainly didn't have enough to eat, which is why she was so thin.

One day, she decided that she would go and visit her great-granddaughter who lived in another village some miles away. She

26

called her dogs to her and told them, "You stay here and guard the house. Don't wander away, and make sure that you come only if you hear me calling you."

Needless to say, the two dogs understood her perfectly and always obeyed her instructions, so the old woman knew it would be safe to leave the house. She fastened the door, cut herself a stout walking stick and set out on her journey.

She hadn't gone far, though, when she saw a sleek fox with long whiskers and sharp teeth and, even worse, the fox saw her. He came up to her, licking his lips, and said in his sly voice, "Ah, a frail old woman, and I feel so hungry. I'm sure you couldn't put up much of a fight and I know that you couldn't run fast enough to escape me, so I think I'll eat you."

"No, wait," said the old woman. "Of course I'd be no match for you, but you don't want to eat me now, not while I'm so thin. I'm going to visit my great-granddaughter who is sure to feed me well. Why don't you wait and eat me when I'm on my way home? I'll make a much better meal for you then."

To her surprise – and, to be honest, to mine as well – the fox agreed to wait until she was on her way back, and so she continued on her journey.

She hadn't gone far, though, when she saw a great strong bear with long sharp claws and, even worse, the bear saw her. He came up, licking his lips, and said, "Ah, a frail old woman, and I feel so hungry. I think I'm going to eat you."

"You don't want to eat me now," said the old woman. "Why, there's no meat on me and I'll scarcely make a mouthful for a fine beast like you. I'm on my way to my great-granddaughter's house and she's sure to feed me up. Why not wait until I'm on my way home? I'll be a much better meal for you then."

Well, I'm astonished to say that

the bear
also agreed to wait
until she was on her way home
and allowed her to go on her way.

But it wasn't her day, because she hadn't gone very much further
when a tiger came bounding along the path and stopped in front of
the old woman.

"Ah, a frail old woman," he said, "and I feel so hungry. I'm sure
you couldn't do anything about it if I decided to eat you all up."

"Of course I couldn't," she replied. "You are big and strong, so
what chance would I have? Why eat me now, though? I'm so thin that
I'd hardly make a snack for you, but I'm on my way to my great-
granddaughter's house and she's a wonderful cook. I'm sure she'll
feed me well and there'll be a lot more meat on me when I return.
Why not wait until then?"

The tiger looked at her and then, I'm astounded to say, he also agreed to wait until she was on her way home. It just goes to show how gullible some animals can be!

The old woman continued along the path and eventually came to her great-granddaughter's house where she was given a wonderful welcome.

"It's so good to see you," her great-granddaughter said, "but you look so pale and thin. I'm sure you aren't getting enough to eat and so you must stay for a few days and let me feed you up."

Already there was a smell of wonderful cooking coming from the kitchen and the old woman didn't need much persuading. She stayed for a week, during which time she had four delicious hot meals each day and lots of snacks in between. She was feeling fitter and certainly looking fatter when the time came for her to take her leave.

She was just saying good-bye when she remembered the animals that would be waiting for her on her way home. She turned pale at the thought.

"Why, great-grandmother, what's wrong? Why do you suddenly look so worried?"

"I've just remembered, I'm going to be eaten," the old woman said, and told her about the fox, the bear and the tiger.

The girl thought for a while and then went round to the back of the house where she had a large, hollow gourd. She brought it round to the front.

"Get into there," she said, "and I'll set you rolling along the path. The animals won't know you're in it and should leave you alone. I'm sure you'll be safe enough that way."

She put the old woman into the hollowed-out gourd shell and gave her a bowl of rice to sustain her on her journey. Then she sealed it up and started it rolling along the path. The old woman inside started singing to keep her spirits up.

> "Rolling gourd, rolling gourd,
> The old woman's gone.
> So I'm eating rice to keep me strong
> As I go rolling along."

In that way she came first to the tiger, who heard the voice coming from the gourd and thought it was an evil spirit. He ran away in a panic.

Then she came to the bear, who listened to the song and when he heard "The old woman's gone" thanked the gourd most kindly for its advice and ambled slowly away.

Finally, when she was almost home, she came to the fox. He looked at the gourd, heard the song and said, "Gourds don't sing and they don't eat rice. Who is in there?"

So saying, he knocked the gourd with his strong legs and it split open. The old woman fell out.

"Ah … hello, old woman. You certainly look like a much better meal," he said. "I've been waiting for you for over a week and I'm very hungry."

He was about to pounce on her when she realized that she was almost home and remembered her dogs. She called for them at the top of her voice and, seconds later, they came bounding into view. The fox took one look at them and, quite forgetting the meal he had planned, ran off as fast as his legs would carry him, pursued by the barking hounds.

The woman went home chuckling to herself at the thought of how she'd tricked all the animals, and soon her dogs gave up chasing the fox and returned to welcome her back.

After her adventures, she decided to stay at home and let her family visit her instead, which they did from time to time. Mind you, I think she must have liked being a little fatter because, from then on, she fed herself very well indeed and could never again be called a "frail" old woman.

Turtle Goes on the Warpath

SKIDI PAWNEE

One day, Turtle decided to go on the warpath against a neighboring tribe. He performed the special war dance, put war paint on his old wrinkled face and started to make his way, slowly and stealthily, toward the enemy camp. However, as he walked along he was aware that he would be alone against a great foe and he needed others to fight with him if he was to have a chance of winning.

He saw Coyote and stopped.

"Where are you
going, Grandfather?" said Coyote.

"I am on the warpath," said Turtle in his slow
deep voice.

"Then I will come and fight with you."

Turtle looked at Coyote, who was sleek and strong,
and asked him, "How fast can you run?"

At this, Coyote set off at great speed, running rings
around Turtle. It was exhausting just to watch him.

"That's much too fast," said Turtle and went on his way.

A little further down the path he met with Hare, who also
inquired, "Where are you going, Grandfather?"

Once again, Turtle replied, "I am on the warpath."

"Then let me come along and fight for you."

Turtle looked at him thoughtfully, then
said, "First let me see how fast you
can run."

Hare was even faster than Coyote.
He ran clean out of sight and back
again in a matter of moments.

"No, that's much too fast, too," said
Turtle sadly and went slowly onward.

The next creature that he met was Eagle, who flew down and perched close to him.

"Where are you going, Grandfather?" he said.

"I am on the warpath."

"But you are alone. Let me come and fight with you, for I am a great warrior."

Turtle looked at him hopefully. "How fast do you fly?" he asked.

Eagle spread his great wings and soared through the air.

"Oh dear – I'm afraid that you're much too fast as well," said Turtle and continued along his lonely way.

Next he met with Raven, who also offered to fight alongside him, but he too could fly very fast. Turtle shook his wise old head sadly and continued on alone.

He hadn't gone much further when he saw a flint knife lying on the ground.

"Where are you going, Grandfather?" said the knife in a hard scratchy voice.

"I am on the warpath."

The knife had grown bored of lying on the ground, so he said, "Then let me come with you."

"Possibly," replied Turtle, "but first show me how fast you can run."

The knife struggled as hard as it could but, try as it might, it couldn't manage to run at all.

"Oh yes," said Turtle, "that's much more like it. Please come with me."

Now, don't ask me how the knife moved, but somehow it did and the two of them continued on their way. Soon they saw a hairbrush that somebody had dropped. It looked at them and with a strange bristly voice said, "Where are you going, Grandfather?"

"Flint Knife and I are on the warpath," came the reply.

"Then do let me come with you. I don't like being left here all alone."

"Maybe we will," said Turtle, "but first you must show us how fast you can run."

The hairbrush turned over on to its bristles, but every time it tried to run, it tripped over them.

"Yes, that will do well," said Turtle. "You may come with us."

The three of them continued on their way when they found an awl, which is a sharp needle-like tool for making holes in leather. "Where

  are you going, Grandfather?" it said in a thin, sharp voice.

"We are on the warpath."

"Then I would like to come with you."

"Can you run fast?" said Turtle.

"Oh no, I'm afraid not. Do you want only those that can move quickly?" came the sad reply.

"No," said Turtle, "not at all. If you cannot run, you are just what we are looking for. Please join us."

The four of them soon came to the edge of the enemy camp, where Turtle gave them whispered instructions.

"There are a great many of them and so we must go in, one by one, and see what damage we can do. First you, Flint Knife."

Flint Knife crept into the camp and among their enemies where somehow he managed to cut the finger of a big strong brave. He slid back stealthily to his friends and told them what he had done.

The next to go in was Hairbrush, and he managed to tangle and pull the hair of another brave. Then Awl went in, and he stabbed the finger of yet another warrior.

Finally, it was Turtle's turn, but he was so clumsy and noisy that the braves caught him before he could do any damage at all. They tied him up and put him in a tipi with a guard outside.

Flint Knife, Hairbrush and Awl decided that they must save him. They crept into the camp but soon they too were captured and the

tribe decided to keep them prisoner and to make use of them.

Flint Knife was carried by a great brave, Hairbrush given to the beautiful daughter of the chief and Awl was used to make holes in soft leather that was used to make fine moccasins.

All that was left to decide was the fate of Turtle.

The tribe gathered in a circle around their enemy and began to talk about making a great fire and roasting Turtle on it.

"Oh yes," said Turtle craftily, "that would be wonderful; I do enjoy being warm and dry. In fact, the only thing I don't like is being wet, and so I ask that you do with me what you will, only, I beg of you, please don't throw me into the lake."

The tribe thought about this and decided that Turtle was a great enemy and should have the worst punishment possible. They seized him, took him to the edge of the great lake and threw him into it, where he landed with a great splash.

Turtle came to the surface and swam until he was well out of reach before he turned to them and grinned.

"Thank you," he called, "thank you so much for throwing me in the lake! You should know that I love water! I was brought up in water! I live in water! There is no place in the world where I am happier than when I'm swimming in water!!"

With that he gave a laugh and swam away, leaving the tribe to realize how easily they had been tricked. Mind you, they still had three very useful prisoners and I don't think that Turtle ever went on the warpath again.

Ananse and the
Impossible Quest

GHANAIAN

One day, the king, who thought himself very wise and powerful, decided he was growing tired of Kwaku Ananse, the spider man. He thought Ananse was getting rather big-headed and a bit too clever for his own good. No matter how difficult the tasks he set for him, Ananse always managed to find an answer. Something had to be done about it … and then the king had an idea.

Ananse was summoned to the palace courtyard and there the king told him he'd been chosen for a very special quest: "There are two very precious things that I wish to have, and I've chosen you, Kwaku Ananse, to get them for me."

"Yes," said Ananse eagerly, "what are they?"

"If I should tell you," the king replied with a sly smile, "I'm sure it would be far too easy for you. So to make it a little more of a challenge for your great wisdom, I am not prepared to reveal what the objects are – only that I want them. If you bring them to me within a week, I will see that you are very well rewarded with land and honor; but if you fail me, you will die."

Kwaku Ananse was deep in thought as he made his way homeward, but walking through the forest he saw the birds flying around and that gave him an idea. He stopped and called all the birds to him.

"I'm on a special mission for the king," he said. "I could be a very good friend to you and all I want now is a small token of your friendship. Fly by my house and each of you leave just one feather. Now off you go, and don't forget."

When Ananse got home he found his wife and son staring at an enormous heap of feathers.

"Don't waste time," he said. "Stick the feathers all over me and make me into a bird."

In no time at all, he was covered in feathers of all shapes, sizes and colors. He looked like the strangest bird you could ever imagine. His two thin arms were just like wings and as he flapped them he began to fly, higher and higher, until he could see the king's palace in the distance.

He flew into the royal courtyard and saw the king with some of his Elders sitting in the shade of a great tree, so he perched on a high branch where he could hear all that was said.

"What's that strange bird?" asked the king.

"Send for Ananse," suggested one of the Elders. "He's sure to know."

"I'm pleased to say that I cannot do that," replied the king, and he explained about the impossible quest he had set Ananse.

"What a clever idea," said the Elders, "and what is it you want him to get for you?"

"Why, he must go to Death's house

and get
me his
golden slippers
and his golden broom.
Nobody goes to visit Death and
returns, so even if he knew what I
wanted, we would still be finished with
him. This way I can put an end to him
whatever happens."

Ananse flew away to the sound of their
laughter. His wife helped him to unstick his
feathers and prepared some food for the
journey, then he set out.

Ananse had been walking for a few hours when he came to a fast-
flowing river. As he looked for a way across, he realized that he was
feeling hungry and thought it would be much easier to carry the food
across in his tummy. He was just about to tuck in when, to his
amazement, he heard the gurgling voice of the rushing water, asking
for a share.

"You never know when you might want a friend," Ananse said to
himself. He threw half of his food into the torrent, which slowed
down a little to reveal a line of stepping stones going across. As soon

as he had eaten his fill, Ananse crossed safely to the other side. Soon he came to the great, gray house where Death lived. He banged on the door and was welcomed inside by an old man. Death didn't have many casual visitors.

"Why not stay the night?" Death asked slyly, after Ananse had introduced himself.

"How very kind of you," said Ananse, knowing full well that if he was silly enough to go to sleep in Death's house, he wouldn't wake up in the morning.

The guest room was dark and dusty, but in the middle of it was a big four-poster bed with a soft feather mattress and warm, cozy covers.

Ananse got into bed and was lying there, pinching himself to stay awake, when he heard the door open.

"Not asleep yet?" Death asked.

"I'm afraid not," said Ananse. "I can never get to sleep without my pair of golden slippers on my feet. I don't suppose you've got any?"

"Well, as it happens, I have. I'll go and get them for you."

So Death brought Ananse the golden slippers.

Don't ask me how Ananse managed to get through that night, but as the morning light crept through the window, he was still wide awake and went down to breakfast clutching the golden slippers.

46

Death was sitting on the porch in a very grumpy mood, which wasn't improved by the irritating buzz of a fly.

"I'll get it," Ananse said, and he picked up the golden broom which just happened to be leaning against the wall. Before Death could say anything, Ananse was running around hitting out at the fly and catching Death with a few hearty smacks in the process. Then, grasping the slippers in one hand and the broom in the other, Ananse chased the fly off the porch and round the corner. Once he was out of sight, he took to his heels and ran just as fast as his legs would carry him, away from Death's house.

It took Death a while to realize he'd been tricked, but then he set off after Ananse, as fast as the wind. Ananse could hear Death just behind him when suddenly he found himself splashing about in water and he knew he was in the river that he had crossed the day before.

"Please, please!" he said. "Remember the delicious food I gave you on my way here? Well, I need your help now. Death is behind me and he'll catch up with me soon unless you could grow into a flood and slow him down."

Quick as a flash, the river became a great deep lake which spread across toward Death and stopped him in his tracks.

Ananse didn't even stop to look back. In fact he didn't stop running until he reached home, and then it was only to put the slippers and the broom in a bag before setting off for the palace.

The king was in his favorite place in the courtyard, sheltering from the sweltering sun. He saw Ananse approaching with a bag that just might contain what he'd sent him for … but how could that be?

"I'm not sure that I've got what you wanted … Could you just tell me what it was?" Ananse was enjoying himself.

With his Elders all around him, the king replied that what he wanted was Death's golden slippers and golden broom. You should have seen his face when Ananse took those very items from the bag! The king was hopping mad, but he had to keep his word and Ananse was given land and power as his reward.

As Ananse was leaving, the king suddenly remembered the strange bird he had seen, and asked if he knew what it was. Ananse thought for a while. He always enjoyed having a quick answer, but this time he had the sense to realize that sometimes it is wise to appear ignorant. So he kept the secret, and I hope you will too.

The Mullah Nasrudin

TURKISH

The Mullah Nasrudin was a big, bearded bear of a man with an answer for everything. It has to be said that he was rather pompous and considered himself very important. He carried himself with great dignity, always dressed in the very best of robes and saw himself as a wise man and teacher, always happy to share his great knowledge – or, at least, what he considered to be knowledge – with anybody and everybody. He had many friends and followers, so wherever he went a crowd gathered, mainly to see what he would get up to next.

The Mullah enjoyed the best of food and drink, and he was in fact very good company, even if he could be rather noisy and a little self-centered. You could say that he was just larger than life and maybe you even know somebody a little bit like him yourself? Whether he was as clever as he thought, I'll leave it up to you to decide.

Late one evening, a group of his friends were on their way home when they were amazed to come across the great man, down on his knees, scrabbling on the ground underneath a street lamp.

"Teacher," they exclaimed in surprise, "what's wrong?"

"It's terrible! I've lost my very best ring, the one with a ruby that was a very special gift. I must find it!"

Needless to say, his friends stopped to help him in the search but, although they looked all around, there was no sign of the ring anywhere.

"When did you see it last?" they asked.

The Mullah thought for a while. "I know I had it on earlier when I was sitting in my backyard," came the reply.

"In your backyard?"

"That's what I said. I was sitting having a little snack and I noticed it was becoming rather loose. I think it must have dropped from my finger."

His friends looked at him. "Did you look for it in your backyard?" they asked.

"Of course not," said the Mullah with great surprise, as though it was the most unlikely thing they could expect from him.

"But, Mullah, have you thought – you probably lost the ring in your backyard?"

The Mullah Nasrudin stood up. "Without a doubt," he said. "I know that."

"Then why are you searching for it here, under the street light?"

"Why, that should be obvious even to you," said the Mullah. "It's

52

very dark in my backyard and the light is so much better here."

A little while later, he chanced to overhear his friends talking and laughing about that evening.

"All was well – I found the ring in my backyard the next day," he said, "when the light was better." He looked around at them and smiled as he went on: "Mind you, I'd have had no difficulty at all in searching in my yard that night, if I'd really wanted to. I don't know whether I've told you before but I'm lucky enough to be blessed with wonderful eyesight. In fact, it is so good that I can see where I am going even when it is completely dark. Even indoors at night, when it's pitch black, I can see as though it's broad daylight."

His friends knew that he was bragging again but they also knew that it was pointless to argue with him when he was in that mood. They would just have to wait their chance, and so, a few nights later, they were delighted to see him wandering around the street in the dark holding on to a bright shiny lamp.

"Great teacher," they said, "the other night you were telling us about your remarkable eyesight. If you can see so well in the dark, why are you bothering to use a lamp?"

They really thought they had caught him that time, but no. Right away he had an answer for them.

"Why?" he said. "To stop others from bumping into me, of course."

As you can see, he had an answer for everything and his fame spread far and wide.

One day, word came to the village where he lived that a great judge was to be appointed and a delegation of people were on their way to see if the famous Mullah Nasrudin might be the man for the job.

"The thing is," his friends said, looking at the well-groomed and expensively dressed bulk of their teacher, "we have heard that they are hoping to find you a humble man, a man of the people, a man who hasn't forgotten his roots."

"Don't you worry, my friends," said the Mullah. "I can be as humble as the next man." And he went into his house to prepare himself for the meeting.

Later that day, when the strangers arrived in the village, they found him sitting on an upturned box, wearing old rags and with a fishing net draped over his big, broad shoulders.

They asked him why he was dressed in this way and he explained, with great modesty, that it was to remind himself of his humble origins.

"Although the world knows me as a great teacher, I am but the son of a poor fisherman and, indeed, I was once a fisherman myself. In those days, I didn't have fine clothes to wear, so what need do I have of them now?"

They were so impressed by this modesty and humility that they decided unanimously that he was the ideal man for the job and, there and then, appointed him Supreme High Judge for the whole district.

It was some time later before he was called upon to preside over his first case, and those who had chosen him were in the courtroom, eager to hear how such a humble man would administer justice. To their amazement, when he strode into the room he wasn't wearing rags and a net at all, but a very stylish new robe, and rather than behaving with humility, he was carrying himself with great importance and dignity.

As he took his seat of justice, they went up

to him. "Mullah," they said, "we don't understand. What about your humble origins as a fisherman, and the son of a fisherman? Why are you dressed in such an expensive way? Where are your rags and net that you drape over your shoulders?"

The Mullah looked them up and down, with a knowing twinkle in his eye and a smile on his lips, before he answered. "My good friends," he said, "that was then and this is now. What need do I have of the fishing net now that I have caught the fish?"

Just how they reacted to this, I don't know, but I do know that Mullah Nasrudin was a good judge. While his ways of considering a case were not always obvious, somehow or other justice was always done.

Brer Rabbit and the Share Crops

AFRICAN AMERICAN

This is a story about Brother Rabbit, or Brer Rabbit, as he's better known. Without doubt, Brer Rabbit can be a bit of a rascal, but he's always got a ready smile and a twinkle in his eye. You can't help liking him, and somehow he always manages to get out of the scrapes that come his way without doing any real harm to anybody.

Once upon a time – and, you know, I do believe it was only the once – Brer Bear and Brer Rabbit decided to be farmers.

Brer Bear had managed to get himself a wonderful spread of a place with acres and acres of good farming land that would grow more or less anything he could wish for, but all that poor old Brer Rabbit could find was just a small scrubby patch of ground that wasn't much use for anything at all.

He decided that he'd have to do something about it and so he put on his best jacket, went along to Brer Bear's house and said, "Good morning to you, Brer Bear. You know, I've been thinking that maybe I should expand my farm a little and so I could be interested in renting your bottom field for the next season – if the price is right."

Brer Bear was sitting out on his back porch in his old rocking chair, enjoying a nice glass of root beer, and he made a great show of thinking about it before he finally said, "Well, I might consider it, Brer Rabbit, seeing as how it's you, but I'm afraid I only rent by shares."

"Just what do you mean by that?" said Brer Rabbit.

"It's quite simple, Brer Rabbit. I let you have the land for free and in return you plant the crop and do all the work. Then when harvest time comes, the two of us share what you've grown."

"Well," said Brer Rabbit, "that seems reasonable enough to me, but how are we going to divide it up fairly?"

"Tell you what," said Brer Bear craftily, "I'll just take all the tops for my share and you can have all the bottoms for yours."

Brer Rabbit put his paw to his head and thought for a good long while before he finally agreed. The two of them shook on the deal and Brer Bear went to his house chuckling to himself because, try as he would, he couldn't think of any crops at all where the goodness might be down at the bottom among the roots and soil … but Brer Rabbit could.

The season went slowly by and harvest time arrived at last. The day came when Brer Rabbit sent one of his sons along to Brer Bear's house to ask him if he'd mind hurrying up and collecting his tops as quickly as he could.

Brer Bear didn't need telling twice and rushed along to the field singing to himself, but the words of the song froze on his lips when he got there and found Brer Rabbit

impatient for him to clear the way so that he could dig up the "bottoms" of his fine crop of … potatoes!

Brer Bear was furious, but it was his own fault and he'd made a deal that he couldn't go back on. While Brer Rabbit watched, he had to cut off all his tops and take them home in a barrow, clearing the way for the harvesting of the potatoes.

A little while later, Brer Rabbit went round to see if he could rent the field again.

"Well," said Brer Bear, "I think you were a bit too clever for me last time so, if I do let you have use of the land, my share will have to be the bottoms and you, Brer Rabbit, will have to make do with the tops."

Brer Rabbit pondered long and hard about it before he eventually agreed and the deal was made.

"I've got you now," Brer Bear thought to himself. The day came at last and Brer Bear followed Brer Rabbit's son to the field, but when he got there his jaw dropped in dismay as he gazed at the fine crop of oats blowing in the gentle breeze, and all he could take of it was the stalks and roots down at the bottom.

Days passed into weeks and weeks into months before Brer Rabbit went round again, but Brer Bear was ready for him.

"I reckon you've done me twice, Brer Rabbit, so this time it's my turn. I'll only let you have the field if I can have the tops and the bottoms. You can have all the middles."

Brer Rabbit tried to argue but there was nothing he could do and so, in the end, he had to agree and, once more, a deal was made.

Brer Bear couldn't wait for the crop to be ready and, a few months later, he thought he'd take a look to see what he was going to get come harvest time. It was a pleasant evening and he was whistling happily to himself as he enjoyed the stroll down to the field; but when he got there, he stopped dead in his tracks and stared in amazement with his mouth wide open before he started shaking his fist in anger.

"Why, that little scoundrel!" he shouted. "He's done me again! He's planted the field with sweetcorn!!"

Now, when sweetcorn grows, right down at the bottom you get the roots, up at the top you get stalks with the stamens that produce pollen, but in the middle, covered with leaves, you get the seeds and they make up the delicious sweetcorn cob.

So Brer Rabbit beat Brer Bear yet again and, you have to admit, it was really Brer Bear's fault!

The Three Sillies

RUSSIAN

Long ago, there lived an old gypsy woman, so old that all she
did was sit by the camp fire each day and leave all the work
to her only son. He was tall and handsome, with long flowing hair
and a ready smile, a good lad who looked after his mother well.
Everything ran smoothly until the day came when he was called up
to do his army service and he had no choice but to go. The soldiers
came for him, cut his hair very short, dressed him in uniform and
marched him away, leaving the old woman by herself.

Time went by; the first year dragged by slowly but then the next one seemed to go a littte faster and, although she missed him, somehow the old woman managed to get by without her son's help.

One evening, she was sitting by the fire preparing vegetables for a stew, when a stranger walked into the camp and straight up to the old woman. He was tall and thin with a bristly chin and, although he was wearing a soldier's uniform, he had a dilapidated look about him.

"Hello, Grandma," he said. "Your son asked me to call by if I should happen to be in the area and so I've made a special journey here. We're soldiers together and I've been home on leave. He sends you his love."

The old woman was delighted with the news, and soon the stranger was enjoying a nice bowl of stew.

"What's life like in the army?" she asked him.

"Oh, it's just terrible. We don't have enough to eat and what we do get is full of gristle and tastes awful. As if that's not bad enough, our clothes are threadbare and our boots are worn through. Just look at the state I'm in."

The old woman looked, and sure enough his clothes were thin and full of holes.

"Is there anything I can do for my poor lad?"

"That's what I'm here for," the soldier replied. "Your son asked if you could give me as much food as you can spare, and his best clothes and boots, so that I can take them back to him."

The old woman didn't need asking twice and went into the back of her wagon where she soon made up a big bundle. The soldier took it from her and hurried out of the camp before she could even ask him his name.

Time went by, as it will, and eventually the son finished his army service and came home to his mother. She was delighted to see that he looked very fit indeed and was well dressed:

"Did you get the clothes and food I sent you?" she asked.

"What clothes … what food?"

"Why, the bundle I sent with the other soldier."

The lad scratched his head: "What other soldier?"

66

His mother began to feel a little apprehensive as she explained what had happened.

"But I never sent anybody," said her son. "They looked after us very well in the army. What was his name?"

The old woman had to admit that she'd never asked it, and the lad was so amazed that she could have been so silly, he became angry with her.

"I've never heard anything like it in my life. You give away food and my best clothes to a stranger, without even asking his name. You're just stupid and I'm not going to stay here with you. I'm going away now and I'll only come back if I can find someone more silly than you."

With that he strode out of the camp.

At first he stormed around a bit, as you do when you lose your temper, but eventually he calmed down and set out on his travels. I'm not sure where he went and how far he journeyed, but I do know that in the end he came to a very wealthy-looking farm.

In the yard he saw a sow with her piglets.

With a smile on his lips and a crafty idea in his mind, he took off his hat and was bowing

down low to these creatures when a fine lady, dressed in the latest fashion, came out of the house.

"What on earth are you doing?" she asked.

"Why, tomorrow is to be our hog's wedding day and I've been sent to ask all the pigs in the district to join them for a wedding feast."

"Don't be silly," said the lady. "They are nothing special. You don't bow to them like that; just pick them up and take them with you – I'm sure they'll enjoy it. I'll find you something to put them in."

The lad watched as she stuffed them into an old sack, and then said, slowly, "You know, I'm not at all sure how I'm going to get them to the wedding. It's quite a long journey and they really ought to travel in style to such a fine event."

"Why, that's easy," she replied. "You must borrow my carriage and travel in that."

So the gypsy hitched up the lady's old horse to the carriage, loaded the sack containing the sow and the piglets on to the back, and hurried on his way before she could realize how he'd tricked her. As he traveled along he had to admit that he'd met someone every bit as foolish as his mother and so he started back toward the camp, although the old horse was very slow.

He was driving along a straight stretch of the road when he saw,

in the distance, a squire mounted on a fine horse galloping toward him.

Quick as a wink, he got down from the carriage and placed his green army cap over an old tree stump. Then, as the squire rode up, he made a great show of struggling to hold it in place.

"What are you doing, gypsy?" the squire asked.

"Why, I've caught myself a firebird – it's here under my hat. If only I could get home and bring back my book of magic, I could put a spell on it. That's the only way to hold such a rare creature."

"Don't worry – I'll watch it for you," said the old squire. "You go and get the book."

"But my old horse is so slow, it could take me a day or more to get there and back."

"Then you must take mine instead. Hitch it to your carriage and you'll go like the very wind."

The gypsy didn't need telling twice and he was soon on his way

with a fine horse, a carriage and a sow and her piglets. I'm sure that I don't have to tell you that he'd no intention of ever returning that way again.

I wonder how long it was before the silly squire looked under the hat or the fine lady realized she'd been tricked?

The lad went back to his old mother and had to admit to her that he'd had no trouble at all finding people far more foolish than she'd ever been. He lived with her happily after that, and if he left from time to time to go on his travels, I'm sure he never returned empty-handed.

Nail Soup

SWISS

As he walked along, all Hans the tramp could think about was how hungry he was and about all his favorite foods that he'd love to be eating, and that just made things worse, so he strode right into the middle of a small town before he realized he was there. It was a pleasant sort of place that he'd never visited before, and there, right in the middle, was a castle.

Hans heaved a sigh of relief because, in those days, the way of it was that if you were in need of a meal, you simply went round to

the kitchen of any big house or castle and you would be sure to get one. So, with a lighter step, our friend Hans walked around until he came to the kitchen door.

As he raised his hand to knock on the door, Hans was thinking about all the delicious food inside and the wonderful meal he was sure to get. He was just about to give a rat-a-tat-tat, when the door was flung wide open and another tramp came hurtling out, almost knocking him flying. The tramp picked himself up, dusted himself down in a resigned sort of way, and then saw Hans looking at him.

"I hope you're not planning to ask for a meal," he said, "because they're as mean as can be in there. I only asked for a few crumbs to eat and the cook threw me out."

"Did he?" said Hans. "We'll see about that. I'm sure I've a trick to beat him."

He searched around and he found an old nail that had been cast from a horse's hoof and then, tucking it into his pocket, he walked boldly up to the kitchen door and knocked on it.

The door was flung wide open and there stood the biggest cook you've ever seen. He had a great black beard almost reaching down to his fat stomach, his face glistened with perspiration from the heat of the kitchen and an enormous apron was wrapped twice around his middle.

"What do you want?" he growled at Hans. "We don't welcome your sort here so don't expect a meal."

"Oh, I'm not wanting any of your food," came the reply. "I just wondered if you could let me have a little pot of boiling water."

"Is that all?" said the cook suspiciously. "What do you want it for?"

"Well," said Hans, "I'm feeling a little peckish and I've a fancy to make myself a nice bowl of Nail Soup. I've got the nail all ready and I'd be happy to let you share it with me if you'd just help me out with the water."

The cook scratched his greasy head.

"I've never heard of such a thing," he said, "but if that's all you want … BOY!!" he shouted. "Bring a pot full of water and set it on the stove."

Up came the little Pot Boy who did all the hard work around the place. He brought a small round-bottomed black iron pot full of water, which was soon steaming on the stove.

Hans dropped the nail into it and slowly stirred it as the water began to bubble.

"Is it ready yet?" said the cook.

Hans took a spoonful and tasted it.

"Mmm," he said, "not bad at all, but it could do with a little salt and pepper to bring out the flavor. Have you got any?"

"Of course," said the cook, who was eager to taste Nail Soup. He

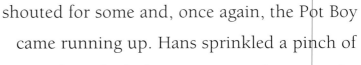

shouted for some and, once again, the Pot Boy came running up. Hans sprinkled a pinch of salt and a little pepper into the pot and cautiously sipped the boiling liquid.

"A nice clear Nail Soup," he said, "but looking at you, Mr Cook, I suspect you might prefer a rich thick one. A little stock would make it much better for you."

"BOY!!!" shouted the cook, and the Pot Boy came running up with the stock pot in which the bones and the goodness left over from the joints of meat were boiled. The thick rich contents were added to the Nail Soup, and so now we have a black pot; in it we've boiling water, a nail, salt and pepper and stock. It was beginning to look and smell quite appetizing but, as I'm sure you and I know only too well, that was really on account of the stock.

Hans tasted it.

"Is it ready now?" The cook was getting hungry.

"Delicious," said Hans, "but when I make soup for the Queen, she tends to prefer Nail and Vegetable. You wouldn't happen to have a few fresh vegetables we could add?"

By now the cook was getting carried away and, not suspecting a thing, he called for vegetables. Carrots, peas, beans, parsnips and potatoes tumbled into the pot and soon a delicious smell began to fill the kitchen. The cook waited as long as he could, then: "Is it ready yet?"

Hans sipped the steaming liquid. "Very tasty," he said, "but I've been thinking about you and I can see that you are a man of taste. As this is going to be your first experience of Nail Soup, you might like to know that the King always asks for Nail, Vegetable and Mixed Meat Soup."

"BOY!!!!" yelled the cook excitedly. "Bring some meat."

Very soon, pieces of chicken, ham and beef were added to the pot and it was all simmering away.

The smell was so delicious, so appetizing, so tempting, that people from all around the castle were drifting into the kitchen, their mouths watering. Hans made them wait, as he slowly stirred the thick, rich soup, until …

"It must be ready now," said the cook, licking his fat lips.

"I'm sure it is," said Hans, "and there's plenty so let's all tuck in, and can' the other tramp have some as well?"

"It's yours really, I suppose," the cook said, "so share it with whoever you want."

They sat around the big wooden kitchen table and everybody had at least two bowlfuls of the delicious soup. The cook even provided some bread and cheese to go with it, and it was such a wonderful meal that afterward they all began to doze.

Hans sat up quietly and shook the other tramp awake. "Come on," he said, "before he finds out."

"Finds out what?"

"Never you mind. Just come on, but don't make any noise."

They crept towards the outside door and had almost reached it when they heard a great bellow from the cook.

He'd reached inside the pot and taken the only thing left in it: that's right – the nail.

Hans and his friend stood frozen to the spot, but they needn't have worried.

"You've forgotten this," the cook said. "You'll need it again, won't you?"

Hans looked at his friend and winked. Then he looked at you and he looked at me, and he winked at us as well.

"Oh no," he said, generously, "I can always get another one. You keep it, then you can make yourself a nice bowl of Nail Soup whenever you want."

Sources

It is the work of storytellers to take a tale and make it their own. The stories in this book are all from the treasure-house of tradition, but I would like to acknowledge how they came to me.

Jack and the Wizard

A Durham-based storyteller with the wonderful name "Sedayne" told this story to his friend and colleague Raymond Greenoaken, also an excellent teller of tales. Raymond told his version at the first night of a story club in Sheffield, and the story lodged in my mind. A good while later it emerged in the form in which it appears here.

The Spirits in the Leather Bag

I first heard this traditional Asian story told by Jim Hatfield. He is an excellent performance poet and storyteller based in Shropshire, and a few years ago he spent some time in the East, where he found this story.

The Frail Old Woman

This has its basis in "The Old Woman and the Fox" collected by Shamita Dasgupta and Sayantani Dasgupta, and is included in their collection *The Demon Slayers and Other Stories*, published by Interlink Books, New York, in 1995.

Turtle Goes on the Warpath

This is based on a story collected by Stith Thompson and included in *Folk Tales of the North American Indians*, published by J. G. Press, North Dighton, Massachusetts, in 1995.

Ananse and the Impossible Quest

The episode of Ananse being covered in feathers and, thus disguised as a bird, eavesdropping on the king (or, in some cases, God) to find out the details of a task, is to be found in various sources. The story of the quest to obtain Death's slippers and broom is based on "Kwaku Ananse and the Unknown Assignment" in Peggy Appiah's wonderful book *Tales of an Ashanti Father*, published by André Deutsch, London, in 1967. This story also begins with the feather episode.

The Mullah Nasrudin

The last ten to fifteen years have seen a great renaissance in the art of storytelling, and I have been introduced to many interesting fictional characters. Just who was the first person of my acquaintance to tell stories of Mullah Nasrudin, I don't know, but the three episodes that make up this tale come mainly from story sessions. There are some great stories in the collections of Idries Shah published by the Octagon Press, London.

Brer Rabbit and the Share Crops

I had heard this tale a number of times, and even told a version of it, before I found it as a Brer Rabbit story in *A Treasury of American Folklore* by B. A. Botkin, published by Crown Publishers, New York, in 1944.

The Three Sillies

While there are similarities with other stories, this version is based on "Three Nincompoops," a story collected by Yefim Druts and Alexei Gessler, and included in *Russian Gypsy Tales* by James Riordan, published by Cannongate Press, Edinburgh, in 1986.

Nail Soup

This is one of those stories that all storytellers seem to know, and I really cannot say when and where I first came across it. Until recently I've told it as "Stone Soup" and then my sister-in-law said she knew it as "Nail Soup," and I rather liked that. It's a story known right across the countries of Europe.

BAREFOOT BOOKS publishes high-quality picture books for children of all ages and specializes in the work of artists and writers from many cultures. If you have enjoyed this book and would like to receive a copy of our current catalog, please write to our New York office: Barefoot Books, 41 Schermerhorn Street, Suite 145, Brooklyn, New York, NY 11201-4845 email: ussales@barefoot-books.com website: www.barefoot-books.com

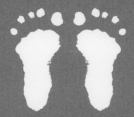